Sönke Albers (Ed.)

Cross-functional Innovation Management

Cross-functional Innovation Management

Perspectives from Different Disciplines

Edited by Sönke Albers

With contributions from

Sönke Albers · Ramaiya Balachandra ·Steffen Blaga
Alok K. Chakrabarti · Arnoud De Meyer · Holger Ernst · Günter Fandel
Santiago Garcia Echevarria · Sam Garg · Hansjörg Gaus
Hans Georg Gemünden · Ashok K. Gupta · Jürgen Hauschildt
Manjulika Koshal · Manfred Krafft · Hartmut Kreikebaum
Katrin Krieger · Wilhelm Krull · Martin Kuder · Heribert Meffert
Heiner Müller-Merbach · Vithala R. Rao · Mark P. Rice · Sören Salomo
Henrik Sattler · Gerhard Schewe · Helmut Schmalen · Reinhart Schmidt
Hans-Horst Schröder · Bernd Skiera · Martin Spann · Thorsten Teichert
G. L. Tembe · Jürgen Weber · Ursula Weisenfeld · Peter Witt
Heiko Kay Xander · Cornelia Zanger · Eric Zayer

To Klaus Brockhoff
for his 65. Birthday

Die Deutsche Bibliothek – CIP-Cataloguing-in-Publication-Data
A catalogue record for this publication is available from
Die Deutsche Bibliothek http://dnb.ddb.de

Prof. Dr. Sönke Albers, Chair of Innovation, New Media and Marketing at the Institute of Innovation Research at Christian-Albrechts-University at Kiel, Germany.

1st Edition October 2004

Gabler is a company of Springer Science+Business Media.
www.gabler.de

Registered and/or industrial names, trade names, trade descriptions etc. cited in this publication are part of the law for trade-mark protection and may not be used free in any form or by any means even if this is not specifically marked.

Cover design: Ulrike Weigel, www.CorporateDesignGroup.de
Printing and binding: Lengericher Handelsdruckerei, Lengerich
Printed on acid-free paper.
Printed in Germany

ISBN 3-409-12627-9

Univ.-Prof. Dr. Dr. h.c. Klaus K. L. Brockhoff

Preface

On October 16, 2004, Klaus Brockhoff will be 65 years of age. This event marks the end of an active position and the beginning of an Emeritus professorship in Germany. After almost four decades of being active in research he has built up a large network of friends, colleagues, and academic students. They want to commemorate his birthday with the dedication of this *Festschrift*.

Originally, his first two academic students, Helmut Schmalen and I planned to edit this *Festschrift*. Unfortunately, Helmut Schmalen died before starting with the work on this volume. Nevertheless, in order to give tribute to his work on diffusion, I invited an academic student of his to write a review article on all the achievements Helmut Schmalen and his students gained in diffusion research.

This book is a rather unique *Festschrift*. First of all, it is in English because Klaus Brockhoff has so many close friends, coauthors, and collaborators all over the world who wanted to contribute to this *Festschrift* that I decided to publish the book in the international language of science so that everybody can read and enjoy it. Second, the *Festschrift* is entirely devoted to the field of technology and innovation management which is the field that Klaus Brockhoff has made popular in Germany, and institutionalized in a way that you now find a substantial number of professors for innovation management at German universities. Although this is his most visible life achievement, Klaus Brockhoff was active in many other areas of business administration and can be considered to be one of the very rare species of researchers nowadays who overlook many fields of general business administration. As a consequence, he has inspired researchers from very different fields. However, all these people who wish to honor him with this *Festschrift* agreed to devote an article on aspects of their discipline with respect to innovation management which indeed represents a discipline crossing all other functional areas within business, thereby linking otherwise specialized researchers of several fields. In total, this *Festschrift* comprises 27 articles from close friends, from colleagues from Bonn, Kiel and Vallendar, as well as academic students whom he promoted. The book is divided into 6 parts looking at innovation management from different perspectives.

The *Festschrift* commences in Part 1 with articles on innovation and strategy by some of his colleagues and their academic students from Kiel, where he spent most of his academic career. Innovations are not all alike! Maybe the degree of innovativeness matters. Therefore, Jürgen Hauschildt and Sören Salomo discuss the relationship between the degree of innovativeness and success. Jürgen Hauschildt's academic students contribute two articles. Hans-Georg Gemünden reviews the work on the effects of innovation networks while Gerhard Schewe investigates the barriers of entry in innovative markets. Three other contributions from long-standing friends deal with strategic aspects of innovations in specific industries and geographical areas. Hartmut Kreikebaum discusses organizational determinants of innovation processes in pharmaceutical companies while Santiago Garcia Echevarria describes the impact of IT technologies on new business designs. Arnoud de Meyer (together with Sam Garg) with his extensive experience in the Asian market investigates whether there is an Asian cultural factor (Asian'ness factor) that affects the implementation success of innovation.

Part 2 is devoted to the process of research and development (R&D) within innovation management. Hans-Horst Schröder digs deep into knowledge management and proposes a new system that provides early information on emerging technologies based on knowledge discovery in databases. Managing R&D-projects is a challenging task. Ramaiya Balachandra reports on recent advances in project selection, project management, project termination and global R&D, closing with a brief look at the future in R&D and new product development management.

Part 3 is devoted to marketing aspects of innovation which has long been the main research area of Klaus Brockhoff. His former doctoral student Henrik Sattler reports on the use of conjoint analysis to new product development and its predictive validity. Vithala R. Rao who was one of the researchers originally introducing conjoint analysis to the marketing community and once a visiting professor at Kiel, investigates how we can model perceptions, preferences, and choices for bundles of multi-attributed items. Klaus Brockhoff's academic student, Holger Ernst, deals with virtual customer integration into the innovation process. Manfred Krafft and Katrin Krieger go further and investigate whether customer relationship management may be utilized to get interesting information from customers. While single experts may not always be able to make valid forecasts on the success of new product ideas, Bernd Skiera and Martin Spann investigate whether this can be achieved by combining the knowledge of many experts in the form of a virtual stock market where new product ideas are traded.

Once an innovation is generated it has to be penetrated into the markets. Sönke Albers therefore suggests a new method of how to forecast the diffusion of a product prior to launch based on analogue innovations. During the last 30 years Helmut Schmalen and his students at the University of Passau have published many articles on the diffusion problem ranging from estimation to deriving optimal marketing-mix strategies. Since his articles have only been published in German journals and because of his untimely death there is little chance to make the English-speaking world familiar with this research. I therefore asked his doctoral student Heiko Xander to write a review article on the diffusion research carried out in Passau. This article is published under Helmut Schmalen's and Heiko Xander's name to acknowledge Schmalen's contributions posthumously.

Ursula Weisenfeld, another academic student of Klaus Brockhoff, takes on the field of diffusion and discusses how risk attitudes and information provision may enhance the diffusion of genetically modified food. If the product has already established itself in the market, companies may want to get information about the attitudes of customer segments along the life cycle. Cornelia Zanger, who received her first academic training in Kiel after the German reunification, describes how this life cycle research can be carried out for a car model.

Klaus Brockhoff has always tried to make research and development accountable. Therefore, a chapter on controlling and funding innovations must not be missed. Part 4 comprises articles on these aspects. Reinhart Schmidt, his long-standing colleague at Bonn and Kiel, discusses how corporate governance should be changed to allow for innovations in companies. Peter Witt, his colleague at WHU (Vallendar), investigates the appropriateness of corporate venture capital. Jürgen Weber, also a colleague from his current institution WHU, demonstrates (together with Eric Zayer), why the German understanding of a controller is particularly helpful for enriching the evaluation of innovations.

Klaus Brockhoff has also contributed to the understanding of the research process at universities and foundations. Therefore, Part 5 is devoted to this topic. Thorsten Teichert, his last academic student, provides the results of a bibliometric analysis of innovation research as published in Research Policy. Günter Fandel (together with Steffen Blaga) describes the production process at universities. Very often, innovative research needs impulses from the outside. Wilhelm Krull as chairman of the Volkswagen Foundation describes how foundations can subsume this role. Heribert Meffert describes how foundations themselves can be subjected to innovation.

Klaus Brockhoff not only wanted to derive recommendations for firms in innovation management, rather he also frequently published recommendations on public policy with regard to innovation. This *Festschrift*, therefore, concludes with articles in Part 6 dealing with the public sector. Heiner Müller-Merbach describes how appropriate indicators for national economic performance can be created which are not dependent on size. Alok Chakrabarti (together with Mark Rice) discusses the changing role of universities in developing entrepreneurial regions and the results that have been achieved in Finland and the US. Ashok Gupta (together with G.L. Tembe and Manjulika Kostal) concludes on the interaction potential between industry and publicly funded R&D labs in India.

The editor thanks all authors of the articles for their contributions to this *Festschrift* thereby honoring Klaus Brockhoff. This collection of articles represents part of his network in Germany and throughout the world. We all want to congratulate Klaus Brockhoff on his 65th birthday and to wish him all the best for his future with many interesting challenges and enjoyable activities.

We would also like to thank the company "BSH Bosch und Siemens Hausgeräte GmbH" for its kind donation that made the publication of this *Festschrift* for Klaus

Brockhoff possible. Moreover, I wish to thank my assistant Jan Becker for all his work in coordinating the editing activities, formatting and proofreading of all articles.

The authors and the editor of this *Festschrift* would be very pleased if this collection of articles on technology and innovation management provides new impulses for research and implementation. Hopefully, they are also a source of inspiration for Klaus Brockhoff himself. In any case, we would appreciate it very much if this *Festschrift* is distributed very widely and further contributes to the establishment of technology and innovation management as a valuable discipline in business administration.

Kiel, October 2004 Sönke Albers

Content

Part 1: Innovation and Strategy

Part 2: Innovation and Research & Development

Part 3: Innovation and Marketing

Part 4: Innovation and Controlling and Finance

Part 5: Innovation, Foundations, and Universities

Part 6: Innovation and National Economic Performance

Part 7: Klaus Brockhoff

Sönke Albers and Jürgen Hauschildt

A Tribute to Klaus Brockhoff

Prof. Dr. *Sönke Albers* and Prof. Dr. Dr. h.c. *Jürgen Hauschildt*, Institute of Innovation Research, Christian-Albrechts-University at Kiel

1 Stations of His Life

Klaus Brockhoff was born in **Koblenz** at the beginning of the Second World War on October 16, 1939. He grew up in the same city to which he returned in 1999 after almost 40 years elsewhere. He was conditioned early by his father's occupation who was a wholesaler for fine wines. Although he could have taken over his father's business he decided to go into academia. As a very bright student at school he realized that business is not an art but something which can be studied thoroughly. Nevertheless, he always benefited greatly from the practical experience gained when working as a salesperson for his father's company during his student years.

After completing his studies of economics at the universities of **Bonn** and **Cologne** in 1962, he started his academic career in Bonn as a research assistant with Prof. Dr. **Horst Albach**, one of the most famous professors in business administration in the last decades in Germany. Horst Albach, himself, was a student with the equally important **Erich Gutenberg** who introduced microeconomics into the German business administration research community. After completing his Ph.D. in 1966 he complemented his studies with a diploma in business administration from the University of **Münster**.

Because of the high quality of his dissertation, he was offered a position for a "**habilitation**" by Horst Albach. In Germany, a habilitation is a postdoctoral degree which serves as an additional requirement to become eligible to apply for a full professorship. During his time as a doctoral student, he was also involved in compiling reports on spendings for Research & Development (R&D). He continued this work by devoting his habilitation thesis to the field of R&D. With an article in the prestigious international journal, *Econometrica,* he was accepted to spend a year as a visiting scholar with a grant by the German National Science Foundation (DFG Deutsche Forschungsgemeinschaft) in **Berkeley** in 1967-68. This was a very exciting year because the student rebellion began in the US and especially in Berkeley during that time. Klaus Brockhoff completed his habilitation in 1969 with a book on the evaluation and selection of research and development (R&D) projects and programs.

After his habilitation Klaus Brockhoff went into industry. He was hired by **Battelle Research Lab**. Because of his talent in managing people he soon became a manager of this company. He applied for positions as a professor at the very early age of 30. He received an offer from Christian-Albrechts-University at **Kiel** in 1970 during a very turbulent period two years after the student rebellion in 1968. But even the students were very keen to hire him because he had already published an article on the optimal size of a firm in the socialist economy and they thought he would be a proponent of this type of economy. This was, however, a misunderstanding on their part but a stroke of luck for Kiel because he laid the foundation for Kiel's good reputation in business administration which has steadily improved over the years. He succeeded **Walter Braun** who became the minister of education for Schleswig-Holstein.

In his first years he taught a broad spectrum of business administration topics so that these lectures could complement the limited economics program offered at that time. During his research on R&D he realized that any planning effort is only worthwhile if the response or future development can be forecast in an acceptable way. Therefore, he engaged in efforts to investigate the forecasting performance with the help of the Delphi-method. At that time, he was very keen on computer support. Hence, he hired people that could implement experimental computer environments. His efforts were recognized by **Prognos AG** in **Basel**, a very well-known consulting firm, in offering him the position of vice-president. However, he was more interested in an academic career and stayed with the University of Kiel after being able to renegotiate more favorable terms.

Not earlier than 1978, a **program for business administration** was introduced (with the intervention of minister Walter Braun) which required the enlargement of the faculty by three professors of business administration. One of them was **Jürgen Hauschildt** who became a long-standing friend of Klaus Brockhoff. With this introduction the program was organized along the functions of a company. Therefore, he had to decide which function to teach. Because of his early interest in new products, he chose Marketing. As a result, his research focused on marketing for almost 10 years.

In 1980, Brockhoff received an offer for a chaired professorship of business administration from the University of **Vienna**. He faced a difficult choice because Vienna not only offered the atmosphere of a cosmopolitan city but also a chair with no specialization requirements. However, he decided to continue with his specialization in marketing and R&D in order to intensify and focus his efforts.

In the mid-eighties Klaus Brockhoff's interest in research and development awoke again but broadened to technology and innovation management. Together with Jürgen Hauschildt, he initiated a **research center** under this new heading by assigning an assistant to it and trying to raise funds from the German National Science Foundation and other foundations. He was convinced that technology and innovation management was a very important cross function that business schools have to teach and to do research on. In order to attain support for establishing chaired professorships for this field he initiated, together with Hauschildt, a so-called **focus program** (Schwerpunktprogramm) by our German National Science Foundation. This program attracted many people active in this field and who have also contributed to this book.

In 1989 Klaus Brockhoff received an offer from **INSEAD (Fontainebleau)** to become the next dean which was indeed a great honor and endowed him with the respect that he already had earned among his fellow scientists. The state of Schleswig-Holstein was seriously concerned about the danger of Kiel losing its good reputation should he leave. They, therefore, offered him a regular **Institute of Innovation Research** with research capacity and funds. This coincided with the establishment of a "**Graduiertenkolleg**" (seminar for doctoral students) on Business Administration for

Technology and Innovation (funded by the German National Science Foundation) of which he became the chairman.

Klaus Brockhoff's engagement for the Graduiertenkolleg led to a sharp increase of doctoral students. Now he was able to direct a large research group which provided the critical mass for research on innovation management that was needed so much. Because of his management capabilities he was very successful at running the seminar - so much so that it was granted funding over the maximum length of time, namely 9 years, and initiated 72 dissertations.

At the height of his career in Kiel he accepted an offer from the first private business school in Germany, **WHU – Otto Beisheim Hochschule in Vallendar** (formerly in Koblenz). This was a very attractive challenge. WHU offered him a professorship of business and asked him to take over the position of rector. Interestingly, he followed his former academic student, Sönke Albers, 15 years later. Over the years, WHU has become a well-established business school and has gained worldwide reputation. When he finishes his term as rector in September 2004 the school will have nearly doubled the number of professorships, the budget, and the students. He has also been able to establish an Executive MBA–program in Vallendar. The WHU is now entering top positions in various rankings. Even though he is fully occupied by the many demands of such a position he still continued his research and activities to promote academic students.

Klaus Brockhoff has promoted five academic students. **Helmut Schmalen** was the first under his supervision. He was originally an assistant to Walter Braun but continued with Brockhoff. Schmalen was interested in the diffusion of innovations as modeled by the Bass-Model. This area lies in the intersection of R&D and marketing. Schmalen finished his habilitation in 1978 and became a professor of marketing at the University of Passau where he stayed until his untimely death in 2002. The second academic student, **Sönke Albers**, was hired in 1974 from Hamburg where he finished a dissertation on airline crew scheduling but continued with research interests in product positioning leading to a number of joint publications. Albers finished his habilitation in 1982, became the first professor at WHU in Koblenz and later a marketing professor at Lüneburg University before he returned to Kiel where he became a colleague of Brockhoff for almost a decade. In the late eighties, he promoted the third academic student **Ursula Weisenfeld** who did her research in the area of innovation management in the biotech industry. Later, she became a professor of marketing at Lüneburg University. The fourth academic student is **Holger Ernst** who followed him from Kiel where he finished his habilitation in 2000 and became a professor at WHU after rejecting another offer from a well-known public university. The fifth and last academic student, **Thorsten Teichert**, finished his habilitation at WHU in 2001 and went then to the University of Bern from where he left to go to the University of Hamburg in 2004.

Klaus Brockhoff's life achievements have been recognized several times. In 1991, he was awarded the prestigious **Max-Planck-Prize**. His contributions to the innovation management have led to the **Karl-Heinz-Beckurts-Prize** which is a very esteemed prize for life achievements. In 1997, he was elected as a member of the **Berlin-Brandenburg Academy of Science** followed by the election into the **European Academy of Science and Arts** in 2000. His outstanding contributions to the discipline of business administration have recently been acknowledged in 2003 by an **honorary doctorate** by the University of Bern.

2 Mapping His Research Track

Up to 2003, Klaus Brockhoff had published an impressive *oeuvre* of 21 books and 265 articles. A person who becomes professor at 30 years of age and who has always documented and published his scientific ideas thoroughly certainly offers sufficient material for an appreciation of his scientific career, which goes above and beyond a modest compilation of life stations. However, this **abundance of publications** does not make life easy for the observer. A long, continuous creative period enables Klaus Brockhoff to make important contributions on a wide variety of subject areas. Klaus Brockhoff has used the opportunity of an undisturbed development of our subject area to deal with different topics throughout his career and to continuously link them. A laudation, which has to concentrate on extracting the main ideas, will have to ignore one or the other contribution which fails to commit itself to a clear classification.

A person who completed his diploma in economics in Bonn and later another diploma in business administration in Münster, and commenced with a scientific career in the sixties, had naturally enough a microeconomic perspective and focused on the most promising direction of our discipline towards decision orientation. Moreover, as the first disciple of Horst Albach and being mathematically talented, it was expected that he would also deliver contributions to optimizing processes in different functional areas of the firm which in those days were considered evidence of scientific talent. Klaus Brockhoff, however, went his own way which he followed consequently throughout his career. In his Ph.D. (1966) he focused on the **company as a coherent unit**. Is company growth determined by changes in the assortment? A person who poses such questions wants to explain, first of all, before recommending actions. Consequently, he transferred the problem in the first step into an **econometric model**. With this modeling, Brockhoff seems to fulfill the expectations of roles at that time. What is new, however, is that this model was **empirically tested** with data from both the automobile industry and the chemical industry. However, he does not limit himself to the simple relations between company growth and changes in the assortment. Rather, the economist in Klaus Brockhoff also incorporates the changes in national income in his model.

A focus on the enterprise, a consideration of the overall economic environment, the formal modeling of hypotheses and large-scale empirical tests – **these features of his Ph.D. became the brand names of Klaus Brockhoff's scientific work**.

In his Ph.D., Klaus Brockhoff became aware of the special significance of new products in an assortment. One of the most important findings of his Ph.D.-thesis was the observation that "the survival of individual enterprises is dependent on the introduction of new products" (161). This fact directed his further scientific activity to the following two major research areas:

- First, to product policy as a task of **marketing** and
- Second, to product innovation as a task of **technology management**.

In his **habilitation thesis,** *"Planning Research in Enterprises"*, he concentrates first of all on the mostly un-investigated field in business administration, research and development. It is remarkable that the title of the first edition was changed in his second edition. With *"Research Projects and Research Programs – Their Evaluation and Selection"* as a new title, Klaus Brockhoff takes a clear decision theory-oriented position and suggests which objects R&D management should focus on. The breaking down of the subject into two aspects – project level and program level – later becomes a general paradigm. He, first of all, considers the assessment of individual research projects and then the planning of the whole research program of an enterprise.

In this work, the variety of the problem aspects that is worked out in detail is fascinating: from a business administration point of view the investment perspective is in the foreground which is also in clear contrast to the then dominating practitioner concepts of evaluating research projects and programs. However, it is indisputably an investment problem of itself which, due to the degree of innovativeness, poses special problems of measuring and evaluation. Brockhoff addresses this challenge and discusses in detail the estimation problems which arise: the consideration of complex objectives and influences which emanate from the area of complex information processes. His differentiated observations on the consideration of time in the planning models were groundbreaking.

You just have to realize the boldness of this emerging scholar: In the sixties, research and development was the natural domain of scientists and engineers. And then a young economist turns up, opposes the use of "tradition and rules of thumb" (Preface) by **the evaluation and selection of research projects and programs,** and instead of this propagates **optimizations** using concepts of investment theory. That must have seemed "inappropriate, interfering, amateurish and unqualified or exotic" (preface 5th edition, R&D). With this, Klaus Brockhoff disputed implicitly the technological definition monopoly of industry researchers and assigned R&D to be the subject of hard-headed business objectives.

It could have been expected that the guild of R&D specialists would close ranks against him. However, this was not the case. Simply because Brockhoff had rendered them a great service: research and development were no longer the playgrounds of genius inventors or tolerated sheds for tinkering around, but are beyond dispute established and institutionalized as operational functions. Their contribution to the success of the business can be quantified and rewarded. Researchers and developers do not have to fear being a victim of an arbitrary budget cutback anymore, because it can be shown that they represent important immaterial investments and not lost consumption expenditures.

A scholar who, after his call to Kiel, had to teach business administration as a minor in the economics program had to prove himself in many subject areas which are highly specialized today. Broad knowledge in general business administration was required. The paradigm at that time demanded a preoccupation **with decision and planning problems**. Klaus Brockhoff made it his duty to supply his students with contemporary lectures and published textbooks on operations research and forecasting methods for planning purposes. Here, he could use his body of knowledge in formal methods: here, he was mainly application-oriented.

However, a new direction began to emerge. In the seventies, at the initiative of Eberhard Witte, a **focus program** by our German National Science Foundation was set up which brought closer together colleagues working on model-theoretical and empirical issues under the subject "Empirical Decision Theory". They met three times a year and discussed theoretical approaches, methodological challenges and empirical findings. Brockhoff's contribution was an experimental examination on **Delphi forecasts** through computer dialogs. This focus program achieved its aim. Henceforth, theoretical and empirical research were no longer understood as opposing research tasks but as complementary ones, just as Klaus Brockhoff had practiced it in his doctoral thesis. Now the combination of explanation and optimization was indisputably considered to be the appropriate program for a scientifically oriented business administration – in agreement with international standards.

During the years of his activities in Kiel – firstly in the general field of business administration, and secondly in the field of marketing – Klaus Brockhoff did not lose sight of research and development management. He always emphasized that the management of R&D is closely related to marketing because the production of new products and their introduction to the market are activities, which can be allotted to both of his special research areas. Nevertheless, it appeared as if it would have to remain a fringe area. Klaus Brockhoff was not just encouraged by business practitioners. At the end of the seventies when he suggested to the local economy to support the introduction of a new discipline of "Management of Research and Development", he received the response that this was something that should be left to the experts in practice. However, early in the eighties several developments took place simultaneously, which provided him the opportunity once again of devoting himself to his favorite subject.

Under the new keyword "**Innovation management**", his efforts on researching the management of research and development were redefined. Innovations were receiving more and more attention from the economy and politics. It was possible to found a small research unit for innovation management which put the coming research work on a solid financial ground. The re-negotiations of his contract in Kiel after Klaus Brockhoff received the call from INSEAD in Fontainebleau allowed him to transform the small research centre into an **Institute for Innovation Research in Business Administration.** This expansion of the Institute for business administration implied that a **new chair** had to be filled: Klaus Brockhoff's dreams were finally realized: He became the first chaired professor for Technology and Innovation Management in Germany.

It was sheer luck that Jürgen Hauschildt was also searching for new tasks in his subject "Organisation". He was able to integrate his theoretical and empirical experience from the collaboration on Witte's project "Columbus" into the new institute. Klaus Brockhoff and Jürgen Hauschildt headed the Institute for Innovation Research in Business Administration together, offered a special business administration program "Innovation management", founded and coordinated the already mentioned DFG-focus program "Theory of Innovation in Enterprises" which worked in the same spirit as its predecessor. This successful development was finally crowned when a postgraduate seminar ("Graduiertenkolleg") with the topic "Business Administration for Technology and Innovation" was founded. The seminar, which was run by Klaus Brockhoff, was a great success. Its duration was extended to the longest possible period of nine years. More than 300 publications resulted from this, among them 72 monographs in the field of technology and innovation management.

The **great life achievement** of Klaus Brockhoff is to be seen exactly here: he established an independent subject area for business administration. The setting up of similar chairs at other German-speaking universities can be traced back to his involvement.

With these impressive management achievements, his self-conception as a researcher was extended. He began his activity as a **specialist** for R&D management, but comprehends himself today as a **generalist** for strategic technology management. Although his most important work was originally entitled "Research and Development – Planning and Control", the number of chapters about operative and tactical planning was relatively reduced in contrast to chapters about fundamental and strategic planning in the course of the five editions.

However, Klaus Brockhoff's development is not to be concluded with this labeling: In his latest publications, he integrated his earlier reflections on information behavior with that of technology management. What was dealt with in his habilitation thesis as "Organization of Information Flow" is seen more comprehensively today: research and development serve the production of new knowledge and are thus elementary tasks of **knowledge management**. Klaus Brockhoff extended this production perspective, in which he placed knowledge utilization on equal grounds next to knowledge production. As a result of this, he achieved a totally new understanding of management tasks for research and development.

3 Particular Highlights

3.1 Management of Research and Development

About 160 contributions of the scientific *oeuvre* of Klaus Brockhoff are devoted to the field of research and development management respectively technology management. In contrast to the dominating trends especially in the American literature, **the individual innovation process** is not the center of his reflections. This topic of his publications comprises only a fifth of his *oeuvre*. His preferred focus is the **research and development program of the entire company** with about 60% of his publications. Klaus Brockhoff, however, does not deny his training as a qualified economist: A further fifth of his publications focuses on **research and development issues at a macro level**: economic studies on different industries, economic surveys on governmental promotion policy, on training, on the protection of intellectual property, on measuring of national research and development activity and its productivity.

From the basis of his habilitation thesis, which was published in two editions, Klaus Brockhoff provided an abundance of contributions which deal with the forecasting, the budgeting and, the controlling of research and development expenditures. Many of these individual publications then entered into his classical textbook "*Research and Development – Planning and Control*", which is now available in its fifth edition. The main chapters of this book demonstrate the foci of his research:

A person who wishes to control an operational unit of a company by the use of planning has to define the tasks very precisely and measure the characteristic control variables. Brockhoff examined different **measuring conventions of input and output variables** in various publications. This includes reflections on deflation indices of R&D expenditures, comparisons of official statistics from different countries, revealing problems with measuring patents, discussions about identifying R&D expenditures in annual reports, suggestions on how to determine the degree of innovation as well as contributions on measuring the innovation success by means of product innovation rates based on the share of turnover coming from new products.

Under the keyword "**strategic planning**", Brockhoff's publications on S-curves, technology portfolios and on technology management are well-known. He was interested in particular in the coordination of **marketing with technology management**. This becomes a serious problem when technological change forces a previously dominating technology to be relinquished for the sake of another one. Brockhoff is especially fascinated by the mastering of information problems such as the measurement of marginal effectiveness and efficiency, the technologically influenced constraints and the analysis of competitors' activities. His special interest was the systemizing of concepts for the illustration of technology pressure, market pull and project volumes in **portfolios**. Many colleagues and students of Klaus Brockhoff learnt and adopted this matrix illustration which he liked so much to use. In everyday life of research, we spoke of Klaus Brockhoff's "four field economy" in this context, with which the majority of problems and relations could be clearly categorized at different degrees of abstraction.

The keyword "**operative planning**" comprises two large topics, which have been systematically investigated by Klaus Brockhoff: budgeting and estimation of production functions from research and development.

With the area of **budgeting**, the technological ideas are turned into financial demands. The procurement of financial resources for projects and programs is the operational consequence of the forecasting of technological developments. Technological forecasts have to be accompanied by estimates of market opportunities. An insight has to be gained into the anticipated cash-flows. The entrepreneur has to commit himself to what can be afforded and what should be funded additionally. With the budgetary decision, research and development becomes an investment, i.e. to a principally future-oriented and, at the same time, a financial activity. Budgeting has to free itself from its past orientation which still predominates the thinking in the real world, when practitioners measure the R&D budget as so-called "research intensity" in percentage of turnover (of the past).

This investment perspective of research and development has an important consequence: this immaterial investment object has to stand up to comparison with other investment objects. Should financial resources flow more into material investments or in other immaterial investments, such as advertising? The decision is taken by comparing the **marginal productivities**. Klaus Brockhoff estimates the relationship between input and output with the help of a Cobb-Douglas production function by using data from the chemical industry. The significant finding was that the marginal productivity of research and development in this industry is greater than that of advertising.

Under the keyword "**tactical planning**" Klaus Brockhoff's publications deal with project evaluation, project sequence planning and project termination. Here, Klaus Brockhoff carries out his investigations at the level of the projects. His topology and critical judgment of **project evaluation procedures** are considered standard knowledge of R&D project management today.

Based on tangible findings on strengths and, above all, on weaknesses of industrial research and development, Brockhoff developed sophisticated reflections on **project sequence planning**, in particular for parallel versus sequential project planning. In this respect, he is increasingly interested in shortening the length of the development process.

Finally, he also looked at the correction of misjudgments under the keyword of **project termination**. Empirically, this problem is approached by determining the influencing factors of project success or failure. So appealing this approach may be, for Klaus Brockhoff, a theoretical concept offers a better basis for a project termination decision. He developed a rule which is based on dynamic optimization and applies the principle of decision trees.

In **controlling,** planning and control are systematically linked to each other. It is only consistent that Klaus Brockhoff does not just limit himself to deriving recommendations on forecasting and decision-making, rather he suggests to constantly pose the question of what has been achieved. This issue does not occur after completion of a project but consistently during the progress of the projects. It is necessary to determine the deviations between actual and plan with respect to the **technical specifications**, to the costs and the deadlines, as well as to introduce the necessary corrections as early as possible.

Klaus Brockhoff personally regretted not having had sufficient time to extend his main textbook on research and development to the topics of organization and leadership. This is surprising because he himself had supplied very important preparatory work on **interface management**. This has to do with the **hierarchy-free coordination** of company sub-sectors. Moreover, this has to do with quite a fundamental issue, which reaches far beyond the traditional coordination of company function areas: coordination between cooperating firms, company subsidiaries, strategic business units, projects up to the coordination of individual members of a project team. Again and again, Klaus Brockhoff discussed the various possibilities of a hierarchy-free coordination: through programs and plans, incentive systems, transfer prices, co-location, job rotation, training, not to mention the hierarchy-supplementing instruments such as liaison officers, staff activity, steering committees and other commissions. Friends and academic students are already looking forward to a new chapter in the next edition of "Research and Development" on this subject.

3.2 Information, Forecasting and Decision Support

Beginning with his habilitation thesis on the evaluation and selection of research projects and research programs, Klaus Brockhoff became interested in the problem of suitable **data bases for planning** very early in his career. On the one hand, he surveyed to what extent planning and forecasting are carried out for certain problem areas and certain methods. On the other hand, he dealt with objects for which future success was very difficult to forecast. Based on the finding that the combination of several different forecasting procedures results in better forecasts than with just one method, emphasis was put on the derivation of group forecasts at the end of the sixties, e.g. the **Delphi-method**. Here, the deviating judgments of persons have to be anonymously justified so that a consensus is reached after several rounds. This method which is especially important for investment management fascinated Klaus Brockhoff and he therefore attempted to examine it with respect to its validity. For this, he programmed a respective computer dialog and then came to the devastating conclusion that even bank managers were not in the position to better forecast short-term interest rates with this system than by simply using the past value. As in many other fields, his reflections flowed into his books. For this reason, his monograph, *Forecasting Procedures for Enterprise Planning,* was a standard textbook for many years.

After a thorough investigation and construction of a topology of information behavior, he was engaged increasingly in the improvement of **information bases for decision-making**. His application fields were, first of all, the consumer information sector and, second, sales support. He implemented an information system for customers for a used-car dealer and investigated whether their information behavior reveals the importance of different car attributes. Nowadays, this is a matter of course by Internet systems such as mobile.de. However, without the earlier research, it would not be known that the sequence in which the consumers ask for details, provides information that can be used for market research purposes.

3.3 Marketing

Even though the primary interest of Klaus Brockhoff is research and development, he was also intensively concerned with marketing. Both fields complement each other. Research planning has to do with the development of technologies for products or for the products themselves. How their sales develop over time decides in the end on the product's success. In so far, it is no surprise that Klaus Brockhoff was preoccupied throughout his career with product policies - a subject which belongs to the core of marketing.

Klaus Brockhoff started brilliantly with the publication of an article in the highly reputated journal, *Econometrica,* with which he gained a high popularity at the age of 28. This article reports the most important results of his doctoral thesis about company growth and assortment changes based on a statistical estimation of **life cycles of products**.

Just to explain and make forecasts how the sales and profit would develop over time was not challenging enough for Klaus Brockhoff. He also wanted to tackle the **optimal design of product attributes**. Starting from the idea that products are subjectively perceived and therefore product positioning has to be realized in the perceived attribute space, he developed, together with Sönke Albers, a procedure with which it is possible to find the optimal positions for new products. He also examined methods to determine ideal points. Later, he included conjoint analysis and choice models. His **textbook** "Product Policy" is still the only textbook on this topic in the German-speaking world and is now published in its fourth edition.

Besides the field of product policy, Klaus Brockhoff, with his micro-economic background, also analyzed **pricing policy**. Here, from the Gutenberg school the double kinked price-response function emerged which he had extended to the case of a duopoly while he was working on his Ph.D. After he had dealt with ideal points in the problem of product positioning, he investigated how appropriate price-response functions should look. He returned to testing Gutenberg's price-response function once again when, for the first time in the history of the cigarette market, the price of cigarettes changed in the course of the introduction of the brand WEST.

When private television stations became popular in Germany, he analyzed the sector of **television advertising** more intensively. For the first time, television stations had the opportunity to determine the duration of the broadcast advertising blocks, while the audience could zap from one station to the next. Therefore, Klaus Brockhoff conducted research on what the consequences of these changes would be.

3.4 General Business Administration

Even though Klaus Brockhoff's research is concentrated in the fields of technology and innovation management and marketing, excursions into many other research areas can be discovered in the course of his career. He was and is one of the last researchers who can be endowed with the predicate of an expert researcher in all fields of **general business administration**. He dealt with such diverse fields such as fee regulations for sewage treatment systems, stakeholder reports on social auditing, planning the portfolio of securities, and the optimal company size in a socialist economy. He was concerned again and again with legislative projects for example, with fee regulating for deep-sea mining.

Another of his **research areas** was the **university** itself. He took a closer look at teaching methods and discussed if case studies were better than the systematic presentation of materials. Moreover, he also examined to what extent the education at universities should be differentiated and what effect the introduction of a scientific procedure would have. Additionally, he discussed the planning and regulation of universities, first of the public and then the private ones. At the same time, the regulating of trust funds had always interested him.

A person who has such a broad approach to business administration is also in the position to preoccupy himself with the **history of his subject**. Therefore, he presented the achievements of Gutenberg's theoretical reflections and the overall achievements of business administration. Finally, he compiled important contributions from the earlier business administration period in a book and described them in their context to today's reflections in order to facilitate the access to historical sources.

4 Manager of Research and Science Politician

Klaus Brockhoff is not only an important scientist but also well-known for his contributions as a **manager of research** and as a **science politician**. Before he became a professor in 1970, he worked as a manager for the research lab Batelle. Before he left, he was responsible for more than 30 scientists and the acquisition of enough projects to fund them. This is comparable to the position of a partner with large consulting companies. Thus, he was already a very experienced research manager before he entered academia.

He was able to make use of this experience when he became the **dean of the faculty of economics and social sciences** of Christian-Albrechts-University at Kiel at a very early age from 1971-73. As a result of his many interactions within the university, he gained wide respect not only among his fellow scientists but also with the university administrators. Because of his experience in applying for funds, he was able to get funds constantly from our German National Science Foundation and the Volkswagen Foundation.

Klaus Brockhoff was very persistent in establishing the discipline of technology and innovation management. When the first Graduiertenkollegs were announced by our German National Science Foundation he was the first to apply for it and was granted one such Graduiertenkolleg for the maximum time of 9 years. He was chairperson and also a very effective manager of a research unit with 7 professors and more than 20 doctoral students in addition to his regular duties at the university. During the same time, he was able to acquire funds for **visiting professorships**. As a result, he invited a number of researchers with whom he collaborated intensively. These include researchers like Alok Chakrabarti, Vithala Rao, Alan Pearson, Ashok Gupta, Ramaiya Balachandra, and Kjell Grønhaug. Given his enormous experience in funding he was elected to the **board of trustees of the Volkswagen Foundation** in 1997.

He was very active in the organizations of his own profession. From 1982-83, he was the **chairman of the division of marketing professors** within the association of professors of business administration of German speaking universities. From 1989-91 he was elected to the position of the **chairman of that association**. During his tenure, he was accompanied by Jürgen Hauschildt as the Vice-Chairman, he had to deal with all the questions resulting from the reunification of Germany. Eventually, it was in 1999 that he and others were able to establish a new division of professors for technology and innovation management. Because of his merits and efforts he was elected as **honorary chairman**.

He was also very active among business managers. In 1983, he founded the **Kiel Association for Business Administration** together with entrepreneurs and managers in order not only to support the research at the University of Kiel but also to disseminate knowledge from science into practice. In 1989, he founded the **Marketing-Club** Schleswig-Holstein which is an association of top executives in marketing. The umbrella organization of all German Marketing Clubs awards a marketing prize every year to a company that applies marketing philosophy successfully. Because of the tremendous success of the "**Schleswig-Holstein Music Festival**" he promoted the application of this organization which eventually **was awarded the price. This award was a great acknowledgement of all his initiatives.**

Throughout his career, he has earned an excellent reputation as a political advisor for science related-issues. As a result, he was appointed as a **member to the "Wissenschaftsrat"** which is a steering committee for a variety of science-related decisions. It consists of the ministers of education of the 16 German states and 16 additional scientists. It decides on priorities of funding university projects with federal money and consults the ministers in their decisions.

He has another ability, namely, to manage the funds of scientific foundations. Over 20 years, he has managed all the funds of university-related foundations in Kiel and was able to outperform the regular rate of return for foundations. Therefore, he is now responsible for the **fund management** of the Volkswagen Foundation.

From 1999 to 2004, he has been **rector of WHU** and has successfully governed this institution. Under his rectorship the school could be enlarged by 60% with respect to funds, professorships, and students. He is one of the rare species who can do both high-level research and also manage such units.

Part 1:

Innovation and Strategy

Jürgen Hauschildt and Sören Salomo

„Too many innovations, all at once..."

Relationship between Degree of Innovativeness and Success of Innovations

Prof. Dr. Dr. h.c. *Jürgen Hauschildt*, Emeritus, Institute of Innovation Research, Christian-Albrechts-University at Kiel, and Dr. *Sören Salomo*, Chair for Technology and Innovation Management, Technical University of Berlin.

1 Is more innovative better?

Politicians and public opinion seem to be driven by innovation euphoria. The idea of a positive and linear relationship between the degree of innovativeness and the innovation success is widely accepted: More innovative projects are more successful! Consequently, substantial or breakthrough change instead of incremental development is demanded for companies, universities and for society in general. Progress is associated and conceptually mixed with discontinuity. The degree of innovativeness becomes a key variable (Salomo 2003; Schlaak 1999). It is the degree of novelty of a product or process innovation which is relevant, i.e. a subjective assessment of the amount of change before and after a deliberate innovative activity.

Is the basic proposition realistic that projects with high degrees of innovativeness also promise a higher return on investment than projects aiming only at incremental change? Brockhoff remains sceptical. He illustrates his ideas with a quotation from the biography of Rudolf Diesel (Brockhoff 1999, 237): American diesel engine producers, who were initially less successful, [...]*"wanted to introduce too many innovations, all at once, into their new constructions and entered the market too quickly"*[1] (Diesel 1983, 298).

2 State of the art of empirical research: Negative and zero relationships

Brockhoff's scepticism seems to be supported by the results of empirical research analysing the relationship between the degree of innovativeness and innovation success:

- Crawford published a seminal paper in 1979 dealing with this relationship. He gathered 32 relevant studies which were available at that time. Out of these, seven studies were chosen as adequate for a systematic assessment. Following his calculations, 36% of all innovation processes were failures (Crawford 1979). Although he did not focus on the degree of innovativeness, this result certainly implies **some doubt about the naïve innovativeness performance relationship**. Whether innovativeness is really positively related to performance is even more questionable as "non-failure" projects not necessarily result in successful innovations.

[1] Translation from German: Die zunächst wenig erfolgreichen amerikanischen Dieselmotorenfabrikanten „[...] haben in ihrer neuen Construction zuviel Neuerungen auf einmal einführen wollen und haben dieselben zu früh in die Praxis hinausgegeben".

- In a systematic review of the relevant innovation management literature, also including German studies, Schlaak (1999) identifies 18 studies explicitly reporting results for the innovativeness success relationship. 11 studies present results confirming a **negative relationship**, two cases show both positive and negative relationships and five studies either report no or an inverse u-shaped relationship (Schlaak 1999).
- It is interesting to note that a negative relationship between innovativeness and success is mainly reported in studies dating several years back. Research building upon data from the past 15 years show more differentiated results. Improvements in measurement approaches and econometric methods applied may help to explain this shift in results. Specifically the increased diffusion of multivariate analyses may help to better isolate individual effects of innovativeness as it allows controlling for other performance antecedents (Gatignon and Yuereb 1997; Swink 2000; Salomo, Steinhoff, and Trommsdorff 2003). Following the meta analysis presented by Henard and Szymanski (2001) the correlation between the degree of innovativeness and innovation success is on average .25. However, correlation varies significantly between all studies included in the meta analysis from -.62 to .81. Research using path models to explain the performance effects of innovativeness generally present a direct but **not very strong impact** of the degree of innovativeness on innovation success (Schlaak 1999; Hauschildt 1999).
- However, most recent research continuously shows no performance effect of innovativeness (Atuahene-Gima and Evangelista 2000; Tatikonda and Rosenthal 2000; Salomo, Gemünden, and Billing 2003) or reports a positive impact only in the case that adequate **innovation management tools** are applied highly in innovative projects (Olson et al. 2001).

Finally, asking experienced R&D managers repeatedly reveals that: "One third of the projects are outright failures, one third is successful and the outcome of the residual projects is still and may be for a long time unknown".

Overall, empirical research does not confirm a positive relationship between innovativeness and innovation success. Rather, negative relationships seem to dominate. In the case that positive relationships are detected they remain very weak.

If these results are replicated it seems to be legitimate to ask, whether radical innovations really pay off. If substantial or "game changing" innovations do not show a positive performance relationship it may be a more rational strategy to rely on less radical innovations.

However, before drawing such a conclusion we need to assess whether the reported empirical results are not biased or otherwise distorted. **No or negative relationships between degree of innovativeness and innovation success may result from conceptual or methodological problems of the respective research.**

3 Problems with the conceptual model in empirical research

(1) To begin with, results suggesting a negative relationship between innovativeness and performance are not totally unexpected. Risk and complexity increase with stronger degrees of innovativeness. Hence, overcoming or managing these barriers increases costs and reduces innovation success.

Innovation management can generally be understood as coping with complexity through application of resources. Innovations are complex because of the vagueness of the problem structure and scope, and the uncertainty of potential outcomes. The unpredictability of the problem components and the conflicts inherent in the problem further add to the complexity. The management of innovation has to reduce this complexity. With increasing degrees of innovativeness, complexity can be expected to increase disproportionately. At the same time, the risk of failure increases.

In order to reduce complexity, resources need to be allocated. Due to the innovative character of the problem this includes specifically human resources. Team members need to intellectually tackle the problem, they need to choose a creative approach in order to generate and accumulate new knowledge, and they also need to tenaciously solve conflicts. Additionally, innovations often demand handling new materials, tools and external partners. Such a new process needs time and incurs costs. Specifically time requirements are often underestimated. Thus, increasing degrees of innovativeness go along with increased resource requirements, and following the relationship of innovativeness and complexity we expect radical innovation to disproportionately demand resources.

Pursuing highly innovative projects inevitably involves incorrect assessments on all relevant levels of the problem and, thus, reduced effectiveness and efficiency of the innovative efforts:

- The danger of technical, market related, financial or organizational failure increases when pursuing highly innovative projects. Failure in these dimensions results in projects not meeting their effectiveness objectives. In other words, this would correspond to lacking benefits from innovation in the project profit loss account.
- As projects strive to meet their goals and intend to reduce the risks more resources will be deployed for the innovative task. Consequently, costs increase and meeting efficiency objectives becomes more difficult. Again, this would correspond to increased costs in the project profit loss account.

Overall, the innovation success is reduced and may even turn out to be negative. At least the subjective performance evaluation will be affected by these mechanisms as effectiveness and / or efficiency outcomes do not meet expectations.

This corresponds well to Brockhoff's idea (Brockhoff 1999, 236):

"Increased newness of product innovations can substantiate the expectation that an increased share of the market potential is obtainable within the planning period. However, there is some reason to believe that the growth rate of these market returns will decrease. As the increase in risks follows the increase in newness, most probably disproportionately, an optimal degree of innovativeness can be derived."[2]

Following this rational, degree of innovativeness and innovation success should display a u-shaped relationship. Assuming linear relationships and testing the propositions accordingly will inevitably result in non-findings.

(2) Assessing radical innovation with the same measurement instrument which was designed to evaluate projects on the basis of previous performance probabilities is not possible. Technological breakthrough and the creation of totally new markets do not only promise a significant return but may allow success that goes far beyond every expectation. The introduction of the PC, the diffusion of mobile telephones or the success story of the anti-baby pill may serve as examples. Each of these cases allowed the leading firms financial returns which were never expected from an ex ante perspective. A rational assessment of opportunities and risks would have probably resulted in totally unrealistic and mostly useless expectations. Firms embarking on such a high risk radical innovation path had a vague expectation of a tremendous success without at least in the beginning being able to provide realistic figures of what this success could result in. And, indeed, some of these entrepreneurs and companies made their hopes for extraordinary success become true. In the long run, reality probably even exceeded their most optimistic hopes.

In other words, some innovations have the potential for success exceeding by far the most extreme level on a performance scale developed and used for the majority of incremental and moderate innovations. These innovations demand a different measurement scale both for the degree of innovativeness and for the innovation success. They are very rare and exceptional events which do not follow the rules developed for the standard game. Simply looking for the relationship between innovativeness and innovation success may not be sufficient to capture these rare events. They may never enter the sample. And even if the sample should include some of these cases they would probably be identified as outliers and eliminated from further analysis. Hence,

---

[2] Translation from German: „Zunehmender Neuigkeitsgrad von Produktinnovationen kann die Erwartung begründen, innerhalb des Planungshorizonts auch größere Anteile des Marktpotentials zu gewinnen. Vermutlich wird aber die Zuwachsrate dieser Ertragserwartungen sinken. Gleichzeitig aber steigt das Risiko [...] vermutlich mit steigendem Neuigkeitsgrad überproportional an. [...] Daraus lässt sich ein optimaler Neuigkeitsgrad ableiten."

results indicating no or negative relationships between innovativeness and success may be explained by an analysis focussing on only a narrow window of reality, excluding so called outliers.

(3) No or negative relationships between innovativeness and success may also be explained by varying types of degree of innovativeness.

Innovation projects tackling moderate degrees of innovativeness last, on average, between two and three years when excluding part of the fuzzy front end before official problem definition. Radical Innovations often need between 7 and 15 years of development (Leifer et al. 2000). During the course of this long lasting development process the degree of innovativeness will be assessed differently. One can expect that the objectives for the degree of newness will be determined along with the problem definition and latest when the project is officially installed. Cyert and March (1963) suggest that such problem definition will initially follow neighbouring and recently defined problems. This may result in underestimating the degree of innovativeness at the beginning of the process. Specifically, this can happen because most peripheral and following problems will only be identified, excluded or included after thorough intellectual occupation with the innovative task.

This has significant consequences: At the beginning of an innovation process an articulated degree of innovativeness is a development objective, at the end of the process it becomes a result. It is not at all clear which of these two very distinct concepts are evaluated in the above mentioned empirical research. Further, it remains questionable whether the respondent is able to recall the initial intended degree of innovativeness when interviewed towards the end of the innovation process. Respondents may even rationalize their performance assessment with respect to the finally realized degree of innovativeness. Research analyzing the relationship of innovativeness and success will not deliver valid results on an aggregate level if the time of measurement is not reported, and varies between different studies. There is some reason to believe that the above mentioned studies assess different degrees of innovativeness.

(4) The direct relationship between innovativeness and success is also subject to moderating and mediating effects from a variety of different other variables. Between determining a degree of innovativeness as an objective and achieving market success with the innovation, several management activities influence the development process. Adequate econometric methods would enable an assessment of the individual direct and indirect performance effect of innovativeness. However, this would require controlling for all management instruments identified as relevant by the multiplicity of innovation management studies – a research endeavour by far exceeding sample sizes and research resources typical and possible in management research.

4 Problems related to the research methods

The conflicting and rather diffuse results presented by empirical research on the relationship of innovativeness and innovation performance may by partly explained by methodological problems. Reviewing these potential problems allows first, to gain a better understanding of the research results and second, it offers insights into promising methodological approaches for further research on this important topic.

4.1 Measurement of degree of innovativeness

Building on the results presented by Schlaak (1999) and Salomo (2003) degree of innovativeness is best understood as a multidimensional phenomenon. Apart from the two "classical" market and technology dimensions the degree of innovativeness is also determined by different aspects of internal and external resource fit. However, most empirical research investigating degree of innovativeness ignores such a multidimensional perspective and even reduces this construct to a single item. Often, innovativeness is only measured as a dichotomous variable rating innovation either as incremental or radical. Such a measurement approach does not account for the complexity of the phenomenon and allows no valid assessment of the degree of innovativeness.

As the degree of innovativeness can be assessed in different dimensions, investigating a relationship between innovativeness and success on the aggregated level may not be adequate or meaningful. Innovativeness measured in several sub-dimensions may still form a continuous scale from incremental to radical. Each level of innovativeness will then result from a combination of different degrees of newness of each sub-dimension. However, if the performance relationship of each sub-dimension varies or even conflicts, the aggregated measure of innovativeness may not always show a linear relationship with innovation success (Salomo 2003). In order to really assess the relationship of innovativeness and success not only valid measurement but also transparency about type and combination of each sub-dimension with its individual performance relationship is required.

Validity of construct measurement is further determined by the research design with respect to the type and number of informants. Although at least the technology dimension of innovativeness should allow an objective assessment of the amount of change, innovativeness is mostly a question of individual perception. Evaluating innovativeness is consequently related to a subject and may vary all dependent on the perspective of each individual. Empirical research needs to account for these circumstances by controlling for a potential informant bias. However, such a measurement approach is not a standard procedure as most studies still rely on information obtained by only one person (Ernst 2001). Although a multi-informant design not per se secures validity, there is some reason to believe that innovation team members with different functional backgrounds may assess each sub-dimension of innovativeness differently. Also, accounting for the potential difference between expected and realized degree of innovativeness it seems necessary to control the hierarchical position of informants. The assessment of these degrees of innovativeness will probably vary between management and team members.

Following the general approach of collecting data with self-administered questionnaires introduces the risk of halo effects. Although personal interviews may help to control such a source of bias, most of the above-mentioned empirical research relies exclusively on questionnaires.

4.2 Measurement of innovation success

Adequate performance assessment of innovation projects has already been discussed in great detail and needs no replication (Hauschildt 1991). However, it is remarkable that most of the empirical research ignores this discussion and relies on rather basic measurement of innovation success – another reason why results on the relationship of innovativeness and success are not satisfying.

Additionally, the performance assessment of radical innovation may face a specific problem. Projects aiming at radical innovations generally run for many years before market launch of the new product is realized. This creates a dilemma for empirical research which wants to analyze such projects: In order to assess innovation management activity in detail and with little bias, research needs to gather the data close to the relevant events. But a valid performance assessment including market information is only possible to a limited extent at that time. On the other hand, capturing success measures at a much later project stage together with much earlier process activities will inevitably increase a bias through post hoc rationalization and hindsight effects.

Empirical research normally chooses to follow the first path in this dilemma and tries to evaluate innovation success by comparing realized results with individual expectations. Classical performance indicators based on accounting measures (e.g. RoI) are not available early enough and, thus, excluded. Innovation performance is not assessed through objective indicators but relies on subjective evaluation to what extent objectives are achieved. Innovations of different size, complexity, radicalness, and performance outcome are levelled. The scale used to assess success is censored upwards for radical innovations. Hence, a positive performance relationship of very innovative ventures can not be detected.

4.3 Sample selection problems

Most empirical researcher follow beaten tracks when building their sample (Ernst 2001). It is a typical approach to contact companies with the request to select an innovation project which best fits to the respective research question. The researcher has only limited influence on this selection procedure and runs the risk that only projects of incremental or moderate degree of innovativeness enter the sample (Salomo 2003). Information about radical innovations often touches critical technology and market related aspects which may significantly determine the future competitive position of the company (Leifer 2000). Disclosing information about less critical but also less innovative projects is probably preferred. Additionally, the development of radical innovation is characterized by strong uncertainties and unexpected discontinuities which further reduce the willingness to disclose information. Biased sample selection can also be expected because of the generally long project duration of radical innovations. With increasing project duration, identifying competent team members becomes more difficult. It is much easier to convince a team member who has followed a complete project to participate in the data collection then someone who only feels competent for a specific part of the overall project. Overall, several reasons add to the hypothesis that highly innovative or radical innovations have been excluded from most empirical research in innovation management. This reduction in variance with respect to the degree of innovativeness may also explain the mixed results on the relationship of innovativeness and success.

5 Reorientation: Is the perspective of empirical research on innovation success adequate?

Innovation management research mainly focuses on projects as a level of analysis. Innovations are understood as individual processes or projects for which degree of innovativeness and innovation success can be assessed independently from other innovations. Apart from this dominant perspective, research also identifies organisations as relevant entities of analysis, in which individual innovation processes are embedded. However, these institutional aspects are generally only assessed in terms of a contingency for individual innovation processes, their degree of innovativeness and innovation success.

Nevertheless, the overall innovation performance of the company is determined by the total of all individual innovations pursued. This supports the idea of striving for success with every individual innovation project. Consequently, each project manager has to be in charge of her or his individual project. From the aggregated perspective, i.e. the perspective of the top management, this is different: Here, not the individual success but rather the overall performance of all projects is relevant. The top management perspective is a portfolio perspective. Somehow exaggerated, in case only one out of 100 projects is successful, but this project easily covers all the costs of the failures, top management will be praised. All failures will probably be of no further interest – with some reason as the top management is mainly accountable for the bottom line. This separates them from civil servants.

Taking such a portfolio approach puts the reported probabilities of failure as a measure of innovation success into perspective. Not only the very fact of success but specifically the size of financial return is of utmost importance. But neither the size of success nor the real costs of failures are in the focus of the above-mentioned empirical studies. The performance assessment of innovation portfolios is generally missing. Research evaluates individual projects like an audit authority and does not evaluate the overall innovation program like an investor. It focuses on the individual responsibility of a project manager and not on the bottom line responsibility of the top management. Only if the portfolio consists of one project, both perspectives are identical.

As a conclusion, research focussing on individual projects when investigating innovation success is by far too limited and not sufficiently precise. This suggests a different starting point for further research as well as a reorientation of innovation management and controlling in practice.

6 Consequences

6.1 For the management of innovation

(1) Without deliberate and thorough assessment of the intended degree of innovativeness at the beginning of each innovation process, every project runs the danger of stumbling unprepared into highly innovative or even radical innovations. The amount of complexity will generally be underestimated which again will result in insufficient resource allocation for development. Such projects run the risk of missing project deadlines and miscalculating project costs. This may even be followed by early project termination. Even if such projects survive, one can probably expect higher costs, compared to a situation of better initial planning. Additional risks may concern customer relationships. Too early market launch may result in call back activities, reclamation, and repair – all with negative effects on customer satisfaction and supplier image.

Underestimating a high degree of innovativeness is probably the rule, not the exception (Schlaak 1999). This is specifically true for smaller companies. Incorrect evaluation of technological and operational problems will expose these to greater risks. But also larger companies may derive from an incorrect initial assessment of the degree of innovativeness. Research aiming at improving the measurement of innovativeness consistently shows that radical innovation is not only determined by technological and market related criteria but includes far reaching changes also in other functional areas (Salomo 2003; Garcia and Calantone 2002; Danneels and Kleinschmidt 2001; Schlaak 1999): With higher degrees of innovativeness change also occurs

- in manufacturing (new production methods and processes),
- in procurement (new suppliers, new materials),
- in the formal and informal organization (new positions, new behaviour, new culture).

After a radical innovation, the company will have changed significantly. Such an innovation will probably affect a larger number of participants: civil service, standardization and regulatory bodies, transfer systems, control systems, support, and communication systems.

In order to evaluate the degree of innovativeness a special measurement instrument is needed. Hauschildt presented already in 1990 a preliminary checklist using 24 items which was developed together with practitioners. This initial innovativeness scale has since then been refined through several empirical studies (Hauschildt 2004). Salomo (2003) builds upon this research and presents a measurement instrument, validated through a multi-informant design, which can be used to assess the degree of innovativeness including radical innovations.

(2) Planning of degree of innovativeness must be followed up by adequate use of innovation management instruments and tools. Potential effectiveness and efficiency losses are best explained using extreme examples: Tackling radical innovations with tools designed for incremental innovations will put effectiveness at stake. Applying management approaches adequate for radical innovation to incremental innovations will result in an efficiency loss.

(3) Thorough evaluation of the degree of innovativeness is also a prerequisite for professional portfolio management. Such assessment aims at creating an optimal mix of newness in the portfolio. This assumes that the degree of innovativeness is positively correlated with risk. Companies balancing their portfolio mix along projects with different degrees of innovativeness will be able to minimize risk and maximize their portfolio performance (Markowitz 1959).

Such a portfolio approach requires a sufficiently large number of innovation projects in order to apply the empirically derived probabilities of success. If a large industrial company reports over 900 R&D projects in its annual report (Thyssen Stahl AG 1995) and if we assume a success rate of about 30%, at least 270 of these projects promise not to be a failure. Small and medium sized companies, however, will have a much harder time to match these requirements.

6.2 For the innovation controlling

Our discussion of the relationship between the degree of innovativeness and innovation success also results in a re-orientation of the innovation controlling. With no doubt planning and controlling quality, time and cost objectives at the individual project level is still the central task of the innovation controlling (Littkemann 1998). This follows from our previous argument that each successful individual project adds to the overall innovation success of the company. However, individual project controlling needs to be completed by project controlling.

In practice, this includes that innovation controlling while still monitoring individual projects must tolerate individual failures in case the overall portfolio is able to support the costs of these failures. This has important consequences:

- Companies need a structured performance assessment of both individual projects and of innovation portfolios. Such a performance assessment needs to account for costs and revenues – not only costs! The importance of an individual project is not determined exclusively by the overall project costs but also by its (potential) revenues. In other words, a project is not important because it consumes a large amount of money and other resources.
- The performance assessment needs to account for the interdependencies between projects. If failure projects enhance the performance of other projects both individual assessments need to be adjusted. In other words, the costs of failures must (partly) add to the costs of successful projects. If that is not possible in individual cases, a lump-sum for imputed risks may be implemented. Such an extra charge would highlight that successful innovations can only thrive in companies with a critical number of dedicated individuals, who are well aware of the fact that a great success may not be within the reach of everybody.

A precise profit and loss accounting for innovation projects has an important human resource management implication: The individual performance assessment of innovation team members will become more just. At least the superficial dichotomous separation of project managers into "winners" and "losers" will become more accurate. Companies which aim at a fair performance assessment and openly disclose the results secure the entrepreneurial spirit even of those who have experienced a failure.

6.3 For the innovation management research

(1) Research and practice must be interested in standardizing the measurement of degree of innovativeness and innovation success. The measurement must be improved.

- Simple dichotomies, like separating projects only into incremental or radical innovations, are neither adequate for gaining a better understanding of relevant issues through research nor adequate for management of innovation projects in practice.
- Scales building on perception of informants should increasingly be substituted or complemented by objective attributes of the innovation. In case subjective measures are inevitable they should at least control for subjective bias. In terms of a multi-informant design independent assessment of the same issue by more than one informant may help to improve measurement.
- Measurement of a complex phenomenon using only one variable is normally not an adequate approach. The reality of innovation has too many facets, which makes assessment of only one or two dimensions insufficient.

(2) It is not sufficient only to ask for project success as a matter of fact. The relevant question from a managerial perspective includes the amount or degree of the success. This again, requires project accounting systems which do not exclusively focus project costs but also include projects earnings. Such a performance assessment can include side- and follow-effects of individual projects and must secure comparability by relating success to the resource input.

Improving and standardizing measurement needs to statistically control for the time dimension. A measurement of constructs which change their properties over time will only allow comparison of different projects when the time of measurement is controlled. Project success could e.g. generally be assessed "two years after market launch". According to the most probably biased impression of the authors, this corresponds well with a commonly used key date in practice.

(3) The portfolio perspective of performance measurement demands a re-orientation: Research should follow practice by not only assessing individual project success but also by measuring portfolio performance. Research investigating the relationship of degree of innovativeness and innovation success consequently becomes more complex. One portfolio may contain innovations of different maturity levels: Recently initiated but still rather fuzzy projects, projects during development, recently launched products, mature products and even degenerated products which may once have been innovations. All different projects in a portfolio may vary with respect to their degree of innovativeness. Suppose, it is the aim of a company only to introduce its "own" innovations. This company would present itself as a network of different actual and past innovation processes, all experiencing different innovation life cycles. Such a

long-term perspective on innovation is neither common in practice nor research. In other words, success of innovations is generally assessed much too early and, thus, incomplete. Investigating the relationship of innovativeness and innovation success should not take a short term perspective. Basic knowledge about innovation life cycles of projects in a portfolio is still lacking.

Understanding innovation activity of a company as a network of different innovation projects which complement each other, which run parallel or follow each other but with different life-spans, suggests that a company can be viewed as an innovation system. First, this implies that the time horizon needs to be stretched far into the future. The future presents itself as a continuous stream of innovations. Success of the company requires successive but also interdependent innovation projects which may complement or even enforce each other. This perspective requires partly a return of the instruments of strategic management, including the various versions of portfolios. However, research needs to add a further dimension to the classical portfolios, covering the development of performance expectation over time. Brockhoff (1999, 235) discusses this problem of the "relevant time horizon" in portfolios and complains that it is mostly ignored, [...] *"that at least a basic distinction between short term and long term activities within this horizon is necessary"*.[3]

We suggest even further differentiating activities, including sophisticated measures of degree of innovativeness and innovation success. This additionally requires further efforts in perfecting measurement of these central constructs.

7 References

Atuahene-Gima, K. and F. Evangelista (2000): Cross-Functional Influence in New Product Development: An Exploratory Study of Marketing and R&D Perspectives, *Management Science*, 46, 1269-1284.

Brockhoff, K. (1999): *Forschung und Entwicklung – Planung und Kontrolle*, 5th ed., Munich/Vienna.

Crawford, C.M. (1979): New product failure rates – facts and fallacies, *Research Management*, 22, 9-13.

Cyert, R.M. and J.G. March (1963): *Behavioral Theory of the Firm*, Englewood Cliffs N.J.

[3] Translation from German: [...] „dass innerhalb dieses Horizonts wenigstens grob kurz- und langfristige Aktivitäten zu unterscheiden sind".

Danneels, E. and E.J. Kleinschmidt (2001): Product innovativeness from the firm's perspective: Its dimensions and their relation with project selection and performance, *Journal of Product Innovation Management*, 18, 357-373.

Diesel, E. (1983): *Diesel – Der Mensch, das Werk, das Schicksal*, Munich.

Ernst, H. (2001): *Erfolgsfaktoren neuer Produkte – Grundlagen für eine valide empirische Forschung*, Wiesbaden.

Garcia, R. and R. Calantone (2002): A critical look at technological innovation typology and innovativeness terminology: a literature review, *Journal of Product Innovation Management*, 19, 110-132.

Gatignon, H. and J.-M. Xuereb (1997): Strategic Orientation of the Firm and New Product Performance, *Journal of Marketing Research*, 24, 77-90.

Hauschildt, J. (1991): Zur Messung des Innovationserfolges, *Zeitschrift für Betriebswirtschaft*, 61, 451-476.

Hauschildt, J. (1999): Widerstand gegen Innovationen – destruktiv oder konstruktiv?, *Zeitschrift für Betriebswirtschaft*, Additional Issue 2, 1-21.

Hauschildt, J. (2004): *Innovationsmanagement*, 3rd ed., Munich.

Henard, D.H. and D.M. Szymanski (2001): Why Some Products Are More Successful Than Others, *Journal of Marketing Research*, 38, 362-375.

Leifer, R., C.M. McDermott, G. Colarelli O'Connor, L.S. Peters, M.P. Rice, and R.W. Veryzer (2000): *Radical innovation – how mature companies can outsmart upstarts*, Boston, MA.

Littkemann, J. (1998): Die Innovationsabrechnung als Zweck des Rechnungswesens? Eine Analyse zur abrechnungstechnischen Behandlung von Innovationen im externen und internen Rechnungswesen, *Der Betrieb*, 51, 1973-1979.

Markowitz, H.M. (1959): *Portfolio Selection – Efficient Diversification of Investments*, New York.

Olson E.M., O.C. Walker, R.W. Rueckert, and J.M. Bonner (2001): Patterns of cooperation during new product development among marketing, operations and R&D: Implications for project performance, *Journal of Product Innovation Management*, 18, 258-271.

Salomo, S., H.G. Gemünden, and F. Billing (2003): Dynamisches Schnittstellenmanagement radikaler Innovationsvorhaben, in: Herstatt, C. & Verworn, B. (Ed.): *Management der frühen Innovationsphasen – Grundlagen, Methoden, neue Ansätze*, Wiesbaden, 161-194.

Salomo, S., F. Steinhoff, and V. Trommsdorff (2003): Customer Orientation in Innovation Projects and New Product Development Success – the Moderating Effect of Product Innovativeness, *International Journal of Technology Management*, 26 (5/6), 442-463.

Salomo, S. (2003): Konzept und Messung des Innovationsgrades – Ergebnisse einer empirischen Studie zu innovativen Entwicklungsvorhaben, in: Schwaiger, M. and D. Harhoff: *Empirie und Betriebswirtschaft*, Stuttgart, 399-427.

Schlaak, Thomas M. (1999): *Der Innovationsgrad als Schlüsselvariable – Perspektiven für das Management von Produktentwicklungen*, Wiesbaden.

Swink, M. (2000): Technological Innovativeness as a Moderator of New Product Design Integration and Top Management Support, *Journal of Product Innovation Management*, 17, 208-220.

Tatikonda, M.V. and S.R. Rosenthal (2000): Technology Novelty, Project Complexitity and Product Development Project Execution Success: A Deeper Look at Task Uncertainty in Product Innovation, *IEEE Transactions on Engineering Management*, 47, 74-87.

Thyssen Stahl AG (1995): *Geschäftsbericht 1994/95.*

Hans Georg Gemünden

Innovation Networks

The Karlsruhe and Berlin Studies

Prof. Dr. *Hans Georg Gemünden,* Chair for Technology and Innovation Management, Technical University of Berlin.

1 Introduction

Klaus Brockhoff has stimulated my empirical research in innovation management in many ways: by his interesting research questions, his challenging standards, his rigorous scientific methods, and by the unique research culture and network of researchers he created. One stream of my research is particularly positively influenced by him, i.e. the research on innovation networks. The initial ideas of this research were born in Kiel in conversations with Klaus Brockhoff and Jürgen Hauschildt. It got its seed funding from their research programme "theory of innovation in the firm", financed from the German National Science Foundation (DFG). With this article I want to give an overview of this research, its research questions, methods and results.

Figure 1: *Overview of the inter-organisational studies at Karlsruhe and Berlin*

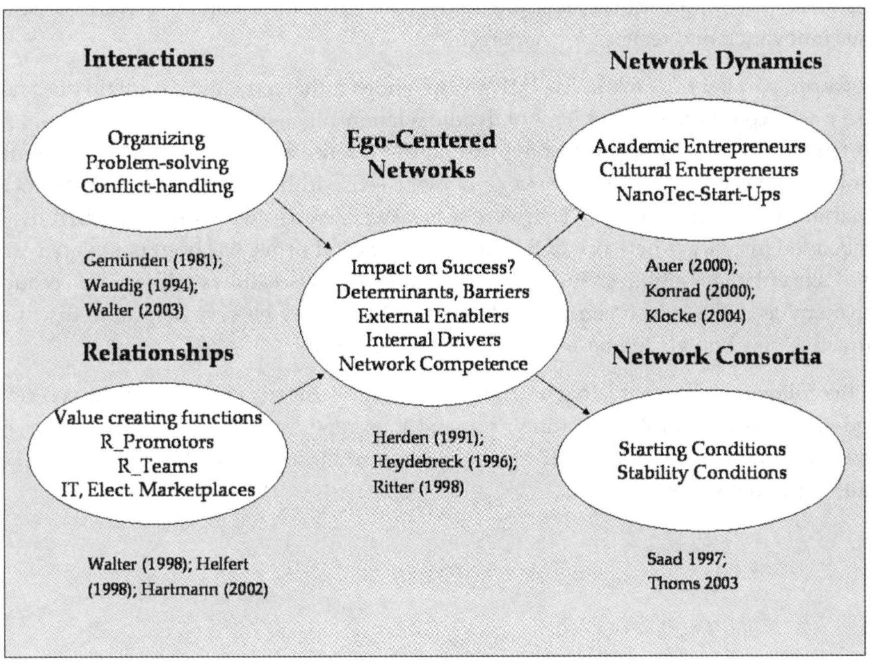

Figure 1 shows the different fields of our inter-organizational research from my research teams in Karlsruhe and Berlin, referencing as main sources the doctoral dissertations and the one habilitation thesis of Walter (2003). The network studies were stimulated by studies on the interaction processes between buyers and sellers when transferring new technologies, and by studies analysing innovation originating from dyadic long-term B2B-relationships. Prominent themes in these two research streams have been the innovating persons, particularly *relationship promoters* (Gemünden 1981, 1988, Gemünden and Walter 1996, 1998, Walter 1998, 1999, Walter and Gemünden 2000) and *relationship teams* (Helfert 1998, Helfert and Vith 1999, Helfert and Gemünden 2001), the *interaction patterns* of the technology transferring partners (Gemünden 1985, Waudig 1994; Walter 2003), the *value creating functions* (Gemünden 1994, Walter, Ritter and Gemünden 2001, Walter and Ritter 2003), the relationship-specific antecedents of customer involvement (Ritter and Walter 2003, Walter 2003), the influence of *IT-competence* on B2B-relationships (Ryssel, Ritter and Gemünden 2004, Walter and Ritter 2004), and the role of *electronic marketplaces* on B2B-relationships (Hartmann 2002, Hartmann, Ritter and Gemünden 2004). This research on dyadic relationships documents the importance of *strong ties,* i.e. close relationships with customers and suppliers are very important for the innovation function of a firm. Value is not only created through mere transactional buying and selling. Rather, close relationships support mutual learning and exchange of information relevant for strategic innovation and technology management.

However, parallel research in the IMP group[1] showed that a dyadic paradigm does not take into account the *connectedness* of dyadic relationships with other relationships. Important constructs like competition, brokerage and more complex multi-party inter-organizational coordination problems, only make sense if third parties beyond the focal dyad are taken into account. Therefore a *network approach,* which sees the B2B-dyad embedded in a larger network of B2B-relationships and firms, has been postulated and used since the late eighties. Such a network approach also allows taking into account the many *weak* ties which companies have and which may be very helpful to discover attractive new knowledge-bases or new application fields.

In the following chapters I first want to show the results of our research on ego-centred networks of a focal innovating firm, and then report research on the dynamics of innovation networks, and finally some findings from our research on consortia, i.e. multi-party networks.

1 The IMP (International Marketing and Purchasing) group is an informal cooperation of researchers from different European countries. It is well known for its annual conferences on interactions, relationships, and networks. Gemünden (1997) summarizes methodological characteristics of the contributions to the 12 first conferences.

2 Shaping Networks: The Drivers and Barriers of a Single Firm's Innovation Network and its Influence on Innovation Success

When we started our research on innovation networks in the late eighties we saw them as a potential *external resource* for the generation of new ideas, the development of new designs, and the successful marketing of innovations to challenging customers who profit from new functionalities, higher performance, and/or lower cost-in-use. Figure 2 documents our view of innovation networks. (See Gemünden 1995, 1999, Gemünden and Heydebreck 1994, 1995a, 1995b, 1996, 1997, Gemünden, Heydebreck and Herden 1992, Gemünden and Ritter 1998b for this hypothesis and the following findings).

Figure 2: *The firm in its innovation network*

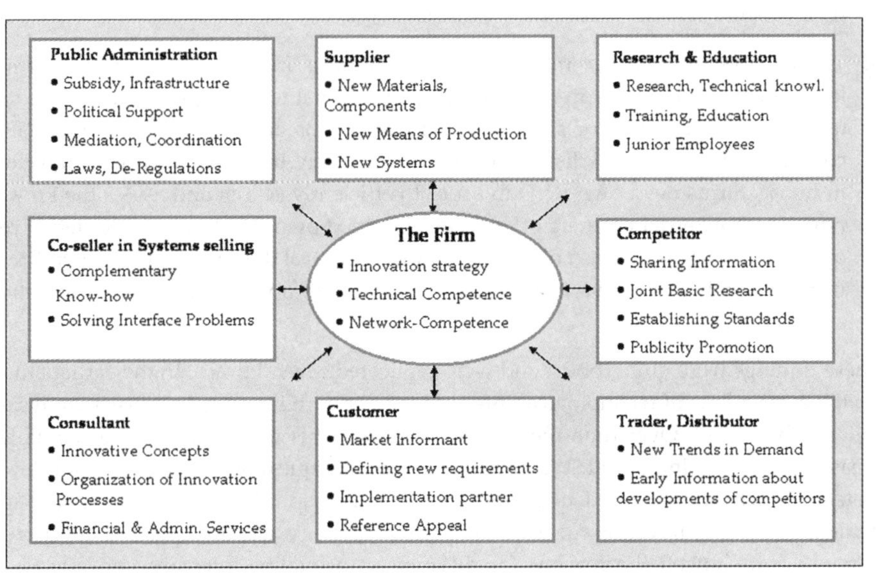

The conditions for the exploitation of these external resources were analysed in a series of quantitative analyses. Among these were the large cross-sectional Lake Konstanz and Black Forrest studies with more than 1,300 innovation networks, the high-tech studies (IT hard- and software, bio-tech, sensory industry, medical engineering, and

East German study after the re-unification) with another 400 networks, the Sweden study on 79 start-up networks, and the network competence study in mechanical and electrical engineering.

Three basic results emerged from theses studies:

- Cooperation with external partners raises success of product *and* process innovations. The exploitation of innovation networks creates value. A firm can get a competitive innovation advantage if it systematically develops and exploits its innovation networks.
- Especially important innovation partners are customers and research institutions. Our findings mirror many other studies on lead-users and technology transfer institutions which show that these two external groups are particularly useful for the firms. It is important to note that we did not interview universities, or applied research and technology transfer institutions like the Fraunhofer Institutes or the Steinbeis Foundation, but the *firms* who are their clients. From their perspective such partners create value through technology transfer, contract research, consulting activities, and recruiting of young skilled and motivated industry researchers and R&D-managers. The more such links firms have established, and the closer their cooperation, the higher their value creation.
- The positive influence of innovation cooperation is independent from the firm's level of expenditures for in-house R&D. The external technologies which firms acquire from other firms or from research institutions and universities are usually complementary to the skills which the firms already have or which they develop in-house. Firms need own R&D in order to efficiently search and assess the know-how which external partners offer. They also need own R&D in order to define requirements and interfaces appropriately and to control their work. Thus, own R&D increases their absorptive capacity, to integrate and appropriate externally delivered knowledge.

These findings were quite robust and were replicated several times. In the earlier studies the correlations of technological interweavement with innovation success were significant, but small. Over time the effects increased. This had different reasons. First, measurement was improved. We posed more specific questions, and used interviews instead of self administered questionnaires. Second, additional constructs were included, like e. g. innovation focus of competitive strategy, which explained additional variance and showed the reasons for differences in quality, intensity, and effects of innovation networks. Third, the empirical object of analysis changed itself: Firms exploited external innovation resources much more systematically, the activity level and quality of their networking increased, more value was created in cooperation with external partners. Therefore innovation networking became a strategically more important variable and the differences between well and poorly managed firms increased.

A more detailed analysis of potential *moderating influences* showed the following tendencies:

- The importance of equipment suppliers and consultants is higher for process innovations than for product innovations. Process innovations usually require a critical size (and age) of an innovating firm. Therefore the effects of cooperation with consultants and equipment suppliers are higher for bigger firms.
- The importance of universities and research institutions is higher for topics with a higher degree of innovativeness. For incremental innovations universities and research institutions do not play a central role. But if products and processes are more fundamentally changed, particularly by *new technologies,* i.e. new materials, new architectures, new technological principles, then universities and research institutions become very important partners. Their effect is then at least as strong as the effect of challenging and innovating customers. It is important that *both* conditions are given: 1. Challenging customers for which new technologies create additional revenues or significant cost reductions are the market base to finance supplier's investments in innovative competences and the positive growth perspective of innovating customers helps the innovating supplier to attract additional external financial resources. 2. By mobilising a network of external technological resources these suppliers – which are the focal firms of our analysis – can fulfil the needs of their customers better than their competitors. They can grow quicker and with less capital compared to the strategy of generating all know-how internally. The transfer of new technologies from universities and research institutions to the market is accelerated by a chain or network of such dynamic firms.

We further consistently found that *small and medium sized enterprises (SMEs) face much higher cooperation barriers,* particularly with universities and research institutions. However, if SMEs had been willing and able to cooperate then they did profit in the same way from these external resources as large firms. This raised the question whether a *stimulation* of external cooperation could increase innovation success and growth of SMEs.

Important external enablers of innovation networks for small and young high-tech firms are *venture capitalists* and *technology centres.* Research results from the Sweden-study (Gemünden and Heydebreck 1995b) show that SMEs in Technology Centres (TC) or in Portfolios of Venture-Capitalists (VC):

- develop larger and more intensively interwoven networks,
- achieve higher innovation success, and
- grow distinctly faster.

The result for the innovation network is documented in figure3. Different reasons may explain these findings. As a selection effect firms which have higher growth motivation and higher capabilities will have a better chance to get venture capital or a place in a technology centre. Also firms in a technology park or in a portfolio of a venture capitalist get access to their already existing networks. A third effect could be that the firms may better learn to develop their network skills in TC or VC environments by observing good practices or asking peer firms and consultants for advice. The selection explanation is confirmed by the finding that entrepreneurs who stress their independence engage themselves less in co-operation than those entrepreneurs who are primarily profit and growth oriented. The latter group has a better match with VCs.

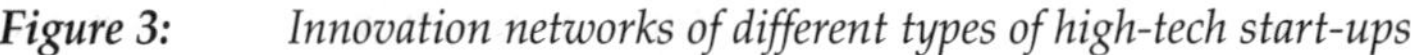

Figure 3: *Innovation networks of different types of high-tech start-ups*

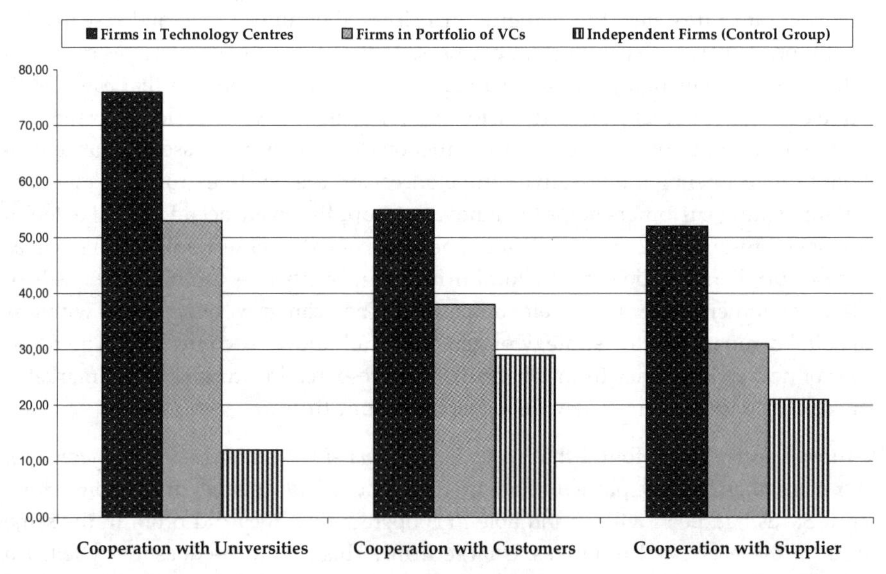

Regarding internal drivers, *innovation strategy* was identified as a major shaper of innovation networks (Gemünden and Heydebreck 1995a). Technology leaders and customer specific developers lay more stress on innovation. They invest heavily in research and development and differentiate themselves with new products and processes. They are especially active networkers, followed by technology-based cost leaders. Firms without a strong strategic focus support hardly any innovation cooperation. Innovation strategy is not only a driver of the innovation network; it also moderates the effect of innovation networks on firm success. Firms with a technology-based strategy gain much more firm growth from cooperation with universities and research institutions than firms with other strategies.

Figure 4: *Antecedents and effects of network competence*

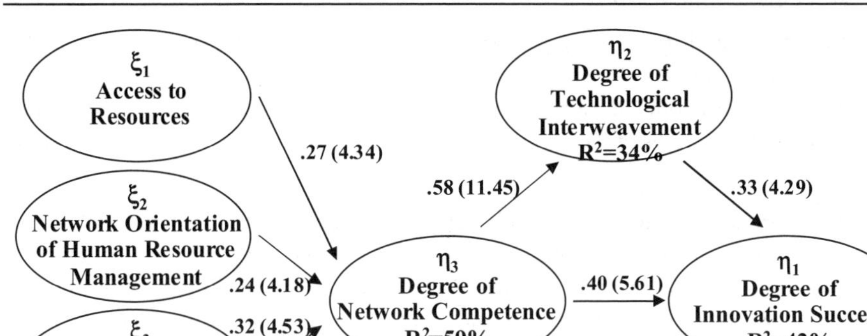

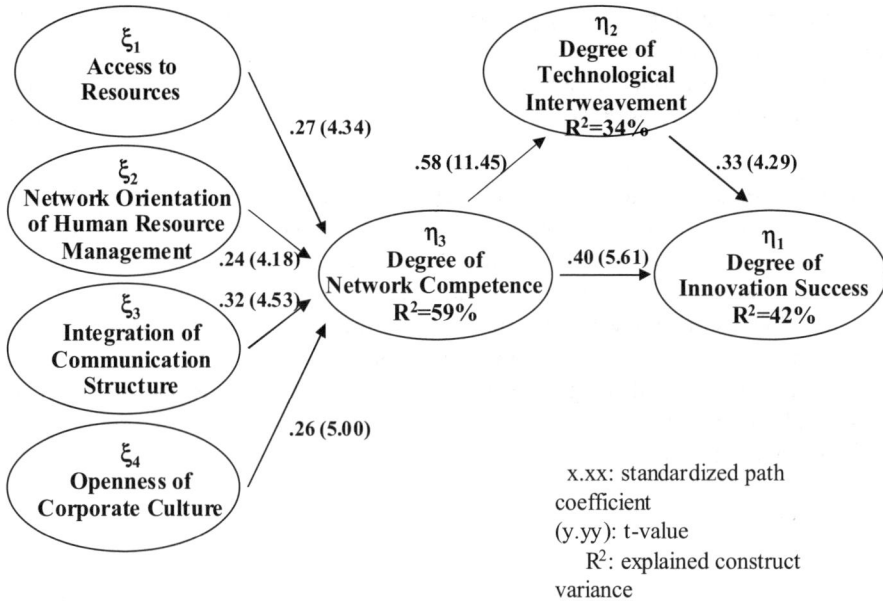

Source: Ritter and Gemünden 2003

Another very important internal driver is *network competence* (Ritter and Gemünden 2003, 2004, Ritter, Wilkinson and Wesley 2002). Network competence is a two-dimensional construct that can be defined as (a) the degree of network management task execution and (b) the extent of network management qualifications. It has a strong positive influence on the extent and quality of inter-organizational technological collaborations and on a firm's product and process innovation success. Four organizational antecedents have a significant impact on a company's network competence: access to resources, network orientation of human resource management, integration of intra-organizational communication, and openness of corporate culture. Access to resources (financial, physical, personnel, and informational) enables people to execute the network management tasks intensively and goal-oriented and helps them developing their qualifications. Through a high degree of network orientation of human resource management in terms of personnel selection, development and assessment, a firm is able to enhance their network competence by hiring and developing necessary human resources. A high integration of formal and informal communication structures makes important information available to those dealing with an external partner. That information may support task execution and qualification development. Finally, openness of corporate culture increases network competence by giving employees the necessary flexibility, spontaneity and responsibility to develop inter-organizational relationships. Figure 4 summarizes our findings.

In further analyses Ritter (1999) and Ritter and Gemünden (2004) showed that the direct and indirect effects of network competence and extent of networking on innovation success are of about the same size as investments in internal R&D. They further identified *innovation focus of the business strategy* as a fifth antecedent of network competence.

Thus, firms are advised to analyze their network competence in order to identify potential areas for improvements. This analysis can be based on the developed model, i.e. analyzing task performance and qualifications. Network management cannot be delegated to a well-defined small group within the firm. Looking at the antecedents it becomes obvious that the whole organization is either prepared for the network economy or not. Improvements can be made by making resources available to network management, by strengthening the network orientation of the human resource management, by increasing the inter-departmental communication, and by promoting an open corporate culture.

3 Understanding and Managing Network Dynamics: The Development of a Single New Firm's Innovation Network and its Influence on Innovation Success

Dynamics of innovation networks have been analysed in three empirical studies on start-ups. Academic technology-based start-ups (Walter, Auer and Gemünden 2002), cultural businesses (Konrad and Gemünden 2002) and nano-tech start-ups (Klocke, Gemünden and Ritter 2002, 2003). All three studies document that external networks are crucial for the development of start-ups. Their dynamics are driven by the entrepreneurial posture of the top manager or the top management team. Figure 5 shows a typical result from these studies. It is a not yet published analysis. The result differs from Walter, Auer and Gemünden 2002 because size and age are not included as controls since they are also influenced by entrepreneurial activities: The higher the level of entrepreneurial activity, the higher and quicker the growth of a firm.

Figure 5: *Determinants and impact of entrepreneurial activities of tech-transfer firms*

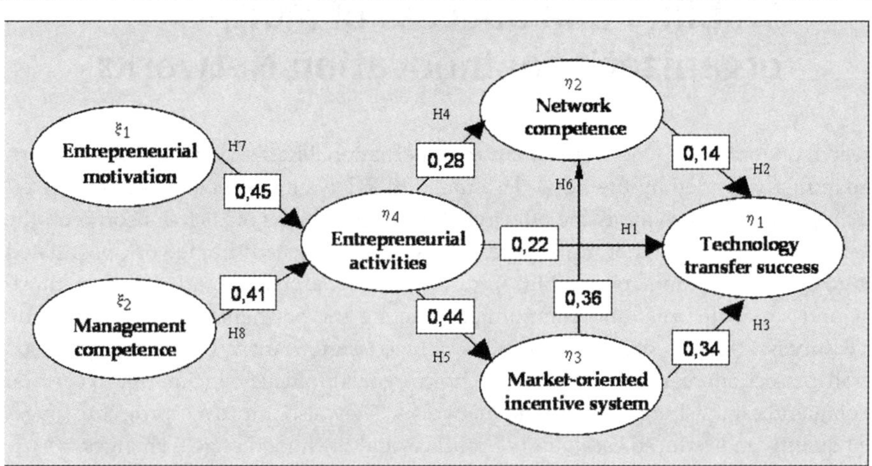

The entrepreneurial activities – promoting opportunities, building capabilities, and accomplishing objectives – foster the establishment of a market-oriented incentive system with material, immaterial, and long-term incentives. They also support the development of a high network competence of the firm with intensive networking activities, high network skills, and a profound network knowledge, so that the innovation network of the firm quickly develops in terms of quantity and quality. The model explains 32% of variance of the logarithm of sales of the last 5 years. The model has the same structure in case a subjective assessment of technology transfer success is taken as the dependent variable.

The analysis of cultural entrepreneurs organizing music and theatre performances showed a similar influence pattern: entrepreneurial activity positively influences the quality of the relationship portfolio of the firm, a market oriented entrepreneurial culture, and the commercial performance of the firm.

The findings from the nano-tech start-ups show that these firms quickly develop innovation networks which do not grow quantitatively, but qualitatively. The cooperation gets more formal, shifts from mere R&D-cooperation to production and market-oriented cooperation, and increase in size per cooperation. It is interesting to note that not only cooperation with customers and universities and research institutions are important for such nano-tech start-ups, but also cooperation with other nano-tech start-ups are very critical for firm development. The reason is that this cooperation enables the firm to develop a system which can be sold as an integrated product. We also found that nano-techs which received venture capital and/or were spin-offs from research institutions developed quicker and better.

4 Orchestrating Innovation Consortia: Stability and Success of Multi-organizational Innovation Networks

Research on multi-party networks analyzed international R&D-cooperation in the software industry funded by the EU programme ESPRIT (Gemünden et al. 1999). The research question was: What is the effect of starting conditions of such consortia on the development and success of multi-party projects? The research framework postulated that goal-fit (clarity and compatibility), resource-fit (competence and complementarities), and social fit (trust and commitment) among the partners should significantly drive success. All six starting conditions showed significant positive influences on overall project success, effectiveness (technical goals), efficiency (time and cost), on learning and establishing international networks. They also improved project management quality, and reduced escalation of conflicts and likelihood of goal changes.

Figure 6 shows the results of an exploratory path analysis. As an extension of the published analysis, three new factors in the formation stage have been included: strategic relevance of the cooperation, thoroughness of partner search, and perceived intercultural problems between the partners. Strategic relevance has a strong influence on the intensity of partner search; it also shows a small but significant direct influence on project success holding constant all other influences. Unexpected is the negative effect of strategic relevance on trust. A higher amount at stake seems to create more caution and less trust. Higher search quality leads to more competent partners. It also has a direct positive influence on project success. Intercultural problems can not be avoided by a more thorough search. It was a political goal of the EU that project partners from so called "cohesion" countries should be included in the funded EU consortia. Our analysis shows that higher intercultural problems were associated with lower goal-clarity and a higher likelihood of escalation of conflicts. Summing up the indirect effects of intercultural problems a substantial source of project risk arises. Klaus Brockhoff has criticized this "political marriages" when we talked about EU funded research consortia. This re-analysis confirms his point of view.

Figure 6: *Influence of starting conditions of international R&D consortia*

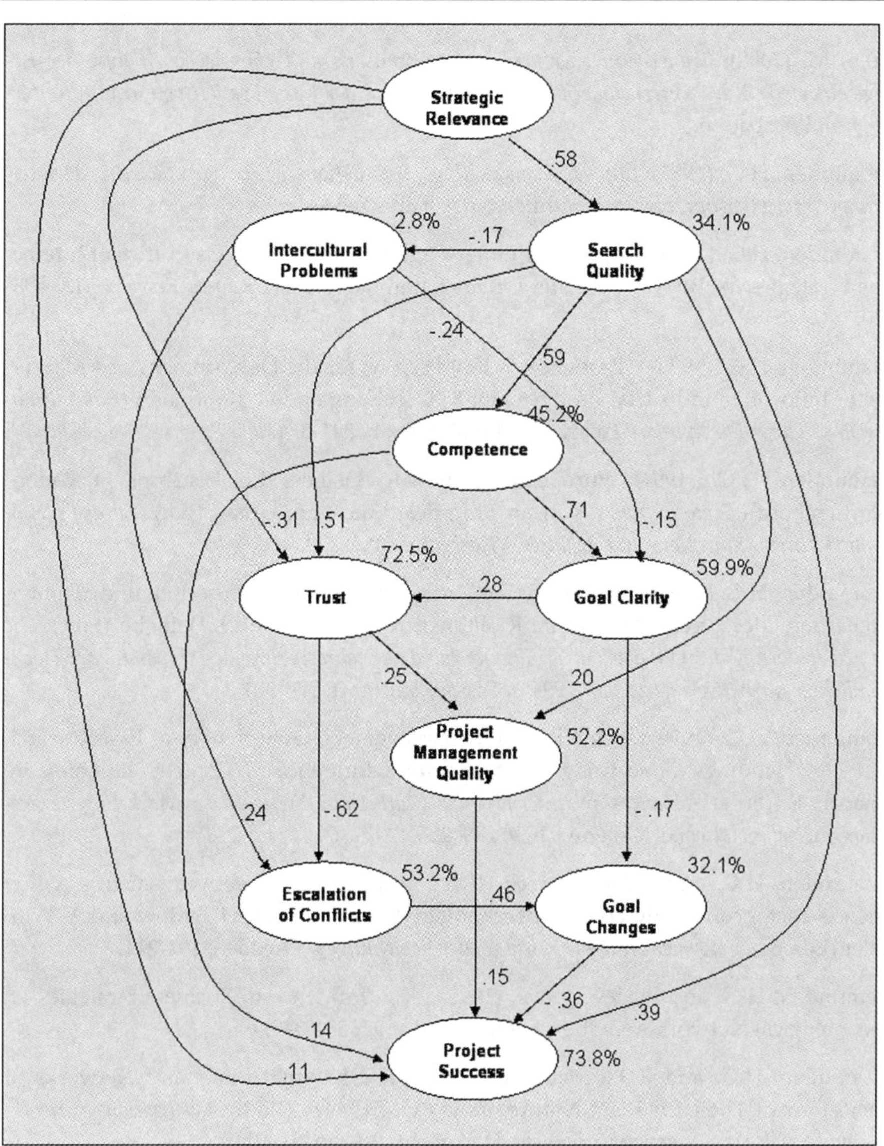

The framework developed in this study has been used in a recently finished study on stability and value creation of telematic service consortia (Thoms 2003). Thoms found positive evidence that goal fit, competences, and resources had a positive effect on task-fulfilment of these consortia which in turn created trust, value and commitment.

5 References

Auer, M. (2000): *Transferunternehmer. Eine theoretische und empirische Analyse der Erfolgswirksamkeit des unternehmerischen Verhaltens und der Organisation von Transferunternehmen.* Wiesbaden.

Gemünden, H.G. (1981): *Innovationsmarketing - Interaktionsbeziehungen zwischen Hersteller und Verwender innovativer Investitionsgüter.* Tübingen.

Gemünden, H.G. (1985): Coping with Inter-Organizational Conflicts - Efficient Interaction Strategies for Buyer and Seller Organization. *Journal of Business Research.* 13, 405-420.

Gemünden, H.G. (1988): „Promotors"- Key Persons for the Development and Marketing of Innovative Industrial Products, in: K. Gr¢nhaug and G. Kaufmann (Eds.): *Innovation. A Cross-Disciplinary Perspective.* London et al., 347-374.

Gemünden, H.G. (1994): European Business-to-Business Relationships of Baden-Württemberg's Firms - Results of an Empirical Study, in: Urban (Ed.): *Europe's Economic Future: Aspirations and Realities.* Wiesbaden, 187-209.

Gemünden, H.G. (1995): Technologische Verflechtung, Innovationserfolg und „Dimensionierung" des Unternehmens, in: R. Bühner, K.D. Haase, and J. Wilhelm (Eds.): *Die Dimensionierung des Unternehmens. Tagungsband zur Jahrestagung des Verbandes der Hochschullehrer für Betriebswirtschaft 1994 in Passau,* Stuttgart, 279-301.

Gemünden, H.G. (1999): Technological Interweavement - A Summary of Past Research and New Findings Concerning the Moderating Influence of Context Variables, in: Ghauri, P. (Ed.): *Advances in International Marketing. From Mass Marketing to Relationships and Networks.* Greenwich, 9, 199–225.

Gemünden, H.G. and P. Heydebreck (1994): Technological Interweavement - A Key Success Factor for Newly Founded Technology-Based Firms, in: J. Sydow and A. Windeler (Eds.): *Management interorganisationaler Beziehungen.* Opladen, 194-211.

Gemünden, H.G. and P. Heydebreck (1995a): The Influence of Business Strategies on Technological Network Activities. *Research Policy,* 24, 831-849.

Gemünden, H.G. and P. Heydebreck (1995b): The External Links and Networks of Small Firms - Their Role and Nature, in: D.P.O. Doherty (Ed.): *Globalisation, Networking, and Small Firm Innovation. London,* Dordrecht, Boston, 87-100.

Gemünden, H.G. and P. Heydebreck (1996): Technology Interweavements - A Key Success Factor for New Technology-Based Firms, in: Oakey, R. (Ed.): *New Technology-Based Firms in the 1990s.* Volume II. London, 80-92.

Gemünden, H.G. and P. Heydebreck (1997): Technological Interweavement: A Means to Achieve Higher Efficiency in Production Processes, in: Oakey, R.P. and M. Mukhtar (Eds.): *New Technology-Based Firms in the 1990s*. Volume III. London, 140-150.

Gemünden, H.G., P. Heydebreck, and R. Herden (1992): Technological Interweavement: A Means of Achieving Innovation Success. *R&D Management*, 22, 359-376.

Gemünden, H.G., M. Högl, T. Lechler, and A. Saad (1999): Starting Conditions of Successful European R&D-Consortia, in: K. Brockhoff, A. Chacrabarti, and J. Hauschildt (Eds.): *The Dynamics of Innovation. Strategical and Managerial Implications*, Berlin, Heidelberg, New York, 237-275.

Gemünden, H.G. and T. Ritter (1998a): Managing Technological Networks: The Concept of Network Competence, in: Gemünden, H.G., T. Ritter, and A. Walter (Eds.): *Relationships and Networks in International Markets*, Devon, 294-304.

Gemünden, H.G. and T. Ritter (1998b): The Impact of Radical Environmental Change on a Company's Network Activities. An Empirical Study in East and West Germany, in: Urban (Ed.): *From Alliance Practices to Alliance Capitalism*, Wiesbaden, 95-130.

Gemünden, H.G., T. Ritter, and P. Heydebreck (1996): Network Configuration and Innovation Success - An Empirical Analysis in German High-Tech Industries. *International Journal of Research in Marketing*. 13, 449-462.

Gemünden, H.G. and A. Walter (1996): Förderung des Technologietransfers durch Beziehungspromotoren, *Zeitschrift Führung Organisation*, 65, 237-245.

Gemünden, H.G. and A. Walter (1998): The Relationship Promoter - Motivator and Coordinator for Inter-organizational Innovation Co-operation, in: Gemünden, H.G., T. Ritter, and A. Walter (Eds.): *Relationships and Networks in International Market*, Devon, 180-197.

Hartmann, E. (2002): *B-to-B Electronic Marketplaces. Successful Introduction in the Chemical Industry*. Wiesbaden.

Hartmann, E., T. Ritter, and H.G. Gemünden (2004): The Fit between Purchase Situations and B2B E-Marketplaces and Its Impact on Relationship Success, *Journal of Consumer Behaviour* – Special Issue on Relationship Management, in print.

Helfert, G.E. (1998): *Teams im Relationship Marketing. Design effektiver Kundenbeziehungsteams*, Wiesbaden.

Helfert, G.E. and H.G. Gemünden (2001): Relationship Marketing Teams, in: Gemünden, H. G. and Högl, M. (Eds.): *Management von Teams. Theoretische Konzepte und empirische Befunde*, 2nd ed., Wiesbaden, 129-156.

Helfert, G.E. and K. Vith (1999): Relationship Marketing Teams: Improving the Utilization of Customer Relationship Potentials Through a High Team Design Quality. *Industrial Marketing Management*, 28, 553-564.

Herden, R. (1991): *Technologieorientierte Außenbeziehungen im betrieblichen Innovationsmanagement,* Heidelberg.

Heydebreck, P. (1996): *Technologische Verflechtung. Ein Instrument zum Erreichen von Produkt- und Prozessinnovationserfolg,* Frankfurt am Main.

Klocke, B. (2004): *Unternehmens- und Netzwerkentwicklung in High-Tech-Sektoren. Entwicklungsgeschwindigkeit deutscher Nanotechnologie-Start-ups,* Wiesbaden.

Klocke, B., H.G. Gemünden, and T. Ritter (2002): Dynamics of Alliance Networks: Development Speed and Its Determinants Analyzed for a Sample of Nanotechnology Companies. *Competitive Paper at the IMP Asia Conference*, December 11-13, 2002 in Perth (Australia).

Klocke, B., H.G. Gemünden, and T. Ritter (2003): Die Entwicklung des Kooperationsnetzwerkes von Nanotechnologie-Firmen im Zusammenhang mit der Unternehmensentwicklung, in: Achleitner, A.-K., H. Klandt, L.T. Koch, and K.-I. Voigt (Eds.): *Jahrbuch Entrepreneurship 2003/04,* Berlin, 165-186.

Konrad, E. and H.G. Gemünden (2002): Unternehmerische Gestaltung von Kulturbetrieben, *Zeitschrift Führung Organisation.* 71, 380-388.

Ritter, T. (1998): *Innovationserfolg durch Netzwerk-Kompetenz. Effektives Management von Unternehmensnetzwerken.* Wiesbaden.

Ritter, T. (1999): The Networking Company: Antecedents for Coping with Relationships and Networks Effectively, *Industrial Marketing Management,* 28, 467-479.

Ritter, T. and H.G. Gemünden (2003): Network Competence: It's Impact on Innovation Success and its Antecedents, *Journal of Business Research,* 56, 745-755.

Ritter, T. and H.G. Gemünden (2004): The Impact of a Company's Business Strategy on its Technological Competence, Network Competence and Innovation Success, *Journal of Business Research,* 57, 459-563.

Ritter, T. and A. Walter (2003): Relationship-Specific Antecedents of Customer Involvement in New Product Development, *International Journal of Technology Management,* 26 (5/6), 482-501.

Ritter, T., I. Wilkinson, and W.J. Johnston (2002): Measuring Network Competence: some International Evidence, *Journal of Business and Industrial Marketing,* 17, 119-138.

Ryssel, R., T. Ritter, and H.G. Gemünden (2004): The Impact of Information Technology Deployment on Trust, Commitment and Value Creation in Business Relationships, *Journal of Business and Industrial Marketing,*19, in print.

Saad, A. (1998): *Anbahnung und Erfolg von europäischen kooperativen F&E-Projekten.* Frankfurt am Main.

Thoms, U. (2003): *Langfristige Beziehungen zwischen Unternehmen. Zum Wert und zur Stabilität inter-organisationaler Partnerschaften.* Wiesbaden.

Thoms, U., A. Walter, and H.G. Gemünden (2002): *Managing the Stability and Value of Business Networks an Empirical Investigation in the Telecommunication Industry,* Competitive Paper, 18h Annual IMP Conference hosted by the Dijon-Burgundy Graduate School of Management ESC, Dijon, France, 5th – 7th September 2002.

Walter, A. (1998): *Der Beziehungspromotor. Ein personaler Gestaltungsansatz für das Relationship Marketing,* Wiesbaden.

Walter, A. (1999): Relationship Promoters: Driving Forces for Successful Customer Relationships, *Industrial Marketing Management,* 28 (5), 537-551.

Walter, A. (2003): An Examination of Relationship-Specific Factors Influencing Supplier Involvement in Customer New Product Development, *Journal of Business Research,* 56 (9), 721-733.

Walter, A. (2003): *Technologietransfer zwischen Wissenschaft und Wirtschaft. Voraussetzung für den Erfolg,* Wiesbaden.

Walter, A., M. Auer, and H.G. Gemünden (2002): The Impact of Personality, Competence, and Activities of Academic Entrepreneurs on Technology Transfer Success, *International Journal of Entrepreneurship and Innovation Management,* 2, 268-289.

Walter, A. and H.G. Gemünden (2000): Bridging the Gap between Suppliers and Customers through Relationship Promoters: A Theoretical and Empirical Analysis, *Journal of Business & Industrial Marketing,* 15, 86-105.

Walter, A. and T. Ritter (2003): The Influence of Adaptations, Trust, and Commitment on Value-Creating Functions of Customer Relationships, *Journal of Business and Industrial Marketing,* 18 (4/5), 353-365.

Walter, A. and T. Ritter (2004): Information Technology Competence and Value Creation in Supplier-Customer Relationships, *Journal of Relationship Marketing,* in print.

Walter, A., T. Ritter, and H.G. Gemünden (2001): Value-Creation in Buyer-Seller Relationships: Theoretical Considerations and Empirical Results from a Supplier's Perspective, *Industrial Marketing Management,* 30, 353-363.

Waudig, D. (1994): *Verlauf und Erfolg kooperativer Innovationsprozesse zwischen Hochschule und Industrie - Eine interaktions-orientierte Fallstudie anhand eines Kooperationsprojektes HECTOR (HEtergeneous Computers TOgetheR) zwischen IBM Deutschland GmbH und der Universität (TH) Karlsruhe.* Diss. Universität (TH) Karlsruhe.

Gerhard Schewe

Barriers to Entry in Innovative Markets

How to Protect Innovative Products Successfully?

Prof. Dr. *Gerhard Schewe*, Department of Organization, Personnel and Innovation, Westphalian Wilhelms University of Münster.

1 Introduction

The close relationship between technological innovations and corporate success has already been widely studied. It is essential that companies should maintain their competitiveness by improving production and manufacturing technologies, as well as by developing new products and opening up new markets. As far back as 1934, Schumpeter (1934, 98) pointed out that entrepreneurs have to introduce innovations in order to be successful. An innovative company which has become a market leader will naturally be anxious to retain its monopoly for as long as possible, and it will do its utmost to keep competitors out of its market by erecting barriers to entry. The objective of the present article is to examine the instruments that an innovative company can use in order to prevent competitors from entering its market.

The adherents of the theory of Industrial Organization have lavished attention on barriers to entry. One of the pioneers in this field of inquiry was Bain, who defines barriers to market entry as "primarily a structural condition, determining in any industry the intra-industry adjustments which will and will not induce entry" (Bain 1962, 3).

Studies concerned with entry barriers often focus on the costs of market entry (Gallini 1992; Wright 1999; Karakaya 2002). In more recent publications about Industrial Organization these are often considered as sunk costs or irretrievable costs (Baumol, Panzar, and Willig 1982, 290 et sqq.; MacLeod 1987, 142 et seq.). Barriers to entry are generally divided into two main groups: (1) structural entry barriers resulting from the structural conditions within a particular industry, and (2) strategic entry barriers deliberately set up by already established suppliers in order to prevent potential competitors from entering the market (e.g. "limit pricing", "excess capacity", or "product differentiation") (Mathis and Koscianski 1996, 266; Schmidt 1998, 266). Firms with innovative products assume that structural barriers alone will not be sufficient to prevent new competitors from entering the market. In addition to structural barriers, they therefore erect strategic barriers to entry (Nahata 1989, 236 et sqq.). The costs entailed by the erection of strategic barriers depend on the height of the structural barriers already in existence.

The purpose of this paper is not to discuss the concept of entry barriers in detail. Our main interest is in empirical evidence germane to this concept, so we shall concentrate on studies which investigate existing barriers to entry from an empirical point of view. The questions which will remain in the forefront of our attention are as follows: What kinds of barriers can we identify when we look more closely at the markets which have been opened up for innovative products? What kinds of barriers prove most effective when innovative firms endeavor to keep competitors out of their markets?

2 Barriers to market entry

The Industrial Organization's literature has produced a multitude of empirical studies dealing with barriers to entry and their impact on strategic behavior (Scott Morton 2000, 1085 et sqq.; Karakaya 2002 379 et sqq.). Unfortunately, many of these analyses fail to distinguish between different types of barriers. They merely analyze the relation between the earnings situation and the cumulated absolute height of entry barriers (George 1968, 274; Gallini 1992, 52 et sqq.; Quirmbach 1993, 157 et sqq.; Takalo 1998, 229 et sqq.). In such cases, entry barriers are simply described as 'high' or 'low'. The findings reported by the authors of these studies offer no guidance what so ever to marketing managers who want to know how to erect the barriers in question. Should they apply for a patent or take advantage of economies of scale in production or distribution? We therefore confined our attention to studies by authors who adopted a differentiated approach to the problems associated with barriers to entry.

The studies we examined contain an exceptionally wide range of findings, and the authors often use different terms to describe similar phenomena. A further complicating factor is that there is a certain amount of overlapping between the research results (Holtermann 1973, 135; Orr 1974, 62 et sqq.; Harrigan 1981, 410 et seq.). The factors most often mentioned are size advantages, product differentiation, customer preferences and capital requirements (Siegfried and Evans 1994, 194; Kleijweg and Lever 1996, 379; Brockhoff 1999, 303; Ehrmann and Biedermann 2002, 499). However, the authors who distinguish these various types of barrier suggest that the impediments in question are more or less interdependent. In strongly growing markets, a competitor's size advantage may have a particular significance. Existing production and marketing capacities, for instance, may be important factors, and the need to satisfy high capital requirements also implies possible size advantages.

In order to facilitate our critical scrutiny of empirical findings regarding the market entry problem, we therefore elaborated the following principles for a systematic analysis of barriers to entry:

- Unlike other authors, we shall not consider capital requirements as an independent barrier to entry. There are two reasons for this. First, capital requirements are frequently connected with size advantages. Secondly, it is often useful to subsume capital requirements within a larger group of barriers. Thus, to take just one example, a company, in order to gain access to a market, may need additional capital for research and development, production or marketing. In our opinion, this kind of capital requirement ought to be subsumed within a larger class such as 'production capacity barriers' in order to indicate the particular domain in which capital needs to be invested.

- Lack of knowledge sometimes constitutes an effective barrier to entry. An obvious example is provided by a situation where an entirely new product is launched. All the barriers constituted by insufficient knowledge can therefore be lumped into a category which we shall label 'novelty barriers'. The types of impediment that fall into this category include lack of technological know-how, insufficient information about production techniques, and lack of information about customer preferences.

With these principles in mind, we carried out a detailed scrutiny of several empirical studies, giving special attention to their findings concerning barriers to entry. The following studies were subject of this meta-analysis: Bain (1962), Comanor and Wilson (1967), Esposito and Esposito (1971), Holtermann (1973), Khalilzadeh-Shirazi (1974), Orr (1974), Duetsch (1975), Stonebraker (1976), Schmalensee (1978), Salop (1979), Harrigan (1981), Oster (1982), Yip (1982 a), Spital (1983), Zörgiebel (1983), Duetsch (1984), Hilke (1984), Urban, Carter, and Mucha (1985), Schnaars (1986), Anderson and Coughlan (1987), Gorecki (1987), Lieberman (1987), Perillieux (1987), Schwalbach (1987), Shapiro and Khemani (1987), Dunne, Roberts, and Samuelson (1988), Smiley (1988), Karakaya and Stahl (1989), Pickford (1991), Bunch and Smiley (1992), Siegfried and Evans (1994), Harabi (1995), Kleijweg and Lever (1996), Mathis and Koscianski (1996), Singh, Utton, and Waterson (1998), Scott Morton (2000), Garcia Marinoso (2001), and Karakaya (2002). We found that the obstructions in question could be classified as follows:

- *Economies of scale*: Barriers are created by high demand growth, high capital requirements, a high volume of investment, high production rates or additional capacity.
- *Patenting*: If an innovative company applies for a patent it is difficult for competitors to use the same technology. They have to develop something similar or apply for a license.
- *Lack of product compatibility*: If products manufactured by different firms are mutually incompatible, buyers may face high switching costs.
- *Corporate image*: A barrier may be created by the good reputation enjoyed by a firm.
- *Product differentiation*: Innovative product differentiation may enhance customer loyalty if a manufacturer possesses reliable information about his customers' preferences.
- *Distribution system*: There is a distribution barrier wherever established suppliers have succeeded in building up an efficient distribution system which sells products to large customer groups through limited distribution channels.
- *Degree of novelty*: A company may be handicapped by a lack of know-how if its rivals introduce technological innovations, start using new production techniques or succeed in carving out new markets.

Using this system of classification, we shall now consider how effective such barriers are in deterring competitors from market entry. In our analysis, the independent variables will be the aforementioned barriers to market entry. The dependent variable is the possibility that a firm will be able to breach barriers to entry by launching a product similar to the one marketed by its rival. This is illustrated in figure 1:

Figure 1: *Theoretical model*

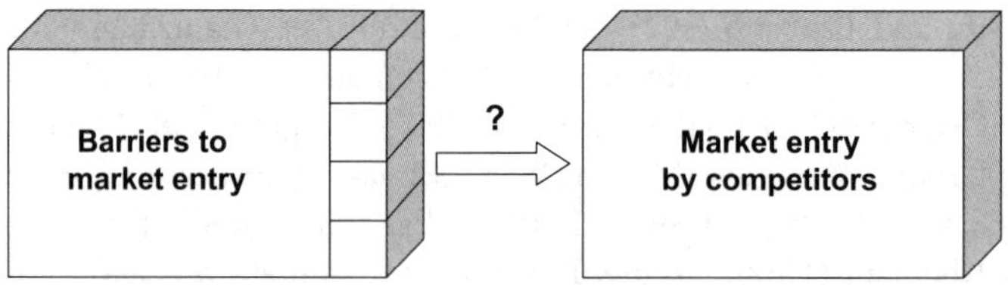

Barriers to market entry → ? → Market entry by competitors

3 Empirical design

Our empirical study is based on 88 interviews conducted in firms whose innovative products were sponsored by Germany's Federal Ministry of Economic Affairs. Most of these enterprises were middle-sized companies in the electrical engineering and mechanical engineering industries. The interviews focused on specific government-sponsored innovation projects and related management activities. Special attention was given to the erection of barriers to market entry. We also looked at the competitive environment, examining cases where rival non-innovative products were fairly similar to innovative ones. Such similarities indicate the effectiveness of the barriers to entry erected by innovators. Table 1 shows how we measured the barriers that were examined in the course of our analysis.

In order to measure the dependent variable, we analyzed competitors' products which are comparable to those manufactured by innovators. In each case two aspects of the competitors' product were considered: (1) the degree of similarity to the innovative product with regard to its applications, and (2) the degree of similarity to the innovative product with regard to the technology employed by the manufacturer. Both variables were judged by the innovative companies. Table 2 shows the measurement instructions in detail.

Table 1: *Measuring instructions for the barriers to market entry*

Factors / measurement variables	*Measuring instructions / scale*
Economies of scale:	
Size of the series	– Size of the innovative production series (5-point scale where 1 = unimportant and 5 = very important).
Size of the market	– Size and growth of the innovative market (5-point scale where 1 = unimportant and 5 = very important).
Patenting:	
Patent protection	– Filing of a patent application by the innovative firm (2-point scale where 0 = no patent and 1 = patent protection).
Lack of product compatibility:	
Switching costs	– Level of switching costs for the user of the innovative product (5-point scale where 1 = very high and 5 = very low).
Ease of application	– Ease of application of the innovative product (5-point scale where 1 = very low and 5 = very high).
Customer needs	– Adaptation of the innovative product to specific customer needs (5-point scale where 1 = very low and 5 = very high).
Corporate image:	
Corporate image	– Importance of the firm's reputation for the product's success (5-point scale where 1 = very low and 5 = very high).
Product differentiation:	
Distribution capacity	– Suitability of the existing distribution system for selling the innovative product (5-point scale where 1 = very low and 5 = very high).
Customers	– Familiarity with the customers who might buy the innovative product (5-point scale where 1 = very low and 5 = very high).
Distribution system:	
Distribution channels	– Existence of a well-established system of distribution channels (2-point scale where 0 = no well-established system and 1 = existence of a well-established system).
Degree of novelty:	
Product's novelty	– Degree of novelty of the innovation compared with that of products already on the market (5-point scale where 1 = very low and 5 = very high).
Development time	– Development time compared with that of other innovative products developed by the firm (5-point scale where 1 = very short and 5 = very long).
Development costs	– Development costs compared with those of other innovative products developed by the firm (5-point scale where 1 = very low and 5 = very high).

In order to analyze our data we use LISREL modeling. Since it integrates factor analytic and regression models, LISREL analysis is appropriate for analyzing the relations between unobservable or theoretical variables like barriers to entry. The parameters of the LISREL model were estimated with the aid of the "Unweighted Least Squares" (ULS) method, which is recommended for small samples and cases where a normal distribution of the variables cannot be assumed.

Table 2: *Instructions for measuring the effectiveness of barriers to market entry*

Factors / measurement variables	*Measuring instructions / scale*
• Effectiveness of barriers to entry:	
Applicatory similarity	• Degree of similarity between the competitor's product and the innovative one with regard to applications (5-point scale where 1 = no similarity and 5 = close similarity).
Technological similarity	• Degree of similarity between the competitor's product and the innovative one with regard to the technology employed (5-point scale where 1 = no similarity and 5 = close similarity).

Our LISREL model shows the following overall fit indices:

- Using the two-step approach adopted by Anderson and Gerbing (1988, 411 et sqq.), we first conducted several chi-square difference tests (SCDT) for the structural models M_t (our theoretical model of interest), M_s (the saturated structural model in which all parameters relating the constructs to one another are estimated), M_c and M_n (the next most likely constrained and unconstrained theoretical alternatives to M_t). Between models M_t and M_s the SCDT is not significant, i.e. there is no significant difference between the chi-squares of the models M_t and M_s. However, when we test chi-square differences between M_t and M_c, we find that the SCDT is significant. Finally, there is no significant SCDT between models M_t and M_u. The results of this series of tests therefore indicate that our model is well specified and represents an acceptable fit. There is no model with a better chi-square and fewer degrees of freedom than model M_t.
- The reliability coefficients of the measurement variables (squared multiple correlation) show values between zero and one. The theoretical constructs of our model have now been measured with sufficient precision.
- The total coefficient of determination for structural equations is 0.931.
- The model as a whole explains 88.8% of variance (AGFI-Index).

- The normalized residuals have a value of less than two.
- With none of the supposed connections between the latent variables, the modification indices indicate an incorrect specification.

4 Results

Since there is only one dependent when we have the variable 'Effectiveness of barriers to entry', the LISREL model only enables us to calculate direct effects. This means that direct and total effects are identical. Table 3 presents the results of the parameter estimate.

Table 3: *Results of LISREL modeling*

Barriers to entry (independent variables)	*Effectiveness of barriers to entry (dependent variable)*
Economies of scale	+ 0.50
Patenting	+ 0.20
Lack of product compatibility	+ 0.17
Corporate image	+ 0.08
Product differentiation	- 0.11
Distribution system	- 0.22
Degree of novelty	- 0.42

The results show that there are only three entry barriers which have proved effective in keeping competitors out of a market: (1) product differentiation, (2) efficient distribution channels, and (3) the novelty of an innovative product. Contrary to what many people assume after reading the specialist literature on industrial organization, economies of scale and patenting do not afford sufficient protection to innovative products.

5 Discussion

Our findings tally with those reported in some other studies. Orr (1974, 62 et sqq.) and Smiley (1988, 172), for instance, arrive at conclusions similar to our own. They both show that some entry barriers are more effective than others. In their view, high capital requirements and high marketing expenditure may have a deterrent effect on rival companies, but R&D intensity and economies of scale are ineffectual.

Let us now look more closely at our results. The effectiveness of a high degree of novelty comes as no surprise in view of the findings reported in other empirical studies (Mueller and Tilton 1969, 570 et sqq.; Harrigan 1981, 400 et sqq.; Siegfried and Evans 1994, 142). In all probability, competitors will be deterred by innovative products containing highly complex components.

In the early stages of our analysis, we assumed that innovative products would not be particularly novel in cases where competitors succeeded in making inroads into the market. In order to test this assumption, we contacted innovative companies confronted with rival products similar to their own. We asked them to assess their competitors' research and development facilities, and in 75% of the cases we studied, the interviewees said that their competitors' ability to attack their markets had nothing whatever to do with R&D. In most cases, a rival's success in overcoming entry barriers was attributed to the fact that an innovative product was not particularly novel and therefore easy to imitate.

The deterrent effect of efficient distribution channels also merits some comment. There is little doubt that such channels give innovative companies a competitive edge over their rivals. This phenomenon has already been observed by the authors of other empirical studies, but most of the barriers described by these authors are considerably higher (Anderson and Coughlan 1987, 78; Karakaya and Stahl 1989, 85 et seq.; v. d. Oelsnitz 2000, 152) than the ones we apprehended.

Our findings concerning economies of scale contradict claims made in other empirical studies (Duetsch 1984, 483 et sqq.; Dunne, Roberts, and Samuelson 1988, 503 et sqq.; Shapiro and Khemani 1987, 21 et sqq.). Unlike other authors, we believe that economies of scale, far from acting as a deterrent, actually encourage rival companies to look for ways and means of breaking into new markets.

In order to attain this objective, however, rival firms must be in a position to achieve economies of scale. We therefore asked innovative companies about the size of rival firms which had broken into their markets by imitating innovative products (Table 4).

In almost 50 % of the cases we considered, the rival company is much bigger than the innovative company. It therefore comes as no surprise that the rival firms classified as 'larger' or 'much larger' benefit from economies of scale. Economies of scale achieved by an innovative company are unlikely to constitute a barrier to entry, especially if the rival firm is much bigger than the innovative one. We agree with Yip (1982 b, 85 et sqq.), who argues that under certain circumstances an entry barrier, instead of keeping rivals out, may constitute a "gateway to entry" for competitors who are anxious to break into new markets: "If barriers are a wall, existing skills and resources are a platform. Thus, entrants can go beyond reducing the height of barriers and can, in fact, obtain an advantage over incumbents" (Yip 1982 b, 87).

Table 4: *The respective sizes of innovative and rival companies*

Size of rival company	*Percentages*
Much smaller than innovative company	11.1 %
Smaller than innovative company	13.3 %
Same size as innovative company	8.9 %
larger than innovative company	17.8 %
much larger than innovative company	48.9 %

Not only do entry barriers show competitors where there are advantages to be gained (Brockhoff 1991, 91 et sqq.); they also indicate – albeit indirectly – the entry strategies that rival firms will have to adopt in order to get into the markets they covet. Initially, competitors confronted with barriers to entry will therefore assess their capacity to overcome the obstacles put in their path; then, if they judge this capacity to be sufficient, they will do their utmost to break into the markets they are interested in.

Table 5: *Patent protection and market entry by competitors*

Market entry by competitors?	*Patent protection?*		*Sum*
	Yes	*No*	
Yes	28	17	45
No	20	23	43
Sum	48	40	88

It is surprising that even a barrier created by patenting will encourage rival firms to attack a market dominated by an innovative company. In 57,5 % of the cases where innovative products were protected by patents, competitors succeeded in breaking into the innovator's market (see Table 5).

Only 54.6 % of the innovative companies tried to protect their products by applying for patents. Three conclusions seem to emerge from this. First, relatively few firms believe in the effectiveness of patenting. Secondly, it would be a mistake to assume a close correlation between patent applications and a high degree of novelty. Thirdly, we are fully justified in affirming that in many cases barriers to market entry, far from acting as a deterrent, actually encourage rival firms to look for ways and means of penetrating the markets they covet.

By revealing the functions fulfilled by innovative products, patent specifications give useful technological information to competitors, who are then in a position to decide whether it would be feasible to develop similar products without incurring the risk of a lawsuit for patent infringement. Many innovative companies are now aware of this major drawback and therefore prefer not to register patents for their products.

In view of the above findings, we feel obliged to challenge the traditional version of the entry barrier paradigm, viz. the idea that barriers to entry can only act as a deterrent to competitors. As we have already pointed out, the impediments in question must be regarded as information signals which help rival firms to adopt appropriate entry strategies. Our data indicate that this is particularly true of barriers created by economies of scale or patenting. If barriers to entry can be shown to have a deterrent effect, this only means that so far none of the competitors has managed to break through them.

6 Implications for patent policy

The implications for corporate patent policy are obvious. Since in many cases patents no longer fulfill the purpose for which they were originally designed, it is essential to establish patenting guidelines for innovative companies (Brockhoff, Ernst, and Hundhausen 1999, 605 et sqq.).

Before filing a patent application, an innovative firm ought to consider whether the product it is planning to launch is really suited to the consumer's needs. The innovator should never forget that technology-push innovation rarely enables an enterprise to achieve market success (Brockhoff 1984, 337 et sqq.), though demand-pull innovation often does. If a business files patent applications indiscriminately, its R&D department will tend to give priority to the technicalities of patenting instead of focusing its efforts on the development of products that fit the consumer's needs.

In this context, the findings of Grefermann et al. (1974, 48) merit close attention: 21% of the companies surveyed said their decision to push ahead with plans to develop a new product was primarily motivated by the desire to obtain a patent on their invention. It is surprising that in 45 % of the cases studied, those responsible for product development failed to take account of the market situation when they had to weigh up the advantages and disadvantages of going ahead with a project. Since patenting was their top priority, they took the line that a successful innovative product is not something that sells well, but something that qualifies for a patent.

As the development costs of innovative products are relatively high, one would expect innovative firms to apply for patents in order to prevent competitors from encroaching on their markets. Yet, as we have already said, our data show that there is no significant correlation between patent applications and the degree of novelty of the products manufactured by the firms we surveyed. The absence of such a correlation is no doubt due to two facts. First, many innovators realize that a high degree of novelty and technological complexity will be sufficient to protect their products from imitation. Secondly, they are also aware that patent applications may diminish the effectiveness of entry barriers created by a high degree of novelty.

Since patents do not afford sufficient protection to the markets of innovative companies, such firms should only apply for patents in cases where patenting might offer special advantages of another kind; and their patent departments ought to turn their energies to the collection and analysis of information pertaining to areas of technology in which their R&D departments are particularly interested for commercial reasons.

7 References

Anderson, E. and A.T. Coughlan (1987): International Market Entry and Expansion via Independent or Integrated Channels of Distribution, *Journal of Marketing*, 51, 71-82.

Anderson, J.C. and D.W. Gerbing (1988): Structural Equation Modeling in Practice, *Psychological Bulletin*, 103, 411-423.

Bain, J. S. (1962): *Barriers to New Competition*, 2nd print, Cambridge, MA.

Baumol, W.J., J.C Panzar, and R.D. Willig, (1982): *Contestable Markets and the Theory of Industrial Structure*, New York et al.

Brockhoff, K. (1991): Competitor Technology Intelligence in German Companies, *Industrial Marketing Management*, 20, 91-98.

Brockhoff, K., H. Ernst, and E. Hundhausen (1999): Gains and Pains from Licensing - Patent-Portfolios as Strategic Weapons in the Cardiac Rhythm Management Industry, *Technovation*, 19, 605-614.

Brockhoff, K. (1984): Probleme marktorientierter Forschungs- und Entwicklungspolitik, in: J. Mazanec et al. (Eds.): *Marktorientierte Unternehmungsführung*, Vienna, 337-374.

Brockhoff, K. (1999): *Produktpolitik*, 4th ed., Stuttgart.

Bunch, D. and R. Smiley (1992): Who Deters Entry? Evidence on the Use of Strategic Entry Deterrents, *Review of Economics and Statistics*, 74, 509-521.

Comanor, W. and T.A. Wilson (1967): Advertising, Market Structure and Performance, *Review of Economics on Statistics*, 49, 423-440.

Duetsch, L.L. (1984): Entry and the Extent of Multiplant Operations, *Journal of Industrial Economics*, 32, 477-487.

Duetsch, L.L. (1975): Structure, Performance and the Net of Entry into Manufacturing Industry, *Southern Economic Journal*, 41, 450-456.

Dunne, T., M.J. Roberts, and L.W. Samuelson (1988): Patterns of Firm Entry and Exit in U. S. Manufacturing Industries, *RAND Journal of Economics*, 19, 495-515.

Ehrmann, T. and R. Biedermann (2002): Die Markteintrittsstrategie der Selbstbeschränkung und das Warten auf die Wachstumschance: Ein Beitrag zur Betriebswirtschaftslehre der Unternehmensgründung, *Zeitschrift für Betriebswirtschaft*, 72, 497-512.

Esposito, F.F. and L. Esposito (1971): Foreign Competition and Domestic Industry Profitability, *Review of Economics and Statistic*, 53, 343-353.

Gallini, N. (1992): Patent policy and Costly Imitation, *RAND Journal of Economics*, 23, 52-63.

Garcia Marinoso, B. (2001): Technological Incompatibility, Endogenous Switching Costs and Lock-In, *Journal of Industrial Economics*, 49, 281-298.

George, K.D. (1968): Concentration, Barriers to Entry and Rates of Return, *Review of Economics and Statistics*, 50, 273-275.

Gorecki, P.K. (1987): Barriers to Entry in the Canadian pharmaceutical Industry: Comments, Clarifications and Extensions, *Journal of Health Economics*, 6, 59-72.

Grefermann, K. et al. (1974): *Patentwesen und technischer Fortschritt, Bd. 1: Die Wirkungen des Patentwesens im Innovationsprozess*, Göttingen.

Harabi, N. (1995): Appropriability of Technical Innovations: An Empirical Analysis, *Research Policy*, 24, 981-992.

Harrigan, K.R. (1981): Barriers to Entry and Competitive Strategies, *Strategic Management Journal*, 2, 395-412.

Hilke, J.C. (1984), Excess Capacity and Entry: Some Empirical Evidence, *Journal of Industrial Economics*, 33, 233-240.

Holtermann, S.E. (1973), Market Structure and Economic Performance in U. K. Manufacturing Industry, *Journal of Industrial Economics*, 22, 119-139.

Karakaya, F. (2002), Barriers to Entry in Industrial Markets, *Journal of Business & Industrial Marketing*, 17, 379-389.

Karakaya, F. and M. J. Stahl (1989): Barriers to Entry and Market Entry Decision in Consumer and Industrial Goods Markets, *Journal of Marketing*, 53, 80-91.

Khalilzadeh-Shirazi, J. (1974), Market Structure and Price-Cost Margins in United Kingdom Manufacturing Industries, *Review of Economics and Statistics*, 56, 67-76.

Kleijweg, A.J.M. and M.H.C. Lever (1996): Entry and Exit in Dutch Manufacturing Industries, *Review of Industrial Organization*, 11, 375-382.

Lieberman, M.B. (1987): The Learning Curve, Diffusion, and Competitive Strategy, *Strategic Management Journal*, 8, 441-452.

MacLeod, W.B. (1987): Entry, Sunk Costs, and Market Structure, *Canadian Journal of Economic*, 20, 140-151.

Mathis, S. and J. Koscianski (1996): Excess Capacity as a Barrier to Entry in the US Titanium Industry, *International Journal of Industrial Organization*, 15, 263-281.

Mueller, D.C. and J. Tilton (1969): Research and Development Costs as a Barrier to Entry, *The Canadian Journal of Economics*, 2, 570-579.

Nahata, B. (1989): On the Definition of Barriers to Entry, *Southern Economic Journal*, 56, 236-239.

Orr, D. (1974): The Determinants of Entry: A Study of the Canadian Manufacturing Industries, *Review of Economics and Statistics*, 56, 58-66.

Oster, S. (1982): Intraindustry Structure and the Ease of Strategic Change, *Review of Economics and Statistics*, 64, 376-383.

Perillieux, R. (1987): *Der Zeitfaktor im strategischen Technologiemanagement*, Berlin.

Pickford, M. (1991): Further Empirical Evidence from New Zealand on Strategic Entry Deterrence, *Massey Economic Papers*, 9, 27-54.

Quirmbach, H. (1993): R&D: Competition, Risk, and Performance, *RAND Journal of Economics*, 24, 157-197.

Salop, S.C. (1979): Strategic Entry Deterrence, *American Economic Review*, 69, 335-338.

Schmalensee, R. (1978): Entry Deterrence in the Ready-to Eat Breakfast Cereal Industry, *Bell Journal of Economics*, 9, 305-327.

Schmidt, F. (1998): *Institutionelle Markteintrittsschranken, potentielle Konkurrenz und Unternehmensverhalten: Ein Beitrag zur Endogenisierung der Marktstruktur.* Berlin.

Schnaars, St.P. (1986): When Entering Growth Markets: Are Pioneers better than Proachers?, *Business Horizons*, 29, 27-36.

Schumpeter, J.A. (1934): *The Theory of Economic Development*, Cambridge, MA.

Schwalbach, J. (1987): Entry by Diversified Firms into German Industries, *International Journal of Industrial Organization*, 5, 43-49.

Scott Morton, F. (2000): Barriers to Entry, Brand Advertising, and Generic Entry in the US Pharmaceutical Industry, *International Journal of Industrial Organization*, 18, 1085-1105.

Shapiro, D. and R.S. Khemani (1987): The Determinants of Entry and Exit Reconsidered, *International Journal of Industrial Organization*, 5, 15-26.

Siegfried, J.J. and L.B. Evans (1994): Empirical Studies of Entry and Exit: A Survey of the Evidence, *Review of Industrial Organization*, 9, 121-155.

Singh, S., M. Utton, and M. Waterson (1998): Strategic Behavior of Incumbent Firms in UK, *International Journal of Industrial Organizations*, 16, 229-251.

Smiley, R. (1988): Empirical Evidence on Strategic Entry Deterrence, *International Journal of Industrial Organization*, 6, 167-180.

Spital, F. (1983): Gaining Market Share Advantages in the Semi-Conductor Industry by Lead Time in Innovation, in: Richard S. Rosenbloom (Ed.): *Research on Technological Innovation, Management and Policy, Vol. 1*, Greenwich et al., 55-67.

Stonebraker, R.J. (1976): Corporate Profits and the Risk of Entry, *Review of Economic and Statistics*, 58, 33-39.

Takalo, T. (1998): Innovation and Imitation under Imperfect Patent Protection, in: *Journal of Economics*, 67, 229-241.

Urban, G.L., T. Carter, and Z. Mucha (1985): Market Share Rewards to Pioneering Brands: An Exploratory Empirical Analysis, in: Howard Thomas et al. (Eds.): *Strategic Marketing and Management*, Chichester et al., 239-252.

von der Oelsnitz, D. (2000): Strategische Interaktion zwischen Eintrittszeitpunkt und Eintrittsbarrieren, in: D. von der Oelsnitz (Ed.): *Markteintritts-Management: Probleme, Strategien, Erfahrungen*, Stuttgart, 137-160.

Wright, D. (1999), Optimal Patent Breath and Length with costly Imitation, *International Journal of Industrial Organization*, 17, 419-437.

Yip, G.S. (1982 a): *Barriers to Entry: A Corporate Strategy Perspective*, Lexington, MA.

Yip, G.S. (1982 b): Gateways to Entry, in: *Harvard Business Review*, (Sept.-Oct.), 85-92.

Zörgiebel, W. (1983): *Technologie in der Wettbewerbsstrategie: strategische Auswirkungen technologischer Entscheidungen untersucht am Beispiel der Werkzeugmaschinenindustrie*, Berlin.

Hartmut Kreikebaum

Innovation Processes in Pharmaceutical Companies

Organizational Determinants

Prof. Dr. *Hartmut Kreikebaum*, Department of International Management, European Business School at Oestrich-Winkel.

1 Introduction

When I first met Klaus Brockhoff in early 1970, we both held positions in prevalent non-academic institutions dealing with research and development problems. He was still active on the staff of Battelle Institut, Frankfurt, I had just joined the strategic planning department of Boehringer Ingelheim. Since then, we share a common interest in problems of industrial R&D, and we also join in an internationally oriented perspective.

The international competitive strength of a country depends on its ability to build up centers of strategic competence. Multinational companies pursue the strategy to locate R&D as well as product development in areas which offer the best conditions for innovation and knowledge generation on a worldwide basis. Germany was always known for important technical innovations (Albach 1994, 50–64). It still possesses two specific sectoral clusters of global importance: metalworking and machinery on the one side, and the chemical industry, including pharmacy and biotechnology, on the other. Around 360 biotechnological companies, targeting at the development of new therapeutic substances and pharmaceutical products, underline Germany's leading position in this field within Europe.

In his textbook "Management von Innovationen" Brockhoff (1996, 61–64)presents successful and less successful innovation projects in their different phases of defining, selection, implementation, and market introduction. Two cases deal with specific problems of developing new products in pharmaceutical companies: the selection of an antivirus drug (parallel or sequential development) and the decision of in-licensing a medicine for treatment of pyelonephritis.

In our paper, we focus on the same topic: studying R&D product portfolio decisions within the pharmaceutical industry. Building-up a flexible organization is a prerequisite for successful innovation strategies. We will analyze the relevant organizational factors determining the success of research and development (R&D) according to recent developments in selected (mainly) German companies.

Challenging innovation processes depend upon strategic thinking, creativity and commitment of the workforce, as well as organizational responsiveness. Chapter 2 includes an update of new traits in R&D strategies within the pharmaceutical industry. Innovation processes always present a challenge to the structural status quo of a firm, if a 'partisan strategy' (Kriegesmann 2004, 16) is envisaged. In chapter 3, we will treat some personnel implications of a flexible R&D organization. Problems of building-up an innovative R&D structure are being discussed in chapter 4. This multiple task includes an active boundary spanning between R&D, production, and marketing, improving communication patterns, and reducing coordination times as well as the innovation cycle itself. We will deal with these problems in chapter 5.

2 Research and development in the pharmaceutical industry

It is fascinating to watch the dramatic changes in the legal, societal, and economic conditions of the pharmaceutical industry in Germany which have taken place during the last decade. Independent of their size, all pharmaceutical firms are forced to reach value through innovation by a growth oriented product portfolio. The worldwide operating enterprises within the pharmaceutical industry are striving for a larger percentage of patented and exclusive products. In order to reach this strategic goal, they heavily rely upon their R&D basis, but also on in-licensing of promising products and on strategic alliances with other companies. The ten largest pharmaceutical corporations in the world market emerged from previous mergers and acquisitions, with Glaxo-SmithKline on top of this list, followed by PfizerWarnerLambert, AstraZeneca, Aventis, Merck, Novartis, and others. A rather unique example of a fully family-owned company with global extension is presented by Boehringer Ingelheim.

The total human pharmaceutical market is divided in patent-protected medicines (with a protection duration of 20 years), which are subject to medical prescription, and multisource drugs, i.e. generics or copycat products. The research-based pharmaceutical companies (especially in Germany) complain an unfavorable political structure that brakes medical-pharmaceutical progress by government-backed promotion of parallel imports and generics, cost and containment measures within the healthcare system, and even considering of reference pricing for patent-protected products. They demand a risk premium for the high risk of inventing a new, innovative medicine instead of "a price cut in the form of official encouragement for non-creative copycat products" (Boehringer Ingelheim 2003a, 3).

There is no doubt about the tendency of an increasing substitution of prescription medicines by generics and OTC-products. This development leads to a shortened product life cycle of patent products and reduces the time span for amortizing risky investment in R&D-activities. On the other hand, there exists no alternative to highly effective substances and innovative medications, providing a distinct benefit to the patients. This benefit may consist in a permanent healing from a special disease or in the treatment of actual pain. In the case of intestine cancer, the "success" of a new drug may be a longer life for the patient, even for a few months, like in the case of Genentech's new product Avastin. In fighting chronic obstructive pulmonary disease, ALTANAS'S newly developed Daxas (Roflumilast) causes a significant reduction of the rate of exacerbation and leads to a daily improvement of health conditions. The discovery of marketable active substances requires fast growing R&D expenditures. Between 1977 and 1997, the average R&D cost for developing a new product amounted from USD 54m to USD 600m (according to Vasella 1998, 144). This is due to new analytical methods as well as higher regulatory requirements and additional requests for product quality. Strategic investments in new technologies add to R&D expenditures.

Product innovations played a vital role from the beginning of pharmaceutical research. The development of new medicines, however, has not always been the result of a combined effort of different departments or researchers. A historical review of Bayer reveals, for instance, that its first pharmaceutical product Phenacetin was invented by chance in 1888 as an 'artificial fever drug'. It broke the monopoly of quinine, which was produced from the hardly accessible cinchona bark and contributed decisively to fighting the worldwide influenza epidemic between 1889-92. Ten years later, Felix Hoffmann discovered acetylsalicylic acid, the basic ingredient of aspirin, the first global drug used against rheumatism, fever, and in cardiology (worldwide known as 'ASS'; see Verg, Plumpe, and Schultheiss 1988, 90–97, 134–141). Strategic thinking in R&D starts with scanning the environment for innovation processes by applying information networking and knowledge management. It centers upon a long-range viewpoint instead of short-term action, thus overcoming, e.g., a narrow outlook for 'German products' only. Furthermore, the innovation strategy must be linked to the corporate strategy process at the earliest stage deemed possible. Another topic, hence, is presented by the need for a constructive cooperation with nature, including a strategic partnership with the bioscience network as a new target.

Increasing R&D productivity requires excellent and competent researchers. Whether pharmaceutical companies are successful in their innovation effort is primarily a question of attracting highly skilled scientists from all over the world. Staffing R&D teams as centers of excellence remains a major responsibility of corporate management. I shall treat this problem in the following chapter.

3 Staffing R&D teams as centers of excellence

"The first and overriding condition for innovation success is to have excellent, competent researchers" (Albach 1994, 27). With this first sentence Albach sums up his recommendations for firms on how they should manage R&D teams for better performance. His recommendations are derived from an international study performed by the Berlin Academy of Sciences and Technology, dealing with the cultural factors influencing costs and time to market of technical innovations. Technical innovations are being defined as new products or new technological production processes. They usually start with an invention and development phase, in the case of fundamental innovations as well as mere improvement innovations, i.e. ingenious new solutions to an existing problem or a creative imitation. The study group collaborated the hypothesis that the creativity in R&D labs of truly European firms draws upon highly talented personnel and highly diversified human resources. Its results are based upon eight in-depth case studies, including the development and marketing of oral conceptives by Schering (Albach 1994, 922–1012).

In general, the innovative personality is characterized by a distinctive creativity and a high degree of motivation concerning hard work. In comparison to others, creative people are able to generate more spontaneously new and original products than others. They possess knowledge that is open to divergent rather than convergent thinking. Expert knowledge represents the crucial prerequisite for innovation. According to these case studies of the Berlin Academy, most of the university graduates in natural sciences working in the labs of five large German and Swiss companies received their professional training in their home countries. The main reason behind these findings may be that the chemical sciences in these countries are being regarded as excellent compared to other nations (Albach 1994, 27). And, since R&D represents a key factor to the global future, the ethical drug industry heavily depends upon promising scientists from centers of excellence all over the world. Therefore, human resource management has to operate on a global screening base.

Two factors determine the R&D team's composition: the chosen product portfolio and the prescribed phases of development. First of all, pharmaceutical companies try to discover and develop products satisfying medical needs with a high therapeutic value for the patient. Their product lives correspond with the indication area. In prescription medicines, this can be, for instance, respiratory, urology, rheumatology, HIV AIDS, cardiology and central nervous system (e.g. Parkinson's disease). Consumer health care products may treat, e.g., cough and cold, gastrointestinal problems, or strengthen the immune system (natural health products). So-called ethical products try to satisfy high unmet needs posed by complex diseases like Alzheimer or diabetes. Promising targets for pharmacological intervention can only be identified if researchers get more insight into the pathophysiological processes at a molecular level (Boehringer Ingelheim 2003b, 4 et sq., 20 et sq.). In order to reach an increased R&D productivity, pharmaceutical companies are forced to implement key enabling technologies like genomics (sequencing of the human genome) proteomics (the large-scale study of the complete protein complement of the genome), molecular biology and genetic engineering. They all enable the production of proteins or antibodies as an alternative to extract protein from donor blood, thus avoiding the risk of infection with serious diseases such as hepatitis B/C or HIV. This targeting new territory of genomics, proteomics, and bioinformatics requires a new type of R&D personnel: people who are highly skilled in new areas of basic research in genomics, proteomics, and bioinformatics on one side, and utilizing selected new technologies in close collaboration with the therapeutic area expertise on the other. Boehringer Ingelheim, e.g., carries out genomics/ proteomics projects in all therapeutic product lives, i.e. respiratory and autoimmune diseases, oncology, metabolic, cardiovascular and viral diseases as well as diseases of the central nervous system. Furthermore, the research staff has to be familiar with the new scientific discipline of bioinformatics, to cope with the unprecedented data volumes in biology. Bioinformatics has become an integral part of all biotechnical approaches (Boehringer Ingelheim 2003b, 30 et sqq.). Genomics and proteomics are not only used in the first stages of drug discovery, but also in toxicology and in the rather new field of pharmacogenetics and in pharmacokinetics, where genes involved and drug metabolism are investigated. The application of these new technologies requires R&D people specifically trained in bioinformatics to advance genomics projects within their teams to new strategic targets.

As a global leader in the field of human vaccines against influenza, hepatitis, meningitis and polio Aventis addresses its efforts on quite another area of R&D (Aventis 2003b, 20 et sq.; also see Aventis 2003a, 20–28). With its system of prevention and disease management, the company is engaged in significant public health initiatives such as Aventis Pasteur, one of the largest private AIDS virus vaccine research programs, and in cancer care. The 'Maison des Cancérologues de France' enables an exchange of knowledge between leading experts in cancer treatment and oncologists. In its new center of excellence it offers a two-year post-graduate study program in oncology. Furthermore, it provides an interdisciplinary approach by including psychological and social dimensions of cancer. Highly trained pharmacists are needed for piloting a program called "Patient Self-Management: Diabetes", combating the effects of diabetes on America's workforce. About 5.700 people are working in research and development of Aventis' branded prescription drugs. The company's Drug Innovation & Approval organization is responsible for delivering the pipeline, increasing innovation and productivity, and optimizing the product value.

A second influencing factor of staffing R&D teams may be seen in the structure of an innovation process. Contrary to the three phases in the automotive industry (analysis of basic technology, product and production development, market launch), innovating prescription drugs usually includes more phases and other strategic decisions (Albach 1994, 83–86). The first two phases consist of the synthesis of the compound and isolation of the new substance, followed by pharmacological screening and chemical testing. The third phase serves as a time of economic screening. Clinical testing I, II and III takes up the bulk of time (between five to seven years), starting with resorption and metabolism in body, followed by testing for chronic toxicity (including teratogenicity and mutagenicity) and effectiveness. Galenic testing (dose tiration), submission and registration are the next two phases, before market analyses lead to a market introduction of the ethical drug in individual countries.

Representatives of many disciplines are closely cooperating during the different stages of development, especially chemists, pharmacologists, physicians, biologists, technicians, and chemical research assistants. They contribute to a firm's position of strength, based upon a flow of new products out of clinical testing. Novartis, e.g., reports about a present bulk of 80 substances in the pipeline (Schmidt 2000). The marketing intelligence function requires additional input from corporate marketing and competitive intelligence staff people. Information retrieval specialists are needed during almost all phases of the innovation process. Market penetration of the registered product requires a sales organization including clinic assistants visiting decision-makers in health centers, ambulances, hospitals, and other medical institutions.

Staffing R&D teams in a pharmaceutical company is directly in line with its specific product strategies. Innovative products determine the business success of the firm. The future challenge of innovation increases with the yet unknown technologies for which a company cannot rely on existing knowledge and experience. In order to activate the innovative potential constantly, the human resource department has to provide employees and leaders with a sense for achieving challenging business targets in a world of change. Their business-related competences include the ability to create or improve innovative processes, systems, and products.

At the Schering Corporation, cross-functional mobility as well as geographical mobility are regarded as an essential part of personnel measures. (Schering 2003a, 17–20) Global players will look out for the creative personality beyond their geographical frontiers. Since different developmental cultural factors may act as constraints on creativity, removal of such barriers will be another important task in order to increase the outcome of new drugs and process ideas (Albach 1994, 91–124). The generation of ideas and discovery of new drugs as a dominant factor of innovation success may still be dominated by individual scientists, assisted by a research team. Innovative teams are necessary in the predevelopment and the development phases to organize the time-consuming and complex research process. In an empirical study of the desired profile of R&D team members in different countries, Brockhoff (1990, 90 et sqq.)discovered remarkable similarities as well as striking differences. It is not at all disputed that managers should act primarily as generalists. American firms, however, preferred an R&D specialist, and so did German companies. Japanese firms, on the other side, prefer outsiders.

4 Building-up an innovative organization

Innovation strategies depend upon innovative organizational frameworks. This statement expresses Chandler's "structure follows strategy"-thesis in a first approximation. It postulates an overall flexible organizational structure for implementing strategic product and process innovations. I will focus on two problems, which are of special interest in this realm. Firstly, I shall discuss the question why the innovative team should present the core organizational pattern of the R&D organization. Chapter 4 treats some problems of coordinating internationally dispersed R&D laboratories in selected German companies.

According to a widespread belief, markets are shaped by men and innovative products are invented by individuals. The Bayer Corporation, heavily engaged in developing pharmaceutical products since 1888, states its experience in summa as follows: "Bayer has reached its present position, because in its history there have always been individual persons who thought and acted innovatively" (Verg, Plumpe, and Schultheiss 1988, 609). Especially many American managers share the opinion that "creative ideas are developed by individuals and not by teams" (Albach 1994, 126). The creative individual seems to be an ideal of the innovative company. The "person in the driver's seat" is being regarded as the backbone of the innovative organization's existence.

There is no doubt about the fact that a team does not exist without its individual members and even the inventor genius depends upon the assistance of other people. It is not trivial, however, that "teamwork" accompanies R&D activities in pharmaceutical firms from the very beginning. When Carl Duisberg introduced the idea of an "Etablissementserfindung", he based it upon the "Etablissement" as a guiding organizational concept of Bayer's new scientific main laboratory at Elberfeld in 1891 and a first expression of the later teamwork concept (Verg, Plumpe, and Schultheiss 1988, 98–102). Duisberg, who became the leading founder of Germany's big chemical industry, already foresaw the future importance of innovative teams in his first year as CEO of the Bayer Corporation. They demand for strong commitment, the integration of the different team members in the innovation process, competence, leeway and knowledge (Albach 1994, 135–162).

Since innovation always represents elements of confrontation of the new technology and products with the established technology and product portfolio, a dedicated commitment of the team is the most important factor of success of an innovative technology and product line. The 'strategic intent' of top management seems to be a prerequisite for a committed R&D team. If it is properly communicated, it helps to overcome frustration to work and secures the company's success.

Many modern pharmaceutical firms recruit their researchers on a global-wide scale. At Boehringer Ingelheim's Research Institute of Molecular Pathology in Vienna, for instance, around 120 biologists, biochemists, and medical doctors originating from 27 countries carry out basic research in the field of molecular genetics, cell cycle regulation, and developmental biology, in order to understand fundamental mechanisms of diseases and identify cell cycle targets for innovative therapies. Expertise across a broad range of disciplines is also being provided in Boehringer's Drug Discovery Center for Oncology, covering teamwork along the entire drug discovery chain from molecual and cell biology, biochemistry, assay robotics, medicinal chemistry and pharmacology, up to immunology (Boehringer Ingelheim 2003b, 12–27). Successfully integrating many disciplines as well as research people in a multinational team requires that all team members communicate in the same language and are top experts in their special field. They also need leedway, i.e. the freedom to follow different ideas in the invention phase and to enjoy autonomy in the later phases of the innovation process, regarding time and budget decisions. Above all, an innovative research team needs a solid knowledge base.

5 Interface management from an international perspective

According to empirical studies, interface management indicates a prerequisite of an innovative organization and represents especially in international companies a yet unresolved problem. "Quite a number of firms face severe problems in managing the interfaces among laboratories, and between laboratories and the other departments of a company" (Brockhoff 1998, 83). As Brockhoff points out, organizational interfaces describe a non-hierarchical coordination between two or more individuals or groups. This specific type of social relation is defined by six elements: autonomy of the organizational units, equal position, interactional relations, enforced interaction, existence of conflicts regarding goals, knowledge and distribution of resources, and common superiors (Brockhoff and Hauschildt 1993, 399; see also Hauschildt 1997, 108 et sqq.).

Company experiences indicate that interface management should already start in the first place of innovation, the so-called fuzzy-front-end of development. This procedure guarantees a lower degree of risk and a higher project efficiency (Herstatt and Verworn 2004, 20).

Innovation processes are highly complex and depend upon an open flow of information among the departments of a company. Managing information networking on an interdepartmental basis and resolving conflicts between the cooperating organizational units is of crucial importance for a successful implementation of innovation strategies within a global perspective. Internationalization of R&D activities originally started with introducing local transfer units which assisted production of pharmaceuticals in a foreign country, with the company headquarters in the home country being in full charge of all functions. This policy changed completely at the beginning of the nineties, when total R&D functions and therapeutic lines were transformed into separate foreign institutions. The foundation of autonomous R&D organizations abroad started in the biochemical field due to a liberal handling of registration, e.g., in the United States. According to von Boehmer's study , the all-round R&D unit with a regional focus represents the most frequently used organizational alternative. Other types like local problem solvers, applied researchers (without development), or all-round R&D units with global market orientation seem to be rather unimportant (von Boehmer 1995, 74 et sqq., 110).

Interface management problems may arise along the same functional line within the global R&D structure and between different functional departments of a firm. The global R&D structure depends upon the task assignment to foreign R&D laboratories, the chosen locus of coordination, and the level of performance (Brockhoff 1998, Chapter 5, 55–81). Its specific characteristics should not be treated as a pure alternative between centralization or decentralization, but should also include a mixed mode decision-making alternative. Based upon the optimum laboratory size and the necessity of coordinating R&D activities as guiding principles, Brockhoff (1998, 68)proposes a taxonomy of nine cases, according to the chosen locus of decision making (headquarters, foreign site and mixed mode decisions) and locus of performance (central, decentral, and division of labor).

A challenge to interface management is presented by all models that are subject to conflicts arising from the need of intense communication and interaction. This is especially the case in joint decision-making including or excluding central laboratory involvement. Conflicts may arise due to cultural divergence, information asymmetries, and different strategic perspectives. Insufficient market knowledge and disturbed communication patterns seem to indicate a severe split between decision-makers in management positions and R&D staffs in British as well as German companies (see von Boehmer 1995, 121–123, and Brockhoff 1990, 34–37). A special cultural conflict between the headquarters and the internationally dispersed local sites arises in the case of insufficient sensitivity of expatriates. In our study of 123 decision-makers in Germany as well as in the United States, for 67.1% of the German and the American partners centralized decision-making in multinational firms represents the adequate means to create a sensitive understanding for ethnical conflicts in the host countries. Both sides agreed that culture-bound conflicts are able to be solved by integrating local representatives and expatriates in a durable dialogue. 86.6% of the German interview partners as well as 63.4% of the American managers agreed that involving the expatriates in decisions of local importance would reduce tensions between different cultural values. Furthermore such integrating processes could strengthen the degree of cultural sensitivity on the headquarters' side.

An overwhelming sample majority of 91.5% (German corporations) respectively 82.9% (American firms) backed the positive effects of integrating local managers in corporate decision-making processes. Against this background, the originally in Latin America developed "dependencia"-thesis could be rejected. Especially in R&D, training of local staff members is being regarded as an important means to bridge existing technological gaps (Kreikebaum, Behnam, and Gilbert 2001, 61–78, 111–119; also see Gilbert 1998, 104–120). Interface management especially aims at integrating knowledge between the R&D department on the one side and the production and marketing departments on the other side (Albach 1994, 198–210). Particularly the information flow between R&D and production plays a vital role from the very beginning of an information process, as production generally prefers existing products while seems to be reluctant towards new ones.

Boehringer Ingelheim solves this problem by totally integrating operations into the development process (Boehringer Ingelheim 2003b, 14 et sq., 22 et sq., 45). The core R&D team thus aims at minimizing time to market, with operations balancing between minimum cost, necessary quality and sufficient supply security. Relying on equal responsibilities on both sides, the interface is regarded as a smooth transition. However, when the various research sites lost their local production responsibilities after having completed the production reallocation projects, handling the interface between R&D and production became a problem of communication.

Since the marketing department is intensely involved in the innovation process, a free information flow between R&D, production, and marketing comprising all stages of the development process becomes inevitably necessary. Thus, a company-wide information system not only assists the interface management on a country level of communication, it additionally links the pharmacology, the medicinal, and the biotechnology functions at the different sites. This way, not only the time to market, but also the risk of innovation failure can be reduced.

As Brockhoff (1998, 83–93)has pointed out unavoidable interfaces could be managed by using two instruments: interface management as a fulltime engagement, either by appointment or by following from a process of social learning, or a complementary interface management. When the R&D structure relies upon networking or competence centers, full time project leaders or process promoters have to be employed to coordinate the projects of various laboratories in different countries. Complementary investments of interface management have to focus on the organizational structure (teambuilding and the readiness to interpret subcultures) as well as on organizational processes (like joint formation of shared values and objectives). The concrete selection of a specific instrument heavily depends on the hierarchical level of coordination, the type of interaction, the reason why the interface exists, as well as on other specific task characteristics like the degree of novelty and the time domain of a common duty.

6 Summary

A critical review reveals some open questions and yet unsolved problems. In a first step, I will describe a few week points. In a second step, some new concepts to cope with failure development on selected problem areas will be discussed.

Taking a long-range view in innovation processes instead of short-term thinking still remains an ongoing task and thus a challenge for every organization planner. The abandonment of a strategic viewpoint inevitably leads to a predominant concentration on short-term goals and action-mindedness. Renouncing innovation strategies seems to be an important barrier to implementing innovations. Therefore, scanning the environment for weak signals announcing technological and scientific changes remains a permanent duty for strategy teams. Thus, the main task of these teams consists of identifying and evaluating new developments in certain therapeutic fields on a company-wide basis. All in all, networking with the outside world defines a permanent task for a key player in immunology, oncology, and inflammation, for instance.

Another organizational weakness consist of the desiderative cooperation of applied clinical research on the one hand and external basic research on the other hand. This may result from the NIH ('Not-invented-here') syndrome as well as from the lack of interdisciplinary, trench fighting or budget restrictions. Regarding the well-known grievances in cancer research, Germany tends to become an imitator state, compared with the United States. Establishing a "Competensive Cancer Center" according to the U.S. model represents a necessary step into the right direction. Furthermore, it would secure a close cooperation between basic research in a country-wide institution and pharmaceutical corporations working and researching in this field of interest. The recently founded center for clinical research and development (ZAFES) at the Goethe University in Frankfurt may be regarded as a necessary link between universities, the pharmaceutical industry, and biotechnology and may serve as a promising "think tank" (Meichsner 2004, 50–53).

The health problems of developing nations represent another challenge. Infection diseases like AIDS, tuberculosis and malaria cause a death-rate of about six million people in these countries. The WHO model "drugs for neglected disease initiative" only marks one example of new civil alliances like public-private partnerships, which are able to fill this gap. Global funds represent a new instrument in attacking this new problem of joined innovation.

7 References

Albach, H. (1994): *Culture and Technical Innovation. A Cross-Cultural Analysis and Policy Recommendations*, Berlin, New York.

Aventis (Ed.) (2003a): *Annual Report 2002 on Form 20-F*, Strasbourg.

Aventis (Ed.) (2003b): *Sustainability Report*, Strasbourg.

Boehringer Ingelheim (Ed.) (2003a): *Annual Report 2002*, Ingelheim.

Boehringer Ingelheim (Ed.) (2003b): *R&D – key to the future*, Ingelheim.

Brockhoff, K. (1990): *Stärken und Schwächen industrieller Forschung und Entwicklung*, Stuttgart

Brockhoff, K. (1998): *Internationalization of Research and Development,* Berlin et. al.

Brockhoff, K. (Ed.) (1996): *Management von Innovationen. Planung und Durchsetzung – Erfolge und Misserfolge,* Wiesbaden.

Brockhoff, K. and J. Hauschildt (1993): Schnittstellen – Management – Koordination ohne Hierarchie, *Zeitschrift für Organisation,* 22, 396–403.

Gilbert, D.U. (1998): *Konfliktmanagement in international tätigen Unternehmen. Ein diskursethischer Ansatz zur Regelung von Konflikten im interkulturellen Management.* Sternenfels.

Hauschildt, J. (1997): *Innovationsmanagement.* 2nd ed., Munich.

Herstatt, C. and B. Verworn (2004): Früh die Weichen für neue Produkte stellen, *FAZ,* 69, March 22, 2004, 20.

Kreikebaum, H., M. Behnam, and D.U. Gilbert (2001): *Management ethischer Konflikte in international tätigen Unternehmen,* Wiesbaden.

Kriegesmann, B. (2004): Mut zur Partisanenstrategie, *FAZ,* 15, January 19, 2004, 16.

Meichsner, B. (2004): Der schnellste Weg zum innovativen Arzneimittel. Das „beste" aus drei Welten, *Forschung Frankfurt,* 1, 50–53.

Schering (Ed.) (2003a): *Corporate Human Resource Strategy. Leading people worldwide,* Berlin.

Schering (Ed.) (2003b): *Annual Report 2002,* Berlin.

Schmidt, S.L. (2000): *Megamerger in der pharmazeutischen Industrie. Ein Beitrag zur Strategieforschung,* Bern, Stuttgart, Vienna.

Vasella, D. (1998): Industry dynamics and change in the pharmaceutical industry, *CEMS Business Review,* 2 (3), 143–147.

Verg, E., G. Plumpe, and H. Schultheis (1988): *Meilensteine. 125 Jahre Bayer,* Leverkusen.

von Boehmer, A. (1995): *Industrialisierung internationaler Forschung und Entwicklung – Typen, Bestimmungsgründe und Erfolgsbestimmung,* Wiesbaden.

Santiago García Echevarría

The Impact of IT Technologies on the New Business Designs

An Empirical Approximation and Proposals for Change

Prof. Dr. Dr. Dr. h.c. *Santiago Garcia Echevarria,* Department of Business Sciences and Director of the Institute of Management and Organization, University of Alcalá (Spain).

1 Introduction

IT technologies play an increasingly important role in the processes of change within business institutions and in particular in management processes. The problem of integrating modern IT technologies into business management presents a very large deficit that has a decisive effect upon companies' results.

The new business designs rest on two basic pillars. Firstly, the debate on leadership and the definition of people's powers and responsibilities, ensuring their own development and that of the company, is gaining increasing importance. Secondly, the new business designs are increasingly involved within the context of the development of ICT management technologies. These two pillars, **people and technology**, are indisputably the very essence of the new business designs.

Without doubt the **people dimension** in leadership and in the development of their powers and responsibilities has not, until recently, been a strong point in business design. They have instead been more oriented towards a functionalism based on the idea of the management "system" in which traditional management design has been the motive force behind business management. In general terms innovation in **management technology** has been sadly lacking and has been predominantly based on a series of financial indicators without ICT technology enhancing decision-making processes. In the last ten years transactional processes have dominated IT technology within companies. Here will we focus the contribution on the IT integration in management.

The scarce resources available to a company and its environment are aimed at measuring human action. This today is the key element in the new business designs and their objective is to adopt, **through the development of people**, decisions that enable **both their skills and resources to be used more efficiently**.

These two pillars aim to discover the available potential within both people and resources (Pümpin and García Echevarría 1990) to foment a shared **dialogue** enabling the information dealing with the results of human action within the company to be evaluated in the most objective manner possible (Pümpin and García Echevarría 1993).

2 IT technologies' unidimensionality versus their globality in business management

Doubtlessly a company's reality and that of any of its ambits is dependent on how its manager perceives it and especially it depends on the instruments used to measure it and the technology utilized to perform the evaluation. This then is the perceivable reality, as we will see later, of a company since 49% of the management information available for evaluating the company's business performance is unidepartmental (Cardona 2003), in other words, it is unidimensional. Therefore, there is a real danger that the company's reality is seen only from the point of view of a **unilateral executive** who is involved in the management of the functions of his/her own responsibility and of the IT instruments being used which in turn, are highly oriented towards his/her function.

Another important aspect of the new business designs springs from the need of all of the people involved in management to have a **global vision** of the business project: of the business in its totality. The dynamics of change, the complexity of management systems and the growing and complex interrelationships within the business, as well as between the business and its environment, impose the need for criteria and evaluations originating from this global vision concerning the business' positioning and orientation. It is true, however, that a partial vision specific to each of the company's areas and functions is the cornerstone of an executive's daily actions, but the criteria for measuring the performance of management, the evaluation of the results contributes to the global result. Therefore, the evaluation criteria, the means used to measure performance, do not depend only upon the executive responsible for the functioning of a specific area, of one reality, but it also depends on this other, more abstract reality, that of **the totality of the company's activities**, with its numerous people, functions and highly differentiated resources and skills. Reality is essentially multidisciplinary and multicultural throughout the company as a whole. As can be observed on a daily basis, the same reality within a company, of a process or situation can be perceived differently by each of the people who managed it and who suggest decisions to solve the company's problems. Risk is perceived in highly different ways depending on which executive evaluates it and therefore, the success or failure of a company's management can also be estimated in different ways.

Currently, great emphasis is been laid upon a traditional phenomenon corresponding to the growing number of interfaces as both the key element of business management and as a manner of measuring management itself. The solution is only possible when the management project and results are shared, as well as **responsibilities** within the dialogue between the different managers who enjoy different levels of approximation to that particular reality. It is "**Living, interdisciplinary**" organizations and not unifunctional "**structural organisations**" that today generate business dynamics (Pümpin and García Echevarría 1990). However, these dynamic organizations must develop within an established institutional "**corporate order**" within which people develop and leadership emerges, enabling the company to discover its line, function and process with its global criteria and management principles so that the executive can go beyond his/her own functional management and act under his/her own initiative and responsibility.

This contribution however is not going to discuss the problem related to the first fundamental pillar that of leadership for the development of people as a fundamental element in the new business designs. In this paper, we are going to focus on the second pillar, which corresponds to the **advance of ICT technologies** for management. It is this advance and not the techniques themselves that enable companies to break down the figure of the "**partial manager**" , and make a great contribution to a company's managers being able to evaluate the different perceptions of the reality of risk and the reality of the decisions from a position where they **"share"** these responsibilities and decisions (interdisciplinarity). Given its increasingly interfunctional nature, reality is too complex and can only be evaluated by managers who, together, share, discuss and take decisions, assuming joint responsibility for the company's future. This then, represents without doubt, the new break with the current business reality.

3 What role does ICT technology innovation play in current business management?

The last ten years have been characterized by the rapid development of technologies for business management, something without precedent in previous designs. In part, these information communication technologies (ICT) involve information techniques, but above all, they involve new conceptualizations in **"person-resources"** interrelationships and their skills and capacities. On the one hand, they are tools that help to provide a better integrated company management based on the relatively secure, rapid availability of information that in general terms, is also shared. On the other hand, the orientation of managers towards a process-based management system, the availability of ERP techniques and the development of different technologies such as CRM, MIS, etc, mean that for the first time, there are significant tools available that provide easier solutions to business management from the interdisciplinary dimension, a dimension wherein lie the greatest challenges for business success, whose fruits are greater productivities. If we take into account that in the studies undertaken , 96%

of managers would be satisfied if they had 16 indicators for measuring and evaluating the results of a company's management, we must regard this as a relatively poor challenge, given a company's complexity (Cardona 2003)

Technologies provide the tools for the new design concepts of business management since they enable the degree of integration of different areas of management, to be added or removed and **interfaces,** interrelationships between different areas and processes, to emerge. In the real business world, 49% of companies have only information that merely covers single departments, information that is handled by the functional managers themselves. This, therefore, is an extremely poor conceptual situation in which to evaluate the failure or success of the business management. Only 13% of managers have information covering four or more departments at their fingertips (Cardona 2003). Indisputably, these management technologies as well as the new business concepts that will be developed, overlap traditional functional areas and in particular (something that is highly significant from the leadership point of view) break down power structures, affecting aspects of business activity. The above implies changes in the way of thinking and a new understanding of the term **"manager"**, his/her field of action and a new involvement of his/her specific field of responsibility within the business as a whole. This new understanding of what a company represents, in terms of business management, and **shared dialogue** where management responsibilities are shared, is a more integrated, more globalized way of thinking that is far more precise in identifying problems and in taking decisions from the point of view of the different evaluations undertaken by the different managers presenting different degrees of approximation to business realities.

Management technologies (ICT) are, and will continue to be, **management tools** that use different techniques from different disciplines, ranging from IT to statistics, or to fields within the worlds of finance and physics. What has happened is that in recent years these ICT technologies have, as a consequence of the integrating nature of their own design, been the motor of new conceptual and organizational business approaches, something that is not limited to business management but also characterizes modern science in the field of the human genome (Hudson 2003), in the field of aviation and in other fields and disciplines (Forman 2003). The search for **integrating technology,** giving rise to the need for new conceptual approaches so that different **"views"** of a problem can be shared by different researchers, is not exclusive to business management. This innovative process is what is both enriching and what gives momentum to the development dynamics of science and reality.

Information and communication technologies in the ambit of business management motivate innovation processes and new, highly innovative forms of organization that are much closer to reality, especially that of people but also closer to the reality of each area and ambit. This enriches people and processes enabling large increases in productivity to be achieved, due to the sharing of business management.

4 The impact of technological innovation upon processes of change within the company

Current processes of change make new innovative management designs obligatory and are of an unknown disruptive nature (Gutenberg 1957) oriented towards "**management productivity" in other words the development of methodologies that enable business performance to be measured, based on an evaluation and measurement that promotes performance in all ambits"** (Fernández de Lis 2003).

The search for a **greater symmetry in information and communication** within the company is based on the following key elements to increase **"executive productivity"** and **"management productivity"** :

- Firstly, the availability of new business concepts based on a shared global vision of both the **business orientation** and conceptualization of its strategy and organizational design.
- It also rests on new patterns of human behavior that foment **dialogue** and **sharing**. Previous to this, **values must be shared** within these human relationships. Dialogue and sharing are the basis of **leadership** and also of the development of attitudes and aptitudes that enable people to become involved and share their individual visions so that through dialogue they approach more closely to the company's real context and problems.
- On the basis of a better knowledge of the complex system that is the company's socio-economic reality and that of its people, information can be shared on the basis of a real **"network"**, of efficient communication, breaking down figure of **"a manager who is bound to his/her own functionality"** .
- The complexity of the change demands shared solutions based on dialogue between the different managers of specific functionality. In this manner, the aim is to achieve the integration of the different visions of the company's reality and to foment cooperation between the different know-hows thus reducing time, problems, and costs while producing knowledge.

Without technological innovation in business management, it is not possible to assimilate change and therefore, it is not possible to give form to the latent technical know-how available within the company.

5 The present situation of technological innovation in business management

The evaluation that has been performed in an empirical study on a global level presents the problem that in business management **"managers do not believe in technology"** (Fernández de Lis 2003). This mainly deals with the problems with the information and communication technologies that support the new management technologies. One of the key problems is that within the company the **interface** between Information Technology as a functional area and the other areas of management activities, does not function fruitfully and as a result, has led to **"company managers viewing investments in technology with a certain degree of skepticism..."** (Fernández de Lis 2003).

A degree of skepticism towards technology has arisen due to the fact that investments in IT techniques are at the most leading to (they are thus evaluated) cost reductions or to some specific increases in **"functional productivity"** but not to a greater achievement in results from the market and client management aspects. This is an orientation of marketing and commercial innovation. In other words, in the terms previously mentioned, IT techniques are oriented towards the productivity relationship denominator, towards the rational consumption of resources and not towards the numerator, i.e. the business and the client. The blame for this problem is claimed to be a lack of **"understanding between managers and the IT department"** (Fernández de Lis 2003). In other words, this problem is due to the fact that the **interface** between a function, IT, as the basis for IT innovation, which is the predominant interpretation, and other specific functions in the business areas, has still not been discovered. This is the reason why this study advances the fact that **"business managers and IT managers do not share a common language and executives must find a common meeting ground"** (Fernández de Lis 2003). It is interesting to observe the statement in this evaluation of the survey's results affirming that **"if you ask an executive if he/she needs technology, he/she will answer that he/she does. However, if you ask him/her what is for, he/she will be unable to answer"** (Cardona 2003). The above situation arises in the case of managers who in their area of responsibility, judge or evaluate it from different perspectives.

Information and communication technology is not conceptually integrated into either decision-making processes or business management, precisely because of that mastery of the technical relationship and functionality, with managers who only perceive, evaluate and judge their own functionality within the company, be it in IT, marketing or any other type of technique. Moreover, this can be observed in the statement made that **"technology is indeed important, but not as an isolated element"**. This means that technology has to be integrated, something that fits with the results of another different study proposing that **"companies do not know how to measure their per-**

formance" (Cardona 2003). And it affirms that only 6% of large companies have an established procedure to evaluate the results of their management.

The results of this research, coinciding with the previous ones, indicate that the level of management information and communication available is not incorporating technologies as a basis for **sharing** the reality that is assumed to exist in decision-making among the different observers.

Figure 1: *Key indicators*

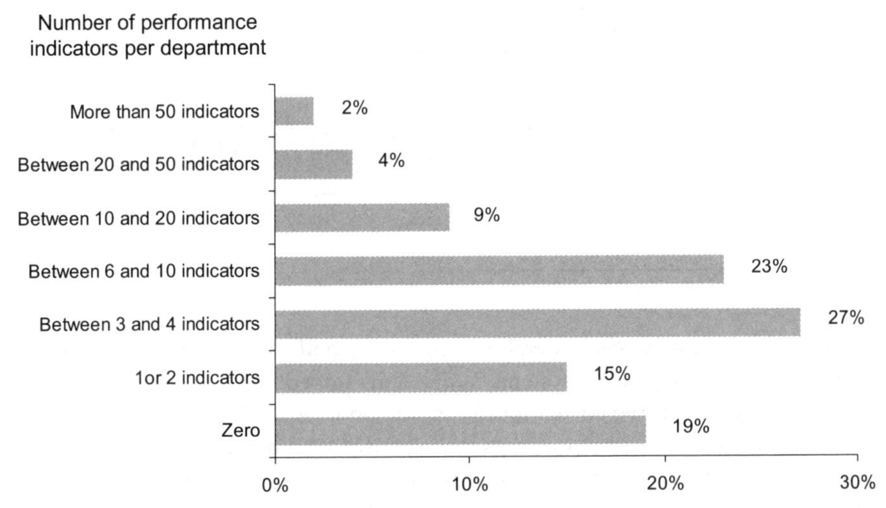

Therefore, as can be observed in Figure 1, the majority of business management measurement systems use between 3 and 10 indicators at most for the highly complex system that is a company. Only 9% of companies use between 10 and 20 indicators.

The most serious problem arising from the deficient integration of technologies is that which can be observed in Figure 2, the lack of a shared vision of information. In Figure 2 we can observe that we still have functional managers whose decisions lack a global orientation. In 49% of the companies a management evaluation measurement system with a unidepartmental nature still predominates, thus giving an erroneous measurement of their management. This constitutes one of the greatest barriers when establishing a shared dialogue between managers both in terms of interpretation, of its functional and global reality in risk taking and evaluating possible decisions for the company as a whole.

Figure 2: *Scope of the information*

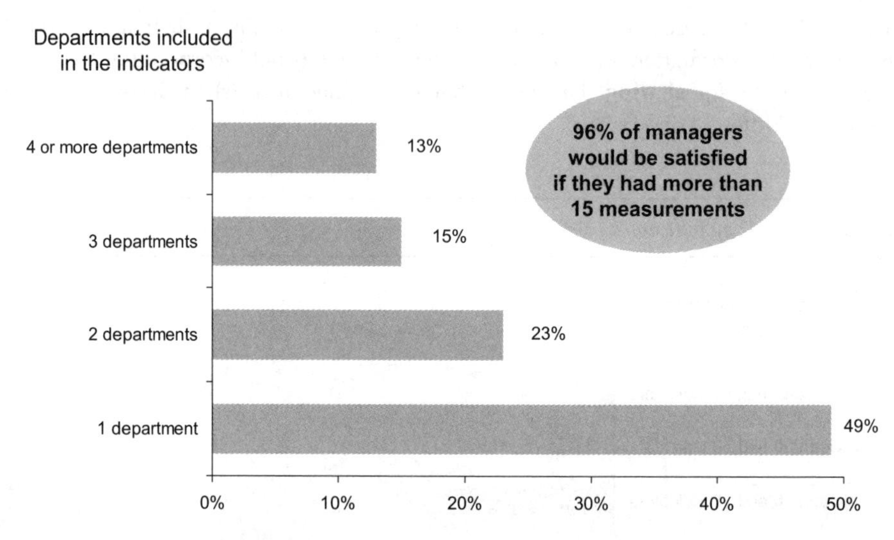

The lack of innovation when integrating information and communication technologies within the new management systems is a serious impediment to undertaking processes of change within the current business situation. Figure 3 shows the generalized dissatisfaction existing within business management with regard to the availability of information and to the means of communication that new technologies provide enabling them to share, evaluate and discuss a company's real processes. Many of the serious problems within the world of business that have arisen in recent years, irrespective of certain penal questions, have been business errors caused fundamentally by this **unidepartmentality** or by the predominance of functional management taking into consideration risks and possibilities that have resulted in serious business crises due to serious strategic errors, a lack of dialogue and a lack of shared information.

Perhaps one of the problems that **"enterprise governance"** presents is that the success of a company depends on its ability to integrate its managers into the shared project, into its global orientation. The current situation of technological innovation in management affects a highly generalized business reality that is searching for a **new conceptualisation** of its strategies and management which will make the integration of the new technological opportunities possible, a conceptualization that will involve highly different multidisciplinary techniques. However, the essence of the fundamental problem lies in **Heisenberg's** statement that reality is what the observer sees and if this observer is not a multiobserver he/she is going to find difficulties in approaching it and will be even less able to take the correct business decisions. We are dealing with a new orientation of Business Culture.

Figure 3: *Managers' evaluations of performance measurements*

- 30% of managers are dissatisfied with their measurement and methodologies
- 15% of managers are satisfied
- 58% of managers use less than 5 indicators
- 49% of companies input information manually
- 25% of companies devote 2/3 days per month to measuring and monitoring performance related information

The most advanced areas in the development of indicators that enable performance to be measured are those of sales and marketing. 13% of sales directors of the 1,000 largest European companies have at their disposal the correct measurement tools in order to evaluate the results (Cardona 2003).

6 How to design the integration of information and communication technology into business management: concepts and tools

The designs for **new business dynamics** (Pümpin and García Echevarría 1990) must include:

- A greater capacity for integration among individual observers (managers) in business processes
- Improved communications through manager integration and multiobservation
- Greater realism in business management, in economic, social and human terms

This is undoubtedly the indirect effect promoted by the historical development of new management technologies as tools within the conceptual change undergone by a company, its managers' behavior and all of its human resources. We might state that instead of people being replaced by technology, what in fact occurs is a new discovery of the individual as a key to the success of a company's processes of change. Not only do the new information and communication technologies integrated into the multidisciplinary and multicultural processes of business management enable a company's reality to be analyzed from its global perspective, responding to functional or partial criteria or perspectives, but they also aim to specify where the fundamental developments, barriers, efficiencies and inefficiencies lie as well as specifying the scope of their application.

Figure 4: *Dimensions of knowledge and the application of its technologies*

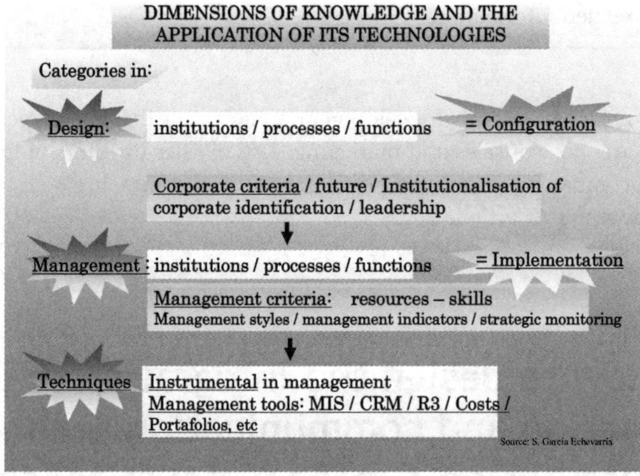

Figure 4 illustrates the three large dimensions affecting the integration of know-how and of technologies into business management:

- Firstly, the dimension that affects how the **institutions** themselves are designed and configured. Given the fact that the technologies are not neutral, they need to be given their own identity and, based on their integration within the conceptualization undertaken by the company, so must their processes and functions.
- However, not only is it the **corporate dimension**, its values and its norms, but, above all, the management **operating process** of the company's economic and social activity that involve the ambit of how to manage people as well as the ambit of functional management of which they are a part.

- The third dimension is the **instrumentalist dimension**, the availability of the necessary tools in order to adapt them to the new conceptualization of the corporation and the processes designed by the company.

This demands radical change not only in thought patterns but also in how the vision of the company and the strategic and organizational designs are designed.

Figure 5: *Interdisciplinary/intercultural knowledge within the company*

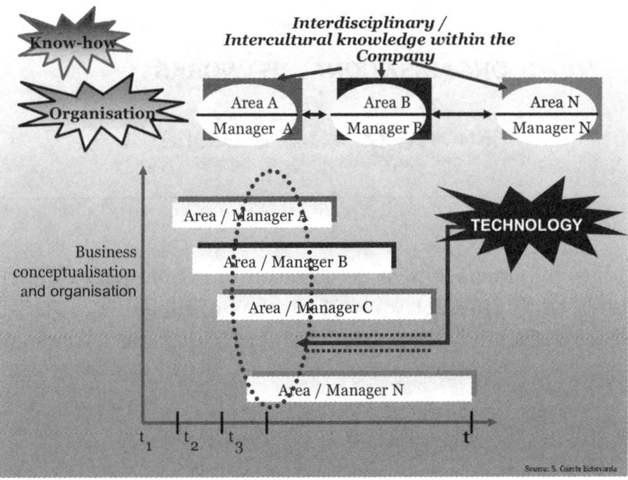

An approach, a simultaneous way of thinking (Figure 5) is needed. All business and indeed, scientific activity is based upon the knowledge available to different people, different managers. The objective is to integrate this knowledge by sharing it, thus making a response to the company's socio-economic reality possible. This socio-economic reality is always an interdisciplinary and intercultural reality within the company. Therein lie difficulties; the difficulty of having people who are able to lead different disciplines and cultures as well as different manners of observing the aforementioned reality. The process of change in the conceptualization and organization of a company must need be oriented towards simultaneity and technology. Technology allows information to be available, as can be seen in figure 5, concerning shared areas. This is when technology becomes a tool for dialogue with regard to the integration of people and resources, of visions and evaluations. Technology is only integrated into business management when it enjoys a simultaneous conceptual and organisational design and both values systems and objectives are shared.

Figure 6: *Knowledge and innovation in business management*

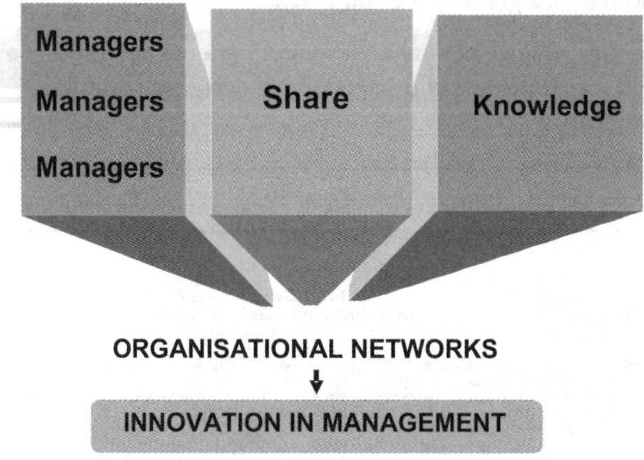

Innovation in business management is the result of people with different functionalities and cultures, with different ways of perceiving situations, risks and capacities, sharing knowledge. Therefore, organizational forms enabling technologies to be used are needed.

7 Integrating information and communication technologies' organizational designs in executive management processes

As has been stated, the key element for integrating modern business management technologies lies firstly, in the company's organizational scheme. A conceptualization of a company's organization, its strategy and its organizational structure in terms of hierarchies or matrices make it impossible to integrate modern **"multiobserver"** technologies into its management. When we talk of **networked organizational structures** we are talking of a means of **simultaneous thinking** in which technology is the instrumental element in promoting the integration of people and knowledge. Thus in conceptual terms, it makes possible a dialogue process that enables accepted values and objectives to be shared, while simultaneously sharing responsibilities. The break with the figure of the **"uniobserver"** and the search for **"multiobservers"** in each and every process will allow a closer approximation to the reality of the world of business and economics.

Figure 7: *Changing organizational forms*

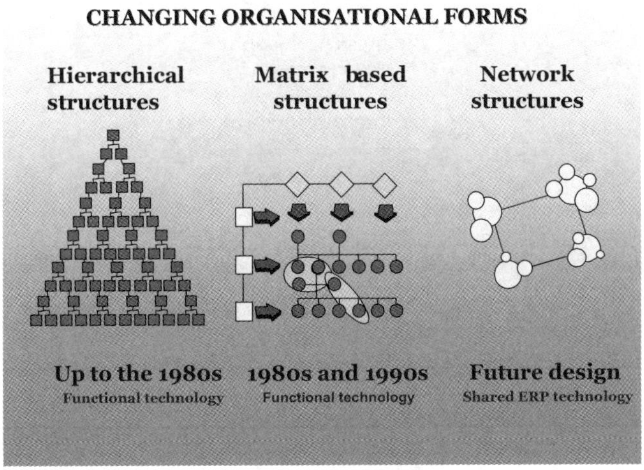

This is because designs which are primarily institutional and corporate, spring from the necessity to share the values system, so that conceptualising globally, a **business philosophy** that enables the design of **corporate principles** is generated. These principles are the element that allows knowledge to be integrated with the support of the technologies once that a vision is shared. Figure 8 illustrates this **corporate and institutional dimension** which is the **sine qua non** condition for the authentic introduction of modern technologies into business management. If this is not the case, there is no **"common language"**, and it will therefore be extremely difficult to share situations and risks. But the **"common language"** is **"the language for sharing values"**, values that have been integrated into the business culture. Therefore, this is not a technical IT problem about which the IT specialist can talk with the financial or sales director, rather it is an issue of sharing values, reinforced by technology, which enables objectives to be shared with the other people involved in the same business project.

Figure 8: *Institution and organisation: technological integration systems*

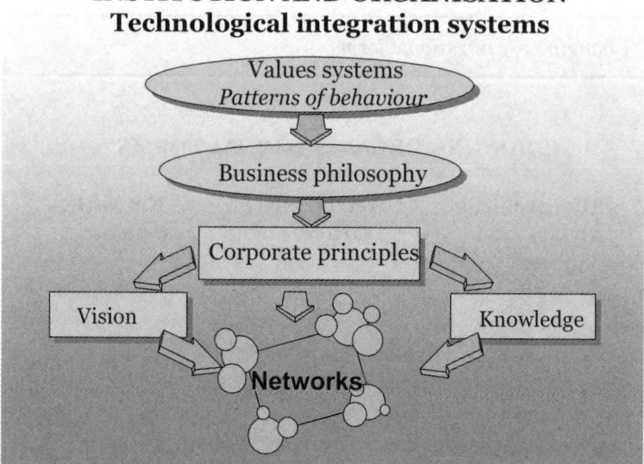

Figure 9: *Globalisation*

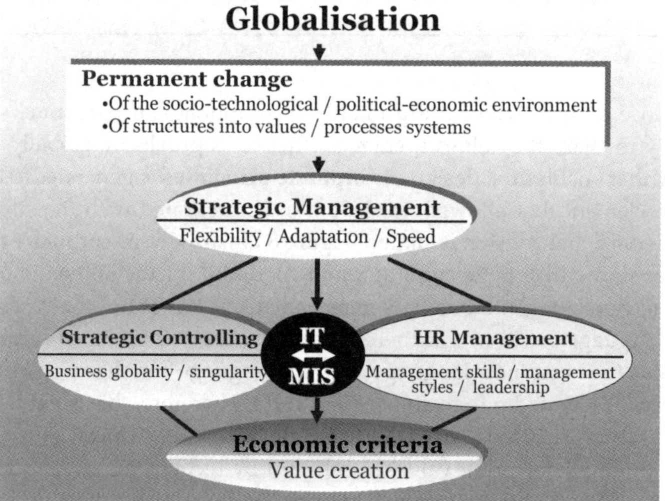

These information and communication technologies integration processes within business management are increasingly necessary taking into account the globalisation dimensions, not only in terms of economic, political and social activity, but also because all business activity, as a consequence of information and communication technologies, must involve itself in this global system. This in turn, means that processes are increasingly complex and demanding. The search for the ability to be in a constant state of change in order to adapt to these socio-political environments as well as to the values systems' structures themselves demands the integration of new management technologies.

8 Conclusions

Managing a company that responds successfully to the permanent, deep changes in its environment needs the two columns mentioned at the beginning of this contribution:

- Firstly, there is a leadership column, the management of human resources and the integration of the individual (Marr and García Echevarría 1997).
- The second is measurement, the indicators of success or failure in the management of available resources and skills. Technology, in this case, denominated ITC, MIS or any of the others that could be mentioned, aim to facilitate the integration of both of the above in order to provide the economic and social conditions for value creation.

This affects all levels of company. The above refer to the management ambit with regard to the availability of resources and their skills, to the design of processes and to areas of business. Therefore, more "**stable**" measurement indicators than those currently available are needed. Furthermore, objectives whose aim is to provide standards of reference for human behaviour are necessary in order to define the future positions of both the company and its activities.

We are dealing with a profound **cultural change within the company**. This is not merely the effect of information and communication technologies; therein lies the error, it is rather an unprecedented cultural change. Information and communication technologies, that serve multidisciplinarity and multiculturalism as the defining tool in a new way of measuring a conceptualization of a company, facilitate the progress of the **captive observer, of the functional manager** of one single reality towards multiobservation, towards a globality seen from different perspectives towards approaching this reality through a shared project. These are the new business designs and the technology's contribution to this new situation.

9 References

Cardona, J.(2003): Las empresas no saben medir su rendimiento. Valoración del Informe IDC y Business Objects de junio 2003, *La Gaceta de los Negocios,* September 11, 50.

Fernández de Lis, P. (2003): "Los directivos no se creen la tecnología". Valoración del Informe Gartner, *El País,* October 26, 36.

Forman, P. (2003): Hoy la Ciencia se valora simplemente como un componente de la tecnología, *El País,* November 12, 33.

Gutenberg, E. (1957): *Grundlagen der Betriebswirtschaftslehre.Bd I: Die Produktion,* 1st ed. (Spanish publication: Fundamentos de la economía de la Empresa-Bd I: La Producción, Buenos Aires).

Hudson, Th. (2003): La excelencia y el liderazgo internacional son claves para atraer inversiones en ciencia, *El País,* November 26.

Marr, R. and S. García Echevarría (1997): *La dirección corporativa de los Recursos Humanos,* Díaz de Santos (Ed.), Madrid

Pümpin, C. and S. García Echevarría (1990): *Dinámica empresarial-Una nueva Cultura para el éxito de la empresa,* Díaz de Santos (Ed.), Madrid.

Pümpin, C. and S. García Echevarría (1993): *Estrategia Empresarial-Cómo implementar la estrategia en la empresa,* Díaz de Santos (Ed.), Madrid.

Arnoud De Meyer and Sam Garg

Innovation Management in Asia

Some Preliminary Findings

Prof. Dr. *Arnoud De Meyer* and *Sam Garg*, Department of Technology Management and Asian Business and Comparative Management, INSEAD at Fontainebleau (France).

1 Introduction

The need to innovate for an organisation is not new. Since the early days of management studies (be it by the management classics e.g. Taylor, Fayol or Schumpeter) the need to innovate for an industrial organisation has been emphasized. And since the early sixties, with the first studies by Burns and Stalker (1961), the SAPPHO studies in the UK (Science Policy Research Unit 1972) or the project management studies carried out in relation with NASA in its efforts to launch the Gemini and Apollo cabins (Allen 1977), scholars and practitioners have developed an impressive set of materials about innovation management. The question we want to raise here in this paper is whether these results are universally applicable or whether there are some geographical differences in the way these results have to be implemented.

The existing literature has obviously pointed out that there are cultural influences in the way one implements management techniques. But we want to go one step further and understand whether a specific context, e.g. East and South Asia, influences the way one manages innovation. In particular we want to explore through a series of case studies to what extent the specific East and South Asian context creates additional or different hurdles for innovation and how eventually companies have overcome these hurdles. Based on these case studies we have indeed been able to distinguish five categories of hurdles for innovation and have discovered some ideas on how companies have overcome these hurdles. These hurdles are: inadequate development resources, ineffective market input, a strong role for the government in the industrial environment impeding innovation, the negative impact of a perception of 'Asian'-ness and a lack of appreciation for intangibles.

2 Motivation for the study

If we exclude Japan from East and South Asia (which we will do for the rest of this paper) one can easily argue that the interest in innovation is a fairly recent preoccupation. While there may have been some lip service paid to the need to innovate in earlier years, it is really the aftermath of the Asian financial crisis in 1997, the emergence of China, and to a lesser extent India, as economic powerhouses and the reduction of protective trade barriers in the second half of the nineties that led to the realisation in East and South Asia that innovation was going to be an important challenge. China's rise is currently probably the single most important factor driving the interest in innovation in Asian companies and by Asian governments. It has become the low cost manufacturer centre for Asia as a whole and will probably remain an exporter of price deflation for the coming years. India's position, while today far less strong, can be expected to be similar towards the end of this decade. This implies that other Asian countries like Korea, Thailand, Malaysia or Indonesia have lost some of their competitive advantage. Moreover the added capacity in China and India may lead to a global overcapacity in some sectors (though not in all as the recent shortage in steel illustrates), even further downgrading the competitive position of South East Asian countries. Their reaction could of course be to increase trade protection but this does not seem to be a long-term solution for them. Innovation is one way of escaping a competitive battle based on cost differentials.

The same obligation to innovate existed and exists for firms located in Europe or the United States, but probably in an even stronger form. These companies download some of the need to innovation to their suppliers, many of whom are located in Asia. Outsourcing of development and innovation has gained in popularity in the developed nations and Asian companies benefit from this new demand. But this leads to an additional need to understand how the process of innovation should and can be managed.

A third reason why innovation has become mandatory is that in Asia itself we witness the development of a growing middle class with its own sophistication and increased disposable income. Their quest for products and services which are more than a mere copy of what exists in Japan, Europe and the United States is growing and they look for solutions which are adapted to their specific needs and fit well the local context.

Finally the financial crisis of 1997 has led to a greater transparency, lower trade barriers, improved legal frameworks. The networking that traditionally led to a competitive advantage through information asymmetry has become less important. Merit has become somewhat more important than connections in doing business in Asia and in such an environment innovation becomes a more important driver of competitive advantage.

Given this rise in importance for innovation we asked ourselves whether the management of innovation in Asia would require a different approach. We still assumed that the fundamentals of innovation management such as for example the need to create a clear strategic context and leadership, an investment in creativity enhancement and good project management, the management of the information flows, paying attention to protection of the ideas in order to be able to get the rent on one's investment in R&D, connecting the market to the innovators and implement innovation through an integrated organisation would still hold. But we also suspected that some of the traditional lessons on how to manage innovation would be more difficult to implement or would require some adaptation.

3 Methodology

Since this was clearly exploratory research, we decided to study the research question through some desk research and the development of case studies as well as the analysis of existing case studies. These case studies were complemented with interviews with privileged observers of the innovation in industry, government and academia. We decided to have as much variety as possible in the case studies in terms of geographical origin and industry. In Table 1 we have listed the 14 case studies that form the basis of this paper. We are still in the process of collecting additional materials and plan a large scale survey of managers and executives in Asia for further research.

Table 1: *List of the exploratory case studies*

Name	*Location*	*Activity*
Aapico Hitech	Thailand	Automotive components
Asiainfo Holdings	Mainland China	Internet provider
Giordano	Hong Kong	Ready made fashion
AU optronics	Taiwan	Flat panel displays
Shin Satellite	Thailand	Telecommunication
Netizen Funds	Korea	Internet based finance
Electronics industry	Taiwan	Electronic components
Pinoy2Pinoy	Manila	SMS based service providers
Biocon	India	Bioengineering
MyWeb	Singapore, Malaysia, China	Electronic set top boxes
Banyan Tree Hotel & Resorts	Singapore	Hospitality
National Library Board	Singapore	Information services
Hewlett Packard[1]	Asia	Electronic products
Philips[2]	Singapore	Electronic products

[1] We considered only the activities of the Asian based part of the organisation
[2] We considered only the activities of the Asian based part of the organisation

4 Observations about the hurdles

Before we address some of the preliminary results of the exploratory study we need to make an important caveat. We did not study, neither through the case studies nor through the desk research, breakthrough innovations. – That does not mean there are none but we did not have them in our sample. – In most of the cases we observed opportunistic adaptations of products or services to the local markets, or exploitation of local market advantages. For example we studied the case of Banyan Tree (De Meyer, Williamson, and Chua 2003), a Singapore based chain of hotel resorts. It would be difficult to argue that such a chain of luxurious and well-located holiday resorts is a breakthrough innovation. But what this company has done is to redefine completely what the customer will experience during a long weekend in one of its resorts. This redefinition puts the emphasis on the individual experience under the aptly chosen slogan 'a sanctuary for the senses' and takes advantage of the quite exquisite physical environment of some Asian islands, as well as the image of personalised service that is often identified with Asia. This way the company offers a new value proposition in the way Kim and Mauborgne define value innovation (Kim and Mauborgne 1997).

A second caveat is that indeed many of the lessons we learned the last 30 years about innovation management do indeed apply. The case on MyWeb.com (De Meyer and Chua 2000), a small producer of electronic set top boxes which enable access to Internet via TV monitors, is an almost classic story on an entrepreneurial venture and the company's final demise is largely due to the same reasons why start-ups go under anywhere in the world. But let's focus on what the additional hurdles can be.

4.1 Inadequate resources

Contrary to what one may perceive when one is confronted with the absolute numbers of populations or engineers and scientists in China, India or South East Asia, there is quite a dearth of capable technologists in many of these countries. In Table 2 we have listed the number of engineers and scientists per million people as well as the number of Internet users as a percentage of the population, based on data provided by the World Bank for 2002. It is clear that the last number was outdated the moment it was collected, but it does give a proxy for the technical development of these countries. It is noticeable that the number of engineers, while large in absolute terms, is still low in proportion to the total population in countries like China, Thailand, Indonesia or India and this in comparison with Japan or the United States. Even in Korea or Singapore we have still a significant lower number of engineers compared to these two countries. The comparison of % of Internet users is slightly different, but still the differences are noticeable. While we do not have hard data on the qualifications of the technical staff, we did perceive through the interviews that companies in Asia are confronted with both shortage and lack of quality of training.

Table 2: *Technical resources in some selected countries*

Country	*Engineers per million*	*Internet users (%)*
China	459	2
Japan	4960	37
Korea	2138	40
Singapore	3282	29
Hong Kong	93	38
Thailand	102	4
Indonesia	n.a.	1
India	158	0
U.S.A.	4103	34

Source: World Bank.

Engineering capability is one aspect of resources. Finance is another. Several times we were told that the Asian financial markets simply miss the sophistication and the willingness to invest in innovation. Risk management is not one of the strengths of Asian financial institutions and the consequence of this is a lower propensity to invest in innovative projects. In one of the cases we were told that as a consequence the cost of capital could be about 1% to 1.5% higher than for a similar project in the United States. While this difference may seem low, it can make a significant difference in international competition.

Beyond the human and financial resources we discovered two aspects of what one may call an inadequate mindset. While a mindset is not necessarily a traditional resource, the right mindset is a conditio sine qua non for successful innovation and can thus considered to be a resource.

First many of the managers in Asia, in particular the ones that have been successful in the past, have a clear mindset that drives them in the direction of cost reduction, as opposed to new value creation. They simply have been too successful with it in the past, and often perceive low labour cost and access to cheap natural resources still as the cornerstone of their competitive advantage. Making the mental switch from being a receiver of technology and a producer for a principal in the industrialised world towards a proactive innovator for local and international markets is not an obvious move.

Secondly many Asian mangers still think too often in terms of product maps as opposed to process and process capabilities maps. Subcontractors are used to get blueprints of products that they need to build. Innovators often have to recombine their process capabilities in order to design and develop new solutions for new needs. The difference between the early chip factories in Singapore and Taiwan can illustrate this. In Singapore the chip making industry bought turnkey factories but there was little local knowledge about the intricacies of wafer production. In Taiwan the wafer production was often developed by engineers who had spend the better part of their professional life in the United States and who had developed an intimate knowledge about the production processes. The first group thought in terms of products and off the shelf technology. The second group had a clear map of the process capabilities needed to have a continuous evolution of wafer production. It is this second group that has been more successful in the short and medium term in rolling out innovations.

4.2 Ineffective market input

The observations we could make through desk research and case studies can be summarised as follows:

- The average Asian company has a limited understanding of or experience with marketing. Many of the companies in our sample, whether it is the automotive producer Aapico, Shin satellite in Thailand or Biocon (De Meyer and Bhardwaj 2003a) in India, had excellent technological capabilities but little knowledge about brand building, developing sophisticated distribution channels or even advertising.
- A substantial disadvantage for innovation by Asian companies is that they are quite far removed from the sophisticated consumer markets in industrialised countries. Tokyo, which is the trend-setting market for Asia, the United States or some of the leading markets in Europe are far removed. Asian companies need to have an extremely long marketing arm to be able to tap into the intimate market knowledge that is needed to develop new products or services.
- There are sophisticated local markets in development. Singapore, Hong Kong or Taipei offer lots of opportunities for fashion designers. Hand phones (the local English for a mobile telephone) are indeed that: a short walk through the streets of Asian capitals will enable you to see hundreds of young and not so young typing SMS on their telephones at sometimes amazing speeds with their hands and fingers. Manila is by far the most sophisticated market in the world for SMS as we described in the case Pinoy2Pinoy (De Meyer and Bhardwaj 2003b). But these are to

some extent still embryonic markets and not mature enough to be a source for products that can be rolled out worldwide.

- Many of the Asian markets are still quite closed if not parochial. There are historical reasons for that. Quite some Asian nations have had a less than happy relationship in the past or are culturally quite far apart from each other. The differences between the multicultural society in Singapore and its two Islamic neighbours are quite substantial. And the historic differences between China and Japan still influence the buying patterns in both countries (Klein and Ettenson 2000). This renders it perhaps difficult to develop Asian wide products for Asian wide markets.
- Finally there is an absolute lack of reliable market data. In many cases it is just absent. In other cases it may be available, but no one trusts its. The lack of accuracy on market data in China has been well documented.

4.3 The strong historic role of the Government impeding innovation

Virtually all Asian governments have played and play a strong role in the development of the local economy. That role is often one of leadership for the industry. Governments have chosen in the past sectors in which they wanted their national champions to be present, and more often than not they have a strong stake in the leading companies (either through direct participation in the equity or by having a strong voice in their management). This may have been an appropriate policy for an economy that needs to catch up or that is acting as a subcontractor for principals in other parts of the world. But when it comes to driving innovation this is definitely less indicated. Governments have no particularly good track record in choosing winners in terms of innovation. And innovative Asian companies are confronted with the following additional hurdles:

- The regulatory environment favourable to innovators and entrepreneurship is often lacking: innovators need good protection of intellectual property rights (IPR) and in particular the enforcement of these rights; they need also a legislation that enables the fast creation of companies, but if the innovation is not successful they equally need legislation that allows them to stop the business in an efficient and clean way.
- The public sector is in many Asian countries still one of the most important purchasers. Local governments tend to be conservative in their procurement and do not favour local innovators over well-established international brands.
- Pro-business policies and regulations have often favoured local entrepreneurs that took advantage of information asymmetry through their good contacts with the

government: they did not need to innovate, simply to set up a company and create jobs. Favouring insiders with trade protection and insider information does not favour necessarily innovative developments.

4.4 Perception of a certain 'Asian'ness

Many aspects that are associated with Asia or Asian cultures impede innovation or make it more difficult to penetrate new markets with Asian innovations. First there is the structure of local companies. While it would be dangerous to make too sweeping generalisations, we have observed that in many cases firms in Asia are either family owned or have a strong family culture. This leads to a certain authoritarianism, and organisations with subservient and sometimes disengaged employees. Limited authority is delegated and the top, wanting to keep control over the firm, becomes a bottleneck in decision-making and the stimulation of creativity.

Secondly Asian goods were often perceived in industrialised countries to be shabby goods. Asian factories are often seen as suitable for low-cost but also low-value work. This perception is still prevalent and in the interviews we were offered several anecdotes how senior managers in European headquarters would confound the manufacturing capabilities of a Thai or Malaysian company with the cute perceptions they had about holiday experiences they had enjoyed in those countries.

This perceived low quality in export markets is sometimes reinforced by a low self-perception. It may be a somewhat irrelevant example but we are still stuck by the observation that in many Asian capitals the mannequins used in fashion houses have Caucasian traits (barring those countries where this is explicitly forbidden). This is an example to us of how Asian companies still don't see their own markets as mature and leading.

In one of the discussions we had about the results of our case studies it was pointed out to us that part of the Asianness that had a negative effect on the urge to innovate had to do with the traditional attitude of Chinese towards innovation. It is true that deep in history the Chinese Empire contributed a lot to the world (going from book printing over irrigation techniques to explosives). But most of the times these inventions were solely to the benefit of the Emperor and the Courts. It took European entrepreneurship to turn book printing into a commercial international success. The question was raised whether this earlier attitude would still have an impact on the attitude of today's entrepreneurs towards innovation. We have at this stage no answer to this question but it is an interesting hypothesis.

Finally there is often a misunderstanding of what entrepreneurship really is. We were often told how great and strong the entrepreneurship is among Chinese. But a careful examination of many success stories about Chinese entrepreneurship reveals that in fact these are success stories about trading and real estate deals. There is nothing wrong with that but it is not about value creation through innovation, R&D and operations.

4.5 Lack of appreciation for intangibles

Finally we observed in our discussions and case studies a very strong lack of appreciation for the intangible side of innovation: brand building is often neglected, or reduced to finding a cute name; lip service is paid to the protection of intellectual property rights, but nobody seems to care a lot about copying of software or other intangible content. Only hard tangible products seem to have real value in many eyes. Perhaps it has something to do with the fact that till now Asian companies had a very strong negative trade balance concerning intellectual property rights. They had to pay the royalties and the licenses and they did not receive a lot. Appreciation for the intangibles may rise the moment these companies can get some benefit from it. But the consequence today of this past attitude is that local innovators hesitate to innovate because they have limited means of protection and thus not get the rent on their investment in R&D.

A second aspect of this lack of appreciation for intangibles is the absence of good design capabilities. Asian companies invest in development, carry out marketing, apply the latest techniques of finance, but often do not have the design capabilities that help to set a product apart. Japan is currently developing as a design powerhouse in Asia and is determining the fashion and the trends. But in the rest of Asia, be it Seoul, Singapore, Hong Kong or Shanghai there is no critical mass in good designers, be it within the companies or on a free-lance basis.

5 What do companies do about it?

The most interesting part of our exploratory research was the discovery that the companies, we prepared case studies about, had actually taken interesting actions to overcome some of these hurdles. In the following paragraphs we want to share some of the examples of the actions.

5.1 Mobilising the resources you don't control

Most successful companies in our limited sample had had access to a network of foreign talent and had kept earlier networks alive. Senior management in Aapico, a Malaysian based company producing automotive components, Biocon, a bio-engineering company in Bangalore, or Asiainfo, a Chinese internet provider had all worked and/or studied abroad in Australia, the UK or the USA and had kept their networks they had built during these days quite well alive. This also applied to the management of Shin satellite, a provider of satellite services in Thailand. The lack of resources, the difficulty to find reliable or relevant market data can be overcome by having an overseas network of information providers.

Aapico is also an example of the use of two other tools to increase the technical capabilities of the company: intensive internal training programmes in order to support the development of technical resources and exploiting the advantages of a partnership with a principal from which one can learn a lot. Aapico organised itself in shuch a way that it could learn a maximum from its partners and customers and was implicitly applying quite some suggestions made by Doz and Hamel about value adding learning partnerships (Doz and Hamel 1998). The same leveraging of partnerships can be observed in the case of the Taiwanese electronic component industry. The links that these companies had through their management and collaborators that had spent many years in the United State were extremely helpful to compensate for the lack of technological resources in Taiwan itself (and for that matter in the subsidiaries of these Taiwanese companies in the PRC).

Finally companies like Biocon in India or the companies active in Manila's SMS based sector were all benefiting from the positive externalities they enjoyed in the networks. Biocon is an interesting example of this in the sense that they stimulated the creation of other bio-engineering firms in Bangalore, a city that is normally better known for its software development and service industries. And like in many sectors where there are high network externalities, the service providers of SMS based services in Manila reinforced each others value to the mobile consumer. The more services offered in the network, the more value the individual service has. But it also becomes simpler for a small company to launch a company with a limited service offering because it benefits from the existence of other companies.

5.2 Overcoming the distance to the customer

Two strategies seem to have the potential to be successful. The first one was to develop products in the local market that could have a chance to become international successes. In the case of Pinoy2Pinoy, i.e. the spectacular development of SMS based services in Manila, the technology is independent from the local market and the demand for SMS based services is probably universal. Only due to a combination of circumstances Manila developed into a lead market for these services, but if the local firms have the guts and the vision to go beyond their local markets they have the potential to exploit a home-grown and home based experience into internationally attractive products. Netizen Funds, an experiment in Korea to use internet to solicit film fans to contribute to the production costs of movies in which their adored actors would play a main role was another idea that may have international appeal and application. The challenge is to find applications which are neutral with respect to culture and infrastructure but where the home market has a slight advance in time over other countries and markets.

A second approach consisted of setting up listening devices or learning experiments in other markets. Giordano's first attempt to go into Europe when it started in Germany can be labelled as such a learning experiment. MyWeb fund raising efforts in the United States were partially also an effort to become part of the knowledge network in California. Both proved in the end not to be successful but if well organised such experiments can have a huge learning value.

5.3 Stimulating the creativity and overcoming the Asian'ness'

There is no quick fix to this, because it does require a long term investment in educational systems and a change of mindset in the companies itself. We nevertheless observed an array of actions that could help overcome an attitude of inferiority or a lack of creativity.

- Creating a sense of urgency does help to stimulate creativity. China is perceived to threaten every economic actor. In some cases the Asian financial crisis of 1997 was used to implement drastic changes or to go against the perceived common wisdom. Aapico used the crisis in 1997 to actually strengthen its position, invest in capacity, rationalise the market and emerge as a winner.
- Creating multicultural teams as we observed in the Taiwanese Electronics industry proved to be very effective to limit the influence of Asianness.
- Giordano invested quite strongly in understanding the creative process of design and implemented this within its organisation.
- Some companies embarked on international partnerships in order to complement the lack of creativity and freewheeling attitude they lacked in their own organisation. Some of the partnerships that Singapore companies created with Israeli companies through the SIIRD are illustrating this.

- Finally several companies implemented consciously organisational changes that would limit the bottleneck at the top and the hierarchical systems present in many Asian companies.

5.4 Managing the government

Here we observed three strategies. Some companies rendered the local government more or less irrelevant by developing an international network. By playing in many different courtyards, you make the court master of each of the individual courts less important. A second strategy consisted of heavily lobbying the government in order to get some legislation that would open up the country. A third strategy consisted of consciously looking for the location and the government that would impose the least constraints and that would be the most progressive. An example of this is the attitude of the Singapore government towards stem cell research and the consequent establishment of a number of bioengineering laboratories in this country. Similarly the development of Bangalore as a heaven for IT companies or Hyderabad for biotech companies are results from a similar open research and development climate.

5.5 Believing in intangible assets

Two of the case studies (Giordano, and Banyan Tree Hotels and Resorts) invested heavily in brand building and with reasonably good results. Other companies e.g. Biocon or MyWeb implemented a well thought through portfolio of protection mechanisms, including patents and trade secrets. But all still wrestled with the need to go through a drastic change of mindset. This change is favoured once the companies itself can start deriving benefits from the sales of intangible assets.

6 Conclusion and further work

In the previous pages we have given a short overview of some very interesting preliminary work about how to apply innovation management within an Asian context. Through our desk research, case studies and interviews, we developed some insights about what is different about implementing the traditional lessons about innovation management in an Asian context. The first observation we made is that there is a lot of similarity and that the lessons we know about innovation have a high universal value.

But there are some specific hurdles to their implementation in Asia. This is important to Asian companies, but also from a more general point: innovation management is partially context specific (and not only culturally determined).

The work is obviously not finished. We are preparing additional case materials and are carrying out a survey of managers in Asia about these hurdles and the solutions to overcome them.

7 References

Allen T.J. (1977): *Managing the Flow of Technology,* Cambridge: MIT Press.

Burns, T. and G.M. Stalker (1961): *The Management of Innovation,* Oxford.

De Meyer, A. and S. Bhardwaj (2003a): *Biocon,* INSEAD case study, Fontainebleau.

De Meyer, A. and S. Bhardwaj (2003b): *Pinoy2Pinoy,* INSEAD case study, Fontainebleau.

De Meyer, A. and C.H. Chua (2000): *MyWeb.com: Bringing the Internet to the Living Room (A1),* INSEAD Case study, Singapore.

De Meyer, A., P. Williamson, and C.H. Chua (2003): *Banyan tree Resorts and Hotels : Building an International brand from an Asian Base,* INSEAD case study, Singapore.

Doz, Y. and G. Hamel (1998): *The Alliance Advantage: the Art of creating Value through Partnering,* Boston.

Kim, W.C. and R. Mauborgne (1997): Value Innovation: the Strategic Logic of High Growth, *Harvard Business Review,* 75 (1), 102-113.

Klein, J. and R. Ettenson (2000): Branded by the Past, *Harvard Business Review,* 78 (6), 28.

Science Policy Unit (1972): *Success and failure in Industrial Innovation, Report of project SAPPHO,* London.

Part 2:

Innovation and Research & Development

Hans-Horst Schröder

Early Information (EI) Based on Knowledge Discovery in Databases (KDD)

Prof. Dr. *Hans-Horst Schröder*, Department of Technology and Innovation Management, RWTH Aachen.

1 Introduction

The environment in which companies operate has changed dramatically over the last three decades. While the first few decades after the Second World War were characterized by supplier-dominated markets involving excess demand and continuous growth, markets in the last two decades have tended to be buyer-dominated, where supply exceeds demand and where growth is erratic. In addition, new technologies have become available, which affect almost all aspects of life. Furthermore, the relatively stable socio-political regimes characterizing the post war-period have been followed by unstable settings giving rise to discontinuities and sudden changes. Finally, and perhaps most pervasively, globalization has brought about an enormous increase in the action sets available, as well as in the horizons which have to be considered when deciding about these actions.

Accompanying these developments, the complexity and dynamics of the environment in which companies operate have increased considerably. This, in turn, has resulted in strong pressure to reduce planning horizons, raising serious problems for the management of technology and innovation which, by their very nature, require long-term consideration and long-range planning. The necessity for a long-range view arises, in particular, for breakthrough innovations based on radically new technologies. These offer a large number of (often unforeseeable) applications and require far-reaching pre-marketing activities, e.g. changes in the innovation's environment and in the education of potential users.

Two strategies might be employed to cope with the pressure on time horizons that results from the changes in a company's environment: a **fatalistic** one - "Take it as it is and adapt by reducing the planning horizon" - with potentially disastrous long-term effects upon technology and innovation and an **active** one - "Counteract these tendencies by improving the information system and intensifying the environmental intelligence efforts". In the past, theory as well as practise have focused on the fatalistic strategy, and have attempted to improve a firm's capability to adapt to reduced planning horizons by increasing its flexibility. While flexibility with respect to innovation has been achieved, above all, by speeding up development, flexibility with respect to technology has been primarily achieved by the development and utilization of flexible manufacturing techniques and processes and by process reorganization.

Comparatively little attention has been paid to the active strategy of improving the effectiveness of information systems. Among the few attempts to improve information about future long-range environments with potentially great impact, two concepts - Business Intelligence (BI), or, more specifically, Technology Intelligence (TI) (Brockhoff 1991; Lichtenthaler 2004), and Early Information (Systems) (EI(S)) (Schröder, Jetter, and Schiffer 2003)- may be discerned. While the former aims primarily at the early detection of **trends**, the latter, which is the subject of this article, focuses more upon the identification of **structural changes** and the **emergence of new patterns** by unveiling **weak signals**, i.e. indicators of potential discontinuities with a considerable impact on the existence and success of the company (for the concept of weak signals, see Ansoff (1976) and Konrad (1991); for a detailed discussion of the phenomenon "weak signals" and its operationalization, see Zeller (2003, 77 et sqq. and 172 et seq.).

EI, which is used in the following as a generic term covering early warning ("Früh-warnung") and early detection ("Früherkennung"), as well as early reconnaissance ("Frühaufklärung") (Schröder and Schiffer 2001, 972 et sqq.), has focused so far upon "drawing knowledge out of people´s heads" thus making available existing knowledge for technology and innovation planning purposes. Schröder, Jetter, and Schiffer (2003, 85 et sqq.), e.g., have designed and implemented employee-based EISs for SME´s that facilitate the integration of knowledge stored in employees' heads. Ahn and Meyer (2000) have proposed to use the knowledge of informants, i.e., experts in specific environmental domains. Sepp (1996, 65 et sqq.) and Schlüter (2004, 61 et sqq.) have finally suggested stakeholder-based EISs, which serve to exploit the knowledge of the various stakeholder groups about potential imminent discontinuities for improving early information.

Some research has also been undertaken with the objective of exploiting the information potentially contained in well structured, external data banks, especially patent banks. Several researchers have designed patent indicators for technological developments and have developed methods for patent analyses based on quantitative patent statistics (Brockhoff 1992; Ernst 1996, 29 et sqq.; Faix 1998, 177 et sqq.). Furthermore, Walter, Gerlitz, and Möhrle (2003) and Zeller (2003) have recently proposed concepts and tools for text analyses of patent documents, complementing the concepts proposed by Peiffer (1994, 46 et sqq.) for technology reconnaissance. Little effort, however, has been made in general to exploit the data contained in less structured data sources. Especially textual data, which have become accessible via the World Wide Web and which may be of great importance for early detection of discontinuities, have almost completely been omitted.

On the other hand, the concepts and techniques developed in the emerging field of **Knowledge Discovery in Databases (KDD)** under the heading "data mining" have recently been extended to cover text analyses, too. Since these concepts and techniques - similar to the concepts suggested for patent analyses - attempt to transform implicit knowledge hidden in large databases into explicit knowledge, but - dissimilar to those concepts – also process text documents in addition to data in numerical format, they may offer a breakthrough for EI. Thus, it is the objective of this article to link these two approaches which have so far been developed independently of one another and to show that the procurement and analysis of EI may be considered a special case of KDD. This is the core idea elaborated in the following section 2 which, furthermore, contains brief descriptions of KDD and EI. Based on this analysis, section 3 presents an integrated KDD-based concept for EI(S) that incorporates KDD concepts and methods into EI(S) and at the same time links human-based EIS approaches with EDP-based approaches. The article ends with some reflections on the usefulness of the concept presented and its consequences for the design and establishment of EI(S).

2 EI(S) and KDD - a Conceptual Comparison

KDD has been defined as "... the non-trivial process of identifying valid, novel, potentially useful, and ultimately understandable patterns in data." (Fayyad, Piatetsky-Shapiro, and Smyth 1996, 6). Similarly, **EI** may be considered to be the process of identifying, diagnosing, evaluating, and providing long-range planning information with a lead time sufficient to exploit profit opportunities and to avoid potential risks (Schröder and Schiffer 2001, 975 et sqq.). EI includes initiation of adequate (re)actions and focuses, as mentioned earlier, on the detection of weak signals.

Due to the process orientation of both concepts, a comparison of their activities promises to be informative. This comparison will be conducted in the first part of this section, whereas in the second part, the main features of both concepts will be compared with each other.

2.1 Process-Oriented Comparison

The KDD literature abounds with descriptions of the KDD process (for a summary, see Säuberlich 2000, 22 et sqq.). Though they differ in the specification of individual activities and their aggregation to process phases, they may be summarized in the **generic 3-phase KDD process model** with a pre-processing, a processing and a post-processing phase, as shown in Figure 1:

- The **pre-processing** phase serves to define and to prepare the data to be analyzed. It includes the selection of the domain for investigation, the definition of the data format(s) which may be processed, the choice of the specific databases to be analyzed, and the transformation of the data into the format required for processing them. The decisions about data domain, data format and data origin are of particular importance because they strongly affect the content of the pre-processing activities required and the analyses feasible in the mining phase: While the concepts and methods designed for data mining in its narrow traditional sense are appropriate for structured numerical data, specific concepts and methods summarized under the collective term "**text mining**" have to be applied for unstructured textual data.

- The selection of data analysis methods and their application form the core of the **processing or data mining phase**. In accordance with the generic functions of data mining, three types of methods are available: segmentation methods (including classification as well as clustering techniques), methods for the discovery of dependencies between the data, and methods for the detection of deviations from previous patterns and of significant structural changes in the database. Usually, parameters have to be specified as a prerequisite for these activities.

Figure 1: *EI and KDD Process*

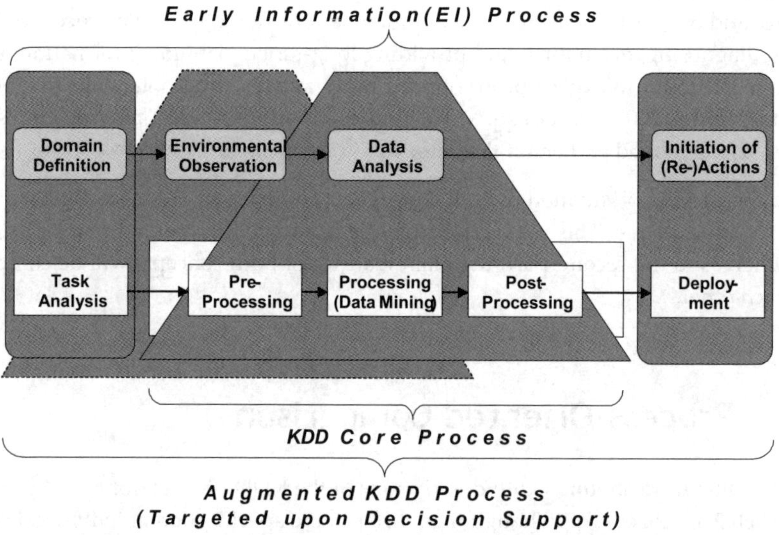

- The interpretation of the computed results is the core activity of the **post-processing phase**. This includes selection and aggregation of the computed results, as well as selection of their mode of presentation, e.g. tabular or visual format. Furthermore, the results have to be disseminated to the persons to whom and organizational units to which they are pertinent.

This core process of KDD has been augmented by Säuberlich (2000, 33 et seq.), from a decision support point of view, by a task analysis phase preceding the core process and a deployment phase following it. The **task analysis phase** contains all the activities necessary to specify the information requirements for the decision at hand. In particular, this includes an understanding of the application domain and definition of the application goals. Furthermore, initial data may have to be collected. The **deployment**

phase comprises the activities required to transform the results into the decision and decision subject context. This augmented model will form the basis for the following discussions.

While there are much fewer proposals in the pertinent literature for modelling the EI process than there are for the KDD process, their diversity is hardly less (e.g. Peiffer 1992, 262 et sqq.; Sepp 1996, 206 et sqq.; Schröder, Jetter, and Schiffer 2003, 28 et sqq.). Again, however, the different models can be easily summarized in a **generic 4-phase EI process model** consisting of domain definition, environmental observation, data analysis, and initiation of (re-)actions, as shown in Figure 1 (Schröder and Schiffer 2001, 975 et sqq.):

- **Domain definition** includes the structuring of the company's environment and the selection of those sections that are to be observed. Although domain restriction contradicts the experience that events with great potential impact upon the company may occur in **all** segments of its environment, it is indispensable from a practical point of view (for the resulting "dilemma of EI" see Schröder and Schiffer 2001, 975).

- **Environmental observation** serves to identify weak signals and comprises two types of activities: environmental scanning, serving to detect weak signals, and environmental monitoring, serving to intensify (or abandon) them. Furthermore, identification of weak signals requires the evaluation of the data collected in order to decide which of them represent weak signals and should be monitored thoroughly.

- **Data analysis** encompasses the explanation of the phenomena observed, the prediction of their future development and the evaluation of their impact upon the company's goals and strategies. It aims at identifying those weak signals that require (re-)action.

- **Initiation of (re-)actions** includes the identification of the proper addressees, as well as the transmission of the early information in a format which suits their needs, abilities and preferences. It bridges the gap between discrete strategic planning cycles and continuous EI activities.

From the foregoing descriptions of the KDD and the EI processes, the following **conclusions** may be inferred (for another comparison see Zeller (2003, 145):

- Domain definition within the EI process resembles task analysis within the KDD process. While task analysis in KDD, however, is mostly concerned with setting goals for individual KDD processes, domain definition within EI focuses upon determining the area in which the general goals of EI are to be realized.

- Environmental observation within EI overlaps with task analysis and pre-processing, as well as with processing within KDD: whereas environmental observation includes the initial data collection and data exploration of the task analysis phase, evaluation of the data collected requires the data cleaning, data integration and especially data transformation activities of the pre-processing phase, as well as most of the activities of the data mining phase. The overlap, however, is only partial. For environmental scanning and monitoring, forming the core of the environmental observation phase, there is, in general, no counterpart within the KDD process. Moreover, the contents and the relative importance of the activities shared by the environmental observation phase of EI and the pre-processing and data mining phases of KDD differ as will be shown in the following sub-section.

- The activities in the data analysis phase of the EI process largely coincide with the KDD core process. As will be shown in the next sub-section, too, however, while the activities are identical, the objects upon which they operate tend to be different.
- The activities in the initiation phase of EI strongly resemble the activities of the deployment phase within KDD.

Thus, although there is no perfect 1:1-relationship between the EI and the KDD processes, there is sufficient similarity between them on the activity level to justify interpretation of the EI process as a KDD process variant; the differences in the phase models mainly spring from different aggregations of these activities to process phases. Hence, the central hypothesis that EI may be considered a specific manifestation of the general KDD process, is supported by the process comparison.

2.2 Feature-Oriented Comparison

Both EI and KDD operate on large data sets. While the database for EI, however, is (at least in principle) unbounded and dynamic, the database for KDD tends to be bounded - usually to internal data assembled in data warehouses - and static. Furthermore, whereas EI is mainly concerned with fuzzy, qualitative, unstructured, usually textual data from external sources, KDD preferentially operates on unambiguous, "hard" quantitative data in structured format. The latter assertion also holds for text mining within KDD: documents which represent the basic unit of textual databases are modeled as vectors in multi-dimensional Euclidean space in order to be processed by text mining techniques (for alternative approaches to modeling documents, see Feldmann and Dagan 1995; Ahonen et al. 1998; Witten et al. 1999).

Both EI and KDD attempt to transform data into information by uncovering hidden information and making implicit knowledge explicit. While the latent knowledge, which EI is interested in, will usually become overt after some time, the knowledge unveiled by KDD, however, may remain latent forever, if not revealed by a KDD initiative. Furthermore, EI is solely interested in deviations from patterns over time, whereas KDD also searches for static, time-invariant relations (for goals of KDD analyses, see Nakhaeizadeh, Reinartz, and Wirth 1998, 3 et sqq.). Finally, while KDD is not usually interested in individual items of a given database, EI attempts to detect weak signals and, is, hence, targeted at identifying individual data.

Both concepts do not specify precise information requirements at the outset, thus giving leeway for the selection of methods for generating knowledge and presenting the results. Whereas EI, however, is solely concerned with time-related data and, therefore, confined to methods and techniques involving time considerations, KDD may focus on time-independent data as well. In addition, EI is mainly interested in content, while KDD is much more concerned with (formal) structure. Similarly, whereas KDD is dominated by considerations concerning the development, selection and application of adequate methods, EI is dominated by considerations about reality. Finally, due to the erratic appearance of weak signals, EI is a continuous process, whereas KDD processes usually are performed in discrete intervals.

The comparison shows that both concepts, in addition to sharing most of their activities, also share essential features: they search for latent information without articulating specific information needs; they deal with large databases, and they allow a high degree of operational latitude. Therefore, EI(S) can be considered a special variant of the KDD process. The comparison, however, also identified several differences: EI and KDD differ with respect to their specific goals, their scope and the type of data they use, the relevance of time and dynamics, and their regard for content and individual items. Hence, the KDD methodology has to be adapted in order to be applicable to EI.

3 ProFIS - an Integrated Approach to Early Information

ProFIS was developed within the collaborative research centre "Models and Methods for Integrated Product and Process Development" supported by the German Research Foundation. Its development was guided by **four principal goals: ProFIS was required to be comprehensive, integrative, flexible, and suitable for SMEs**. Comprehensiveness refers to the phenomena included, e.g. the various dimensions of the environment, to the activities considered, e.g., scanning and monitoring, and to the sources included, e.g., knowledge in electronic databases and in human minds. The integration requirement implies that ProFIS was required to integrate the available approaches for EI, e.g. the human-orientated and the EDP approach, the various techniques applied, e.g. techniques for data and text mining, or the various core concepts employed, e.g. early warning, early detection and early reconnaissance. The flexibility requirement implies usefulness for different users, different conditions of use and different types of early information. It is closely related to the goal of suitability for SMEs, which implies simplicity (without compromising methodological rigor), few resource requirements and consonance with the strengths of SMEs, e.g. their flexibility and proximity to customers.

Figure 2: *ProFIS Modules*

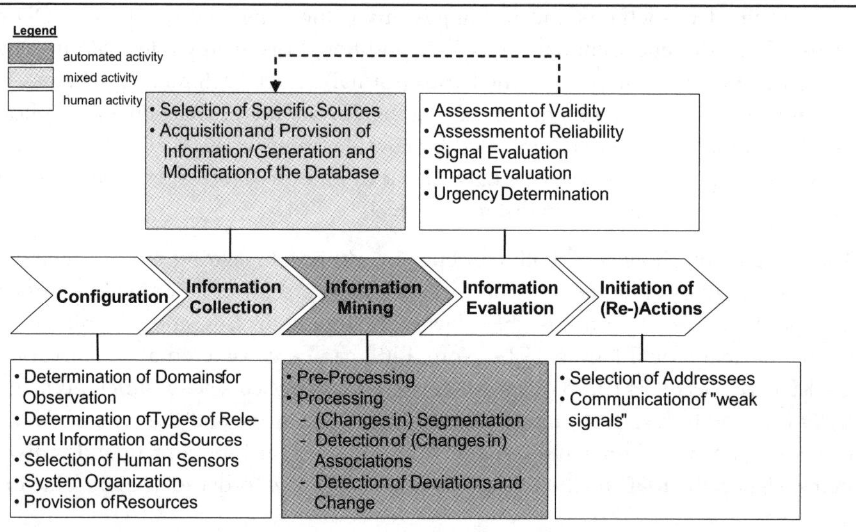

ProFIS employs modular design principles: as Figure 2 shows, it consists of five modules, three of which - information collection, information mining, and information evaluation - are passed regularly. While the first module, (system) configuration, is passed in principle only once before regular operations start, the last module - initiation of (re-)action(s) - is performed whenever weak signals are detected that require immediate action(s). Figure 2 shows furthermore that three of the five modules - configuration, information evaluation and initiation of (re)actions - are the domain of human beings, whereas one - information mining - is automated. In the remaining module - information collection - human and EDP operations are performed in parallel.

3.1 System Configuration

In addition to the domain definition phase of the standard EI process described in section 2.1, the configuration module of ProFIS also includes determination of the types of information and sources to be processed by the EI system, selection of human sensors, organization of the system and provision of resources, in particular the EDP hardware and software required to run the system.

Whereas domain definition is concerned with determining and structuring the area to be observed, **determination of the types and sources of information to be processed** refers to the data input to the system. ProFIS has been designed as an **open system** with respect to both aspects. While the focus is on environmental observation, the methodological approach is broad enough to encompass internal phenomena, e.g. potential results of in-house R&D activities or the loss of key researchers approaching retirement age, too. Furthermore, ProFIS is capable of processing any data provided by any source over a wide variety of formats. Though its focus is on textual data, numerical data may be processed, too. The data may be provided by human beings (e.g. employees or members of pressure groups) in free format, as well as by internal and external databases (e.g., patent databases) in fixed or variable formats. Since the system also processes HTML-formatted data, most of the data available in the WWW may be included. The user decides which types of data and sources s/he wants to include.

Human sensors may be selected internally from a company's staff, as well as externally from institutions and persons with a superior reputation in the domains selected and the motivation to supply early information. Likewise, information brokers (Zelewski 1987) and consultants, for instance, may be employed as human sensors. Thus, in addition to the "employee concept", both the "expert sensor concept" ("Informantenkonzept") and the "stakeholder concept" can be implemented.

ProFIS supports selection of internal sensors by offering the **staff assessment module SAM**. Employing fuzzy set concepts, SAM computes EI aptitude scores for each employee and each environmental segment based on his or her position and function in the company as well as on his or her private reading habits and personality (for details, see Freund and Wassenhoven 2004, 412 et sqq.). While information about reading habits is provided by employees, information about personality features is supplied by on-line administration of the 16 PFr test ("16-Persönlichkeits-Faktoren-Test"; Schneewind and Graf 1998) which is well-known in psychological personality theory.

With regard to the **organization** of the EI process, ProFIS assumes, in principle, sequential organization, as shown in Figure 2. Although sequential in principle, however, the process provides for several feed back loops. The most important one is the loop from information evaluation to information collection, accounting for the dependence of data collection on the results of previous data analyses. An important example for this feed back loop is the transition from scanning to monitoring. Based on research which demonstrates the positive effects resulting from the establishment of committees with members from all functional areas affected, as well as from top management (see e.g. Schröder, Jetter, and Schiffer 2003), ProFIS assumes the establishment of such a committee for controlling the EI process, in particular for information evaluation.

Organization of the EI system is closely related to **provision of resources** because it implies broadly defined resource requirements, in particular with respect to staff. In addition to staffing and providing the EDP infrastructure necessary for operating EI –

systems, provision of resources in general also includes provision of the mining software required (for an overview of presently existing packages, see Säuberlich 2000, 56 et sqq.). Since hardware and software requirements of ProFIS are low, and since the mining software required is included, no additional support for this task is provided.

3.2 Information Collection

Input information may be provided manually by entering reports and news about potential weak signals into the system, or automatically by importing data from internal or external databases. **Manual input** is provided as a rule by human sensors both internally and externally, but can be provided by other employees, too. The entering of information may be supported by specific forms that ensure systematic inclusion of additional background information, such as the source(s) of the information, the time up to when the discontinuity will occur, the suspected impact on the company, and potential measures to be taken (see, e.g., the trend description form in Krystek and Müller-Stewens 1993, 188 et seq.).

For **automatic input,** information retrieval is used, i.e. the search for documents which satisfy a given information need of the user, as well as the ordering of these documents according to their importance (Zeller 2003, 121 et seq.). **Search machines**, in particular Google, are employed to search for documents with pre-specified contents. The documents to be processed may either be selected from the documents found in accordance with the order of relevance established by the search machine, or stochastically, thus accounting for the possibility that weak signals may arise from any segment of the environment. In addition, **information agents** are employed to search for information from pre-defined sources, e.g. URLs of patent offices, research institutions or competitors. Both manual and automatic provision of input data may occur undirected or directed, e.g., in reaction to the identification of a weak signal. Thus, ProFIS supports scanning, as well as monitoring

3.3 Information Mining

The ProFIS module information mining contains all the activities required for preprocessing and for processing the information collected. It is the KDD core of the EI – system, in principle capable of processing both numerical and textual data. Due to the focus of EI on textual data, however, only the textual part of the mining module will be described in this section.

ProFIS employs a simple automated **"word bag" approach with elimination of stopwords**, i.e. "function words and connectives such as articles and prepositions that appear in a large number of documents and are typically of little use in pinpointing documents that satisfy a searcher's information need" (Chakrabarti 2003, 48) **for modelling the documents as space vectors** (for a comparison of "word bag" and "phrase bag" approach, see Scott and Matwin 1999). In the prototype at present under construction, **no stemming**, i.e. a reduction of suffixes and a replacement of inflected words by their common root (Scott and Matwin 1999, 381) is performed. It is, however, planned to include stemming in a future extended version.

The different words in the text base remaining after the elimination of stop-words form the set of textual elements and determine the dimensionality of the space vectors representing a specific document. **Each individual document vector is defined by assigning weights** to all the words contained in the set of textual elements. The weights are computed as the product of **term frequency TF** and **inverse document frequency IDF**. Term frequency TF is defined as the relative frequency of the occurrence of a term in the (reduced) document; inverse document frequency is given by the inverse of the relative frequency of the documents containing the word considered in the database. While TF is used to measure (on a semantic level) the significance of a word for a single document in which it appears, IDF serves to decrease the weight of textual elements that occur in many documents without contributing much to their content.

The **processing sub-module** of ProFIS **encompasses all types of mining activities** mentioned in section 2.1. **Segmentation** is realized by automatically **classifying** the documents with the aid of naïve Bayesian classifiers into user-defined categories (for alternative segmentation methods and techniques, see Nakhaeizadeh, Reinartz, and Wirth 1998, 11 et sqq.; Chakrabarti 2003, 81 et sqq.); there is no restriction imposed by ProFIS on the categories selected. Naïve Bayesian classifiers have been chosen in spite of their relative inefficiency in comparison to other algorithms for classifying (see e.g. Dumais et al. 1998, 151 et sqq.; Nigam, Lafferty, and McCallum 1999, 64 et sqq.) because they are easy to compute and communicate - qualities which were considered essential in view of the requirement of SME suitability. User-supplied training documents for each of the environmental segments defined serve as a reference basis for the classification process. Documents can be assigned to one or more segments of the environment.

Identification of associations and **detection of deviations and structural changes** are executed jointly by analyzing time series of the support and the confidence of associations automatically extracted from the text base. Defining an **association (rule)** in a text base as a rule of the type 'If X, then Y' where X and Y are certain subsets of textual elements in the text base, its **support** is defined as the proportion of documents in the text base that contains the subset X, whereas its **confidence** is defined as the relative proportion of documents among those documents containing X, that also contains Y (for more rigorous definitions see Säuberlich 2000, 110et seq.). In addition to extracting association rules with strongly decreasing and increasing support and confidence,

ProFIS supports the analysis of pre-defined **fictitious** associations over time, e.g., the co-occurrence of the words "propulsive power" and "fuel cells".

Using this feature and establishing hierarchies of indices (or keywords), the employment of **concept hierarchies** is possible, too, in order to exploit the information contained in indices or keywords which are often supplied together with documents (e.g. with patent data). A concept hierarchy is " ... a directed acyclical graph ... of concepts ... [where] ... an arc from concept A to B denotes that A is a more general concept than B" (Feldman and Dagan 1995, 113), e.g., transportation vehicle → bicycle → mountain bike. Due to the hierarchical nature of concept hierarchies, tagging a document with a certain concept or keyword implies tagging it with all concepts or keywords below it. Concept hierarchies may be used for detecting structural changes and the emergence of new patterns by comparing relative entropies of observed and expected (distributions of) concepts or keywords.

Information mining in ProFIS is usually realized for the **whole** set of documents stored in the database, thus offering the possibility to relate events from different environmental segments to each other which often intensifies the strength of weak signals. This global approach, however, implies the risk of missing weak signals from specific areas which might get drowned in the mass of data. The global approach also tends to neglect the different quality of the documents available, e.g., the correctness of data provided by patent offices and of data from dubious URLs. Therefore, ProFIS, in addition to global analyses, also offers the possibility of analyzing **sub**sets of documents. Subsets may be generated by several criteria, among which the environmental segments and the source of the documents are of particular relevance: While the former criterion supports focused analyses of specific areas, the latter may be used to tackle the problem of differing data quality.

3.4 Information Evaluation and Initiation of (Re-) Actions

Evaluation of the information acquired by information mining requires, above all, **determination of the relevance of changes and deviations identified**. While this task is demanding in EI in general, it is even more demanding in KDD-based EI, because mining operates on the semantic level, while evaluation is concerned with the pragmatic level of information. Therefore, many categories, associations and deviations detected by information mining techniques may be meaningless for the substantial problem area of interest. The sorting out of irrelevant phenomena may be facilitated by differentiating between the analyses according to information sources, as mentioned in the preceding subsection. Thus, it may be advantageous, e.g., to separate the evaluation of data provided by human sensors from those collected in the WWW.

In addition to assessing the problem relevance of the mining results information evaluation encompasses **analyses of** the remaining **potential weak signals,** as described in section 2.1. Finally, for those early signals which require immediate (re-)action, the activities summarized in the initiation phase of the EI process have to be performed.

It is the exception rather than the rule that information detected by KDD-supported EI results in straightforward initiation of actions. More often, the information is used to either turn from scanning the environment to monitoring specific areas or topics or to re-formulate the areas and topics observed. This way, a **continuous process alternating between information collection, information mining and information evaluation** is initiated. The process starts with an extremely open and fuzzy enquiry, which induces a correspondingly hazy information retrieval. The documents collected are processed by employing information mining techniques. The mining results are evaluated and then serve to reduce the fuzziness of the enquiry and the haziness of the information retrieval. This sequence will be repeated over and over again until it converges towards a specific phenomenon satisfying the requirements of weak signals.

Information evaluation is a human domain. Therefore, the functionality of ProFIS in this module is restricted to presenting the mining results in a clearly structured and easily understandable format.

3.5 Evaluation of ProFIS

The preceding discussion showed that ProFIS covers all environmental dimensions, encompasses all activities in the EI process, and includes all information sources which might be relevant for EI. Thus, the **first goal of comprehensiveness** can be considered **achieved**. Furthermore, ProFIS merges human-orientated EI with information technology-driven EI and offers techniques for textual as well as for numerical data. Its focus on the detection of weak signals is broad enough to encompass early warning as well as early detection and early reconnaissance. Consequently, the **second goal of integration** may be considered **achieved, too**. Finally, configuration of ProFIS is mostly user-driven, thus providing the possibility to adapt to specific conditions of use and different types of information processed as well as to different types of information sources and formats. Therefore, the **third goal of flexibility** can **also** be considered **achieved**. **Questions** may **arise**, however, **as to the** achievement of the **fourth goal of SME suitability**: ProFIS assumes not only availability of large data sets and EDP infrastructure, but also employment of sophisticated information mining methods and availability of internal expertise for evaluation of the mining results and maintenance of the continuous EI process described in the preceding sub-section. Whereas data requirements and methodological sophistication are accounted for by automation, lack of internal expertise and motivation of SME management to maintain the EI process may form a serious barrier to the application of ProFIS in SMEs.

In addition **two "caveats"** should be kept in mind:

- ProFIS is a **concept** rather than a tool ready for application. At present, it is at the prototype stage and still has to prove its usefulness in reality. In particular, its ability to bridge the gap between semantic and pragmatic levels of information still has to be demonstrated.
- ProFIS has not yet satisfactorily solved the **conflict between recall** or effectiveness, i.e. the ability to retrieve all relevant documents, **and precision** or efficiency, i.e. the ability to find only the relevant documents (for precise definitions of these measures, see Chakrabarti 2003, 53 et sqq.): enlarging the database and employing full text modeling (instead of indexing) does tend to increase effectiveness but simultaneously tends to decrease efficiency.

4 Conclusions

Many companies today are confronted with a widening gap between the actual information available and the data containing potential information. This general observation is particularly true for early information, the importance of which is growing steadily due to the ever increasing complexity and dynamics of the environment in which companies operate. The KDD–concept, developed recently for extracting information from large databases, may be an instrument to counter this development.

Based on unveiling the similarities between EI and KDD, both on the process and on the features level, it has been shown that KDD promises to improve EI, in particular when textual data is to be processed. Several approaches and techniques developed within KDD for modeling and categorizing textual documents, as well as for extracting relations between (types of) textual data in the database and for detecting deviations from expectations, may also be applied for EI. Furthermore, ProFIS - a concept integrating the KDD process and instruments into EI - has been presented for merging the unique abilities of human beings with the power of modern information technology for the benefit of EI. ProFIS has been shown to be a comprehensive, integrative and flexible concept, that might be applied by large companies as well as by SMEs.

Although ProFIS might help to close the gap between information and data in EI, it is not without its deficiencies. As mentioned before, it operates in its automated part, in particular in text mining, solely on a **semantic** level, employing rather crude measures for the potential significance of textual phrases on a pragmatic level. More research is needed to bridge the gap between the semantic and the pragmatic levels of textual information. More research is also needed for solving the conflict between effectiveness and efficiency. In particular, research aimed at unveiling the information patterns of weak signals, enabling a more directed search may prove to be useful. Last but not least, the completion of the prototype currently under construction is urgently required for testing the concept developed regarding its effectiveness. In spite of these deficiencies, the integration of KDD concepts and instruments may be an attractive approach towards narrowing down the gap between the information needed and the data available in EI.

5 References

Ahn, H. and C. Meyer (2000): Das Informantenkonzept: Ein Beitrag zur strategischen Frühaufklärung in KMU, *Industrie-Management*, 5, 32-36.

Ahonen, H., O. Heinonen, M. Klemettinen, and A.I. Verkamo (1998): Applying Data Mining Techniques for Descriptive Phrase Extraction in Digital Document Collections, *Proceedings of the IEEE Forum on Research and Technology Advances in Digital Libraries*, Santa Barbara, CA, 2-11.

Ansoff, H.I. (1976): Managing Surprise and Discontinuity- Strategic Response to Weak Signals, *Zeitschrift für betriebswirtschaftliche Forschung*, 28 (2), 129-152.

Brockhoff, K. (1991): Competitor technology intelligence in German companies, *Industrial Marketing Management*, 20, 91-98.

Brockhoff, K. (1992): Instruments for patent data analyses in business firms, *Technovation*, 12 (1), 41-58.

Chakrabarti, S. (2003): *Mining the Web*, San Francisco, Cal.

Dumais, S. et al. (1998): Inductive Learning Algorithms and Representations for Text Categorization, *Proceedings of 7th ACM International Conference on Information and Knowledge Management (CIKM-98)*, Bethesda, MD, 148-155.

Ernst, H. (1996): *Patentinformationen für die strategische Planung von Forschung und Entwicklung*, Wiesbaden.

Faix, Axel (1998): *Patente im strategischen Marketing*, Berlin.

Fayyad, U.M., G. Piatetsky-Shapiro, and P. Smyth (1996): From Data Mining to Knowledge Discovery: An Overview, in: Fayyad, U.M. et al. (Eds.): *Advances in Knowledge Discovery and Data Mining*, Menlo Park, Cal. et al., 1-34.

Feldman, R. and I. Dagan (1995): Knowledge Discovery in Textual Databases (KDT), *Proceedings of the 1st International Conference on Knowledge discovery (KDD'95)*, Montreal, 112-117.

Freund, M. and R. Wassenhoven (2004): Ansatz eines Frühinformationssystems zur Schaffung einer strategischen Wissensbasis, in: Chamoni, P. et al. (Eds.) *Proceedings Multikonferenz Wirtschaftsinformatik (MKWI) 2004*, Duisburg/Essen, 407-419.

Konrad, L. (1991): *Strategische Früherkennung*, Bochum.

Krystek, U. and G. Müller-Stewens (1993): *Frühaufklärung für Unternehmen*, Stuttgart.

Lichtenthaler, E. (2004): Technology intelligence processes in leading European and North American multinationals, *R&D Management*, 34 (2), 121-135.

Nakhaeizadeh, G., T. Reinartz, and R. Wirth (1998): Wissensentdeckung in Datenbanken und Data Mining: Ein Überblick, in: Nakhaeizadeh, G. (Ed.): *Data Mining*, Heidelberg, 3-33.

Nigam, K., J. Lafferty, and A. McCallum (1999): Using Maximum Entropy for text Classification. *Proceedings of Machine Learning for Information Filtering Workshop*, IJCAI '99, Stockholm, 61-67.

Peiffer, S. (1992): *Technologie-Frühaufklärung*, Hamburg.

Säuberlich, F. (2000): *KDD und Data Mining als Hilfsmittel zur Entscheidungsunterstützung*, Frankfurt a.M.

Schlüter, C.K. (2004): *Strategische Frühinformationssysteme für KMU*, Diss. RWTH Aachen.

Schneewind, K.A. and J. Graf (1998): *16-Persönlichkeits-Faktoren-Test, Revidierte Fassung*, Testmanual, Bern et al.

Schröder, H.-H. and G. Schiffer (2001): Konzeptionelle Grundlagen der strategischen Frühinformation, *wisu*, 30 (7), 971-978.

Schröder, H.-H., A. Jetter, and G. Schiffer (2003): *Strategische Frühinformation*, TCW-report 38, München.

Scott, S. and S. Matwin (1999): Feature Engineering for Text Classification. *Proceedings of ICML-99, 16th International Conference on Machine Learning*, Bled, Slovenia, 379-388.

Sepp, H.M.(1996): *Strategische Frühaufklärung*, Wiesbaden.

Walter, L., A. Gerlitz, and M.G. Möhrle (2003): Semantische Patentanalyse mit dem Knowledgist und PIA., *Proceedings des 25. Kolloquiums der TU Ilmenau über Patentinformation*, Ilmenau, 235-248.

Witten, I.H. et al. (1999): Text mining: A new frontier for lossless compression, *Proceedings Data Compression Conference*, Los Alamitos, Cal., 198-207.

Zelewski, S. (1987): Der Informationsbroker, *DBW*, 47, 737-748.

Zeller, A. (2003): *Technologiefrühaufklärung mit Data Mining*, Wiesbaden.

R. Balachandra

Recent Advances in R&D and New Product Development Projects[1]

Prof. Dr. *R. Balachandra,* Department of Information, Operations and Analysis, Northeastern University at Boston (U.S.A.).

[1] This is a revised and updated version of a paper presented at the ICMORD Conference, New Delhi, India, 2003.

1 Abstract

The fast pace of technology, the increasing pressure to introduce new products into the market at an ever-increasing pace, and the globalization of R&D need new approaches to manage projects in New Product Development and R&D. This paper is a brief review of the recent advances in areas such as project selection and project management. The paper is structured in four sections – project selection, project management, project termination and global R&D, closing with a brief look at the future in R&D and NPD Project Management. The paper will provide a comprehensive review of the recent research in this important field in the past two decades.

2 Introduction

The art and science of managing R&D projects and New Product Development (NPD) projects have seen vast changes in recent years with a better understanding of the underlying processes and the changing market and technological environments. Great progress has been achieved in selecting and managing R&D projects and the related New Product Development projects. The approach to selecting R&D and NPD projects has shifted from treating individual projects in isolation to treating them as a collection or portfolio of projects, emphasizing the link between projects and their outcomes and the strategic goals of the organization.

The increasing globalization of commerce and the opening up of international borders have greatly facilitated the movement of technology across borders. The growth and prevalence of faster electronic communication and the Internet have helped in spreading the R&D effort across continents. It is not unusual to find R&D and NPD teams distributed around the globe pursuing common projects. The movement towards outsourcing has provided an impetus for outsourcing many facets of R&D to countries with high skilled personnel but with lower wages. Management of such projects requires special skills and processes where the managers have to be sensitive to the cultural differences of the members of the project teams.

Faster life cycles and globalization of commerce are exerting increasing pressures on firms to develop new products faster and introduce them into global markets. Developing new products faster requires a focused effort in R&D and in New Product Development activities.

There is a growing realization that not all projects are the same and the approach to managing R&D projects has to be tailored to fit the nature of the project. Projects differ on three identifiable dimensions. The success factors (those factors that indicate whether the project will be successful commercially) are different for different types of projects. The type of project also dictates the issues that should be emphasized. Consequently the management of a project has to be appropriate to suit the nature of the project.

As this brief introduction shows, there have been many advances in the practice of managing R&D and NPD projects in recent years. Technology, techniques, better understanding of the underlying nature of projects and the opening of borders, has vastly changed the environment of R&D and NPD projects. This paper attempts to provide a comprehensive review of the advances in this field in four major areas – project selection, project management, project termination, and globalization. Since most R&D projects lead to new products/processes, we include projects of both types (R&D and NPD) in this review. Also, these projects pertain to the commercial sector and not to the sponsored or government research projects. There are many differences in selecting and managing the projects in the two arenas.

3 Project Selection

Most innovative firms focus on developing competitive products to enhance their share of the market and/or profitability. There is always pressure to come up with ideas for new products or processes. These ideas come from a variety of sources both within and from outside the company.

In most cases the resources needed to pursue all the ideas generated are much larger than what the company can afford. The firm, therefore, needs to select from among the large number of ideas generated those ideas that lead to potential profits for the company. But this is a difficult choice. Many facts about the idea and the resulting product are still not known. There are many uncertainties. The uncertainties are usually of three kinds– market, technology and environment. Market uncertainty arises from the fact that the new product may not be as widely received as the firm expects. Technology uncertainty arises when the technology for the product may not be fully developed and there may be problems in making the technology work for this application. Environmental uncertainty arises when some new unanticipated regulations are introduced by regulators or supply conditions change. Additionally organizational uncertainties may also exist. These pertain to the abilities of the organization to successfully complete the project.

While choosing the idea for further work one must carefully choose those ideas that have a good chance of success in the market. The choice will be dependent upon a careful evaluation of the planned product's success in the market, which in turn depends on a number of factors. Some of these factors are quantifiable (albeit as educated guesses) while many others are qualitative and prone to be highly subjective.

The earlier project selection models focused on ranking the projects subjectively based on the relevant factors for an organization. For example, some firms may give a heavier weight to market factors while some others may emphasize the technology factors. The ranked projects were then allocated funds from the budget until the budget was exhausted. This procedure had a number of problems – the actual funds needed for a project did not enter the picture for ranking the projects. If there were disagreements on the ranking among the executives the senior person's opinion counted the most.

To minimize the differences in ranking, Souder developed the Q-Sort method. In this procedure, executives divide the set of projects into three groups – excellent, OK and no good. If there is common agreement among all the executives, then that grouping is used for the final allocation. If there were disagreements then the controversial projects would be discussed in detail until there is a consensus. (Souder and Manadakovic 1996)

The inherent subjectivity in ranking and sorting methods led to the development of more objective procedures. Scoring methods attempt to reduce the subjectivity. In these methods, a number of factors are identified (specific to a firm) that are considered important for the success of the project. The factors are then assigned weights based on their relative importance for the success of the project with reference to the organization. Each project is rated on the factors and assigned a score (usually on a scale of 1 to 5). The sum of the individual factor scores multiplied by the weight for the factor gives the total score received by the project. The projects are now ranked according to the total score and the top scoring projects are selected for allocating funds. (See Henriksen 1999)

The methods described above do not optimize the R&D project portfolio. Linear programming and integer programming models have been developed that try to select the optimum set of projects to maximize the expected returns within a given R&D budget. The models get more complex with the inclusion of probabilities and time-phased investments. (See Bard and Balachandra 1997, for a model using Integer Programming for reallocating budgets after identifying failing projects.)

One weakness with these methods is that they do not consider the interaction effects of projects. The successful completion or even the fact that a project is active may sometimes influence the success of another project. This interaction effect is not easily taken into account. Complex programming models have been developed to include such interactions. For a recent review of the many project selection approaches see Martino (1995).

Though these models help in identifying the most suitable projects for funding, there are a number of weaknesses with these models. First, the models are based on estimates of a number of items that are not easily known. This is true of any NPD or R&D

project. Similarly, the technology involved in the project may not be successfully developed in the time frame. Even assuming that these difficulties can be overcome, there is a more severe problem. The projects selected do not necessarily strengthen the overall long-term goals of the firm. The procedures do not allow one to include the goals of the firm into the selection of the projects.

A recent development to handle these issues is the portfolio approach to project selection and budget allocation. (Roussel et al. 1991, Edgett et al. 1998). This approach takes on a number of different forms. A common thread in all these approaches is to identify two major dimensions that are considered important for achieving the goals of the firm. Some typical dimensions used by a number of US firms are:

1. Strategic intent, market segments
2. Market risk, technology risk
3. Market attractiveness, financial attractiveness
4. Importance to firm, ease of execution etc.

The projects under consideration are plotted on a 2x2 matrix with these dimensions, after evaluating each project on the dimensions. The projects are usually represented by circles with the projects' budgets scaled to the areas of the circles. (See Figure 1 for an example.)

Figure 1: *An example of a Typical Portfolio Representation*

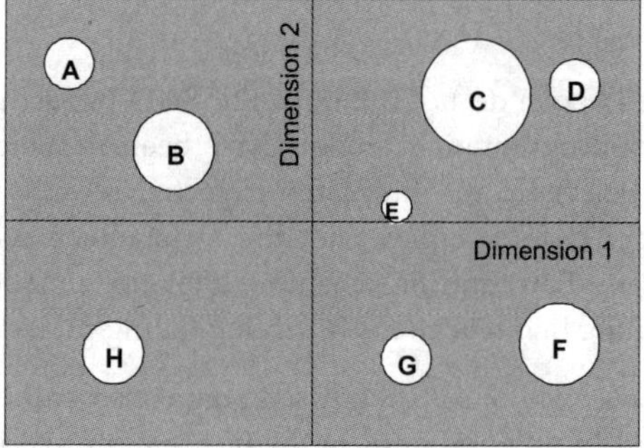

The size of the circles represent the budget allocation

This approach gives a good picture of the portfolio. It shows how the projects are positioned in terms of the two chosen dimensions. (See Edgett et al. 1998, for a discussion of NPD portfolios.) However, if these dimensions are not the critical dimensions that the firm is concerned about, the picture does not really help in determining the types of projects that the firm should be undertaking. It cannot fully show whether there is an overemphasis on certain types of projects and no or under emphasis on certain other types that may be critical for the firm's long-term success.

Recent work is focusing on developing on optimum R&D project portfolios. Ringuest and Graves (1999) have looked at portfolio formulations taking into account the risk involved with each project. Beaujon et al. (2001) have suggested approaches to balance R&D portfolios on different criteria. Chien (2002) has developed a framework for evaluating R&D project portfolios so that the right projects will be selected, while Mikkola (2001) looks at how the portfolio approach impacts on innovations in the organization.

One of the key weaknesses of the R&D project selection and management research in the past has been that all projects are considered in the same manner. Most research in this field consisted of generating a number of factors that are supposed to be important for the success of a project. Using survey methods the researchers collect information about a number of projects (regardless of the type) from a number of different companies. The projects are then coded and subjected to statistical analysis to determine the critical factors for success or failure. (See Balachandra 1989 for an extensive discussion of this approach). Though this method produces a number of factors that appear critical, a careful study of a number of research results showed that there was no agreement on the factors. A study by the author (Balachandra and Friar 1997) showed that there were over 100 factors described by various researchers. Some conclusions were contradictory too. For example, some studies would say that doing an initial thorough market study is highly critical for success of a project, while some other studies dismissed the need for any market study.

This led to the development of a contextual framework for R&D and NPD projects. This framework consists of three dimensions – market, technology, and innovation and can be represented as a cube, called the contextual cube for NPD and R&D projects. (See Figure 2.)

This framework suggests that all projects are not the same. There are differences in the projects depending on the combination of the three dimensions. It also follows that the success factors and the way the projects should be managed depend on the project's position in the contextual cube. Products geared for newer markets have different success factors than projects aimed for existing or older markets. Such differences exist for projects located in other parts of the cube. Shenhar (1996) suggests a similar framework for general projects using two dimensions – size of the project, and the scope of the project.

Figure 2: *Contextual Nature of NPD Projects*

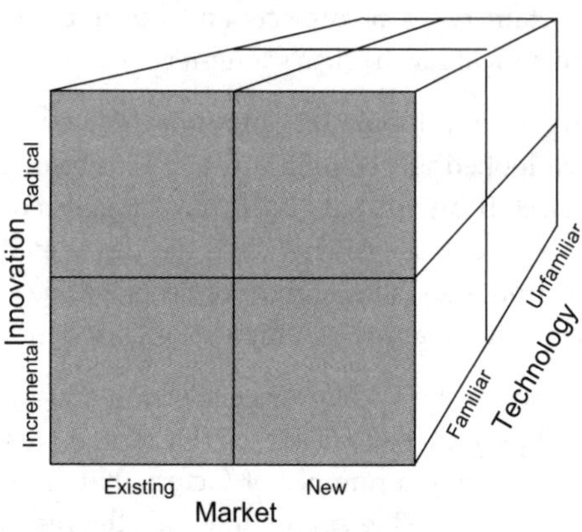

With this understanding, the approach taken for project selection as well as for developing an optimum portfolio needs considerable change. For example, instead of using one set of factors to evaluate projects, we need to develop different sets of factors to evaluate different types of projects. Thus a development project with an incremental innovation, using old established technology, aimed for an already established market should be focusing more on detailed market studies, a more systematic project organization with a higher degree of cost control. On the other hand, a project with innovative technology aimed for a completely new or not yet developed market requires very little market study (as there is yet no market to study), and a more flexible project organization with less controls (to encourage the creativity of the personnel). See Balachandra and Friar (1999).

This approach also helps in identifying the most suitable set of projects that a firm should be focusing on. Depending on the goals of the firm, the focus on projects could be to have a variety of projects fulfilling different niches of market and technology or simply focus on the current niche. For example, one firm's strategic focus could be to extend the product line of an established product while also focusing on new technologies to replace older technologies in its products. An example of applying this approach is shown in Figure 3.

A recent study has shown that in some industries the development of technology and the development of the market for the products of the technology are phased. First there is a great spurt in technology development resulting in many advances in the technology itself. The market at this stage is very fragmentary. After some time with the stabilization of the technology, the market explodes resulting in a large number of products with many variations using the technology. During this time the technology remains relatively static. Not many new developments in technology take place during this time.

Figure 3: *Representation of NPD Portfolio*

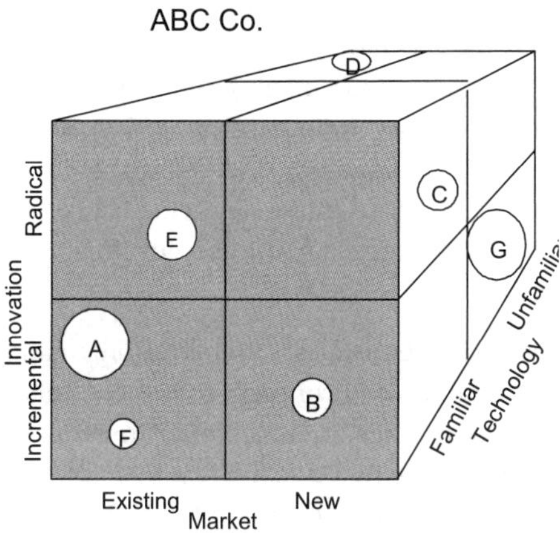

Then the market achieves some sort of stability where marginal improvements to existing products are developed and marketed. During this time the technology starts moving ahead rapidly to develop technologies that will move the products into the next phase. The whole process can be described as a double helix of development. (See Balachandra et al. 2004 for a more complete description of this movement and its application to the PC industry.)

With the existence of this dynamic, the nature of the R&D and NPD project portfolio should change depending on the phase of the cycle the firm finds itself in. In the early stages of a technology, the portfolio should emphasize technology development projects. In the latter period the focus should be on developing incremental variations of existing products. The budget allocation should reflect the changing focus.

Project selection continues to be a major problem in R&D management. Though there have been many techniques developed to optimize the projects for a firm, there are too many uncertainties in the process. The models and their outcomes are as good as the information.

4 Project Management

The field of managing R&D projects is vast. In the early days of corporate R&D where individuals and not companies departments got involved with research, managing the projects was relatively easy. An engineer or researcher was assigned to one project and his/her progress was monitored by the manager. The manager took care to select the appropriate person to do the job based on the qualifications and experience. As research got larger, new approaches to managing the projects had to be developed. (For a good discussion of this issue see Roussel et al. 1999.) Research and development became a team effort. Instead of managing individuals, teams of personnel had to be managed. But there was a difference. Unlike workers on a factory floor, the researchers were highly educated. New approaches had to be developed to motivate the researchers to accomplish the desired goal.

Managing professionals and scientists is different from managing other personnel. They need to be provided with an environment that is conducive for creative work. At the same time, the budget and other organizational constraints should not be forgotten. When the balance between the two is lost it results in uneconomic performance for the group. For example, take the case of Xerox's PARC facility set up sometime in the late 1980s. It had a brilliant team of scientists and engineers who produced some of the most outstanding technology for the computers – Graphical User Interface (GUI), hyperlinks and many other innovations. The scientists were given a free reign without much regard to how the results were going to be exploited by the company. Consequently, Xerox did not use much of the research output from this lab. (For a good description of the PARC laboratory see Hiltzik 2000).

Much work has been done in the past regarding managing professional engineers and scientists. (See Jain and Triandis 1999). The lessons from these studies are well known. One of the major factors is encouraging communication between individuals and groups. Allen (1982) suggests that the layout of the laboratory should be designed to facilitate such communication. Another factor that is considered important is the presence of a "Gate Keeper." A gatekeeper is a person who is relatively well informed in related and sometimes even unrelated areas. In addition he/she is recognized as a source of information in a number of areas by the researchers. (Tushman and Katz 1980)

But the problem in most of these approaches is that they treat all R&D activities as the same. But they are not, as mentioned in the previous section. R&D and NPD projects may be categorized on the differences in three key dimensions – technology, innovation and market. We will briefly describe each of these.

The technology involved in the project may be completely new to the organization or the organization may be familiar with it. In the former case the organization may have to either procure the technology if it already exists with another organization, or in case it is completely new, may have to develop it new. In either case, there is much uncertainty both in terms of time and money. On the other hand, if the organization is familiar with the technology and has already used it in some products, then the time and budgets can be set with a higher degree of certainty.

The type of innovation involved in the project could also range between what is termed "incremental," and "radical." Incremental innovations require marginal improvements for the product, while radical innovation implies a completely new product. A newer version of an existing product is an incremental innovation, while a product designed completely new is a radical innovation. An improved toothpaste is an incremental innovation, while the program to operate on-line auction (e-bay) was a radical innovation.

The result of the R&D effort aimed at a market that is already well established, we call it "Existing Market." In this case, one has to study closely the trends in the market and the potential demand. The market research has to be more rigorous. On the other hand, if the result of the R&D effort is aimed at a non-existing market, we call it "New Market." For example, "e-bay" was a product for a new market. There were no online auctions until that time. Nobody could even guess what the market size was going to be. There was even a question about whether any one would trust the seller and buy items without having ever seen them.

These differences in the characteristics of the projects do produce differences in managing the projects. For example, an NPD project for an incremental innovation with familiar technology and designed for an existing market will need extensive market research. It will be possible to do so, as the market has already been identified. Similarly, as the technology is known and it is an incremental innovation, the work on the project can go more smoothly. It can even be planned to be completed in a given time. The budgets can be set very clearly, and the time schedules can be set with relatively precise dates. Consequently managing such projects require a more bureaucratic approach with defined budgets and schedules, and people held responsible for not meeting time and cost constraints. Examples of such projects are in the area of new versions of an established product – like one of the many Sony Walkmans.

On the other hand, if it is a project dealing with unfamiliar technology for a still non-existing market, and possibly a departure from existing designs, a different approach has to be taken to manage the project. There may be no detailed market research as the product and its market are still unknown; no specific time schedules can be set as the path to completion is undefined, and has to be left to the ingenuity of the researchers. In this case, one may need a more flexible approach to managing the project with flexible budgets and time schedules. Imposing a bureaucratic approach will lead to failure of such a project. New technological projects belong to this type. (See Balachandra and Friar 1997 for a fuller discussion of these issues.) This theme has been explored well by a number of new studies in the general project management area where the classification criteria are different. (See Shenhar 1996).

5 Project Termination

The next important area in the field of R&D project management is the termination issue. Not all projects undertaken are completed successfully. As a matter of fact, hardly one out of 100 ideas are successfully introduced into the market and become successful in the market.

The life of a project goes through a number of stages. See Figure 4 for a representation of the different stages. Most projects start out as ideas and have to be nurtured through the different stages. At each stage there is a filtering process where some are discontinued (terminated) while a few make it to the next stage. Typically, each stage requires more resources, and consequently only those projects that are considered to have a greater potential for success are allowed to continue.

Figure 4: *Stages in the Life of an R&D or NPD Project*

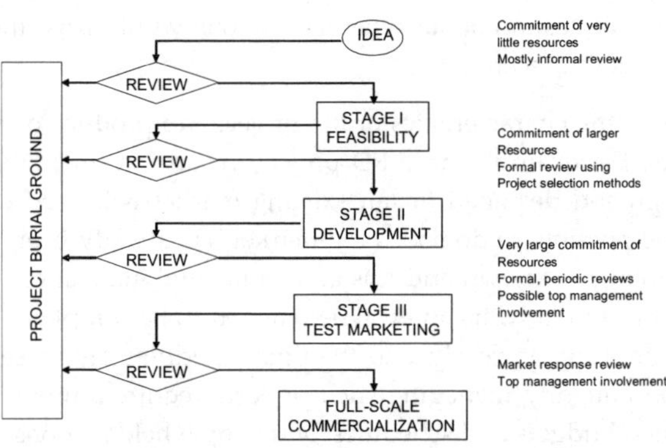

Source: Balachandra, R. *Early Warning Signals for R&D Projects,* Lexington: Lexington Books, 1989.

Many different approaches are available for filtering projects at each stage (Balachandra 1989; Cooper et al. 2002). The evaluation of projects at each stage is almost akin to project selection. However, there are differences.

At the beginning of the project's selection into the portfolio of projects, there is very little 'good' information about the project's technological and market strengths. Many of the assessments are guesses. As the project proceeds some of the information gets better; more market information is available and the technology will be better understood. Therefore the assessment about the project is made differently.

This is the approach suggested by Cooper's "Stage Gate" Process (Cooper et al, 2002)). In this procedure different stages are defined for the life of the project and at each stage assessments are made for the project to determine whether the project should be allowed to continue or should be terminated.

One of the important fields of research in this area is to determine the factors that can be used as indicators for the potential failure of a project. A large study comprising over 100 projects in the US led to the determination of a set of factors that had a greater chance of predicting whether an industrial R&D project was going to be successful or not. (See Balachandra 1989 for a complete discussion of this field.)

A number of factors were identified in this study as being capable of predicting the failure of an ongoing R&D project. This study was replicated in a number of other industrial countries (Japan, Germany and the UK). These inter-country studies showed that the factors were relatively common except for a few minor differences. (See Balachandra and Brockhoff 1995; Balachandra 1996; Balachandra, Brockhoff, and Pearson 1996).

Although these factors help to identify projects in trouble (or projects that have a lower probability of being successful), one cannot rely completely on evaluations using these factors alone. The factors usually are identified from a study of a number of projects that may be of different types. Therefore the factors that are identified by these studies are descriptive of a composite set of projects and may not be applicable to a particular type of project.

More research is needed in this area to identify the signaling factors indicating success or failure for different types of projects.

6 Globalization of R&D

In the past two decades, R&D has tended to become global in many large corporations. Large international corporations such as IBM, Microsoft, and Hitachi have established regional research centers all around the globe. The major objective of setting up these operations is to draw the technical skills of the local scientists to achieve faster research in many areas. More and more companies are following this lead. See Gunasekaran (1997) for a comprehensive discussion of some of the important issues in globalizing R&D.

The major issues in globalization are

1. Division of the work between the corporation's R&D facilities and the regional laboratories.
2. Coordinating the research efforts between the labs, central R&D facility and the business units that are the potential users of the research.
3. Managing the projects from the central corporate offices.
4. Degree of autonomy to be given to the regional labs.

Different organizations have taken different approaches to handle these issues. At one extreme, each regional laboratory is completely autonomous. It identifies the projects it will undertake, decide on the budget for each project, assign the research staff for the project, and monitor and manage the project. The only control the corporation has is on the budget. It may also play a major role in defining the scope of the research areas based on the skills available locally.

At the other extreme, the regional laboratory is just an extension of the central R&D facility and everything is controlled from the central office. The manager of the laboratory reports directly to the corporation's R&D Vice President on a very frequent basis. This system is feasible as the communication between the regional lab and the central office can be extremely efficient due to the advent of modern telecommunications – international phones, Internet and international video conferencing.

Recent research in this area suggests that the nature of the relationship between the central corporate office and the regional labs create problems. Asakawa (2001b) discusses the tensions that arise between the head quarters and the subsidiary labs from the Japanese multinational's perspective. The dynamics between the head quarters and the subsidiary labs should be carefully monitored to produce effective results (Asakawa 2001a). The exact nature of the relationship between the head quarters and the subsidiary labs should be based on a number of factors. The most important factors are:

1. The nature of research that will be done in the regional labs. Is it basic research, new product development or just incremental improvements for the local market?
2. The type of personnel that can be hired.
3. The nature of communication facilities available.
4. The type of regulations regarding intellectual property.
5. The type of trade regulations between the country and the country of the corporation.

A number of recent studies have shown that frequent communication between the corporate office and the regional labs is the most effective way of managing the regional labs (McDonough 1997). In spite of the progress in the Internet, it has been found that telephone is still the most effective communication method. Personal visits are nearly not as useful and productive, though it provides a sense of closeness between the local researchers and the corporate officers.

Globalization of research is still in a nascent stage. Many companies are establishing regional laboratories in different countries. Some have been very successful – IBM's labs in Europe have been very productive even earning Nobel prizes.

7 Future of R&D Management

R&D management is at a threshold now. Increased globalization and the rapid expansion of technologies throughout the developing countries has made managing R&D and the research labs extremely important for firms attempting to go global. The advanced countries such as the US, Japan and Germany are setting up to be more intellectual property developers and leave the more mundane tasks to other countries where the labor is cheaper. A classic example of this trend is in the hard disk drive industry. Most of the manufacture of the disk drives is in Singapore and the Far East. (See McKendrick et al. 2000.) Practically all the R&D and development activities for the hard drive are in the US and in Japan.

There is a recent trend where some of the development activities are also being moved to the Far East where the manufacturing is, as the skill levels get better and the infrastructure for R&D activities improves. If this trend continues it will be not be surprising to see many major international corporations setting up their research laboratories in countries such as India. Already firms such as GE, Intel and other technology firms have established R&D laboratories in India to do original research. These activities will force R&D managers to take a closer look at managing R&D activities in far away locations.

8 References

Allen, T.J. (1977): *Managing the Flow of Technology,* Cambridge, MA: MIT Press.

Asakawa, K. (2001a): Evolving headquarters-subsidiary dynamics in international R&D: the case of Japanese multinationals, *R&D Management,* January, 31 (1), 1-14(14).

Asakawa, K. (2001b): Organizational tension in international R&D management: the case of Japanese firms, *Research Policy*, 30 (ER5), 735-757.

Balachandra, R. (1989): *Early Warning Signals for R&D Projects*, Lexington MA: Lexington Books.

Balachandra R. (1996): A Comparison of R&D Project Termination Factors in Four Industrial Nations, *IEEE Transactions on Engineering Management*, 43 (2).

Balachandra R. and K. Brockhoff (1995): Are R&D Project Termination Factors Universal? *Research • Technology Management*, 28 (4).

Balachandra, R., K. Brockhoff, and A. Pearson (1996): R&D Project Termination: Process, Communication and Personnel Changes, *Journal of Product Innovation Management*, 13 (3).

Balachandra, R. and J. Friar (1997): Factors for Success in R&D Projects and New Product Innovation: A Contextual Framework, *IEEE Transactions on Engineering Management*, EM-44 (3), 276-287.

Balachandra, R. and J. Friar (1999): Managing New Product Development Processes the Right Way, *Information • Knowledge • Systems Management*, 1 (1), 33-43.

Balachandra, R., M. Goldschmitt, and J.F. Friar (2004): The Evolution of Technology Generations and Associated Markets: A Double Helix Model, *IEEE Transactions on Engineering Management*, 51 (1), 3-12.

Bard, J.F., R. Balachandra, and P.E. Kaufman (1988): An Interactive Approach to R&D Project Selection and Termination," *IEEE Transactions on Engineering Management*, 35 (3), 139-146.

Beaujon, G.J., S.P. Marin, and G.C. McDonald (2001): Balancing and Optimizing a Portfolio of R&D Projects, *Naval Research Logistics*, 48 (1), 18-40.

Chien, C.F. (2002): A portfolio-evaluation framework for selecting R&D projects, *R and D Management*, 32 (4), 359-368.

Cooper, R. G., S.J. Edgett, and E.J. Kleinschmidt (2002): Optimizing the stage-gate process: what best-practice companies do-I, *Research • Technology Management*, 45 (5), 21-27.

Edgett, S.J., E.J. Kleinschmidt, and R.G. Cooper (1998): *Portfolio Management for New Products*, New York.

Gunasekaran, A. (1997): Essentials of international and joint R&D projects, *Technovation*, November, 17 (11), 637-647+725(11).

Henriksen, A.D. and A.J. Traynor (1999): A Practical R&D Project-Selection Scoring Tool, *IEEE Transactions on Engineering Management*, 46 (2), 158.

Hiltzik, M.A. (2000): *Dealers of Lightning: Xerox PARC and the dawn of the computer age,* New York.

Jain, R.K. and H.C. Triandis (1997): *Management of Research and Development Organizations: Managing the Unmanageable,* 2nd ed., New York.

Martino, J.P. (1995): *Research and Development Project Selection,* New York.

McDonough III E F. and K.B. Kahn (1997): Using "Hard" and "Soft" Technologies for Global New Product Development, *IEEE Engineering Management Review,* 25 (3), 66.

McKendrick, D.J., R.F. Doner, and S. Haggard (2000): *From Silicon Valley to Singapore: Location and Competitive Advantage in the Hard Disk Drive Industry,* Palo Alto, CA.

Mikkola, J.H. (2001): Portfolio management of R&D projects: implications for innovation management, *Technovation,* 21 (7), 423-435(13).

Ringuest, J.L. and S.B. Graves (1999): Case, Randolph H., Formulating R&D Portfolios that Account for Risk, *Research • Technology management,* 42 (6), 40.

Roussel, P.A., K.N. Saad, and T.J. Erickson (1991): *Third generation R&D: managing the link to corporate strategy,* Boston, Mass.

Shenhar, A.J. and D. Dvir (1996): Toward a typological theory of project management," *Research Policy,* 25, 607-632.

Souder, W.E. and T. Mandakovic (1986): R&D Project Selection Models, *Research Management,* July/August, 36-42.

Tushman, M. and R. Katz R. (1980): External communication and project performance: An Investigation into the role of gatekeepers. *Management Science,* 1071-1085.

Part 3:

Innovation and Marketing

Henrik Sattler

Applications of Conjoint Analysis to New Product Development

Prof. Dr. *Henrik Sattler*, Institute of Marketing, Retailing and Management Sciences, University of Hamburg.

1 Introduction

There is no doubt that firms in order to achieve growth are increasingly developing new products (Brockhoff 1999). However, the success of new products is uncertain. In many product categories new product failure rates are around 80% (Ernst&Young and Nielsen 1999). Often 50 million € or more are spent for the introduction of new products (Aaker 1991; Mortimer 2003; Sattler 1997). Moreover, unsuccessful product introductions can have negative spillover effects, e.g. substantial losses of brand equity (Keller and Sood 2003; Sattler 2001).

In order to increase new product success firms are looking for customer integration within the new product development process. One critical step in new product development (NPD) is selecting from among multiple possible product concepts the one that the firm will carry forward into the marketplace. There is a need for low-cost, parallel testing of the appeal of new product concepts, the results of which closely mirror ultimate market performance (Dahan and Srinivasan 2000). An instrument very often applied for such testing is conjoint analysis (CA).

Applications of CA within the NPD process include the estimation of partworth utilities for certain levels of product attributes (assuming that a product consists of a bundle of product attributes, Brockhoff 1999; Lancaster 1971) in order to forecast the overall preference of customers for new product concepts. The basic procedure shall be illustrated by a meanwhile classical application of conjoint analysis published in the *Zeitschrift für betriebswirtschaftliche Forschung* by Albers and Brockhoff (1985). The new product concept under consideration was a particular food described by four product attributes, i.e. package shape (3 levels), package pictures (3 levels), brand (2 levels), and price (3 levels). Respondents were given a fractional factorial design of 9 product concepts, each of which was described by the levels of the features it contained, and were asked to rank order the product concepts in order to indicate their preference for the new products. It was assumed that the overall preference was an additive sum of the partworth utilities of the product attributes. Each attribute was represented by a series of dummy variables. A regression model was used to estimate the contribution of each attribute to overall preference. In this manner partworths were obtained for each respondent enabling to simulate choice probabilities for new products concepts. In the almost 20 years since the article by Albers and Brockhoff (1985) was published much has changed.

This article deals with academic and commercial applications of CA within the NPD framework. With respect to the academic applications we focus on the recent relevance of CA in general, product categories where NPD-CA is applied to and major improvements academic research has made since the article by Albers and Brockhoff (1985). CA is also of great practical relevance as shown in the studies by Wittink and colleagues (Wittink, Vriens, and Burhenne 1994; Wittink and Cattin 1989). In the past twenty years, CA has benefited from the communication between academics and practitioners. Academic method development has led to new practical applications and practice has inspired academics to address requirements that have emerged from real-life problems. However, little information is available on current commercial use of CA. The latest extensive study of this kind (Wittink, Vriens, and Burhenne 1994) is based on data that are more than ten years old. Thus, the study by Wittink, Vriens, and Burhenne is updated with respect to some questions of general interest with a particular focus on NPD.

2 Academic Applications of Conjoint Analysis to NPD

2.1 Review of the EBSCO Research Data Base

Conjoint analysis has caused a lot of interest in academic marketing research (Green and Srinivasan 1990; Green, Krieger, and Wind 2001). In order to get a systematic picture of recent academic CA applications a literature review of all peer reviewed journals covered by the EBSCO research data base was conducted. The review focuses on the last five years, i.e. from January 2000 to February 2004 (for the time before see e.g. Green, Krieger, and Wind 2001; Green and Srinivasan 1990; Sattler and Hensel-Börner 2000). Within the EBSCO data base a search of all peer reviewed journals covering some type of NPD CA application was done. The search includes the words "conjoint", "conjoint analysis" and "conjoint measurement". From the articles identified only those were selected which covered some type of empirical NPD applications of CA as a main focus of the paper. Applications of CA which clearly focused on a subject outside NPD (e.g. pricing) were excluded.

As a result of this review 46 applications of CA to NPD were found. This means that on average almost every month one NPD-based CA application article appears in an international peer reviewed journal. With 8 applications in 2000, 11 in 2001, 10 in 2002, 15 in 2003 and 2 in the two month investigated in 2004 there seems to be at least no decrease in the number of academic applications.

Furthermore, it is interesting to look at the academic NPD-CA fields of application (see Table 1). Most striking is the high relevance of the service sector with 58.7% of all 46 applications identified. Another 30.4% of the applications deals with durables such as automobiles and consumer electronics. Only 10.8% of the NPD-CA applications refer to fast moving consumer goods.

Table 1: *Academic Fields of NPD-CA Applications (January 2000 to February 2004)*

	Number of Applications (n=46)
Automobiles	6
Consumer Electronics (including PCs)	5
Other Durables (Furniture, Sport Articles)	3
Food	5
Banking	4
Choice of Occupation	3
Education	4
Environment and Urban Planning	3
Health Care	4
Restaurants	2
Tourism and Recreation	4
Web Design	3

2.2 Advances of Academic Applications

Besides the number and fields of application it is of particular interest which are the major improvements academic applications of CA achieved since the application published by Albers and Brockhoff in 1985. In this article we focus on three issues (for a more comprehensive discussion see e.g. Hauser and Rao 2004):

- Improvements in the validity of CA,
- improvements in visualising new product features, and
- integration of a large number of product features.

2.2.1 Validity

The motivation for the academic development of CA stems basically from several theoretical advantages over traditional methods of measuring customers' preference structure, especially over self-explicated approaches (Green and Srinivasan 1990). The advantages include a larger similarity to real choice situations, less chance of receiving only socially accepted responses, and better range sensitivity. All these issues are supposed to increase the (predictive) validity of CA. However, a comprehensive analysis of academic studies published in peer reviewed journals by Sattler and Hensel-Börner (2000) comparing the validity of CA against self-explicated approaches fails to confirm the superiority of conjoint measurement. Instead, the majority of empirical comparisons (18 out of 23, i.e. 78%) found either non significant differences between methods or even higher predictive validity or reliability for self-explicated approaches. Attempts to explain these results by factors such as the type of CA measure, experimental design, sample size, sampling procedure, product category and the number of attributes failed.

Table 2: *Validity (Hit Rate for Several Holdouts) of Discrete Choice CA*

	Hit Rate				
	Discrete choice CA HB	*ACA*	*Self-explicated*	*Self-explicated ACA*	*Random*
	84%	78%	75%	68%	50%
Discrete choice CA HB					
ACA	***				
Self-explicated	***	*			
Self-explicated ACA	***	***	***		
Random	***	***	***	***	

n.s. = non significant * $p < 0.10$ ** $p < 0.05$ *** $p < 0.01$

Source: Hartmann and Sattler (2004)

As the review by Sattler and Hensel-Börner (2000) includes only studies until 1999 it does not cover the latest academic developments. In particular it neglects discrete choice CA and advanced estimation procedures such as latent class regression models (LC) or hierarchical bayes (HB) (Gensler 2003). It seems that these developments can improve the validity of CA applications substantially (Gensler 2003; Haaijer, Kamakura, and Wedel 2000; Hartmann 2004; Hartmann and Sattler 2004). Results of the most comprehensive empirical study to date are shown in Table 2. The study deals with a NPD for pay-TV programs. As can be seen from Table 2 discrete choice CA estimated with a HB approach achieves with 84% of correct predictions the highest hit rate, significantly higher (p<0.01) than the hybrid CA method adaptive conjoint analysis (ACA; Green, Krieger, and Agarwal 1991), a certain self-explicated approach (Hartmann and Sattler 2004), and a model based on the self-explicated data collection part of ACA (Green, Krieger, and Agarwal 1991). In contrast, ACA just slightly outperforms the first self-explicated approach under consideration.

Thus it might be concluded that NPD applications of CA are in particular promising for discrete choice CA methods.

2.2.2 Visualising New Product Features

For measuring consumers' preference structures particular problems appear for products with really new products features, i.e. really new products. Existing market research techniques, such as CA, forecast considerably less accurate for really new products than for incrementally new products (Hoeffler 2003). Customers have limited knowledge about really new product features and therefore must construct preferences at the time of measurement. When preferences are measured in this way, rather than retrieved from something the consumer already knows, the resulting product features' importance weights are unstable and can easily change by small changes in measurement procedure (Hoeffler 2003).

In order to overcome these problems several internet-based product concept testing methods have been developed that incorporate virtual (instead of physical) prototypes of new products (Brockhoff 1999; Dahan and Hauser 2002; Toubia et al. 2003). Static as well as dynamic presentations of product features can demonstrate how the new product works through a simulated video clip of its operation. Meanwhile, interactive web-based CA exploiting new capabilities to present product features, product use, and marketing elements in streaming multimedia presentations (Dahan and Srinivasan 2000; Dahan et al. 2002) are available. In a method called information acceleration described by Urban, Weinberg, and Hauser (1996) the virtual product presentation is combined with a complete virtual shopping experience. Several empirical studies have demonstrated that the incorporation of (web-based) virtual product features can enhance the predictive validity of CA compared to traditional types of product feature presentation (Dahan and Srinivasan 2000; Dahan et al. 2002; Ernst 2001).

However, it has to be taken into consideration that customer integration via CA – even with the new possibilities of a virtual presentation of product features – not always supports the development of really new products (Brockhoff 1999).

2.2.3 Dealing with a Large Number of Product Features

Business-to-business companies and complex durable goods manufacturers as well as firms offering complex services require preference measurement methods that can handle a large number of product features. As Dahan et al. (2002) pointed out there is a growing tendency in the product development process to integrate more product attributes in order to handle more customers needs.

For traditional full profile CA it has been recommended to use no more than 6 attributes (Green and Srinivasan 1990). Otherwise severe problems concerning respondents' information overload are very likely (Green and Srinivasan 1990; Wittink, Vriens, and Burhenne 1994). Furthermore, it is probable that a large number of attributes lead to the statistical problem of too few degrees of freedom for individual parameter estimation (Green and Srinivasan 1990; Wittink, Vriens, and Burhenne 1994). At least the information overload problem applies in the same way for discrete choice CA if more than 6 attributes are used.

In order to handle a large number of product attributes several methods have been developed, including several types of hybrid CA (Green, Caroll, and Montemayor 1981; Green 1984; Johnson 1987; Green and Krieger 1996; Srinivasan and Park 1997; Hensel-Börner and Sattler 2000). Hybrid CA is a combination of a self-explicated approach and some type of CA. Today, ACA is one of the most popular method for hybrid CA among researchers as well as managers (see chapter 3), especially for applications with many attributes. Recently, new methods for adaptive question selection have been developed to minimize the uncertainty in parameter estimation. In this *polyhedral adaptive conjoint estimation* each question constraints the feasible set of partworths for product attribute levels (Dahan et al. 2002; Hauser and Rao 2004). This method is now available as an option within ACA.

3 Commercial Applications of Conjoint Analysis to NPD

In order to get more insight in the commercial applications of CA to NPD we conducted an empirical survey (which was part of a more comprehensive study by Hartmann and Sattler 2002). We address the following issues:

- What significance does the commercial use of CA in general have (with respect to the share of institutes conducting CA and the number of CA studies per year applied)?
- What significance do commercial NPD applications of CA relative to other marketing problems investigated with CA have?
- What are the methods of CA most often applied?
- How many product features are included?

Some of these questions are an update of the study conducted by Wittink, Vriens, and Burhenne 1994, the latest comprehensive study covering commercial applications of CA.

3.1 Research Design

The sample consists of market research institutes in Germany, Austria, and Switzerland. According to the study by Wittink, Vriens, and Burhenne (1994) Germany is the country in Europe, where CA is most often applied, with more than one third of the projects reported all over Europe. The authors report no differences between Germany and the total sample. Therefore it can be argued that the trend of the results could hold elsewhere in Europe, too.

The main source of the sample were the member listings of the ESOMAR (European Society for Opinion and Marketing Research) and the German BVM association (Berufsverband Deutscher Markt- und Sozialforscher e. V.), the client list of Sawtooth Software's European agent SKIM (as far as it is published), and a list of the top 50 German market research institutes (by turnover in 2000). Companies offering only qualitative research or field services were excluded. The gross sample resulted in 224 institutes, 186 being German (compared to a German gross sample of 136 in Wittink, Vriens, and Burhenne 1994), 20 Austrian, and 18 Swiss. The numbers of institutes in the three countries correspond roughly with their population sizes (82, 8, and 7 million, respectively).

The market researchers in the sample received a questionnaire of two pages together with a cover letter explaining the purpose of the study. Field work took place from mid-September to mid-November 2001. 57 institutes answered the mailing, i. e. a 25.4% response rate compared to 29% (Wittink, Vriens, and Burhenne 1994) and 24% (Wittink and Cattin 1989) in earlier studies. Three of the questionnaires were unusable, leaving a net sample of n=54. The response rate is spread evenly across the three countries. Our research covers almost as many institutes as previous studies, although those studies were aimed at a substantially larger target population (59 institutes across Europe participated in the study by Wittink, Vriens, and Burhenne 1994, and 66 institutes from the USA participated in the study by Wittink and Cattin 1989).

In total 304 CA studies in the past 12 months were reported. Since each respondent was asked to describe a maximum number of 5 studies in detail, the particulars of 121 of the 304 studies were given. The studies were weighted by the number of studies conducted by the institute divided by the number of studies described in detail.

3.2 Results

3.2.1 Significance of Commercial Use of CA in General

65% of the net sample conducted CA-studies during the past 12 months. This is a major increase compared to 37% that reported CA-studies in the five-year period from 1986 to 1991 (Wittink, Vriens, and Burhenne 1994). Evidently, in the last 10 years CA has become a widespread tool across marketing research institutes.

The median number of studies conducted in the past 12 months by those 35 institutes that conducted any study is 4.0 with an average of 8.7, compared to slightly more than 3 projects per year in the 1986 to 1991 period (Wittink, Vriens, and Burhenne 1994). Thus, not only the number of institutes offering preference structure measurement has increased drastically but even more so the number of studies per institute. This results in a total of 304 studies in the past 12 months.

Still, practitioners estimate that the number of studies in this field will increase further, both in their own institute and in the German-speaking market in general. 56% (64%) of the respondents reported that there would be rather more or definitely more studies conducted in their institute (in the market). 35% (33%) estimated a constant trend in their own institute (in the market), whereas just 9% (3%) expected a downward trend.

3.2.2 Significance of Commercial NPD Applications of CA

Having a closer look at NPD it turns out that NPD is one of the most significant commercial CA applications. The main goal of the studies, which was mentioned most often (multiple answers possible, results weighted), was NPD (46%) and pricing (48%), followed by segmentation (21%) and brand equity measurement (16%). With less than three answers, measurement of customer satisfaction, promotion effectiveness and advertising effectiveness seem to be of minor importance. Wittink, Vriens, and Burhenne (1994) used slightly different categories but the focus seems to be basically unchanged with the exception of brand equity measurement which is a new application of this type of study. Applications of NPD CA seem to remain basically unchanged over time.

3.2.3 Type of CA Method Most Often Applied

The methodology used most often (multiple answers possible, results weighted) was discrete choice CA (47 %) followed by ACA or related methods (34 %). In the third place was traditional CA (20 %), i.e. ranking or rating of concepts. Less often self-explicated methods (14 %) or paired comparison (8 %) were implemented. Compared to the results by Wittink, Vriens, and Burhenne 1994 (ACA 42 %, traditional full-profile CA 24 %, 15 % trade-off matrix, 4 % paired comparison, 5 % combination, 10 % others (hybrid)), the software package ACA is still strong but has lost its first position to discrete choice CA methods like Choice Based Conjoint (CBC), offered by Sawtooth. Thus, our study confirms the surmise that discrete choice CA will become the dominant CA method (Haaijer, Kamakura, and Wedel 2000).

However, these results are strongly moderated by the aims of the studies (Table 3). For NPD traditional CA is still the type of method most often applied. The overall dominance of discrete choice CA results mainly from its use for pricing studies. The small number of discrete choice CA aimed at NPD is surprising, because this type of CA method seems to have the highest validity (see above) and commercial software is available, e. g. from Sawtooth Software. It seems that many market research companies are not aware of the latest developments. In addition, many companies stated that discrete choice CA needs a very high level of personal training and requires a high amount of investments in software compared to traditional CA.

Table 3: *Aims of Studies by Type of Method Applied*

	Total (n=121)	*Traditional CA (n=24)*	*Discrete choice CA (n=56)*	*ACA (n=41)*
NPD	46%	61%	26%	61%
Pricing	48%	36%	75%	28%
Segmentation	21%	41%	11%	22%
Brand equity measurement	16%	17%	10%	20%

Base: 121 studies described in detail, weighted

3.2.4 Number of Product Features

As pointed out in chapter 2 for situations with substantially more than 6 product features the application of ACA (or other hybrid CA) or self-explicated approaches is recommended. For traditional CA as well as discrete choice CA no more 6 product attributes should be used. These recommendations have been widely cited and used in academic applications of CA (e.g. Herrmann, Schmidt-Gallas, and Huber 2000) Pullman, Dodson, and Moore 1999).

However, for commercial applications of CA these recommendations are not adhered to very often, at least not for traditional CA. As can be seen from Table 4, 65% of all traditional CA applications use more than 6 attributes and 48 % use even more than 10 attributes. The percentage of studies with many attributes (as well as the mean number of attributes and the median) are substantially lower for discrete choice CA, but still 24 % of the discrete choice studies employ more than 6 attributes. In all these cases, severe biases in estimating preference structures are likely because of respondents' information overload (see above). Even if a bridging design is applied several validity problems remain (Green and Srinivasan 1990).

Table 4: *Number of Attributes*) Implemented in a Study by Method*

	Total *n=121 (n=54)*	*Traditional CA* *n=24 (n=13)*	*Discrete choice CA* *n=56 (n=13)*	*ACA* *n=41 (n=25)*
Mean number of attributes	14 (18)	26 (30)	9 (8)	14 (14)
Median number of attributes	8 (14)	11 (18)	6 (7)	14 (14)
Percentage of studies with more than 6 attributes	55% (75%)	65% (70%)	24% (49%)	85% (93%)
Percentage of studies with more than 10 attributes	40% (54%)	48% (56%)	13% (18%)	62% (66%)

*) Number of attributes for NPD applications only are shown in parentheses
Base: 121 studies described in detail, weighted

The highest percentage of studies applying more than 6 (and also more than 10) attributes use ACA. This is consistent with recommendations (Green and Srinivasan 1990) and also with empirical results finding an increase in the application frequency of ACA as the number of attributes increases (Wittink, Vriens, and Burhenne 1994).

Comparing the results for NPD applications of CA with all types of CA applications (Table 4) reveal some, but no major differences.

4 Summary

Applications of CA to NPD are highly relevant. This article focuses on academic as well as commercial applications. The main results can be summarized as follows:

- On average almost every month one NPD-based CA application article appears in an international peer reviewed journal.

- NPD-based academic applications of CA are most often applied in the service sector.
- The most promising method in terms of (predictive) validity seems to be discrete choice CA.
- Interactive web-based CA exploiting new capabilities to present product features, product use, and marketing elements can enhance the validity of CA.
- There are several procedures to incorporate a large number of product features in applications of CA in order to handle more customers needs. However, in commercial applications of CA these procedures are often not used; still traditional CA is used for applications with substantially more than six product features.
- Based on a comprehensive sample of market research institutes it could be shown that in the last 10 years CA has become a widespread tool across marketing research institutes. Not only the number of institutes offering preference structure measurement has increased drastically, but even more so the number of studies per institute. Still, practitioners estimate that the number of studies in this field will increase further.
- NPD is one of the most significant commercial CA applications.
- The CA methodology currently used most often within commercial applications is discrete choice CA, even more often than ACA, the dominant tool in the last decade. However, for NPD applications of CA still traditional types of CA are dominant.

5 References

Aaker, D.A. (1991): *Managing Brand Equity: Capitalizing on the Value of a Brand Name*, New York.

Albers, S. and K. Brockhoff (1985): Die Gültigkeit der Ergebnisse eines Testmarktsimulators bei unterschiedlichen Daten und Auswertungsmethoden, *Zeitschrift für betriebswirtschaftliche Forschung*, 37, 191-217.

Brockhoff, K. (1999): *Produktpolitik*, 4th ed., Stuttgart, New York.

Dahan, D. and J.R. Hauser (2002): The Virtual Customer, *Journal of Product Innovation Management*, 19, 332-353.

Dahan, D. and V. Srinivasan (2000): The Predictive Power of Internet-Based Product Concept Testing Using Visual Depiction and Animation, *Journal of Product Innovation Management*, 17, 99-109.

Dahan, D., J.R. Hauser, D.I. Simester, and O. Toubia (2002): *Application and Test of Web-based Adaptive Polyhedral Conjoint Analysis*, MIT-Working Paper.

Ernst, O. (2001): *Multimediale versus abstrakte Produktpräsentationsformen bei der Adaptiven Conjoint-Analyse. Ein empirischer Validitätsvergleich*, Frankfurt.

Ernst & Young and Nielsen (1999): *New Product Introduction: Successful Innovation/Failure: A Fragile Boundary*.

Gensler, S. (2003): *Heterogenität in der Präferenzanalyse - Ein Vergleich von hierarchischen Bayes-Modellen und Finite-Mixture-Modellen*, Wiesbaden.

Green, P.E. (1984): Hybrid Models for Conjoint Analysis: An Expository Review, *Journal of Marketing Research*, 21, 155-169.

Green, P.E. and A.M. Krieger (1996): Individualized Hybrid Models for Conjoint Analysis; *Management Science*, 42, 850-867.

Green, P.E. and V. Srinivasan (1990): Conjoint Analysis in Marketing: New Development with Implications for Research and Practice, *Journal of Marketing*, 54, 3-19.

Green, P.E., J.D. Caroll, and M. Montemayer (1981): A Hybrid Utility Estimation Model for Conjoint Analysis, *Journal of Marketing Research*, 45, 33-41.

Green, P.E., A.M. Krieger, and M. Agarwal (1991): Adaptive Conjoint Analysis: Some Caveats and Suggestions, *Journal of Marketing Research*, 28, 215-222.

Green, P. E., A.M. Krieger, and Y. Wind (2001): Thirty Years of Conjoint Analysis: Reflections and Prospects, *Interfaces*, 31 (3, Part 2 of 2), 56-S73.

Haaijer, R., W. A. Kamakura, and M. Wedel (2000): Response Latencies in the Analysis of Conjoint Choice Experiments, *Journal of Marketing Research*, 37, 376-382.

Hartmann, A. (2004): *Kaufentscheidungsprognose auf Basis von Befragungen*, Wiesbaden.

Hartmann, A. and H. Sattler (2002): *Commercial Use of Conjoint Analysis in Germany, Austria and Switzerland*, Research Papers on Marketing and Retailing, No. 6, University of Hamburg.

Hartmann, A. and H. Sattler (2004): Wie robust sind Methoden zur Präferenzmessung?, *Zeitschrift für betriebswirtschaftliche Forschung*, 56, 3-22.

Hauser, J.R. and V.R. Rao (2004): Conjoint Analysis, Related Modelling, and Applications, in: Y. Wind and P. E. Green (Eds.): *Market Research and Modelling: Progress and Prospects*, New York et al.

Hensel-Börner, S. and H. Sattler (2000): Ein empirischer Validitätsvergleich zwischen der Customized Computerized Conjoint Analysis (CCC), der Adaptive Conjoint Analysis (ACA) und Self-Explicated-Verfahren, *Zeitschrift für Betriebswirtschaft*, 70, 705-727.

Herrmann, A., D. Schmidt-Gallas, and F. Huber (2000): Adaptive Conjoint Analysis: Understanding the Methodology and Assessing Reliability and Validity, in: Gustafsson, A., A. Herrmann, and F. Huber (Eds.): *Conjoint Measurement: Methods and Applications*, Berlin, 253-278.

Hoeffler, S. (2003): Measuring Preferences for Really New Products, *Journal of Marketing Research*, 40, 406-420.

Johnson, R.M. (1987): Adaptive conjoint analysis, in: Sawtooth Software (Ed.): *Proceedings of the Sawtooth Software Conference on Perceptual Mapping, Conjoint Analysis, and Computer Interviewing*, 1, 253-265.

Keller, K.L. and S. Sood (2003): Brand Equity Dilution, *Sloan Management Review*, 45 (1).

Lancaster, K. (1971): *Consumer Demand: A New Approach*, New York.

Mortimer, R. (2003): Fool's gold for marketers?, *Brand Strategy*, 168, 20-22.

Pullman, M. E., K.J. Dodson, and W. L. Moore (1999): A comparison of conjoint methods when there are many attributes, *Marketing Letters*, 10 (2), 1-14.

Sattler, H. (1997): *Monetäre Bewertung von Markenstrategien für neue Produkte*, Stuttgart.

Sattler, H. (2001): *Markenpolitik*, Stuttgart et al.

Sattler, H. and S. Hensel-Börner (2000): A Comparison of Conjoint Measurement with Self-Explicated Approaches, in: A. Gustafsson, A. Herrmann and F. Huber (Eds.): *Conjoint Measurement. Methods and Applications*, Berlin et al., 121-133.

Srinivasan, V. and C.S. Park (1997): Surprising Robustness of the Self-Explicated Approach to Customer Preference Structure Measurement, *Journal of Marketing Research*, 34, 286-291.

Toubia, O., D.I. Simister, J.R. Hauser, and D. Dahan (2003): Fast Polyhedral Adaptive Conjoint Estimation, *Marketing Science*, 22, 273-303.

Urban, G.L., B.D. Weinberg, and J.R. Hauser (1996): Premarket Forecasting of Realy-New Products, *Journal of Marketing*, 60, 47-60.

Wittink, D. R. and P. Cattin (1989): Commercial Use of Conjoint Analysis: An Update, *Journal of Marketing*, 53, 91-96.

Wittink, D. R., M. Vriens, and W. Burhenne (1994): Commercial Use of Conjoint Analysis in Europe: Results and Critical Reflections, *International Journal of Research in Marketing*, 11, 41-52.

[illegible] and H. Seifert (1990), [illegible] [illegible] Conjoint Analysis [illegible] [illegible]

[illegible]

[illegible]

[illegible]

[illegible] (1988), [illegible] Marketing Research [illegible]

[illegible] New York.

[illegible] Marketing Research [illegible]

[illegible] and [illegible] (19[illegible]), A Comparison of Conjoint [illegible] [illegible] Journal [illegible] 10 (2), [illegible]

[illegible] (1989), [illegible]

[illegible] (1991), [illegible]

[illegible] (19[illegible]), A Comparison of Conjoint [illegible]

[illegible]

[illegible]

[illegible]

[illegible]

Vithala R. Rao

Bundles of Multi-attributed Items

Modeling Perceptions, Preferences, and Choice

Prof. Dr. *Vithala R. Rao,* Deane W. Malott Professor of Management and Professor of Marketing and Quantitative Methods, Johnson Graduate School of Management, Cornell University at Ithaca (U.S.A.).

1 Introduction

A commonly used paradigm for studying consumer choice in marketing research is: Information -> Perception -> Preference -> Choice---> Satisfaction/Subsequent Choice. In this paradigm, firms' marketing mix decisions provide the input to the information used by consumers in forming perceptions of choice alternatives. Different transformation functions can exist in the way consumers form perceptions and preferences based on the information on alternatives due to individual (consumer) heterogeneity. The ultimate choices made by an individual consumer will be affected by a host of situational factors such as budget and availability of items. Brockhoff is one of the first to model the product positioning problem for a single product (Albers and Brockhoff 1977). See Kaul and Rao (1995) for a review of the analytical techniques used for analysis of consumer perceptions, preferences, and choice in the context of product positioning and design. While various analyses can be conducted with revealed choice data, our focus in this paper is on stated judgments, stated preferences, and stated choices.

Much of the past research has focused on the choice of a single item (from a set of competing items) and it is only recently that researchers have become fascinated with studying the choice issues for bundles[1] of items. Products and/or services that are offered as bundles include fly-cruise vacation packages, season tickets for entertainment or sports events, computer hardware and software packages, stereo component packages, courses offered at a University, meal specials in restaurants, etc. A number of diverse reasons from the perspectives of both sellers and buyers are cited to explain why bundling is becoming an accepted business practice in the marketplace. One main reason for creating a bundle is to take advantage of any complementary or substitute relationships among the bundle items and attributes.

Any item of choice is normally described as a vector of multiple attributes (two at the minimum such as price and quality). In the research on single item choices, the attribute information is collapsed into a single measure for the deterministic component of utility for the item and a random utility framework is used to derive probabilities of choice of a single item (McFadden 1986). This measure is usually a weighted linear function of the attribute scores and the weights are either ascertained from individuals or estimated from data on choices or preferences.

But, when one deals with a bundle, one has a matrix of information on items by attributes and this matrix needs to be collapsed into a single measure for the bundle as a

[1] There is a growing body of literature on choice of multiple product categories (Ainslie and Rossi 1998, Manchanda, Ansari and Gupta 1999, Russell and Petersen 2000, Deepak, Ansari, and Gupta 2002, and Singh, Karsten, and Gupta 2003). In a way, one can look at an individual's marketplace (revealed) choice of a set of brands from different product categories at a point in time as a bundle. But, we will confine our paper to stated choice and judgments in this paper.

whole. The research problem, then, is one of finding the appropriate mapping function from items to the bundle; further, this mapping function needs to consider the relationships among the items as well as the relationships among the attributes. The extant research has utilized various approaches to this mapping problem (see Chung and Rao 2003 for a quick review).

Against this background, this paper will focus on the following topics: (i) Defining a bundle; (ii) Modeling bundle perceptions; (iii) Modeling bundle preferences; (iv) Modeling bundle choice; and (v) Future research directions.

2 Defining Bundles

Several definitions for a bundle exist. The most frequently cited definition by bundle studies is from sellers' perspective due to Guiltinan (1987), who defines bundling as the practice of marketing two or more products and/or services in a single "package" for a special price. However, this definition fails to emphasize one important feature, namely, the multi-attributed nature. Given this, we define a bundle as a subset of items offered in a single package, each of which is described on a number of attributes; therefore, a bundle can be abstracted as a product with multiple levels of some attributes. In some situations, an item in a bundle cannot be decomposed into attributes and can only be looked at holistically. Further, situations arise in which the attributes of items within a bundle are not (fully) comparable.

For analysis and modeling purposes, bundles[2] can also be divided based on three criteria: (i) degree of product homogeneity across items in the bundle; (2) whether the bundling is implicit or explicit; and (3) who (buyer or seller) forms the bundle.

The first criterion is quite critical to bundling research. We call products that can be characterized by the same set of product attributes (or dimensions) as homogeneous products and products that cannot be characterized by the same product attributes as heterogeneous products. Typically, homogeneous products belong to the same product category (or fulfill the same consumer need), while heterogeneous products do not belong to a single category but to multiple categories. Basically product heterogeneity is a matter of degree since in many categories, especially emerging new markets like hi-tech industry, it is often the case that some products hold unique attributes compared to other products.

[2] A more general way of looking at bundles is with the concept of mixtures. In a mixture, the individual items occur with different proportions. When these proportions are either 1 or zero, the mixture becomes a bundle. An example of a mixture is a portfolio of stocks or a blend of wines.

We first consider the criterion of product heterogeneity. If the components of a bundle are relatively homogeneous, we characterize such a bundle as an assortment. In this kind of a bundle, the components can be directly compared in terms of the basic attributes that are shared by all components. An example of an assortment is a set of magazines subscribed by a consumer. However, if the bundle consists of heterogeneous products, the attributes of the various items cannot be directly compared. The components of such a bundle are functionally quite different from each other, but together they work as a system. Hence, each component not only contributes to utility on its own, but becomes quite valuable when combined with the other components. For example, bundling a PC system comprising a monitor, PC and printer is a predominant practice in computer industry. It should be noted that a package of items, each of which has only unique attributes is strictly not a bundle but can be treated as a multi-attributed product.

The second criterion of implicit bundling or explicit bundling refers to the physical aspect of packaging items. If a set of products is prepackaged and physically sold together as a bundle (either offered by the manufacturers or suppliers, or put together by the buyers), we call such cases as "explicit bundling". But even though no physical bundles are being offered, some buying and selling practices can be conceptually treated as bundling. We call these "implicit bundling". Examples of implicit bundling that are buyer determined are purchases made on promotions and loss-leader strategies, whereas tie-in sales are examples of implicit bundling which is determined by the seller.

Third, based on who actually puts together the bundles, bundling can be thought of as either seller determined or buyer determined. In general, the seller has three alternative strategies to market his/her products/services: (i) *Pure Components:* The seller only sells various components separately, but not as a bundle; (ii) *Pure Bundling:* Under this strategy, the seller markets various components as a bundle only and does not sell individual components separately. Examples of this practice include manufacturers selling only certain stereo systems, some computer workstations and the like; and (iii) *Mixed Bundling:* In this option, the seller markets the bundle as well as the individual components; the bundle price may or may not be the simple sum of the components that comprise the bundle[3]. In the case of mixed bundling, examples of both options - seller supplied and buyer assembled - can be found. While all these three bundling strategies are used in marketing, there is no data on the extent to which each strategy is followed and the profiles of the firms that use them. In the case of pure bundling employed by the seller, the buyer does not have many options to determine bundles. The buyer's options are limited to buying a pre-packaged bundle offered by the seller or not buy at all. However, when the seller is pursuing a pure components strategy or mixed bundling, the buyer can purchase the components and put together a bundle

3 If the bundle price is greater than the sum of the individual component prices, the bundling strategy is known as premium bundling.

(other than the one offered) according to her preference or needs. In this situation, however, no discount is generally possible for the buyer. An example would be the purchase of various components of a hi-fi system by a customer.

A product (or service) mixture is perhaps a more general way of looking at bundles. In a mixture, the individual items occur with different proportions. When these proportions are either 1 or zero, the mixture becomes a bundle. An example of a mixture is a portfolio of stocks or a blend of wines.

3 Modeling Bundle Perceptions

To fix ideas, let us assume that we are interested in identifying how the perceptions of a group of homogeneous subjects are formed for m bundles of fixed size[4] k ($1 < k \leq n$), formed from a set of n multi-attributed items, each described on r attributes. Let the perceptual space of the n items be denoted by the nxr matrix, $X = (x_{jp})$; for simplicity, we assume this space to be common across all the subjects in the study. Let α_{bj} denote the presence or absence of the j-th item in b-th bundle; it is either 1 (included in the bundle) or 0 (not included in the bundle). The sum of α_{bj}-values over j will be k, the size of the bundle. (If the bundle is a mixture, then α_{bj}s can be proportions.)

The research questions with respect to mapping perceptions of bundles are:

(i) What is the dimensionality of the perceptual space of the m bundles?

(ii) What is the relationship of the perceptual space of the bundles to that of the individual items?

In general, when individuals consider bundles, they may create some summary measures for each attribute for the bundle such as the mean value of the attribute for the bundle and dispersion of the attribute across the items in the bundle. In this situation, a perceptual space of bundles is of dimensionality 2r, the entries will be mean and dispersion of the bundle on each attribute. The entries are derived from the X-matrix and the bundle compositions.

However, the problem of finding an appropriate space for bundles is an open issue. Empirical and theoretical research is called for on the above questions.

---

4 While we consider bundles of fixed size, the discussion easily extends to bundles of varying sizes.

4 Modeling Bundle Preferences

While the problem of finding the perceptual space of bundles is quite intricate, modeling of preference (or utility) of a bundle is somewhat less complicated. If there is no issue of complementarity or variety, the preference (utility) for a bundle can be simply the sum of preferences (utilities) of the items in the bundle. We describe two specific bundle preference models.

Complementarity Model: Using the vector model of preferences for single items, we can write the preference (or deterministic component of utility) for the j-th item as: $Y_j = \sum w_p x_{jp}$, where w_p is the weight an individual assigns to the p-th attribute.

Now consider the b-th bundle defined by α_{bj} values. Under the assumption of no complementarities, the preference (or the deterministic part of bundle utility) for the b-th bundle BV_b can be written as: $BV_b = \sum \alpha_{bj} Y_j = \sum w_p V_{bp}$; where $V_{bp} = \sum \alpha_{bj} x_{jp}$, which is simply the (sum of the scores of the items included in the bundle on the p-th attribute (or a weighted sum in case of mixtures).

One way to incorporate complementarities or substitutions in this formulation is to specify the weights (w_ps) as functions of the sum scores on other attributes. A simple formulation for this is:

$$w_p = w_{p0} + \sum c_{sp} V_{bs}.$$

Here the parameter c_{sp} measures the degree of relationship between the attributes s and p in the preference for the bundle. We can divide the pairs into three categories: reinforcing (P^+), neutral (P^0), and counteracting (P^-). A reinforcing pair of attributes is complementary in the formation of preference, a neutral pair exhibits no relationship, and a counteracting pair shows a substitutive relationship. The parameters, c_{sp} for the set of pairs in P^0 will be zero. As an illustration, consider the case of a faculty group in a university department (or a "bundle" of faculty members) and three relevant attributes of research, teaching, and service. The pairs of attributes (research and teaching) and (service and teaching) can be reinforcing while the pair, (research and service) can be neutral. In this illustration, the three pairs of attributes are symmetric; but in general a pair of attributes need not be symmetric; for example, the effect of research on teaching can be complementary while that of teaching on research can be substitutive. The above formulation can accommodate any asymmetries in the attribute relationships; thus, for a pair of attributes s and p, c_{sp} need not be equal to c_{ps}.

The complementarity model for the preference (utility) for the b-th bundle will be as follows:

$$BV_b = \sum_{p} w_{p0} V_{bp} + \sum_{s,p \in p^+} (+1) c_{sp} V_{bs} V_{bp} + \sum_{s,p \in P^-} (-1) c_{sp} V_{bs} V_{bp}.$$

Balance Model: While the complementarity model deals with relationships between pairs of attributes, Farquhar and Rao (1976) developed a balance model which deals with the relationships among the items in the bundle for a given attribute. They consider means and dispersions of items in a bundle on an attribute and classify the essential attributes (those that matter or whose with a non-zero weight) into four categories, two for means and two for dispersions. The two categories for the means are desirable and non-desirable, where higher (lower) means are preferred in a bundle for the desirable (non-desirable) attribute. They labeled the categories for dispersions as counter-balancing and equi-balancing, where higher (lower) dispersions are preferred for a counter-balancing (equi-balancing) attribute. The attributes will have differential weights. Calling the attribute categories as B_d for desirable, B_n for non-desirable, B_e for equi-balancing, and B_c for counter-balancing, the model for preference (utility) of the m-th bundle according to a balance model is:

$$BV_b = \sum_{p \in B_c} (+1) w_p D_{pb} + \sum_{p \in B_e} (-1) w_p D_{pb} + \sum_{p \in B_d} (+1) w_p S_{pb} + \sum_{p \in B_n} (-1) w_p S_{pb}$$

where S_{pb} and D_{pb} are respectively sum and dispersion of the items in the b-th bundle on the p-th attribute.

Several applications of the balance model have appeared in the literature; these include: evaluation of packages of television programs (Farquhar and Rao 1976), acquisition of one forms (Rao, Mahajan, and Varaiya 1991), and measurement of brand equity in acquisitions (Mahajan, Rao, and Srivastava 1994).

5 Modeling Bundle Choice

During the last twenty years or so, researchers have utilized revealed choice data to understand preference as contrasted with that of studying stated preference. The focus was directly on choice based on the random utility framework. This framework requires the specification of the deterministic component of utility; which is equivalent to the modeling of preference. This approach has been applied to a limited set of choice problems for bundles. The approaches to bundle choices adopted in the marketing literature so far[5] can be classified according to the type of units for utility analysis; component-based and attribute-based approaches (Chung and Rao 2003). The attribute-based approaches can be further classified by the type of comparability of bundle components, homogeneous and heterogeneous components. Figure 1 shows this classification and relevant studies for each approach.

Figure 1: *Five Approaches to Modeling Bundle Choices*

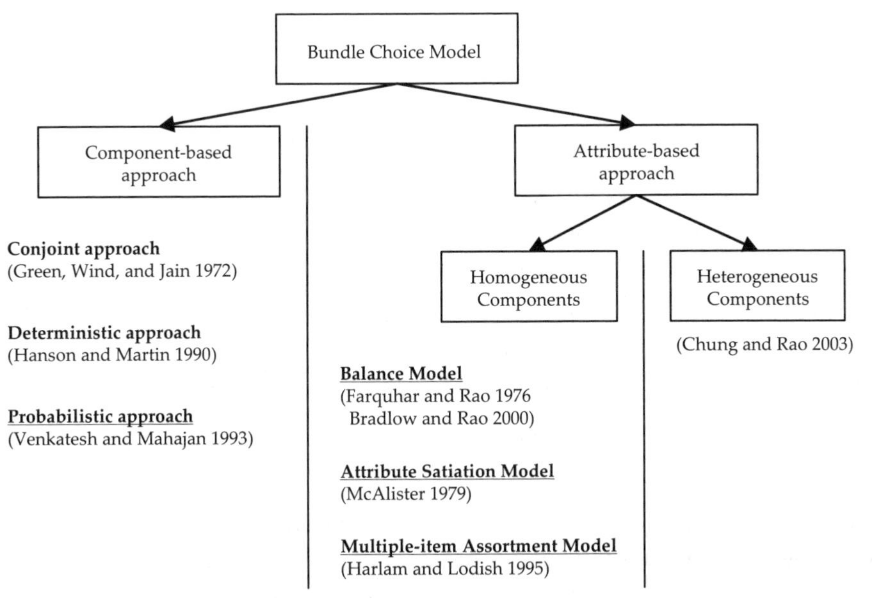

Source: adapted from Chung and Rao (2003).

Component-based approaches to bundle choice consider individual products (components) of a bundle as the ultimate unit of analysis in describing the utility of a bundle. In this stream, complementarity among the components is described directly in terms of the products. Three methods are employed in this approach; these are (1) the conjoint modeling (Goldberg, Green, and Wind 1984; Green and Devita 1974; and Green, Wind, and Jain 1972), (2) mixed integer linear programming (Hanson and Martin

[5] We confine the review of the extant research to research on bundling. Some research on non-bundling problems such as variety seeking behavior observed over time consumer purchasing (Lattin 1987) is not discussed due to the limitation of space, even though those ideas are somewhat similar to the extant bundle utility models.

1990), and (3) the probabilistic model (Venkatesh and Mahajan 1997; Ansari, Siddarth, and Weinberg 1996; and Venkatesh and Mahajan 1993).

The general choice model developed by Chung and Rao (2003) is applicable to bundles of heterogeneous products. It considers the issue of comparability of attributes across components in the bundle by classifying attributes as fully comparable, partially comparable and non-comparable. Their resulting specification for bundle utility is:

$$BV_b = \alpha_0 + \sum_{p_1 \in A^1} \left[\beta_{p_1} S^b_{p_1} + \gamma_{p_1} D^b_{p_1}\right] + \sum_{p_2 \in A^2} \left[\beta_{p_2} S^b_{p_2} + \gamma_{p_2} D^b_{p_2}\right] + \sum_{p_3 \in A^3} \alpha_{p_3} C^b_{p_3} \qquad (2)$$

where:

BV_b = the value of alterative b for individual i
A^g= the set of attributes characterized by comparability type g; g=1,2,3.

$$g = \begin{cases} 1 & \text{if the attribute is fully comparable;} \\ 2 & \text{if the attribute is partially comparable; and} \\ 3 & \text{if the attribute is noncomparable;} \end{cases}$$

p_g = an attribute in the group of comparability type g; g=1,2,3.
$S^b_{p_g}$ = a weighted sum of the ratings of relevant components for bundle b on attribute p weighted by the corresponding category importance,
$D^b_{p_g}$ = a weighted sum of squares of the differences between the ratings of relevant components in bundle b and the mean rating of bundle b on attribute p_g, weighted by the corresponding category importance.

Using stated choice data obtained in an experimental context, the authors provide a comprehensive comparison of several choice models for bundles and demonstrate that their general formulation performs much better on various criteria of fit and prediction.

For modeling purposes, it will be useful to consider how interdependence can be described in terms of the attributes of the items in the bundle. Mathematically, the general functional form for the utility of a bundle is:

$$U(b) = \text{main effect}(1) + \text{cross-attribute effect}(2) + \text{cross-item effect}(3) + \text{general cross effect}(4)$$

$$= \sum_{c,p} X_{cp}\beta_{cp} + \sum_{c} \alpha_c\, g(X_{c1}, X_{c2}, \ldots, X_{cP}) +$$

$$\sum_{p} \alpha_p\, f(X_{1p}, X_{2p}, \ldots, X_{Cp}) + \sum_{\substack{c \neq c' \\ p \neq p'}} \alpha_{cpc'p'}\, h(X_{cp}, X_{c'p'})$$

where X_{cp} is the score on the p-th attribute for the c-th component of the bundle, b and αs and βs are parameters. Further, g(.), f(.),and h(.) are the measure functions for the corresponding interdependences (2), (3), and (4), which will be detailed later.

Table 1: *Four components of bundle utility*

	Within items	*Across items*
Within attributes	Main effects (1)	Cross-item effects (3)
Across attributes	Cross-attribute effects (2)	General cross effects (4)

The main effects are the independent contributions of the levels of all bundle components on any attribute to the total utility of the bundle. Cross-attribute effects (2) are the additional contributions to the utility of the bundle produced by the interaction among attributes within bundle items (or components). Cross-item effects (3) are the extra contribution to the utility of the bundle produced by the differences among the levels of items within attributes. The final one, general cross effects (4) are the extra contribution to the utility of the bundle produced by the interaction among attributes across bundle components (or differences among the levels of components within attributes). Therefore, the first two effects arise directly from the components of the bundle while the last two effects are due to interdependence among the components of the bundle.

5.1 No interdependence model: the models for the within item effects

If only main effects (1) and cross-attribute effects (2) contribute to the utility of a bundle, the utility of a bundle is simply the sum of the utilities of the items in the bundle. In this situation, any choice model for a bundle is not different from the standard choice model for a single multi-attributed product, which has been fully studied by most of standard choice models for multi-attributed products. In this case, the utility model for such bundles is as follows:

$$U(b) = \sum_{c,p} X_{cp}\beta_{cp} + \sum_{c} \alpha_c g(X_{c1}, X_{c2}, \ldots, X_{cP})$$

Typically, the model formulates g(.) as interaction terms as $X_{cp}X_{cp'}$ for any attribute pair, p and $p' \in A_{b_c}$ where A_{b_c} is a set of attributes for bundle component c of bundle

b. Then, the g(.) measure for the c-th component is $\sum_{\substack{p \neq p' \\ p,p' \in Ab_c}} \alpha_{cpp'} X_{cp} X_{cp'}$. The corresponding specification for the utility of the b-th bundle when there are no interdependence among products is: $U(b) = \sum_{c,p} X_{cp}\beta_{cp} + \sum_{c} \sum_{\substack{p \neq p' \\ p,p' \in Ab_c}} \alpha_{cpp'} X_{cp} X_{cp'}$.

5.2 Interdependence model: the models for the across item effects

If interdependence among products exists due to cross-attribute effects (3) or general cross effect (4), the utility model for bundles differs from the standard choice model for a single product. The extant bundle studies suggest a variety of different measures to interdependence among bundle components according to the types of effects generating interdependence among products. We will summarize such approach as below.

5.2.1 Interdependence within attributes

Most of assortment choice models focus on how to incorporate interdependence among products within attributes balance and attribute satiation. Three modeling approaches can be identified: *the distance approach, the frequency approach,* and *the interaction approach.*

1) The distance approach

Interdependence among products within attributes has been studied by several bundle choice models. Some studies describe interdependence within attributes by using a concept of balancing (Chung and Rao 2003; Bradlow and Rao 2000; Harlam and Lodish 1995; Farquhar and Rao 1976) and satiation (McAlister 1982). These models develop a variety of measures to capture the interdependence among products within attributes.

We suggest a general measure, distance based balancing measures, for the interdependence among bundle components within attribute p, $f_b(X_{1p}, X_{2p}, \ldots, X_{Cp})$ below.

$$f_b(X_{1p}, X_{2p}, \ldots, X_{Cp}) = (X_{bp} - X_p^*)^2$$

where X_{bp} is the position of bundle b or a component of bundle b on attribute p and X_p^* is the position of a reference point on attribute p.

We can treat other measures for $f_b(X_{1p}, X_{2p}, \ldots, X_{Cp})$ developed by the existing models for bundles as special cases of this measure. For example, Attribute satiation model

(McAlister 1979, 1982) uses cumulative levels of attribute p for bundle b as the position of bundle b on attribute p and the levels of saturation on the attribute as the position of reference points and does not use main effects and cross-attribute effects.

2) Frequency approach

Harlam and Lodish (1995) suggest a different type of measure, WITHIN, based on the frequency of choosing a certain level of attributes over time for balancing effects. Their balancing measure (WITHIN) for the interdependence among bundle components within attribute p, $f_b(X_{1p}, X_{2p}, \ldots, X_{Cp})$ can be expressed as below.

$$f_b(X_{1p}, X_{2p}, \ldots, X_{cp}) = \sum_c 1(X_{cp}, X_p^*) \text{ for all attribute level } X_p^*$$

$$1(X_{cp}, X_p^*) = \begin{cases} 1 \text{ if attribute level } X_p^* \text{ of product c bought by an individual i is equivalent to an} \\ \quad \text{attribute level } X_p^* \\ 0 \text{ otherwise} \end{cases}$$

Basically, their idea of modeling interdependence is similar in spirit to that of balancing model (Farquhar and Rao 1976).

3) Interaction approach

Even though none of bundle choice models employ interaction terms for interdependence among products within attributes, it is still possible to use interaction terms for interdependence among products within attributes. However, this approach seems not handy since it requires more number of terms as the number of bundle components increases and it is less parsimonious compared to the distance approach.

5.2.2 Interdependence among products across attributes

The value of a product can be increased or decreased not only by the interdependence within attributes but also the interdependence across attributes. Interdependence across attributes across bundle components can be modeled by the interaction terms of product attributes among bundle components (Green and Devita (1974)) as:

$$h(X_{cp}, X_{c'p'}) = X_{cp} X_{c'p'}$$

Then, the interdependence among products across attributes (4) can be modeled by

$$\sum_{\substack{c \neq c' \\ p \neq p'}} \alpha_{cpc'p'} X_{cp} X_{c'p'}$$

Interdependence across attributes has not been well examined in the choice literature. More studies on this type of interdependence are needed in the bundle literature.

6 Future Research Directions

This paper has laid out in a concise manner various issues in the research on bundles. It is perhaps fair to say that bundling research is in its early stages in marketing. Various directions for future research can be identified. First, new ways of modeling interdependence among the items included in the bundle need to conceptualized and modeled. Second, a comprehensive comparison of the extant criteria used in modeling interdependence will help identify which criteria are probably more reasonable than others. Third, much of the research on bundling looked at an individual's evaluation of a bundle and did not consider the issue of group decision making which arises in a business to business context or eve in a household context; the existing models will need to be modified to accommodate the effect of interactions among group members while evaluating bundles. Fourth, while there have been some attempts to estimate individual-level parameters to determine preference heterogeneity, computational methods need to be developed to explore this issue further. Fifth, as pointed out earlier, studies are needed that utilize bundling models in various managerial decisions such as cross-selling and market structure of multiple category–based bundles consisting of heterogeneous product categories; the extant models looked at the managerial issues of optimal pricing and market segmentation. Sixth, opportunities exist to study how individuals create bundles in a sequential manner; various concepts of anchoring and adjustment may be relevant for this research direction. Finally, there exist significant opportunities to adapt the models covered here to the cross-category analyses using revealed choice data; here newer methods may be needed to estimate the underlying attribute structure as well as weights in the bundle utility models.

Acknowledgment:
I thank Jaihak Chung of Sogang University, Seoul, S. Korea for his help with this paper.

7 References

Ainslie, A. and P.E. Rossi (1998): Similarities in Choice Behavior Across Product Categories, *Marketing Science*, 17 (2), 91-106.

Albers, S. and K. Brockhoff (1977): A Procedure for New Product Positioning in an Attribute Space, *European Journal of Operational Research*, 1, 320-328.

Ansari, A., S. Siddarth, and C.B. Weinberg (1996): Pricing a Bundle of Products and Services: The Case of Nonprofits, *Journal of Marketing Research*, 33, (February), 86-93.

Bradlow, E. and V.R. Rao (2000): A Hierarchical Bayes Model for Assortment Choice, *Journal of Marketing Research*, 37 (May), 259-268.

Chung, J. and V.R. Rao (2003): A General Choice Model for Bundles with Multiple Category Products: Application to Market Segmentation and Pricing of Bundles, *Journal of Marketing Research*, 40 (May), 115-130.

Deepak, S.D., A. Ansari, and S. Gupta (2002): *Investigating Consumer Price Sensitivities Across Categories*, Working Paper, University of Iowa.

Farquhar, P.H. and V.R. Rao (1976): A Balance Model for Evaluating Subsets of Multiattributed Items, *Management Science*, 22 (January), 528-539.

Goldberg, S.M. P.E. Green, and Y. Wind (1984): Conjoint Analysis of Price Premiums for Hotel Amenities, *Journal of Business*, 57 (Suppl. 1, Part 2), S111-S132.

Green, P.E. and M.T. Devita (1974): A Complementarity Model of Consumer Utility for Item Collections, *Journal of Consumer Research*, 1 (December), 56-67.

Green, P.E., Y. Wind, and A.K. Jain (1972): Preference Measurement of Item Collections, *Journal of Marketing Research*, 9 (November), 371-377.

Guiltinan, J.P. (1987): The Price Bundling of Services: A Normative Framework, *Journal of Marketing*, 51 (April), 74-85.

Hanson, W.A. and R.K. Martin (1990): Optimal Bundle Pricing, *Management Science*, 36, 2 (February), 155-174.

Harlam, B.A. and L.M. Lodish (1995): Modeling Consumers' Choices of Multiple Items, *Journal of Marketing Research*, 32, (November), 404-418.

Kaul, A. and V.R. Rao (1995): Research on Product Positioning and Design Decisions, *International Journal of Research in Marketing*, 12 (4), 293-320.

Lattin, J.M. (1987): A Model of Balanced Choice Behavior, *Marketing Science*, 6 (Winter), 48-65.

Mahajan, V., V.R. Rao, and R.K. Srivastava (1994): An Approach to Assess the Importance of Brand Equity in Acquisition Decisions, *Journal of Product Innovation Management*, 11, 221-235.

Manchanda, P., A. Ansari, and S. Gupta (1999): The 'Shopping Basket': A Model for Multicategory Purchase Incidence Decisions, *Marketing Science*, 18 (2), 95-114.

McAlister, L. (1979): Choosing Multiple Items from A Product Class, *Journal of Consumer Research*, 6 (December), 213-24.

McAlister, L. (1982): A Dynamic Attribute Satiation Model of Variety Seeking Behavior, *Journal of Consumer Research*, 9 (September), 141-50.

McFadden, D. (1986): The Choice Theory Approach to Market Research, *Marketing Science*, 5 (4), 275-297.

Rao, V.R., V. Mahajan, and N.P. Varaiya (1991): A Balance Model for Evaluating Firms for Acquisition, *Management Science*, 37 (3), 331-349.

Russell, G.J. and A. Petersen (2000): Analysis of Cross Category Dependence in Market Basket Selection, *Journal of Retailing*, 76 (3), 367-392.

Singh, V.P., K. Hansen, and S. Gupta (2003): *Modeling Preferences for Common Attributes in Multi-Category Brand Choice*, Working paper, Cornell University.

Venkatesh, R. and V. Mahajan (1993): A Probabilistic Approach to Pricing a Bundle of Prices or Services, *Journal of Marketing Research*, 30 (November), 494-508.

Venkatesh, R. and V. Mahajan (1997): Products with Branded Components: An Approach for Premium Pricing and Partner Selection, *Marketing Science*, 16 (2), 146-165.

Holger Ernst

Virtual Customer Integration

Maximizing the Impact of Customer Integration on New Product Performance

Prof. Dr. *Holger Ernst*, Department of Technology and Innovation Management, Otto Beisheim Graduate School of Management (WHU) at Vallendar.

1 Introduction

The successful development and launch of new products and services is the major driver of sustained business performance in many industries (Brockhoff 1999; Han, Kim and Srivastava 1998). The development of new products, however, has been notoriously plagued with high flop rates (Crawford 1987; Urban and Hauser 1993). The failure of new products must be mainly attributed to the inability of firms to design new products according to customer preferences (Ernst 2002b; Henard and Szymanski 2001). This is particularly a challenging task in markets, which are characterized by a large distance between firms and their customers, the existence of strong intermediaries such as retailers, a high number of potential customers and rapidly changing customer preferences (Ernst and Gulati 2003). It is therefore an important challenge for management to improve the interaction with customers during new product development (NPD) in order to reduce failure rates and to increase the financial returns from high investments in the development of new products and services (Brockhoff, 2003; Brockhoff 1998).

The impact of customer integration on new product performance needs to be conceptually understood as an optimization problem, because the benefits of customer integration need to be weighed against the costs of customer involvement in NPD (Brockhoff 2003; Brockhoff 1998; Brockhoff 1997). Costs of customer integration into NPD can possibly result from the selection of inappropriate customers as development partners, the orientation towards niche markets, the failure of missing the right point for a design freeze during development, distorted communication between supplier and customer and opportunistic behavior of customers (Brockhoff 1997). This theoretical notion has been confirmed by empirical research showing that the impact of customer integration on new product performance is non-linear, i.e., too much customer integration can reduce the economic performance of new products (Ernst 2001). The integration of customers into NPD, therefore, needs to be managed carefully in order to maximize the positive contribution of customer input into NPD from the supplier's perspective (Brockhoff 1998; Brockhoff 1997; Ernst 2001). Important clues for management to achieve this objective come from empirical research on success factors of new products.

Empirical research shows that the successful integration of customers into NPD requires three main elements. First, the involvement of very innovative or so-called 'lead users' has been repeatedly found to positively impact new product performance (Gruner and Homburg 2000; Lilien et al. 2002). 'Lead users' are characterized by two elements: a) they face needs that will be general in the marketplace, but they face them months or years before the bulk of that marketplace encounters them, and b) they are positioned to benefit significantly by obtaining a solution to these needs (v. Hippel 1986). 'Lead users' provide insights in future market needs; they often develop own innovations related to these new market needs and they provide the richest information for NPD (Lilien et al. 2002; v. Hippel 1986).

Second, the involvement of customers in the early and later stages of the NPD process has been found to impact new product performance (Gruner and Homburg 2000). Customer input is especially valuable in the early stages of the NPD process, because the 'relative advantage' of the new product over existing products as perceived by the customer needs to be identified as a guideline for the subsequent development phase (Ernst, 2002a; Kim and Wilemon 2002). The 'relative product advantage' is one of the most important success factors of new products (Montoya-Weiss and Calantone 1994; Rogers 1995). Customer feedback is further important during the testing and validation stage prior to market launch. Customers provide important information about the new product performance under 'real-life' conditions. This information is valuable for the supplier regarding the final new product design and the ultimate launching decision (Brockhoff 1998). Existing empirical research suggests that customer involvement in the development phase does not impact new product success (Gruner and Homburg 2000). This has been mainly attributed to the fact so far that customers lack the technical knowledge to provide relevant input in this phase of NPD (Brockhoff 1997; Gruner and Homburg 2000).

Third, a large extent of communication between the NPD team and the 'area of usage' on the customer side throughout the NPD process is a success factor of customer integration into NPD (Kirchmann 1994). The 'area of usage' refers to the area on the customer side where the new product is eventually used in daily operations. Only members of the 'area of usage' are capable to assess the true 'relative product advantage' and to provide the NPD team with the required design specifications. The level of communication and the amount of information shared and used between the NPD team and the 'area of usage' can be enhanced by using design tools as, for example, quality function deployment (Griffin and Hauser 1996; Ottum and Moore 1997).

The Internet offers new opportunities to better integrate customers into NPD because of its three core characteristics: efficiency, direct and interactive communication and customization (Ernst and Gulati 2003). First, the basic proposition of the Internet is that information can be efficiently provided and accessed by multiple users. Firms can therefore more quickly and less costly interact with their customers in NPD (Ernst and Gulati 2003). This reduces development time and cost, allows testing more design options with customers and makes it possible to continuously update customer requirements along the entire NPD process. Furthermore, more comprehensive and realistic information about product concepts or product attributes can be provided by using multiple media, for example, pictures, sound, videos etc., in the Internet (Dahan and Hauser 2002; Ernst 2000). This leads to a better assessment regarding new and complex product features because the customer can more easily recognize and hence assess the benefits of a new product concept (Ernst 2000).

Second, a further fundamental feature of the Internet is that direct and interactive peer-to-peer communication is possible (Ernst and Gulati 2003). Firms have the choice to either actively approach their customers regarding NPD, for example, by means of an idea contest, or they can passively use the information provided by customers, for example, by means of a suggestion or complaint box on their web page. Interactions between customers can either be initiated by the firm, for example, in 'on-line' focus groups (Dahan and Hauser 2002), or passively monitored by the firm, for example, in existing 'on-line' customer communities (Kozinets 2002). Direct and interactive communication at various levels greatly enhances the value of customer input in NPD for the firm (Dahan and Hauser 2002).

Third, a final fundamental characteristic of the Internet is the possibility to precisely target individual customers or customer segments (Ernst and Gulati 2003). Individual information about customers can be used to identify design features that differentiate the new product from competing products and add most value to the individual customer. New products can therefore be customized to customer segments and even to single customers. Furthermore, important customers for NPD, such as 'lead users' or 'opinion leaders', can be identified which provide the most valuable information for NPD (Ernst et al., 2004). These customers are of particular use for NPD because they provide the best ideas for new products and they are the first to anticipate future market needs (v. Hippel 1986).

The internet therefore seems to offer the opportunity to improve the impact of customer integration on NPD performance (Dahan and Hauser 2002; Ernst and Gulati 2003; Nambisan 2002). This could be achieved, if the internet facilitated the implementation of the previously discussed key success factors of customer integration into NPD, i.e. the identification and integration of 'lead users' in NPD, the efficient integration of customers in the early and the later phases of NPD and the direct communication between NPD team and the 'area of usage' along the entire NPD process. It will be explored conceptually in the following paragraph, if virtual customer integration (VCI) into the NPD process has this potential to increase NPD performance.

2 VCI in Multiple Stages of New Product Development

The options for using VCI vary according different stages of the NPD process. A typical NPD process with its main phases was chosen to illustrate VCI and its key benefits (Cooper, Edgett, and Kleinschmidt 2002; Ernst 2002a). Table 1 summarizes the key aspects.

Table 1: *VCI in Multiple Stages of New Product Development*

	Idea Generation and Assessment	*Concept Definition & Project Selection*	*Development*	*Testing*	*Market Launch*
Key Idea	Customers as 'idea generators' and 'consultants' for idea assessment and selection	Customers as 'consultants' for concept assessment and selection and 'co-creators' for concept refinement	Customers as 'co-creators' in development and 'consultants' for the assessment and selection of design options	Customers as 'potential buyers' for the assessment of market potential	Customers as 'first buyers' to speed up the diffusion of the new product in the market
Customer Input	- Ideas for new products - Assessment of ideas - Suggestions for improving existing products - Complaints about existing products	- Assessment of product concepts - Refinement of product concepts	- Ideas and suggestions for development - Assessment of design options during the development process	- Assessment of product acceptance - Estimation of market potential	- Product purchase and communication of user experience
Key Benefits	- Increased number of ideas - Use of customers' creativity - Early customer feedback for idea assessment - Identification of valuable customers for new product development (e.g. 'lead user')	- Identification of relative product advantage (value proposition) - Mass customization - Increased number of testing options - Reduced market risks - Customer feedback in the most critical stage of new product development - Better market information for early termination decisions	- Use of customers' creativity and expertise - Continuous customer feedback - Testing of more design options - Reduction of development risk - Improved decision making (continuation or termination)	- Efficient application of various market research tools - Realistic presentation of the new product's functionalities	- Efficient identification and use of 'opinion leaders' or 'innovators' - Reduction of entry barriers for very innovative products - Speeding up the diffusion process - Generation of strong 'pull-effects' from the market - Increased customer retention - Pre-announcements to influence buying decisions
Industry Examples	Ben & Jerry's; Peugeot; Audi; P&G; Henkel; Grohe	Adidas; Audi; Bosch & Siemens Household Appliances; P&G	Texas Instruments; Volvo; Audi; Adidas; Nokia; Amazon; Mars; Blair Witch Project; Freytag; Swarowski; Dietrich	Market Research Firms; Harry Potter; Mars	Blair Witch Project; Harry Potter

Stage 1: Idea Generation and Idea Assessment

Idea generation is the starting point of the NPD process. The number of ideas generated is important because ideas are the fundamental source of innovation (Kim and Wilemon 2002). Ideas need to be assessed in order to pick the most promising ideas for the next phase of NPD (Cooper, Edgett, and Kleinschmidt 2002). The traditional way that most firms have followed in this stage has major shortcomings. Ideas are often generated only within the firm, as for example in the R&D and the Marketing department. This approach neglects the creativity of customers, which may also have great ideas for new services and products (Brockhoff 2003). Second, internally generated ideas are frequently assessed from an internal point of view only. This is highly problematic because the customers' assessment may be quite different. Early customer feedback can avoid the danger that ideas are pursued further, which are likely to be rejected by the market. It can further open up the possibility that ideas are refined by customers, which increases the probability that an idea becomes a market success (Thomke and v. Hippel 2002).

VCI is a great vehicle for firms to tap on their customers' ideas for new products or services by providing their customers a section on the firms' web page where customers can articulate and describe new ideas and give suggestions for improving the firms' existing products (Ernst and Gulati 2003). Customers can further make complaints about the firms' existing products. Complaints are often a great source for the firm to generate new ideas. Ideas for new products need to be screened by the firm at a first milestone of NPD in order to decide whether it should further pursue with the idea or not. The customer assessment of the idea is a very important evaluation criterion at this early stage (Cooper, Edgett, and Kleinschmidt 2002).

The German car manufacturer Audi collects ideas from customers in its 'virtual lab'. Audi has, for example, generated new ideas for infotainment hardware and infotainment services for all its cars in various internet-based idea contests. In this idea contest, customers could describe their own vision of infotainment systems in the future. The ideas were assessed by a cross-functional team within Audi. More than 70% of a total of 342 ideas were classified as having a high or a very high application potential and are likely or very likely to be used in future Audi products (Bartl 2004).

VCI has the advantage that the number of ideas entering NPD increases. Further, the firm gets access to the creative potential of its customers and must not only rely on its internally generated ideas (Ernst and Gulati 2003). This is important because successful new products have often resulted from customers' ideas. Further, 'demand-pull' innovations which are derived from customer needs are often more successful compared to 'technology-push' innovations where the latter type of innovation only anticipates an existing customer need (Brockhoff 1999). Firms can use the Internet to let customers assess the ideas, which have been developed inside the firm, and those ideas, which came externally from customers. The interactive discussion among customers leads to the further refinement of individual ideas (Dahan and Hauser 2002). VCI enables the efficient identification and early integration of important 'lead users' in NPD. 'Lead users' are a great source for innovative ideas and they provide the most valuable input for assessing and refining new product ideas and concepts early in NPD (Lilien et al. 2002; v. Hippel 1986).

Virtual stock markets can be used in the internet to identify 'lead users' for integration in NPD (Ernst et al. 2004). Virtual stock markets have been developed for forecasting purposes (Spann and Skiera 2003), however, they can also be used for expert identification, as for example 'lead users'. The basic idea behind virtual stock markets is that traders are asked to trade with new product ideas or concepts. Traders are rewarded based on the value of their portfolio at the end of the trading period. Traders therefore have the incentive to maximize their portfolio rather than supporting an idea or product concept they favor individually (Spann and Skiera 2003). It has been shown empirically that trading performance in a virtual stock market correlates with 'lead user' characteristics. There is a significantly higher number of 'lead users' among the top traders in virtual stock markets. Thus, internet-based virtual stock markets are an effective and efficient tool to identify 'lead users' for NPD (Spann et al. 2004).

Stage 2: Concept Definition and Project Selection

Once ideas have been developed into more detailed product concepts, these product concepts have to be defined and assessed (Cooper, Edgett, and Kleinschmidt 2002). This stage is considered to be the most critical in NPD because at the end of this phase, management has to make a crucial decision, i.e., either to terminate or to continue with the project (Cooper, Edgett, and Kleinschmidt 2002; Ernst 2002a). Moving the product concept into the development stage causes high subsequent investments in R&D and project management that are – in the light of opportunity cost – lacking for other projects. Careful portfolio management and project selection is a critical success factor of innovations (Ernst 2002b; Montoya-Weiss and Calantone 1994). Absolutely essential in this stage is the assessment of the product concept from a customer perspective. Only product concepts that have a unique selling proposition, which is perceived and valued by the customer, should be continued (Ernst 2002a). It is well established that this unique selling proposition is an important success factor of new products (Montoya-Weiss and Calantone 1994; Rogers 1995). The main management challenge in this stage is that usually multiple product concepts are feasible and that professional customer feedback must ideally be obtained for all of them. This is especially required when market uncertainty is high, for example, in emerging markets (Bower and Christensen, 1995). Many firms, however, refrain from getting sufficient customer feedback in this early stage of NPD because of time and resource constraints. This shortcoming frequently leads to wrong or incomplete project selection at the end of the concept definition phase (Cooper, Edgett, and Kleinschmidt 2002).

VCI is a better way to design new products or services for mass-customization early on in the NPD process (Ernst and Gulati 2003). New products and services can be tailor-made for individual customers or customer segments. The early and intensive interaction with customers enables the firm to identify those product attributes, which differentiate the new product sufficiently to provide added value to the customer while at the same time achieving the necessary economies of scale. Well-established market research tools for product design, for example conjoint analysis, can be conducted via the Internet (Dahan and Srinivasan 2000). The results yield important information for NPD, especially the relative importance of individual product attributes that impacts the emphasis of subsequent research and development efforts. VCI further leads to an increased number of testing options for ideas and new product concepts. This is particularly important where customer requirements are difficult to assess and where customer input is very fragmented. More testing options reduce the risk of focusing to early on a product design, which later proves to be unsuccessful in the market. VCI allows getting better customer feedback, particularly for highly innovative product ideas. The potential benefits of these innovations to the customer can be better communicated in a rich media environment as the Internet (Dahan and Hauser 2002; Ernst 2000). VCI thus leads to higher market research quality early in NPD, which helps management to select the most promising new product concepts for further development or to terminate unpromising product concepts early in the NPD process (Cooper, Edgett, and Kleinschmidt 2002; Ernst 2002a).

Figure 1: *The Virtual Lab at Audi – Product Configurator*

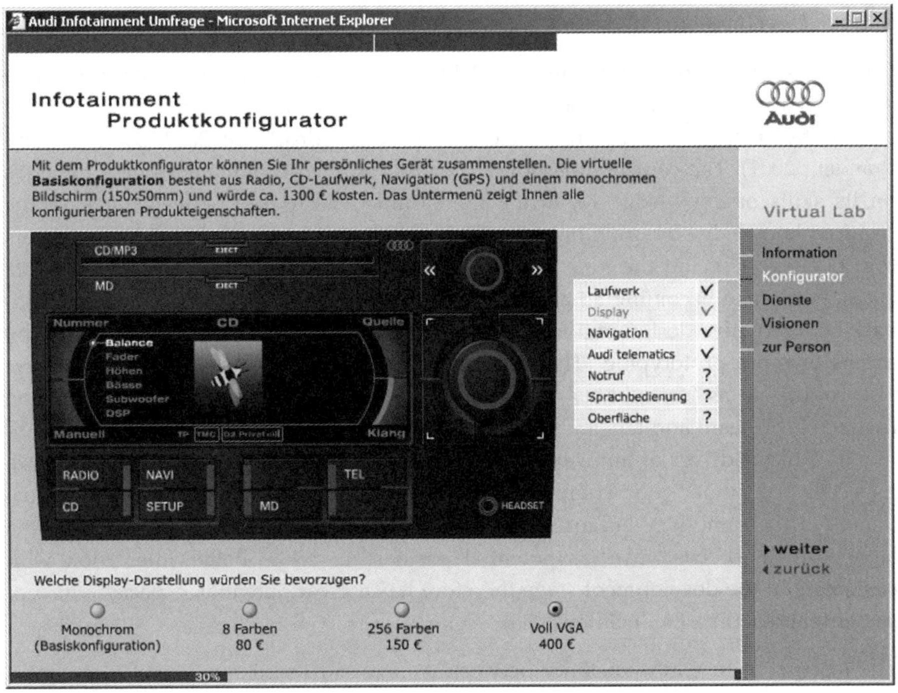

The German car manufacturer Audi regularly tests multiple product options for different car components over the web in its 'virtual lab' (Bartl 2004). Within four weeks, Audi got detailed feedback from thousands of customers on various product and design options regarding future infotainment systems and services in its cars. A cross-functional team of Audi engineers and Marketing managers had developed various product and design options for infotainment hardware and infotainment services. Customers could build their own infotainment system in the 'virtual configurator' (figure 1). Rich media, for example, professional graphical and textual illustrations and audio sequences, was used in order to create a realistic environment for the customer. Customers further had the option to re-configure the infotainment system to achieve a certain end price for which the probability of purchase was highest. This information was very valuable for Audi to assess the customers' willingness to pay for infotainment systems and services in general and specifically for certain infotainment components. Audi received valuable feedback from its customers resulting in important implications for NPD. The development team was able to drop specific products and services due to insufficient customer interest and to focus subsequent R&D effort on those infotainment elements, which were perceived as most valuable by the customer (Bartl 2004).

Stage 3: Development

Customers must also be integrated into NPD during the development phase. The role of the customer can change, as the customer becomes a 'co-creator' who actually contributes to the development of the new product (Brockhoff 2003; Sawhney and Prandelli 2001). The contribution of the customer in the development phase depends on its skills or knowledge regarding the product. Firms can actively increase the required knowledge by providing so-called tool kits, which can be used by customers to actively co-develop the new product together with the firm (v. Hippel and Katz 2002). Further to becoming an active 'co-creator' in NPD, continuous customer feedback on alternative design options can be gathered by the NPD team, for example, by means of rapid prototyping (Thomke and v. Hippel 2002). Customers can therefore also contribute as 'consultants' to the development phase in NPD. The interaction between NPD team and the 'area of usage' of the intended innovation has been identified as a major driver of innovation success on industrial markets (Kirchmann 1994). Especially, consumer good companies find it very difficult to interact with their customers in the same way because they are far away from their customers and face a large number of customers as potential partners in NPD. Better interaction with customers in the development stage therefore has a great potential, especially in consumer markets (Ernst and Gulati 2003).

The Internet reduces the distance between a firm and its customers. VCI enables a closer and more efficient interaction between the NPD team and the customer actually supposed to use the innovation (Dahan and Hauser 2002). This is important because it is ensured that the new product is developed according to customer requirements.

VCI further allows the testing of various design options, which substantially reduces market risk, particularly when customer requirements are very unclear in emerging markets (Bower and Christensen 1995). Customer preferences can be updated along the entire development process. This ensures that changes of customer requirements can be incorporated into the final design of the new product (Ernst 2002a). Further, if customer requirements cannot be matched and the market is likely not to materialize as predicted, the NPD project can be terminated. This saves resources and frees resources for more promising NPD projects (Cooper, Edgett, and Kleinschmidt 2002). Furthermore, the virtual input of knowledgeable customers as 'co-creators' leads to the identification of new design options, the refinement of existing design options or the development of other solutions to existing design problems (Ernst and Gulati 2003).

Some innovative firms from various industries are already interacting with their customers over the web in the development phase. VCI for development has been known for digital products, especially software. However, customers can also participate in the development of non-digital products over the web (Dahan and Hauser 2002; Ernst and Gulati 2003). Audi, for example, uses the 'virtual configurator' (figure 1) to integrate customers during the development phase (Bartl 2004). Customers can assess various design options as 'consultants' to the NPD team. They can further add and describe their own ideas regarding the improvement of the product design. This has helped Audi to refine the initially developed product concept, to update customer preferences regarding the product concept and the design options, to generate additional customer input during the development phase and to generate ideas for new product concepts. According to Audi, the interaction with customers has improved decision making in the development phase, for example, regarding the optimal design and pricing of new products and services and the termination or continuation of NPD projects depending on customer assessment (Bartl 2004).

Stage 4: Testing

The final product concept needs to be tested prior to market launch. This is important for the estimation of the new product's acceptance and its market potential (Brockhoff 1999). Classic methods of market research, for example surveys, test market simulators, test markets etc. are often expensive and time-consuming (Brockhoff 1999; Urban and Hauser 1993). These problems are even more of concern when the new product is launched internationally and when individual segments of customers are targeted.

Many of the classic market research tools can be applied in the Internet including virtual test markets, which substitute or complement test market simulators or real test markets (Dahan and Hauser 2002; Kozinets 2002). It has also become possible to simulate the Marketing-Mix in a virtual environment (Urban, Weinberg and Hauser, 1995). Various new tools, for example 'web-based conjoint' or 'user design', have been developed to test product concepts virtually (Dahan and Hauser 2002). These virtual market research techniques have the advantage that they are more efficient compared to conventional off-line market research procedures. Substantial efficiency gains compared to conventional ways to interact with customers in the testing phase in NPD can be realized by means of VCI (Ernst and Gulati 2003).

Stage 5: Market Launch

The launch of a new product or service is an important success factors, especially in consumer goods industries (Brockhoff 1999). A high number of firms typically spend more money on launching the new product than on its development (Urban and Hauser 1993). Management attention therefore increasingly focuses on improving this phase of NPD. The following three areas are of particular importance: First, the fast diffusion of the new product is mainly facilitated by the firm's ability to identify and target a specific segment of customers, so-called 'opinion leaders' or 'innovators' (Rogers 1995). These customers are the first buyers of the new product and they report their experiences with the new product to other customers. Finding these innovative customers and integrating them into NPD has been a difficult and cumbersome task in the past. Second, the pre-announcement of new products has become a regular practice in many industries (Ernst and Schnoor 2000). This tactic should mainly deter customers from buying existing products and encourage them to wait for the new product. Highly innovative products often have experience or belief attributes, which increase the buying risk for the customer. Pre-announcements with detailed information about the new product can be used to reduce this risk for the customer. Companies spend increasingly more on pre-announcement campaigns and it is questionable if the returns justify these huge investments (Ernst and Schnoor 2000). Third, many firms lack access to the end consumer because of intermediaries like retailers. This limits the firm's ability to directly interact with customers during the launch and after-launch phase to fully maximize the returns from the innovation in the marketplace.

VCI enables the firm to efficiently identify and target 'opinion leaders' or 'innovators'. For example, firms can use 'virtual stock markets' on their web page or in appropriate 'on-line' customer communities for this purpose (Bartl, Ernst, and Füller 2004). The application of 'virtual stock markets' has shown that a large percentage of 'innovative' customers can be identified very efficiently (Spann et al., 2004). Monetary rewards seem to play only a minor role in attracting these customers for 'virtual stock markets' or other forms of VCI; the entertainment and fun factor appears to be more important (Bartl, Ernst, and Füller 2004). Once these 'innovative' customers are identified, they can be integrated into NPD in order to design the final product and to support the launching campaign. The integration of these 'innovative' customers speeds up the diffusion of new products (Rogers 1995).

Firms can further use VCI to pre-announce their new products prior to market launch. An internet-based pre-announcement campaign could signal to customers that the company is determined to deliver the promised product in time. Rich media can be used in the Internet to provide the necessary amount of information about the new product to the customer, which helps to reduce the buying risk, especially for very innovative products without prior user experience (Brockhoff 1999). For example, the film 'Blair Witch Project', an innovative film concept, had been pre-announced in the Internet months before the film came into the theaters. The film was talked about well in advance before it was actually released and it became a great commercial success.

VCI can also support the launch of highly innovative products. The benefits of these innovations to the customer can be better communicated in a rich media environment as the internet (Dahan and Hauser 2002). Additionally, the market can be systematically prepared by providing relevant information about the new product prior and during market launch. This helps to educate the customer and to lower perceptual barriers, which will eventually lower market entry barriers (Rogers, 1995). This strategy is known from the industrial goods industry where suppliers integrate their customers into NPD in order to engineer customer needs and to successfully introduce an innovation customers had not initially demanded (Temaguide 1998).

VCI generates 'pull effects' in markets with strong intermediaries, especially retailers. It reduces the distance between firm and the end user. This lowers the existing power of intermediaries and could ultimately lead to more direct sales to the customer who becomes increasingly used to interact with the firm over the Internet. Furthermore, VCI can lead to increased customer retention. If customers are involved in NPD, they are very likely to buy the new product and to communicate their experience to other potential buyers. An additional effect could be an increased brand loyalty, which reduces the likelihood of switching to a different brand. In this sense, VCI can improve existing customer relationship management activities of firms.

3 Summary and Conclusion

VCI has a great potential for improving customer integration into NPD. Figure 2 summarizes the main advantages of VCI. The ability to customize communication with multiple types of customers in the Internet allows the establishment of a fully customer-centric approach in NPD. Customers can individually be integrated into NPD depending on the activity to be performed by the customer. The separating line between an organization and its customers disappears and organizations move towards becoming really customer-centric (Ernst and Gulati 2003). At the same time, the communication is interactive and efficient, fully leveraging the generic advantages of the Internet. VCI should therefore lead to the development of better products, the reduction of flop rates and hence to higher sales and profits for the firm.

It has become clear that the Internet offers many opportunities for firms to interact with their customers along the entire NPD process. Recognizing the value of customer input in all phases of NPD leads to the continuous integration of specific customers into NPD across various stages. The perception of 'customer' turns into a perception of 'partner' in NPD. The 'partner' can take on different roles in NPD depending on its input (Brockhoff 2003; table 1). Customers as 'idea generators' provide ideas and suggestions in the first phase of NPD. After that, customers become 'consultants' where they have to refine ideas and to assess first product concepts. Customers can become 'co-creators' in the development phase where they become actively involved in the development of the new product. Further, customers provide assessments of various design options as 'consultants' in the development phase. Then, customers become 'potential buyers' as they have to express their likelihood of purchase of the new product. Finally, customers can take the role of 'first buyers' who are the first to buy the new product shortly after it has been launched. This role concept suggests that one customer can take on all roles from 'idea generator' to 'first buyer' or that there are various customers in each of the aforementioned roles in NPD. Ultimately, the 'partner' becomes a virtual 'member' of the firm's NPD team (Ernst and Gulati 2003).

Figure 2: *Key Advantages of VCI*

1. Support of mass customization of new products and services
2. Continuous update of customer requirements along the entire NPD process from idea to market launch
3. Substantial efficiency gains (especially time and money) compared to conventional methods of customer integration in NPD
4. Increased number of testing options for ideas and new product concepts which reduces market risk
5. More accurate assessment of the market potential of highly innovative new product concepts and better preparation of the market for highly innovative new products
6. Generation of 'pull effects' in markets with strong intermediaries (especially retailing) through direct interface with end user
7. Identification of important customers for NPD (especially 'lead users' and 'opinion leaders')

To fully leverage the benefits of VCI, management should obey five core fundamental principles when implementing VCI in the firm (Ernst and Gulati 2003). First, VCI requires a significant cultural change in the firm. The firms' openness towards and its acceptance of customer input into NPD, especially in the R&D department, is a basic requirement for the successful implementation of VCI. Second, the most value of VCI to the firm lies in the first three stages of NPD. Customer input in these stages of NPD has the highest potential value for new product success (Ernst 2002a). Third, VCI needs to be institutionalized within the firm and cross-functional processes must be defined aligning VCI with the existing internal processes. Fourth, adequate incentives need to be established in order to motivate customers to participate in NPD. This is particularly relevant when customers become partners in NPD and substantially contribute to the innovation, for example with new ideas or new solutions. Having the right incentives is of major importance, if a long-term relationship to specific customers ought to be established. Fifth, 'off-line' and 'on-line' procedures to integrate customers into NPD should complement each other. The extent of 'off-line' and 'on-line' integration of customers depends on various factors, especially the product's characteristics and the input required from customers (Ernst and Gulati 2003).

Figure 3: *Maximizing the Impact of Customer Integration on NPD Performance by VCI*

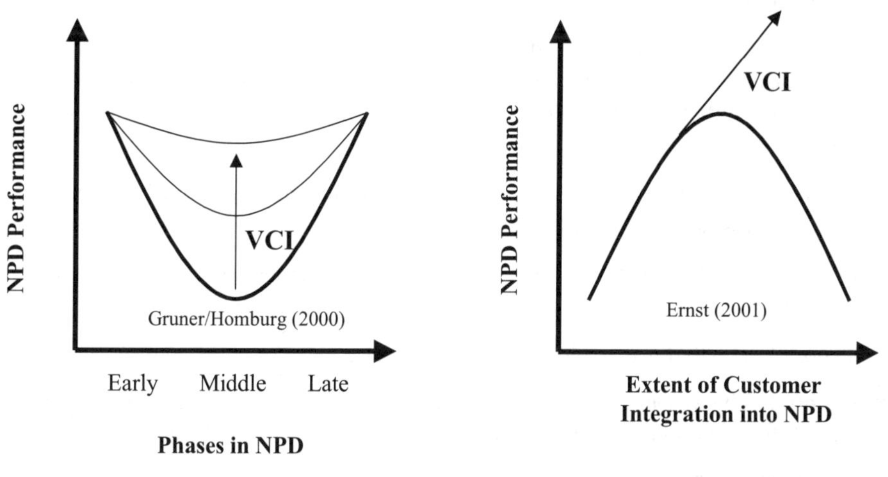

It has been argued at the outset of this paper that customer integration into NPD has to be understood as an optimization problem (Brockhoff 1997). Customer integration into NPD needs to be carefully managed in order to maximize its impact on NPD performance. Core success factors of customer integration into NPD are the involvement of 'lead users', the integration of customers in the early and later phases of NPD and the extent of communication between NPD team and the 'area of usage' along the entire NPD process (Ernst 2002b; Gruner and Homburg 2000; Kirchmann 1994; Lilien et al. 2002). It has been shown that VCI can help firms leveraging these success factors of customer integration in NPD even better. The internet in this sense becomes a core enabler of successful customer integration into NPD. Furthermore, VCI has the potential to even achieve more valuable customer input in the development phase. Positive effects of customer integration in the development phase have not been shown empirically in the traditional 'off-line' world yet (Gruner and Homburg 2000). Figure 3 summarizes this argument in a graphical way suggesting that VCI is a promising approach to solve the optimization problem of customer integration into NPD and to maximize the positive contribution of customers to the successful development and launch of new products.

4 References

Bartl, M. (2004): *Virtuelle Kundenintegration in die Neuproduktentwicklung*, PhD dissertation (forthcoming), Vallendar.

Bartl, M., H. Ernst, and J. Füller (2004): Community Based Innovation – eine Methode zur Einbindung von Online Communities in den Innovationsprozess, in: C. Herstatt and J. Sander (Eds.) (2004): *Produktentwicklung mit virtuellen Communities*, Wiesbaden, 141-167.

Bower, J.L. and C.M. Christensen (1995): Disruptive technologies: Catching the wave, *Harvard Business Review*, 73 (1), 43-53.

Brockhoff, K. (2003): Customers' perspectives of involvement in new product development, *International Journal of Technology Management*, 26 (5), 464-481.

Brockhoff, K. (1999): *Produktpolitik*, 4th ed., Stuttgart.

Brockhoff, K. (1998): Der Kunde im Innovationsprozeß, Berichte aus den Sitzungen der Joachim Jungius-Gesellschaft der Wissenschaften e.V., 16 (3), Hamburg.

Brockhoff, K. (1997): Wenn der Kunde stört - Differenzierungsnotwendigkeiten bei der Einbeziehung von Kunden in die Produktentwicklung, in: Bruhn, M. and H. Steffenhagen (Eds.): *Marktorientierte Unternehmensführung*, Wiesbaden, 183-202.

Cooper, R.G., S.J. Edgett, and E.J. Kleinschmidt (2002): Portfolio Management - Fundamental to New Product Success, in: Belliveau, P. and A. Griffin, and S. Somermeyer (Eds.): *The PDMA Toolbook for new product development*, 331-364.

Crawford, C.M. (1987): New Product Failure Rates: A Reprise, *Research Management*, 30 (4), 20-24.

Dahan, Ely and John R. Hauser (2002): The Virtual Customer, *Journal of Product Innovation Management*, 19 (5), 332-353.

Dahan, Ely and V. Srinivasan (2000): The predictive power of internet-based product concept testing using visual depiction and animation, *Journal of Product Innovation Management*, 17, 99-109.

Ernst, Holger (2002a): Management der Neuproduktentwicklung, in: Albers, S. and A. Herrmann (Eds.): *Handbuch Produktmanagement*, 2nd ed., Wiesbaden, 333-358.

Ernst, Holger (2002b): Success Factors of New Product Development: A Review of the Empirical Literature, *International Journal of Management Reviews*, 4 (1), 1-40.

Ernst, Holger (2001): *Erfolgsfaktoren neuer Produkte. Grundlagen für eine valide empirische Forschung*, Wiesbaden.

Ernst, H. and R. Gulati (2003): *Virtual Customer Integration. Bringing the Customer back into the Organization*, Working Paper, Vallendar/Evanston.

Ernst, H. and A. Schnoor (2000): Einflussfaktoren auf die Glaubwürdigkeit kundenorientierter Produktvorankündigungen: Ein signaltheoretischer Ansatz, *Zeitschrift für Betriebswirtschaft*, 70 (12), 1331-1350.

Ernst, H., J.H. Soll, and M. Spann (2004): Möglichkeiten zur Lead-User-Identifikation in Online-Medien, in: C. Herstatt and J. Sander (Eds.): *Produktentwicklung mit virtuellen Communities*, Wiesbaden, 121-140.

Ernst, O. (2000): *Multimediale versus abstrakte Produktpräsentationsformen bei der adaptiven Conjoint-Analyse. Ein empirischer Vergleich*, Franfurt am Main.

Griffin, A. and J.R. Hauser (1996): Patterns of Communication Among Marketing, Engineering, and Manufacturing – A Comparison between two Product Teams, *Management Science*, 38 (3), 360-373.

Gruner, K. and C. Homburg (2000): Does Customer Interaction Enhance New Product Success, *Journal of Business Research*, 49 (1), 1-14.

Han, J. K., N. Kim, and R. K. Srivastava (1998): Market orientation and organizational performance: Is innovation a missing link?, *Journal of Marketing*, 62 (4), 30-45.

Henard, D. H. and D. M. Szymanski (2001): Why some new products are more successful than others. *Journal of Marketing Research*, 38 (3), 362-75.

Kim, J. and D. Wilemon (2002): Focusing the fuzzy front-end in new product development, *R&D-Management*, 32 (4), 269-279.

Kirchmann, E. (1994): *Innovationskooperationen zwischen Herstellern und Anwendern*, Wiesbaden.

Kozinets, R.V. (2002): The Field Behind the Scene: Using Netnography for Marketing Research in Online Communities, *Journal of Marketing Research*, 34, 61-72.

Lilien, Gary L., Pamela D. Morrison, Kathleen Searls, Mary Sonnack, and Eric von Hippel (2002): Performance Assessment of the Lead User Idea-Generation Process for New Product Development, *Management Science*, 48 (8), 1042-1059.

Montoya-Weiss, M. and R. Calantone (1994): Determinants of New Product Performance: A Review and Meta-Analysis, *Journal of Product Innovation Management*, 11, 397-417.

Nambisan, S. (2002): Designing Virtual Customer Environments for New Product Development: Toward a Theory, *Academy of Management Review*, 27 (3), 392-413.

Ottum, B.D. and W.L. Moore (1997): The Role of Market Information in New Product Development, *Journal of Product Innovation Management*, 14, 258-273.

Rogers, E.M. (1995): *Diffusion of Innovations*, 4th edition, New York, London.

Sawhney, M. and E. Prandelli (2001): Beyond Customer Knowledge Management: Customers as Knowledge Co-Creators, in: Y. Malhotra (Ed.): *Knowledge Management and Virtual Organization*, Hershey.

Spann, M. and B. Skiera (2003): Internet-Based Virtual Stock Markets for Business Forecasting, *Management Science*, 49 (10), 1310-1326.

Spann, M., H. Ernst, B. Skiera, and J.H. Soll (2004): *Identification of Lead Users in Consumer Goods Markets via Virtual Stock Markets*, Working Paper, Frankfurt/Vallendar.

Temaguide (1998): *Supplier-Customer partnership in the innovation process CD-Rom*, Brighton, Kiel, Madrid, Manchester.

Thomke, S. and E. von Hippel (2002): Customers as Innovators, *Harvard Business Review*, 80 (April), 74-81.

Urban, G.L. and J.R. Hauser (1993): *Design and Marketing of New Products*, 2nd edition, Upper Saddle River, NJ.

Urban, Glen L., Weinberg, B. and John R. Hauser (1995): Premarket forecasting of really new products, *Journal of Marketing*, 60, 47-60.

Von Hippel, E. (1986): Lead Users: A Source of Novel Product Concepts, *Management Science*, 32 (7), 791-805.

Von Hippel, E. and R. Katz (2002): Shifting Innovation to Users via Toolkits, *Management Science*, 48 (7), 821-833.

Manfred Krafft and Katrin Krieger

Successful Innovations Driven by Customer Relationship Management

Prof. Dr. *Manfred Krafft*, Institute of Marketing at Westphalian Wilhelms University of Münster, and Dipl.-Kffr. *Katrin Krieger*, Bain & Company, Inc., PhD candidate at the Department of Technology and Innovation Management, Otto Beisheim Graduate School of Management (WHU) at Vallendar.

1 Innovation - the customer view ignored?

Capabilities to innovate are the source of business success; in particular if companies are facing an environment characterized by high levels of technological and market uncertainty caused by shortened product life cycles or customer needs that are continuously changing. Some of the most spectacular success stories are driven by innovative ideas, e.g. the introduction of the four-wheel-drive (Quattro) in a passenger car by Audi or the launch of the Walkman by Sony. In addition to the demand for innovation from business practitioners, the requirement of being innovative can be derived from established scientific concepts, e.g., the idea of "creative destruction" – a process of destroying old structures or products and creating new ones for future growth (Forster and Kaplan 2001). Despite the fact that the importance of innovations for company success is basically accepted, the percentage of innovation projects that fail is still alarming (Christensen and Raynor 2003). But what makes the difference between success and failure in the innovation process? One, maybe the most important answer, focuses on the customer: The customer view is often misread or even ignored; declining sales due to a missing customer acceptance of the product (see Brockhoff 1999 for a definition) innovation is the consequence.

Reviewing the former empirical research in the field of innovation management (see Ernst 2002 for an overview of the empirical literature on success factors of innovations), we found that most of the studies consider market/customer orientation: But without specific focus, market/customer orientation is only one of many factors affecting the success of innovation projects, with the consequence that the results referring to the market or customer remain on quite an abstract level. Summarizing the findings of these studies, the amount and quality of the market/customer information flow as an input factor to the innovation process and the correspondence of customer needs with the product innovation as an output factor of the innovation process have been identified as aspects that are of specific importance for the innovation success. In this respect, only a few studies focus on the innovator/customer relationship and consider the form of the customer integration into the innovation process in more detail. The results of these studies are of specific interest for the described research problem: They offer a better understanding of the role of the customer as a driver for innovation success. The work by Urban and von Hippel (1988), Gales and Mansour-COLE (1995), or Lilien et al. (2002) belong for example to this second type of studies in the English-speaking area, as well as Kirchmann (1994) or Gruner and Homburg (1999) in the German literature. The relevant findings are reviewed in Figure 1.

Figure 1: Main findings in the field of innovation and customer management

Customer-related success factors for innovation projects:

- High level of customer integration in the innovation process in terms of frequency and number
- Systematic customer integration in early and late stages of innovation processes
- Integration of specific customer segments in the innovation process, e.g., lead users or customers with high levels of usage and/or profitability
- Systematic utilization of the customer as a source for innovative ideas
- Information flows between the technical specialists of the B2B-customer and the innovator

Recent empirical studies of success factors offer some isolated answers regarding the questions of the intensity, the time and the type of customer integration in the innovation process. But so far, there exists no complete framework considering the impact of customer-oriented strategies, processes, structures, and technologies on the success of innovation projects. In addition, although the single stages of the innovation process (e.g., (1) concept development phase, (2) product development phase, and (3) implementation phase) are assumed to require a **varying degree of customer involvement**, they have not been analyzed in detail so far. In summary, the negative side of a lacking or insufficient market or customer orientation in the innovation process is identified by many studies, but an extensive instruction how innovators can implement this insight and manage their customer relationships successfully is still missing. A starting point to solve this problem is a comprehensive concept that has been discussed by marketing researchers in the recent years and that focuses directly on the relationship between suppliers and their customers, namely **customer relationship management** (CRM). The background and the components of CRM will be discussed in the next section.

2 Customer focus - how to build valuable customer relationships?

2.1 Background of customer relationship management

As pointed out in the last section, market and customer orientation has already been proved to be crucial success factors for innovation projects. To understand the background of these concepts, their impact on business performance and finally their role in the development process of the CRM concept, the relevant marketing literature has been screened:

Reviewing prior research on market orientation, two main perspectives can be distinguished: On the one hand, researchers suggested a philosophical approach on market orientation, focusing on the companies' attitudes, while on the other hand, research efforts are based on market orientation representing a company's behavior. Narver and Slater (1990) support the second approach and define market orientation as a concept consisting of the components customer orientation, competitor orientation and interfunctional coordination. According to Kohli and Jaworski (1990), market orientation should be implemented via three distinct steps of knowledge processing: (1) market intelligence generation, (2) intelligence dissemination throughout the company, and (3) organization-wide responsiveness to this intelligence. The concept of customer orientation is closely related to the idea of market orientation, being defined as a component of the broader market orientation approach (Narver and Slater 1990) or even used synonymously (Ruekert 1992).

The CRM concept represents a more far-reaching approach than the introduced market/customer orientation theories, going beyond the sheer gaining of customer information and managing long-term valuable customer relationships instead. In this context, Helfert, Ritter, and Walter (2001, 2) remark: "the overall market orientation of firms needs to be translated on a relationship level to be effective". Grönroos (1997) refers to CRM as a new marketing paradigm, which – in contrast to the transactional marketing with a focus on **initiating** transactions with mostly unknown customers – concentrates on **establishing, developing** and **maintaining successful long-term** relationships with **well-chosen** customers (Morgan and Hunt 1994). Other researchers assess the superiority of the CRM concept according to the respective situation and define CRM as a strategic choice (e.g., Reinartz, Krafft, and Hoyer 2004). CRM is based on the assumption that transactions in the past will have an effect on transactions in the future. The classical transactional marketing, being an inside-out approach, gives the product a special emphasis, while relationship marketing, being an outside-in approach, puts the customer in the focus of attention (Bruhn 2003; Krafft and Götz 2003).

The relationship marketing concept was first mentioned by Berry (1983) in the early 1980s in the service area and by Jackson (1985) in the industrial marketing area and considers the firm's relationships with customers as well as with all other stakeholders. Today, after 20 years of research and business practice, relationship marketing and CRM (with focus on the customer as stakeholder) are accepted parts in standard marketing textbooks. The fundamental elements of CRM are briefly classified in the next section.

2.2 Elements of customer relationship management

Central subject of CRM is a business relationship. The business relationship is characterized as a planned series of exchange episodes between a producer and a customer (Anderson 1995). The understanding of CRM as a **comprehensive** concept leads to the conclusion that the implementation of CRM will affect different dimensions of a company, which should be adjusted to the requirement of the specific customer relationship: CRM "is a journey of strategic, process, organizational, and technical change whereby a company seeks to better manage its own enterprise around the customer" (Brown 2000, XV). It follows that CRM can be covered best conceptually by the four dimensions (1) strategy, (2) process, (3) structure, and (4) technology (Rigby, Reichheld, and Schefter 2002):

1. As a **strategy**, CRM means the alignment of the whole company to the customer. In this dimension, the targets are defined and the long-term direction of the company is confirmed. The CRM strategy determines the priority of customer value management.
2. Dwyer, Schurr, and Oh (1987) emphasize the **process** dimension and define five general phases to develop a buyer/seller relationship. First of all, the process dimension affects marketing, customer service, and sales as processes with direct customer contact; but apart from that, all core processes of a company should be examined, as long as they influence customer benefit. New product development has to be considered as one focal issue. The process dimension of CRM includes tools that help to implement the principles of CRM in the organization.
3. According to the basic rule "structure follows strategy", CRM represents a customer-focused organizational **structure**, with cross-functional coordinated teams that cope with market needs.
4. The link between the process and the technology dimension of CRM becomes obvious: CRM **technology** is an important enabler of CRM processes.

The CRM tools of the process dimension are key success factors in the CRM implementation; they support the relationship building and handling between producer and customer. In this context, the value-oriented **customer segmentation** and prioritization is identified as an effective CRM tool leading to economic success (Reichheld 1996). The communication process in CRM is handled through **multi-channel management**, enabling an interactive contact between customer and supplier (Peppers, Rogers, and Dorf 1999). According to Ling and Yen (2001, 84), "CRM begins with in-depth analysis of customer behavior and attributes to achieve complete knowledge on the customers, their habits, desires, and their needs". This leads to CRM being a solution that focuses on managing the information flow between customer and producer and allows a successful **knowledge management** (Soo et al. 2002). It becomes obvious that CRM tools are interrelated: The maintenance of the customer data through knowledge management is the starting point for the segmentation of the customer base; the choice of the right contact channel depends on the specific customer segment, and via multiple channels, the relevant knowledge on customers can be gained. Table 1 shows that several authors in the field of CRM develop principles and activities, which refer to the CRM tools knowledge management, segment management and multi-channel management.

Table 1: *Derivation of CRM tools*

CRM principles leading to CRM tools (by author)	*Knowledge management*	*Segment management*	*Multi-channel management*
■ PINTO 1998	In-depth understanding of customer behavior and value	Lifetime value per customer	Wide range of customer contact points
■ PEPPERS, ROGERS, AND DORF 1999	Identify (collect information)	Differentiate (identify top customers)	Interact (offer alternative means of communication)
■ BERRY 2000	Tracking buying patterns	Targeting profitable customers	Opening lines of communication
■ DILLER 2000	Information about customers	Investments in customers, customization for single clients	Interaction with customers, integration of customers
■ GRÖNROOS 2000	Developing a customer database	Segmentation based on customer relationship profitability	Seeking direct contacts with customers
■ HOMBURG AND SIEBEN 2000	IT-usage to gain and process customer information	Economic efficiency, systematization, individuality	Selection of optimal customer touch points

3 CRM - the missing link to superior innovation management?

3.1 CRM and innovation - basic assumptions

Research object of CRM is the customer relationship and consequently – in the innovation process – also the customer/innovator relationship during every single stage of an innovation project. Combining innovation management with the fundamental ideas of CRM, the main question is **if** and **how** customer relationship management can influence the success of innovations. So far, the impact of a comprehensive CRM concept on innovation success and finally company performance has not yet been investigated. Preliminary findings in the field of customer/market orientation and innovation suggest there is a relationship, but yet, there is no clear evidence for the connection between CRM and innovation success. We propose that the CRM concept can be a useful company-wide strategy to align product innovations to customer needs, providing a customer-centric organizational structure and technology to support the innovation process. In addition, it is supposed that specific CRM processes are valuable tools to pick the right customer to interact with during different stages of the innovation process, provide and combine interfaces to the customers that are adapted to innovation-phase-specific requirements, and enable a knowledge management system to gain relevant customer information for the innovation project.

We developed a framework – see Figure 2 for an illustration – that builds on the characteristics of a comprehensive CRM concept, touching the four dimensions of strategy, structure, process and technology. Process as a central CRM dimension is operationalized in this model through the application of the following CRM tools: knowledge management, segment management, and multi-channel management. Each stage of the innovation process requires specific customer involvement: It is expected that a **stage-specific degree of implementation** of the CRM tools positively affects innovation success. The following sections will address these effects in detail.

Figure 2: Model – CRM elements affecting innovation success

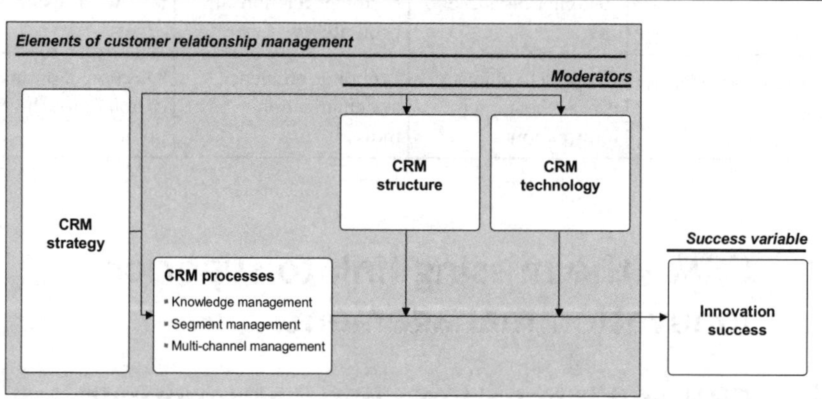

3.2 CRM strategy provides the framework for customer focused innovations

In these days of rapidly shrinking product lifecycles, a continuous flow of innovation is the lifeblood of many companies. One could argue that the strategic orientation of a company should provide an environment that enables new product development. To align the product innovation to customer needs in order to be successful, the application of a CRM strategy is expected to provide such an environment. The CRM strategy, generally defined as a long-term guideline to reach a company's target, is supposed to determine the fundamental orientation of the CRM processes, CRM structures, and CRM technologies. The CRM strategy shapes all procedures where the firm deals with the customer. It is characterized by the idea of a consistent alignment of all activities to the life cycle of a customer. Therefore, the success of CRM is measured by metrics such as customer satisfaction, customer loyalty and customer retention and finally their impact on company success. Implementing CRM in the innovation process, the innovation success becomes the central goal. In addition, the definition of the CRM strategy has to be followed by a company-wide communication in order to be successful.

3.3 CRM processes support a customer-centric innovation process

3.3.1 Knowledge management to gain relevant customer information for innovation projects

The central role of developing market knowledge competence in the innovation process is stressed by many studies (Li and Calantone 1998). E.g., Rogers (1982, 111) points out "the most innovative firm in an industry is likely one that best manages its [...] information flows". Knowledge management as a focal CRM tool comprises the creation, control and development of customer knowledge of a company that is internally available, as well as the management of this customer knowledge, which has to be generated externally and that is hypothetically also a successful tool to gain customer knowledge that is relevant for the innovation project. Knowledge on customer behavior, desires, and needs is a main driver for CRM **and** for innovation management (Rogers 1982; Ling and Yen 2001). Srivastava, Shervani, and Fahey (1998) emphasize CRM's impact of learning about customers' needs through ongoing interactions over time on internal processes such as the new product development process.

The main target of knowledge management as a major CRM tool is to enable all employees to make their business decision on the basis of the complete knowledge available in the company. But many times, appropriate processes to **gain relevant data,** analyze the information, and use the knowledge for internal core activities is missing. Systematic knowledge management as a focal CRM component may be a solution. According to Kohli and Jaworski (1990, see section 2.1), knowledge management comprises the acquisition and dissemination of customer information as well as the organization-wide responsiveness to it. These three steps can be interpreted in the light of CRM and innovation:

1. Customer information acquisition: Via building long-term customer relationships, a company can use every single contact with the customer to gain information. Usually, a part of the requested information for the innovation process is already available in the organization through ongoing business activities. This implies that customer knowledge can be combined from different sources. If the desired customer information is not available in the organization, strong relationships to customers can be used to satisfy information needs through an interaction with customers during the innovation process.
2. Customer information dissemination: "Organizational learning is the means by which knowledge is preserved so that it can be used by individuals other than its progenitor" (Sinkula 1994, 36). The process step of information dissemination underlines the importance that all relevant information has to be available to all employees that are involved in the innovation process.
3. Organization-wide responsiveness to customer information: The final step is the application of relevant customer knowledge in the innovation project.

Overall, knowledge management as a CRM tool can provide relevant customer information, serves to disseminate crucial information to the innovation team and helps innovation projects to succeed. CRM technologies supporting such customer knowledge management processes are discussed in further detail in section 3.5. Considering the requirements of every single stage of the innovation process, the implementation of this CRM tool especially at the beginning of the innovation process (concept development phase) seems to be helpful to assess the need for innovations in a systematic way. In the product development phase, which is more technically oriented, customer knowledge management seems to be less important, apart from testing prototypes by customers. In the implementation phase, the innovator needs customer knowledge management to evaluate the market acceptance of the innovation.

3.3.2 Segment management to develop innovations for the most valuable customers

CRM also facilitates a more sophisticated customer segmentation: Customer value-based segmentation follows the idea of selecting only the most valuable customers for an interaction during the innovation process and the adjustment of the innovation to their needs. In addition, integration of customer segments should be differentiated across the stages of the innovation process, and misleading customer feedback has to be identified (Brockhoff 1997). But who are the right customers to be involved at different stages of innovation processes – especially from the firm's perspective? Based on the relevant literature, four interesting types of customers were identified:

First of all, a main principle of CRM is the identification of the **economically most valuable** customers. The so-called Pareto law (in many cases, 20% of the customers account for 80% of revenues or profits of a company) demands almost for a segmentation of the customer base on economic criteria. Krafft and Albers (2000) provide an overview of different segmentation approaches and show that portfolio and scoring methods are appropriate for a segmentation of customers considering their economic value. Taking into account the needs of profitable customers when creating product innovations seems to be very promising. These customers seem to be valuable partners for interaction in all stages of the innovation process. Understanding innovation management as an investment decision, segmenting will help to allocate company resources: Spend more R&D budget to grow profitable segments, control costs of low-margin customers, and terminate unattractive relationships.

Apart from economic value, each customer has information potential: "The **information potential** of the customer is obtained from the total useful information received by the company from the customer within a certain period of time" (Huber, Herrmann, and Morgan 2001, 48). Especially in the concept and the product development phase of an innovation process, relevant expertise of customers can be used as a valuable source. A well-known example for using customer knowledge in the innovation process is the lead user concept. Lead users are "in advance of a market with respect to a given important dimension which is changing over time" (Urban and von Hippel 1988, 570). They can provide indications of prospective customer needs and enable an efficient new product development. But the lead user group is not the only interesting segment in the innovation process; any customer expertise or their knowledge as a user can contain important advice to innovation projects (Brockhoff 1997).

In the context of innovations, the consideration of the impact of **opinion leaders** on buying patterns of their social system (e.g., family, friends, neighbors) seems to be a valuable point of departure for successful innovations (Childers 1986). If the innovator manages to convince opinion leaders of the quality of the innovative product, then the opinion leaders will influence the potential customer base. That is why an interaction with opinion leaders can be very attractive in particular in the implementation stage of the innovation process.

Another central aspect in CRM is reaching **relationship quality**. A win-win situation between customer and producer forms the basis for a close, long-term relationship (Grönroos 2000). Customers in such a relationship of high quality show satisfaction, trust and commitment (Smith 1998). The integration of this customer segment in all stages of the innovation process has the advantage that the more loyal customers are more willing and prepared to share their knowledge with the producer.

In summary, from an innovator's perspective, customers should be categorized based on their profitability, their knowledge, their opinion leader potential or their loyalty to the company. The degree to which customers should be involved in innovation processes differs across the stages of this process.

3.3.3 Multi-channel management to integrate customers in the innovation process

Direct interaction processes through multiple channels are an integral part of the CRM concept (Parvatiyar and Sheth 2000). CRM requires an interactive, two-way communication between supplier and customer. The supplier has to keep in steady contact with his customers and should provide incentives to motivate esteemed customers to get active. Apart from customer interaction, the integration of valuable customers in core processes of an organization is desired from a CRM perspective. A principle of customer integration is to solve problems in cooperation with customers. Customer interaction and integration can be understood as communication processes that support a knowledge sharing between producer and customer (Gales and Mansure-Cole 1995). Each contact provides the opportunity to gain valuable data and to enhance the relationship with those customers. The systematic integration of traditional and new electronic communication channels to manage the dialog with the customer can be defined as **multi-channel management** (Brown 2000). Knowing that all information is consolidated across channels, customers and suppliers have the chance to choose the most appropriate communication channel for a specific situation.

In the context of innovation management, multi-channel management as a central CRM tool provides the innovator with the opportunity to adapt the contact channel to the kind of information s/he needs for the specific innovation stage and to the kind of customers s/he wants to involve. For example, the channel "complaints office" may have stored valuable hints for new product ideas that can be used in the first phase of the innovation process, while face-to-face contacts may be most appropriate for prototype testing in the product development phase. Similarly, the specific advantages of the internet can be utilized in order to test innovations on a larger scale in the implementation stage. To summarize, we propose that multi-channel management is positively linked to innovation success. However, multi-channel approaches have to be differentiated across the separate stages of the innovation process to generate maximum profitability. And, as in any use of qualitative research (e.g., focus groups), the innovator has to identify and select valuable and relevant information. We propose that qualitative studies are most appropriate in early stages of the innovation process, while large quantitative analyses are more adequate in later stages.

3.4 CRM helps to structure organizations around customer-oriented innovations

If a company switches from a transactional perspective to a relationship orientation, the organizational structure has to be adapted accordingly to become customer-centric. Based on conceptual reasoning and empirical findings, we propose that a customer-oriented organizational structure provides an appropriate frame to support the implementation of knowledge management, segment management and multi-channel management processes.

As the given tasks of a company are usually too broad to be handled by a single person, division of labor and therefore specialization is required (e.g., Brockhoff 1985). Coordination between departments and specific employees is essential to reach the company's targets. Brockhoff and Hauschildt (1993) examined tools to coordinate functional departments that depend on an interaction with each other but do not have the same supervisory managers. In the innovation context, a CRM-oriented organizational structure serves to align multiple interfaces between hierarchical and functional positions and thus provides a platform for employees with complementary capabilities and access to different information. In particular, "[o]rganisational structure has also been shown to be a factor influencing the amount of corporation across the marketing-R&D interface, and thus the chance of new product success" (Calantone, Di Benedetto, and Divine 1993, 340). Involved areas are technical functions like R&D (see Brockhoff 2003 for a definition) and customer facing functions like marketing or customer service. Following the principles of the CRM concept, the involvement of technical and marketing-oriented functions in innovation projects promises to increase success of these projects. CRM-oriented organizational structures help to support the collaboration between relevant functions in the innovation context and thereby increase the chance of innovation success (Sethi, Smith, and Park 2001).

Understanding organizational structures as a system of rules that adjust the behavior of employees to the company's strategic targets (Chandler 1969), the connection between rewards and structures becomes obvious. By providing appropriate incentive schemes, an innovator can stress the importance of CRM-activities to the employees. It has been shown that the likelihood of a more profitable execution of CRM processes increases, if employees are rewarded adequately (Reinartz, Krafft, and Hoyer 2004).

In summary, we propose that the degree of interfunctional collaboration and the company's support of CRM compatible behavior are critical moderators of the link between CRM processes and innovation success. An empirical study that we currently conduct shows preliminary evidence that successful innovators integrate CRM and new product development by means of organizational structures and systems.

3.5 CRM technology accelerates the innovation process

Software companies like Siebel, Oracle, SAP, and PeopleSoft have built a CRM market of approximately US$ 20 billion in 2002 (Gartner, Inc.). Usually, the implementation of CRM leads to an investment in a technological CRM infrastructure. Talking about CRM technology, one can distinguish between front-end systems and back-end systems (Wilson, Daniel, and McDonald 2002):

- Front-end systems: Electronic communication channels, rather than traditional channels, build the front-end to the customer and help to manage one-to-one contacts to the customer. Front-end systems are technological enablers of multichannel management as a CRM tool.
- Back-end systems: CRM analytics enable organizations to aggregate relevant customer data, analyze this data, perform predictive modeling, distribute the analysis throughout the organization, and apply the results to every customer interaction – e.g., the interaction during innovation processes (Bromberger 2004). Back-end systems provide technological support needed for knowledge management and segment management systems, being the "users" of customer information. Especially, the application of conventional methods to gain and analyze customer data – e.g., by means of traditional market research tools – are insufficient to satisfy the high requirements on the quality of customer information data in the innovation process: Conventional methods focus on analyzing aggregated data to provide reports for highly technical users, while CRM analytics offer user-friendly knowledge about customers in real-time. Central elements of back-end systems are data warehouses to collect customer information and data-mining systems to examine customer information (e.g., run "what if" scenarios).

To conclude, CRM technology is considered to be a moderator on the effect of CRM systems and tools on the success of innovation projects.

4 Conclusion

The capability of organizations to launch innovative products is more important than ever to be successful in the long run. Customer relationship management has been presented in this chapter as a concept that may be useful to systematically identify interesting innovations, increase success of innovation projects and improve innovation management. In our contribution, we have pointed out the following:

In order to understand CRM as a comprehensive model, four elements are considered essential for innovation success, namely CRM strategy, CRM process, CRM structure, and CRM technology. By successfully implementing these four elements, the innovator is able to listen to the right customers at different stages of the innovation process, while innovative ideas, concepts, and finally products are developed. Our conceptual results indicate that the implementation of knowledge management, segment management and multi-channel management as CRM tools in every single stage of the innovation process leads to successful innovations. Unfortunately, empirical investigations of the effects discussed in this chapter have not yet been conducted. Future research should fill this gap of the current literature.

5 References

Anderson, J.C. (1995): Relationships in business markets – Exchange episodes, value creation, and their empirical assessment, *Journal of the Academy of Marketing Science*, 23 (4), 346-350.

Berry, L.L. (1983): Relationship marketing, in: Berry, L.L., G.L. Shostack and G. Upah (eds.): *Emerging perspectives on services marketing*, Chicago (IL), 25-28.

Berry, L.L. (2000): Relationship marketing of services – Growing interest, emerging perspectives, in: Sheth, J.N. and A. Parvatiyar (Eds.): *Handbook of relationship marketing*, Thousand Oaks (CA)/London/New Delhi, 149-170.

Brockhoff, K. (1985): Abstimmungsprobleme von Marketing und Technologiepolitik, *Die Betriebswirtschaft*, 45 (6), 623-632.

Brockhoff, K. (1997): Wenn der Kunde stört – Differenzierungsnotwendigkeiten bei der Einbeziehung von Kunden in die Produktentwicklung, in: Bruhn, M. and H. Steffenhagen (Eds.): *Marketingorientierte Unternehmensführung. Reflexionen – Denkanstöße – Perspektiven, Festschrift für Heribert Meffert zum 60. Geburtstag*, Wiesbaden, 351-370.

Brockhoff, K. (1999): *Produktpolitik*, 4th ed., Stuttgart/Jena.

Brockhoff, K. (2003): Exploring strategic R&D success factors, *Technology Analysis & Strategic Management*, 15 (3), 333-348.

Brockhoff, K. and J. Hauschildt (1993): Schnittstellen-Management – Koordination ohne Hierarchie, *Zeitschrift für Führung + Organisation*, 62 (6), 396-403.

Bromberger, J. (2004): *Customer Relationship Management mit Unterstützung von Internettechnologien*, Wiesbaden.

Brown, S. (2000): *Customer relationship management – A strategic imperative in the world of e-business*, Chichester.

Bruhn, M. (2003): *Relationship marketing – Management of customer relationships*, Halow.

Calantone, R.J., A.C. di Benedetto, and R. Divine (1993): Organisational, technical and marketing antecedents for successful new product development, *R&D Management*, 23 (4), 337-351.

Chandler A.D. (1969): *Strategy and structure - Chapters in the history of the American industrial enterprise*, Cambridge (MA).

Childers, T.L. (1986): Assessment of the psychometric properties of an opinion leadership scale, *Journal of Marketing Research*, 23 (May), 184-188.

Christensen, C.M. and M.E. Raynor (2003): *The innovator's solution - Creating and sustaining successful growth*, Boston (MA).

Diller, H. (2000): Customer loyalty - Fata morgana or realistic goal? Managing relationships with customers, in: Hennig-Thurau, T. and U. Hansen (Eds.): *Relationship marketing - Gaining competitive advantage through customer satisfaction and customer retention*, Berlin/Heidelberg/New York, 29-48.

Dwyer, R.F., P.H. Schurr, and S. Oh (1987): Developing buyer-seller relations, *Journal of Marketing*, 51 (April), 11-27.

Ernst, H. (2002): Success factors of new product development – A review of the empirical literature, *International Journal of Management Reviews*, 4 (1), 1-40.

Foster, R.N. and S. Kaplan (2001): *Creative destruction. Why companies that are built to last underperform the market – And how to successfully transform them*, New York.

Gales, L. and D. Mansour-Cole (1995): User involvement in innovation projects - Towards an information processing model, *Journal of Engineering and Technology Management*, 12 (1/2), 77-109.

Grönroos, C. (1997): Value-driven relational marketing – From products to resources and competencies, *Journal of Marketing Management*, 13, 407-419.

Grönroos, C. (2000): *Service marketing and management - A customer relationship management approach*, Chichester.

Gruner, K. and C. Homburg (1999): Innovationserfolg durch Kundenbindung, *Zeitschrift für Betriebswirtschaft*, 67 (special issue 1), 119-142.

Helfert, G., T. Ritter and A. Walter (2001): *How does market orientation affect business relationships?*, 17th Annual IMP Conference at the Norwegian School of Management, Oslo.

Homburg, C. and F.G. Sieben (2000): Customer Relationship Management - Strategische Ausrichtung statt IT-getriebenem Aktivismus, in: Bruhn, M. and C. Homburg (Eds.): *Handbuch Kundenbindungsmanagement. Grundlagen – Konzepte – Erfahrungen*, Wiesbaden, 473-501.

Huber, F., A. Herrmann, and R.E. Morgan (2001): Gaining competitive advantage through customer value oriented management, *Journal of Consumer Marketing*, 18 (1), 41-53.

Jackson, B.B. (1985): *Winning and keeping industrial customers - The dynamics of customer relationships*, Lexington (MA)/Toronto.

Krafft, M. and S. Albers (2000): Ansätze zur Segmentierung von Kunden – Wie geeignet sind herkömmliche Konzepte?, *Zeitschrift für betriebswirtschaftliche Forschung*, 52 (September), 515-536

Krafft, M. and O. Götz (2003): Customer Relationship Management öffentlicher und privater TV-Sender, in: Wirtz, B.W. (Ed.): *Handbuch Medien- und Multimediamanagement*, Wiesbaden, 337-363.

Kirchmann, E.M.W. (1994): *Innovationskooperation zwischen Herstellern und Anwendern*, Wiesbaden.

Kohli, A.K. and B.J. Jaworski (1990): Market orientation – The construct, research propositions and managerial implications, *Journal of Marketing*, 54 (April), 1-18.

Li, T. and R.J. Calantone (1998): The impact of market knowledge competence on new product advantage – Conceptualization and empirical examination, in: *Journal of Marketing*, 62 (October), 13-29.

Lilien, G.L., P.D. Morrison, K. Searls, M. Sonnack, and E. von Hippel (2002): Performance assessment of the lead user idea-generation process for new product development, *Management Science*, 48 (8), 1042-1059.

Ling, R. and D. Yen (2001): Customer relationship management - An analysis framework and implementation strategies, *Journal of Computer Information Systems*, 41 (3), 82-97.

Morgan, R.M. and S.D. Hunt (1994): The commitment-trust theory of relationship marketing, *Journal of Marketing*, 58 (July), 20-38.

Narver, J.C. and S.F. Slater (1990): The effect of a market orientation on business profitability, *Journal of Marketing*, 20 (October), 20-35.

Parvatiyar, A. and J.N. Sheth (2000): The domain and conceptual foundations of relationship marketing, in: Sheth, J.N. and A. Parvatiyar (Eds.): *Handbook of relationship marketing*, Thousand Oaks (CA)/London/New Delhi, 3-38.

Peppers, D., M. Rogers, and B. Dorf (1999): Is your company ready for one-to-one marketing?, *Harvard Business Review*, 77 (January-February), 3-12.

Pinto, S.K. (1998): Realizing the power of customer relationship management, *Journal of Database Marketing*, 6 (1), 70-82.

Reichheld, F.F. (1996): *The loyalty effect – The hidden force behind growth, profits and lasting value*, Boston (MA).

Reinartz, W., M. Krafft, and W.D. Hoyer (2004): The CRM process – Its measurement and impact on performance, *Journal of Marketing Research*, 41 (in press).

Rigby, D.K, F.F. Reichheld, and P. Schefter (2002): Avoid the four perils of CRM, *Harvard Business Review*, 80 (February), 101-109.

Rogers, E.M. (1982): Information exchange and technological innovation, in: Sahal, D. (Ed.): *The transfer and utilization of technical knowledge*, Lexington (MA): Lexington, 105-123.

Ruekert, R.W. (1992): Developing a market orientation – An organizational strategy perspective, *International Journal of Research in Marketing*, 9, 225-245.

Sethi, R., D.C. Smith, and C.W. Park (2001): Cross-functional product development teams, creativity, and the innovativeness of new consumer products, *Journal of Marketing Research*, 28 (February), 73-85.

Sinkula, J.M. (1994): Market information processing and organizational learning, *Journal of Marketing*, 58 (January), 35-45.

Smith, J.B. (1998): Buyer-seller relationships - Similarity, relationship management, and quality, *Psychology & Marketing*, 15 (1), 3-21.

Soo, C., T. Devinney, D. Midgley, and A. Deering (2002): Knowledge management - Philosophy, processes, and pitfalls, *California Management Review*, 44 (4), 129-150.

Srivastava, R.K., T.A. Shervani, and L. Fahey (1998): Market-based assets and shareholder value - A framework for analysis, *Journal of Marketing*, 62 (January), 2-18.

Urban, G.L. and E. von Hippel (1988): Lead user analysis for the development of new industrial products, *Management Science*, 34 (5), 569-582.

Wilson, H., E. Daniel, and M. McDonald (2002): Factors for success in customer relationship management (CRM) systems, *Journal of Marketing Management*, 18 (1/2), 193-219.

Bernd Skiera and Martin Spann

Opportunities of Virtual Stock Markets to Support New Product Development

Prof. Dr. *Bernd Skiera* and Dr. *Martin Spann*, Department of Electronic Commerce, Johann Wolfgang Goethe-University at Frankfurt.

1 Introduction

Although the Internet has not fulfilled all expectations of the stock markets, it has been adopted by many consumers and companies all around the world. Recent studies report a 53.5% adoption rate among consumers in Germany (Eimeren et al. 2003) and a 60% adoption rate among consumers in the United States (Rayport and Jaworski 2001). In Western Europe alone, more than 250 Mio. consumers are expected to have access to the Internet in 2005 (European Information Technology Observatory 2004). Worldwide business-to-business electronic commerce is expected to be greater than 1 Trillion USD in 2003 (Rayport and Jaworski 2001). This wide acceptance of the Internet alters product development (Dahan and Hauser 2002). Yet, new product development still remains difficult and costly (Di Benedetto 1999, Brockhoff 1999). The flop rates of newly launched products remain high over the years, often surpassing 50% (Urban and Hauser 1993). Hence, even small improvements in the new product development process can have a major effect on companies' profits and competitive advantage if this flop rate is reduced.

Therefore, new methods to improve new product development are of high relevance for companies. Virtual stock markets could be such a method. They have recently gained much attendance (Spann and Skiera 2003c, Wolfers and Zitzewitz 2004, Polk et al. 2003) and even the Pentagon considered virtual stock markets as a tool to better forecast economic and political stability (Hulse 2003). The basic idea of virtual stock markets is to make future events or market situations expressible and tradable through virtual stocks (Spann and Skiera 2003b, Forsythe et al. 1992). Thereby, the cash dividend (payoff) of such shares of virtual stocks depends on a particular outcome, e.g., the success of a software development project (Ortner 2000), product sales (Plott 2000), goodness of new product concepts (Chan et al. 2002) or new product sales (Spann and Skiera 2003a). Studies show that virtual stock markets might have the potential to support new product development successfully (Spann and Skiera 2003a). Yet, none of those studies provided a comprehensive analysis about the particular stages of new product development that might be supported. In addition, little is known about the factors that influence the forecasting accuracy of virtual stock markets.

Therefore, the aim of this paper is to analyze the opportunities of virtual stock markets to support new product development and to empirically determine factors that influence the forecasting error of virtual stock markets. For that reason, we analyze in Section 2 the impact of the Internet on new product development. Section 3 describes virtual stock markets and their opportunities to support the different stages of the new product development process. In Section 4, we describe an empirical study that uses virtual stock markets to forecast the success of new products, compare forecasting accuracy with those of expert judgments and analyze the factors that influence forecast accuracy. Section 5 summarizes the implications of the paper.

2 Opportunities of the Internet for New Product Development

Brockhoff (1999) proposes to distinguish five stages of the new product development process, namely (i) idea generation and screening, (ii) development of product concepts, (iii) research & development, design and engineering of product prototypes, (iv) product testing and (v) product launch. Others share this point of view (Urban and Hauser 1993, Dahan and Hauser 2002). Therefore, we use these five stages to structure the different ideas that have been proposed to support new product development (see Figure 1).

Figure 1: Opportunities of the Internet to support stages of new product development

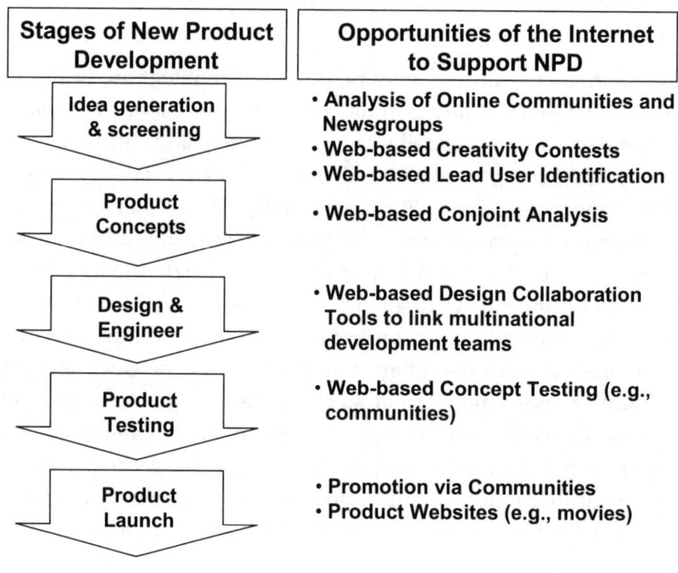

Figure 1 provides an overview of the opportunities of the Internet to support new product development. The idea generation and screening stage can be supported in several ways by the Internet. Online communities and newsgroups can be systematically analyzed for new product ideas. In addition, creativity and idea generation contests can be easily organized via the Internet (Ernst et al. 2004). Thereby or in connection with an online survey, a company can try to identify lead users, which it can then use as a source for new product ideas (Urban and Von Hippel 1988, Brockhoff 2000).

In the product concept stage, consumer preferences for different new product concepts can be evaluated via web-based preference elicitation tools such as conjoint analysis. Thereby, the presentation of new product concepts as well as the preference elicitation method can be conducted completely online, saving time and money, as well as making use of the graphic and audio capabilities of the world wide web to depict virtual products and product features (Dahan and Hauser 2002, Dahan and Srinivasan 2000, Ernst and Sattler 2000). In addition, the computational capabilities of the Internet allow to dynamically adapt web-pages in real time (Toubia et al. 2003).

Web-based design collaboration tools, such as computer aided design (CAD) and computer aided manufacturing (CAM), linked to a company's knowledge management system, can support interaction between multi-regional and multi-national R&D-teams. Further, such tools and online communities in a company intranet as part of its knowledge management system can enhance collaboration between different departments engaged in the design and engineering stage of the new product development process (Grover and Davenport 2001).

Product prototypes can be tested among an online community as part of the product testing stage (Panten et al. 2001). Web-based preference elicitation tools can be applied at this stage as well.

The launch of a product can be supported by specific product websites (e.g. for movies), which inform consumers about the product and thereby help to reduce buyer uncertainty for fairly new products. Further, new products can be promoted via online communities and newsgroups (Albers et al. 1998). In addition, product placements in Online games can provide a new opportunity to promote products.

3 Virtual Stock Markets and Their Use in New Product Development Stages

The idea of virtual stock markets is to bring a group of participants together via the Internet and let them trade shares of virtual stocks. These stocks represent a bet on the outcome of particular future events and their value depends on the realization of these events. Once the occurrence of the particular event is known, each share of virtual stock receives a cash dividend (payoff) according to that particular event (e.g., $1 for each unit sold). As those "stocks" are actually securities because their terminal values are contingent upon the outcome of an uncertain event, some authors use the label "security" (Dahan and Hauser 2002, Chan et al. 2002). However, in accordance with the major part of the literature dealing with virtual stock markets (e.g., Forsythe et al. 1992, Forsythe et al. 1999, Spann and Skiera 2003b), we use the denomination "stocks" because that makes the concept easier to understand for the major part of the participants.

Such types of virtual stock markets were first applied in the form of a political stock market to predict the outcome of the Bush vs. Dukakis US presidential election in 1988 (Forsythe et al. 1992). Afterwards, virtual stock markets were used to predict the results of many other elections (Forsythe et al. 1999, Spann 2002). Later on, researchers started to apply virtual stock markets to solve business problems. Ortner (2000) uses virtual stock markets for the success of a software development project, Plott (2000) for predicting product sales and Spann and Skiera (2003a) for forecasting new product sales. Most recently, the Pentagon intended to use virtual stock markets to derive forecasts concerning foreign policy events, e.g., a coup d'état in certain countries (Polk et al. 2003, Spann and Skiera 2003c).

The basic idea behind virtual stock markets is that the price of one share of a virtual stock should correspond to the virtual stock market's aggregate expectations of the event outcome because participants of the virtual stock markets use their individual assessment of the particular event to derive an individual expectation of the cash dividend of the related share of virtual stock. According to the Hayek hypothesis, the market mechanism should be the best way to aggregate the individual assessments, because the price mechanism on a competitive market is the most efficient instrument to aggregate the asymmetrically dispersed information of market participants (Hayek 1945, Smith 1982).

Virtual stock markets can be used as an information gathering tool to support new product development. The different opportunities of virtual stock markets to provide market intelligence in the new product development process are displayed in **Figure 2**, again using the distinction into five stages proposed by Brockhoff (1999).

In the idea generation and screening stage an online community can be created, which is organized around existing products that are traded on a virtual stock market. One example is the Hollywood Stock Exchange (www.hsx.com) that performs a virtual stock market on the success of new movies and contains a major virtual community dealing with movie related topics. Thus, trading on the virtual stock market stimulates consumers to express and discuss new product ideas as well as new product success factors in the online community. The systematic analysis of this community can produce new product ideas (Ernst et al. 2004). Further, participants of this virtual stock market can be analyzed in order to detect lead users (Spann et al. 2003).

In the product concept stage, a virtual stock market can try to assess consumers' aggregated preferences for different new product concepts taken up ideas that have been proposed by Chan et al. (2002). One major problem of the design applied by Chan et al. (2002) is that the payoff value of stocks and thus the assessment of product concepts could be biased by a self-fulfilling prophecy (Spann and Skiera 2003a). The reason is that Chan et al. (2002) use the final price in the stock market as payoff value. Spann and Skiera (2003a) propose a design modification of a payoff based on the results of two parallel experimental groups that might solve this problem if each group's final stock price is used as the payoff for the stock prices of the other group.

At the design and engineering stage, different design and development solutions can be evaluated at a virtual stock market on a company's intranet. Thereby, the assessments on the feasibility and efficiency of different construction and manufacturing solutions can be traded by one or several R&D-teams. Further, the inclusion of members for the marketing department as traders can add market-related information. Virtual stock markets might especially be beneficial in such situations because the aggregation of the individual estimates will not be biased due to different positions in a company's hierarchy (Spann 2002). Spann and Skiera (2003a) show in a different context that even virtual stock markets with only 12 participants are large enough to get good results.

***Figure 2:** Opportunities of Virtual Stock Markets to Support New Product Development*

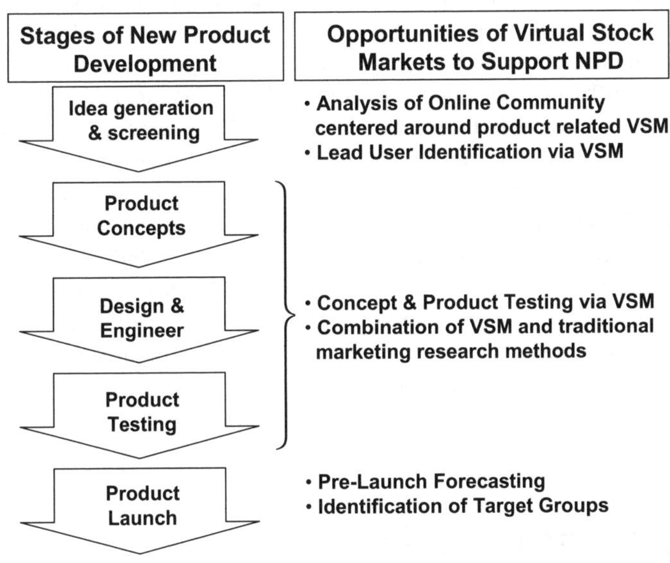

Product prototypes can be tested in a virtual stock market so that participants can trade their assessments on the market success of these different prototypes (Chan et al. 2002). Thereby, additional information could be elicited by combining a virtual stock market with traditional survey and focus group methods on the same set of consumers, because trading in the virtual stock market can stimulate consumers to focus on the subject and quantify their assessment of market success (Spann and Skiera 2003b).

Virtual stock markets can be used for pre-launch forecasting of a product's market success. Such forecasts are very useful for a company in order to optimize their product-launch related marketing instruments. For example, a movie studio can use this information to decide on promotions and advertising related to the movie's release. Movie exhibitors can plan on whether to display the movie in large or small theatres. (Spann and Skiera 2003b). Further, an analysis of traders' portfolios and trading behavior might be useful for the analysis of target groups (Spann and Skiera 2003a).

Compared to other knowledge gathering techniques applicable in the new product development process, virtual stock markets offer the following advantages (Spann and Skiera 2003b, Dahan and Hauser 2002): First, they allow for an almost real-time reaction of stock prices to additional information and, hence, a very quick prediction of the impact of that information on future market situations. Second, it does not burden the researcher with the task of weighting and aggregating different expert judgments as this is achieved by the trading mechanism implemented in the virtual stock market. Participants, for example, weight their assessments by the volume and the price of the purchase or sale order they place or accept. Third, once established, a virtual stock market can operate at rather moderate operating costs, e.g. for repeated new product concept tests. Fourth, a virtual stock market provides participants with an incentive to reveal their true assessments (Forsythe et al. 1999), if an adequate remuneration is properly linked to the participants' performance on the virtual stock market. Hence, whereas many consumer surveys remunerate consumers for their participation at a survey, a virtual stock market usually remunerates participants for their successful participation (Spann and Skiera 2003b, Dahan and Hauser 2002). Wertenbroch and Skiera (2002) show, for example, that consumers' willingness-to-pay differs significantly according to the incentive structure being provided. Finally, participants in a virtual stock market might have more fun than their counterparts partaking in consumer or expert surveys (Dahan and Hauser 2002).

4 Empirical Study

The goal of the following empirical study is to analyze the use of a virtual stock market to predict the success of new products prior to their launch. Thereby, we analyze the feasibility, the forecast accuracy and the factors influencing forecast accuracy of a virtual stock market to predict the success of new products, namely the success of movies in Germany. Movies face high financial stakes for production and marketing, a significant failure rate, and rather unstable market conditions. (e.g., Sawhney and

Eliashberg 1996 or Eliashberg et al. 2000). Hence, we look at a virtual stock market that has been used as a pre-launch forecasting tool in the product launch stage.

4.1 Design of the Study

We conducted the movie exchange (www.CMXX.com) seven times for the prediction of movies, using our own virtual stock market software (the first round also included the chart position of 11 pop music singles in Germany which we omit for our analysis). We conducted a virtual stock market for the prediction of the box-office success (number of visitors) of movies in Germany. During the seven rounds of CMXX, virtual stocks for ten to fifteen movies were traded in each round. In total, virtual stocks were traded for eighty-one movies. At the end of CMXX, each share of movie stock received a cash dividend (payoff) according to the total number of visitors of the respective movie in Germany until the end of the specific round.

Prices were limited to $3,000 (virtual) in the first round, and $3,500 (virtual) in the following rounds for movie stocks, considering that more than 3,000,000 and 3,500,000 movie visitors were unrealistic in Germany. In the first round, CMXX provided non-monetary incentives in the form of a "Golden Record" and ten music CDs for the participant with the highest portfolio value, five and three music CDs respectively for the participants with the second and third highest portfolio values. Four sets of movie merchandise were given to randomly chosen participants ranking fourth to one hundredth according to final portfolio value. In the second to seventh rounds, the participant with the highest portfolio value in each round received an annual ticket for a large German movie exhibitor; the participants with the second and third highest portfolio value received ten free movie tickets and a set of movie merchandise, respectively. Table 1 provides an overview of the design of the movie exchange.

4.2 Forecast Accuracy

The price of a share of a movie stock represents a prediction of the number of visitors for the selected movie up until the end of the specific round. Thus by multiplying the stock price with 1,000, the forecast of a movie's number of visitors can be easily derived.

Table 1: *Design of the Movie Exchange*

Step	*Decisions*
Choice of Forecasting Goal	Forecasting the number of movie visitors in Germany
	Payoff function: Movie visitors in Germany: 1 virtual Euro per 1,000 visitors of a movie
	Duration: First round: 22 January – 5 February 2001; [Second to seventh rounds: Duration of one month each between May and October 2001]
	Open to the public; participants can join at any time
Incentives for Participation and Information Revelation	*Composition of Initial Portfolios / Endowment:*
	Endowment of 100 shares of each type of movie stock and $500,000 [$250,000] (virtual) per participant
	Provision of loans up to $500,000 [$250,000] (virtual) at no interest rate per participant
	Remuneration / Incentive Mechanism:
	Nonmonetary rewards
	Rank-order tournament: Rewards for participants with the highest, second highest and third highest increase in (virtual) portfolio value (annual movie ticket, 10 free movie tickets, movie merchandize)
	Time interval: Whole virtual stock market duration
	Incentives not based on performance: First round: Lottery for four rewards among participants ranked fourth to one hundredth
Financial Market Design	Double auction trading mechanism with open order book
	Trading times: Twenty-four hours a day, seven days a week
	No short trading
	Order types: Limit and market without temporal restriction
	No position limits, maximum price limits of 3,000 [3,500] for movie stocks
	No trading fee

In each round, the movie exchange attracted around fifty actively trading participants. The forecasts derived from CMXX used the price of the last trade of a specific type of stock before trading was stopped at the end of a specific round. CMXX faced the problem that it included movies with very few visitors and presumably little information available among the participants (e.g., the movie "althan.com" had only 20,000 visitors compared to 2,296,000 visitors for "Unbreakable"). Consequently, forecast accuracy for the less publicized movies below 100,000 visitors was rather bad with an absolute percentage error of above 100% each (see Table 2).

Table 2: *Forecast Error of Movie Exchange*

APE	*Round 1*	*Round 2*	*Round 3*	*Round 4*	*Round 5*	*Round 6*	*Round 7*	*Overall*
Movie 1	**.024**	26.889	**.096**	**.050**	**.048**	**.012**	**.030**	
Movie 2	2.776	**.232**	.061	**.198**	**.010**	5.000	**.028**	
Movie 3	**.332**	**.031**	**.400**	**.130**	**.032**	**.252**	**.505**	
Movie 4	.190	**.570**	1.667	**.956**	**.170**	**.018**	**.031**	
Movie 5	**.057**	**.307**	**.123**	2.824	.333	.053	**.190**	
Movie 6	**.141**	**.222**	**.208**	**.055**	**.102**	**.189**	n.a.	
Movie 7	9.667	**.170**	**.378**	**.407**	5.600	1.000	**.281**	
Movie 8	.705	2.784	7.214	**.297**	**.153**	**.250**	2.049	
Movie 9	3.516	**.005**	**.074**	**.835**	**.701**	n.a.	**.040**	
Movie 10	.630	3.839	2.258	2.390	3.115	**.080**	**.500**	
Movie 11	.250	**.263**	49.000	1.041	1.935	n.a.	**.013**	
Movie 12		13.318		1.174		.479	3.895	
Movie 13		**.118**						
Movie 14		**.133**						
Movie 15		5.507						
MAPE	*1.663*	*3.626*	*5.589*	*.863*	*1.109*	*.733*	*.687*	**2.119**
Median	*.332*	*.263*	*.378*	*.621*	*.170*	*.220*	*.190*	**.263**
Min	*.024*	*.005*	*.061*	*.050*	*.010*	*.012*	*.013*	**.010**
Max	9.667	*26.889*	*49.000*	*2.824*	*5.600*	*5.000*	*3.895*	**49.000**

Bold print: Movies having over 100,000 visitors.
n.a.: Movie release postponed.
APE: Absolute Percentage Error.

4.3 Performance Compared to Expert Judgments

The performance of the CMXX results is compared to corporate expert predictions from the management of a large German movie exhibitor that we were able to collect for the first two rounds but not for additional rounds (see Table 3). We compare the predictions of CMXX directly. The expert predictions were provided approximately one week before the end of each round of CMXX and were not made available to the participants of CMXX. The CMXX hit rate in the first round was six out of ten for movies (for the eleventh movie the CMXX prediction and the expert prediction were identical). In the second round, the CMXX hit rate was eleven out of fifteen in comparison to the expert predictions from the movie exhibitor. Table 3 compares the Mean Absolute Percentage Error (MAPE) of CMXX to that of the expert predictions for movies having over 100,000 visitors. The forecasts of CMXX are significantly better than those of the experts, indicating that either CMXX performed well and/or that the experts performed poorly.

Table 3: *Comparison between Predictions of CMXX and Experts (Movies > 100' visitors)*

Instrument	CMXX: MAPE	Experts: MAPE	CMXX % improvement (p-value)[a)]
Round 1*	13.83%	47.46%	70.86% (.331)
Round 2*	20.50%	115.73%	82.29% (.010)
Round 1+2*	18.59%	96.20%	80.68% (.005)

[a)] Percentage of improvement of CMXX over alternative expert judgments:
= [MAPE Expert – MAPE CMXX] / MAPE Expert (two-tailed paired t-test for difference)

* Movies having over 100,000 visitors.
MAPE: Mean Absolute Percentage Error.

4.4 Factors Influencing Forecast Error

The results of our empirical study demonstrate, that virtual stock markets can sometimes produce rather weak results. Therefore, it is important to derive factors which can indicate the expected forecast accuracy of a virtual stock market. In this section we will analyze the influence of different exogenous and endogenous factors on the forecast error of the movie exchange. Exogenous factors are the ones which are not derived from the virtual stock market itself, but rather depend on the product being used on the virtual stock market: the distribution intensity of movies in the form of the number of screens a movie is released on opening weekend as well as the genre of a movie (see Table 4). Endogenous to the stock market is the stock price volatility of a specific stock on the last 5 days of trading at the virtual stock market.

Table 4: *Coding According to Genre of Movie*

Movie Genre	Action/Thriller	Drama/Romance	Comedy	Rest
Number of Movies	22	18	26	15
ANOVA (Impact of genre on forecast error): F-Value = 1.116, p-value = .348				

Table 5 displays the estimation results for the influence of endogenous and exogenous factors on the forecast error of all 81 movies traded at the movie exchange. Thereby, only price volatility and the number of movie screens at the opening weekend exert a significant influence. However, these two variables (one exogenous and one endogenous) display a significant negative correlation (Pearson: -.400 (p-value: .000)). Thus, both, the exogenous factor of the number of screens, as well as the endogenous factor of price volatility can indicate the expected forecast accuracy of the virtual stock market. If we omit from the 81 movies the 20% having the highest price volatility, then the mean forecast error reduces from 211.9% to 97.13%. The cut of value for the price volatility is a coefficient of variation of 0.509 or 50.9% in this case. Analogously, if we omit from the 81 movies the 20% having the lowest number of screens on opening weekend, then the mean forecast error reduces from 211.9% to 69.79%. The cut of value for the number of screens is 119 in this case. The latter results are in line with the forecasting errors (71.1%) of Sawhney and Eliashberg (1996) in a study to predict the box-office revenues for ten movies.

Table 5: *Estimation Results for Factors influencing Forecast Error of Movie Exchange*

Parameter value (standardized)	*Model 1*	*Model 2*	*Model 3*
Constant (p-value)[a]	(.008)	(.000)	(.613)
Price volatility (p-value)[b]	.153 (.199)		.277 (.012)
Number of Screens (p-value)	-.289 (.024)	-.319 (.004)	
DV_Action_Thriller (p-value)	-.252 (.078)		
DV_Drama_Romance (p-value)	-.227 (.123)		
DV_Comedy (p-value)	-.229 (.127)		
R^2	.171	.102	.077
F-Value (p-value)	3.084 (.014)	8.955 (.004)	6.584 (.012)
N = 81 Movies			

[a] Constant: No value for standardized parameters.
[b] Measured as coefficient of variation.

5 Summary and Conclusions

The results of the empirical study show that virtual stock markets can provide better predictions than expert judgments. Yet, there is no guarantee that virtual stock markets lead to good results and the empirical study shows that virtual stock markets might also provide some rather weak forecasts. The promising result, however, is that the forecasting error might be further reduced by recognizing the factors that had a negative influence on forecasting accuracy in previous virtual stock markets. Therefore, the repeated use of virtual stock markets allows to develop good indicators for the expected forecast accuracy and the price volatility might serve as a general indicator for a VSM's predictive validity.

Virtual stock markets seem to provide promising opportunities to support the new product development process and the recent publications indicate that the use of virtual stock markets might provide many benefits for companies. As most of these opportunities have gained very little attention in literature, virtual stock markets might be a rich field for further studies in the area of new product development. The availability of a flexible software solution (www.virtualstockmarkets.com) will support research in this area.

6 References

Albers, S., C. Paul, and M. Runte (1998): Virtuelle Communities als Mittel des Absatzes, in: O. Beisheim (Ed.): *Distribution im Aufbruch. Bestandsaufnahmen und Perspektiven*, Munich.

Brockhoff, K. (2000): Produktinnovation, in: Albers, Sönke and Andreas Herrmann (Eds.): *Handbuch Produktmanagement*, 2nd ed., Wiesbaden.

Brockhoff, K. (1999): *Produktpolitik*, 4th ed., Stuttgart et al.

Chan, N.T., E. Dahan, A. Kim, A.W. Lo, and T. Poggio (2002): *Securities Trading of Concepts (STOC)*, Cambridge, MA.

Dahan, E. and J.R. Hauser (2002): The Virtual Customer, *Journal of Product Innovation Management*, 19 (5), 332-53.

Dahan, E. and V.S. Srinivasan (2000): The Predictive Power of Internet-Based Product Concept Testing Using Visual Depiction and Animation, *Journal of Product Innovation Management*, 17 (3), 99-109.

Di Benedetto, A.C. (1999): Identifying the Key Success Factors in New Product Launch, *Journal of Product Innovation Management*, 16 (6), 530-44.

Eimeren, B., H. Gerhard, and B. Frees (2003): ARD/ZDF-Online-Studie 2003. Internetverbreitung in Deutschland: Unerwartet hoher Zuwachs, *Media Perspektiven* (8), 338-58.

Eliashberg, J., J.-J. Jonker, M.S. Sawhney, and B. Wierenga (2000): MOVIEMOD: An Implementable Decision-Support System for Prerelease Market Evaluation of Motion Pictures, *Marketing Science,* 19 (3), 226-43.

Ernst, H., J.H. Soll, and M. Spann (2004): Möglichkeiten der Lead-User-Identifikation in Online-Medien, in: Herstatt, C. and J. Sander (Eds.): *Produktentwicklung mit virtuellen Communities,* Wiesbaden.

Ernst, O. and H. Sattler (2000): Validität multimedialer Conjoint-Analysen. Ein empirischer Vergleich alternativer Produktpräsentationsformen, *Marketing ZFP,* 22 (2), 161-72.

European Information Technology Observatory (2004): *10th Edition,* Frankfurt/M.

Forsythe, R., F. Nelson, G.R. Neumann, and J. Wright (1992): Anatomy of an Experimental Political Stock Market, *American Economic Review,* 82 (5), 1142-61.

Forsythe, R., T.A. Rietz, and T.W. Ross (1999): Wishes, Expectations and Actions: A Survey on Price Formation in Election Stock Markets, *Journal of Economic Behavior & Organization,* 39, 83-110.

Grover, V. and T.H. Davenport (2001): General Perspectives on Knowledge Management: Fostering a Research Agenda, *Journal of Management Information Systems,* 18 (1), 5-21.

Hayek, F.A. von (1945): The Use of Knowledge in Society, *American Economic Review,* 35 (4), 519-530.

Hulse, C. (2003): Pentagon Prepares a Futures Market on Terror Attacks, *The New York Times,* 29. July 2003.

Ortner, G. (2000): Aktienmärkte als Industrielles Vorhersagemodell, *Zeitschrift für Betriebswirtschaft - Ergänzungsheft,* 70 (1), 115-25.

Panten, G., C. Paul, and M. Runte (2001): Virtuelle Communities, in: Albers, S., M. Clement, K. Peters and B. Skiera (Eds.): *Marketing mit Interaktiven Medien. Strategien zum Markterfolg,* 3rd ed., Frankfurt/M.

Plott, C.R. (2000): Markets as Information Gathering Tools, *Southern Economic Journal,* 67 (1), 1-15.

Polk, C., R. Hanson, J. Ledyard, and T. Ishikida (2003): The Policy Analysis Market: An Electronic Commerce Application of a Combinatorial Information Market, *ACM Conference on Electronic Commerce,* San Diego.

Rayport, J. and B.J. Jaworski (2001): *E-Commerce,* New York.

Sawhney, M.S. and J. Eliashberg (1996): A Parsimonious Model for Forecasting Gross Box-Office Revenues of Motion Pictures, *Marketing Science,* 15 (2), 113-31.

Smith, V.L. (1982): Microeconomic Systems as an Experimental Science, *American Economic Review*, 72 (5), 923-55.

Spann, M. (2002): *Virtuelle Börsen als Instrument zur Marktforschung*. Wiesbaden.

Spann, M., H. Ernst, B. Skiera, and J.H. Soll (2003): *Identification of Lead Users via Virtual Stock Markets*, Frankfurt/M.

Spann, M. and B. Skiera (2003a): Einsatzmöglichkeiten virtueller Börsen in der Marktforschung, *Zeitschrift für Betriebswirtschaft*, forthcoming.

Spann, M. and B. Skiera (2003b): Internet-Based Virtual Stock Markets for Business Forecasting, *Management Science*, 49 (10), 1310-26.

Spann, M. and B. Skiera (2003c): Taking Stock of Virtual Markets. How can Internet-Based Virtual Stock Markets be Applied for Business Forecasting and Other Forecasting Issues, *ORMS Today*, 30 (5), 20-24.

Toubia, O., D.I. Simester, J.R. Hauser, and E. Dahan (2003): Fast Polyhedral Adaptive Conjoint Estimation, *Marketing Science*, 22 (3), 273-303.

Urban, G. and E. Von Hippel (1988): Lead User Analyses for the Development of New Industrial Products, *Management Science*, 34 (5), 569-862.

Urban, G.L. and J.R. Hauser (1993): *Design and Marketing of New Products*, 2nd ed.

Wertenbroch, K. and B. Skiera (2002): Measuring Consumer Willingness to Pay at the Point of Purchase, *Journal of Marketing Research*, 39 (May), 228-41.

Wolfers, J. and E. Zitzewitz (2004): Prediction Markets, *Journal of Economic Perspectives*, forthcoming.

Sönke Albers

Forecasting the Diffusion of an Innovation Prior to Launch

Prof. Dr. *Sönke Albers,* Institute of Innovation Research, Christian-Albrechts-University at Kiel.

1 Problem

Companies that want to grow face a fundamental dilemma: They can only increase their current base of sales substantially if they introduce really new products into the market. However, the risk of a market failure also increases with the degree of innovativeness of the product (Booz, Allen & Hamilton Inc. 1982). Really new products are those which are defined as being not only new to the company but also new to the market (Garcia and Calantone 2002). In this case, the pioneer has to develop the whole market and cannot draw inferences from experiences which another competitor has already made. Hence, the pioneer has to forecast the development of the new category in the market. Of course, future entrants may take away market share from the pioneer. In any case, the first and most important task for a pioneer is to forecast the diffusion of his innovative product category (Thomas 1985).

Forecasting is a topic that Klaus Brockhoff (1977) has been made popular in Germany. However, he has also shown the many pitfalls when being involved in a practical forecasting task. Forecasting the diffusion of a really new product category prior to introduction is in particular very difficult. We can not base our forecast on any past data. In addition, we cannot ask people if and when they would like to adopt the new product. It is highly unlikely that people can imagine what the innovative product can do for them. When cellular phones were first introduced to the market, for example, T-Mobile (Deutsche Telekom AG) thought that its market potential was limited to business users that needed a cellular phone because they did not have much time and had to use such a device while on their business trip. Nowadays, with millions of teenage users they have realized that cellular phones are needed also for people who have a lot of free time and need entertainment. While some techniques for information acceleration (Urban et al. 1997) have been developed, there is general agreement that these techniques do not help much when predicting the diffusion of really new categories because the respondents have no clear idea of how the product may evolve and change their life. The only way is a subjective judgment that is based on analogous products or services (Thomas 1985 and Easingwood 1989). However, this leads to the question what the most analogous product or weighted set of analogous products is. Furthermore, we must decide what kind of information we have to look for to be able to develop a suitable forecast of the diffusion. In more detail, a company is interested in forecasting not only the market potential that can be reached in the very end, but also the diffusion speed which decides both on the break-even time and the profitability of an innovative product.

2 Literature review

In the last decades, the Bass model has evolved as the dominant model for explaining and predicting the diffusion of innovations (Bass 1969). It is characterized by an s-shaped penetration of the innovation in the market over a period of time. This shape results from a distinction between innovators and imitators. The first group of people is assumed to adopt an innovative product primarily because of its benefits while the imitators adopt it mostly because of social pressure suggesting that such a product belongs to the usual set of products that a person has to possess (Brockhoff 1999, 121). The Bass model of diffusion can be described mathematically as follows:

$$(1)\quad x_t = \left(p + q \cdot \frac{X_{t-1}}{m}\right)(m - X_{t-1}) \qquad (t = 1,\dots,T)$$

The resulting development of cumulative sales over time (expressed as penetration of market potential) is depicted in Figure 1.

Figure 1: *Different shapes of the Bass diffusion curve*

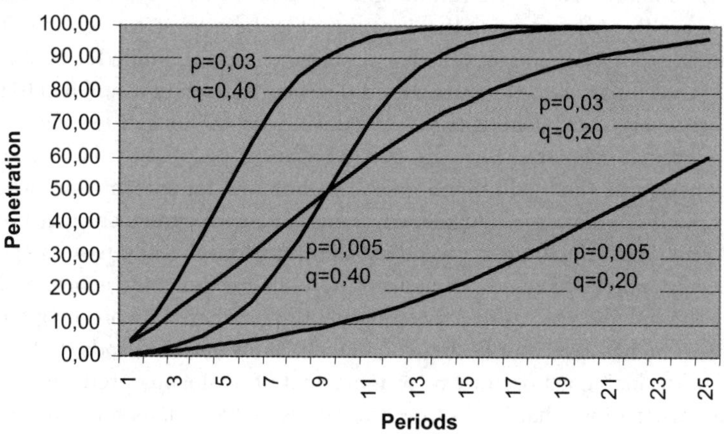

The shape of the function depends on the following parameter values:

x_t: Sales units in period t,

p: innovation coefficient,

q: imitation coefficient,

m: market potential,

X_{t-1}: Cumulative sales units up to period t-1.

Knowing these parameter values one can reconstruct a variety of diffusion curves which is depicted in Figure 1 for different values.

This function has been shown to provide a very good fit to many diffusion patterns of innovations observed in the past (Lilien, Rangaswamy, and Van den Bulte 2000). Therefore, we can try to forecast the diffusion of a really new product prior to its introduction by taking the parameter values of a diffusion of an analogous product that is as similar as possible. This can be done in the following different ways:

1. First of all, the user may select a product which he or she feels is the most similar one in terms of diffusion. There are some articles that support this by providing a rather large number of estimates for a variety of products (e.g. Lilien, Rangaswamy, and Van den Bulte 2000, 300-302). In addition, there is also a large number of articles that have already appeared and give information on the parameter values of specific innovations (for an overview, see Mahajan, Muller, and Wind 2000).

2. Because of the high number of already published articles, a person who is searching for the parameter values of the most analogous product has enormous difficulties in finding all the results. As a consequence, meta-analyses have appeared that provide an analysis of the results of published studies. Sultan, Farley, and Lehmann (1990) have condensed the results derived so far. Their main result is:

   (2) $p = 0.03\,,\ q = 0.38.$

   The meta-analysis also regresses the parameter values p, q, and m on a set of factors that vary over the studies. These may be different product groups or different geographic regions. With this information, we can adjust the overall mean values as given in (2) by product- or region-specific factors. The meta-analysis also accounts for differences in the design of the underlying studies. By adjusting it we can correct possible study biases. Sultan, Farley, and Lehmann (1990) describe in more detail how to proceed in order to get estimates for p and p of analogous products.

3. Another way is not to explain different values of p, q, and m as published in the various articles but to directly derive the parameter values from more than one time series of diffusion data as well as from a larger cross-section of related products. This has been done for the first time in the context of international diffusion (Gatignon, Eliashberg, and Robertson 1989). They have pooled the data for a product across several different countries. While their primary goal was to explain differences in the adoption behavior across countries we may draw inferences from it if we want to introduce the same product in another country. Then we only have to correct country-specific diffusion patterns and can forecast the diffusion of a product in a new country. This has been done in particular in the field of cellular phone services that have been introduced in some countries with a long lag. Many global telecommunication companies like T-Mobile have used similar approaches to forecast the diffusion in the emerging countries in Eastern Europe before enter-

ing the business there. Over time these approaches have become more and more sophisticated. Ihde (1996) has taken the Generalized Bass Model (Bass, Krishnan, and Jain 1994) and estimated the coefficients p, q, and m (relative to the population) of a pooled data base of the diffusion of cellular telephone services in 17 European countries. In addition, he specified a variable market potential depending on the price of the service. All three parameters are specified as functions of variables that may explain differences between the countries. He considered variables like the penetration of information services (telephone, radio, TV, newspapers), the penetration of cars, the urbanization, the amount of air traffic kilometers, and the rate of employed women. His findings are depicted in Table 1:

Table 1: *Diffusion curve parameter values for cellular phone services depending on characteristics of 17 European countries*

Explaining Variables	*Hypothesis*	*Regression Coefficient*	*Significance*
Innovation coefficient p		0.0235	0.00
Imitation coefficient q		0.3047	0.00
Car penetration and urbanization	+	0.3163	0.48
Information services penetration	-	-0.2259	0.39
Competition	+	0.1023	0.09
Rate of employed women	+	1.5583	0.05
Air traffic kilometers	+	-0.0749	0.12
Market potential saturation level m_0		1000	
Scaling parameter b_0		-1.5176	0.00
Price	-	-0.5231	0.00
Exports and Imports	+	0.2357	0.43

Source: Ihde 1996

Later on, this approach was extended to an analysis across 6 different products and 31 different countries (Talukdar, Sudhir, and Ainslie 2002).

4. Pooling data across several entities has also been applied to a different set of products in order to explain differences in the values of the parameter values caused by the presence of certain generic product attributes. Bähr-Sepplfricke (1999) collected data for 20 different consumer durables and telecommunication services. She characterized these products by generic attributes like the product reduces housekeeping time or entertains people or can be bought as a gift. By jointly analyzing these panel data she was able to derive the overall mean parameter values for p, q,

and m as well as their dependence on product attributes. The results are described in Table 2:

Table 2: *Diffusion curve parameter values depending on characteristics of 20 different products*

Explaining Variables of Market Potential	*Coefficient*	*Significance*
Constant Market Potential m	59.1577	0.000
Explaining Variables of Innovation Coefficient	*Coefficient*	*Significance*
Constant Innovation coefficient α_0	0.0097	0.000
Price development	-0.0064	0.000
Continuous Expenses	-0.0029	0.000
Cost Savings	-0.0027	0.000
Time Savings	-0.0029	0.000
Can be bought as gift	-0.0030	0.000
Technical Risk	-0.0030	0.000
Explaining Variables of Imitation Coefficient	*Coefficient*	*Significance*
Constant Imitation coefficient β_0	0.3297	0.000
Price development	0.0637	0.000
Continuous Expenses	0.0811	0.000
Cost Savings	0.0620	0.000
Time Savings	0.0313	0.009
Can be bought as gift	0.0503	0.000
Technical Risk	-0.0208	0.093
Overall Explained Variance	84.86%	

Source: Bähr-Sepplfricke 1999

Now, the idea is to take the innovation which is to be introduced into the market, characterize it by its generic attribute levels, and insert the values into the equation resulting from Table 2 (Bähr-Sepplfricke 1999). Unfortunately, a cross-validation of her analysis did not provide very satisfactory predictions.

5. Instead of searching for the most analogous product, one may combine the forecast of several analogous products. It is a general result that a combination of forecasts outperforms single method forecasts (Meade and Islam 1998). One way may be to select a number of analogous products, to assign weights to the various products and base the forecast on a weighted mean of the parameter values p, q,

and m. A more sophisticated method has been proposed by Bayus (1993) when he attempted to forecast the diffusion of High-Definition Television. First of all, he estimated the parameter values p, q, and m as well as three other parameters characterizing the development of the prices over time. Second, he clustered the products according to these six parameter values. Third, he asked the managers for weights that they would assign to the clusters such that the weighted combination of the clusters would characterize High-Definition TV as best as possible.

These methods rely on sound estimates of p, q, and m. Unfortunately it was established that the parameter values are not independent estimates but depend on the length of the time series and are related to each other (Van den Bulte and Lilien 1997). In particular, they found that with every additional period the m is close to the last value. Only if the time series includes the peak period with the sales maximum then the estimate for m gets stable. But even in this case it is not clear what the ultimate value will be and therefore a validation is often not possible. In addition, Van den Bulte and Lilien (1997) found that p and q depend heavily on the chosen M. On average, an increase of the last observed number of adopters (via more periods of observations) by 10% leads to an increase of m by 5%, a decrease of q by 10%, and an increase of p by 15%. Therefore, it is better to derive information that is independent of each other. If one wants to calculate weighted averages, then it is not clear whether the derived values are still related in a true way to each other. In addition, if one adjusts the parameter values according to the findings of meta-analyses with respect to a product or regional scope then it is also not clear whether the resulting values fit together. In the following, I therefore propose an alternative method that is based on independent information that describes the diffusion of an innovation.

3 Independent descriptors of diffusion processes

As the method of computing weighted averages of p, q, and M for a set of analogous products or the adjustment of these values of meta-analyses lead to values that are no longer related in a proper way to each other, it is necessary to base the inference from analogous products on information that is independent of each other. This should not be done on the basis of parameter values estimated with the help of statistical procedures but on the basis of parameter values that describe the structure of those diffusion curves. Therefore, it is suggested here to take the following descriptors for the analysis:

- Period of peak sales,

- Sales as a percentage of cumulative sales at peak period,
- Sales at peak period.

The period of peak sales has long been recognized as an important descriptor of diffusion processes. The earlier a category or product reaches its peak sales, the earlier the company reaches it break-even point. The peak sales period characterizes the diffusion speed and can be derived by determining the first derivative of the diffusion function (1), setting it to zero and solving it for the period t_{max} (Bass 1969):

$$(3)\quad t_{max} = \ln\left(\frac{q}{p}\right) \Big/ (p+q)$$

Sales as a percentage of cumulative sales at peak period t_{max} describes an important aspect, namely whether the diffusion curve (see Figure 1) represents a steep or flat diffusion. Given a certain level for absolute cumulative sales, the company achieves in the first case very few sales in the very first periods, it is uncertain for a long time whether the product will really take off (Golder and Tellis 1997), and does not reach the break-even point early. The steeper the diffusion is, the more the pioneer must rely on imitators that have to be addressed via mass advertising in an appropriate way. In the case of a rather flat diffusion, the company has higher planning certainty and achieves profitability faster.

With these two descriptors it is possible to fully infer the diffusion speed and the respective diffusion shape of a product. This is plausible because we can rewrite the basic diffusion model by Bass (1) in terms of a normalized market potential of M = 1:

$$(4)\quad f_t = (p + q \cdot F_{t-1})(1 - F_{t-1})$$

f_t : Increase of market potential penetration in period t,

F_t: Market potential penetration in period t.

For estimation purposes, it has been established that it is better to use the formulation in the time domain that means to describe the full diffusion process without knowledge of the previous adoption rate (Srinivasan and Mason 1986):

$$(5)\quad F_t = \frac{1 - e^{-(p+q)\cdot t}}{1 + \left(\frac{q}{p}\right) e^{-(p+q)\cdot t}}$$

Now, the ratio of sales to cumulative sales at peak period is given by:

$$(6)\quad \frac{f_{tmax}}{F_{tmax}} = \frac{F_{tmax} - F_{tmax-1}}{F_{tmax}} = 1 - \frac{F_{tmax-1}}{F_{tmax}}$$

Note that our two descriptors define two equations (5) and (6) with two unknown parameter values p and q. While it is not possible to derive a closed form solution for p and q, the parameter values can easily be derived with the help of EXCEL's "Solver".

The third descriptor can be used to calculate the market potential because a characteristic of the Bass model is that the adoption process is symmetric, and therefore market potential of adopters is twice as high as adoption in the peak period:

(7) $m = 2 \cdot$ Sales at peak period.

Of course, this information is problematic for inference purposes because the market potential varies according to the nature of the product. However, it is possible to express market potential as a percentage of the maximum addressable potential. In the case of household products this is the number of households in an economy.

Finally, it is emphasized that this procedure only provides valid forecasts until the peak period. Especially, when the diffusion is asymmetric (Easingwood, Mahajan, and Muller 1983), then the sales of all periods after peak will be biased. However, firms are mostly interested in learning something about the early periods: Can they expect an early take-off? Is the diffusion steep or flat and what level of penetration can be achieved until that period? Therefore, as my proposed procedure is not influenced by any asymmetric shape I think that it will provide valuable information.

In the following, I will investigate whether the inference procedure works well in terms of achieving a good R^2 until the peak period. If this is the case, the method is worthwhile. The subsequent section provides the data necessary for deriving the information to infer from analogous products.

4 Predictive Validity of the Inference Method

In order to assess the predictive validity of this approach, I use a data set provided by Lilien, Rangaswamy, and Van den Bulte (2000) to compare my inferred prediction of the diffusion curve with the one resulting from the best fitting parameter values as also given there (note that the results refer to a statistical estimation in the adopter domain while my inference proposal is based on the time-domain). However, I only include those data series that show a curve which is approximately s-shaped.

Table 3: *Predictive Validity of Inferred Compared to Estimated Diffusion Curves*

	Explained Variance up to Peak Inferred	*Explained Variance up to Peak Estimated*	*Explained Variance all Periods Inferred*	*Explained Variance all Periods Estimated*
oxygen steel (USA)	87.55%	61.82%	25.20%	48.85%
oxygen steel (Japan)	85.81%	47.63%	25.20%	55.36%
plastic milk contai. 1 gl.	32.53%	33.08%	27.28%	56.51%
plastic milk cont. 0,5 gl.	71.49%	55.36%	38.51%	49.58%
steam & motor	89.96%	0.80%	29.14%	21.16%
Scanning stores (FRG)	95.53%	48.30%	96.34%	47.35%
Scanning stores (DK)	96.83%	-9.42%	-6.61%	-51.82%
CT scanners (50-99)	91.71%	22.47%	10.22%	10.89%
Ultrasound	88.30%	79.96%	46.71%	70.64%
Mammography	95.62%	93.12%	29.32%	90.93%
hybrid corn	95.02%	87.94%	85.00%	88.56%
artificial insemination	93.32%	70.06%	44.63%	52.74%
bale hay	96.40%	11.33%	79.98%	1.22%
bed cover	2.78%	36.90%	-39.71%	23.68%
Blender	71.87%	63.83%	66.39%	48.14%
can opener	16.96%	26.73%	43.53%	50.79%
electric Coffeemaker	9.38%	43.24%	47.77%	69.80%
coffeemaker ADC	98.58%	-93.07%	19.92%	-12.59%
curling irons	33.81%	-59.24%	-23.30%	38.41%
Dishwasher	83.28%	73.46%	62.95%	65.63%
Disposer	52.12%	-32.95%	18.80%	-27.67%
clothes dryer	10.68%	24.75%	-27.99%	31.73%
hair dryers	66.14%	42.32%	53.10%	9.39%
steam iron	74.61%	45.25%	50.26%	77.49%
microwave	75.42%	70.22%	82.08%	77.05%
Refrigerator	24.13%	12.14%	-64.76%	30.46%
Camcorder	54.93%	-22.74%	41.78%	-32.91%
clothes washer	7.42%	16.03%	9.56%	17.83%
home PC	99.74%	-0.88%	-165.52%	5.93%
telephone answering device	36.45%	42.33%	0.14%	52.12%
television BW	99.12%	3.18%	24.15%	72.93%
TV color	78.85%	12.35%	-155.33%	22.71%
VCR	99.53%	-7.15%	89.03%	1.22%
cordless telephone	71.33%	39.87%	-10.11%	19.13%
cellular telephone	54.93%	40.60%	41.78%	44.65%
Radio	29.03%	-3.52%	14.50%	-28.43%

In my proposal, I just focus on the part until the peak of the sales curve has been reached because diffusion may be asymmetric (Easingwood, Mahajan, and Muller 1983) which is hard to predict prior to launch. In addition, managers are first of all interested to learn about the diffusion until peak sales. In the meantime, they may be able to influence sales in a variety of ways such that sales beyond the growth phase are not an important managerial issue. Therefore, I compare the fit of the curve resulting from my inference proposal with the least squares estimates for the period up to peak sales. This is done on the basis of the explained variance R^2 of the sales data. In a second step, just to get insights into the predictive validity of the whole diffusion curve, I computed the respective R^2 for the complete data series. The results are given in Table 3.

As one can see from the results, the predictions are quite accurate. As actual diffusion curves are very often asymmetric my proposal achieves a better fit up to the peak sales period than the curve fitted with least squares in the adopter domain for the whole data series. Only when we consider the whole curve the prediction is frequently less valid. In any case, this method shows a valid way of forecasting a diffusion curve based on just three descriptors.

5 Meta-Analytic Information

From section 4, we can conclude that the proposal to generate the diffusion curve forecast from three descriptors on analogue products produces valid forecasts. As a consequence, this section provides results on the descriptors for a total of 34 products (data provided by Lilien, Rangaswamy, and Van den Bulte 2000). The results are given in Table 4.

Either the user wants to take a weighted combination of products or one can run a meta-analysis on the basis of a characterization of the products according to their generic attributes like in Bähr-Sepplfricke (1999). Let us apply the first case and forecast the sales of VCR by a weighted combination of products. Of course, the determination of appropriate weights is a highly subjective process but is by far better than guessing the penetration directly. Let us assume that the diffusion of VCRs behaves like a combination of 40% TV Color, 30% Radio, and 30% telephone answering device.

If we take the values for the three analogous products from Table 4, the calculation of weighted averages of the descriptors leads to the following values: Sales peak after 6.7 periods, sales as a percentage of cumulative sales up to peak period = 34.33%, and market potential = 83.37. The determination of a weighted mean of market potential is only possible if this is expressed in terms of penetration of population. Based on these estimates the coefficients p and q can be inferred and are reported in the second row of Table 5. On this basis, we can predict the respective diffusion curve with the help of function (5). The fit as measured by the explained variance is $R^2 = 0.83$ for the periods up to sales peak and $R^2 = 0.8416$ for all periods. If we had taken alternatively the weighted average of the three coefficients p, q, and m directly, we obtain the parameter values reported in the first row.

Table 4: *Inferred Coefficients of Diffusion Curves for different Products*

	Peak Sales period	*Ratio Sales to Cumulative at Peak*	*Inferred Market Potential*	*Inferred Innovation Coeff. (p)*	*Inferred Imitation Coeff. (q)*	*Estimated Market Potential*
oxygen steel (USA)	15	22.65%	72.40	0.0005	0.4596	60.5
oxygen steel (Japan)	5	38.24%	61.20	0.0161	0.7521	81.3
plastic milk containers 1 gl	10	23.30%	82.32	0.0044	0.4610	100.0
plastic milk containers ½ gl	23	16.12%	34.24	0.0002	0.3247	28.8
steam & motor	16	23.99%	56.16	0.0002	0.4888	86.7
Scanning stores (FRG)	13	25.94%	19.546	0.0005	0.5292	16702
Scanning stores (DK)	5	50.05%	2.122	0.0047	1.0837	2061
CT scanners (50-99)	7	36.33%	57.80	0.0039	0.7490	57.9
Ultrasound	12	21.88%	122.49	0.0022	0.4378	85.8
Mammography	11	26.09%	88.04	0.0015	0.5293	57.1
hybrid corn	12	38.61%	122.01	0.0000	0.8142	100.0
artificial insemination	7	26.47%	68.00	0.0139	0.4977	73.2
bale hay	10	28.89%	90.00	0.0016	0.5897	92.2
bed cover	19	10.34%	77.40	0.0045	0.1935	72.2
Blender	21	22.78%	51.80	0.0000	0.4637	54.5
can opener	7	17.11%	59.60	0.0384	0.1892	68.0
electric Coffeemaker	11	10.67%	106.80	0.0250	0.1095	100.0
Coffeemak. ADC	4	48.29%	46.80	0.0174	0.9931	32.2
curling irons	4	42.47%	43.80	0.0284	0.8091	29.9
Dishwasher	24	10.47%	59.20	0.0014	0.2059	47.7
Disposer	25	10.97%	63.80	0.0009	0.2175	50.4
clothes dryer	23	9.44%	89.00	0.0026	0.1812	70.1
hair dryers	6	25.36%	56.00	0.0282	0.4230	51.6
steam iron	7	18.23%	72.40	0.0353	0.2361	100.0
microwave	15	20.37%	86.40	0.0009	0.4106	91.6
Refrigerator	17	12.50%	144.00	0.0038	0.2395	99.7
Camcorder	11	30.01%	47.18	0.0007	0.6172	30.5
clothes washer	25	8.53%	133.60	0.0110	0.0330	100.0
home PC (millions of units)	3	60.73%	15.28	0.0235	1.3200	25.8
telephone answering device	7	34.68%	73.48	0.0048	0.7081	69.6
television BW	3	63.26%	52.80	0.0191	1.4173	96.9
TV color	4	42.75%	52.40	0.0278	0.8182	100.0
VCR	7	42.22%	72.00	0.0017	0.8953	76.3
cordless telephone	11	29.94%	62.80	0.0007	0.6154	67.6
cellular telephone	11	30.01%	47.18	0.0007	0.6172	45.1
Radio	10	22.74%	134.55	0.0048	0.4479	100.0

Compared to the method based on descriptors, rather poor fits of R^2 = -14.07% for the periods up to the sales peak and R^2 = 36.18% for the whole time series result. In order to better assess the quality of the proposed method, it is finally compared to the best fitting curve as derived from nonlinear least squares for the periods up to sales peak. The consequences of the poor fit can best be realized by computing the resulting net present values of the three methods up to the sales peak. The proposed method provides a value (14,911) very close to the true value (16,392) while the direct method predicts a net present value that is twice as high as the true value which may lead to completely different managerial conclusions.

Table 5: Evaluation of the proposed inference of diffusion parameters

Method	*Innovation Coeff. p*	*Imitation Coeff. q*	*Market Potential m*	*Explained Variance (to Peak Period)*	*Explained Variance (Time Series)*	*Net Present Value*
Weighted Average of Coefficients	0.0140	0.674	90.88	-14.07%	36.18%	32.694
Weighted Average of Descriptors	0.0063	0.695	83.37	83.00%	84.16%	14.911
Nonlinear Least Squares Estimation	0.0016	0.845	83.36	99.83%	82.21%	15.437

6 Summary

Deriving forecasts for innovative durable product categories prior to launch is a very difficult task. Except for product modifications or new bundles of known attributes, we cannot ask the potential user because he cannot imagine the future benefits of such an innovation. Therefore, companies depend on subjective judgment based on analogous products. In principle, this is possible because the diffusion of nearly all innovations follows an s-shaped trend which can be modeled with the help of the Bass model. Very often, there is no direct analogue so that it may be advisable to combine several semi-analogous products to a weighted average. Unfortunately, the coefficients of the Bass model depend on each other and cannot be combined independently.

Instead of using the innovation and imitation coefficient p and q, it is proposed in this paper to describe the diffusion curve by the period in which sales peak and the ratio of sales in the peak period to cumulative sales up to this point of time. It is shown how the parameter values for p and q can be derived from the two descriptors. Based on the additional assumption that penetration in the peak period is 50%, it is also possible to infer the saturation level for cumulative sales. It has been shown that this method reproduces the respective diffusion curves of 34 products very accurately up to the peak period. This finding also implies that predictions should focus on the diffusion up to the peak period because the rest is of minor interest to companies.

In order to help managers with forecasts this article provides the values of the three descriptors for 34 different product categories. Any person who wants to derive analogous products can use this data base and combine the products such that the weighted average of the descriptors of these products is as similar to the category for which the forecast is needed. This is a method that is easy to apply, uses all the experience of the past and shows high face validity.

7 References

Bähr-Seppelfricke, U. (1999): *Diffusion neuer Produkte: Der Einfluss von Produkteigenschaften*, Wiesbaden.

Bass, F.M. (1969): A New Product Growth Model for Consumer Durables, *Management Science*, 15, 215-227.

Bass, F.M., T.V. Krishnan, and D.C. Jain (1994): Why the Bass Model fits without Decision Variables, *Marketing Science*, 13, 203-223.

Bayus, B.L. (1993): High-Definition Television: Assessing Demand Forecasts for a Next Generation Consumer Durable, *Management Science*, 39, 1319-1333.

Booz, Allen & Hamilton Inc. (Ed.) (1982): *New Products Management for the 1980*, New York.

Brockhoff, K. (1977): *Prognoseverfahren für die Unternehmensplanung*, Wiesbaden.

Brockhoff, K. (1999): *Produktpolitik*, 4th ed., Stuttgart.

Choffray, J.M. and G.L. Lilien (1986): A Decision-Support System for Evaluating Sales Prospects and Launch Strategies for New Products, *Industrial Marketing Management*, 15, 75-85

Easingwood, C.J. (1989): An analogical approach to the long term forecasting of major new product sales, *International Journal of Forecasting*, 5, 69-82.

Easingwood, C.J., V. Mahajan, and E. Muller (1983): A Nonuniform Influence Innovation Diffusion Model of New Product Acceptance, *Marketing Science*, 2, 273-295.

Garcia, R. and R. Calantone (2002): A Critical Look at technological Innovation Typology and Innovativeness Terminology: A Literature Review, *Journal of Product Innovation Management*, 19, 110-132.

Gatignon, H., J. Eliashberg, and T.S. Robertson (1989): Modeling Multinational Diffusion Patterns: An Efficient Methodology, *Marketing Science*, 8, 231-247.

Golder, P.N. and G.J. Tellis (1997): Will It Ever Fly? Modelling the Takeoff of Really New Consumer Durables, *Marketing Science*, 16, 256-270.

Ihde, O.B. (1996): *Internationale Diffusion von Mobilfunk: Erklärung und Prognose länderspezifischer Effekte*, Wiesbaden.

Lilien, G.L., A. Rangaswamy, and C. Van den Bulte (2000): Diffusion Models: Managerial Applications and Software, in: V. Mahajan, E. Muller, and Y. Wind (Eds.): *New-Product Diffusion Models*. Boston et al., 295-311.

Mahajan, V., E. Muller, and Y. Wind (Eds.) (2000): *New-Product Diffusion Models*, Boston et al.

Meade, N. and T. Islam (1998): Technological Forecasting – Model Selection, Model Stability, and Combining Models, *Management Science*, 44, 1115-1130.

Srinivasan, V. and C.H. Mason (1986): Nonlinear Least Squares Estimation of New Product Diffusion Models, *Marketing Science*, 5, 169-178.

Sultan, F., J.U. Farley, and D.R. Lehmann (1990): A Meta-Analysis of Applications of Diffusion Models, *Journal of Marketing Research*, 27, 70-77.

Talukdar, D., K. Sudhir, and A. Ainslie (2002): Investigating New Product Diffusion across Products and Countries, *Marketing Science*, 21, 97-116.

Thomas, R.J. (1985): Estimating Market Growth for New Products: An Analogical Diffusion Model Approach, *Journal of Product Innovation Management*, 2, 45-55.

Urban, G.L., J.R. Hauser, W.J. Qualls, B.D. Weinberg, J.D. Bohlmann, and R.A. Chicos (1997): Information Acceleration: Validation and Lessons From the Field, *Journal of Marketing Research*, 34, 143-153.

Van den Bulte, C. and G.L. Lilien (1997): Bias and Systematic Change in the Parameter Estimates of Macro-Level Diffusion Models, *Marketing Science*, 16, 338-353.

Helmut Schmalen and Heiko Kay Xander

Marketing-Mix and New Product Diffusion

Determination of Optimal Price and Advertising Strategies with a Heterogeneous Diffusion Model

Prof. Dr. Dr. h.c. *Helmut Schmalen* † and Dr. *Heiko Kay Xander*, Department of Marketing, University at Passau.

1 Basics in Diffusion Research

Capturing the diffusion process of an innovation is of great managerial importance –as shown extensively by Brockhoff (1999) for new product development– whereas first applications of the diffusion phenomenon were applied to the case of intangibles, such as information or diseases. In analogy to the spread of diseases, the sales growth of a new product follows an idealized product life cycle which is explained by the buying behavior in the social system: Following this, in diffusion theory two types of buyers are distinguished: innovators and imitators. Innovators purchase whether or not others buy because they are particularly interested in new products, which is why advertising is of great importance to them. Imitators on the other hand buy because others have bought; they are not concerned about whether these purchasers are innovators or imitators. The decisive point of the imitative behavior lies in the internal factors of the diffusion process: imitative behavior is the result of (1) social influence, meaning that every time a new product finds an additional buyer, the *social pressure* working on the remaining potential imitators is increased and the desire to also own the product becomes more intensive. The growing diffusion of a product also gives potential imitators (2) a feeling of security with respect to the product's quality (*experience in the social system*), which also strengthens the desire to acquire it. And, finally, the increasing product penetration offers potential imitators (3) more *information about the innovation*. Positive information about the new product forces the decision to adopt whereas negative information has a reducing impact (see for these explanations Schmalen and Pechtl 1992). The information that a potential adopter needs to make the adoption decision is transmitted by communication processes (Rogers 2003). Besides mass media communication processes multi-stage interpersonal communication flows increase the dynamics of the spread of an innovation. This multi-stage communication model comprises personal communication channels, like word-of-mouth, and impersonal communication channels, like the observation of the behavior of others.

In diffusion research the behavioral assumptions underlying the spread of an innovation are incorporated in mathematical models (Schmalen, Binninger, and Pechtl 1993). Aggregate models on the group level and disaggregate models on the individual level can be differentiated by the level of perspective on the diffusion process. Whereas the first macroeconomic models embrace simplicity and parsimony in order to be analytically solvable, the latter focus on a more detailed representation of the adoption process by including variables like awareness and learning or forget. The different perspectives led in the past to a discussion about the validity of diffusion models. According to this, the complex phenomenon of innovation diffusion is not adequately represented on the highly aggregated macro-level: therefore, models of innovation diffusion need to capture the behavioral assumptions of diffusion theory in a more realistic way. This is feasible for example by considering the social interaction of different types of adopters as in the model of Schmalen (1979) or by integrating social network theory.

Many aggregate diffusion models refer in their formulation to a model that was first presented by Bass (1969, see for an overview Mahajan, Muller and Wind 2000). In discrete time formulation the original Bass Model captures sales at time t (S_t) as

$$(1) \quad S_t = (\hat{a} + \hat{b}\frac{X_{t-1}}{M})(M - X_{t-1}) \qquad \text{with } X_{t-1} = \text{cumulative sales} = \sum_{\tau=1}^{t-1} S_\tau$$

where M is the size of the market potential and $\hat{a}$ denotes the coefficient of innovation and $\hat{b}$ denotes the coefficient of imitation (Bass 1969); in this interpretation the buying probability of a potential adopter is influenced "externally" ($\hat{a}$) and "internally" ($\hat{b}\frac{X_{t-1}}{M}$). S_t is then the expected value of the total demand at time t. According to this interpretation every buyer is both innovative and imitative (Jeuland 1981). Originally, the Bass Model was used as a forecasting model to predict the penetration trajectory of a new product by providing estimates of sales and of future market development. The extended General Bass Model explicitly captures marketing-covariates (Bass, Krishnan, and Jain 1994). In the literature the interpretation of the Bass Model is widely discussed (see the previous work of Schmalen 1989 or Schmalen and Binninger 1994). One reason for the discussion of the Bass Model is its remaining market potential ($M-X_{t-1}$), which has a homogeneous structure in the original formulation. This homogeneous market potential does not correspond to empirical results where a structured market demand carries out the diffusion process, as documented in a study by Pechtl (1991): Here, for the case of adoption and diffusion of professional software solutions by manufacturers, 5 different types of adopters could be identified that differed in the way they react to social influence. As the parsimonious formulation of the Bass Model is in spite of its user-friendliness not able to explicitly differentiate different types of adopters in a market (see also van den Bulte 2002) we present a model that considers heterogeneity of the demand and integrates marketing-mix variables. This model first was introduced by Schmalen in 1979 therefore representing an early contribution to the discussion of the Bass Model and was extended continuously by anticipating and integrating actual developments in diffusion research (see Schmalen and Xander 2002).

2 A Marketing-Mix Diffusion Model

2.1 Heterogeneity of the Demand

Considering the innovator-imitator dichotomy of the diffusion theory, the spread of a new product is modeled as a multiple stage process within a structured demand. We call this extension of the Bass Diffusion Model the modified Diffusion Model. In this model the total market potential M for a new product is divided into several segments (M_i). In each period, of the segment specific remaining market potential (M_i-X_{it-1}), a fraction h_{it} ($h_{it} = a_i + b_i \frac{X_{t-1}}{M}$) buys the product. As total sales at point in time t we get:

$$(2) \qquad S_{t,\,Modified} = (a_1 + b_1 \frac{X_{t-1}}{M})(M_1 - X_{1t-1}) + (a_2 + b_2 \frac{X_{t-1}}{M})(M_2 - X_{2t-1}) +$$

$$\ldots \qquad + (a_i + b_i \frac{X_{t-1}}{M})(M_i - X_{it-1}) + \ldots + (a_n + b_n \frac{X_{t-1}}{M})(M_n - X_{nt-1})$$

$$\Rightarrow \qquad S_{t,\,Modified} = \sum_i^n S_{it} = \sum_i^n (a_i + b_i \frac{X_{t-1}}{M})(M_i - X_{it-1})$$

with a_i, b_i = segment-specific coefficients of innovation, imitation

M_i= market potential of segment i ($M_i = \alpha_i \cdot M$ with $0<\alpha_i \leq 1$)

M = total market potential ($M = \sum_i^n M_i$)

X_{it-1}= cumulative sales in segment i ($X_{t-1} = \sum_i^n X_{it-1}$)

Adopters in segment i are both innovative (a_i) as well as imitative ($b_i \frac{X_{t-1}}{M}$). Therefore the model captures multiple homogeneous market segments which differ in level of the absolute amount of the coefficients. In one segment i dominates innovative behavior ($a_i > a_{i+1}$), in another segment (i+1) dominates imitative behavior ($b_i < b_{i+1}$). In each period, each segment possesses –in contrast to Bass- its own segment-specific purchasing probability ($a_i + b_i \frac{X_{t-1}}{M}$) and its own remaining market potential (M_i-X_{it-1}). The imitative segment members are influenced by the perception of the aggregated product penetration rate and not by segment-specific penetration rates. In the further investigation, a simplified case is considered with i=1,2; b_1=0; a_2=0 in order to capture the extreme values of the underlying behavioral assumptions. In this case it is

$$(3) \qquad S_{t,\,Modified} = a_1 (M_1 - X_{1t-1}) + b_2 \frac{X_{t-1}}{M}(M_2 - X_{2t-1})$$

In a direct comparison of (3) to the Bass Model (4, below), we now have the dichotomy of innovators and imitators, as intended in the theory (Schmalen 1989):

$$(4) \qquad S_{t,\,Bass} = \hat{a} (M - X_{t-1}) + \hat{b} \frac{X_{t-1}}{M}(M - X_{t-1})$$

For a numerical analysis we specify the models with comparable values of the parameters to get an appropriate solution for the life cycle of a new product. We choose for the Bass Model [modified Diffusion Model] a market potential of M=100.000 [innovators market potential of M_1=20.000, imitators market potential of M_2=80.000]. We set the coefficient of innovation as $\hat{a}$ $[a_1] = 0.025$ and the coefficient of imitation as $\hat{b}$ $[b_2] = 0{,}3$. These are the values determined for black and white TV sets by Bass (1969), where the value for the imitation coefficient also corresponds to an empirical solution depicted by a meta-analysis of Sultan, Farley, and Lehmann (1990).

Figure 1: *Numerical Example of the Bass Model and the Modified Diffusion Model*

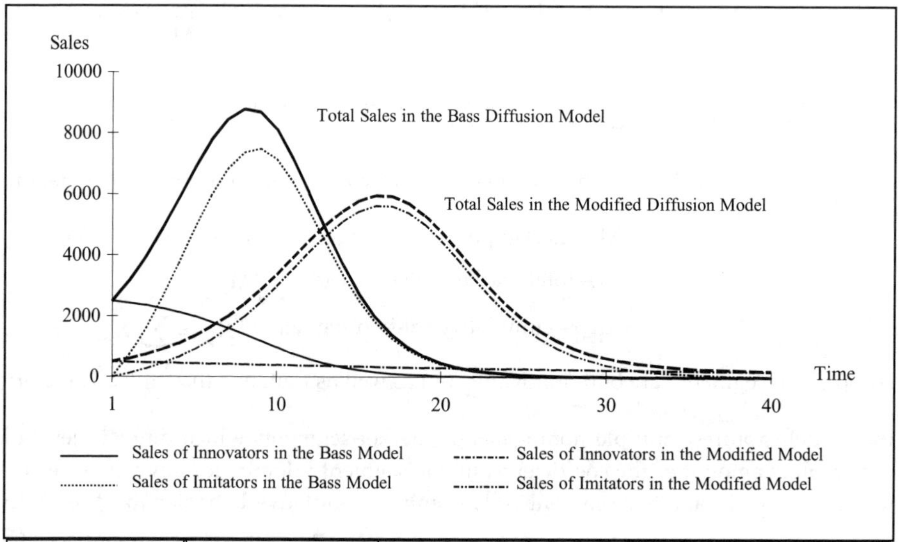

Bass:	$\hat{a} = 0.025$	$\hat{b} = 0.3$	M = 100.000	
Modified:	$a_1 = 0.025$	$b_2 = 0.3$	$M_1 = 20.000$	$M_2 = 80.000$

As Figure 1 shows, innovators and imitators together carry the life cycle of a new product. Owing to their special pattern of behavior, innovators make up the larger part of demand at the beginning of the product life cycle, while imitators come to represent the larger part during later stages. This is consistent with the described communication model above. In the Bass Model, the diffusion process runs faster because at the beginning, the innovators are recruited from the total market potential, which is much bigger than that for the innovator segment in the modified model. The modified model forms a typical product life cycle, as is the case for many empirical data, whereas the Bass Model captures primarily left skewed product life cycles.

2.2 Integration of Marketing-Mix Variables

The integration of marketing-mix variables in diffusion models has a long tradition (see the overview in Krishnan, Bass, and Jain 1999). Here, the adopters differ in the manner they react to various stimuli. According to the results of communication and diffusion research, innovators can be incited to buy a product first of all because of a high degree of novelty (N); secondly, due to extensive advertising (W_t); and finally, due to a favorable price (P_t). Imitators on the other hand are influenced by the degree of product diffusion among innovators and imitators (Y_t, analogous to the Bass model); and secondly, by a favorable price (P_t); while advertisement (W_t) does not have much influence. The purchasing probability of the innovators (h_{1t}) and the imitators (h_{2t}) depends on the marketing instruments presented. For the specification of the purchasing probability we have chosen a Cobb-Douglas function in order to assess the marketing-mix interaction of each instrument. In various studies, different formulations of the price-response functions were also tested (see Schmalen 1995).

(5 a) $$h_{1t} = h_{1t}(N, W_t, P_t) \quad \text{with } 0 < h_{1t} \leq 1$$

(5 b) $$h_{2t} = h_{2t}(Y_t, P_t, W_t) \quad \text{with } 0 < h_{2t} \leq 1$$

In order to assess competitive effects the model here is also extended to the case of a dynamic oligopoly and also considers the cost situation of a firm: The product development costs (E) depend on the degree of newness (N) and the development time (π) (optimal product development strategies are presented in Schmalen 1980). The objective function which is to be maximized addresses discounted profits (G) over a finite time horizon T. We show the equation of the pioneer in the monopoly situation:

(6) $$G = \sum_{t=1}^{T} \left[(P_t - k_t)\cdot S_t - W_t\right]\cdot(1+i)^{-t} - E(N,\pi) \quad \rightarrow \max!$$

with i discounting rate ($i < 1$)
k_t variable costs, that follow an experience curve

As a result of the model's complexity, analytical solutions are not feasible. Therefore, a numerical solution is derived with the help of a heuristic optimization procedure. The optimization procedure is based on an evolutionary algorithm which incorporates the principles of biological evolution: mutation and selection (see for this "mutation method" Xander 2002). The aim of the simulation experiment is then to find profitable courses of action while limiting the scope of search efforts. For this reason, the price and advertising search takes place within the upper and lower limits of a given price class ('$P_t \leq P_t \leq P_t$') and within given upper and lower budgetary limits of advertising ('$W_t \leq W_t \leq W_t$'). The results at the end of the optimization are listed in Figure 2.

Figure 2: *Optimal Price and Advertising Strategies in the Case of a Monopoly*

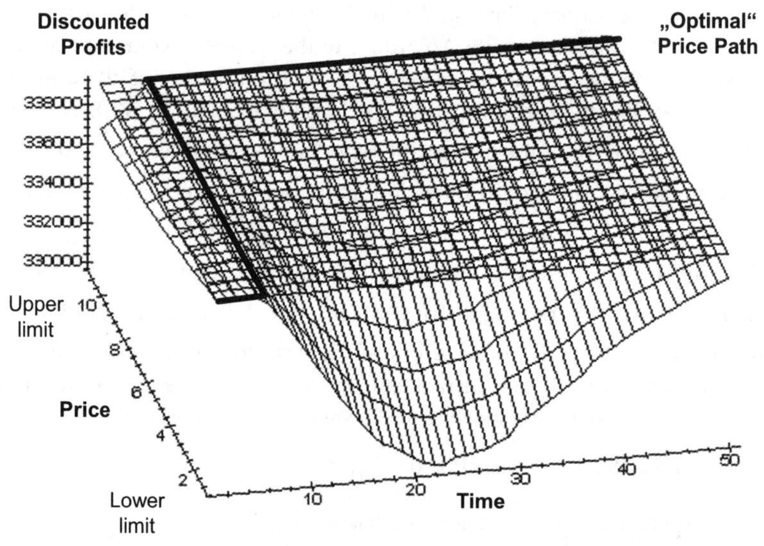

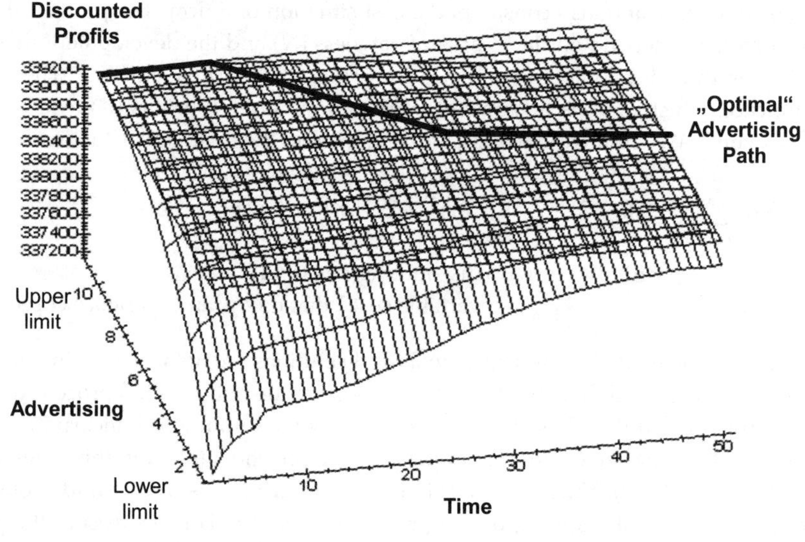

Source: Xander (2003)

3 Optimal Price and Advertising Strategy

3.1 Competitive Effects in a dynamic Duopoly

For the analysis of optimal marketing-mix strategies in a dynamic duopoly we willtest the following hypotheses of a competitor's reactions (see also Schmalen 1982):

1. "Linked competition": the competitor always sets his price 20% below and his advertising budget 20% above the pioneer's ($P_t^2 = P_t^1 \cdot (1-0,2)$; $W_t^2 = W_t^1 \cdot (1+0,2)$).

2. "Informed competition": The pioneer expects the competitor to gain knowledge of his price and advertising strategies and tries to adjust to them in an optimal way. A firm's best decision depends then on the decision of its competitor (($P_t^1 \mid P_t^2$)= opt).

Figure 3: *Marketing-Mix in a Dynamic Duopoly in the case of Linked competition*

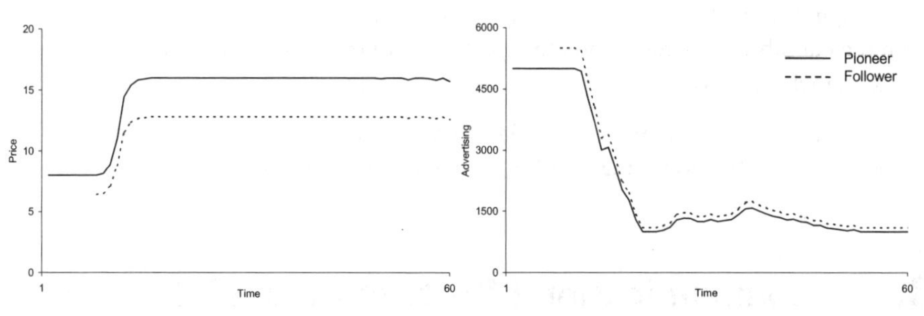

Figure 4: *Marketing-Mix in a Dynamic Duopoly in the case of informed competition*

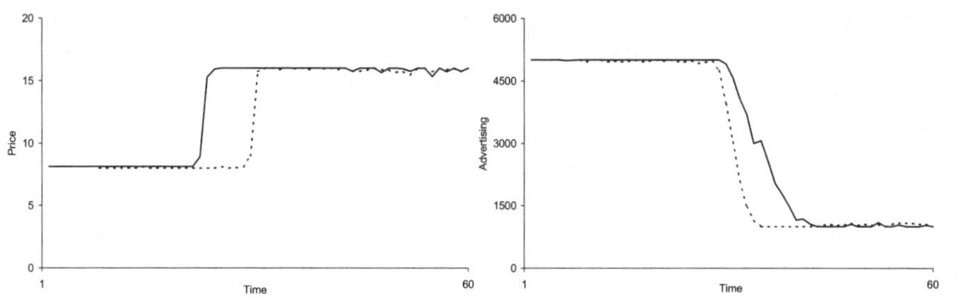

The pioneer's "optimal" mix strategy in the case of linked competition is depicted in Figure 3. A low introductory price and a high introductory advertising budget are recommended for the pioneer. Soon after the competitor enters the market, the price should be raised and advertising be reduced. Introductory pricing and advertising lead to rapid sales growth in the market: large-scale advertising assures extensive purchases by -advertising sensitive- innovators. This and the low price soon stimulate strong demand on the part of –price sensitive- imitators. When the competitor enters the market, the pioneer changes his strategy completely: he "forces" the linked competitor to raise his price and cut his advertising budget. Later on, the pioneer increases his advertising budget again and causes the linked competitor to do the same. The pioneer tries to exploit the competitor.

The assumption of a 20% more efficient competitor seems pessimistic at first from the pioneer's point of view, but in practice, the hypothesis of linked competition is certainly of some empirical relevance (especially in advertising, where competitors often serve as an orientation). The optimal strategy in the case of informed competition (Figure 4) recommends an aggressive market entry for the pioneer and the follower. The reciprocal optimization of both competitors leads to a situation where the mutation method does not find any better solution for either of them. The model is in a stable equilibrium. In this situation, no firm has an incentive to unilaterally deviate from the equilibrium, which leads to a prisoner's dilemma that only can be resolved if both end their aggressive mix-phase sooner (Schmalen 1992).

Further extensions of the model include a variable market potential, the integration of replacement purchases (Schmalen 1987) or the market expansion to different countries.

3.2 Communication Effects in Global Diffusion

In an early extension, the simulation model was used to examine export marketing-mix strategies in the case of two related countries (Sartorius 1983). The home market, where the pioneer first introduces a new product, and the foreign market, where he exports the innovation after a certain period of time. In both markets, the pioneer has to deal with competition. In this study, the two markets are related due to an international communication effect that links the imitators of the markets: In this case, prior adoption of a new product in one country (the home market) affects adoption in other countries (the foreign markets) and vice versa (Table 1). Therefore the buying probability of the imitators depends in the model of Sartorius not only on the home penetration rate but also on the penetration rate of the innovation in the foreign country. This approach is later on often used in the context of international diffusion research.

Table 1: *Demand Functions in Sartorius (1983)*

	Demand home market		Demand foreign market	
Innovators	$S_{1t}^{h}=h_{1t}^{h}\cdot\left(M_{1}^{h}-X_{1t-1}^{h}\right)$	$X_{1t-1}^{h}=\sum_{\tau=1}^{t-1} S_{1\tau}^{h}$	$S_{1t}^{f}=h_{1t}^{f}\cdot\left(M_{1}^{f}-X_{1t-1}^{f}\right)$	$X_{1t-1}^{f}=\sum_{\tau=1}^{t-1} S_{1\tau}^{f}$
Imitators	$S_{2t}^{h}=h_{2t}^{h}\cdot\left(M_{2}^{h}-X_{2t-1}^{h}\right)$	$X_{2t-1}^{h}=\sum_{\tau=1}^{t-1} S_{2\tau}^{h}$	$S_{2t}^{f}=h_{2t}^{f}\cdot\left(M_{2}^{f}-X_{2t-1}^{f}\right)$	$X_{2t-1}^{f}=\sum_{\tau=1}^{t-1} S_{2\tau}^{f}$

Communication effect across countries

To determine an appropriate introduction strategy the following situations of international relationship are distinguished.

1. No communication effect
2. symmetric communication effect

In the first case, where an inter-country communication effect between the imitators is missing, the optimal introductory strategy on the home market is comparable to that in the duopoly case but with a longer advertising period (Figure 5). As we assumed a strong and aggressive competitor, the pioneer is forced to uphold advertising longer. In the foreign country, the pioneer reduces advertising very soon. Because he has no support from a spill-over effect from the home country a prolongation of the high budget advertising phase against the aggressive competitor is not reasonable, as the diffusion process occurs very quickly. Optimal pricing recommends a high price strategy in the foreign market: in the absence of an international communication effect, the loss on the export market is minimized by a high price and low advertisement.

Figure 5: *Marketing-Mix in Cross Country Diffusion without Communication Effect*

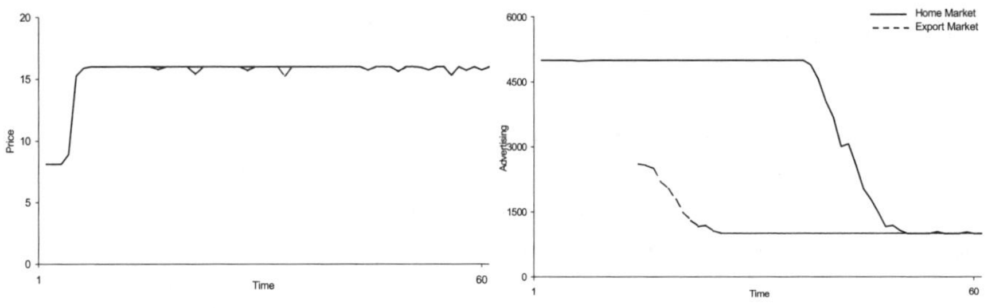

Figure 6: *Marketing-Mix in cross country diffusion with symmetric communication*

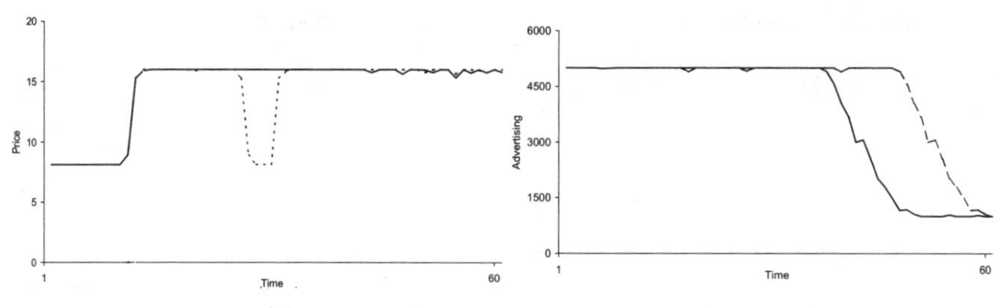

In the case of symmetric communication (Figure 6), the home market penetration price strategy is extended because in an interconnected market situation, the spill-over effect of the home market (high product penetration rate) serves to stimulate the purchases on the export market. In this situation, a positive return on the export market is achieved due to the aggressive marketing strategy, which recommends cutting the price for a short period of time when the competitor enters the foreign market. Advertising on the export market is extended as the pioneer deals with a strong competitor.

Table 2: *Demand Functions in Sein Min (1990)*

	Demand in industrial country		Demand in less developed country	
Innovators	$S^h_{1t} = h^h_{1t} \cdot \left(M^h_1 - X^h_{1t-1}\right)$	$X^h_{1t-1} = \sum_{\tau=1}^{t-1} S^h_{1\tau}$	$S^d_{1t} = h^d_{1t} \cdot \left(M^d_1 - X^d_{1t-1}\right)$	$X^d_{1t-1} = \sum_{\tau=1}^{t-1} S^d_{1\tau}$
Imitators	$S^h_{2t} = h^h_{2t} \cdot \left(M^h_2 - X^h_{2t-1}\right)$	$X^h_{2t-1} = \sum_{\tau=1}^{t-1} S^h_{2\tau}$	$S^d_{2t} = h^d_{2t} \cdot \left(M^d_2 - X^d_{2t-1}\right)$	$X^d_{2t-1} = \sum_{\tau=1}^{t-1} S^d_{2\tau}$
International imitators in less developed country:			$S^d_{3t} = h^d_{2t} \cdot \left(M^d_3 - X^d_{3t-1}\right)$	$X^d_{3t-1} = \sum_{\tau=1}^{t-1} S^d_{3\tau}$

Communication across countries

The simulation model was extended in a similar way by Sein Min (1990) for the case of optimal export marketing-mix strategies in less developed countries. In less developed countries, the market segment of international imitators plays an important role in the diffusion of new products (Table 2). This market segment stimulates diffusion from industrial to less developed countries due to open mindedness and membership in the modern sector of a society. Innovation diffusion then follows a trickle-down process – initiated by the international imitators.

3.3 Diffusion Effects through Repeat Purchases

In their traditional formulation diffusion models only address first time purchases of durables in order to eliminate the problem of repeat purchases. In this context it is important to note that for an ongoing diffusion process, first time purchases are not sufficient to build up a stable product life cycle. Binninger (1993) extended the modified diffusion model by integrating repeat purchases and analyzed their impact on R&D and optimal marketing-mix strategies in the integrated product life cycle concept. Repeat purchases appear in the Binninger model when the product life time (υ) is over and the product has to be replaced. The replacement of products does not necessarily occur for all previous buyers - instead only a fraction c of the previous first time buyers S_t^F repurchase. Repeat purchases S_t^R in a point of time t can –differentiating innovators S_{1t}^R and imitators S_{2t}^R - then be written as:

$$S_{1t}^R = c_1 \cdot S_{1t-\upsilon_1}^F \quad , \text{for } t > \upsilon_1 \qquad \text{innovators repurchases}$$

$$S_{2t}^R = c_2 \cdot S_{2t-\upsilon_2}^F \quad , \text{for } t > \upsilon_2 \qquad \text{imitators repurchases}$$

The repeat purchase rate does not have to be constant over time – instead it can depend on the marketing-mix: $c_1 = h_{1t}^R$ and $c_2 = h_{2t}^R$ (Table 3). Then, the total product penetration rate influences first and repeat purchases of the imitators and -in the simulated cases under consideration (see below)- also the purchasing probability of the innovators. By derivation from the simulation analyses, we present optimal strategies for:

1. Snob effect vs. bandwagon effect (Innovators react negatively vs. positively to raising product diffusion)
2. Different replacement cycles for innovators (υ_1=5; 10) and imitators (υ_2=10; 5)

Table 3: Demand Functions in Binninger (1993)

	Initial purchases S_t^F	for $t \le \upsilon_1, \upsilon_2$	Repeat purchases S_t^R	for $t > \upsilon_1, \upsilon_2$
Innovators	$S_{1t}^F = h_{1t}^F \cdot \left(M_1 - X_{1t-1}^F\right)$	$X_{1t-1}^F = \sum_{\tau=1}^{t-1} S_{1\tau}^F$	$S_{1t}^R = h_{1t}^R \cdot S_{1t-\upsilon_1}^F$	$X_{1t-1} = \sum_{\tau=1}^{t-1} S_{1\tau} - S_{1\tau-\upsilon_1}$
Imitators	$S_{2t}^F = h_{2t}^F \cdot \left(M_2 - X_{2t-1}^F\right)$	$X_{2t-1}^F = \sum_{\tau=1}^{t-1} S_{2\tau}^F$	$S_{2t}^R = h_{2t}^R \cdot S_{2t-\upsilon_2}^F$	$X_{2t-1} = \sum_{\tau=1}^{t-1} S_{2\tau} - S_{2\tau-\upsilon_2}$

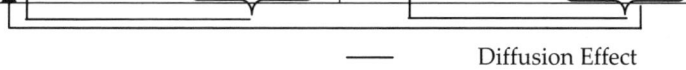

—— Diffusion Effect

In the case where the innovators behave in a snobbish way (S), they have a high purchasing probability when the diffusion rate is still low (Figure 7). In comparison to the "normal" monopoly case (solid line in Figure 9), a high pricing strategy at the beginning of the product life cycle in combination with a reduced advertising strategy is recommended. If the innovators are oriented to product diffusion (bandwagon effect, B) which makes the innovators' demand depend on the penetration rate, initial sales start very slowly so a longer price penetration phase is necessary. In order to stimulate the diffusion process, the high budget advertising phase is extended to the end of the planning horizon because replacement purchases lead to ongoing sales growth (see also Schmalen, Binninger, and Pechtl 1993). Similar results are obtained when looking at differentiated replacement cycle times for innovators and imitators (Figure 8). A longer innovator replacement cycle ($\upsilon_1=10$; $\upsilon_2=5$) leads to a less aggressive marketing strategy than a longer imitator replacement cycle ($\upsilon_1=5$; $\upsilon_2=10$). In the latter case, an early loss of innovator repurchases therefore demands the support of a low penetration price strategy and high volume advertising budget.

Figure 7: Marketing-Mix with repeat purchases and snob (S) vs. bandwagon (B) effects

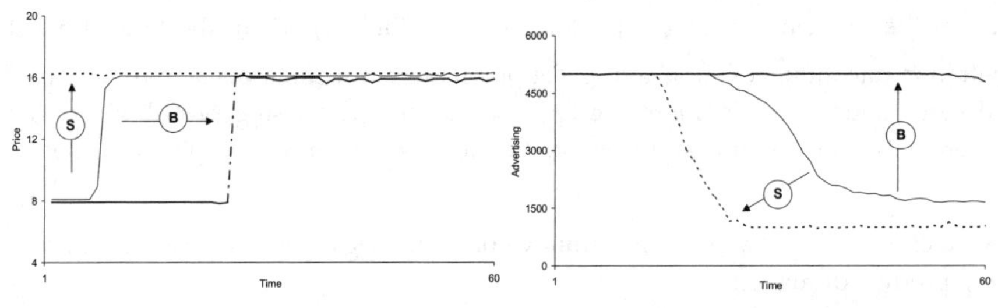

Figure 8: Marketing-Mix with repeat purchases and different replacement cycle times

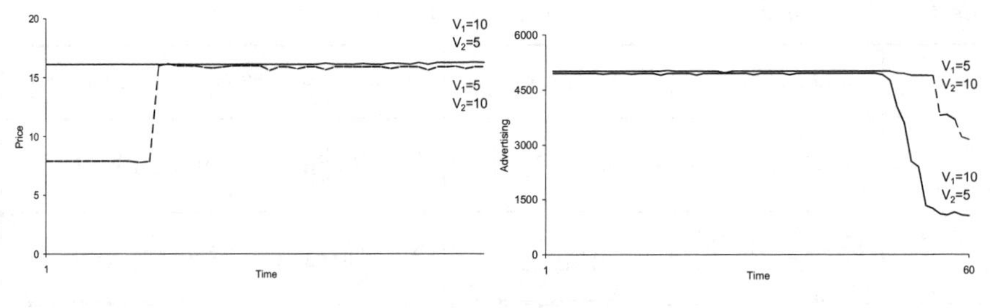

3.4 Substitution Effects in Multi-Product Diffusion

The recent extension of the modified diffusion model by Xander (2003) captures multi-product diffusion. As new products are neither introduced into a vacuum nor do they exist in isolation, the relationship to other existing products has to be considered. Products can have a complementary or a substitutive relationship to other goods, whereas the first enhances and the latter delays the diffusion of an innovation. In this model extension, substitution effects and market expansion effects occur (see also Mahajan, Sharma, and Buzzell 1993). Introduction of a new product expands the existing market; at the same time substitution effects between the products lead to a decrease of the future demand. When considering an existing product A in a given market, the following is valid: with the introduction of a differentiated product B, an expansion effect arises through activation of the innovator market potential of B (Table 4). Initial sales in this innovator segment (S_{3t}) lead at market introduction time z^B not only to an initial diffusion effect but also to a substitution effect in the imitator's remaining market potential. Alternatives A and B compete against the remaining market potential of the imitators: $(M_2 - X^A_{2t-1} - X^B_{2t-1})$. Whereas in the former model formulations, competition occurred within the same product class and concerned brands, the approach presented here considers different product features and qualities of competing product classes. For total sales of alternative A and alternative B we get:

$$S^A_t = S_{1t} + S^A_{2t} \quad \text{and} \quad S^B_t = S_{3t} + S^B_{2t}$$

For the depiction of optimal marketing-mix strategies in the multi-product situation, different cases will be analyzed:

1. Products are offered by independent producers, given quality B > quality A
2. Products are offered by independent producers, given quality A > quality B

Table 4: Demand Functions in Xander (2003)

	Demand Product A		Demand Product B (for t>z^B)	
Innovators	$S_{1t} = h_{1t} \cdot (M_1 - X_{1t-1})$	$X_{1t-1} = \sum_{\tau=1}^{t-1} S_{1\tau}$	$S_{3t} = h_{3t} \cdot (M_3 - X_{3t-1})$	$X_{3t-1} = \sum_{\tau=z^B}^{t-1} S_{3\tau}$
Imitators	$S^A_{2t} = h^A_{2t} \cdot (M_2 - X^A_{2t-1} - X^B_{2t-1})$	$X^A_{2t-1} = \sum_{\tau=1}^{t-1} S^A_{2\tau}$	$S^B_{2t} = h^B_{2t} \cdot (M_2 - X^A_{2t-1} - X^B_{2t-1})$	$X^B_{2t-1} = \sum_{\tau=z^B}^{t-1} S^B_{2\tau}$

--- Substitution Effect —— Diffusion Effect

In the case that the later introduced product B is of a higher quality, an intensive penetration phase for the first product is recommended that lasts over the market entry time of B (Figure 9). Due to the fact of the superior standard of the second product, here a high price strategy is optimal because the innovators of product B are attracted by the high quality and their purchase reinforce the imitators' demand for B. Both price strategies are combined with the –already known- introductory advertising strategy, which recommends for B a longer high level advertising phase. In the opposite case (Figure 10), where A has the higher quality, the same explanation as in the first case is valid: innovators are attracted by superior quality which is why a high price is possible. But for the later introduced product B, a price cut does not seem to be the right strategy; instead, the high price remains optimal even with the lower quality. The high price strategy is therefore also recommended in the low quality situation. Obviously the differentiation of the later introduced product demands a continuous high price in order to reduce losses resulting from the shorter market phase.

This model situation was also applied to the case of optimal marketing-mix strategies for successive generations of an integrated monopolist (Schmalen and Xander 2002).

Figure 9: Marketing-Mix for independent producers, given quality B > quality A

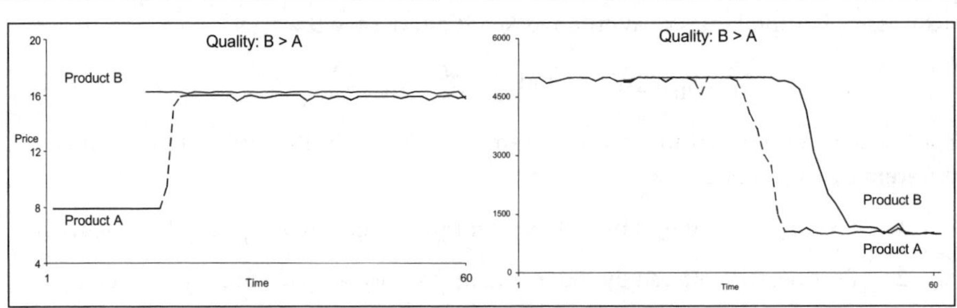

Figure 10: Marketing-Mix for independent producers, given quality B < quality A

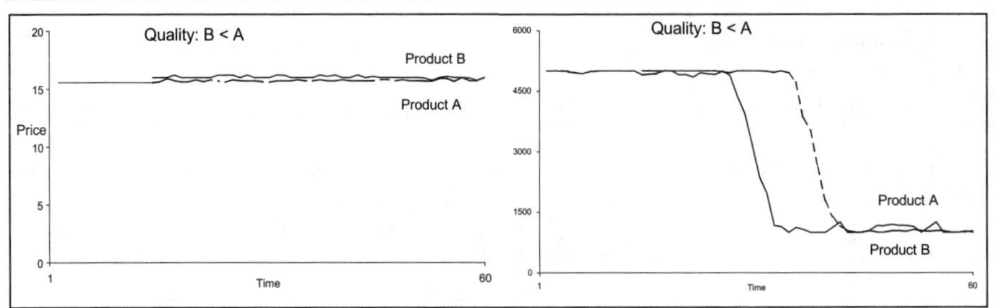

4 Conclusion

With the model presented here, we show that the explicit differentiation between imitators and innovators matters not only for descriptive (length and magnitude of the product life cycle) and methodological purposes (interpretation of innovator and imitator dichotomy), but also for normative purposes (optimal marketing-mix strategies). The models results are theoretical results, meaning that they depend on the range of the values considered. Nevertheless, the model's sensitivity is a proof of its capability to adapt very well to different market scenarios, so that the use of a simulation model provides rich insights into the complex market phenomenon of innovation diffusion. The model and the relevant extensions represent nearly 25 years of diffusion research of the Chair of Marketing at the University of Passau, Germany.

5 References

Bass, F.M. (1969): A New Product Growth Model for Consumer Durables, *Management Science*, 15 (5), 215-227.

Bass, F.M., T.V. Krishnan, and D.C. Jain (1994): Why the Bass Model fits without decision variables, *Marketing Science*, 13 (3), 203-223.

Binninger, F.-M. (1993): *F&E- und Marketingmanagement im integrierten Produktlebenszyklus. Eine computergestützte Simulationsanalyse*, Regensburg.

Brockhoff, K. (1999): *Produktpolitik*, 3rd ed., Stuttgart, New York.

Jeuland, A.P. (1981): *Parsimonious Models of Diffusion of innovation. Part B: incorporating the variable of price*, Working Paper University of Chicago, Chicago.

Krishnan, T.V., F.M. Bass, and D.C. Jain (1999): Optimal Pricing Strategy for New Products, *Management Science*, 45 (12), 1650-1663.

Mahajan, V., S. Sharma, and R. Buzzell (1993): Assessing the Impact of Competitive Entry on Market Expansion and Incumbent Sales, *Journal of Marketing*, 57, 39-52.

Mahajan, V., E. Muller and Y. Wind (Eds.) (2000): *New-Product Diffusion Models*, Boston.

Pechtl, H. (1991): *Innovatoren und Imitatoren im Adoptionsprozess von technischen Neuerungen*, Bergisch-Gladbach, Köln.

Rogers, E. (2003): *Diffusion of Innovations*, 5th ed., London.

Sartorius, B. (1983): *Exportmarketing für neuartige Gebrauchsgüter auf verbundenen Märkten. Eine computergestützte Simulationsanalyse*, Passau.

Schmalen, H. (1979): *Marketing-Mix für neuartige Gebrauchsgüter*, Wiesbaden.

Schmalen, H. (1980): Optimale Entwicklungs- und Lizenzpolitik, *Zeitschrift für Betriebswirtschaft*, 50 (10), 1077-1103.

Schmalen, H. (1982): Optimal Price and Advertising Policy for New Products, *Journal of Business Research*, 10 (1), 17-30.

Schmalen, H. (1987): *Modelle absatzwirtschaftlicher Diffusionsforschung: Darstellung und computergestützte Analyse*, Vortrag vor der Kommission Marketing, Schloss Gracht.

Schmalen, H. (1989): Das Bass Modell zur Diffusionsforschung, *Zeitschrift für Betriebswirtschaft*, 41 (3), 210-226.

Schmalen, H. (1992): *Kommunikationspolitik: Werbeplanung*, 2nd ed., Stuttgart.

Schmalen, H. (1995): *Preispolitik*, 2nd ed., Stuttgart, Jena.

Schmalen, H. and F.-M. Binninger (1994): Ist die klassische Diffusionsmodellierung wirklich am Ende?, *Marketing ZFP*, 16 (1), 5-11.

Schmalen, H. and H. Pechtl (1992): *Technische Neuerungen in Kleinbetrieben. Management von Forschung, Entwicklung und Innovation*, Stuttgart.

Schmalen, H. and H. Xander (2002): Produkteinführung und Diffusion, in: Albers, S. and A. Herrmann (Eds.): *Handbuch Produktmanagement*, 2nd ed., Wiesbaden, 441-468.

Schmalen, H., F.-M. Binninger, and H. Pechtl (1993): Diffusionsmodelle als Entscheidungshilfe zur Planung absatzpolitischer Maßnahmen bei Neuprodukteinführungen, *Die Betriebswirtschaft*, 53 (4), 513-527.

Sein M. (1990): *Exportmarketing im Wirtschaftsverkehr zwischen Industrie- und Entwicklungsländern*, Passau.

Sultan, F., J. Farley, and D. Lehmann (1990): A Meta-Analysis of Applications of Diffusion Models, *Journal of Marketing Research*, 27, 70-77.

van den Bulte, C. (2002): *The Bass Diffusion Model is not a Mixture of Innovators and Imitators*, Working Paper The Wharton School, University of Pennsylvania.

Xander, H. (2002): *Evolutionäre Optimierung mit MUTABA (mutativ-biologischer Algorithmus)*, Diskussionspaper No. 5, Rechts- und Staatswissenschaftlichen Fakultät, Ernst-Moritz-Arndt University, Greifswald.

Xander, H. (2003): *Marketing-Mix Strategien in umweltfreundlich-differenzierten Märkten. Simulation und Optimierung eines lebenszyklusübergreifenden Diffusionsmodells*, Wiesbaden.

Ursula Weisenfeld

Risk, Information and the Diffusion of Innovations

The Example of Genetically Modified Food

Prof. Dr. *Ursula Weisenfeld*, Department of Marketing and Technology Management, University at Lüneburg.

1 Introduction

In September 1998 Nestlé introduced the snack 'Butterfinger' into the German market only to withdraw about a year later. The product was labeled as containing genetically modified (GM) maize. This GM marked product was an unsuccessful innovation in the German market and Greenpeace blamed the failure on consumers' resistance to genetically engineered food. One aim of the product's introduction was to test the market for its acceptance of GM food. However, as will be shown in this article, such an introduction needs to be carefully planned, especially if the key characteristic (genetically modified) is best to be avoided for many people. As a sweets product the Butterfinger candy bar is also or even primarily targeted at children which has been criticized by Greenpeace. The target group for such a product needs to be chosen carefully: those consumers who either have an understanding of what genetically modified means or who are willing to be taught what it means might then display a level of knowledge that permits them to make an informed choice. The source of such an information needs to be highly credible which means it is not advisable to rely solely on the company's communication but rather to engage in collaboration with respected organizations in the field.

2 Change Agents and the Diffusion of Innovation

Asymmetry of Information

In his article on 'Technology Management in the Company of the Future' Brockhoff (1996, 177) states that 'new technologies may be regarded as information' and points out the importance of information asymmetry for the strategic management of technology.

Imperfect information exists in all markets. Some economic agents are more or less informed than others about price, quantity, quality or other relevant market data, thus information is said to be asymmetrical. The more informed party can communicate information by 'signaling', and the less informed can screen for information to decrease the asymmetry. When the buyer is uncertain about, for instance, characteristics of an innovation, the seller can use signals like pre-announcing of the new product (Eliashberg and Robertson 1988), advertising (Nelson 1970, 1974) or price (Gerstner 1985) to indicate the quality. In the case of an innovation one can expect the asymmetry of information to be significant: innovations are associated with uncertainty (Pearson

1990) regarding the underlying technology and regarding the acceptance, usage and diffusion in markets. Scientists and developers will be better informed about the technology but they will be less well informed with regard to user needs and usage patterns. Communication can help to understand the potential benefits and risks of an innovation and to learn about the effects an innovation has on various stakeholders. Thus, communication plays a key role because innovations are not simply adopted but adapted to everyday lives and vice versa (Gristock 2000).

Perceived Risk of GM Food

Genetically modified food clearly is an area where perceived risks influence the diffusion of innovations. The retailing industry in Europe, starting in the UK in 1998 (for example Sainsbury's, Tesco) and spreading to continental Europe (for example Carrefour, Migros, Rewe, Aldi) adopted a restrictive policy on GM food (European Commission, Directorate-General for Agriculture 2000). The industry by and large declared their own brands free of GM ingredients, hoping to gain a competitive advantage through signaling the *absence* of a certain characteristic. Objections to GM food are based on grounds such as social or ethical but the key issue is the perceived risk associated with GM innovations. While the technology has been adopted widely in the farming sector, particularly in the USA, consumers especially in Europe do not only ignore GM food because of lack of benefits but actively seek to avoid genetically modified food owing to perceived high risk (Moon and Balasubramanian 2001). If this perceived risk of the innovation is seen as justified by stakeholders or change agencies, they may aim at preventing the diffusion of the innovation. If on the other hand change agencies see the perception of the risk as unjustified , they may aim at accelerating the process. An important question is how to overcome this barrier to product evaluation. This is not to manipulate consumers to buy something they don't want, rather, it is about the transmission and reception of information: which signals should a change agency send out to *initiate* information processing?

Information and Perceptions

Information is vital to the perception and acceptance of innovations in the market place. In fact, Rogers (1983) defines diffusion as the 'process by which an innovation is communicated through certain channels over time among the members of a social system' and communication as the 'process in which participants create and share information with one another in order to reach a mutual understanding'. Particularly in the case of controversially discussed technologies, the perceptions of chances, risks and hazard, held by various stakeholders (scientists, managers, 'the public') may differ to a great extent and the perceptions of the risks should be taken into account when assessing innovation risks (Keizer, Halman, and Song 2002). These perceptions usually will be based on incomplete information. Over time, perceptions and evaluations may change subject to additional information (Chatterjee and Eliashberg 1990, Roberts and Urban 1988). Such a change may lead to a perceived lower probability of negative outcomes (risk reduction effect) or may lead to the recognition of risks not considered previously (risk recognition effect). The strength and direction of these effects have an impact on the adoption behavior: consumers may buy or wait for next generation products (leapfrogging). This phenomenon of deferring the purchase of a product in anticipation of future developments, has been discussed e.g. by Weiss and John (1989) and Weiber and Pohl (1996). More knowledge about an innovation may lead to a better understanding of benefits as well as risks and this increased knowledge may affect buying behavior. A change agent, defined as 'an individual who influences clients' innovation decisions in a direction deemed desirable by a change agency' (Rogers 1983) may aim at lowering the perceived probability of certain negative outcomes and achieve a risk reduction effect. Alternatively, the change agency may aim at drawing attention to risks not considered previously, thereby achieving a risk recognition effect. In both cases, it is important to improve information and communication. However, there are limitations to effective and transparent information:

Political-Economic Structures

Respective efforts will work differently in different political-economic structures: while organic food is affordable and has a growing market in industrialized countries, GM food such as the 'golden rice' might offer solutions to problems in the developing world. Thus, Green, Harvey and McMeekin (2002) propose that different paradigms of 'food consumption and production systems' (FCPS) exist and that advocating single strategies without considering their suitability at different geographical scales are unhelpful with regard to sustainability. But in a global world political-economic structures and systems are linked, change agents are driven by different agendas and often act on a worldwide basis. Opposition to GM food may well affect attitudes in the developing world: Zambia's president, Levy Mwanawasa banned the import of 'poisonous' GM corn and soy despite severe starvation. Next to alleged health risks, another reason is seen in the threat to export of agricultural products to Europe, if imported GM seeds contaminate local fields (Economist 2002).

The Use of Public Relations Strategies

Public Relations strategies are used by proponents and opponents alike. These include practices such as:

- Using supposedly independent experts
- Minimizing public participation in debates on technology
- Not disclosing funding sources
- Using language selectively
- Omitting certain information.

Providing the same information to different consumers still will lead to different attitudes: prior knowledge, personal characteristics etc. account for differences in information processing and attitude formation. Thus, different receivers need to be addressed appropriately. Successful communication with consumers who differ with regard to level of understanding and experience requires appropriate rather than homogeneous information. However, suggestions such as 'use of heavy point-of-purchase promotion', 'keep it a non-issue' or 'use one-sided message emphasizing benefits' (Wansink and Kim 2001) may not be appropriate strategies for achieving credibility but rather may be counter-productive to a successful engagement with the public.

Influencing Diffusion

If an innovation does not pose a special risk deriving from the (controversially discussed) *technology* and it offers benefits to (certain) consumers, how can change agents aiming at promoting the diffusion of this innovation signal its quality? Rogers (1983) identified five factors, which have an impact on the acceptance of an innovation in the market place: relative advantage of the innovation, compatibility with existing values, complexity, divisibility and observability. Stewart, Harding and Day (2002) discussed these factors with regard to *farmers* adopting new agricultural biotechnology and pointed out the importance of consumer acceptance. Wagner Weick and Walchli (2002) applied the factors to the adoption of genetically engineered food in the market place. The authors conclude that in order to promote the diffusion, strategies such as developing new products that offer benefits to the end consumer, increasing efforts to study health and environmental impacts and labeling are important. While these are relevant, if not necessary strategies, *effective communication* of e.g. specific benefits or new knowledge about impacts is crucial for the success of these strategies. The *perception* of advantage, compatibility and complexity can be influenced by sending, withholding and manipulating information, particularly if it is difficult for users to assess the quality of an innovation.

3 The crucial role of information

Often, products have *attraction* characteristics (characteristics of a product which are perceived as being desirable by a given consumer) and *avoidance* characteristics (the consumer seeks to avoid the product owing to the risk associated with the characteristic), and the decision process involves making trade-offs. This can lead to cognitive dissonance (Festinger 1957). In the case of genetically modified food such negative consumer attitudes can translate into a willingness to pay to avoid these products (Burton et al. 2001; Moon and Balasubramanian 2001). For innovations, novelty implies lack of experience and uncertainty regarding the characteristics. Information is crucial to the process of getting aware of and evaluating the innovation. However, reception and effectiveness of information vary:

Consonant and Dissonant Information

Preconceptions influence the interpretation of information. In what follows it will be distinguished between different kinds of information: information that supports the evaluation of a specific characteristic shall be designated as *consonant* while information that challenges the evaluation of a characteristic shall be denoted *dissonant*. Suppose a person prefers organically grown (OG) food and rejects genetically modified (GM) food (alternatively: prefers GM and rejects OG). Conflicting information might produce cognitive dissonance when buying organically grown food (see Table 1).

Table 1: *Organically Grown as Attraction and Genetically Modified as Avoidance Characteristic*

Characterist	*Attraction:*	*Avoidance:*
Information	*OG*	*GM*
Consonant	III: 'OG is good' 'a growing body of scientific evidence is indicating that organic food is healthier than conventional produce. Researchers from the University of Copenhagen recently reported that organically grown produce has higher levels of nutrients when compared with conventional produce'[c]	II: 'GM is bad' 'Commercialization of the tomatoes is dangerous because they contain antibiotic-resistant marker genes which some researchers say may remain in the human gut and enable dangerous organisms to develop antibiotic immunity'[b]
Dissonant	IV: 'OG is bad' 'According to recent data compiled by the U.S. Centers for Disease Control (CDC), people who eat organic and "natural" foods are eight times as likely as the rest of the population to be attacked by a deadly new strain of E. coli bacteria (0157: H7)...organic and "natural" food consumers also face increased risk of illness from toxins produced by fungi—and some of these toxins are carcinogenic'[d]	I: 'GM is good' 'The FDA today announced that FLAVR SAVR, a new tomato developed through biotechnology, is as safe as tomatoes bred by conventional methods'

[a] http://www.fda.gov/bbs/topics/NEWS/NEW00482.html

[b] http://userwww.sfsu.edu/-rone/GE%20Essays/GEF%20labelling.htm

[c] http://www.purefood.org/newsletter/organicview21.cfm

[d] http://www.hudson.org/american_outlook/articles_fa98/avery.htm

Statements as shown in Table 1 often are commented on. These comments might refer to the contents or to the source or both. This information itself on (contents and/or source of) information again might be subject to comments. Thus, patterns of information evolve which reflect and enhance camps. These in turn could have an impact on how information is perceived, processed and used in making a choice. For example statement IV of Table 1 has been said to be part of 'a nasty campaign against organic food' and the source has been described as being 'Dennis Avery (who was in the Agriculture Department under Reagan, who now works at the right-wing Hudson Institute)' (Meadows 2000). Similarly people could comment on the scientific reputation of the researchers from the University of Copenhagen (statement III) or the scientific basis of the FDA statement (I). Are the researchers at the forefront of research, what is their standing in the scientific community, are they influenced by politics of their institute, do institutes attract scientists with certain attitudes (self-selection)? For example, if Greenpeace attracts scientists who are against the introduction of GMO and companies attract scientists who are in favor of GMO, the policies and attitudes of the respective organizations are reinforced. Who funded the research and how does the funding body exercise influence on the way research has been performed or even on the interpretation and disclosure of results? In general, for every information the impartiality and the capabilities of its sender could be questioned.

Genetically Modified as a Credence Quality

The acceptance and effectiveness of information regarding the innovation may depend on the kind of qualities concerned. While *search qualities* and *experience qualities* (Nelson 1970) can be verified, credence qualities (Darby and Karni 1973) pose a problem in that the consumer cannot check the characteristic and information concerning that characteristic is difficult to verify. For example, for consumers it is usually not possible to verify whether a plant has been organically grown. Sellers might build up a reputation for being reliable or they might join an association that on the basis of respected rules certifies the product's characteristic. Signals involve costs (Kirmani and Rao 2000), either up-front (advertising, acquiring a certificate) or only in case of a default (guarantee). These signals are sent to address the *quality* of a product. However, in the case of an avoidance characteristic, signaling explicitly needs to address the associated *risks*. The issue of an avoidance characteristic in GM food is very strong. The presence or absence of this characteristic (genetically modified) is not easily revealed, hence it is a credence quality. Quite often it is an unwanted characteristic and thus the possibility of its occurrence in food is dissonant to the attitudes of the respective buyer. In the ,Guide for Companies in the Agro-Food Sector to Communicate on Genetic Engineering to the Public', Menrad et al. (1998, 3) point out that 'Particularly for food the availability of pilot products may help to overcome acceptance barriers, because food is not only purchased but also consumed and therefore affects the consumers' sense of taste'. However, the *consumption* of GM food can only account for search and experience characteristics, it does not help regarding credence characteristics (long-term effects of GM Food).

4 A Framework for Signaling in the Case of Avoidance Characteristics

The processing of information varies according to the receivers' characteristics and situational factors. Different levels of understanding and experience as well as differences in risk attitudes are key reasons for the diversity of attitudes towards GM food.

In what follows, the emphasis lies on three of the many factors possibly influencing the processing of information and thus, the achievement of desired effects: the perception of and attitude towards *risk,* the actual and perceived *expertise* of an individual and the *credibility* of the information source.

With regard to genetically engineered food, risks to human health and the environment are discussed intensively and in a highly controversial way, the expertise of end consumers with regard to food production and genetic modification is low, the credibility of parties involved is being questioned. Companies have been blamed of not having responded to customers' and in general the public's concerns in a sensible way. Food scandals contributed significantly to the rise of concern about health and distrust into scientists, companies and politicians.

The Perception of and Attitude towards Risk

Signals to overcome an avoidance characteristic need to address the risk associated with this characteristic. In this context it is important to differentiate between technical risk, perceived risk and risk tolerance. A technical definition of risk is the expected value of the negative outcomes (the hazards) resulting from a decision. This scientifically assessed risk involves an element of judgment (Fischhoff, Slovic, and Lichtenstein 1983). The risks as assessed by experts will vary, however, there usually will be a consensus view of these risks. The outliers expressing dissent might be right or wrong, they might base their voiced disagreement on a different (scientific) judgment, they might have different values and priorities leading to different reference systems, or the voiced dissent might involve politics. The acknowledgement of a scientist will depend on his legitimacy, on his scientific reputation and on the lack of evidence of politics involved. For convenience, the risk as perceived in consensus by the experts of a domain shall be denoted *scientifically assessed* risk, r_s. This technical concept of risk being of limited use for policy making (Kasperson et al. 1988), the perception of risk by lay people needs to be considered in risk communication (Renn 1990). Public perceptions and evaluations of different risks are not directly comparable to each other, rather, people often feel differently about risks for which the products of frequency and consequence are the same (Litai, Lanning, and Rasmussen 1983). Thus, when discussing the perception of a risk, it is important to look at the nature of that risk. While r_s represents one consensus view of the scientific community, the *perceived* risk r_p varies with the interest for and understanding of science and the reference frame. The way a decision situation is being described influences the *tolerance* of the involved risk r_t (Tversky and Kahneman 1981). People's attitudes about the cause of a risk also shape the acceptance of the risk. For example, if the technology in question is desirable the associated risks are likely to be perceived as less serious (Renn 1990) and may be tolerated.

If $r_p > r_s$,

a change agent may give information to achieve a risk reduction effect,

if $r_p < r_s$,

the change agent may draw attention to risks not considered previously. The latter is exemplified in social marketing campaigns against smoking or the abuse of alcohol. In the case of GM food it would apply to certain *products* that are perceived as harmful by the change agency.

If, however, $r_t < r_p$, r_s

the question is whether the tolerance level could (and should) be changed ('life is risky'), or the attractiveness of alternatives could be lowered ('a rotten tomato poses a higher risk to health'). When advocating the extreme version of the precautionary principle, the tolerance level is zero. According to several studies (Moses 1998, Eurobarometer 2000) consumers in Europe and increasingly in the USA perceive risks associated with GM food to an extent that they seek to avoid that characteristic. Scientists point out that the products derived from genetic modification are no more harmful than ordinary products (Gassen 2000), and that, owing to the fact that these products undergo extensive testing they should be comparably safe (in any case, testing food for health hazards is not easy (Katzek 2000)). Thus, there are differences between risk as viewed by members of the scientific community and as perceived by the general public. Hence, for change agents advocating the technology and its innovations, communicating results of scientific studies as well as information on the competence and trustworthiness of the information sender is the primary task.

Table 2 differentiates between stakeholders on the basis of perceived and tolerated risks and gives examples. Those stakeholders, whose perceptions are similar to the scientifically assessed risks are denoted 'informed'. They may or may not be in favor of the innovation, depending on their risk tolerance.

Informed adopters balance chances and risks: While respecting ethical aspects and biosafety concerns, the FAO requests the recognition of 'biotechnology's potential for increasing food supplies and alleviating hunger'(FAO 1999) , and 'A Nobel prize laureate, Dr. Norman E. Borlaugh, has defended the utilization of Genetically Modified Organisms or GMOs to boost food production in the world' (Okoko 2000). Informed avoiders don't tolerate risks: Greenpeace advocates the strict version of the precautionary principle. Non-carers don't know about the risks but they don't care either. Badly informed avoiders don't know about the risks but they rather don't try.

Table 2: *Adopters, Avoiders and Non-Carers of GM Food: Examples*

Perceived risk / *Tolerated risk*	$r_p = r_s$	$r_p > r_s$
$r_t >= r_p$	Informed adopters FAO, third world nutritionists: we acknowledge the presence of risks, but we balance that against chances	Non-carers Consumers: we don't know much about GM and for us GM is not an important characteristic
$r_t < r_p$	Informed avoiders Greenpeace: we do not want GM food, it cannot be proved to be risk-free (precautionary principle)	Badly informed avoiders Consumers: we don't know much about GM and we perceive significant risks which we do not tolerate

The Actual and Perceived Expertise of an Individual

In order to address the risk of an avoidance characteristic appropriately, a sender needs to consider the receivers' knowledge about the characteristic. In the case of innovations, the knowledge is likely to be scarce. Crucially, the narrower the consumers' knowledge regarding the innovation, the slower the rate of adoption will be (Gatignon and Robertson 1985, 853). Furthermore, self-assessed knowledge and objective knowledge may not correspond. Alba and Hutchinson (1987) reviewed empirical results on the effects of expertise on consumer behavior. They conclude that sub-optimal decisions may occur owing to an abbreviated search process (overestimated expertise) or to poorly processed information (belief in knowing the content). In a review of empirical studies Alba and Hutchinson (2000) conclude that the correspondence levels between confidence and accuracy of knowledge are only moderate. This overconfidence of consumers has an impact on consumer decision making. The discrepancy between self-assessed knowledge and objective knowledge might be particularly high for credence qualities (Park, Mothersbaugh, and Feick 1994).

In a survey of 600 residents of New Jersey, Hallman and Metcalfe (1993) found that 55% of the respondents rated their understanding of science and technology as good, 25% rated it as very good, and 91% of the respondents felt that they had an adequate or very good understanding of how food is grown and produced. However, in the same study 28% said that they had eaten fruits or vegetables produced by cross-fertilization or cross-breeding (when practically all fruits and vegetables on the market are produced that way) and 17% said that they had eaten fruits or vegetables produced by genetic engineering (when at the time of the survey no such product was available to the consumer). Similarly, a study undertaken for the European Commission in 1997 found that consumer understanding of biotechnology is not well developed (Moses 1998). If this were indicative for a general pattern of knowledge in the area of food production information on GM Food would have to take into account that level of knowledge.

The Credibility of the Source of Information

If signals are to be successful the source needs to be credible. Expertise and trustworthiness are key elements of the concept of credibility (Goldsmith, Lafferty, and Newell 2000): while expertise refers to the knowledge of the subject, trustworthiness indicates how much the source is believed to be honest (McGinnies and Ward 1980). Thus, if the source of information is known to perform state of the art research on GMO and it is believed that the information sent is not biased owing to politics involved, the source can be said to be credible.

The New Jersey survey of public perceptions of agricultural biotechnology reported that scientists are the most credible and companies involved in genetically engineered products are the least credible source of information (Hallman and Metcalfe 1993). The credibility of the source is key for the acceptance and processing of the information. If there is a discrepancy between the scientifically assessed risk and the risk as perceived by an individual, the individual might be inclined to reassess its perception through information acquisition. In this case, changing one's risk perception towards the scientifically assessed risk is the result of an attempt to reduce cognitive dissonance. For that to happen the dissonance has to be high enough. If scientists explain the scientifically assessed risk and it is lower than consumers perceive it to be, the dissonance introduced by this will be higher the trustworthier that scientist is to the person.

Signaling Emphases

These factors (receivers' characteristics, i.e. risk attitude and expertise, and credibility of source) can act as barriers or promoters in the search for and processing of information and therefore have implications for signaling (Table 3).

1. If people perceive high risks, communication of *scientifically assessed 'facts'* can introduce dissonance which in turn might be reduced through changing one's opinion (Festinger 1957). This information ('facts') might be misinterpreted or distrusted which is why information on the *credibility of the source* is important.

2. If the tolerance level for the risk involved in a product is low compared to the perceived risk that person seeks to avoid the product. Here, *information on the risk of alternatives* or on *risk in general* ('no risk-free world') is appropriate.

3. Knowledgeable' people might not look for information or process information superficially. Information stemming from organizations and individuals who are not perceived as representing the consensus view of experts might be disregarded by the scientific community and vice versa: information stemming from the (con-

sensus) scientific community might be disregarded by outliers. Arousing *interest in the new information* itself as well as providing *information on* the (high) *professional standing of the source* are ways to increase the likelihood of processing the information.

Table 3: *Screening and Signaling in the Case of Genetically Engineered Food*

Key variable, Situation	*Screening might involve…*	*Signalling should involve…*
r_p ($>r_s$) the person perceives the risk to be higher than the scientifically assessed risk, key issue: risk perception	Search for facts re genetic engineering, Search on information sources	Communicating facts re genetic engineering, Information on credibility of sources
r_t ($<r_p$) the person's tolerance for the risk is lower than the perceived risk, key issue: risk tolerance	N.A. (search for food which has not been genetically engineered)	Communicating facts re food safety in general, Teaching about risks
(3) High expertise	Shallow information search and processing	Motivating for processing the 'new' information, Information on the professional standing of the source
(4) Low expertise	Lack of confidence in ability to understand information	Providing confidence in the ability to process information from that source
(5) Trust in information source	Preference for that source	Reinforcing the credibility: e.g. information on corporate social responsibility
(6) Distrust in information source	Neglect of information source	Information on credibility of source: information on corporate social responsibility, Partnering with credible organisations,

4. On the other hand, people perceiving themselves as having no expertise might think that they are not able to judge and thus not engage in information search at

all. In this case it is important to conduct the information transfer in a way that takes into account the background knowledge (Nyyssoenen 2000)

In both these cases, the *motivation* to search and process information should be enhanced.

5. High credibility of the information source is likely to lead to a preference for that source as well as to an increased likelihood of accepting the respective information. High credibility needs to be reinforced over time, taking into account progress in science as well as changing perceptions and evolving needs in society. *Information on the sender* is crucial to *keep up* high credibility.
6. If an individual does not trust the source of information he or she might not be willing to process information. Thus, information on the credibility of the source is as important as the information itself. The sender could increase the credibility of information and its trustworthiness by co-operating with trusted information sources. Venkatesh and Mahajan (1997) discuss partner selection decisions when a brand is sold with branded components (co-branding). Similarly, a company might co-operate with a respected research organization and incorporate relevant research results in their message.

These signals: communicating facts, teaching about risks, displaying and advertising high corporate social responsibility, and co-operating all are long-term measures to change the perception of an avoidance characteristic. In the case of credence qualities they involve up-front costs as default in claims can rarely be proven.

5 Conclusion

The concentration process in the industry led to companies influencing and managing the value chain from doing research, developing seed and chemicals to marketing products. Thus, emphasis has been on developing or strengthening core competencies, assuring acquisition of knowledge, and external growth. The marketing side however has been largely neglected, resulting in a failure to communicate risks and benefits. The protests of opponents such as Greenpeace, Friends of the Earth, consumer organizations and the like had a cascading effect on upstream activities (European Commission, Directorate-General for Agriculture 2000). Companies try to create attraction characteristics and usually communication is about these attraction characteristics: they 'engineer consent'. Groups who are critics of these companies try to pick on or create avoidance characteristics and usually their communication is about these avoidance characteristics: they 'engineer dissent'. However, a company's true engagement requires signaling not about the overall quality of the product but about the risks associated with it. Thus, instead of engineering consent (or dissent) it is important to be open about interests and to promote transparency. In an attraction world, signaling of quality involves using established means such as advertising and guarantees. In an avoidance world, signaling to change the perception of a single characteristic involves addressing the risk associated with that characteristic. Distinguishing between search, experience and credence characteristics helps understanding signaling of quality in an 'attraction world'. The concept of avoidance characteristics however implies that signaling needs to address risk explicitly and that change agents need to aim at transparency. The question why people want to avoid certain characteristics led to the analysis of risk and expertise. Categorizing people with regard to their knowledge about the subject and their perception of risk and credibility of information source leads to a definition of priorities in communication.

6 References

Alba, J.W. and J.W. Hutchinson (1987): Dimensions of Consumer Expertise, *Journal of Consumer Research,* 13, 411-454.

Alba, J.W. and J.W. Hutchinson (2000): Knowledge Calibration: What Consumers Know and What They Think They Know, *Journal of Consumer Research* 27 (September), 123-156.

Brockhoff, K. (1996): Technology Management in the Company of the Future, *Technology Analysis & Strategic Management,* 8 (2), 175-189.

Burton, M., D. Rigby, T. Young, and S. James (2001): Consumer attitudes to genetically modified organisms in food in the UK, *European Review of Agriculture Economics* 28 (4), 479-498.

Chatterjee, R. and J. Eliashberg (1990): The Innovation Diffusion Process in a Heterogeneous Population: A Micromodeling Approach, *Management Science,* 30 (9), 1057-1079.

Darby, M.R. and E. Karni (1973), Free Competition and the Optimal Amount of Fraud, *Journal of Law and Economics,* 16, 67-88.

Economist (2002): *GM crops in Africa. Better dead than GM-fed?*, September 21, 94.

Eliashberg, J. and T. Robertson (1988): New Product Preannouncing Behavior: A Market Signaling Study, *Journal of Marketing Research,* 25 (August), 282-292.

Eurobarometer (2000): *The Europeans and Biotechnology,* Eurobarometer 52.1, European Commission, March 15.

European Commission, Directorate-General for Agriculture (2000): *Economic Impacts of Genetically Modified Crops on the Agri-Food Sector.* http://europa.eu.int/comm/agriculture/publi/gmo/fullrep/.

FAO (1999): *Biotechnology in agriculture,* http://www.fao.org/WAICENT/FAOINFO/AGRICULT/magazine/9901sp1.htm.

Festinger, L. (1957): *A Theory of Cognitive Dissonance,* Stanford, CA.

Fischhoff, B., P. Slovic, and S. Lichtenstein (1983): 'The Public' vs 'The Experts': Perceived vs. Actual Disagreements about Risks, in: Covello, V.T., W.G. Flamm, J.V. Rodricks, and R.G. Tardiff (Eds.): *The Analysis of Actual Versus Perceived Risks,* Volume 1 of Advances in Risk Analysis: Society for Risk Analysis, 235-249.

Gassen, H.G. (2000): Possible Health Risks of GM Foods, OECD: *Assessing the Safety of GM Food,* The OECD Edinburgh Conference on the Scientific and Health Aspects of Genetically Modified Foods, 28 February to1 March.

Gatignon, H. and T. Robertson (1985), A Propositional Inventory for New Diffusion Research, *Journal of Consumer Research,* 11, 849-867.

Gerstner, E. (1985): Do Higher Prices Signal Higher Quality? *Journal of Marketing Research,* 22 (May), 209-216.

Goldsmith, R.E., B.A. Lafferty, and S.J. Newell (2000): The impact of corporate credibility and celebrity credibility on consumer reaction to advertisements and brands, *Journal of Advertising,* 29 (3), 43-54.

Green, K., M. Harvey, and A. McMeekin (2002): *Transformation in Food Consumption and Production Systems,* manuscript, CROMTEC Manchester School of Management.

Gristock, J. (2000): *Systems of Innovation are Systems of Mediation: A discussion of the critical role of science communication in innovation and knowledge-based development,* Working Paper, SPRU Science and Technology Policy Research, University of Sussex, August.

Hallman, W.K. and J. Metcalfe (1993): *Public Perceptions of Agricultural Biotechnology: A Survey of New Jersey Residents,* Rutgers State University of New Jersey.

Kasperson, R.E., O. Renn, P. Slovic, H.S. Brown, J. Emel, R. Goble, J.X. Kasperson, and S. Ratick (1988): The Social Amplification of Risk: A Conceptual Framework, *Risk Analysis,* 8 (2), 177-187.

Katzek, J. (2000): *Outline of the research project and experiences with long-term monitoring of products (pharmaceuticals, food additives and fat substitute olestra),* workshop held at the University of Darmstadt, http://homepages.tu-darmstadt.de/~gassen/Workshop/ProcKatz.html.

Keizer, J.A., J.I.M. Halman, and M. Song (2002): From experience: applying the risk diagnosing methodology, *Journal of Product Innovation Management,* 19, 213-232.

Kirmani, A. and A.R. Rao (2000): No Pain, No Gain: A Critical Review of the Literature on Signaling Unobservable Product Quality, *Journal of Marketing*, 64, April, 66-79.

Litai, D., D.D. Lanning, and N.C. Rasmussen (1983): The Public Perception of Risk. Covello, V.T., W.G. Flamm, J.V. Rodricks, and R.G. Tardiff (Eds.): *The Analysis of Actual Versus Perceived Risks*, Volume 1 of Advances in Risk Analysis: Society for Risk Analysis, 213-224.

McGinnies, E. and C.D. Ward (1980): Better liked than right: trustworthiness and expertise as factors in credibility, *Personality and Social Psychological Bulletin*, 6, 467-472.

Meadows, D.H. (2000): Refuting the Media Lies About the Dangers of Organic Food, *The Global Citizen*, March 9, http://www.purefood.org/Organic/organiclies.cfm.

Menrad, K., K. Koschatzky, S. Massfeller, and E. Strauss (1998): *A Guide for Companies in the Agro-Food Sector to Communicate on Genetic Engineering to the Public*, European Commission EUR 18359

Moon, W. and S.K. Balasubramanian (2001): Public Perceptions and Willingness-To-Pay a Premium for Non-GM Foods in the US and UK, *AgBioForum*, 4, 221-231.

Moses, V. (1998): *Looking at the biotechnology consumer*, European Commission, Directorate Science Research and Development, EUR 18492.

Nelson, P. (1970): Information and Consumer Behavior, *Journal of Political Economy* 78, 311-329.

Nelson, P. (1974): Advertising as Information, *Journal of Political Economy*, 82, 729-754.

Nyyssoenen, H. (2000), *Design and accessibility of baby food labelling from the consumers' point of view, Study of the labels of infant formulae and cereals in Belgium, Britain, Finland, Spain and Sweden*, project B5-1000/98/000064, introduction, http://www.ekl.oulu.fi/-research/babyfood/reports.html)

Okoko, T. (2000): Nobel Laureate Hails GMO Technology, *Panafrican News Agency*, June 7, http://www.africanews.org/PANA/news/20000607/feat12.html.

Park, C.W., D.L. Mothersbaugh, and L. Feick, (1994): Consumer Knowledge Assessment, *Journal of Consumer Research*, 21 (June), 71-82.

Pearson, A. (1990): Innovation Strategy, *Technovation*, 10 (3), 185-192.

Renn, O. (1990): *Risk Perception and Risk Management: A Review*, Risk abstracts, Institute for Risk Research, University of Waterloo, Ontario.

Roberts, J.H. and G.L. Urban (1988): Modeling Multiattribute Utility Risk, and Belief Dynamics for New Consumer Durable Brand Choice, *Management Science*, 34 (February), 167-185.

Rogers, E.M. (1983): *Diffusion of Innovations*, 3rd ed., New York, London.

Stewart, P.A., D. Harding, and E. Day (2002): Regulating the new agricultural Biotechnology by managing innovation diffusion, *American Review of Public Administration,* 32 (1), 78-99.

Tversky, A. and D. Kahneman (1981): The Framing of Decisions and the Psychology of Choice, *Science,* 211 (January), 453-458.

Venkatesh, R. and V. Mahajan (1997): Products with branded components: An approach for premium pricing and partner selection, *Marketing Science,* 16 (2), 145-165.

Wagner Weick, C. and S.B. Walchli (2002): Genetically engineered crops and foods: back to the basics of technology diffusion, *Technology in Society,* 24, 265-283.

Wansink, B. and J. Kim (2001): The Marketing Battle over Genetically Modified Foods: False Assumptions about Consumer Behavior, *American Behavioral Scientist,* 44 (8), 1405-1417.

Weiber, R. and A. Pohl (1996): Das Phänomen der Nachfrageverschiebung, *Zeitschrift für Betriebswirtschaft,* 66, 675-696.

Weiss, A.M. and G. John (1989): *Leapfrogging Behavior and the Purchase of Industrial Innovations,* Report No 89-110, Technical Working Paper, Marketing Science Institute, Cambridge, MA.

Cornelia Zanger, Martin Kuder, and Hansjörg Gaus

Characterizing Customer Groups During the Life Cycle of a Car Model

Results of an Empirical Study

Prof. Dr. *Cornelia Zanger*, Dr. *Hansjörg Gaus*, Department of Marketing and Retailing, Chemnitz University of Technology, and Dipl.-Kfm. *Martin Kuder*, BMW AG.

1 Introduction

The world auto market is, with regard to its volumes, an extraordinarily important product market: in the year 2001, 55 million cars were sold worldwide (VDA-Jahresbericht 2002, 32). Due to a tremendous growth of competitive pressure, the manufacturers since the mid 1990s face significant challenges (Hünerberg, Heise, and Hoffmeister 1997, 3-27): e.g., the lapse of the advantages for manufacturers in their home markets because of their *existing* competitors' global business policies, the global market entry of *new* competitors (Korea, Malaysia) or saturation tendencies in the triad markets. In addition to the growing competitive intensity, manufacturers are expanding their product programs (Diez 2000, 54 and 347) which means it is becoming increasingly difficult for individual companies to have a range of products that the customers can distinguish clearly from the competition.

From the diverse challenges the auto industry is confronted with results a growing rivalry: even in such a situation the challenge for the automobile manufacturers is to retain the existing customers and to attract new ones. Hence, in the form of customer orientation, a prominent factor of performance is arising which means that marketing activities play a key role for a company's success. Another important implication is the necessity to give up a static view of customer groups. Especially in such a situation it is inadequate to regard customer structures independent from the dimension of time – implicitly assuming a given product would attract the same purchaser structure at any given time of its market life. Moreover, a dynamic, phase-specific conception is required which allows to study the changes the customer structures are underlying over time as a basis for market segmentation. The application of such a conception in marketing is crucial for ensuring that customer groups can be addressed more precisely through measures of marketing action - resulting in an increase of a company's economic performance.

Therefore, the close surveillance of customer structures during the life cycle presently is a highly interesting issue for marketing research. One reason for this point of view is the assumption that in business research the scientific potential of the life cycle concept is still waiting to be fully utilized - even if there is a growing number of studies in this field (Mahajan, Muller, and Bass 1990, Mahajan, Muller, and Srivastava 1990 and Meffert and Burmann 2000). Furthermore, it has been emphasized in recent publications (Bauer and Fischer 2000, Backhaus and Gruner 1997) that due to the raise in spending for the development of new products, the management of product life cycles is one of the most challenging tasks for the future.

This article is aimed at reducing the gap between the scientific and practical interest in product life cycles on the one hand and the availability of empirical results on the other hand. In order to provide a theoretical foundation for the considerations of this article, we will critically review Rogers' (1962/1995) prominent adoption model and examine if it can be adapted to the understanding of automobile purchases. The identification of necessary modifications leads to the design of an empirical study. In a descriptive analysis it is evaluated if the assumption of the existence of customer groups that can be clearly distinguished from each other at different stages of the product life cycle is supported and - since this is the case - to point out to implications for product planning and marketing action in the car industry.

2 Analytical Framework

The life cycle concept - especially that of a product life cycle - forms the theoretical backbone of this article. The sales volume generated by a given product over time allows to draw a curve which can be subdivided into different stages form the market introduction until the exit (Brockhoff 1974). The shape of this product life cycle curve does not follow a natural law, it can, in contrast, be influenced. The focus of this article is to learn about differences in the groups of customers during different stages of such a life cycle curve. The most appropriate theoretical model for such a customer-oriented point of view is Rogers' (1995) adoption model which explicitly allows to categorize adopters of innovations (including products) in different phases of the life cycle. However, because of Rogers' special conception of innovations, the limitation of his model to first time buyers, the focus on innovativeness as the only differentiating variable, and the assumption of a normal distribution of the curve, this model needs some modifications to be applicable on data from the car industry.

Crucial for the transferability of the adoption model to automobile purchases is the identification of other relevant motivational constructs besides "innovativeness". For this very reason, a literature review was done which concentrates on empirical evidence concerning hypothetical constructs like activation, emotion, involvement, motive, attitude, value, and personality which are used prominently for the explanation of consumer behaviour (Trommsdorff 2002).

The basic idea underlying the study outlined in this article is to look out for so called "predisposition profiles" of car purchasers during the product life cycle. To be able to identify such profiles, the question has to be answered which constructs should be used to generate them. The decisive criteria were that a construct must have an empirically evident explanatory power for the decision to buy a car and that it is relatively stable over time. The results clearly show that in this context the concepts of attitude (e.g., Unger 1998, Häubl 1995), value (e.g., Zanger, Baier, and Gaus 2004, Gaus and Zanger 2004, Gaus 2000), and personality are the most promising ones but our study focuses exclusively on the values of car buyers. The value construct was preferred over the attitude construct due to its superior stability over time and over the personality construct because the latter is conceptually not as clearly defined as both others, values and attitudes, are. An additional element of our analytical concept are demographic data of the car buyers which are only used as passive segmentation variables in order to describe the (value-based) motivational predisposition profiles.

Since the decision to buy a certain car model is not only limited to the perception of the core product itself but relies on a more holistic picture of the offer created by the marketing mix activities of an automobile manufacturer, all of the "four Ps" (Kotler 2003) have to be taken into account to properly understand product life cycles in the car industry. Concrete activities, however, usually are limited to a short period of time during the whole life cycle of a car model. From this assumption, the conclusion is drawn to regard the marketing mix instruments of Product, Price, and Promotion (or better: communication) as varying over time. Only the fourth "P", namely Place, is regarded as relatively stable over time because changes in the organization and financing of distribution systems in the car industry usually are largely expensive and time consuming operations. Therefore, inducing selective and quick variations in the use of the instrument "Place" proves to be quite difficult.

An additional and also very important assumption which results from the review of data provided by a car manufacturer as well as from everyday experience is that characteristic patterns of the marketing mix instruments can be observed empirically which are typical for certain stages in the life cycle of a car model.

The following Figure 1 illustrates the analytical framework outlined above.

Figure 1: *Illustration of the analytical framework*

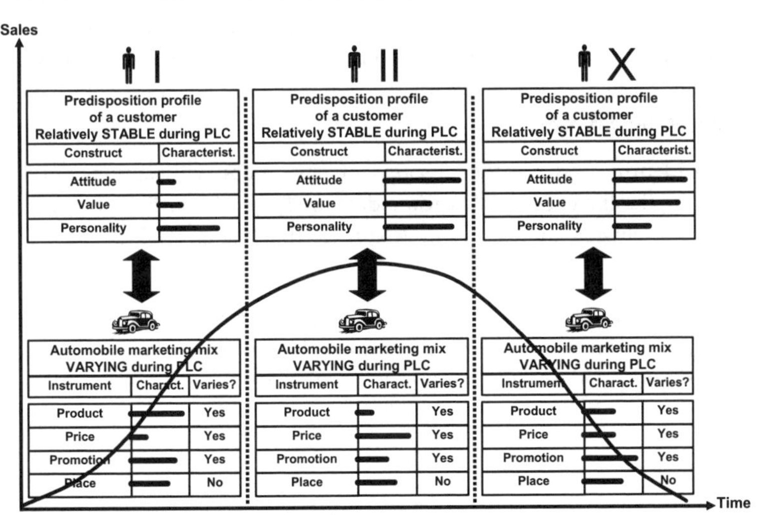

When a customer decides to buy a new car, he goes through a decision process. We argue, that he tries to find that offer (i.e., the combination of the four Ps which is changing during the life cycle of a car model) which best fits to his predisposition profile. This means, the customer compares the offers characterized by a distinct pattern of the marketing mix instruments with his own needs which, in the present study, are traced through his values (especially domain-specific values related to the purchase, use, and maintenance of cars: see Gaus 2000). Hence, the purchase decision can be viewed as the result of a "matching" process between the customer with his needs and expectations towards a car on the one side and a specific "package" of marketing instruments on the other side. From the idea of such a matching process going on constantly follows the proposition of the existence of groups of customers with relatively homogenous predisposition profiles. Its members have in common that they decide to buy a car model at a specific point of its life cycle.

3 Analyses and Results of an Empirical Study

Since the present study has been conducted in cooperation with the car manufacturer BMW AG (Munich), it was possible to use mass data on car purchases from the company's own market research. These data which are gathered by questionnaires distributed annually to large random samples of BMW's buyers were very well suited to our purposes, since they not only allowed to follow the life cycle of a car model (based on data representative for the sales of the BMW 3-series in Germany from 1994 to 2000) but also contained extensive data on car buyers' values and their demographic attributes. The data file which was used for the data analyses reported below consisted of 2310 buyers of the BMW 3-series.

In order to identify and describe groups of customers with similar predisposition profiles during the life cycle, multivariate data analyses - in particular combinations of factor analyses, cluster analyses, and ANOVAs (Backhaus et al. 2003) - have been performed.

These analyses were based on a list of 16 statements representing car-related values (see Table 1) which in the questionnaire were to be answered using a four-point scale (from "1 - completely agree" to "4 - completely disagree").

Table 1:	*Car-related values (Source: BMW AG)*

1. A car gives me the feeling of independence and freedom.
2. I prefer to care for my car myself.
3. For me, my car is a way of expressing my individuality and personality.
4. I see a car as a means of transport; the element of driving pleasure plays an inferior role for me.
5. When buying a car, I always look for a model that is very progressive.
6. When buying a car, I would like to have the feeling that the producer has tried to find unique technical solutions.
7. Friends and colleagues often ask me for advice when buying a car.
8. I like to have a car that catches people's attention.
9. The car that I drive must show my social status.
10. I like to look at beautiful cars.
11. When buying a car, I choose the cheapest model which fulfils my requirements
12. I like to drive fast.
13. In my opinion, cars are the main cause of environmental problems.
14. I like cars that are unusual.
15. The interior of a car should have a homelike atmosphere.
16. I would like a car that includes every possible safety feature, even if it meant sacrificing some other features of the car.

The following Table 2 shows the results of an exploratory factor analysis (principal component analysis, VARIMAX rotation) which led to the reduction of the 16 car-related values to four higher-order factors which were labelled "Status Orientation", "Innovation Orientation", "Hedonistic Orientation", and "Rationalism". Three of the value items were omitted from the final factor model due to their low communalities as recommended by Backhaus et al. (2003, 317).

Table 2: Results of the factor analysis of the car-related values (only factor loadings > .2 are reported)

Item No.	Keyword	Factor 1 Status Orientation	Factor 2 Innovation Orientation	Factor 3 Hedonistic Orientation	Factor 4 Rationalism
9	Social Status	**.82**			
3	Personality and individuality	**.81**			
8	People's Attention	**.79**		.27	
1	Freedom and independence	**.51**	.26		-.40
6	Unique technical solutions		**.74**		
5	Very progressive model		**.73**		
16	Every possible safety feature		**.64**		
14	Unusual style	.21		**.73**	.22
10	I like watching beautiful cars		.29	**.65**	
12	I like to drive fast			**.59**	-.23
13	Main cause of environmental problems				**.72**
11	Buy cheapest model			-.35	**.53**
4	Car is mainly means of transport	-.29		-.34	**.46**

Source: own computation

On the basis of the resulting factor scores for the four-factor solution cluster analyses were carried out in order to identify groups of customers with similar predisposition profiles using the stepwise clustering procedure (Backhaus et al. 2003; Gaus 2000, 148-151) illustrated in Figure 2.

Figure 2: *Stepwise cluster analysis procedure*

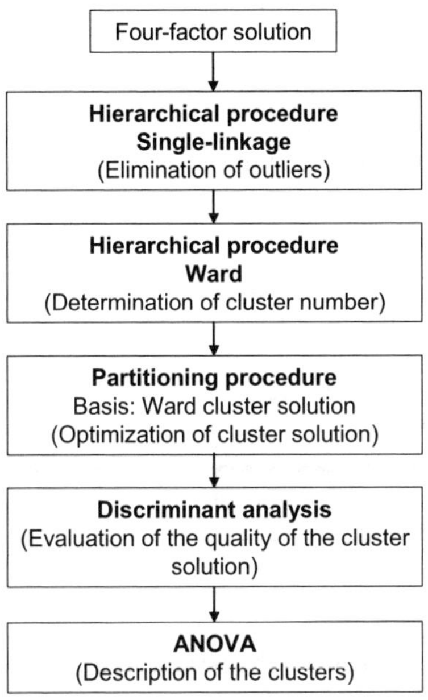

Source: Gaus 2000, 149

The cluster solution finally accepted for interpretation differentiates between five groups of BMW customers which were labelled "**Young Status Seekers**", "**Rationalists**", "**Hedonists**", "**Brand Loyal**", and "**Car Enthusiasts**". The description and interpretation of these groups show that the cluster analysis results are practically significant (Hair et al. 1995, 22) which means they are an adequate starting point for our life cycle analysis. Another highly important finding concerning our main research interest is that for each cluster one particular year in the product life cycle of the BMW 3-series can be identified in which significantly more cluster members bought such a car than in any other year (see Figure 3). The "basic purchases" box in the illustration symbolizes the fact that not all the members of a cluster have purchased a BMW in the group's "peak year" but that considerable numbers of them bought their car in a different year instead.

Figure 3: *"Peak years" of the individual clusters during the life cycle*

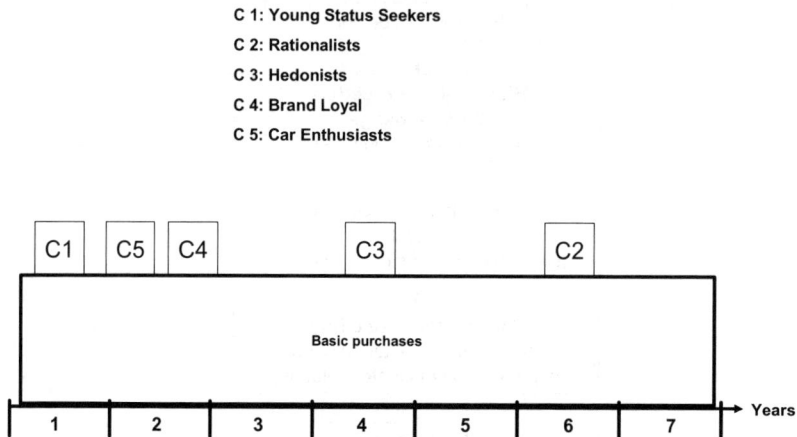

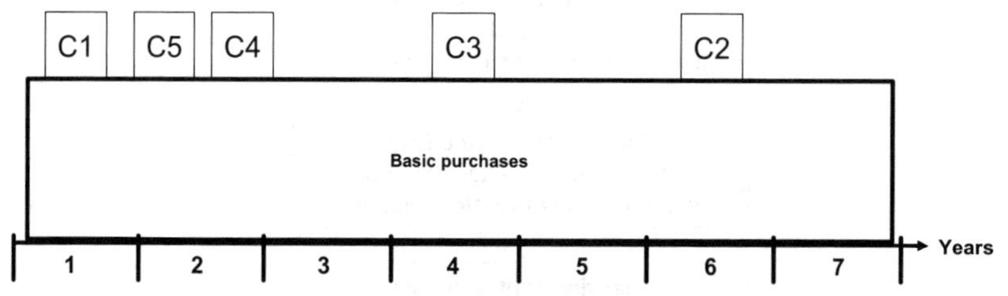

Source: own computation

For **Cluster 1 (Young Status Seekers)** the peak year is the first year of the product life cycle. The members of this cluster which are obviously fond of new car models strongly agree with the Status values and strongly disagree with Innovation and Rationalism values.

The peak year of **Cluster 2 (Rationalists)** is the sixth year which means a clear shift in the second half of the life cycle has to be recognized. It is no surprise that hedonistic values are clearly rejected while Rationalism values are important for this cluster.

Cluster 3 (Hedonists) shows a clear emphasis of the fourth year which marks the middle of the life cycle and also the subsequent years five to seven are clearly represented more frequently than the preceding three years. The members of this cluster are strongly motivated by the Hedonistic as well as the Rationalism values, an orientation resulting in attempts to get luxury cars at moderate costs which can more easily be satisfied in the later stages of a car model's life cycle.

The customers from **Cluster 4 (Brand Loyal)** which are predominantly interested in Innovation values and are strongly opposed towards Rationalism and Status values bought their car most frequently in the second year and also quite often in the first year of the life cycle.

The **Car Enthusiasts** in **Cluster 5** not only follow an outstandingly strong Status orientation but also highly agree with Innovation values. Altogether, this cluster shows a strong tendency to purchase in the first three years of the life cycle with a peak in the second year.

After obvious support for our assumption that different predisposition profiles lead to specific purchasing patterns during the product life cycle had been identified, in a second step of the descriptive analysis it should be examined if the variations in the marketing mix activities concerning the three Ps "Product", "Price" and "Promotion" ("Place" is omitted for the reasons mentioned above) were matching with the "peak years" of the individual clusters. The following Figure 4 uses the example of **Cluster 1 (Young Status Seekers)** which has its peak of purchases in the first year of the life cycle to illustrate how this analysis was conducted.

Figure 4: *Matching cluster "peak years" and marketing mix activities*

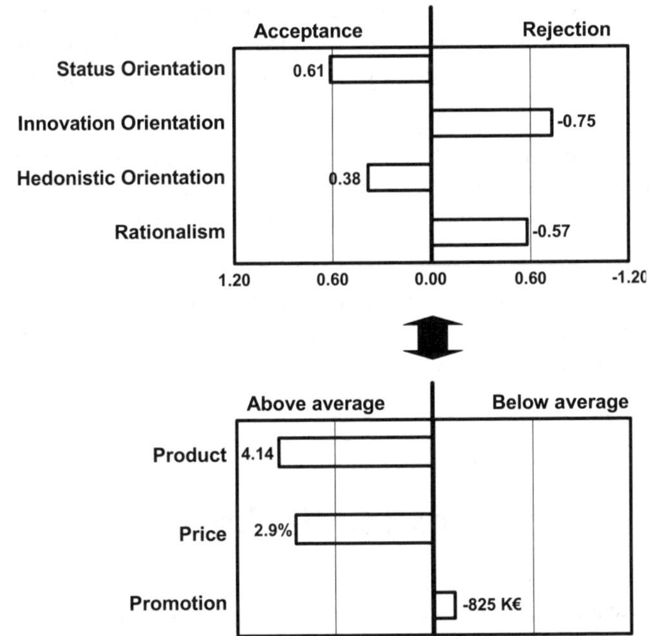

Source: own computation

Product: The indicator used to measure the variations the product (BMW 3-series car) itself underlies during the period of study was the number of the different types of engines that were newly introduced in every single year of the life cycle. This variable was chosen because it is valid, significant, and easy to compute. The resulting value for the average of product measures was 1.86 per year. Thus, the result for the indicator for year one which is calculated by subtracting the average value from the observed value is **4.14**, since five new engines were introduced in that year.

Price: Similarly to the marketing mix instrument Product, Price also is subject to significant changes during the life cycle. The average price increase during the seven years was roughly 2.2 percent but in the year of the introduction of a new model (year one), the price rise was much higher with 5.1 percent resulting in a deviation from the average value of **2.9** percent.

Promotion: The gross media spending of the advertising activities were chosen as an appropriate indicator for the instrument Promotion. Even this figure shows a significant correlation with the life cycle stage with average spending of 17.4 million EURO per year on the BMW 3-series and 16.5 million EURO in year one which means a deviation from the average of **0.825** million EURO.

With regard to the factor scores of the car-related values, the customers in **Cluster 1** most strongly agree with the Status values, an orientation which can be expressed with a vehicle which is clearly distinguished from the average car. Thus, the wish to satisfy Status values fits the relatively high value for the marketing mix instrument Product very well.

Additionally, the relatively high refusal of the Rationalism values is compatible with a relatively small price-sensitivity as indicated by the fact that the high price rise in year one does not deter the members of **Cluster 1** from purchasing in an early stage of the product life cycle.

Thus, the exemplary results for **Cluster 1** illustrating the "matching" technique used in our descriptive analysis prove to be plausible and interpretable which can be stated for the **Clusters 2 to 5** in a similar way.

4 Implications for Marketing Action

In this last section, we want to address some implications that result from the aforementioned analyses as it seems obvious that the optimisation of the marketing mix activities during a product's life cycle provides valuable potentials to improve a company's sales and profits.

As illustrated in Figure 5, the empirical life cycle function according to Brockhoff (1974) can - from the point of view of an automobile manufacturer - not be regarded as ideal. A closer look at the rate of capacity utilization, especially in the second half of the life cycle, clearly shows the necessity of measures to modify the shape of the curve in a favourable way.

Figure 5: *Supporting the sales in the second half of the product life cycle*

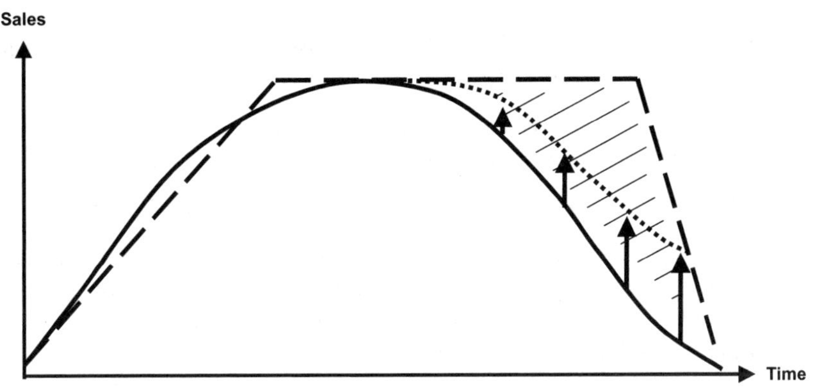

In the illustration the continuous line symbolizes an empirical life cycle curve. In addition, the production capacity is indicated by the broken line, while the dotted line shows the potentially beneficial effect of marketing action to stabilize sales in the second half of the life cycle.

A prominent challenge a car manufacturer is confronted with is to generate marketing activities which attract new customers in the later stages of a product life cycle - especially from the competitors' brands - and at the same time do not irritate the existing buyers of the own brand. Our empirical findings reported in this article suggest to efficiently address groups of potential buyers at a certain point during a product's life cycle by using marketing mix combinations that best fit their respective predisposition profiles.

5 References

Backhaus, K., B. Erichson, W. Plinke, and R. Weiber (2003): *Multivariate Analysemethoden*, 10th ed., Berlin et al.

Backhaus, K. and K. Gruner (1997): Die Beschleunigung von Produktlebenszyklen, *Zeitschrift für Betriebswirtschaft*, 1, 157-187.

Bauer, H.H. and M. Fischer (2000): Die empirische Typologisierung von Produktlebenszyklen und ihre Erklärung durch die Markeintrittsreihenfolge, *Zeitschrift für Betriebswirtschaft*, 9, 937-958.

Brockhoff, K. (1974): Produktlebenszyklen, *Handwörterbuch der Absatzwirtschaft*, in: Tietz, B. (Ed.): Stuttgart, 1763-1770.

Diez, W. (2000): *Automobilmarketing: erfolgreiche Strategien, praxisorientierte Konzepte, effektive Instrumente*, Landsberg am Lech.

Gaus, H. (2000): *Wertesystem-Segmentierung im Automobilmarketing*, Wiesbaden.

Gaus, H. and C. Zanger (2004): Werte und Automobilkauf: Erklärungsansätze, empirische Ergebnisse und Implikationen für die Markenkommunikation, in: Zanger, C., S. Habscheid, and H. Gaus (Eds.): *Bleibt das Auto mobil? Mobilität und Automobil im interdisziplinären Diskurs*, Frankfurt am Main et al.

Häubl, G. (1995): *Standortentscheidungen und Konsumentenverhalten*, Wien.

Hair, J.E., R.E. Anderson, R.L. Tatham, and W.C. Black (1995): *Multivariate Data Analysis with Readings*, 4th ed., Englewood Cliffs.

Hünerberg, R., G. Heise, and M. Hoffmeister (Eds.) (1997): *Internationales Automobilmarketing: Wettbewerbsvorteile durch marktorientierte Unternehmensführung*, Wiesbaden.

Kotler, P. (2003): *Marketing Management*, 11th ed., Upper Saddle River.

Mahajan, V., E. Muller, and F.M. Bass (1990): New Product Diffusion Models in Marketing: A Review and Directions for Research, *Journal of Marketing*, January, 1-26.

Mahajan, V., E. Muller, and R.K. Srivastava (1990): Determination of Adopter Categories by Using Innovation Diffusion Models, *Journal of Marketing Research*, February, 37-50

Meffert, H. and C. Burmann (2000): Product Life Cycle Management: Grundmodell und neuere Entwicklungen, *Texis*, 2, 6-10.

Rogers, E.M. (1962): *Diffusion of Innovations*, New York: The Free Press.

Rogers, E.M. (1995): *Diffusion of Innovations*, 4th ed., New York: The Free Press.

Trommsdorff, V. (2002): Konsumentenverhalten, 4th ed., Stuttgart.

Unger, M. (1998): *Die Automobil-Kaufentscheidung*, Frankfurt am Main et al..

Verband der Automobilindustrie e.V. (VDA) (2002): *Jahresbericht 2002* (www.vda.de).

Zanger, C., G. Baier, and H. Gaus (2004): Wertesysteme und Automobilkauf: Eine empirische Untersuchung, in: Wiedmann, K.-P. (Ed.): *Fundierung des Marketing: Verhaltenswissenschaftliche Erkenntnisse als Grundlage einer angewandten Marketingforschung*, Wiesbaden, 207-230.

Part 4:

Innovation and Controlling and Finance

Reinhart Schmidt

Corporate Governance and Product Innovation

Some Results from an International Study

Prof. Dr. *Reinhart Schmidt*, Department of Finance and Banking, Martin-Luther-University at Halle-Wittenberg.

1 Introduction

Research on the relationships between corporate governance and innovation is the result of a new broader view which seems to be needed in order to secure the progress, effectiveness and efficiency of innovations. The academic work by Klaus Brockhoff can demonstrate the development of such a broader view in the area of innovation.

In the fifties and early sixties of the 20th century the theory of the growth of the firm was on the agenda of management scientists. With his doctoral dissertation Brockhoff (1966) was one of the first researchers applying the theory of growth by empirically investigating the influence of changes in the product portfolio on corporate growth.

The next step was to analyze research as the main source of growth and to derive optimal R&D programs. Here he started with theoretical work, conducted many empirical studies and wrote the well-known textbook (Brockhoff 1999). He then detected marketing as a further source of growth, from which one of the few textbooks on product policy emerged (Brockhoff 1988). The link between R&D and marketing and the discussion of resulting interface problems was a further step (Brockhoff 1989). Finally, a still broader view resulted from the integration of R&D and the theory of innovation, an example is the cooperative work on the strategic and managerial implications of the dynamics of innovation (Brockhoff, Chakrabarti, and Hauschildt 1999).

The research on the management of innovation mostly looks at a single innovation and how to promote a special idea (see e.g. Hauschildt 1997). On the other hand, a broad corporate view requires the integration of the inner and outer environment of the firm as well. This can be reached by referring to the theory and practice of corporate governance and thus by looking at corporate governance as an instrument of innovation management.

Tirole (2001) defines "**corporate governance as the design of institutions that induce or force management to internalize the welfare of stakeholders**". This broad definition, with its reference to stakeholders and not only to shareholders, shows the connection with the general theory of organization. From the theoretical point of view corporate governance is connected with principal-agent-theory (Vives 2000) and thus incorporates aspects of organization and decision theory. Thus, the usage of corporate governance for innovation management can have qualitative and quantitative aspects.

Relationships between corporate governance and innovation can be influenced by country-specific corporate governance systems and by industry-specific requirements concerning the characteristics of innovations. Therefore research on these relationships is desirable in order investigate whether specific corporate governance systems are more or less suitable for a specific industry. With respect to international competitiveness, the adequate formation of a corporate governance system – mainly based upon legal requirements – may thus enable specific countries to attract specific industries. This idea led to the organization of the international empirical study "Corporate Governance and Product Innovation" (COPI) which has been conducted from 1999 to 2002 by a joint group of researchers from six European countries and which has been financially supported under the "Targeted Socio-Economic Research Programme" by the European Commission.

Innovations can be divided into process innovation, product innovation, and organizational innovation. Implications for public policy in the European Union are especially wanted for those innovations which are able to create new jobs. Therefore **product innovations** have been preferred in the European project – though in some industries, like in banking, product innovation often is closely linked to process innovation.

After a theoretical discussion of the relationships between corporate governance and innovation we present and discuss some detailed results from those parts of the overall project which have been derived at the University of Halle with respect to German pharmaceuticals and banks.[1] Finally, we take a broader view and refer to newest developments of corporate governance with respect to innovations in business practice.

2 Theoretical Relationships between Corporate Governance and Innovation

The existing corporate governance systems refer to some common concepts, but the systems mainly show country-specific characteristics. There are a lot of elements by which such systems can be described – see the attempt of an *empirical* classification of more than 30 corporate governance codes by using cluster analysis (Schmidt 2003). On the other hand, one can try to distinguish between types of corporate governance and financial systems which are based upon the dominance of insiders or outsiders within the financial system: "control-orientated" versus "arm's length" systems (see Berglöf 1997). Tylecote and Conesa (1999) call these two systems "insider-oriented" and "outsider-oriented", respectively.

For some people the distinction between insiders and outsiders seems to be linked to the separation between one-tier-systems and two-tier-systems of corporate governance. It must be stressed that these two classifications are independent. Outsider-orientation will be mainly found in the Anglo-Saxon world with its one-tier system but also a German listed company with its two-tier system can be oriented toward outsiders (see as an example the case of Schering below).

---

[1] The author wants to thank Birgit Maczulaitis for her intensive work in the research project.

O'Sullivan (2000) has criticized the Anglo-American governance debates that they are only concerned with the distribution of residual returns and do not ask "how these residuals are generated through the development and utilization of resources." Therefore she links innovation and resource allocation to governance. She especially looks at the relationship between organizational control and innovation and derives the role of the specific industry, the change inherent the innovation process, and the change of corporate governance institutions as important determinants of a corporate governance system. Later Lazonick and O'Sullivan (2000) propose that a corporate governance system should **support innovation by generating financial commitment, organizational integration, and strategic control.** And their paper ends with the statement: "It should be clear that corporate governance is not about aligning incentives of shareholders and managers. Corporate governance is the relation between resource allocation and economic performance on a national, regional, and even global scale."

Tylecote and Conesa (1999) develop a theory which requires to dealing with three types of problems in order to get an effective corporate governance system for innovating firms – they propose novelty, visibility and appropriability as the important factors:

Industries vary in the degree of **novelty**. The higher the novelty of technologies and markets, the more firms need a corporate governance system which integrates industry-specific expertise. Information and communication technology and biotechnology and by them affected pharmaceuticals thus need such expertise.

Industries also show differences concerning the **visibility** of the process of innovation. Low visibility means that performance cannot be properly monitored without high firm-specific perceptiveness in the corporate governance system. Tylecote and Conesa (1999) state a requirement for visibility with respect to physical capital, research (basic and applied) and development, training, design and engineering, and marketing. An outside observer will ask for disclosure of information; if such information is not required by law only insiders can sufficiently evaluate the relevant variables.

Industries can be different with respect to the **appropriability** of innovations. This concept looks at the possibilities to ensure the returns of an innovation. Innovation leads to "spill-overs" to others (besides the shareholders), especially to the employees and customers or suppliers. These groups become beneficiaries of the innovation, patenting is a means of potentially excluding such spill-overs. Alternatively the shareholders can establish a coalition with the other stakeholders. Two extreme approaches can be defined due to Tylecote and Conesa (1999) as a result: (1) Shareholders are the only group of stakeholders whose interests must be considered; (2) 'Enfranchised stakeholders' are forming a coalition with the maximization of the total return to this coalition as the main objective.

Outsider-oriented corporate governance systems should be preferred if industry-specific expertise is needed, which also implies emphasis on shareholder value. Insider-oriented systems are better if firm-specific expertise is relevant, stakeholders must be included.

The main implication of these theoretical considerations is that there is no single ideal corporate governance system. Under the view of innovation, the adequate corporate governance system depends on the characteristics of innovation in a special industry (Tylecote 1999). This means that already the general structure of a "national" corporate governance system may be more or less attractive for a specific industry.

3 Empirical Evidence

The empirical basis for the following presentation and discussion has been taken from the COPI project. The research was executed as a joint European research project in six countries under the coordination of Andrew Tylocete from Sheffield University Managemen School. Researchers from France, Germany, Italy, The Netherlands, Sweden, and United Kingdom cooperated in a 36-months-project from 1999 to 2002.

3.1 Aims and Structure of the Research Project

The objective of the project was:

- to improve scientific understanding of the relationships between corporate governance and product innovation;
- to enable managers, institutional investors, other stakeholders in industry (e.g. banks and trade unions), and policymakers to take steps to improve national and European performance in product innovation in the high and medium technology industries, which are crucial to competitiveness now and in the future. In order to do this it will be necessary to explore which corporate governance regimes are highly conducive to successful product innovation - in the specific circumstances of each firm, industry and country;
- to understand what legal and other measures at national and EU level are appropriate to encourage the development - or continuation - of such corporate governance regimes, and which should be avoided;
- to show company management, shareholders and other stakeholders what they can do to help develop a corporate governance regime suitable to their circumstances.

Furthermore, the objective was to test a contingency theory of the effects of corporate governance on product innovation: It is hypothesized that the effects of a given corporate governance system are a function of certain characteristics of the industry's technologies and pattern of technological change – besides national and corporate culture.

Four partly overlapping project phases were distinguished in order to arrive at overall results:

1. Reviewing the specific characteristics of the **corporate governance systems** in each of the six countries (see for Germany: Ehrentreich and Schmidt 1999).
2. Reviewing the trends of **innovation with respect to selected industries**. The following six high and medium technology industries were analyzed: motor vehicles, machine tools, fine chemicals, pharmaceuticals/biotechnologies, software, and banking. These sectors seem to be crucial to European competitiveness now and in the future.
3. Conducting **case studies** for six to nine companies from two to three preselected industries per country. For instance, the German research group investigated three companies from machine tools (Freiberg), three banks and two pharmaceutical firms (Halle).
4. Developing, sending out and evaluating coordinated **questionnaires** to a sample of companies. The questionnaires contained exactly the same questions for all countries and industries, some industry-specific questions were added. Every company from the drawn samples got three questionnaires which were sent to different persons within the same company: the first was concerned with shareholder relationships, the second addressed problems of R&D (for banks: IT), the third contained questions concerning personnel. In special cases a fourth questionnaire – subsidiaries' relationships with headquarters – was used.

3.2 General Results from Six European Countries

Meanwhile there exist specific evaluations which apply the theoretical concept of novelty, visibility and appropriability to one country. For example, Visintin (2001), one of the researchers of the international project, has shown that the *Italian* corporate governance system can be characterized by high firm-specific perceptiveness, high inclusion of shareholders, but low industry-specific expertise. And – as a consequence – for Italy she states an industrial specialization in industries with low novelty, low visibility, and low appropriability.

The **results of the international study** have been condensed to a final report to the European Commission. The main findings have been summarized by the project coordinator as follows (Tylecote 2002):

"1. Different sectors do indeed present different combinations in the intensities of the three variables; some, software at least, have high novelty *and* low visibility, high need for reconfiguration *and* high spill-overs. All sectors, even that with the highest visibility (pharmaceuticals), require considerable firm-specific perceptiveness from at least their principal shareholders.

2. While it is generally true that the one outsider-dominated corporate governance and financial system (the UK) is relatively high in industry-specific expertise, it shows less of this than the USA. Likewise our insider-dominated corporate governance and financial systems vary substantially in firm-specific perceptiveness, and in stakeholder inclusion; and this, almost regardless of how far they have moved towards outsider-domination. These variations have the effects predicted.

3. The five countries with insider-dominated corporate governance and financial systems are shifting at various speeds towards the outsider end of the continuum. France is well in the lead, Italy and the Netherlands in the rear. These changes are having broadly the predicted effects.

4. Some of the 'new' (or 'renewed') institutional shareholders associated with the move to outsider-domination have shown the ability to develop a high degree of industry-specific expertise *and* firm-specific perceptiveness. The latter in particular is related to their degree of 'engagement' with firms in which they hold a major stake."

A policy recommendation is to encourage engagement by "new" institutional shareholders which actively evaluate and influence a company's innovation policy by their industry-specific *and* firm-specific knowledge. Thus, a change from old insider shareholders to "new" institutional shareholders can ensure an optimal use of shareholders' knowledge for corporate innovation policy.

3.3 Some Results for German Pharmaceuticals and Banks

The two industries which have been investigated at the University of Halle, pharmaceuticals and banks, are of different economic importance and they differ with respect to the role of R&D, the possibilities to protect innovations and the legal form of the companies.

German *industrials* are mainly organized as sole proprietorships, partnerships, or companies with limited liability (GmbH or Aktiengesellschaft), thus enabling to select between different systems of corporate governance. And the selection of the *banks* has to consider that the German banking system can be characterized by the three sectors which are mainly different with respect to the legal form, ownership, and corporate objectives: the private banking sector, the cooperative banking sector, and the sector of savings banks. Thus, the legal form of the company can be of great importance for the corporate governance system – a fact which is often neglected by comparative reviews in the Anglo-Saxon world.

Questionnaires were sent out in the year 2000 to 96 pharmaceutical companies which belong to the German association of research-based pharmaceuticals, 27 answered. The banks were selected from the list of the 100 largest German banks, a preselection led to 55 companies from which 24 answered. Though in all cases the names of the contacted persons had been checked in advance by phone calls, we got back all three questionnaires per company only in much fewer cases. The main reason may be that the companies were asked questions which seem to touch very sensitive areas. Nevertheless, due to the intensive preparation of the procedure our response rate was much higher than the average response rate of the COPI project participants.

The following tables present some results from the pharmaceutical sample. The investigations are based upon a scale from 1 (lowest) to 7 (highest) for the importance of an item.

Table 1: *Priority given to different stakeholders in the company's corporate strategy (scale from 1 (low) to 7 (high))*

Type of stakeholder	Mean value		Standard deviation	
	5 years ago	today	5 years ago	Today
Shareholders	5.23	**5.77**	1.92	1.64
Employees	5.15	**5.69**	1.63	1.03
Labor unions	2.85	2.69	1.63	1.60
Dealers and distributors	4.23	4.62	2.09	2.02
Customers	6.00	**6.38**	1.00	0.65
Preferred suppliers	4.85	5.23	1.63	1.64
Other suppliers	4.15	4.23	1.46	1.42
Providers of debt capital	2.54	2.69	2.10	2.10
Government	3.77	4,15	1.36	1.41
Ecological pressure groups	3.15	3.62	1.57	1.94
Society at large	4.38	5.00	1.12	1.29

Source: results from own COPI study (NOB=13 German pharmaceutical companies)

A first comparison is concerned with the influence on corporate strategy. Table 1 shows the priority given to different stakeholders in the company's corporate strategy. The most important stakeholders are and have been the customers: this can be confirmed by the importance of targeted research and development of concerning specific diagnostic or therapeutic fields. Then the (direct) interests of the shareholders are considered. The employees are slightly behind on rank 3 with a high value as compared to some other countries. Taking customers and employees together, the long-term character of strategic thinking and acting becomes apparent – independently of eventual short-term pressures from the shareholders.

Table 2: *In-depth understanding of problems by different shareholders in German pharmaceutical companies (scale from 1 (low) to 7 (high))*

Problem area	Type of shareholder	Mean value		Standard deviation		NOB
		5 years ago	Today	5 years ago	today	
General situation	largest	5.31	**5.85**	1.44	1.14	13
of the industry	average	4.55	5.27	1.51	1.40	11
Key technologies	largest	5.33	**5.58**	1.56	1.62	12
of the industry	average	4.45	4.91	1.78	1.79	11
Financial position	largest	5.69	**5.69**	1.32	1.38	13
of the company	average	4.90	5.20	1.45	1.48	10
Short-term technology	largest	5.00	**5.62**	1.96	1.66	13
Strategy	average	4.20	4.90	1.99	1.79	10
Longer-term technology	largest	5.23	**5.46**	1.96	1.94	13
Strategy	average	4.09	4.64	2.02	2.06	11
Quality and competence	Largest	5.54	**5.77**	1.27	1.24	13
of the top management	Average	4.91	5.00	1.45	1.48	11

Source: results from own COPI study

The results confirm former results of the author when he asked corporate finance directors in 1996 (Schmidt 1998): "There is empirical evidence that German companies are well aware of short-term pressures from the financial markets and that they have established mechanisms to ensure long-term orientation in spite of short-term pressures. This result to a remarkable extent seems to be supported by the system of corporate governance in Germany."

Labor unions and providers of debt capital (banks) show values far below the mid grade 4.00. Concerning banks this means that the high profitability of the pharmaceutical industry allows to avoid bank loans and that the companies want to stay independent from banks. The companies can follow this strategy of independence because in many cases these responding companies are sound family-owned firms.

The in-depth understanding of problems by different types of shareholder is documented in Table 2. The first areas of understanding are industry-specific, the second four are firm-specific.

There is no remarkable difference in the observed or estimated understanding of problems when looking at industry-specific versus firm-specific problems. Moreover, there is no clear ranking of problems that are understood better or worse. Perhaps the estimation character inherent in the question has influenced the answers. But we can state that the shareholders are oriented toward industry-specific and firm-specific problems as well. Differences are obvious concerning the type of the shareholder and the development within the last five years. These results are plausible because of minor knowledge of the average shareholder and because of more effective investor relations and communication by different media.

In the theoretical section the possibilities of appropriability were shown to determine whether shareholders or also other stakeholders will benefit from product innovations. The importance of different factors which allow a protection of product innovations is investigated in Table 3.

Table 3: *Protection of product innovations from competitors within German pharmaceutical companies (scale from 1 (low) to 7 (high))*

Type of protection	Mean value		Standard deviation		NOB	Level of significance
	5 years ago	today	5 years ago	today		
Patents on products	5.63	**6.05**	1.57	1.39	19	0.039
Patents on processes	4.44	4.67	1.79	2.03	18	0.206
Other protection rights	4.53	5.03	1.28	1.42	16	0.071
Expertise of personnel	4.67	5.06	1.49	1.51	19	0.168
Fixed tangible assets	4.41	4.94	1.33	1.25	17	0.142
Brand image	4.63	5.00	1.50	1.45	19	0.149
Distribution network	3.94	4.50	1.89	2.09	18	0.038
Secrecy	5.05	**5.37**	1.08	1.07	19	0.109

Source: results from own COPI study

The important role of patents for the protection of products in the pharmaceutical industry is well-known. But the relatively high value for "secrecy" shows the necessity of an adequate corporate governance system. A Wilcoxon-test for paired samples was applied to test for differences in the mean values of "5 years ago" versus "today". The role of patents and the distribution network have gained more importance on a 5-percent level of significance.

Investigating interaction between a company's departments widens the traditional view of corporate governance which relates the firm to the shareholders or other outside stakeholders.

The perceived distance between actual and ideal intensity of interaction (see Table 4) requires not only the solution of interface problems (as investigated in detail by Brockhoff 1989) but also the review and construction of wider organizational procedures within the corporate governance system.

Table 4: *Actual versus ideal intensity of interaction between departments within German pharmaceutical companies (scale from 1 (low) to 7 (high))*

Intensity of interaction between departments	**Mean value**		**Standard deviation**		**NOB**	**Level of significance**
	actual	**ideal**	**actual**	**ideal**		
Different research units	4.70	6.10	1.34	0.74	10	0.010
Research with development	5.29	6.18	1.40	0.88	17	0.004
R&D with marketing	4.24	5.76	1.25	0.75	17	0.000
R&D with production	3.94	4.75	1.48	1.34	16	0.010
R&D with finance	3.82	4.59	1.67	1.41	17	0.017
Finance with marketing	4.47	5.12	1.55	1.21	17	0.042
Different product divisions	3.38	4.00	1.19	1.60	8	0.059
Different geographical divisions	3.56	4.44	1.51	1.74	9	0.039

Source: results from own COPI study

The high demand for interaction between research and development is plausible. The required intensity of the interaction between R&D and marketing is also known. But the relatively high value concerning the interaction between finance and marketing may give some hints on limited financial resources with respect to expensive marketing activities.

Again, a Wilcoxon-test for paired samples was applied to test for differences in the mean values of "actual" versus "ideal". With respect to seven of the eight types of interaction the companies perceive that there is a significant deviation from the ideal situation – showing the need for better governance.

A correlation analysis of variables from Tables 3 and 4 can confirm the importance of corporate governance for ensuring interaction. The companies which report high actual interaction between R&D and marketing or finance and marketing are protecting their innovations through expertise of personnel (coefficients of correlation 0.751 and 0.620, both significant at the 1%-level).

Governance variables meanwhile have been introduced to test for the intensity of innovation (see the review by Munari/Sobrero 2003). For large US pharmaceutical companies Lacetera (2000) adds three governance variables to innovation-specific variables in order to explain the research intensity. Only a shareholder concentration variable (besides the innovation variables) leads to better regression results. But as a further result, she addresses the **problem of defining relevant institutional and organizational practices** in order to get measurable variables for the statistical analysis concerning the influence of corporate governance.

The conducted **case studies** indeed lead to a deeper insight into firm-specific relationships.. The selection of case studies on German pharmaceuticals concentrated on listed companies because of secrecy problems with non-listed companies. Moreover, the selection should demonstrate that it seems too simple to generally assign German listed companies to the so-called "Deutschland AG" – as many foreign researchers and analysts do. The chosen companies, Schering and Schwarz Pharma, are independent companies. Schering is a large company (from Germany's point of view) with no dominant shareholder and with important own research activities. Schwarz Pharma is a medium-sized listed company which went public in 1995, the family still holds the majority of shares, and until 2000 has had relatively small own research activities.

At **Schering** (see the case study by Maczulaitis/Schmidt 2001) the successful relationship between innovation and corporate governance is apparent. This is reached by having scientists as members of the supervisory board and by creating new organizations as a link to the scientific community. On the other hand, there is a strong informal connection with financial analysts, the investor relations department knows and informs all analysts who are doing research on Schering. In the case of **Schwarz Pharma** the history of the company is important. The company was very successful in importing US products to Germany and grew quickly. Then the analysts criticized the lack of own research activities and the company decided to establish own research – a risky strategy for the company. This change in the strategy demonstrates the pressure from the capital market very impressively.

The selection of the case studies on banking was influenced by the fact that the German banking system consists of three sectors as described above. We decided to investigate one company from each sector.

At the well-known (listed) **Commerzbank** the importance of outside stakeholders is quite remarkable, because innovativeness is identified as one of the criteria which are evaluated by financial analysts. The management board also gets some pressure from the shareholders including fund managers but there are "still no Anglo-Saxon conditions". Because of the central role of IT for bank processes and products the bank has made high outlays for IT and related personnel. A small "research" group of three product scientists exists but there seem to be problems in the acceptance of their proposals. The marketing department plays a strong role in the approval of new product proposals. Innovations at **DZ Bank** (formerly: DG Bank) – the central bank of more than 2,000 cooperative banks in Germany – are mainly initiated by the market, especially by customers, and they are promoted bottom-up in the organization. Here the management board is not an initiative group but it finally decides on proposals. The supervisory board does not play any role in promoting or decision-making with respect to innovations. Though the company's legal form is a joint-stock company one cannot apply the general finding of the international study that shareholders want to decide on innovations. **Sachsen LB** – one of the regional banks ("Landesbank") in the supporting sector for more than 500 German savings banks – was founded in Leipzig/Eastern Germany after the German reunification. The management board decided to concentrate the bank's new development on innovative products – especially in the area of risk management. This strategy had the advantage of avoiding a larger equity base, on the other hand intelligent employees had to be acquired from competitors. Because of the bank's legal form the management board is controlled by an administration board; this board does not have enough inside-knowledge to initiate or control innovations.

As a result from our case studies of three large German banks we can state that the **combination of a company's legal form, the ownership structure and the company's objective system** plays an important role for the relationship between corporate governance and innovation, especially the legal form should not be neglected.

4 Adaptation of the Corporate Governance System to Innovation

In practice companies now recognize the necessity of adapting the corporate governance system to innovation. By these approaches existing organizational bodies are changed with respect to innovation or new bodies are created.

Actual developments in the development of corporate governance show the adaptation of the systems to innovation. In a recent press release of March 23, 2004, the Italian company **Merloni Elettrodomestici** reports an "upgrading" of its corporate governance system with an innovation and technology committee. The task of this committee will be "to define the strategies and investments needed to develop the Company's innovation capability. It will also take action to spread the culture of innovation within the enterprise ...". Besides four members of the board, the new committee includes experts from business practice and universities, and a number of company managers. In this case the committee is created as a new organizational body besides the existing formal corporate governance system of the Italian style.

On the other hand, meanwhile there exist solutions which use the existing formal corporate governance system. If some members of the supervisory board are elected because of their technological expertise – see the case study on **Schering AG** (Maczulaitis and Schmidt 2001) – then this is a first step of incorporating innovative capabilities on the board level. The second step will be the creation of an own body – a board committee – as created by **Procter & Gamble**. The respective committee charter is presented in Figure 1.

Figure 1: *The Procter & Gamble Company Board of Directors Innovation & Technology Committee Charter*

I. The Committee's Purpose. The Committee is appointed by the Board for the primary purpose of overseeing and providing counsel on matters of innovation and technology.

II. The Committee's Duties and Responsibilities. The Committee has the following duties and responsibilities.

1. ***Innovation and Technology Approaches and Plans***. To review and make recommendations to the Board on major strategies and other subjects relating to:

   a) The company's approach to technical and commercial innovation.

   b) The innovation and technology acquisition process to assure ongoing business growth.

   c) Measurement and tracking systems important to successful innovation.

2. ***Other Activities***. To perform any other activities as the Committee deems appropriate, or as are requested by the Board, consistent with this charter, the company's bylaws and applicable law.

3. ***This Charter***. To maintain and update, as appropriate, this charter, which will be published on the company's website.

III. Authority to Retain Experts. The Committee has the authority to select, direct, and, if appropriate, terminate such experts as it deems necessary in the performance of its duties.

IV. Evaluation of the Committee. Periodically, the Committee will evaluate how well it has fulfilled its purpose and will report its findings to the full Board.

Source: Procter & Gamble

Finnalyy, **good governance is incorporated at lower corporate levels**. The Finnish service company **Serco** aims at "Embedding sound governance" and reports: "We treat all our contracts as if they were businesses and therefore apply sound business principles including the establishment of boards at business unit and contract level. ...At individual contract level the board becomes a catalyst for innovation, continual service improvement and business review."

From an international perspective, **codetermination** must be seen as a special factor which influences the structure of a corporate governance system. Jürgens (2002) describes the "crucial role of the works councils and of Volkswagen's corporate governance system". For multinational companies the Schmidt (2004) shows that the worldwide different regulations concerning codetermination may create great problems of coordination, thus also affecting innovations.

5 Conclusion

Relationships between corporate governance and innovation are a new field of research because traditional concepts of corporate governance use a narrow definition of corporate governance and do not consider innovation. The corporate governance approach must be based on a broader theoretical concept which includes the problems of innovation. Meanwhile also the companies have recognized the necessity of adapting the corporate governance system to innovation. Presented examples of these approaches show that existing organizational bodies are changed with respect to innovation or new bodies are created.

The theoretical part of this paper refers to the classification of corporate governance and financial systems as established by Berglöf and to the approaches for a link between innovation and corporate governance by Lazonick/O'Sullivan and Tylecote/-Conesa. Based upon these theories, a research group from six European countries conducted an empirical study on the relationships between corporate governance and product innovation. The results have been derived from a review of the country-specific corporate governance systems and of relevant technologies in the investigated six industries, after that case studies and questionnaires have been used for the empirical study.

For the part of the project which has been conducted at the University of Halle some detailed results are reported and discussed. Case studies of large German banks show that the combination of a company's legal form, the ownership structure and the objective system plays an important role for the relationship between corporate governance and innovation.

The main result of the empirical international comparison is that industry-specific characteristic elements of innovation are adequately considered by only some of the country-specific corporate governance systems. Thus, the institutional properties of a corporate governance system seem to be one determining factor for the international allocation of industries.

Pressure on change in corporate governance systems will come more and more from institutional investors. They have been relatively passive shareholders with relatively few reform proposals. Meanwhile some institutional investors are playing an important role in monitoring companies and making new proposals. A policy recommendation from the international research group is to encourage an engagement by "new" institutional shareholders which actively evaluate and influence a company's innovation policy by their industry-specific *and* firm-specific knowledge. A change from old insider shareholders to "new" institutional shareholders can ensure an optimal use of shareholders' knowledge for corporate innovation.

6 References

Berglöf, E. (1997): Reforming corporate governance: Redirecting the European agenda, *Economic Policy*, 23, 93-123.

Brockhoff, K. (1966): *Unternehmenswachstum und Sortimentsänderungen*, Opladen.

Brockhoff, K. (1988): *Produktpolitik*, 2nd ed., Stuttgart.

Brockhoff, K. (1989): *Schnittstellen-Management. Abstimmungsprobleme zwischen Forschung und Entwicklung und Marketing*, Stuttgart.

Brockhoff, K. (1999): *Forschung und Entwicklung*, 5th ed., Munich.

Brockhoff, K., A. Chakrabarti, and J. Hauschildt (1999): *The Dynamics of Innovation. Strategic and Managerial Implications*, Berlin.

Ehrentreich, N. and R. Schmidt (1999): *The German Corporate Governance System with Special Respect to Innovation*, Betriebswirtschaftliche Diskussionsbeiträge, 34, University of Halle.

Hauschildt, J. (1997): *Innovationsmanagement*, 2nd ed., Munich.

Jürgens, U. (2002): *Corporate Governance, Innovation, and Economic Performance – A Case Study on Volkswagen*, Working Paper, WZB Berlin.

Lacetera, N. (2000): *Corporate Governance and the Governance of Innovation: the Case of Pharmaceutical Industry*, Working Paper, CESPRI, Bocconi University.

Lazonick, W. and M. O'Sullivan (2000): *Perspectives on Corporate Governance, Innovation, and Performance*, Working Paper, INSEAD.

Maczulaitis, B. and R. Schmidt (2001): *Corporate Governance and Product Innovation at Schering AG: A Case Study*, Betriebswirtschaftliche Diskussionsbeiträge, 24, University of Halle.

Munari, F. and M. Sobrero (2003): Corporate Governance and Innovation, in: Calderini, M., P. Gorrone and M. Sobrero (Eds.): *Corporate Governance, Market Structure, and Innovation*, Cheltenham and Northampton, 3-27.

O'Sullivan, M. (2000): The Innovative Enterprise and Corporate Governance, *Cambridge Journal of Economics*, 24, 393-416.

Schmidt, R. (1998): Financial Markets, Corporate Governance and Short-Term Pressures in Germany, in: Demirag, I. S. (Ed.): *Corporate Governance, Accountability, and Pressures to Perform – An International Study*, Stamford and London, 297-332.

Schmidt, R. (2003): International Comparison of Corporate Governance Codes, Principles, and Recommendations by Using Content Analysis, in: Berndt, R. et al. (Ed.): *Leadership in turbulenten Zeiten*, Berlin et al., 71-83.

Schmidt, R (2004), Mitbestimmung in internationalen Unternehmen, in: *Handwörterbuch der Organisation und Unternehmensführung (HWO)*, Stuttgart (in press).

Tirole, J. (2001): Corporate Governance, *Econometrica*, 69, 1-35.

Tylecote, A. (1999): *Corporate Governance And Product Innovation – A Critical Review Of The Literature*, Working Paper, TSER Programme of the European Commission, University of Sheffield.

Tylecote, A. (2002): *Corporate Governance Performance Pressures and Product Innovation*, Final Report (restricted), TSER Programme of the European Commission, University of Sheffield.

Tylecote, A. and E. Conesa (1999): Corporate Governance, Innovation Systems and Industrial Performance, *Industry and Innovation*, 6, 25-50.

Visintin, F. (2001): *Corporate Governance and Product Innovation – An Attempted Explanation of the Italian Industrial Specialisation*, Working Paper, Università degli Studi di Udine.

Vives, X. (2000): *Corporate Governance*, Cambridge.

Peter Witt

External Innovations and Corporate Venture Capital

Prof. Dr. *Peter Witt*, Department of Entrepreneurship, Otto Beisheim Graduate School of Management (WHU) at Vallendar.

1 The theory of external innovations

An innovation is the introduction into the market of a new physical product or of a new technological production process (Albach 1993, 50). The importance of innovations for firms' long-term success has been a topic of interest in business administration for decades. Large companies spend considerable amounts of money on R&D expenditures. In doing so, they create measurable value (Brockhoff 1995). Unfortunately, investments in innovative activity face many uncertainties of considerable magnitude. There is the risk of technological failure, the risk of missing market acceptance, the risk of too short product life cycles to amortize the R&D expenditures (Brockhoff 1967), the risk of imitations by competitors and many other risks. Therefore, technology and innovation management is an important component of strategic planning (Brockhoff 1998) and controlling (Albach 1993, 230-236).

For the purposes of this paper, a distinction between external and internal innovations is useful. While internal innovations stem from inventions and development activities by the innovating firm, external innovations are based on ideas generated and on first steps in the development process taken in another organization (Albach 1993, 64). The big advantages of external innovations over internal ones are the reduced time to market, the opportunity to develop at lower costs, and the reduction of development risks. The major disadvantage is the difficulty to identify and to acquire pre-developed promising technologies. Another disadvantage is the fact that external innovations sometimes face serious barriers to implementation which are caused by so-called "not-invented-here-effects". Empirical studies in different countries have shown that there are striking differences in innovation performance between countries like the U.S., Japan, and Germany. Interestingly, the differences are particularly large for external innovations with German firms facing serious competitive disadvantages. They have higher costs and need more time for external than for internal innovations. In Japan, it is just the opposite (Mansfield 1988).

Existing research on innovation management clearly shows that there is a whole array of instruments for firms to realize external technological innovations. They can further develop inventions made by and acquired from someone else, they can pursue cooperative R&D with other firms (Brockhoff 1992), or they can have specialized institutions to do R&D work for them. This paper will focus on direct equity investments in innovative new ventures, so-called corporate venturing or corporate venture capital investments (Hardymon, DeNino, and Salter 1983, Sykes 1990, Brody and Ehrlich 1998), as one important way of getting access to new technologies and later transforming them into external innovations.

The term corporate venture capital depicts activities by which an established corporation invests corporately owned finance and other resources in a number of high potential new ventures (Maula and Murray 2000, 1). The ventures may be spin-offs from the parent company or independent start-ups. Investments can be made by the established corporation alone or together with other investors, e.g. venture capital firms or other large corporate investors. Corporate venturing can take different forms. The most straightforward one is a direct equity investment by the large company in a start-up. A very off-hands form are investments by the large company in venture capital funds. In between these two alternatives we have indirect equity investments in new ventures, i.e. investments of a legally separate corporate venture capital (CVC) unit that is wholly owned by a large company. It is this third form of "corporate venture capital" or "corporate venturing" that I will focus on in the following paragraphs.

2 Corporate venture capital and innovative activity in large groups

2.1 The history of corporate venture capital

In the U.S., corporate venture capital activities have been observable since at least four decades. In the 1960s and early 1970s, 25 % of the Fortune 500 firms had a corporate venturing program. These were largely disbanded in 1974 and 1975 due to the collapse of the public market for new issues (Rind 1981, 171). When the independent venture capital market started to grow again in the early 1980s, large U.S. groups renewed their interest in corporate venturing until the market downturn in 1987 (Gompers and Lerner 1998, 7). From the beginning of the 1990s on, the cycle of increased corporate venturing activities started again. What distinguished this cycle from earlier ones was the considerably larger scale of activity and the more diverse set of companies involved in these efforts (Block and MacMillan 1993 and Lerner 2000, 2). The surge in U.S. corporate venturing has just recently been stopped by the breakdown of the new economy (Chesbrough 2000, 31-32).

In Germany, corporate venture capital is a comparatively new phenomenon. The oldest German CVC firm is T-Telematik Venture Holding GmbH, a subsidiary of Deutsche Telekom AG and currently the largest German corporate venture capitalist in terms of funds (over 250 million Euro) and the number of employees. Another early market entrant was DaimlerChrysler Venture GmbH, founded in 1997 with a 20 million Euro funds that was later extended to 100 million Euro. DaimlerChrysler closed its CVC firm in 2003. Bertelsmann entered the market in 1998 with a funds of 30 million Euro and the CVC company Bertelsmann Ventures which was largely restructured in the year 2000. In 1999, Siemens Venture Capital GmbH started operations, the second largest player in Germany in terms of the number of employees as of March 2004. The corporate venture capital units which had been created in several strategic business units of Siemens in the following years were later all integrated into Siemens Venture Capital GmbH. In 2000 and 2001, a number of other German CVC firms entered the market. Examples are Deutsche Post Ventures GmbH with a funds of 50 million Euro, BASF Venture Capital GmbH, equipped with a 100 million Euro funds, and Metro Online Ventures, funded with 50 million Euro.

The majority of CVC programs in the U.S. (Albrinck, Hornery, Kletter, and Neilson 2000, 4) and almost all programs in Germany have been created as a legally separate subsidiary (Witt and Brachtendorf 2002, 687). This organizational separation of the corporate venturing activities from the parent company has some theoretical advantages. First, it solves motivational and organizational difficulties in simultaneously operating the existing business and devoting financial means to independent ventures. Second, it facilitates the separate valuation of individual start-ups in the CVC portfolio by outside investors. Third, the separation from the parent company gives the management of the CVC unit the required degree of autonomy to quickly react to market opportunities and to ensure a speedy and efficient selection process for start-ups that frequently also try to get financed by venture capital firms. From an organization theory perspective, the challenge is to "maintain the delicate balance between smothering the venture and letting it run wild" (Simon, Houghton, and Gurney 1999, 157).

An interesting parallel between the developments of the U.S. and the German market for corporate venture capital is the changing level of investment intensity. Whenever capital markets decline, CVC units tend to be dissolved. When stock prices soar, companies create new CVC units. These cyclical rather than long-term investment strategies may indicate insufficient corporate commitment to corporate venturing (Rind 1981, Hardymon, DiNino, and Salter 1983, and Gompers and Lerner 1998). Another explanation is that the financial goals of investing in start-ups may be more important than officially stated, such that the availability of exit options in the near future drives investment behavior. Finally, it could be that the market for corporate venturing is driven by irrational behavior, i.e. group pressure among large firms to do what all the others do regardless of long-term strategic implications.

2.2 Goals of corporate venture capital activities

Larger groups thinking of creating a CVC unit typically are innovative companies. They have central R&D departments and/or R&D departments in their strategic business units. Nonetheless, these groups have experienced that it is impossible to do research on all new technologies that may become relevant for their businesses in the future. Therefore, their most prominent strategic reason to engage in corporate venturing is to get a "window on potential new business growth areas" (Sykes 1990, 38) or, in different terms, a "window on technology" (Winters and Murfin 1988, 208).

A second reason is to transfer part of the innovative and entrepreneurial spirit that characterizes start-ups into the group, i.e. to foster entrepreneurial thinking and to increase the speed of technological development. The large company can keep contacts (and equity stakes) in spin-offs, i.e. new ventures being created by employees who were willing to create a new venture with technology from the company they once worked for. Corporate venturing also serves to educate all employees in the parent company to the dynamics of technology and market development. It serves as a signal for the importance of external innovations, employee initiatives, and entrepreneurial activity. "Communicating the activities of a corporate venture capital program company-wide so that personnel can see firsthand how and why venture companies are formed, nurtured, and succeed or fail, gives invaluable experience and encouragement to intrapreneurs" (Winters and Murfin 1988, 214).

A third goal of creating corporate venture capital units is the need to leverage existing technology and to support the development of markets and technologies around existing core competencies (Chesbrough and Scolof 2000). In some markets like mobile telecommunication or computer chips, new ventures develop applications and services that support the large corporation's growth and that it cannot develop and market at similar speeds on its own. In other industries, complementary technologies need to be developed to create customer benefit for a core technology already owned and marketed by the parent company. A case in point is nanotechnology ventures and the new materials and coatings expertise of large groups in the chemical industry.

A fourth goal of corporate venturing is return on capital. While it is undisputed that equity investments of venture capitalists in start-ups (exclusively) aim at maximizing the return on investment, it is much less clear that the same should hold true for corporate venturing. First, the strategic benefits could be realized within the group even without much return on capital for the CVC firm. Second, achieving financial returns does not mean that strategic goals are met as well. And if corporate venturing produces no more than positive returns on capital, the money can better be invested elsewhere, e.g. in venture capital funds: "The impact of possible capital gains on total corporate results is viewed as minor compared with the potential for development of new business" (Sykes 1990, 38).

2.3 Corporate venture capital and innovation strategies

Many companies want to be innovative and still find it difficult to implement a growth strategy based on innovations. They are said to be "genetically programmed to preserve the status quo" (Stringer 2000, 71) instead of realizing and implementing radically new technologies. This is one reason to pursue corporate venturing activities, i.e.

to utilize the R&D capabilities and ideas of start-ups. Founders of new ventures have little emotional or economic investment in the status quo, they are intrinsically motivated to realize innovations, and they face less regulatory or administrative hurdles (Rind 1981, 173). In terms of an innovation strategy, strategic corporate venturing is a form of outsourcing R&D to smaller entities which are more specialized, more flexible, and more willing to realize innovations.

Venture investments are typically perceived to be riskier than traditional in-house corporate research and development programs (although they do not have to be). They also tend to be focused on markets and technologies which are somewhat remote from the parent company's present activities, ideally in new and complementary technologies (Hellmann 2001). Therefore, corporate venturing is managed differently than conventional R&D. Start-ups being funded by corporate venture capital firms are less subject to a rigid management of R&D costs and enjoy more leeway in their R&D focus (Albrinck, Hornery, Kletter, and Neilson 2000, 3). Failure of a new venture, even if it was selected very carefully, is the norm rather than the exception. In organizational and legal terms, a large group can handle a write-off in a portfolio firm of the CVC unit much easier than the failure of a large R&D project in the own company. And even if the start-up fails as an independent company, the parent can still benefit from the investment if portfolio firms act as agents or catalysts for the introduction of innovative technologies, products, and processes or if they stimulate entrepreneurial activities in the group (Maula and Murray 2000, 2).

One central problem of implementing the parent firm's innovation strategies, at least partly, by corporate venturing programs is the lack of control. R&D takes place in two different companies, the parent company and the new venture. Corporate cultures and working styles may largely differ between the two. The parent cannot tell the start-ups in the portfolio of the CVC directly what to do and what not to do. Every attempt to do so would actually reduce the innovativeness of the entrepreneurs and thus the potential for external innovations: "Most big companies concentrate so much on owning and controlling things, they do not attempt to learn from the ventures they sponsor" (Stringer 2000, 81). Although owning an equity stake in the start-up and sitting on its board of directors, the CVC management faces similar control problems, i.e. a difficult to find balance between autonomy and control (Simon, Houghton, and Gurney 1999).

Another central problem of an external innovation strategy involving corporate venture capital activities is the required degree of fit between the group and the new venture. Without this fit, both partners cannot benefit from each other's competencies and resources. Empirical research in Canada has shown that there are two dimensions of the fit between the parent company and the innovating ventures. The relational fit reflects organizational culture and structure, while the economic fit refers to goals and resources (Thornhill and Amit 2000, 33-35). The worse the fit between the parent company and the new venture, the lower are the chances of success for the individual start-up and for the parent company trying to realize external innovations.

3 Corporate venture capital as a multi-stage principal-agent-problem

3.1 The organizational structure of corporate venture capital programs

Corporate venturing programs as defined in this paper consist of three (legally independent) partners: The parent company, the CVC firm, and a number of start-ups that this CVC company has invested in. For the sake of simplicity and without loss of generality, the theoretical discussion will focus on a situation with just one start-up in the portfolio of the corporate venture capital firm. From an economic perspective, this organizational structure produces a two-stage principal agent situation with a number of interesting agency problems.

On the first stage, there is the parent company investing money in a legally separate unit, the CVC company This investment can take the form of annual budgets or a fund. Obviously, information asymmetries between the parent (principal) providing financial means and the CVC company (agent) investing this money in start-ups are large. Different interests can also prevail. If the CVC manager gets a performance related bonus depending on financial ratios like return on investment while the parent company is mainly interested in reaching strategic goals, the CVC unit may be overly focusing on financially attractive investments and fail to thoroughly search for investments with large strategic value for the group (Block and Ornati 1987). Similarly, if the parent company does not ensure a long-term funding of the CVC unit, this unit will look for short-term gains rather than long-term strategic investments.

On the second stage, the CVC unit is investing money in a start-up. This principal agent situation is well known and has been described extensively in the literature, because it is identical to that of the typical venture capital investment where the VC firm is the principal and the start-up the agent (Admati and Pfleiderer 1994 and Hellmann 1998). Again, information asymmetry and a divergence of interests may prevail. Figure 1 depicts the two stages of principal-agent-relations in corporate venture capital programs.

Figure 1: *Corporate venture capital as a two-stage principal agent problem*

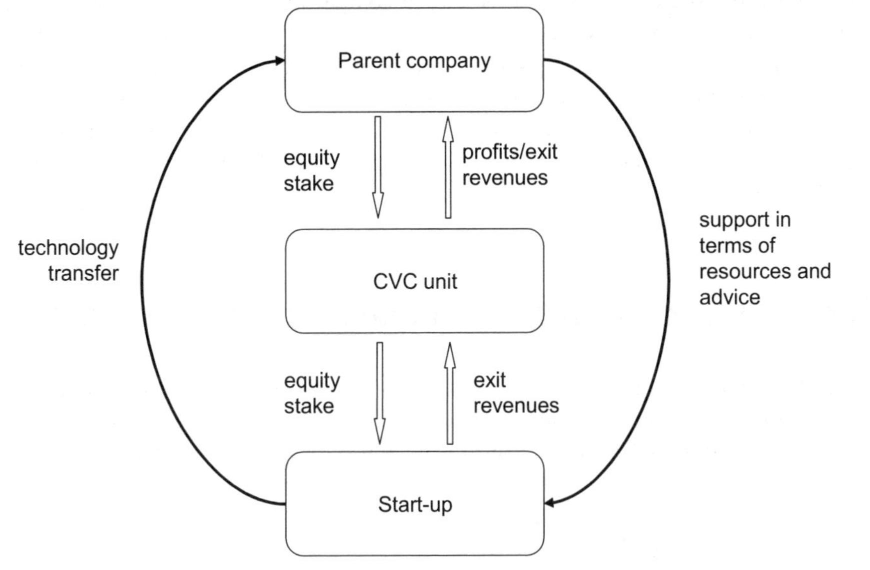

Although it is common to see the investor as the principal and the receiver of capital as the agent, the reverse perspective may be equally relevant because investors could also behave opportunistically. A first important example is the exit planning. Most CVC units promise to realize the exit option that creates the highest value in terms of company valuation. But given the importance of external innovations for the group, entrepreneurs run the risk to be taken over by the parent company if they are very successful, even if another form of exit would provide the entrepreneurs with a higher valuation of their shares. A second example is the commitment and the ability of the investor to provide support, know-how, and access to networks. While CVC units may promise to give similar forms of support as regular venture capitalists and offer the services of the large group as extra benefits, none of the two may be readily available after the investment contract has been signed.

A position of critical importance for the success of corporate venturing is the managing director of the CVC unit. Important qualities to look for are the ability to build bridges between the start-up and the parent company, to recruit teams and to attract talented people. In the theoretical literature, there is a no clear-cut recommendation whether firms should hire internal or external candidates as managing directors of a CVC firm (Albrinck, Hornery, Kletter, and Neilson 2000, 10). External candidates, preferably with a venture capital background, have the advantage that they know capital markets and potential investors very well. They may also bring expertise in screening the deal flow and selecting promising investment opportunities. But their major disadvantage is the lack of knowledge and personal networks within the parent company. Internal candidates can more easily tap into the parent company's resources and know whom to talk to when the start-ups need expertise or support. It is also easier to compensate them along the lines of the group's salary structures. Unfortunately, managers with a professional background that was mainly acquired within the group frequently lack experience in the venture capital business. In particular, they may find it difficult to select promising ventures and to establish contacts to other investors from the venture capital scene.

3.2 The relation of financial and strategic goals

From a theoretical perspective, corporate venture capital as defined in this paper only makes sense if the large companies pursues strategic, i.e. innovation goals when investing in start-ups. If financial returns were the only goal, investments in venture capital funds would appear to be preferable to the creation of a corporate venture capital program. Strategic goals have proven to be much harder to realize than financial goals (Chesbrough 2000, 33). Examples of U.S. corporate venturing programs showed that it is a long road from identifying a potential technological opportunity in a start-up to realizing that potential within the parent company. Most importantly, external innovations from CVC activities take time to mature.

Rind (1981, 178) analyzed a number of U.S. corporate venture capital programs from the 1960s and 1970s and concluded: "Unless it is the firm intention to continue the programme for at least seven years, a venture activity should not be organized." In one of the early large-scale empirical studies on corporate venture capital programs in the U.S., Siegel, Siegel, and MacMillan (1988, 236) found that most CVCs are indeed more concerned with strategic benefit than with financial return. But the study also revealed that the priority for strategic goals led to a neglect of important venture investment criteria. In particular, the CVCs in the sample seemed to be sacrificing financial and entrepreneurial quality criteria to achieve strategic fit for the corporation, a sacrifice the authors stated to be "of dubious value".

While the priority for achieving strategic goals is perfectly justified from the perspective of the parent's innovation strategy, it may still produce competitive disadvantages on the market for new venture equity investments. In particular, the start-up may fear to get deprived of know-how and proprietary technology while being part of the CVC portfolio and thus prefer to sign contracts with other investors: "Entrepreneurs really do fear the loss of proprietary information to the parent" (Hardymon, DeNino, and Salter 1983, 118). In particular, one competitive advantage of venture capital financing is the fact that the investor can credibly claim to be interested in financial returns from exit proceeds only, not in depriving the new venture of its technology.

3.3 Support for start-ups by the group

What the start-up expects from a corporate venture capital funding (besides money) is support and expertise from the group. Direct communication between managers or technical experts in the parent company and the entrepreneurs in the new venture are of crucial importance. Periodic routine reports to the parent or indirect communication via the managing director of the CVC firm cannot ensure that the new venture really benefits from the know-how and the experience of the group. In an empirical study on U.S. corporate venture capital programs, Sykes (1990, 44) found that the most valuable communication was at direct working relationship meetings with individuals in the ventures, rather than at board meetings.

The main theoretical problem with the idea of the group directly and personally supporting start-ups in the portfolio of the CVC unit is the misalignment of incentives. Even if the CVC unit offers to grant the start-up access to the relevant departments in the parent company, it is by no means clear that those departments are willing to co-operate. If the technologies or the products to be developed within the start-up are substitutional rather than complementary to those of the parent company and its strategic business units, quite the contrary happens. The more successful the start-up is, the more likely it becomes that it threatens established business units and thus gets no support at all because it is seen to cannibalize existing businesses (Chesbrough 2000, 34).

In a theoretical model based on principal agent theory, Hellmann (2001) has investigated positive and negative interactions between the start-up and the parent company. He finds that whenever the new venture is a complement to the parent, the optimal financing arrangement is a corporate venture capital contract, i.e. the entrepreneurs choose the strategic investor. But if the venture is a substitute, then the optimal financing is venture capital. The central insight of Hellmann's model is that corporate venture capital firms' quest for synergies, to be found frequently in practice, can turn into a major competitive disadvantage, in particular if the strategic synergy is substitutional in nature and not complementary to existing products and processes within the group.

The principal agent perspective on corporate venturing highlights another potential problem. Support for start-ups by departments or individual persons from the group could easily be combined with attempts to get control over the start-up's activities. Whenever the two partners directly interact and thus leave out the intermediary, i.e. the CVC firm, the parent company could try to increase its influence on the start-up. Empirical studies in the U.S. have shown that such behavior is detrimental to the corporate venturing process. Big companies simply drove away the entrepreneurs and innovators by attempting to guide, control, or influence the commercialization of their ideas (Stringer 2000, 80). Another empirical study conducted in the U.S. found that start-ups with financial support from corporate venturing programs pursued less broad strategies than their resource base and their business model would have allowed because they fear to "infringe on someone else's turf" in the parent company (Shrader and Simon 1997, 47).

3.4 Technology transfer from start-ups to the group

External innovations can only succeed if technological know-how, inventions, or pre-developed products are being transferred from the new venture to the parent company. One obvious way for the parent to do so is to buy technology from the start-up after the first and most risky steps of development have been completed. Another way is to acquire the start-up, i.e. buy the entrepreneurs', the CVC firm's, and all other investors' shares, and integrate the venture as a department or a new strategic business unit into the group (Albrinck, Hornery, Kletter, and Neilson 2000, 9). The major agency problem of transferring technology from a start-up in the CVC portfolio to the parent company is the lack of incentives for start-ups to participate in the deal.

First, selling the core technology or the whole company to the parent largely changes the role of the founders. They either become managing directors of a new strategic business unit in the group und thus lose their entrepreneurial independence. Or they leave the group and do something else. The so-called "serial entrepreneurs" will start new ventures, others may retire or look for a new job. Second, selling technology or the whole company to the large group will only be regarded by the entrepreneurs as a successful exit if the price exceeds the perceived value. There may be other, more attractive exit options like going public, selling the technology or the company to another large group or developing the technology further in the start-up. As Sykes (1990, 42) notes, "the better entrepreneurs (...) don't want to lose the option of taking the venture public at some point." Finally, only if the technology transfer to the parent company is perceived as a well timed deal by all three parties (start-up, CVC unit, parent company), i.e. if everyone agrees on the timing of the actual technology transfer to the group, cooperation and commitment can be expected.

Obviously, corporate venturing programs are trying to overcome the agency problems of technology transfer and exit planning by contractual agreements. Examples are predetermined valuation techniques, staged forms of financing with milestones, and all forms of exit clauses. To ensure that start-ups do not hide successes in technology development or new strategic technology fits to existing businesses in the group, the CVC unit (and sometimes even the parent company) will also implement controlling and reporting systems.

4 Empirical evidence on the German market for corporate venture capital

As the German market for corporate venture capital is small in comparison to the U.S. and has just recently come into existence, little empirical evidence is available. Most existing studies consist of an analysis of individual case studies, recommendations by practitioners, or report on anecdotal evidence. Three more scientific large-scale empirical studies have been published, they will be presented in more detail below. All three are descriptive in nature. To my best understanding, no confirmatory empirical study testing theoretically derived hypotheses on German corporate venture capital programs has been conducted so far (as of March 2004).

The first study to systematically examine the potential of a market for corporate venturing in Germany was Schween (1996). As the empirical analysis was completed before the first legally independent German corporate venture capital program was launched in 1997, Schween's work focuses on venture capital like activities within large companies and their strategic business units. A second study, conducted in 2001, was based on interviews with eight German CVC units (Daniels, Leker, and Seeliger 2002). It focused on the strategic goals and the organizational structure of corporate venturing programs in Germany. The authors state that at the time of their survey, 12 of the 100 largest German companies were found to have active corporate venturing programs. In the most recent and broadest empirical study of the German market for corporate venture capital (Witt and Brachtendorf 2002), 29 private and for-profit CVC units were identified as of June 2001 in Germany. Eight of them had recently terminated their operations, leaving 21 active corporate venturing programs, all of which were included in the survey and agreed to participate. With regard to content, the study covered the whole value chain of corporate venturing activities. It was based on personal interviews with a semi-structured and pre-tested questionnaire.

In the study by Daniels, Leker, and Seeliger (2002), all CVC units reported that getting information on dynamically developing technologies and creating options to buy these technologies later were their most important strategic goals. This result clearly demonstrates that the will to pursue external innovations is a major driver of corporate venture capital activities. With respect to the organization of corporate venturing, the authors derive six critical factors: support by top-management, focus on strategic potential, the creation of interfaces for external and internal ideas, the inclusion of expert knowledge, support of start-ups by experienced managers, and the utilization of the investment know-how of CVC managers.

In the study by Witt and Brachtendorf (2002), getting a window on technology and fostering the parent's innovative abilities were stated to be the most important strategic goals of corporate venturing. Interestingly, the perception of the importance of financial returns differed between the parent company and the CVC unit. While CVC managers felt financial returns to be as important as strategic goals, the parent companies ranked financial returns as less important. Again, this indicates that from the perspective of the large group, the search for external innovations drives corporate venturing activities, not primarily financial motivations. Furthermore, the survey revealed that German CVC units are with one exception organized as limited liability companies (GmbH) managed by a former employee of the parent company, typically an experienced manager with a background in the group's central technology or R&D department. In contrast to recommendations in the literature, most German CVC firms did not hire experienced talents from the venture capital community (Winters and Murfin 1988, 217). The managing director is supported by a small group of investment managers (on average nine people) and directly reports to the executive board of the parent company.

According to the study by Witt and Brachtendorf (2002, 688), German corporate venture capital firms seem to be less autonomous in their decisions than the theoretical literature suggests. While 95 percent of the firms in the sample reported that they could autonomously reject quests for investment by start-ups, many CVC units were not entitled to make investment decisions in new ventures without prior consent of the parent company. Almost half of the CVC firms could not autonomously decide on the timing and the form of the exit. Two thirds of the CVC units had no right to change the investment focus without approval by the executive board of the parent company. 35 percent were not even entitled to decide on syndications, i.e. co-investments with venture capital firms or other strategic investors.

With respect to the cooperation between start-ups and the parent company, the study by Witt and Brachtendorf (2002, 688-690) gives strong support to the notion of serious agency problems in corporate venturing. The study found almost no institutionalized forms of support from the parent company for the start-up. The transfer of know-how and resources was shown to be organized informally and thus to depend largely on the qualifications of the managing director in the CVC unit as the intermediary between the start-up and the parent. All the managing directors of CVC firms in the sample had to report monthly or quarterly to the parent company, in most cases directly to the CFO or the CEO. To avoid envy, they received salaries that are comparable to managers of equal rank in the group. Most importantly, the variable part of their compensations was found to be tied to short-term target agreements rather than the return on investment in the CVC unit or the realization of external innovations in the group. In short and in direct contradiction to suggestions in the academic literature (Siegel, Siegel, and MacMillan 1988, 233), German corporate venture capitalist are treated like other managers in the group and not like independent venture capitalists.

5 Summary and conclusion

Analyzing the reasons for the cyclical nature and the frequent failings of U.S. corporate venture capital programs in the three decades from the late 1960s to the late 1990s, Gompers and Lerner (1998, 9-10) found three major strategic mistakes. First, many programs in the U.S. suffered from a lack of well defined missions, i.e. they sought to accomplish a wide array of not necessarily compatible objectives. Second, senior management showed insufficient commitment to corporate venturing activities and terminated many programs before their strategic goals could ever materialize. Third, many programs inadequately rewarded successful risk taking by the corporate venture capital management team and excessively punished failure.

Looking at the existing empirical evidence on German corporate venture capital programs, which started in 1997 and thus could well have learned from the U.S. role models and U.S. failures, we see a striking similarity of strategic mistakes. According to Witt and Brachtendorf (2002, 686-690), most German corporate venturing programs pursue a confusing mixture of different strategic as well as financial objectives. Many programs were terminated shortly after their inception, mainly because capital markets declined and senior management was dissatisfied with the short-term financial outcomes. And inadequate compensation schemes oriented at salary levels in the parent company instead of venture capital like incentives were found to be the norm rather than the exception.

Given this evidence, it seems fair to conclude that little if any learning from the corporate histories of foreign companies takes place in the corporate venturing activities of large German groups. While these firms state the strategic goal of realizing external innovations to be their most important mission, the (not so long) history of corporate venture capital programs in Germany rather indicates a short-term and cyclical involvement. Perhaps the most disturbing empirical evidence is the fact, that the German market for corporate venture capital, despite its theoretically more long-term perspective, behaves even more cyclical than the German market for venture capital.

6 References

Admati, A. and P. Pfleiderer (1994): Robust Financial Contracting and the Role of Venture Capitalists, *Journal of Finance*, 49, 371-402.

Albach, H. (1993): *Culture and Technical Innovation*, Berlin.

Albrinck, J., J. Hornery, D. Kletter, and G. Neilson (2000): Adventures in Corporate Venturing, *Strategy + Business*, 22, 1-12.

Block, Z. and I.C. MacMillan (1993): *Corporate Venturing – Creating New Businesses within the Firm*, Boston.

Block, Z. and O.A. Ornati, (1987): Compensating Corporate Venture Managers, *Journal of Business Venturing*, 2, 41-51.

Brockhoff, K. (1967): A Test for the Product Life Cycle, *Econometrica*, 35, 472-484.

Brockhoff, K. (1992): R&D Cooperation Between Firms – A Perceived Transaction Cost Perspective, *Management Science*, 38, 514-524.

Brockhoff, K. (1995): Value generation by industrial research, *Technovation*, 15, 591-599.

Brockhoff, K. (1998): Technology management as part of strategic planning – some empirical results, *R&D Management*, 28, 129-138.

Brody, P. and D. Ehrlich (1998): Can big companies become successful venture capitalists?, *The McKinsey Quarterly*, 50-63.

Chesbrough, H.W. (2000): Designing Corporate Ventures in the Shadow of Private Venture Capital, *California Management Review*, 42, 31-49.

Chesbrough, H.W. and S.J. Scolof (2000): Creating New Ventures from Bell Labs Technologies, *Research & Technology Management*, March-April, 13-17.

Daniels, H. von, J. Leker, and C.W. Seeliger (2002): Corporate Venture Capital – der Weg zur erfolgreichen Erschließung neuer Technologien?, *Perspektiven der Wirtschaftspolitik*, 3, 303-316.

Gompers, P.A. and J. Lerner (1998): *The determinants of corporate venture capital success: organizational structure, incentives and complementarities*, Working Paper No. 6725, National Bureau of Economic Research, NBER Working Paper Series, Cambridge, MA.

Hardymon, G.F., M.J. DeNino, and M.S. Salter (1983): When corporate venture capital doesn't work, *Harvard Business Review*, May/June, 114-120.

Hellmann, T. (1998): The Allocation of Control Rights in Venture Capital Contracts, *Rand Journal of Economics*, 29, 57-76,.

Hellmann, T. (2001): *A Theory of Strategic Venture Investing*, Working Paper, Graduate School of Business, Stanford University, February.

Lerner, J. (2000): *A note on corporate venture capital*, HBS case 9-201-036, Boston.

Mansfield, E. (1988): The Speed and Cost of Industrial Innovation in Japan and the United States: External vs. Internal Technology, *Management Science*, 34, 10, 1157-1168.

Maula, J. and G. Murray (2000): *Corporate venture capital and the creation of US public companies: the impact of sources of venture capital on the performance of portfolio companies,* Working Paper, Helsinki University.

Rind, K.W. (1981): The role of venture capital in corporate development, *Strategic Management Journal,* 2, 169-180.

Schween, K. (1996): *Corporate Venture Capital: Risikokapitalfinanzierung deutscher Industrieunternehmen,* Wiesbaden.

Shrader, R.C. and M. Simon (1997): Corporate versus independent new ventures : resource, strategy, and performance differences, *Journal of Business Venturing,* 12, 47-66.

Siegel, R., E. Siegel, and I.C. MacMillan (1988): Corporate venture capitalists: Autonomy, obstacles, and performance, *Journal of Business Venturing,* 3, 233-247.

Simon, M., S.M. Houghton, and J. Gurney (1999): Succeeding at Internal Corporate Venturing: Roles Needed to Balance Autonomy and Control, *Journal of Applied Management Studies,* 8, 145-159.

Stringer, R. (2000): How To Manage Radical Innovation, *California Management Review,* 42, 70-88.

Sykes, H., B. (1990): Corporate Venture Capital: Strategies for Success, *Journal of Business Venturing,* 5, 37-47.

Thornhill, S. and R. Amit (2000): A dynamic perspective on internal fit in corporate venturing, *Journal of Business Venturing,* 16, 25-50.

Winters, T.E. and D.L. Murfin (1988): Venture Capital Investing for Corporate Development Objectives, *Journal of Business Venturing,* 3, 207-222.

Witt, P. and G. Brachtendorf (2002): Gründungsfinanzierung durch Großunternehmen, *Die Betriebswirtschaft,* 62, 681-692.

Jürgen Weber and Eric Zayer

Unexpected Allies in Innovation

An Analysis of the Controller's Contribution to Innovation Processes[1]

Prof. Dr. *Jürgen Weber* and Dipl.-Kfm. *Eric Zayer*, Department of Controlling and Telecommunications, Otto Beisheim Graduate School of Management (WHU) at Vallendar.

---

[1] The authors would like to thank Michelle Mussafi for her thoughtful comments and useful suggestions

1 Introduction

The importance of a constant stream of innovative products to a company's long term success has long been accepted. The same is true of the need for strong management involvement in innovation. While innovation processes have always been considered a challenging terrain for managers, several trends have recently increased the pressure. For one, growing global competition has raised the need for innovation. Second, the increasing orientation of companies towards shareholder value concepts has forced managers to watch the use of funds and innovations' contributions to the company more closely. Tight management is needed to guarantee a steady flow of economically successful innovations that create shareholder value. In consequence, managers face the increasingly complex task of integrating innovation processes into the strategic and operational planning and monitoring systems used in other parts of the company.

In this paper, the authors want to put forth the hypothesis that the performance of innovation processes can be improved by introducing a specialized employee that supports managers. In Germany, there is such a specialized employee: the Controller. While not commonly integrated into innovation processes, Controllers are frequently delegated tasks such as information retrieval and reporting, planning and monitoring and economic evaluation in many other functional areas. Given the challenges management faces in the field of innovation and the heightened importance of proper management, the authors want to critically discuss and evaluate the Controller's potential contribution to the innovation process.

2 Definitions

In this chapter, readers will first be introduced to the authors' concept of Controllers. Further, the innovation process' characteristics will be briefly described. At the end of the chapter, the reader should have a clear impression of the Controller's characteristics, skills, tasks and relationship with management so that his role in the innovation process can be logically derived in Chapter 3.

2.1 The Controller

Although originally an American concept (the term itself betraying its Anglo-American roots), Controller positions are today mostly limited to Central Europe.

Controllers have become a common institution in German companies in the second half of the 20th century and take over a multitude of different tasks there. Hence, it is first necessary to develop a common understanding of Controllers and to differentiate them from managers.

Probably the most apparent distinction relates to the tasks that are attributed to Controllers versus managers. While a manager is expected to exercise leadership, have a vision, make decisions fast and intuitively, manage people and drive them to complete projects successfully, the Controller is a highly specialized employee who works as a supporting and challenging counterpart to the manager to ensure economically sound decisions in three distinct areas: financial and accounting information supply, planning and monitoring processes and analytical economic evaluation.

By comparing Controllers and managers along four dimensions (know-how, character traits, motivational structure and cost), the main differences become apparent. The Controller sets himself apart by his specific ***know-how***. His solid economic and business education and his in-depth focus on financial and accounting aspects set him apart from managers that do not necessarily have the Controller's strong financial know-how but rather come from an engineering or sales/marketing background. His competencies in planning and monitoring processes, financial-information systems and analytical evaluation tools allow Controllers to act as an "economic conscience" and to check plans and projects for their economic viability. This way, they can ensure that only financially profitable projects are implemented. Comparing ***character traits*** reveals that Controllers are commonly perceived as rather unemotional, skeptical, risk-averse, accurate and analytical persons. Being charged with high-level responsibilities and the management of their subordinates, managers typically have little time for in-depth economic analyses and often have to adopt an intuitive, more optimistic "can-do" approach towards problems. In consequence, the Controller can counterbalance the more risk-seeking and more intuitive managers with his more analytical approach to ensure sound decision-making. Further, in the case of disputes, the Controller can contribute economic analyses to create a more objective basis for the discussions. Third, controllers share a common ***motivational structure*** – since they are not directly responsible for the (past) decisions of management, they are more independent in their evaluations than managers that inevitably develop a strong commitment to their projects and that typically have a strong determination to realize their ideas. Hence, Controllers are in a good position to take the role of a critical counterpart and ensure objective, unbiased economic evaluations. Also, in discussions among managers from different departments, the Controller can leverage his uninvolved position and offer a less biased perspective to mediate any potential conflicts. Fourth, Controllers are set apart by their *cost*; in general they are somewhat "cheaper" than managers who carry the full responsibility; therefore Controllers should take over repetitive administrative tasks and free up the managers' time.

As pointed out, the Controller's mission is to ensure financially sound, rational behavior. He does so by a combination of supporting and challenging tasks. The supporting aspect materializes for example when the Controller unburdens the manager from repetitive administrative tasks and frees up the latter's time for more important activities. Another supporting aspect comes to light when the Controller supplements the manager in fields where the Controller's specialized financial and accounting know-how allows him to perform tasks more effectively than the manager. The challenging aspect expresses itself in the Controller acting as a critical counterpart, counterbalancing the manager and challenging his decisions and actions like a devil's advocate. The authors believe that managers accept the Controller's criticalness only because he also delivers directly usable contributions in his supporting function. It is thus important to understand the Controller as a carrier of a bundle of tasks that cannot be split up.

The Controllers' mission as supporting and challenging counterparts that ensure rational behavior has an important implication: there is no static set of specific tasks that can be attributed to Controllers. Rather, their tasks are to a high degree situation-specific and may change over time. Controllers have to actively scan their environment for potential bottlenecks to rational behavior and work to mitigate these in consequence. Among other factors, the manager's business knowledge and leadership style will predominantly influence the Controllers' role (Weber 2002, 72). For example, in the case that a manager is an engineering expert with limited knowledge about financial evaluation, the Controller should not expect to be told what to do; rather, he has to supplement the manager and actively take over tasks relevant to the economic evaluation and then convince the manager of their importance.

One of the strengths of this approach to Controllership is that Controllers' tasks in new functions or in the future can be extrapolated more easily. By analyzing the situational factors and identifying potential bottlenecks to rational behavior, Controllers' tasks can be identified reliably. Hence, the authors will attempt to show typical bottlenecks in the innovation process and derive examples of the Controller's potential contribution.

2.2 The Innovation Process

The focus of this paper is on technical product and process innovations, defined as the successful deployment of an idea that is new to the company (Hauschildt 1993, 11). Technical innovations are the result of a more or less well structured innovation process (also referred to as new product development process) which is defined as the *"(...) sequence of activities and decisions that have the objective to Introduce or deploy a new product"* (Gerpott 1999, 49, translated by the authors). While there are several different depictions for this process (Stippel 1999, 20 for an overview), they typically show a sequence of steps from the innovation strategy and the initial idea for innovation to the commercialization and market diffusion and involve predominantly three departments: R&D, manufacturing and marketing (Schewe 1992, 28).

There is a strong consensus among practitioners and theoreticians that the innovation process is too important for the company to leave to pure chance (Brockhoff 1999a and 1999b) and hence needs proper management. The goal of innovation management must be to guarantee the steady flow of economically successful, innovative products that are necessary for the company to attain its overall long term goals and create shareholder value (Gupta, Wilemon, and Atuahene-Gima 2000, 57 or Stippel 1999, 36). To achieve this objective, innovation management involves both step-specific as well as process-spanning activities and tasks (Stippel 1999, 36).

Figure 1: *The Innovation Process*

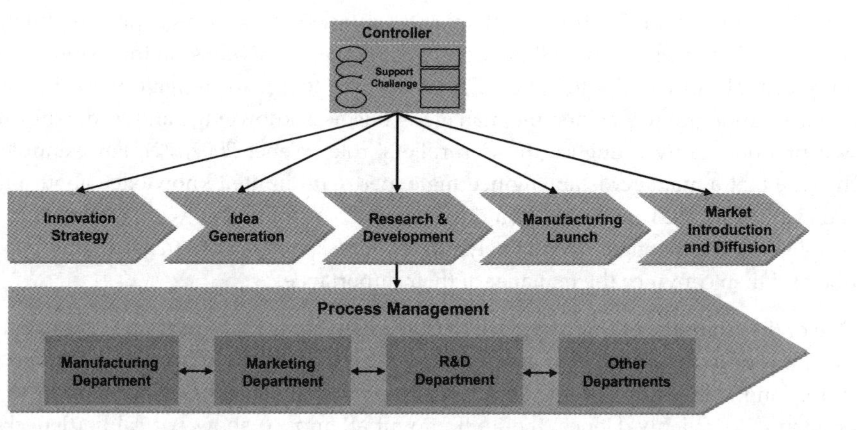

Source: Combines elements of Sabisch 1991; Hauschildt 1993 and Brockhoff 1999b

However, the innovation process is defined by some characteristics that make it a challenging area for management (a more detailed description of potentially relevant particularities will be given in chapter 4.2). The more challenging the process, the more managers need support – thus it is surprising that Controllers are rarely integrated in innovation processes; even in Germany, where Controllers are common in other areas of management. It is probable that innovation managers have no experience working with Controllers and are unsure of their potential benefits and that Controllers on the other hand have been ignoring innovation processes, finding them too technical, too unstructured or too difficult to evaluate. To counter these arguments, the Controller's potential contributions will be identified and evaluated in the subsequent chapters.

3 The Controller's Potential Contributions to the Innovation Process

In the following section, the authors will identify the Controller's potential contribution to the innovation process in his function as a counterpart who supports and challenges the manager. As pointed out before, the Controller can contribute to the individual steps of the innovation process (section 3.1) as well as to the overarching process level (section 3.2).

3.1 Contributions to Individual Process Steps

For the purposes of this analysis, the objectives and main management tasks of each individual process step will be outlined briefly. As pointed out before, the Controller will have to assess the manager's background and leadership and decide where he should best unburden, supplement or challenge the manager to ensure rational behavior. In the following sections, examples of potential Controller contributions will be given. However, this should not imply that the Controller will engage in all of the activities all the time – depending on the manager's abilities and orientation, the Controller will assume different roles and tasks in different situations.

Strategy Phase
In the first process step, the strategy for innovation and technology has to be determined.

The manager can delegate tasks such as information retrieval and editing for the strategic analysis to the more analytical Controller. If the Controller assumes that the manager is too intuitive in his decisions, the Controller can support the manager with analytical tools (e.g. technology-lifecycle or portfolio analysis) to ensure a logical derivation of the strategy (Kreikebaum 1991 or Bürgel, Haller, and Binder 1996).

Given the importance of innovation to the company's long term profitability, the innovation strategy has to be coordinated with the corporate strategy and other related functional strategies, e.g. the marketing strategy (Brockhoff and Chakrabarti 1988). Making use of the Controller's experience with corporate planning, the manager can delegate this task to the Controller to free up his own time for other tasks.

Being more independent than the manager, the Controller can take over an important role in the strategic check-up. He can dedicate more time to check premises and to challenge the quality of analysis and the comprehensiveness of the resulting strategy than the time-pressed manager. Further, the Controller can use his access to information systems to track the strategy's implementation. In the case that relevant new information emerges, the Controller should check whether the strategy is still adequate and push for adjustments when necessary.

Idea Generation Phase
In the following process step, ideas have to be generated, evaluated and selected.

Managers can delegate the set-up of the structured idea generation process to the Controller. Using his experience with coordinating complex processes that span several departments, the Controller can make sure that employees from all relevant departments are integrated into a structured process that provides for the use of creative techniques and a staged evaluation process (Stockbauer 1989, 201 and 210). During the evaluation, the Controller can make sure that the potentially biased manager allows for a balanced evaluation integrating aspects from marketing as well as R&D and manufacturing. The manager can delegate the economic evaluation of ideas to the Controller, leveraging the latter's advantage on the tool side. In addition, the unbiased Controller can act as an economic conscience and make sure that the selected ideas are in line with the previously fixed innovation strategy. Further, the Controller should see that ideas with weak evaluations are excluded from further development to save the company's scarce resources.

Research and Development Phase
In the ***research and development*** process step, a project will be started to generate usable technical knowledge (Gerpott 1999, 28).

The first area where a Controller could contribute in this step is in the internal or external development decision (Gerpott 1999, 227). Essentially, the Controller can counterbalance any biases to keep development internal as he is probably less prone to the 'Not-Invented-Here' syndrome (Mehrwald 1999 for a detailed discussion) than the managers and engineers that are more directly and more emotionally involved.

The Controller's budgeting experience makes him an ideal choice for the handling of the project's budgeting. He can support the bottom-up budget calculations and reconcile these with management's top-down calculations in the ensuing negotiations (Brockhoff 1987; Brockhoff and Chakrabarti 1997 or Brockhoff 2001, 64).

During the process that follows, the manager can assign the administrative monitoring function to the Controller. Profiting from his experience with information systems, the Controller may take on all tasks of recording, analyzing and reporting cost, time and performance information. When the development project reaches its pre-defined gates, the Controller can participate in committee meetings to ensure rational go/no-go decisions, e.g. by challenging overly optimistic sales and cost forecasts (Weber, Hirsch, Linder, and Zayer 2003, 14). Using his more analytical approach, the Controller can calculate the effects of competitor reactions on sales forecasts and improve the quality of cost estimates by using benchmarking studies and historic cost curves. The Controller should make sure that also more intuitive managers incorporate the financial facts into their decisions. Providing a sound financial analysis can be especially helpful when there are conflicting views between different members of the team. By delivering methods and hard facts, the Controller can focus disputes on data and make them more productive. For example, conflicts between marketing and technical departments can be emotionally defused by providing methods such as quality function deployment (Hauser and Clausing 1988) or target costing approaches (Seidenschwarz 1993).

Manufacturing Launch Phase

When the product is transferred from development into production, the Controller can again contribute to supporting and challenging management.

The Controller should be integrated in the make-or-buy decision or when there is a decision between different facilities and methods to prevent potential biases or contortions and ensure proper analysis. After the initial introduction to production, the Controller can use his experience with information systems and ensure that costs and quality are monitored very closely and that deviations from the previously planned target values be reported directly to ensure prompt reactions.

Market Introduction and Diffusion Phase

In the last phase, the proper marketing mix (see Albers 2001, 83 and Albers 1989) has to be decided on.

When the remaining three Ps (price, place and promotion) of the marketing mix's four Ps (McCarthy 1981) have to be decided on, the manager can once more delegate tasks that fall into the Controller's competence areas. For example when determining the innovation's price, the Controller can supply information on marginal costs and target contribution margins as input into price setting and make sure the resulting price reflects the product's competitive environment and the value the product potentially creates for the customer (Kotler and Bliemel 1999, Chapter 17). Also, the manager can have his Controller conduct an economic analysis of planned promotional activities (Schulz-Moll, Esser, and Klein-Bölting 2003, 165). Another example of the Controller's contribution to the marketing mix includes the calculation of contribution margins of different distribution channels which can then be used in decisions concerning the product's distribution.

3.2 Contributions to the Overall Process

So far, the Controller's contribution in distinct process steps has been described. However, it is equally important for a successful implementation that the overall innovation process is well-managed and coordinated (Brockhoff 1986, 354). Three areas will be analyzed for the Controller's contribution on the process level: process management, coordination and champions of innovation.

Process Management

The Controller can trigger innovation processes, e.g. when his revenue extrapolations (based on the current product line up) indicate a gap to the previously fixed targets for that time point. Directing the management's attention to the strategic revenue gap, the Controller creates awareness for the need for innovation (Stockbauer 1991).

Once the need for innovation has been acknowledged, the manager can delegate tasks such as budgeting, objective setting and the process set-up for the overall innovation process to the Controller. During the course of the innovation process, the Controller can deploy his strength of measuring and aggregating information into performance indicators and take on the documentation and monitoring of the implementation. Stippel (1999) presents over 40 specific performance indicators as well as a system that integrates these. By collecting and aggregating data, the Controller enables the manager to gain a quick overview and thus facilitates the manager's job of managing the complex process. Even without direct instruction, the Controller should track the innovation's progress to make sure that the process is on track.

An important aspect of managing the innovation process is to integrate it into the overall company and its overarching planning, monitoring and reporting systems. Being responsible for monitoring and reporting in other areas of the company, the Controller can integrate innovation measures into the overall reporting system. Reporting innovation measures companywide will inevitably direct senior management's attention to innovation processes and help innovation managers focus on important aspects. The idea of using information mostly to direct attention to a problem area is also referred to as "conceptual use of information" (Menon and Varadarajan 1992), according to the old lore: *"What gets measured, gets done"*.

Coordination

The complex innovation process is characterized by a high number of interfaces, e.g. interfaces between the R&D, marketing and manufacturing departments as well as the more indirectly involved departments or interfaces between the individual process stages (Gaiser 1993, 4 or Brockhoff 1989). Coordination of these interfaces is important to guarantee a smooth implementation (Gupta, Raj, and Wilemon 1986). Controllers are known as taking an important stake in the coordination of different entities in the company. Some authors even consider coordination to be the core of the Controlling function (Horváth 2003), while others plainly refer to the Controller as "interface specialist" (Gaiser 1993, 15). While the Controller's tasks go beyond pure coordination, their specific role as coordinators in the innovation process will be highlighted here.

At the outset of the innovation process, the Controller can avail his involvement in the planning cycle and the process set-up to create interfaces between the necessary departments and thus take care of the integration of all relevant groups. During the course of the innovation process, the controller can take advantage of his experience with information systems to organize the flow of information between different departments and provide the team with the relevant information (e.g. process status, the percentage of budgets used or the expected net present value). Empirical studies confirm the need for improved information flows (Littkemann 1997, 185). Another important aspect of the Controller's interface function is to provide a common language to members of the innovation process, since communication problems often prevent understanding between departments (Brockhoff 1989, 73). R&D personnel often speak in very technical terms that are hard to understand for non-experts; marketing also has its own lingo and so does manufacturing. By providing numbers on cost, sales and revenue projections, the Controller can provide a common language, an Esperanto, that the different parties can converse in. Third, the Controller can use his position as an unbiased outsider (i.e. not coming from a marketing, manufacturing or R&D department) and his less emotional personality to moderate in discussions. Empirical evidence suggests that marketing departments typically have a higher relative influence on management decisions than other departments (see Homburg, Weber, Aust, and Karlshaus 1998, 22). The Controller should watch out for such biases and make sure that the best solution for the company overall is chosen.

Champion of Innovation

Schon (1963, 74) was the first to describe the importance of a "champion" (or "innovation promotor") that is not directly involved in the technical innovation work but that helps to sell the innovation within the organization. Over time, several distinct roles for innovation champions have been identified (Witte 1973, Hauschildt and Chakrabarti 1998, Hauschildt and Kirchmann 1998 and Walter and Gemünden 1998). A detailed look at champion literature reveals that the Controller resembles the descriptions of the process promotor (Hauschildt and Chakrabarti 1998) and can thus take an important role in driving innovation processes to success.

In-depth knowledge of the organization and information flows characterize the process promotor. The Controller typically accumulates this kind of detailed know-how during the planning cycle or when designing information systems. This allows him to communicate more easily with members of different departments and across hierarchical levels.

Process promotors are supposed to translate technical lingo into "corporate language" and communicate the innovation's progress in the organization. The Controller not only has good access to different departments and top management, but his economical evaluations can also serve as a commonly understood language. Hence, the Controller can help transmit the innovation's status probably better than purely technically-oriented staff. By making innovations measurable and by reporting performance indicators, the Controller not only creates awareness for innovation at different levels of the organization, but also establishes more trust in the innovation process.

Another important aspect of the process promotor is the ability to transfer vague ideas into actionable objectives with solid processes to achieve these. Considered a planning specialist, the Controller is used to set up structured processes. In addition, his involvement in developing corporate strategy should help him to create a link between corporate strategy and innovation activities. This contribution especially should help keep innovation processes in line with the overall strategy and create shareholder value. The Controller is hence in an ideal spot to fulfill the role of a process promotor.

4 Evaluation of the Controller's Contribution

4.1 Relevance

In the previous chapter, the Controller's potential contributions to the innovation process were identified. However, a question remains: How relevant is the contribution to the innovation process? Evidence can be derived by comparing the Controller's contribution with the success factors that have been identified in previous empirical studies. Since there is a large amount of success-factor studies, Ernst's (2002) meta-analysis, that groups the success factors into five broader categories (new product development-process, organization, culture, senior management and strategy) will be used as a framework for the following discussion. Due to space constraints, the authors had to omit the sources of the original studies – interested readers should refer to Ernst's paper for an overview.

New Product Development Process
In the new product development process category, strong orientation to market demands, good preparatory work, (especially the clear definition of the product), high quality of planning (i.e. the set-up of a structured process) as well as continuous commercial assessment are identified as significant success factors.

While the Controller supports the orientation to market demands only indirectly through his coordination tasks and by ensuring that the marketing department's opinions are integrated adequately in the evaluations, the Controller can contribute strongly to planning, process management and commercial assessment. Being a specialist in the field of planning, the Controller can take over the complete process set-up and planning of (financial) process targets. Given the Controllers' strong competencies in evaluation tools and his direct access to the company's information system, he is obviously in an ideal situation to support the continuous commercial assessment.

Organization

Well operating cross-functional teams, a strong project leader with adequate qualification and authority, high autonomy and responsibility of the team, strong commitment of the leader and intense communication within the team are considered the relevant success factors with respect to the organization of the new product development process.

Although the Controller can do little more than make sure that cross-functional teams are set in place, he can contribute significantly to the remaining 4 success factors. By acting as a supporting and critical counterpart to the project leader, the Controller supplements the manager's technical knowledge with his business knowledge, thus increasing the overall qualification of the project's management. The more the senior management can be sure that the team combines all necessary capabilities for the economic success of the project, the more it will be ready to let the team work autonomously. With his reporting and monitoring activities, the Controller makes the project manager feel more traceable and accountable for his actions, thereby increasing his commitment to the project's success. By easing information flows, offering a common language for communication and moderating in situations of conflict, the Controller can help intensify communication within the team.

Culture

Although only a limited scope of cultural elements have been tested so far, 4 factors have been identified as critical for success in the culture field: a systematic innovation scheme, an entrepreneurial, innovation-friendly climate (indicated by free time for researchers to work on their personal field of interest, support for work on unofficial projects and corporate venture capital) and the existence of innovation champions.

While the Controller's impact on the climate in general is unclear, the Controller can use his process responsibility to create systematic schemes to deal with innovations. Further, the Controller can use his position in the planning and budgeting cycle to ensure that researchers are granted time and resources to fulfill their interests. However, most evident is probably the Controller's contribution as predestined process promoter.

Senior Management

Two main factors concerning senior management appear to be relevant to success: top management's material and non-material support for the innovation and its accountability.

As shown above, the Controller can increase senior management's likeliness to invest significantly into innovation processes by directing their awareness to innovation, supporting innovation personnel in the communication of their needs and by making innovation more controllable. With his information and reporting system, the Controller can increase the accountability of senior management and thus increase pressure on top management indirectly.

Innovation Strategy
In the field of strategy, three main success factors materialize: clear definition of the innovation objectives and the innovation's meaning for the overall company, strategic focus and long term momentum.

Being actively integrated in the definition of innovation objectives and coordinating the corporate and innovation strategy, the Controller not only contributes to the clear and strict definition of objectives but also handles their communication within the organization. In his role as supporting process coordinator, the Controller ensures that the innovation's momentum is maintained throughout the whole process and that it does not get stuck at the transition between two phases or interfaces.

Conclusion
The analysis indicates that the Controller can deliver a significantly positive contribution to 13 of the 17 identified success factors. Hence, it is highly probable that the integration of Controllers improves the success probability of an innovation process.

4.2 Potential Issues

Given the particularities of the innovation process, having a Controller work in the field can also be perilous. Unwanted side-effects can occur if the Controller is unaware of or incapable of dealing with the particularities of the innovation environment. In this section, potential traps for Controllers will be identified and ways to cope with these particularities will be presented.

Short-Term Focus
Controllers often adopt a short-term accounting focus and are often backward-looking in their analysis, e.g. when interpreting historic cost data. This is not compatible with innovation's orientation towards the long-term future. Failure to recognize this aspect could lead the Controller to oppose innovation projects with the rationale that they are not profitable in the short-run. To counter this effect, the Controller has to understand the long-term investment character of innovation and adapt his evaluation and control systems accordingly (Littkemann 1997, 12).

Reluctance to Systems Change
Being used to working in routine areas, Controllers might have difficulties working with innovation processes that are typically singular and unique; two innovation processes seldom are alike. Within the process, untested, new ways to solve a problem might have to be taken and structures and systems that were compatible with former processes might have to be changed. If the Controller opposes necessary changes or is too slow (e.g. to adapt his reporting systems), he can harm the innovation process' success. It is crucial that the Controller accepts the individual process' uniqueness.

While critically challenging the need for change, he has to be ready to adapt to new situations wherever necessary.

Failure to adapt Work Style
Innovation processes can exhibit a complexity that, in combination with the high level of uncertainty, might make them resemble something closer to chaos than to a structured process. Being known for their preference for well-planned, logically-structured, tightly-monitored processes, Controllers may seem to be an unlikely contributor to innovation processes. If they try to directly transfer their preferences and work-styles, they might represent more of a hazard than a benefit for innovation processes. Since complexity and uncertainty render detailed planning next to impossible, detailed planning would not only be a waste of time, but demanding strict compliance with inappropriate plans would certainly discourage managers. Rather, the Controller has to embrace complexity and uncertainties as necessary evils. Instead of fighting them, he should classify processes by their amount of complexity and uncertainty and adapt his systems and tools to the context. The Controller should use tools have been designed to incorporate uncertainty and flexibilities, like for example the "rolling detailing of planning" instead of a fixed plan; modern, less rigid budgeting techniques that are adapted to situations of high uncertainty like "Beyond Budgeting" (Hope and Fraser 2003 and Weber 2003) or evaluation tools like Real Options that can price flexibility (Trigeorgis 1996).

Failure to Recognize Risk
While manufacturing processes are generally well understood and mastered, innovation processes typically exhibit much higher technical, market and economic risks. Failing to recognize the higher levels of risk, the Controller could be a precarious counselor. The Controller has to incorporate the existing risks into his planning (e.g. by making sure that the company's future does not solely depend on the success of a single innovation, using a balanced portfolio approach). In his monitoring task, the Controller should actively look for indicators suggesting a failure to be able to react (i.e. improve or terminate) quickly. In the evaluation of projects, special attention should be placed on risk as opposed to focusing only on revenue aspects. Risks should be mapped and explicitly integrated into the project's evaluation, e.g. by using sales distributions to incorporate sales variability instead of using just average forecasted sales.

Failure to Focus on Appropriate Measures
Controllers, who restrict their reporting to cost information, can represent a real threat to managers trying to control an innovation process. Empirical evidence shows that managers tend to focus their attention on the data that is reported to them, ignoring other, maybe more relevant aspects. Given the higher relative importance of time and performance measures in comparison to cost data in the innovation area, a Controller that reports only cost data would be outright distracting to the manager and would lead the manager to set false priorities. The implication is clear – the Controller has to

adapt his management information and reporting system and include a larger percentage of non-financial data, specifically time and quality data, offering managers a one-stop solution for their information needs.

Failure to Gain Confidence

Potentially the most perilous hazard is the limited acceptance for Controllers and their services in the innovation field (typically most pronounced in the R&D-department). In mild cases, the lack of trust prohibits fruitful cooperation; at the extreme the introduction of an unaccepted Controller could embitter technical experts, sour the atmosphere and lead to decreased effectiveness. Two reasons are generally given for this limited acceptance: First, the R&D employees' disdain for "technical laymen" is assumed to make them dislike Controllers who do not have enough technical expertise to appreciate their work and who probably purely annoy researchers with their administrative demands. Second, cultural differences (e.g. expressed by differing values, objectives, and work styles) are said to weigh on the relationship (Rossel 1998, 327 or Werner 1997, 1).

To counter the first point, the Controller should start showing interest in technical work and accumulate enough technical knowledge to neither be intimidated by researchers' technical explanations, nor to annoy scientists with a lack of understanding. Only if the controller is willing to look, listen and learn can he expect the researcher to make an effort to be open to the business perspective. In order to deal with the presumed cultural differences, Controllers must learn to accept the researcher's peculiarities, as long as they are not in conflict with the economic success of the innovation. Equally, researchers have to be educated to understand the Controllers' contribution and business arguments as well. Mutual insight will most probably improve the relationship over time.

Lack of Acceptance of Mutual Adjustment

Another aspect that could potentially endanger the important but fragile atmosphere in the R&D-department is the Controller's lack of experience with mutual adjustment as the predominant coordination mechanism. Being used to working with plans, it is easily imaginable that Controllers will have significant difficulties when working with R&D employees that are used to setting their own work schedules and changing these flexibly as new information comes up. Falling victim to behavioral patterns and attempting to "over-coordinate" or to plan everything in detail could prove fatal. Instead, Controllers have to be more flexible with individuals that are used to a lot of freedom. Trust is clearly a precondition in this context, but is not be enough. When individuals have larger degrees of freedom in the fulfillment of their tasks, considering behavioral aspects becomes increasingly important. Controllers (in practice and in theory) have to analyze how self-organizing employees can be governed and how tools and information offered by Controllers influence their decisions and behavior (Weber, Hirsch, Linder, and Zayer 2003).

Inadequate Reaction to Measurement Problems

The inability to measure input and output correctly can have two detrimental outcomes: either the Controller spends a lot of time and resources in vain to collect hard data or the Controller resigns since he believes that he cannot control a process that he cannot measure. Two alternative strategies to cope with this issue are suggested here.

The first strategy would be to attempt to alter and improve measurement. Since it can prove difficult to measure innovation processes directly, Controllers can try to improve the portfolio of performance measures by integrating qualitative measures (e.g. the result of peer reviews to assess the long term prospects early on) or by using trailing quantitative measures such as the percentage of sales of new products to total sales or leading quantitative measures such as the R&D pipeline's fill status (Gerpott 1999, 81 or Stippel 1999 for a range of output measures). The second strategy is that Controllers accept the measurement difficulties and shift their attention to challenging the proper use of inputs and process implementation. The logic is that when the right inputs are combined correctly, the output should not be far off the desired state. More time may then be dedicated to pressing control questions, for example the optimal moment for a project termination. Rather than resigning or wasting time to calculate precise project values, the Controller has to accept that a rough estimate is enough and focus on more promising tasks (Littkemann 1997, 14 for a similar argument).

5 Conclusion

In this paper, the authors have attempted to identify and analyze the Controller's potential contribution to innovation processes.

They have introduced readers to their concept of the Controller as a specialized counterpart who ensures rational management behavior. The Controller supports the manager by taking over tasks that he can fulfill more effectively or efficiently to unburden and to supplement the manager. Further, Controllers scan their environment for potential shortfalls in rational behavior and work to mitigate these.

Examples of the Controller's contribution to innovation management have been derived on the level of individual process steps as well as the process management level. It has been shown that in each phase of the innovation process, the Controller can deliver a significant number of contributions. On the process level, the Controller can not only support process management, but also take on a coordination function and promote the innovation's case. Senior level management will appreciate the Controller's work to ensure rational behavior in the area of innovation; managers in the innovation area will probably mostly appreciate the Controller's supporting and unburdening services.

The value of this contribution was shown using empirically identified key success factors of innovation processes. Supporting 13 out of 17 major key success factors directly, the Controller's contribution can be considered positive and valuable. However, the innovation field has characteristics that differentiate it from classical Controller domains – failing to recognize these potential pitfalls would be dreadful for Controllers.

Given that Controllers carefully pay attention not to fall victim to the specific pitfalls of this particular environment, they can deliver a valuable and unique contribution to innovation processes. In consequence, the authors suggest that Controllers be integrated in innovation processes to a larger degree.

6 References

Albers, S. (1989): Gewinnorientierte Neuproduktpositionierung in einem Eigenschaftsraum, *Zeitschrift für betriebswirtschaftliche Forschung*, (41) 3, 186-209.

Albers, S. (2001): Marktdurchsetzung von Innovation, in: Albers, Sönke, Klaus Brockhoff, and Jürgen Hauschildt (Eds.): *Technologie- und Innovationsmanagement. Leistungsbilanz des Kieler Graduiertenkollegs*, Wiesbaden, 79-116.

Brockhoff, K. (1986): Effizienz von Forschung und Entwicklung. Staudt, Erich (ed.): *Das Management von Innovationen*, Frankfurt, 343-355.

Brockhoff, K. (1987): Budgetierungsstrategien für Forschung und Entwicklung, *Zeitschrift für Betriebswirtschaft*, (57) 9, 846-869.

Brockhoff, K. (1989): *Schnittstellenmanagement*, Stuttgart.

Brockhoff, K. (1999a): *Forschung und Entwicklung. Planung und Kontrolle*, 5th ed., Munich.

Brockhoff, K. (1999b): *Produktpolitik*, 4th ed., Stuttgart.

Brockhoff, K. (2001): Innovationsmanagement als Technologiemanagement, in: Albers, S., K. Brockhoff, and J. Hauschildt (Eds.): *Technologie- und Innovationsmanagement. Leistungsbilanz des Kieler Graduiertenkollegs*, Wiesbaden, 17-78.

Brockhoff, K. and A. Chrakrabarti (1988): R&D,Marketing Linkage and Innovation Strategy, *IEEE Transactions on Engineering Management*, (35) 3, 165-174.

Brockhoff, K. and A. Chakrabarti (1997): Take a Pro-active Approach to Negotiating Your R&D-Budget, *Research Technology Management*, (40) 5, 37-41.

Bürgel, H.D., C. Haller, and M. Binder (1996): *F&E Management*, Munich.

Ernst, H. (2002): Success Factors of New Product Development: A Review of the Empirical Literature, *International Journal of Management Reviews*, (4) 1, 1-40.

Gaiser, B. (1993): *Schnittstellencontrolling bei der Produktentwicklung*, Munich.

Gerpott, T. (1999): *Strategisches Technologie- und Innovationsmanagement*, Stuttgart.

Gupta, A., S.P. Raj, and D. Wilemon (1986): A Model for Studying R&D-Marketing Interface in the Product Innovation Process, *Journal of Marketing*, (50) 4, 7-17.

Gupta, A., D. Wilemon, and K. Atuahene-Gima (2000): Excelling in R&D, *Research Technology Management*, (43) 3, 52-58

Hauser, J. R. and D. Clausing (1988): The House of Quality, *Harvard Business Review*, (66) 3, 63-73.

Hauschildt, J. (1993): *Innovationsmanagement*, Munich.

Hauschildt, J. and A. Chakrabarti (1998): Arbeitsteilung im Innovationsmanagement, in: Hauschildt, J. and H.G. Gemünden (Eds.): *Promotoren*, Wiesbaden, 67-88.

Hauschildt, J. and E. Kirchmann (1998): Zur Existenz und Effizienz von Prozesspromotoren, in: Hauschildt, J. and H.G. Gemünden (Eds.): *Promotoren*, Wiesbaden, 89-110.

Homburg, C., J. Weber, R. Aust, and J.-T. Karlshaus (1998): *Interne Kundenorientierung der Kostenrechnung. Ergebnisse der Koblenzer Studie*, Vallendar.

Hope, J. and R. Fraser (2003): *Beyond Budgeting*, Stuttgart.

Horváth, P. (2003): *Controlling*, Munich

Kotler, P. and F. Bliemel (1999): *Marketing-Management. Analyse, Planung, Umsetzung und Steuerung*, 9th ed., Stuttgart.

Kreikebaum, H. (1991): *Strategische Unternehmensplanung*, 4th ed., Stuttgart.

Littkemann, J. (1997): *Innovationen und Rechnungswesen*, Wiesbaden.

McCarthy, J. (1981): *Basic Marketing. A Managerial Approach*, 9th ed., Homewood.

Mehrwald, H. (1999): *Das ‚Not-Invented-Here'-Syndrom (NIH) in Forschung und Entwicklung*, Frankfurt.

Menon, A. and R. Varadarajan (1992): A Model of Marketing Knowledge Use within Firms, *Journal of Marketing*, (56) 4, 53-71.

Rossel, A. (1988): Controlling im F.u.E.-Bereich eines Pharma-Unternehmens. Konzeptionen, *Controller Magazin*, (13) 6, 326-330.

Sabisch, H. (1991): *Produktinnovationen*, Stuttgart.

Schewe, G. (1992): *Imitationsmanagement*, Stuttgart.

Schon, D. (1963): Champions for Radical New Inventions, *Harvard Business Review*, (41) 2, 77-86.

Schulz-Moll, P., M. Esser, and U. Klein-Bölting (2003): Brand Investment Controlling, *Zeitschrift für Controlling und Management*, (47) 3, 165-169.

Seidenschwarz, W. (1993): *Target Costing*, Munich.

Stippel, N. (1999): *Innovationscontrolling*, Munich.

Stockbauer, H. (1989): *F&E-Controlling*, Vienna.

Stockbauer, H. (1991): F&E-Budgetierung aus der Sicht des Controlling, *Controlling*, (3) 3, 136-143.

Trigeorgis, L. (1996): *Real Options. Managerial Flexibility in Resource Allocation*, Cambridge.

Walter, A. and H.G. Gemünden (1998): Beziehungspromotoren als Förderer interorganisationaler Austauschprozesse: Empirische Befunde, in: Hauschildt, J. and H.G. Gemünden (Eds.): *Promotoren*, Wiesbaden, 133-158.

Weber, J. (2002): *Einführung in das Controlling*, 9th ed., Stuttgart.

Weber, J. (2003): Controlling in unterschiedlichen Führungskontexten – ein Überblick, *Zeitschrift für Controlling und Management*, (47) 3, 183-192.

Weber, J., B. Hirsch, S. Linder, and E. Zayer (2003): *Verhaltensorientiertes Controlling*, Vallendar.

Werner, H. (1997): *Strategisches Forschungs- und Entwicklungs-Controlling*, Wiesbaden.

Witte, E. (1973): *Organisation für Innovationsentscheidungen. Das Promotoren-Modell*, Göttingen.

Part 5:

Innovation, Foundations, and Universities

Thorsten Teichert

Mapping Research in Innovation Management

A Bibliometric Analysis of Research Policy

Prof. Dr. *Thorsten Teichert*, Institute for Marketing and Trade, University of Hamburg.

1 An Analysis of Intellectual Structure

Co-citation analysis is an established tool for the investigation of structural patterns within published literature and reveals interrelationships between ideas, authors and "the intellectual structure of scholarly fields" (White 1990, 84). The underlying assumption is that closely related works are frequently cited together by referencing works. As an example, Figure 1 maps co-citations of the German author Brockhoff as received from publications in the leading journal, *Research Policy*.

Figure 1: *Example of an Author Co-Citation Ego-Network*

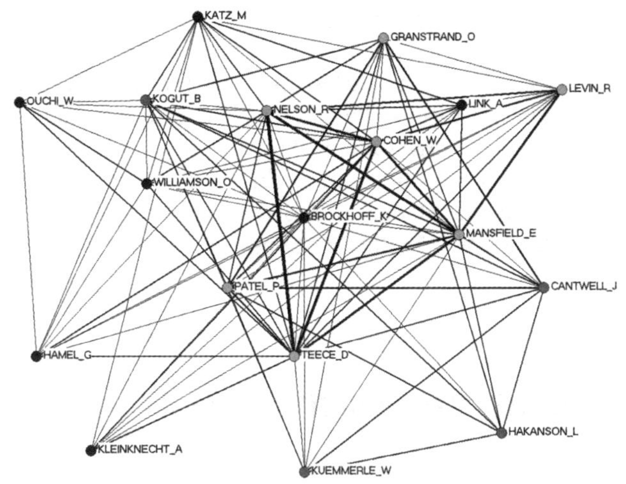

The diagram represents an ego-net and from this it can be seen that Brockhoffs' work is connected to a broad range of authors and key debates. The lines on the diagram illustrate the connections of his contributions (only 5 or more co-citations are shown). More selective or loosely linked co-citation patterns appear on the periphery of such a chart. If this kind of analysis is enlarged to cover entire sets of cited authors, it can provide valuable insights about their relative influence and their interrelations, or the existence of specific "schools of thought". Co-citation analysis has been repeatedly used successfully to map the intellectual structure of many academic disciplines (e.g.: Hoffman and Holbrook 1993; White and Mc Cain 1998). However, it "captures only what citers have recognized them (i.e. the authors) for, not what they have actually done" (White and Mc Cain 1998, 329). Thus, the information clearly cannot resemble a full lifetime's work for authors, but can provide a specific view of the past. Upfront it is to be mentioned that such an analysis neither provides a truly long-term perspective (e.g: Brockhoff 2003) nor an in-depth investigation of specific schools of thought (e.g. for Germany: Albers et al. 2001; Herstatt and Lüthje 2003).

Co-citation analysis can be applied to different levels of aggregation: On the level of single publications, it is long used to analyze relations among specific conceptual ideas or empirical findings (Small 1973). At a highly aggregated level, an analysis of co-cited journals can investigate role patterns in the generation of scientific knowledge (Rost and Teichert 2004). Here we apply an intermediary level of aggregation, i.e. author co-citation analysis (ACA), which evaluates how single actors are positioned relatively to each other in a research field (White 1990).

Bibliometric information about 1.147 articles published in *Research Policy* between 1985 and 2003 was collected from the social science citation index. Since meaningful co-citation profiles can only be calculated for highly cited and co-cited authors, the investigation bases on the top 5% citation receiving first authors (this is common practice to ACA, see e.g. McCain 1990). The analysis is further restricted to those authors, who also get co-cited with least three others. This is because this study is less concerned with specific viewpoints of single authors but more in retrieving schools of thought. A total of 146 authors pass both filters, who represent 6.306 citations or 33% of all cited publications. Finally, author citation co-occurrences were aggregated at the publication level, leading to a total of 4.897 author citations.

2 Overall Research System

An overall view on the structure on co-citations-relations is provided in a novel way by applying social network analysis (Wasserman and Faust 1999). First, a distinction is made to examine the central and peripheral structures of the system. If it exists, the core should be dense and internally cohesive, whilst the periphery, although connected to the core, should be internally loosely coupled or even unconnected. Secondly, a differentiation of subfields present in the co-citation patterns is restricted to the periphery, because it is, by definition, less cohesive than the core. Such a core-periphery structure is very plausible in scientific discourses which often divide into a commonly shared base and separated school of thoughts (e.g: Mullins et al. 1977).

Different algorithms and associated statistical tests are available for detecting a core-periphery structure using the software package UCINET (Borgatti et al. 2002). The commonly used fit function CORR simultaneously considers core and peripheral block interactions (Borgatti and Everett 1999). By applying this procedure, a set of 26 authors is identified as core. Table 1 lists the authors identified above, the number of citing research policy articles and the size of the authors' ego-nets in percent of all other authors. Pavitt receives by far the most number of citations; he is also connected to all other authors in the data set. As well as being editor of *Research Policy*, he is also the most cited author. Six other authors are cited by 100 or more articles and they are connected to well above 80 percent of authors. This highlights their central positioning within the scientific discourse as reflected in publications that appeared in *Research Policy*. The remaining 22 authors are cited by slightly fewer articles and they possess as well smaller ego nets. Here, those both measures of authors' centrality diverge: Authors with identical number of citing articles show different sizes of the ego net. Comparing e.g. Narin with the less cited Arrow, the latter even has a much larger ego-net (80% against 58%). This indicates a more narrow discourse of Narins' works as compared to a broader discourse of Arrows' work. Summarizing, those simple bibliographic measures already indicate that the core authors can be differentiated from each others. The following analyses elaborate on this separation.

Table 1: *Authors of the Core*

	Citing articles	Ego-Net		Citing articles	Ego-Net		Citing articles	Ego-Net
PAVITT_K	212	100%	GRILICHES_Z	89	83%	TUSHMAN_M	65	77%
NELSON_R	171	94%	VONHIPPEL_E	87	78%	HENDERSON_R	65	74%
MANSFIELD_E	149	95%	ROTHWELL_R	82	84%	JAFFE_A	62	78%
TEECE_D	142	97%	FREEMAN_C	79	90%	ABERNATHY_W	61	73%
COHEN_W	132	94%	DAVID_P	79	77%	ARROW_K	56	80%
DOSI_G	123	86%	PATEL_P	77	85%	LEVIN_R	52	74%
ROSENBERG_N	100	86%	SCHERER_F	69	79%	GRANSTRAND_O	50	76%
MOWERY_D	95	95%	NARIN_F	67	58%			

Figure 2 summarizes the intellectual structure within the core. Authors are co-located according to a multidimensional scaling of their interconnectedness in a two-dimensional space. The relative amount of co-citations of two authors is indicated by the thickness of connecting lines, whereby ten or more joint citations are shown. Nodes are displayed as circles if the authors' average cited publication stems from before 1990 or as rectangles if, on average, newer publications than 1990 were cited. The size of the nodes indicates the relative amount of authors' citations. Overall, the graph visualizes the relative positioning of authors within the core. As before (Table 1), the very core consists of Cohen, Mansfield, Nelson, Pavitt, and Teece. Looking at the outer areas of the graph, one can identify certain foci shown in the author co-citations. These include strong connections of Von Hippel with Rothwell; Levin, Scherer and Griliches; Tushman and Abernathy and Narin and Jaffe. This suggests that the core authors are linked to different research streams in the periphery.

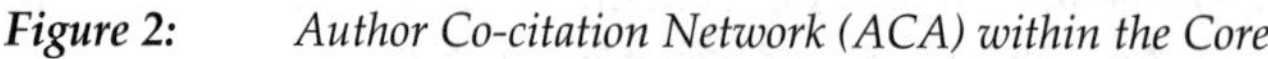

Figure 2: *Author Co-citation Network (ACA) within the Core*

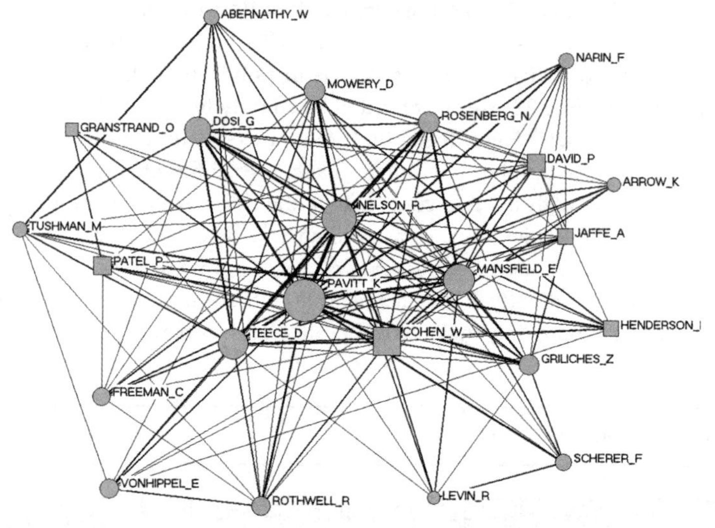

An analysis of the periphery differentiates the subfields present in the co-citation patterns, because the periphery is, by definition, less cohesive than the core. Thus, the closeness of authors is algorithmically related to perceived similarity by citers (McCain 1990). A factor-analytic procedure is applied in which the matrix of co-citation occurrences is used to calculate correlations between the received citations of authors (White and McCain 1998). The preferred solution (Table 2) contains seven factors with a minimum initial eigenvalue of 3.4 and explains 74.4 per cent of the total variance. Of these factors, the first three contribute 59% of explained variance, with the remaining four 15.4%. This indicates differences in the prominence of specific discourses.

Table 2 displays the result of the factor analysis. It lists each author and their primary corresponding factor loadings onto the relevant factors. Values approaching one indicate that the author's co-citation patterns are fully encompassed in the factor and that the discourse the author's work gives is totally represented by the particular research stream. Smaller values indicate that not all co-citation occurrences of an author are explained by the factor. This can either be a consequence of an author's connection to other research streams outside of the discourse of *Research Policy* or of a broader research agenda, as is often the case in the European research tradition. Secondary belongings of authors (also with factor loadings above 0.3) are listed in brackets in the table and indicate that an author's work is specifically related to other factors – i.e. the other research streams within the discourse of *Research Policy*.

Table 2: *Relationships of Periphery Authors to Research Streams (Factor Analysis*)*

Technology Strategy for Single Companies	Loading Factor 1	Research Policy for National Systems of Innova-	Loading Factor 2	Globalization and International R&D Networks	Loading Factor 3
ALLEN_T	0.81	ABRAMOVITZ_M (5,6)	0.64	ARCHIBUGI_D (2,5)	0.71
ANDERSON_P	0.69	ADAMS_J (4,6)	0.63	BARTLETT_C	0.95
BURGELMAN_R	0.76	CALLON_M (7)	0.75	BASBERG_B (2,6)	0.51
CHRISTENSEN C. (7)	0.67	DASGUPTA_P (4)	0.76	CANTWELL_J	0.91
CLARK_K	0.86	FAGERBERG_J (5)	0.76	CHENG_J	0.91
COOPER_A	0.79	FELDMAN_M	0.69	CHIESA_V	0.85
COOPER_R (7)	0.68	FELLER_I (4)	0.69	DEMEYER_A	0.91
CUSUMANO_M	0.82	GIBBONS_M (1)	0.78	DUNNING_J	0.93
EISENHARDT_K (7)	0.62	GRANOVETTER_M (4,7)	0.44	FLORIDA_R	0.80
ETTLIE_J	0.87	GRUPP_H	0.79	HAKANSON_L	0.93
HANNAN_M	0.75	HICKS_D	0.90	HEDLUND_G	0.94
IANSITI_M (4)	0.74	KATZ_J	0.84	HEWITT_G	0.91
KLEPPER_S (5,7)	0.66	KLEVORICK_A (4)	0.78	HIRSCHEY_R	0.83
LEONARDBARTON_D	0.78	KLINE_S (4,5)	0.65	HOWELLS_J	0.88
LEVINTHAL_D	0.69	LUNDVALL_B (5)	0.59	KOGUT_B (4)	0.66
MARCH_J	0.67	LUUKKONEN_T	0.77	KUEMMERLE_W	0.93
MARPLES_D	0.82	MARTIN_B	0.78	LALL_S	0.72
REINGANUM_J (4,7)	0.58	MEYERKRAHMER_F	0.79	MILLER_R (1,5)	0.55
ROBERTS_E	0.79	PRICE_D	0.89	NIOSI_J	0.86
ROSENBLOOM_R	0.72	ROMER_P (5)	0.68	ODAGIRI_H	0.79
SAHAL_D (5)	0.67	SAVIOTTI_P (5,7)	0.47	PEARCE_R	0.90
SIMON_H	0.79	SCHMOCH_U	0.82	RONSTADT_R	0.93
TEUBAL_M (2,5)	0.51	SOLOW_R (6)	0.59	SCHMOOKLER_J (5)	0.64
UTTERBACK_J (5)	0.76	STONEMAN_P (6)	0.54	VERNON_R	0.85
VANDEVEN_A	0.83	STORPER_M (5)	0.54		
WINTER_S (5,6,7)	0.55	TIJSSEN_R	0.77		

Application of Theories of the Firm	Loading Factor 4	Evolutionary Economics of Technological Change	Loading Factor 5	Econometric Applications and Technometrics	Loading Factor 6
ARORA_A (1)	0.65	BELL_M (1,2)	0.66	ACS_Z (2,4)	0.55
BARNEY_J (1)	0.55	CARLSSON_B (1,2)	0.61	AUDRETSCH_D (2,4)	0.42
BROCKHOFF_K (3)	0.58	DEBRESSON_C	0.61	EVENSON_R (2,4)	0.56
COASE_R (1)	0.44	LEE_J (1)	0.57	GEROSKI_P (4)	0.60
GULATI_R	0.84	MALERBA_F (2,6)	0.64	HALL_B (2)	0.77
HAGEDOORN_J	0.80	PEREZ_C	0.69	LERNER_J (2,4)	0.63
HAMEL_G (1)	0.83	RICHARDSON_G (1,4)	0.57	PAKES_A (2)	0.75
KAMIEN_M	0.74	SOETE_L (2,6)	0.48	TRAJTENBERG_M (2,7)	0.57
KATZ_M (7)	0.69				
KLEINKNECHT_A	0.78				
LINK_A (2)	0.72				
OUCHI_W (1)	0.71				
PISANO_G (1)	0.67				
PORTER_M (1,5)	0.55				
POWELL_W	0.67				
PRAHALAD_C (1)	0.59				
SAKAKIBARA_M	0.83				
SPENCE_A (6)	0.77				
VEUGELERS_R	0.67				
WERNERFELT_B (1)	0.55				
WILLIAMSON_O (1)	0.69				

Reinforcing Dynamics and Lock-In Effects	Loading Factor 7
ANTONELLI_C (2,6)	0.52
ARTHUR_W (1,2,5)	0.65
COWAN_R (1,2,5)	0.55
EISENBERG_R (4,6)	0.44
FARRELL_J (1)	0.70
FORAY_D (1,2,5)	0.60

**) Secondary belongings of authors (factor loadings above 0.3) are listed in brackets.*

The above analysis is purposely restricted to peripheral authors. Core authors were excluded as factor variables from the analysis because the magnitude of their influence was shown to distort the matrix to such an extent as to prevent the extraction of meaningful factors. This holds true as well from a content prospective: Schools of thought are expected to jointly rely on the foundations of innovation management but to differentiate between themselves. Nonetheless, it is possible to relate the core authors to specific research streams. Factor values are calculated which indicate the connections between authors of the identified factors and core authors with the results shown in Table 3. For simplification, values below 0.5 are not reported. According hereto, the core authors are most closely connected to the second factor (11 authors with factor values above 1.0), followed by the first factor with 9 authors. In contrast, only five core authors are related to factor 3. Thus, this particular stream references the foundations of innovation research to a lesser degree than the other two. The remaining factors show both positive and negative factor values for core authors, indicating that a subset of core authors is co-cited less than average with works from the specific factor. Accordingly, one can presume a large content distance between parts of the core and research streams which may indicate contested or even incompatible views.

Table 3: *Placement of Core Authors into Research Streams*

AUTHOR	Factor_1	Factor_2	Factor_3	Factor_4	Factor_5	Factor_6	Factor_7	avg_value
TUSHMAN_M	4.79	-1.09		-0.62	-0.81		1.97	0.66
ABERNATHY_W	3.82	-0.77		-0.93			0.98	0.43
HENDERSON_R	3.64	-1.17		0.76	-1.69	1.57	2.64	0.78
VONHIPPEL_E	3.56	1.00			-1.25	-1.36	-1.85	0.00
ROTHWELL_R	3.20	1.29		0.99		-1.73	-3.51	0.04
NARIN_F		4.62		-1.21	-2.97	0.70	-0.89	-0.03
PAVITT_K	2.37	4.12	1.47		4.08	1.45	-2.48	1.61
ROSENBERG_N		3.62				-1.38		0.37
MANSFIELD_E		3.31	2.50	2.07	-2.72	2.33	0.53	1.18
NELSON_R	1.47	2.77		1.34	1.91		1.92	1.39
JAFFE_A	-1.07	2.25			-0.59	1.41		0.47
PATEL_P		1.03	3.95	-0.77	1.82			0.81
GRANSTRAND_O			3.14					0.48
TEECE_D	1.67		1.04	4.62	2.57	-1.17	1.24	1.35
COHEN_W		1.02		4.09		2.47		1.15
MOWERY_D		0.94		1.68	0.50	-0.94	0.85	0.51
ARROW_K		0.51		1.15		0.77		0.27
DOSI_G	1.69			-1.02	4.80		2.51	1.20
FREEMAN_C		0.68		2.36	2.40	-1.81	-1.20	0.34
GRILICHES_Z		0.54				5.77		0.87
LEVIN_R		-0.58		1.12	-0.86	4.16		0.50
SCHERER_F					1.59	3.74	-1.70	0.49
DAVID_P		2.22		-0.73	-0.61	0.53	5.83	0.96
Total	1.09	1.14	0.42	0.72	0.39	0.75	0.32	0.69

Summing up, seven research streams can be set apart for *Research Policy* as a result of this co-citation analysis. The first two factors are distinct both in terms of their prominence and in terms of their connectedness to the core authors. The third factor depicts an internally intense discourse which is more separate from the core, whilst the remaining four factors are less pronounced, as can be seen by the percentage of explained variance. While the fourth factor still contains a high number of authors, these are however only loosely connected to the underlying discourse represented by the factor (average factor loadings below 0.7). Finally, the last three factors are limited both in size (i.e. number of authors) as well as strength (no factor loading exceeds the threshold value of 0.8). Out of those, only factor six connects highly to several authors in the core, while the other discourses are more distant and seem to reflect particular discourses of limited size and influence.

3 Single Research Streams

In this section, the factors extracted above are analysed in further detail to identify potential "schools of thought". The discussion investigates findings presented in section 2 in more detail and enhances them with further analysis. The multidimensional scaling procedure is applied within each factor group to reveal specific substructures. This results in an overall picture of the co-citation patterns within the single research streams which are presented in network diagrams of the same type as Figure 2.

Research streams and author contributions are further assessed by enriching the previous findings with bibliographic data and other author information. Firstly, factor loadings indicate the typicality of co-citations patterns of an author, i.e. how good the factor represents the context within which an author is being referenced. As a second aspect, the number of received citations of an author and his connectedness to other authors (i.e. size of the ego-net) indicates his prominence in a research field. Thirdly, author information such as average publication year and nationality are retrieved as background information. Single works of selected authors are highlighted to validate the aggregated view of the author co-citation analysis (note that this selection is purely illustrative and can by no means be representative). Finally, the fit with core authors (factor values listed in Table 2) examines the embeddedness of the discourses.

3.1 Technology Strategy for Individual Companies

Factor one contains a high percentage of authors with high factor loadings (Table 2) and explains 30 per cent of the total variance. Therefore, this research stream is characterized by a high coherence. Furthermore, authors belonging to this factor are characterized by both the earliest average date of their cited publications (1985) as well as by the highest average number of received citations compared to authors belonging to other factors. In addition, the average citation half-life which describes the rate of obsolescence of scientific literature (Burton and Kebler 1960) lies well above ten years and is highest of all factors. Nearly all authors stem from the US and take mostly a strategic perspective on how to react to technological change cycles from the viewpoint of single companies. Thus, this factor can be described as *"Technology Strategy for Single Companies"*. Looking at selected works of contributing authors can validate this interpretation. Three works stand out, the most cited is Utterback and Abernathy (1975), Clark (1985) as well as Anderson and Tushman (1990) on technological evolution cycles and related product design issues.

Figure 3 summarizes the intellectual structure of this research stream, with greater than two co-citations being shown. It becomes evident that Utterback, Allen and Clark constitute the established core of this research stream with Utterback representing creative destruction and technological change; Allen the intraorganizational management of such technology flows; with Clark connecting the thoughts of Utterback and Allen. This is an intuitive result since in his 1985 article Clark portrays the coevolution of the impact of technological change on product design hierarchies and the mental models of product users. As expected, newer research is located more on the outer (orbits) edges of the co-citation network. However, Eisenhardt has achieved a prominent position in terms of the number of citing articles for her work. In addition, Leonard-Barton visibly extends this research stream with her article on various facets of core capabilities, and several of the more recently cited authors are connected to her. This can be traced back to her prominent article in which she differentiates various facets of core capabilities (Leonard-Barton 1992).

Comparing single authors, the contributions of Allen, Cooper, Simon and a single publication of Marples stand out both in terms of date published as well as citation half-life. They can thus be regarded as early and guideposts' pieces of works. The most prominent author of the first factor is Utterback with 51 referencing articles. However, his co-citation pattern is only partly explained by the factor (with factor loading below 0.8). This indicates a certain dispersion of his referenced work. The same holds true for Eisenhardt, Christensen and Winter, who both possess under-average factor loadings but receive above-average number of citations. Again, we suppose a broad scope of research relations of these authors. In contrast, the first factor represents following authors best: Ettlie, Clark, van de Ven, Marples, and Allen (all of them with factor loadings above 0.8). This implies that their patterns of co-citedness are both highly similar to each others as well as most typical for this factor. Finally, Cooper occupies a surprisingly peripheral position within the network. This clearly shows that the research on success factors in innovation management is not strongly reflected in this journal and the contribution of such a view cannot be assessed with this data set.

Figure 3: *ACA within "Technology Strategy for Single Companies" (Factor 1)*

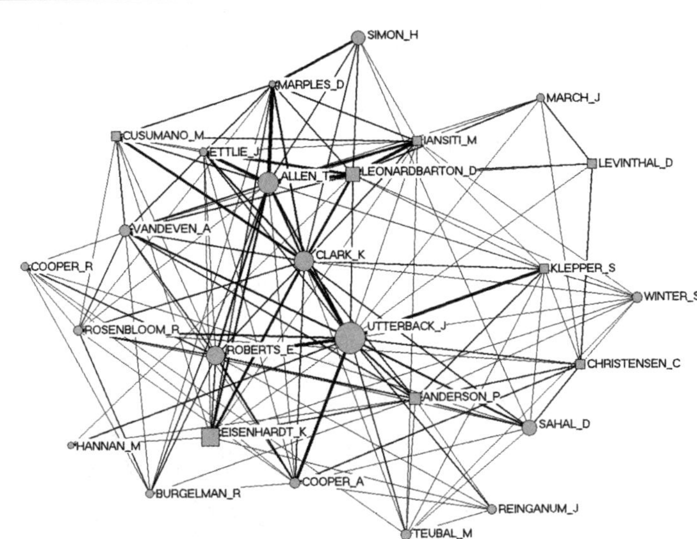

Assessing the connections of authors belonging to this research tradition to our core authors, one can find very intense relationships (Table 3): Factor values show that five core authors are primarily connected to this research stream, whilst secondary connections exist to Dosi, Nelson, Pavitt, and Teece. The three most strongly connected authors are Tushman, Abernathy, and Henderson. These all show a strong stance within this discourse and clearly differentiate themselves from that reflected in factor two (factor values of around –1.0). In contrast, von Hippel and Rothwell are simultaneously connected to the research stream of factor two and this leads us to assume that their ideas contribute to the exchange between these research streams.

3.2 National Systems of Innovation

Table 2 shows that the second factor is characterized by a more diverse group of authors than the first. There are only four (Hicks, Price, Katz, and Schmoch) out of 26 authors who possess a factor loading above 0.8 and in addition, these authors are not the most cited authors for this factor. At first sight it seems to be more difficult to identify the research direction of all authors of this factor. However, certain characteristics are evident. First of all is the predominance of European authors evident, and secondly, from a content perspective, one can identify issues of science evaluation and science policy as common ground. Public funding of basic research is thus a common feature or the related debates on the benefit of government investment. Third in this factor group, most authors are characterized by a high closeness to the journal *Research Policy* itself. For example, two editors of the journal, Callon and Meyer-Krahmer, feature highly in this factor and occupy central positions in this discourse (Figure 4). In addition, about a quarter of the references relate to former articles published as well in *Research Policy,* e.g. Martin and Irvine (1983), Dasgupta and David (1994). Thus, this factor can be described as *"Research Policy for National Systems of Innovation".*

Figure 4: *ACA within "Research Policy for National Systems of Innovation" (Factor 2)*

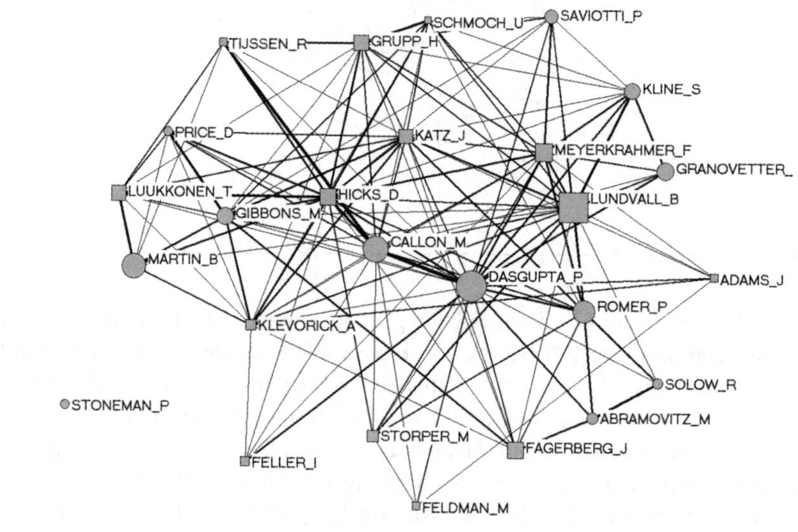

The foundations of the research stream in this second factor can be found in the works of Abramovitz, Gibbons, Price, and Solow, whose contributions stem back to the 1970ies with citation half-lives well above 10 years. Since this research stream is concerned with interorganizational knowledge production networks, it connects to social network theory. Here, Granovetter contributed a sociologist's perspective to the issue of embeddedness. Furthermore, an analysis of the Ego-Net of the authors reveals some other additional central players, with the strongest links for Dasgupta, Hicks and Lundvall (Figure 4). They complement each other in their prominent perspectives on industrial structure, scientometrics and national systems of competencies and knowledge production. By this, it can again be concluded that this research stream constitutes the very core of "research policy". This assessment is further validated by analysing the connections to the core (Table 3). First and foremost, the work of *Research Policy's* past editor Pavitt is closely linked to this stream. He and Narin load with factor values of above 4.0 on the second factor. Following these, the works of Rosenberg, Mansfield, Nelson, and Jaffe are also strongly related (in descending order).

3.3 Globalization and International R&D Networks

The third factor is characterized by particularly strong relationships (Table 2). The majority of these authors (16 out of 24) are represented with factor loadings of above 0.8. This indicates a particularly closed circle. Furthermore, Figure 5 shows a very dense network of co-citations (again, a minimum of two received co-citations is shown) and indicates an internally highly connected discourse.

Figure 5: *ACA within "Globalization and International R&D Networks" (Factor 3)*

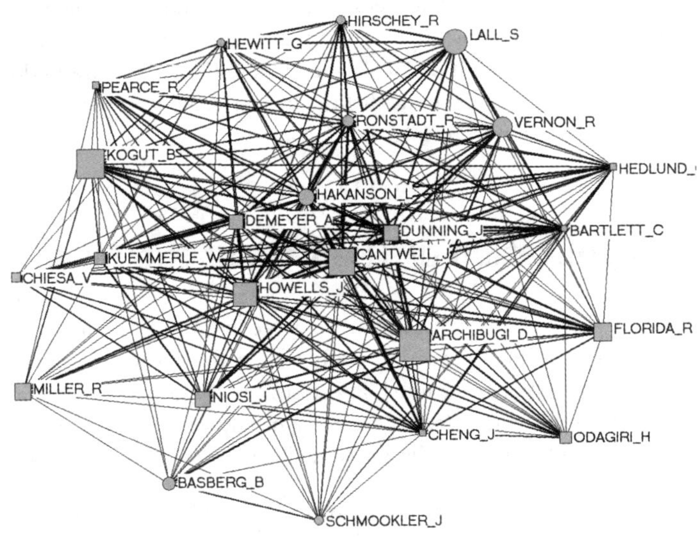

Further analyses show that this research stream is influenced by a large number of more recent ideas. Newer contributions dominate both in terms of centrality and size, as shown by the dominance of rectangles in Figure 5. However, the discourse has roots back to an analysis by Vernon (1966) on the relation between international trade and product lifecycle, and Schmookler's contribution on the driving forces of inventive activities. The often referenced works of Dunning (1994) and Hedlund (1986) extend this view by relating globalisation issues to technology strategy and human resource management. To continue this tradition, the works of the most recent publishing author Niosi relate the issue of internationalization to technology transfer and the learning organization. Accordingly, this research stream can be labelled as "*Globalization and International R&D Network*".

In exploring the structure of the group, Cantwell is highlighted as a prominent representative of this research stream as he is located in the center of the co-citation network (Figure 5). In his highly referenced work, he analyzed the globalisation of technological innovation and derived implications for locating international networks of R&D. It is interesting to note that the three other most cited authors, Archibugi, Howell, and Kogut, also relate to other research streams identified in this study. While the first two authors relate more to an economic perspective, the last's work contributes to broader issues of collaboration and knowledge in the firm. Such a broad perspective can, however, not be identified for most of the other authors of this research field who, as stated above, have high factor loadings indicating a relatively close cluster.

Again this assessment can be extended by looking at connections to the core authors (Table 3). Compared to the other factors, few core authors (5) relate at all to this discourse. Out of those, only two (Granstrand and Patel) are found to be primarily connected to this research stream and it should be noted that Granstrand does not connect to any other factor. Thus, this research stream clearly shows patterns of strong internal coherence and separation from external discourses.

3.4 Application of Theories of the Firm

Factor four stands in clear contrast to factor three in terms of bibliometrics and is characterized by many authors who are loosely tied to their discourse (Table 2). Thus, the co-citation network possesses a much lesser density (Figure 6). Further analysis reveals that these authors are connected to a variety of authors outside this factor. This indicates a broader, but less intense discourse with a high external openness.

A closer view at the authors contributing to this factor reveals representatives from a variety of theoretical lines. Prior work includes that of organizational theorists such as Coase, Ouchi, and Williamson, research on market structure and innovation (Kamien and Spence), the market-based view (Porter) and, Hamel and Wernerfelt on the resource-based view of strategy. Interestingly, these basic theoretical frames of reference all fall into this factor indicating that these theories are often contrasted within *Research Policy* articles. Thus, innovation management can be described as a pluralism of theories applied jointly and complementary to each other. Accordingly this factor has been labelled as "*Application of Theories of the Firm*" in innovation management.

References are highly focused on authors from the US which shows a strong dependency on conceptual discussions and theoretical contributions which have originated in the US. Notable exceptions are Brockhoff (Germany) and Hagedoorn, Kleinknecht, and Veugelers (Benelux). Given that these European authors are referenced for their latter works from the 1990s, a slight shift towards a more European dialog is emerging.

Figure 6: *ACA within "Application of Theories of the Firm" (Factor 4)*

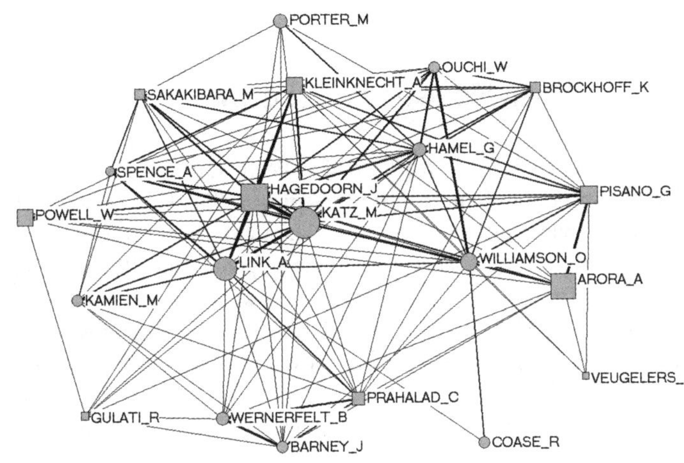

The multidimensional scaling of authors in this factor (Figure 6) reveals an inverse structure of core-periphery positions. Whereas only three authors Hagedoorn, Katz, and Link are located in the center of the network, the most prominent authors are found on the periphery. This lies in accordance to the postulated focus on "theory application" against "theory generation" and indicates contrasting theoretical foundations. The separation is interesting with representatives from the resource based view located in the lower part of the graph and with Porter at the very top. Similarly, the transaction cost perspective is on the right hand side, while the left side represents transaction return considerations stemming from interorganizational networks.

Factor four represents best the authors Hagedoorn, Hamal, Gulati, and Sakakibara (with factor loadings of above 0.8) and these authors can be classified as protagonists in theory application. Interestingly, the latter two are among the youngest referenced work in the sample, hinting slightly towards a trend of theory integration in innovation management. Furthermore, Hagedoorn and Link contribute an especially large amount of more than twenty works. This indicates a high modularity of research contributions and seems to hold true for the entire discourse, since no single work stands out in terms of number of received citations. In summary, theory applications in innovation management may be characterized by modular contributions which discuss and integrate concepts from different theoretical frames.

This integrative perspective is somehow reflected by the positioning of core authors (Table 3), who are more related to this factor than to factor three (*Globalization and International R&D Network*). The two most closely related authors – Teece and Cohen – are connected to several different research streams. Two other core authors can be related to "theory applications", Cohen and Mowery, and again a look at their contributions validates the labelling of this discourse as theory applications.

3.5 Further Research Streams

The fifth factor encompasses works which lie in the tradition of the Schumpeterian view of innovation (e.g. Malerba and Orsenigo 1995). This research stream combines the evolutionary view of technological change with basic consideration about the organisation of industries and a sectoral view of economies (Richardson 1972). Accordingly, it can be termed *"Evolutionary Economics of Technological Change"*. This research stream is characterized as a highly traditional view that contains few new approaches as the high average age of cited work shows. It is less pronounced than the former ones and there are only eight authors featured. Furthermore, no author is highly represented by the factor, with six out of eight authors loading on other factors with factor loadings above 0.3. Thus, this discourse is only loosely coupled and often relates to other research streams. For example, Soete, Perez, and De Bresson discuss the effects of evolutionary changes in the economy on the utilization of technology. In addition, the authors belonging to factor five are also related to factor seven. Finally, Soete's and Malerba's work relies strongly on the application of technometrics and therefore load as well on factor six.

The sixth factor integrates a macroeconomic perspective with a focus on technometrics. Hall and Pakes are the two authors who are best represented by this factor. Measuring R&D output and its economic contributions roots back to early work of Evenson, Pakes, and Traitenberg (e.g. 1990). At the same time, this discourse constitutes a highly active research field as it is characterized by on average youngest date of cited publications and citing articles. In this regard, Audretsch and Lerner provide the newest works to feature here. Audretsch and Feldman's (1996) contributions on R&D spillovers and the geography of innovation deserve mentioning as other examples of prominent work. Overall, this factor shall be characterized as *"Econometric Applications and Technometrics"*. Since it emphasizes a methodological perspective the factor loadings are generally low as the empirical findings of this stream of research will be evident in different conceptual contexts. The main three authors in the factor, Acs, Audretsch and Geroski all feature in factors five to seven. Furthermore, eleven other periphery authors relate to this research stream as well (Table 2), four of them stemming from factor 2 (*Research Policy for National Systems of Innovation*). This shows a strong interlocking between methodological and content perspectives within *Research Policy*. Looking finally at the relationship to the core authors, Griliches, Levin, and Scherer show a strong and exclusive focus on this research stream.

The last factor has the lowest explanatory power and contains the fewest number of authors (six altogether). These are all simultaneously related to at least one other factor (with factor loadings between 0.3 and 0.5). However, a closer analysis on the contents reveals that this discourse is worth mentioning. Two works stand out as foundations of this discourse, the early works of Farrell and Saloner in 1985 on standardization, compatibility and innovation, and Arthur's work in 1989 on increasing returns and lock-in effects. Newer works of Cowan and Gunby (1996) build on this foundation and investigate the effects of positive feedback on technological trajectories and its consequences for management. Furthermore, this research stream can be characterized as a development of the thoughts reflected in factor 5 (*Evolutionary Economics of Technological Change*), as is indicated by their relationship shown in Table 2. In summary, this factor assembles concepts about a new knowledge based economy and can be termed "*Reinforcing Evolutionary Dynamics and Lock-In Effects*". Within the set of core authors (Table 3), David is the protagonist of this research stream. However, Dosi, Henderson, and Nelson and Tushman provide essential contributions to this discourse as well.

4 Conclusions

Author co-citation analysis provides a multifaceted view on the intellectual structure of research in a discipline and here it is successfully applied to innovation management. The analysis of articles from *Research Policy* reveals a core-periphery structure in which seven distinct discourses can be distinguished and positioned against each as represented in Figure 7. Further analysis enables a closer characterization of these research streams, relationships and dynamics.

The discourses on *Technology Strategy for Single Companies* and *Research Policy for National Systems of Innovation* are the two major research streams and complement each other well as fundamental perspectives. The first assumes a single company perspective, while the second relates to entire economic systems. Their dominance in the discipline as a whole is reflected in the way both research streams closely connect to the core. The business-related discourse is also closely related to the discourse *Application of Theories of the Firm* while the economic interpretation is similarly linked to methodological approaches present in the stream *Econometric Applications and Technometrics*. In contrast, the third major discourse *Globalization and International R&D Networks* is relatively autonomous and has few overlaps with the other research streams and the core.

Certain more recent developments also emerge in the analysis. In particular, the discourse on *Reinforcing Evolutionary Dynamics and Lock-In Effects* represents a relatively new perspective that builds on works in *Evolutionary Economics of Technological Change.* In addition, the former features several newer methodological approaches which appear in *Econometric Applications and Technometrics.* These tools and methods are also becoming more prominent and increasingly appear in the discourse on *Research Policy for National Systems of Innovation.*

Figure 7: *Synopsis of the Revealed Intellectual Structure*

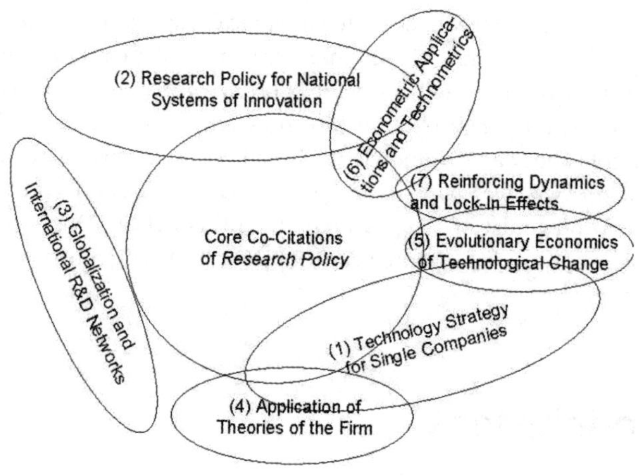

Finally, the analysis has identified some possible areas for future research: First of all, the discourse on *Globalization and International R&D Networks* may be further connected with other research of both the business-level as well as the economic discourses. Secondly, the application of advanced methodologies such as sophisticated patent analysis, which have been identified in the *Econometric Applications and Technometrics* discourse, may be applied to extend research on *Technology Strategy for Single Companies.*

5 References

Albers, S., K. Brockhoff, and J. Hauschildt (2001): *Technologie- und Innovationsmanagement. Leistungsbilanz des Kieler Graduiertenkollegs,* Wiesbaden.

Anderson, P. and M.L. Tushman (1990): Technological discontinuities and dominant designs – a cyclical model of technological change, *Administrative Science Quarterly*, 35 (4), 604-633.

Arthur, W.B. (1989): Competing technologies, increasing returns, and lock-in by historical events, *Economic Journal*, 99 (394), 116-131.

Audretsch, D.B. and M.P. Feldman (1996) : R&D spillovers and the geography of innovation and production, *American Economic Review*, 86 (3), 630-640.

Borgatti, S.P. and M.G. Everett (1999): Models of core/periphery structures, *Social Networks*, 21 (4), 375-395.

Borgatti, S.P., M.G. Everett, and L.C. Freeman (2002): *Ucinet 6 for Windows*. Harvard: Analytic Technologies.

Brockhoff, K. (2003): An utopian View of R&D functions, *R&D Management*, 33 (1), 31-36.

Burton, R.E. and R.W. Kebler (1960): The "half-life" of some scientific and technical literatures, *American Documentation*, 11, 18–22.

Clark, K.B. (1985): The interaction of design hierarchies and market concepts in technological evolution, *Research Policy*, 14 (5), 235-251.

Cowan, R. and P. Gunby (1996): Sprayed to death: Path dependence, lock-in and pest control strategies, *Economic Journal*, 106 (436), 521-542.

Dasgupta, P. and P.A. David (1994): Toward a new economics of science, *Research Policy*, 23 (5).

Dunning, J.H. (1994): Multinational enterprises and the globalization of innovative capacity, *Research Policy*, 23 (1), 67-88.

Hedlund, G. (1986): The hypermodern MNC – a heterarchy, *Human Resource Management*, 25 (1), 9-35.

Herstatt, C. and C. Lüthje (Eds.) (2003), Market Orientation in Innovation Management, *International Journal of Technology Management*, Special Issue 26 (5/6).

Hoffman, D.L. and M.B. Holbrook (1993): The intellectual structure of consumer research – a bibliometric study of author co-citations in the 1st 15 years of the journal of consumer research, *Journal of Consumer Research*, 19, 505-517.

Leonard-Barton, D. (1992): Core capabilitites and core rigidities – A paradox in managing new product development, *Strategic Management Journal*, 13 (Sp. Iss. SI), 111-125.

Malerba, F. and L. Orsenigo (1995): Schumpeterian patterns of innovation, *Cambridge Journal of Economics*, 19 (1), 47-65.

Martin, B.R. and J. Irvine (1983): Assessing basic research – some particular indicators of scientific progress in radio astronomy, *Research Policy*, 12 (2), 61-90.

McCain, K.W. (1990): Mapping authors in intellectual space: A technical overview, *Journal of the American Society for Information Science*, 41(6), 433-443.

Mullins, N.C., L.L. Hargens, P.K. Hecht, and E.L. Kick (1977): The Group Structure of Cocitation Clusters: A Comparative Study, *American Sociological Review*, 42, 552-562.

Richardson, G.B. (1972): Organisation of industry, *Economic Journal*, 82 (327), 883-896.

Romer, P.M. (1990): Endogenous technological change, *Journal of Political Economy*, 98 (5), 71-102.

Rost, K. and T. Teichert (2004): *Scientific Discourse in Management Journals: An Evaluation from the Analytic Network Perspective*, Working Paper, Institute for Innovation Management, University of Bern.

Small, H.G. (1973): Co-citation in the scientific literature. A measure of the relationship between two documents, *Journal of the American Society for Information Science*, 24, 265-269.

Trajtenberg, M. (1990): A penny for your quotes – patent citations and the value of innovations, *Rand Journal of Economics*, 21 (1), 172-187.

Utterback, J.M. and W.J. Abernathy (1975): Dynamic model of process and product innovation, *Omega – International Journal of Management Science*, 3 (6), 639-656.

Vernon, R. (1966): International investment and international trade in product cycle, *Quarterly Journal of Economics*, 80 (2), 190-207.

Wasserman, S. and K. Faust (1999): *Social network analysis*, 5th ed., New York.

White, H.D. (1990): Author co-citations analysis: Overview and defense, in: C.L. Borgman (Ed.): *Scholarly communication and bibliometrics*, Newbury Park, CA, 84-106.

White, H.D. and K.W. McCain (1998): Visualizing a discipline: An author co-citation analysis of information science, 1972-1995, *Journal of the American Society for Information Science*, 49 (4), 327-355.

Günter Fandel and Steffen Blaga

Capturing the Qualities of Students as Inputs and Outputs of Universities

Prof. Dr. *Günter Fandel* and Dipl.-Kfm. *Steffen Blaga*, Department of Production Management, FernUniversität in Hagen.

1 Preliminary remarks

This paper in honor of Klaus Brockhoff and his work on innovation does not contribute directly to this research area. It looks more for an innovative way to apply production theory and correlation calculations in order to comprehend and to describe, how students as inputs and outputs of universities develop in their qualities. As a result of these considerations a production technology will be derived analyzing some interesting aspects of the production of services at universities in an innovative manner. This links to the intention of this volume.

In the literature, there already exist numerous approaches for regarding the efforts of universities in teaching and research as services production and for describing it by models of production theory (Albach et al. 1978; Stieger 1980; Fandel and Paff 2000; Fandel and Blaga 2004). Considerations on the efficiency or on the costs and success of universities were in the foreground of these analyses (Fandel 1995, 2003; Fandel and Paff 2000). The results nowadays form very often the basis for the redistribution of funds among universities (Fandel and Gal 2001).

In university-level education students are normally regarded as the inputs and graduates as the outputs of this services production. From an output-oriented perspective the success of universities is often measured using the level of the withdrawal or dropout rate (Smith and Naylor 2001), the length of the average time taken to complete studies in defined faculties (Hackl and Sedlacek 2002a, 2002b) and the extent to which graduates can be placed in the labor market (Lohmar et al. 1982; BfA 2000). The latter is determined essentially by the grades achieved in the degree examination; it serves as an indication for the assessment of the quality of a graduate from a specific university. In contrast, from an input-oriented perspective the efficiency of a university is judged by how many students it accepts with the given resources and supports in the basic courses (Fandel and Gal 2001). If we concentrate on the input and output aspect simultaneously, education policy expects that, with the existing capacities, a university accepts a large number of students and graduates as many of them as possible. Hereby it is normally assumed that the quality of the teaching process of a university will effect the qualities of its graduates.

One aspect has hardly been examined in these studies: to what extent does the success of universities in teaching, measured by the number and qualities of their graduates, depend on the qualities of the students as external inputs (Maleri 1973), and how do these qualities develop in the course of studying. This addresses the known, but unsolved, problem of university education, whether the qualities of students are features of the inputs or the outputs of universities (Albach et al. 1978). Thereby the qualities of students as inputs could be measured by the grades they have achieved in the school leaving examinations or in the obligatory examinations in the first course of their studies. A more recent investigation by Fries (2002) has shown that the grades achieved in the leaving examinations are by far the best indicators for the study success.

2 Object and basis of the analysis

In the following, it will be examined on the basis of 272 graduates (full-time students) of the Faculty of Economics at the FernUniversitaet in Hagen in the years 2000-2002, how the qualities of the graduates developed from the start of studying to graduation. Especially, three questions should be answered:

1. whether the teaching process of the faculty has remained constant with respect to its quality over the time the graduates passed through (productivity aspect of the process). If so, then changes in the qualities of the students may be mainly attributed to their characteristics as inputs and their efforts during studying,
2. how graduates migrated through different groups of grade levels at the start of studying, in their Part I examinations and in their finals, and to what extent they remained in comparable quality groups throughout their studies (productivity aspect of the quality of inputs), and
3. whether indications can be found that graduates who took longer to study arrived at groups with better grade levels in the subsequent examinations (productivity aspect of time staying in the process).

In order to derive statements on the stability of the quality of the teaching process in the Faculty of Economics at the FernUniversitaet in Hagen the distributions of the grades are examined that define the quality features of the students. Observations on the length of study time and considerations on typical patterns of quality developments during studying are taken into account. Additionally, we will analyze the changes in students' quality ranks from the initial grades beginning their studies to the grades for the Part I examinations and from these to the grades for the final examinations, the degree grades. The more inconspicuous these findings are, or the weaker the displacements in the quality ranks, the more it may be assumed that the quality of a student is more important for his success in studying than particularities of the teaching process. The average grade achieved in the first four obligatory written examinations in the basic courses serves as a quality indicator for graduates at the start of studying (entrance qualification). In contrast to the average grade of the school leaving examinations this has the advantage of a more homogenous quality assessment, because the examinations in the first course of study are largely standardized through the appropriate study letters, which have basically remained the same over time for all students. The grades in the Part I examinations (intermediate qualification) and the degree grades (final qualification) serve as quality indicators on the subsequent educational levels. An argument to use these quality measures is that the Part I grades as well as the final examination grades are composed from a number of written examination grades that can be achieved successively during the studies. Then, as in a credit point system, the partial grades are summed up to an overall grade, when the student has passed the respective part of his study. By this procedure random faults on the award of grades are not very effective.

To study the second question migration matrices are derived based on migrations of students from the entrance qualifications to the Part I grades, and from the Part I grades to the final examination grades, which explain, in analogy to the activity analysis of the production theory, how students with specific Part I grades or graduates with specific final examination grades (intermediate products and final products respectively) are generated from students with different entrance qualifications or Part I examination grades (inputs of different quality). Formally this is a multi-level multi-product manufacturing system. The production function is in principle substitutional, because amounts of students with specific Part I or final examination grades can be composed from amounts of students with different entrance qualifications or Part I grades. The concrete migration matrices then represent, seen from the aspect of an activity analysis, specific production processes, which were realized on the basis of the production interdependencies (Fandel and Blaga 2004).

Table 1: *Distribution of qualities on entrance, Part I and degree*

i	x_i	f_i^E	j	y_j	f_j^V	k	z_k	f_k^D
1	11	0.04	1	5	0.02	1	4	0.01
2	84	0.31	2	69	0.25	2	82	0.30
3	137	0.50	3	174	0.64	3	170	0.63
4	40	0.15	4	24	0.09	4	16	0.06
Σ	272	1.00	Σ	272	1.00	Σ	272	1.00

The average grades for the 272 were available at the form of one decimal place after the point. However, for describing the migration patterns between different quality groups only integers on a scale of 1 - 4 are considered here. While the average grade in the four basic course examinations can be interpreted as the quality of the input "students", and the degree grade as the quality of the output "graduates", the grade for the Part I examinations represents both an output and an input quality.

Table 1 contains the absolute and relative frequencies of the grades of the 272 students at the various grade levels. Because none of the 272 students here had an entrance qualification below "pass", let q^E be the entrance quality with $q^{E_i} = i$, q^V be the Part I quality with $q^{V_j} = j$, and q^D be the degree quality with $q^{D_k} = k$, $i,j,k = 1,\ldots,4$.

In addition, let

- x_i be the number of first semester students whose entrance qualification is the grade $q^{E_i} = i$, $i \in \{1, 2, 3, 4\}$,
- y_j be the number of students with the Part I grade $q^{V_j} = j$, $j \in \{1, 2, 3, 4\}$,
- z_k be the number of graduates with the degree grade $q^{D_k} = k$, $k \in \{1, 2, 3, 4\}$, and

f_μ^v, $v \in \{E, V, D\}, \mu \in \{i, j, k\}$, be the corresponding relative frequencies.

Figure 1 shows the appropriate histograms in absolute frequencies.

Figure 1: *Histograms of the quality distributions in accordance with Table 1*

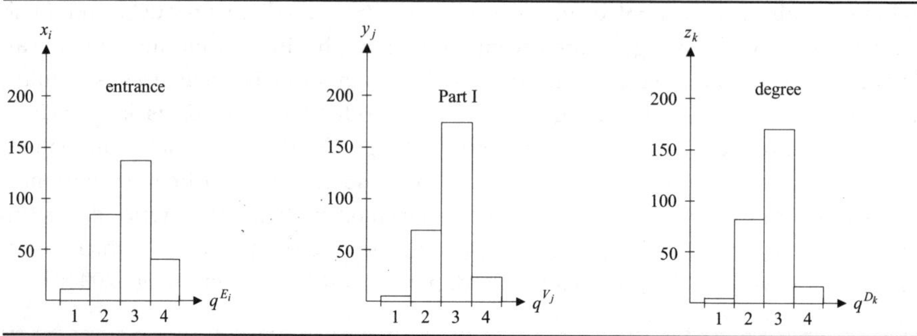

The means of the quality characteristics of the individual education levels are $\overline{q}^E = 2{,}76$, $\overline{q}^V = 2{,}80$ and $\overline{q}^D = 2{,}73$.

If the distribution of the study time is examined, measured in the number of semesters required for graduation, it can be seen that it is mainly located between 9 and 20 semesters. While some students graduate after 8 semesters, others take up to 36 semesters to complete their studies successfully. The average length of study time $\overline{t}$ was 15.8 semesters, or about 8 years. It is interesting that the distribution of the study time shows a similar pattern to that of the graduates from the Vienna University of Economics and Business Administration (Hackl and Sedlacek 2002a, 2002b). Table 2 presents some statistical parameters for the two institutions.

Table 2: *Comparison of statistical parameters with regard to the study times of the 272 graduates of the FernUniversitaet in Hagen and graduates of the Vienna University of Economics and Business Administration*

	FernUniversitaet in Hagen	*Vienna University of Economics and Business Administration*
Mean value	15.8 semesters	15.4 semesters
0% (Min)	8.0 semesters	6.7 semesters
10%	10.2 semesters	10.0 semesters
25% (Q1)	11.7 semesters	11.6 semesters
50% (median)	14.5 semesters	14.2 semesters
75% (Q3)	18.1 semesters	17.5 semesters
90%	21.7 semesters	22.4 semesters
100% (Max)	36.0 semesters	39.2 semesters

3 Effects of the teaching process on the qualities of students

In this section we will discuss whether the qualities of students are influenced through the production process of teaching in the Faculty of Economics at the FernUniversitaet. To demarcate such quality effects of the production system from individual qualities of students as inputs, or of graduates as outputs of the university, the distributions of the grades at the different quality levels entrance grade, Part I and degree are compared with one another (3.1), and the correlations between these qualities are determined (3.2).

We start implicitly from static production conditions on the educational system assuming that the quality of the teaching process of the faculty did not change in the years in which the 272 graduates studied. This may be regarded as critical with respect to the range of 11 years in which 90% of the graduates completed their studies; however, there are plausible clues to this:

- The contents of the study letters relevant to the examinations remained more or less the same throughout this period.
- The support for students has hardly changed in the period considered, because the professors were largely the same, and the support system through mentors in the FernUniversitaet's study centres did not change.
- The award of grades in the written examinations for the entrance qualifications, Part I and final examinations followed a fixed scheme for the attribution of points the students were aware of and from which there have been no deviations in the period under observation.

3.1 Grade distributions

The distributions of the grades shown in Table 1 and Fig. 1 give rise to the following interpretations:

1. The grades are distributed around an average grade, i.e. the degree course is neither too difficult nor too easy.
2. From the beginning of the study to the final degree there is a movement of students from the edges of the grades to the average, i.e. the students' qualities become more homogenous in the course of their studies.
3. The grades in the final examinations are slightly better than the grades in the Part I examinations. This corresponds to the well-known phenomenon in education

systems that marking in later course phases is slightly more generous than in earlier phases.

In addition, the credit point system avoids random faults in awards of grades that can be created through written examinations that differ too much in their contents and scope. So, it is not surprising that the grades for students' entrance qualifications and their Part I and final examination grades, expressed originally in digits are approximately normally distributed. These normal distributions are not, as might be suspected, the result of grade adjustments of specific examination dates. On the contrary, with the 272 successful students the grades come from written examinations that they sat on very different dates. The degree grades are on average slightly better than the grades for the Part I examinations. The reason is that when the final examination grade is determined the grade for the thesis counts double.

These interpretations hardly permit the conclusion that the education system of the faculty has any significant effects on the qualities of students.

3.2 Correlation calculations

If we want to corroborate the supposition that the educational process does not influence the qualities of students we can investigate whether the students' qualities are preserved throughout the different grade levels in such a way that students who are good remain good, while students with poor entrance qualifications tend to achieve poor Part I or final examination grades. The approaches of Kendall and Spearman (Hartung 1984) for calculating non-parametric correlations were used here to determine the dependencies of the Part I grades on the entrance grades, and the dependencies of the degree grades on the entrance grades or the Part I grades, respectively. Tests on the dependencies of the qualities were carried out. The results are summarized in Table 3.

These results substantiate the supposition that students achieve a higher quality rank in the Part I and final examinations the higher their quality rank in the entrance qualification and the Part I grade, respectively. It is to be noted here that the ranks are not places awarded to graduates within the same examination cohorts, but that the ranks of different examination dates are compared with each other. This can certainly be criticized as well; however, this fact endorses the supposition that the assessment of students' qualities from starting studying through the Part I examinations, and from the Part I examinations to the final examinations, is neutral within certain limits, i.e. good students remain good students, and poor students remain poor students.

Table 3: *Results of the correlation calculations for determining the dependencies of qualities for different quality levels for N = 272 graduates*

			q^V	q^D
Correlation calculation according to Kendall (τ_b)	q^E	Correlation coefficient	0.540 (0.616)	0.284 (0.343)
		Significance (bilateral)	< 0.0001	< 0.0001
	q^V	Correlation coefficient	----	0.466 (0.433)
		Significance (bilateral)	----	< 0.0001
Correlation calculation according to Spearman (ρ)	q^E	Correlation coefficient	0.578 (0.786)	0.307 (0.472)
		Significance (bilateral)	< 0.0001	< 0.0001
	q^V	Correlation coefficient	----	0.494 (0.580)
		Significance (bilateral)	----	< 0.0001

The hypothesis that there are no dependencies of these grades on one another is rejected in all correlation calculations on a 99% level of significance. The correlations are even better if the calculations are carried out with the grades in digits as in the original data. Table 3 shows the respective results in brackets. From this it becomes clear that the quality of students tends to be more a quality of these inputs that decides on the success of studying than being determined by the educational process.

4 Development of students' qualities within the educational process

We follow here the usual microeconomic procedure defining goods by their qualities when we like to describe how, among the group of 272 graduates, beginners with a specific entrance quality became students with a specific Part I grade and these then became graduates with a specific degree grade. Let be

r_{ij}, w_{ik} or v_{jk} the number of students turning from x_i with the entrance quality i or from y_j with the Part I grade j, respectively, into y_j with the Part I grade j or into z_k with the degree grade k,

$R = (r_{ij})$, $V = (v_{jk})$, $W = (w_{ik})$ the migration matrices in numbers of students.

Then, the migration matrices in Table 4 show the developments in the qualities of the students through the course of study. Jumping from the input grades immediately to the degree grades shortens the migration movements to one step. This is why the improvements and deteriorations in qualities are higher than in the migration over two levels. However, it is interesting that the migration tends to concentrate more on the main diagonals of the matrices, i.e. the students' qualities tend to be preserved by the educational system, which means that the system is calculable for the students.

Table 4: *Migration matrices $R=(r_{ij})$, $V=(v_{jk})$, $W=(w_{ik})$ for migrations between grades on different levels of evaluations*

Migration matrix $R=(r_{ij})$: from the start of studying to Part I level

	q^{V_j}				
q^{E_i}	**1**	**2**	**3**	**4**	**Sum**
1	3	8			**11**
2	2	42	40		**84**
3		19	107	11	**137**
4			27	13	**40**
Sum	**5**	**69**	**174**	**24**	272

Improvements	48
Neutral migrations	165
Deteriorations	59
Sum	**272**

Migration matrix $V=(v_{jk})$: from Part I level to degree

	q^{D_k}				
q^{V_j}	**1**	**2**	**3**	**4**	**Sum**
1	1	4			**5**
2	3	43	23		**69**
3		33	129	12	**174**
4		2	18	4	**24**
Sum	**4**	**82**	**170**	**16**	272

Improvements	56
Neutral migrations	177
Deteriorations	39
Sum	**272**

Migration matrix $W=(w_{ik})$ from the start of studying to degree

	q^{D_k}				
q^{E_i}	**1**	**2**	**3**	**4**	**Sum**
1	3	6	2		**11**
2		38	43	3	**84**
3	1	32	95	9	**137**
4		6	30	4	**40**
Sum	**4**	**82**	**170**	**16**	272

Improvements	69
Neutral migrations	140
Deteriorations	63
Sum	**272**

The migrations recorded in the matrices in Table 4 conceal individual developments in the qualities of every single student, which can be traced for each graduate n, $n \in \{1,\ldots,272\}$, by the quality triple $q_n=\left(q_n^{E_i}, q_n^{V_j}, q_n^{D_k}\right)$. Assuming the neutrality of the educational process, these triples can now disclose how each student worked on his or her input and output quality respectively while studying, independently of the educational process. The quality triples that can be considered can be composed in step-by-step migration matrices between Part I and degree grade starting from the specific input grade at the beginning of studying, as shown in Table 5. For example, 29 students passed through the quality triple $q=\left(q^{E_2},q^{V_3},q^{D_3}\right)=(2,3,3)$, whereas none of the graduates realized the quality triple $q=(2,2,1)$.

Table 5: Derivation of all feasible quality triples for a course of studying

		q^{D_k}				
q^{E_i}	q^{V_j}	1	2	3	4	Sum
1	1	1	2			3
	2	2	4	2		8
	3					
	4					
	Sum	3	6	2	0	11
2	1		2			2
	2		28	14		42
	3		8	29	3	40
	4					
	Sum		38	43	3	84
3	1					
	2	1	11	7		19
	3		21	80	6	107
	4			8	3	11
	Sum	1	32	95	9	137
4	1					
	2					
	3		4	20	3	27
	4		2	10	1	13
	Sum		6	30	4	40
Sum		4	82	170	16	272

From the 82 students who passed the final examinations with grade 2, 6 students started with the entrance grade 1. In addition, a closer study of the migration matrices shows that, with the exception of the two migrations through the quality triple $q=\left(q^{E_4},q^{V_4},q^{D_2}\right)=(4,4,2)$, there were no students in the groups of the Part I grades or the degree grades respectively who have improved or worsened their grades by more than one grade level. With these two exceptions, all matrix elements outside the main diagonals and the direct conjugate diagonals equal zero. This means that the substitutionalities between the quality levels are considerably restricted, i.e. good graduates are generally recruited from good students.

Only 12 students managed an increase of two grades through the levels of the quality evaluation (not even 5% of all students). If we consider that, from the entrance grade to the Part I grade, and from the Part I grade to the degree grade, grades can remain the same, improve or deteriorate, then nine typical migration patterns can be differentiated shown in Table 6 together with their absolute and relative frequencies.

If we neglect the special cases 1 and 9, because migrations from and to the marginal grades 1 and 4 can each only take place in one direction (that means their percentage terms are smaller, of course) and no changes to or from grades 0 and 5 can take place, then the typical migration patterns confirm the considerations in the previous section that the educational process tends to preserve the qualities of students as characteristics of the inputs.

Table 6: *Typical migration patterns*

Cases	*Absolute frequency*	*Relative frequency in %*
1: $q^{E_i} > q^{V_j} > q^{D_k}$	5	1.84
2: $q^{E_i} = q^{V_j} > q^{D_k}$	33	12.13
3: $q^{E_i} > q^{V_j} = q^{D_k}$	31	11.40
4: $q^{E_i} > q^{V_j} < q^{D_k}$	12	4.41
5: $q^{E_i} = q^{V_j} = q^{D_k}$	110	40.44
6: $q^{E_i} < q^{V_j} > q^{D_k}$	18	6.62
7: $q^{E_i} < q^{V_j} = q^{D_k}$	36	13.24
8: $q^{E_i} = q^{V_j} < q^{D_k}$	22	8.09
9: $q^{E_i} < q^{V_j} < q^{D_k}$	5	1.84
Sum	272	100.00

This picture becomes even clearer if the grade drifts that result from the migration matrices are examined (Fandel and Blaga 2004). Let the (positive) grade drift of quality d be defined by the number n_d of the migrations of students who achieved a grade in an educational level that is poorer by d than the grade in the qualification level immediately preceding; accordingly, a negative grade drift means a grade improvement. So, it holds:

$$n_d = \sum_{i=1}^{4} r_{i,i+d} \quad \text{and} \quad n_d = \sum_{j=1}^{4} v_{j,j+d}\text{, respectively.}$$

For $d = -1$ one obtains, for example, from matrix R in Table 4:

$$n_{-1} = r_{10} + r_{21} + r_{32} + r_{43} = 0 + 2 + 19 + 27 = 48 \ .$$

For $d = 0$ the result is in each case the sum of the matrix elements in the main diagonals (no grade changes between the current and the previous qualification stage). Missing migration movements or grade drifts, however, do not mean that there was no further qualification, but simply state that the Part I or final examinations were passed with the same (equivalent) grade as in the entrance qualification, or in the Part I examinations respectively. Table 7 shows the grade drifts for the matrices in Table 4. Where the grade drift is different from zero the upper number indicates the number and the lower number the percentage figure, measured against the respective column sum.

Table 7: *Grade drifts n_d calculated on the basis of the migration matrices in Table 4*

Drift attribute d \ *Matrix*	*R*	*V*	*W*
+3	0	0	0
+2	0	0	5/2
+1	59/22	39/14	58/21
0	165/61	177/65	140/51
-1	48/17	54/20	62/23
-2	0	2/1	7/3
-3	0	0	0

The original data on the 272 graduates provided only weak indications that students who study longer were able to improve their degree grade in comparison with their entrance grade (time against grades) and that shorter periods for studying can only be realized by the acceptance of poorer grades (substitution of grade for time). The correlation calculations showed only two remarkable phenomena in this context:

1. Of the 137 students who entered the educational system with grade 3 as their entrance grade, those with the better qualities in the degree grade also took less time to complete their studies. It was therefore better for these students to study quickly; those who took longer often performed worse.
2. Of the 170 students who passed their final examinations with grade 3, those who took less time to complete their courses came from a better entrance grade, and

those who came from the weaker entrance grade 4 took longer to achieve this degree grade.

5 Describing the developments of students' qualities by an input-output model

Denote by

$a_{ij} = r_{ij}/x_i$, $b_{jk} = v_{jk}/y_j$ or $c_{ik} = w_{ik}/x_i$ the proportions of x_i or y_j, that move to group y_j or z_k,

$A = (a_{ij})$, $B = (b_{jk})$ and $C = (c_{ik})$ the migration matrices in proportions of students,

$\overline{P}$ the static system of producing services in "teaching" at the Faculty of Economics at the FernUniversitaet;

in addition, let

$$\boldsymbol{x} = (x_1,\dots,x_4)^T, \ \boldsymbol{y} = (y_1,\dots,y_4)^T, \ \boldsymbol{z} = (z_1,\dots,z_4)^T.$$

Then the two-level multi-product manufacturing of generating graduates with specific degree grades from student beginners with different entrance qualities can be described by the implicit production function (Koopmans 1951)

$$f(\boldsymbol{x}, \boldsymbol{y}, \boldsymbol{z}, \overline{P}) = 0$$

with $\boldsymbol{x}$ as input vector, $\boldsymbol{y}$ as intermediate product vector and $\boldsymbol{z}$ as final product vector. The fundamental production structure, and its processes, can be represented through student flow equations or student balance equations of the form

$$\boldsymbol{z} = B^T \boldsymbol{y} \quad \text{and} \quad \boldsymbol{y} = A^T \boldsymbol{x} \quad \text{with} \quad \sum_{i=1}^{4} x_i = \sum_{j=1}^{4} y_j = \sum_{k=1}^{4} z_k = N = 272.$$

If the education system is considered as a one-step multi-product manufacturing, i.e. if the Part I qualification as an intermediate step is dropped, then the production system reduces to:

$$f(\boldsymbol{x}, \boldsymbol{z}, \overline{P}) = 0 \quad \text{and} \quad \boldsymbol{z} = C^T \boldsymbol{x}.$$

Because for every z_k, $k \in \{1, 2, 3, 4\}$, and for every y_j, $j \in \{1, 2, 3, 4\}$, holds

$$z_k = \begin{cases} B_k^T \boldsymbol{y} = \sum_{j=1}^{4} b_{jk} y_j = \sum_{j=1}^{4} v_{jk} & \text{für} \quad \boldsymbol{y} \neq \boldsymbol{0}, \\ C_k^T \boldsymbol{x} = \sum_{i=1}^{4} c_{ik} x_i = \sum_{i=1}^{4} w_{ik} & \text{für} \quad \boldsymbol{y} = \boldsymbol{0}, \end{cases}$$

or

$$y_j = A_j^T \boldsymbol{x} = \sum_{i=1}^{4} a_{ij} x_i = \sum_{i=1}^{4} r_{ij} \, ,$$

the production conditions could be characterized in principle by total substitution. Figure 2 illustrates these circumstances for the recruitment of students with the Part I grade j from beginners with the entrance qualities i or i', $i \neq i'$.

Figure 2: *Recruitment of students with the Part I grade j from beginners with the entrance qualities i or i' respectively*

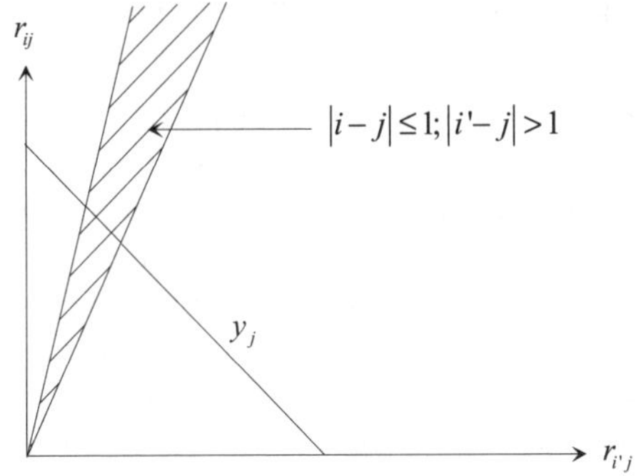

However, the fewer graduates or students with a fixed Part I grade are recruited from groups with an increasing grade difference with respect to the previous qualification (Part I grade or entrance quality), the more it can be assumed that substitutionality is restricted.

For the explicit formulation of the production function it must therefore be assumed that the yield coefficients between the quality levels are widely rigid and that they are smaller the greater the differences are between the quality levels of successive qualification stages. This impression would intrude itself if the migration relations would remain constant over time and the conjugate diagonals of the migration matrices were not or only sparsely occupied. Rigid yield coefficients would correspond to fixed transition probabilities between the quality levels, which could be estimated with the help of the migration matrices; they would cause limitational production relations between the students' groups of different qualities.

On the other side, however, sparsely occupied conjugate diagonals of the migration matrices mean that the education system of the faculty is neutral with regard to the grades, i.e. a graduate's grade quality depends to a very great extent on the grades in the Part I examinations, and these are influenced by the grades at the start of the degree course. This would mean, however, that the qualities of students are more relevant for the final success in a degree course than the quality of the educational process. It would therefore not be surprising that elite universities that select the best students following an entrance examination also produce the best graduates.

6 Limits and extensions

From the aspect of economic theory the description model presented for recording the qualities of students in the services production of "teaching" in universities has some unsatisfactory limitations. However, at the same time they form the starting points for further developments.

The migrations examined in the model can expose particularities how students with specific entrance grades become graduates with specific degree grades via the Part I examinations in a two-level educational process. The corresponding matrices in percentage terms provide information on the yield coefficients needed for determining student flow equations. The contribution of the external input "students" to the success of the universities' services production can be modeled explicitly through this approach, which is widely used in input-output analysis (Koopmans 1951). Time series models with a larger sample size may provide information on whether the yield coefficients remain constant over longer periods or change, i.e. the quality of students varies over the course of time.

One disadvantage of the description model is that it only describes the qualities of graduates through students' entrance grades or Part I grades, without taking into account explicitly how the degree grades depend on the study time. The available data material does not as yet provide an indication for such dependencies. However, larger sample sizes would make it desirable to include this aspect, and to differentiate with respect to students' gender as well. If the original data in tenths of grades are taken as the basis, the distribution of the grade drift can be determined even more precisely in dependence of the study time. This would lead to a so-called diffusion equation, which would generate a stochastic explanation model of the quality changes.

If one starts from the findings that higher grades in studies (beginners, Part I, degree) lead to higher salaries in industry (Bartels 1993)*, then the explanation model derived from the description model can be taken as a basis for formulating a decision model.

* Large law firms determine the initial starting salaries of their lawyers on average so that each point achieved in the second state law examinations is valued at EUR 500.

The faculty could react to students with poorer entrance grades with more intensive support activities in teaching, to increase the yield coefficients of poorer grade classes for better grade classes, and thus to contribute to a greater added value in the educational system. The canvassing potential of these universities would be correspondingly high. If the quality of teaching did not suffer any impairment, a large gain in their reputations would result.

7 References

Albach, H., G. Fandel, and W. Schüler (1978): *Hochschulplanung*, Baden-Baden.

Bartels, J. (1993): *Absolventen des Fachbereichs Wirtschaftswissenschaft – Ergebnisse einer Repraesentativbefragung*, Zentrum für Fernstudienentwicklung – FernUniversitaet – Gesamthochschule – in Hagen, 1993.

BfA (2000): *Analysen zum Arbeitsmarkt / Strukturen der Arbeitslosigkeit: Akademiker/innen, Bundesanstalt für Arbeit*, Landesarbeitsamt Nordrhein-Westfalen, Düsseldorf.

Fandel, G. (1995): *Wirtschaftlichkeitsaspekte einer Hochschule. Inhalte einer gutachterlichen Stellungnahme über die FernUniversitaet*, Weinheim.

Fandel, G. (2003): Zur Leistung nordrhein-westfaelischer Universitaeten – Gegenüberstellung einer Verteilungslösung und der Effizienzmaße einer Data Envelopment Analysis, in: Backes-Gellner, U. and C. Schmidtke (Eds.): Hochschulökonomie - Analysen interner Steuerungsprobleme und gesamtwirtschaftlicher Effekte, *Schriften des Vereins für Socialpolitik*, Neue Folge, 296, 33-50.

Fandel, G. and S. Blaga (2004): Dienstleistungsproduktion in Hochschulen. Zur Beschreibung der Qualitäten der externen Faktoren „Studierende", *Schriften des Vereins für Socialpolitik*, forthcoming.

Fandel, G. and T. Gal (2001): Redistribution of funds for teaching and research among universities: The case of North Rhine-Westphalia, *European Journal of Operational Research*, 130, 111-120.

Fandel, G. and A. Paff (2000): Eine produktionstheoretisch fundierte Kostenrechnung für Hochschulen – dargestellt am Beispiel der FernUniversitaet Hagen, *Zeitschrift für Betriebswirtschaft*, special issue 3/2000, 191-204.

Fries, M. (2002): Abitur und Studienerfolg. Welchen „Wert" hat das Abitur für ein erfolgreiches Studium?, *Beitraege zur Hochschulforschung*, 1, 24. Jg., 30-51.

Hackl, P. and G. Sedlacek (2002a): Analyse der Studiendauer am Beispiel der Wirtschaftsuniversitaet Wien, in: Dutter, R. (Ed.): *Festschrift 50 Jahre Österreichische Statistische Gesellschaft*, Vienna, 41-59.

Hackl, P. and G. Sedlacek (2002b): *Forschungsbericht Studienverlaufsanalyse*, Forschungsbericht der Wirtschaftsuniversitaet Wien.

Hartung, J. (1984): *Statistik*, Oldenburg.

Koopmans, T.C. (1951): Analysis of production as an efficient combination of activities, in: Koopmans, T.C. (Ed.): *Activity Analysis of Production and Allocation*, New York, 33-97.

Lohmar, U., G.E. Ortner, and M. Bayer (1982): *Die deutsche Hochschule zwischen Numerus clausus und Akademikerarbeitslosigkeit. Der doppelte Flaschenhals*, Hannover.

Maleri, R. (1973): *Grundzüge der Dienstleistungsproduktion*, Berlin et al.

Smith, J. and R.A. Naylor (2001): Dropping out of University: A statistical analysis of the probability of withdrawal for UK university students, *Journal of the Royal Statistical Society*, C, 164; 389-405.

Stieger, H. (1980): *Zur Ökonomie der Hochschule*, Gießen.

Wilhelm Krull

Encouraging Change

The Role of Private Foundations in Innovation Processes

Dr. *Wilhelm Krull*, Secretary General of the Volkswagen Foundation.

1 Common wisdom? The meaning of "innovation"

A cartoon in a German newspaper published a few months ago showed an example of a very effective means of cost cutting in electoral campaigns: an advertisement containing one single word: "Innovation!", and the names of all German political parties underneath.

If one changed the names of the political parties, this advertisement would probably work in almost all societies around the world. No doubt, "innovation" has become one of the most popular buzzwords in economy, business, politics, and society at large:

"The word innovation is one of the most overused, underdefined terms in organizational life. No one seems to be sure just what the word means. Is it merely something new to a given organization or a development that challenges the prevailing wisdom in a field? Is it an initiative that achieves a certain cachet as the fashion of the moment or something that changes the course of practice? Although the 'whatever is new to you' definition is by far the most common in studies of private-sector innovation, it fails to take account of the rationale for innovation in the public sector." (Light 1998, XIV).

To understand why and how this word has become a cure-all for societies, a panacea for the economy and science, one has to look back to the beginning of the last century. Before the Second World War a broad definition of "innovation" prevailed, particularly represented by the Austrian economist Joseph Alois Schumpeter (1883-1950). The entirety of new products, processes and technical solutions was perceived as "innovation," Schumpeter's definition also included non-technical, "soft" factors such as institutional frameworks and social conditions between participating organizations and individuals. (Meyer-Krahmer 2003, 6-9). After the war, this definition did not seem to be valid any more: innovation was more or less identical with new products and technologies. Technological achievements and innovation were synonymic.

Today, we have returned to a rather Schumpeterian perception of innovation – from mere product innovation to a systemic, process-oriented approach. It is not self-evident any more that "whatever is new to you" deserves to be acclaimed as an innovation. On the contrary: if a new product or process fails to become "socially robust" and sustainable, it will also fail to become an innovation. Albeit it is new, it will not have a positive influence on science, society, or the economy (Nowotny, Scott, and Gibbons 2001).

As a consequence, facilitating and producing innovation does not only mean to develop new processes and products, it also means to organize bi-directional communication between science and society, it means to create institutional structures that enable researchers to create innovation, it means to bridge the gap between practice and theory, and finally it means to cross borders between countries, but also between disciplines. All of these challenges, of course, interact closely with each other and call for systematic, integrated approaches. In this article, I will argue that private foundations are the most suitable organizations to take on these challenges.

2 Private foundations and their capacity to innovate

Financial constraints in the public sector have led researchers and policy-makers to stress the need for new regulatory frameworks, such as tax incentives, and the provision of fewer bureaucratic procedures, so as to stimulate private initiative, particularly in the field of higher education and research. Given the enormous wealth accumulated in Europe since the Second World War, this seems a timely idea, not least because of the large impending transfers of private property from one generation to another. In Germany, for example, it has been estimated that within the next ten to fifteen years, more than three trillion euros are at stake. This is indeed a unique opportunity for foundations to be established, but also for existing charities to accumulate capital.

But is this opportunity also a universal remedy for science and technological development, for the destitute German higher education and research system? Most probably it is not: if one looks at the 10,000 foundations in Germany, one realizes that only about 13 % provide funds for higher education and research; and that the funds provided by these foundations amount to only 450 to 500 million euros annually. Therefore, private foundations cannot compensate for huge deficits in public spending. Indeed, even the Volkswagen Foundation, which is by far the largest German foundation – it awards some 100 million euros per year –, has explicitly excluded a compensatory function from its portfolio.

2.1 The Volkswagen Foundation

The Volkswagen Foundation is an autonomous non-profit organization incorporated under private law. Independent from the car-manufacturer bearing the same name, it sees its role in facilitating change at various levels of research and research policy-making, by establishing funding initiatives designed to stimulate developments, redress imbalances, and create role models for strategies and structures. Last, but not least, its activities encompass a wide array of incentives for developing a better understanding of Europe and for fostering international collaboration.

The Volkswagen Foundation is economically independent and thereby completely autonomous in its decision making. The capital stock – currently amounting to 2.1 billion euros – must above all serve two objectives: one is to ensure the sustained funding of research initiatives; the other is to maintain the real value of the Foundation's equity in the face of inflationary pressure. It is obviously inadmissible to use any of the Foundation's equity for funding purposes, since this would jeopardize its long-term existence.

Funding, therefore, is financed solely out of the returns on invested capital. In order to make sure that the material value of the Foundation's equity is also at least maintained at a constant level in the future, it is necessary to protect the Foundation's assets against risks such as monetary inflation. This is done by building reserves, within the parameters of fiscal law, by appropriating a proportion of the annual returns on investment for this purpose. However, this is not enough to be able to maintain a constant level of funding for any length of time. This calls for investment not only in interest-bearing securities, but also in intrinsic values like stocks and real estate. The Foundation's portfolio, as required by its statutes, is managed in such a way that the assets are both adequately hedged and at the same time geared to relatively high yield. (Brockhoff 2002, 277 et sqq.; Brockhoff 2003, 221 et sqq.)

Due to its portfolio management, the Volkswagen Foundation has been able to support humanities and social sciences as well as science and technology in higher education and research with more than three billion Euros. This is almost six times the amount of its original endowment in 1962 (which amounted to DM 1.1 billion) and shows how sustainable foundations can contribute to innovation processes.

Of course, portfolio management is only one side of the coin. Leading change and supporting innovation can only be achieved when the yield is used strategically:

"If foundations serve only as passive middlemen, as mere conduits for giving, then they fall short of their potential and of society's high expectations. Foundations can and should lead social progress. They have the potential to make more effective use of scarce resources than either individual donors or the government. Free from political pressures, foundations can explore new solutions to social problems with an independence that governments can never have." (Porter and Kramer 1999, 121-122).

Against this background, the long-term success of any funding agency or private foundation depends upon basing its strategy as well as its funding decisions on top-notch expert advice. For a research funding foundation this encompasses the preparation of new funding initiatives, as well as encouraging individual proposals. However, it is difficult to strike a balance between requirements and criteria when it comes to assessing interdisciplinary proposals. Successful researchers do not only need to have track records of scientific excellence, but also a readiness and ability to develop common approaches, to enter into a process of mutual learning. There will always remain a certain degree of risk, especially in newly developing fields. But where a climate of mutual trust exists between foundation officers and researchers, a readiness to take risks can be turned into mutual advantage.

The initiatives and examples from the work of the Volkswagen Foundation described in this article are intended to show that foundations actually can create an added value, by engaging in this process of mutual risk-taking, by fostering innovation and making an impact on public policy, by the establishment of good practice – or at least, by demonstrating the feasibility of implementing new concepts. Unlike publicly financed agencies, which have to provide equal opportunities for all institutions, and even individuals, and which operate within a framework that involves cumbersome administrative procedures, private foundations can act much more freely, flexibly, and quickly. They do not have to wait for political consensus. They can act autonomously, in supporting the first experiments in new areas, and in being front runners in institutional reform.

3 Trans-disciplinary funding modes and their impact on research communities

Is this advantageous legal form already a value in itself? Arguably it is not. Michael Porter's and Mark Kramer's core argument is that, due to their privileged tax treatment, foundations have to create value by achieving "equivalent [...] benefit with fewer dollars" or "greater [...] benefit at comparable cost." (Porter and Kramer 1999, 126). In other words, a clear-cut strategy is indispensable, and subsequently a deliberately selective distribution of funds.

For funding organizations active in the field of higher education and research such a strategy is badly needed, today more than ever. For decades it has been taken for granted that publicly financed universities are the stronghold of discipline-based teaching and research. The results achieved in improving our knowledge base seemed to justify the increasing tendency towards specialization – and a subsequent concentration of funds for specialized, disciplinary research. However, as the "emphasis has moved away from free inquiry to problem solving and, more generally in the direction of problem-oriented research" (Gibbons, Limoges, and Nowotny 1994, 71), there is an urgent need to stimulate interactions between researchers from different disciplines. Research policy wisdom has been telling us for some time that "new knowledge is usually formed at the boundaries of fields – i.e., in the transition to neighboring fields and neighboring disciplines, not at the disciplinary core where textbook knowledge has its seat" (Mittelstrass 1998, 12). To foster and support this kind of knowledge creation at the boundaries of disciplinary fields is the core element of our strategy – sometimes against considerable opposition from the respective research communities.

3.1 Innovation processes in economy and society

The aim of private funding of trans-disciplinary research must be to overcome this opposition and to introduce new research topics, fields and approaches on the agenda of research communities. In its funding initiative "Innovation Processes in Economy and Society", for example, the Volkswagen Foundation offers support for research which focuses on the complexity of innovation processes, taking into account the multi-faceted interaction between social, economic, and scientific as well as technological factors. At the same time, this funding initiative is targeted at making a contribution to linking up the various approaches in innovation research – which up to now have mainly been explored in separate disciplines – and to promoting the international networking of researchers working in this field. Comparative studies contrasting diverse processes in different contexts, especially in the form of joint research projects receive particular attention. The focus is not confined to an analysis of the technical and organizational innovation processes which take place within and around firms; rather it should concentrate on the scientific, technological, social, political and cultural preconditions of innovation processes, their consequences for society, culture, politics, law and the economy – especially the interdependence of the specific factors at work in these processes.

This gives rise to the question concerning the role innovation processes assume in the shaping of a knowledge based society, and how, in turn, the innovation processes are influenced by the structure of economies and societies. Ambivalent effects as well as the non-intended consequences of innovation processes should also be taken into account. The methodological and theoretical problems facing innovation research should be specifically addressed in the projects, and may re-present the main object of investigation in selected proposals. Terminology, assessment criteria, and procedures are all possible topics, as well as the identification of success criteria for societal discourse on the subject of innovation.

Such an approach is not plain sailing and free of caveats. It excludes disciplinary research on innovation – no matter of how high standing its quality and the participating researchers might be. The terms for funding in this initiative begin with the following sentence: *"Funding will be made available to interdisciplinary research projects dealing with issues of innovation research preferably in international collaboration."* A trans-disciplinary approach is hence a fundamental condition for funding. The dismissing decisions that the foundation and its experts had to make in several cases due to this paragraph in the terms for funding were not at all easy ones: several of the high quality applications we received were mono-disciplinary research proposals. It is, however, rather surprising how small the readiness to engage in trans-disciplinary research projects is in German innovation research. This seems to be the only explanation for the relatively small number of projects funded in this initiative so far.

Surprisingly, the easiest market mechanisms do not work in the starting phases of trans-disciplinary funding initiatives: the customer (i.e. the foundation) asks for innovative products and gives detailed conditions for these products, but it gets offered only off-the-peg clothing. Furthermore, the details in the request for proposals are in some cases deliberately ignored. In the end, the foundation has to justify why it did not buy – or in this case support – a product it has never asked for. Sometimes we even hear that the foundation does spend its money in a wrong way and acts detrimentally with respect to the health of individual disciplines.

This attitude – a striking example of what has been called "destructive opposition" to innovations (Klöter 1997, 150 et sqq.) – is an almost exclusive phenomenon in German humanities and social sciences, and a true restraint in innovation processes. This is much the worse because research funding organizations need external input and constructive criticism. Clearly, Jürgen Hauschildt's statement that the further development of methods to "overcome destructive opposition" and "the deliberate encouragement of constructive opposition" are central tasks for innovation management, does not only apply to the business world. It also applies to institutions funding and to institutions conducting research. (Hauschildt 1999, 235.)

One has to come to the conclusion that trans-disciplinary research only scarcely originates on its own. The readiness to engage in research at the border of one's own discipline, however, is an essential component of innovation processes. This readiness can not at all be taken for granted; on the contrary: it has to be created. Therefore, it remains a central concern of the Volkswagen Foundation to bring together and consolidate research approaches from different disciplines. We cannot enforce innovation, we can only encourage it.

3.2 Bridging the gap

The boundaries between different disciplines are, however, not the only ones to be crossed. It seems to be equally important to bridge the huge gap between theory and practice, between academia and practical application of its insights. Compared to other countries, like the USA for example, Germany lacks the same type of continual and commonplace interaction between academia and practice, marked by mutual exchange and permeability between the two spheres. The initiative "Bridging the Gap" is intended to contribute toward breaking down the conventional partitioning of career patterns already at an early age in favor of interface-biographies.

Successful cooperation between academia and practice can and must be approached from both sides. Therefore, this funding offer is aimed on the one hand at researchers, who, as a follow-up to thematically relevant research work, are now interested in gaining in-depth experience in suitable government and non-government organizations.

On the other hand, suitably qualified staff belonging to such organizations will also be given the opportunity to develop a deepened or new orientation by undertaking work at research facilities engaged in issue-related fundamental and strategic research.

We hope that bringing researchers from universities and other research institutions to government and non-government organizations and vice versa does not only influence their research activities and/or practical decision making, provide insights into the other sphere, and open up new career perspectives. We are also convinced that in the long run this will affect the organization, or research institution itself. It is clear that a foundation cannot support such a program forever. Therefore, it must be our goal to give an impetus which has to be sustained by the organizations and research institutions. Leading change means to initiate it – and to support it. However, in the end it is the institution itself and the people working in it who will have to change: A simple change in administrative and organizational structures doesn't change the mindsets of the researcher, administrator, or politician affected.

4 Leading institutional change

For foundations leading institutional change is, therefore, similar to encouraging and supporting institutions and its leaders to engage in change processes towards achieving research- and innovation-friendly structures. In some of his recent publications, Rogers Hollingsworth, Hollingsworth, and Hage (2003) have found medium scale research organizations to be the most probable environment for achieving major breakthroughs in research and innovation. His studies on research institutions in the field of biomedicine revealed two basic concepts that seem to be institutional conditions sine qua non for ground breaking research: firstly an interdisciplinary organizational structure, and secondly strong leadership connected with very high quality standards.

Research institutions and organizations, however, have reacted to the increasing complexity of knowledge creation and research with an increase in size and diversity. Subsequently, this creates an increase in bureaucracy and hierarchic structures. In other words: the increase in diversity and size creates a decrease in integration and flexibility – and this lack of flexibility and integration inhibits trans-disciplinary research and innovation. The reasons for this are manifold. One thing, however, is clear: if universities want to profit from private funding, they have to be flexible, they have to accept foundations as partners, and have to engage with them in a productive interplay.

4.1 Efficiency through autonomy

For these reasons, foundations are vitally interested in research-friendly, flexible structures at universities and do help them concerning their decision-making and administration: e.g., by helping them to create the structures and processes which make their governance and administration more efficient. All of this serves the need to create a research-friendly environment in which minds and ideas can develop. Thanks to private foundations, which respect an individual university's right to summon its strengths and pull itself out of difficulties, more than twenty of the eighty-five universities are now being supported in reconfiguring their capacity to manage their affairs more effectively.

In the funding initiative "Leistungsfähigkeit durch Eigenverantwortung" (Efficiency through Autonomy) 10 German universities received as much as € 12 million from the Volkswagen Foundation. The aim of this program was to improve the conditions for teaching and research at the respective universities. However, we also wanted to show that administrative and organizational change is possible. Hence, this funding initiative was not designed to start a major redesign of science and research policy in Germany. Rather, the ten universities supported were to become role-models for similar institutions, and of course, also the legislation could learn from their experimental approaches.

4.2 New opportunities for young researchers

The requirements of the 'Habilitation' for a long time have implied that young researchers are dependent upon established professors, whom they serve as 'assistants', before they complete the 'Habilitation' at an average age of forty years. This is clearly too late. It makes our universities less attractive than, for example, those of the United States, which offer talented scholars early opportunities to pursue their research as independent 'assistant professors'.

Even though this deplorable situation is recognized in almost all parts of our research system, the system itself, is not able (or not willing?) to change. And neither are most of its institutions, be it on the funding, or on the researching end. When, for example, in the mid-1980s, the German Science Council recommended a restructuring of doctoral training, neither the Federal States nor the Deutsche Forschungsgemeinschaft, but the Thyssen Foundation, the Bosch Foundation, and the Volkswagen Foundation were the first to offer support to universities willing to implement new thematically focused graduate schools (Graduiertenkollegs).

This lack of readiness and ability to change is also apparent as to new opportunities for young researchers. In order to demonstrate that new career patterns can be integrated into the German system, the Volkswagen Foundation created in 1996 a program for junior research group leaders. More than fifty have been and still are supported. With its newest funding initiative supporting young researchers, the Foundation aims at combining support for both persons as well as institutions. With the "Lichtenberg Professorships" the Volkswagen Foundation will provide support to outstandingly qualified (junior) academics in connection with innovative fields of research located between the disciplines as well as new teaching concepts within the respective research environment. The funding which will be made available for a period of up to eight years is expected to pave an interesting new path in higher education. On the one hand, young scholars will be offered a future perspective on a kind of "tenure-track", and on the other hand institutions will gain a better basis for planning – both from a strategic viewpoint with respect to content and institutional structures as well as concerning personnel development in the sense of long-term capacity building

5 Crossing borders - new approaches to international grant-making

Where public institutions are reluctant to encourage new ideas, private foundations also have a special role to play. They have been actively involved in international cooperation through exchange programs, and by making academics aware of problems in other countries. Often, they are the first to support scholars and researchers from politically sensitive regions. It will in future be even more important for private foundations to support strategically relevant initiatives, including high-risk activities, e.g. focusing on Sub-Saharan Africa, for which it is difficult, if not impossible to gain public support.

5.1 Knowledge for tomorrow

The Volkswagen Foundation's funding initiative "Knowledge for Tomorrow. Cooperative Research Projects in Sub-Saharan Africa" aims at medium-, to long-term cooperation between German and African research workers and is open to all disciplines. By means of providing targeted support to junior scholars and scientists it is intended to create the conditions necessary for a self-sustaining process of development in research and higher education in Africa. The initiative aims at providing a contribution to the development and sustainable reinforcement of research in sub-Saharan Africa. This is to be achieved via research projects developed and carried out by African scholars and scientists in cooperation with German partners, providing junior scientists in Africa with an opportunity to enhance their skills and academic qualification. Besides this Afro-German cooperation, a special focus will be on the development, reinforcement and extension of academic networks inside Africa.

In order to support the mutual identification of future-oriented areas of investigation and the cooperative development of innovative research issues the Volkswagen Foundation sets up and carries out thematic workshops in close cooperation with researchers from Europe as well as from Africa. These meetings will be utilized to discuss the current status of research, identify subjects of investigation, and to explore the possibilities for cooperation that should also embrace other researchers and research locations inside sub-Saharan Africa.

5.2 Common foreign and security policy studies - a joint initiative by three European foundations

Similar challenges are evident here in Europe: Only by giving young people incentives, also financially, to develop intercultural competences and common perspectives can we meet the growing demand for future leaders. These competences are not an end in itself – they are core qualifications to meet future challenges. A good example for such an incentive could look like the initiative "European Foreign and Security Policy Studies" – a joint research and training program which has just been launched by three European foundations (Compagnia di San Paolo, Torino/Italy, Riksbankens Jubileumsfond, Stockholm/Sweden, and VolkswagenStiftung).

The participating foundations are convinced that the national views which dominate academic and practical approaches towards a Common Foreign and Security Policy (CFSP) should recede in favor of a trans-national perspective. The envisioned research and training program aims at developing such a perspective by young researchers and practitioners in their further qualification. The program also aims at mobility across borders and between the academic and practical spheres. The candidates can work at academic institutions of their own choice and appropriate (European) organizations engaged in CFSP. Each participant in the program will be funded for up to two years. At least half of the time should be spent abroad in an academic or practice organization. Individual activities should be combined with the active participation in conferences and summer schools involving the other researchers funded in this initiative. Events should be held every six months. Joint publications and internet presentations could serve as further instruments for supranational networking.

Candidates for funding are young researchers and practitioners who aim at postgraduate or postdoctoral research in the field of CFSP. They should be selected according to personal qualification and the expected quality of the proposed piece of research. Disciplines, nationality, or belonging to an EU member state should not be essential. Candidates who have passed the research and training program should be able to work as university teachers, analysts for institutes or "think tanks", in the media, the civil service, or in political NGOs.

It is a crucial task not only for research and research funding institutions to open up these career perspectives to young researchers. Above all, innovation is created by brilliant minds and their ideas. A well set-up innovation process, on the other hand, will also result in the creation of ideas and, subsequently, of minds who pursue these ideas. Foundations are striving to be part of such a "self-sustaining" innovation process – because we need these ideas in order to further develop our work.

6 Conclusions

Foundations play an important role in innovation processes, and according to their statutes they have to ensure that all funding is used for the purpose for which it was allocated. This also means that they have to ascertain that their funding is used for supplementary activities and does not, for instance, simply serve to bolster the budget of recipient institutions or providers which may lie behind them, such as the state. This constraint, strange as it might sound, creates the inspiring effect that private funding has on the development of research and higher education, but also the willingness of citizens, enterprises and foundations to spend their money for these purposes.

Within what I would call the "Magic Triangle" of successful research and innovation – consisting of risk-taking, flexibility and quality assurance – foundations can encourage, support, and inspire institutions and individuals to build and shape their research environment. Above all, however, "trust" is in the centre of this triangle. The few examples I gave of the work of the Volkswagen Foundation were meant to show that foundations can contribute to this magic triangle by encouraging risk-taking, by stimulating new developments, redressing imbalances, creating role models for an effective change of research strategies or institutional structures, and by contributing to the creation of a more research-friendly society. Due to the perpetuity of their funds, foundations are reliable partners, willing to foster risky projects, and to help researchers to break new grounds. They can help their partners in universities and other research institutions to act, not only to react, in the respective innovation processes, in the development of scholarship, and in selected areas of basic and strategic research.

7 References

Brockhoff, K. (2002): Erhaltung eines Stiftungsvermögens, *Zeitschrift für betriebswirtschaftliche Forschung*, 54, 277-284.

Brockhoff, K. (2003): Optimierung der Vermögenslage einer Stiftung, in: Kötz, Rawert, Schmidt, and Walz (Eds.): *Non Profit Law Year Book*, Köln, 221-234.

Gibbons, M., C. Limoges, and H. Nowotny (Eds.) (1994): *The New Production of Knowledge*, London.

Hauschildt, J. (1999): Opposition to innovations – destructive or constructive?, in: Brockhoff, K. et. al (Eds.): *The Dynamics of Innovation*, Berlin, 217-240.

Rogers Hollingsworth, J., E.J. Hollingsworth, and J. Hage (2003): *Fostering Scientific Excellence: Organizations, Institutions, and Major Discoveries in Biomedical Science*, New York.

Klöter, R. (1997): *Opponenten im organisationalen Beschaffungsprozeß*, Wiesbaden.

Light, P.C. (1998): *Sustaining Innovation. Creating Nonprofit and Government Organisations that Innovate Naturally*, San Francisco.

Meyer-Krahmer, F. (2003): Robinson Deutschland - Innovation in Deutschland, *Spektrum der Wissenschaft*, November, 6-9.

Mittelstrass, J. (1998): 15 Truths about the Future of Universities, in: Mittelstrass, J. (Ed.): *The Future Role of the Universities in the Scientific and Academic System*, Berlin.

Nowotny, H., P. Scott, and M. Gibbons (2001): *Re-Thinking Science: Knowledge and the Public in an Age of Uncertainty*, London.

Porter, M.E. and M.R. Kramer (1999): Philanthropy's New Agenda: Creating Value, *Harvard Business Review*, Nov/Dec, 121-130.

Heribert Meffert

Innovation in Non-Profit-Organizations

The Example of an Operating Foundation

Prof. Dr. Dr. h.c. mult. *Heribert Meffert*, Emeritus, Institute of Marketing at Westphalian Wilhelms University of Münster and President of the Executive Board of the Bertelsmann Foundation.

1 Introduction

Issues relating to the emergence and promotion of innovation in enterprises, as well as their implementation in the market, form a central focus of the theoretical work of Klaus Brockhoff. This relates to integrating effective innovation management with market-oriented management.

In this context, the academic literature has devoted relatively little attention to innovation problems in the non-profit sector. The following paper will consider issues relating to innovation in non-profit-organizations using the example of an operating foundation. Against the background of central developments of the foundation sector in Germany, the organization of innovation processes, diffusion of innovations and significance of brands for successful innovation, will be discussed. This will proceed according to the basic view that as "think-tanks", foundations play the role of change agents in the societal innovation process.

2 The State of Play in the Foundation Sector in Germany

2.1 Core Developments

Measured by the number of foundations established, the foundation sector seems, since the middle of the 1980s, to have overcome its period of stagnation. It is currently experiencing an impressive renaissance. After a first period of increased foundation establishment in the late Middle Ages and a second in the late 19th century as a result of the Industrial Revolution (Smith and Borgmann 2001; Anheier 2001) the foundation sector in Germany has, since this period, found new strength (see Figure 1).

Amongst the many driving forces of this growth which led to the current number of approximately 12,000 German foundations (Anheier 2003), three central factors can be identified which have contributed substantially to the described developments.

For one thing, the supply-side conditions for establishing foundations are currently exceptionally favorable. Never before have there been so many affluent people (Deutsches Institut für Altersvorsorge 2000). This necessary condition is supplemented by motives of private individuals or organizations who have legal rights over this capital, enabling them to make these funds available to a foundation. That is, there is a sufficient basis for wishing to create a foundation. Independent of the individual biographies, a number of reasons can be observed as to why people with potential philanthropic commitment actually go ahead and donate a portion of their wealth for the common good. The fact that there have never before been so many childless couples, is a further probable explanation.

Figure 1: *Number of foundations established over the period 1950 – 2003*

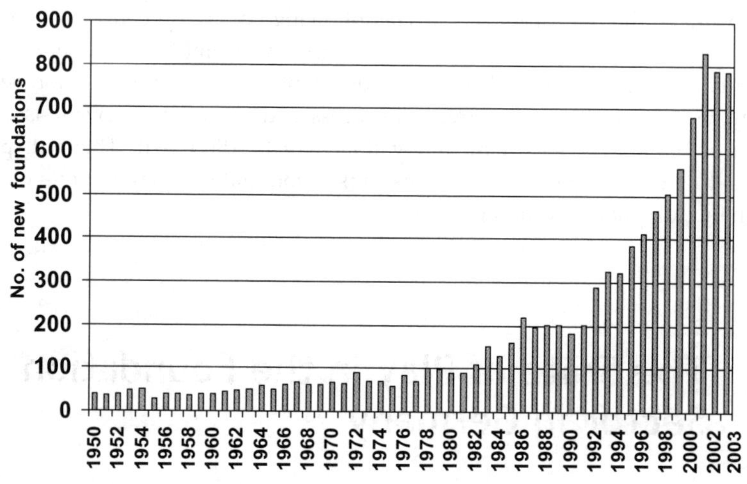

Source: Bundesverband Deutscher Stiftungen e.V. 2001; 2004

Apart from these favorable conditions on the supply side, the behavior of the authorities constitutes a second promotional factor for the development of the German foundation sector. The idea of foundations has been rediscovered not only by potential founders but also by political decision-makers (Bertelsmann Stiftung 1999). This strengthens the sector through successive improvements in the taxation and civil law framework and thus contributes further to growth in the sector.

The outlined supply and the apparent political goodwill face a third factor responsible for growth: the clear demand for the services that foundations can provide. Over the last few years, the debate as to the relationship of state, economy and civil society has achieved a new dynamic. In this context, it is clear that, to an increasing extent, the state is less able to assume responsibility for all spheres of life and that the significance of the civil society will consequently increase in this power triangle.

2.2 Forms and Content of Foundation Work

The concept of a foundation is not legally protected in Germany and, particularly in the countries governed by European civil law, which include Germany, is applied to a number of different types of organization (Toepler 1996, 27). In the following section, a private, non-profit-oriented organization which devotes its wealth to a common cause and whose orientation has been established by a founder's preferences and wishes, will be regarded as a foundation (Anheier 2003, 51). Based on the manner in which they work, foundations can be divided into three basic types.

- Project foundations conceive, initiate and pursue activities on their own initiative, generally in the form of projects. According to their own understanding of themselves, they are often "think-tanks" with the objective of securing the future viability of society. The Körber Foundation and Bertelsmann Foundation are both examples of this type.
- Grantmaking foundations approve funds on application made by third-parties. They often award prizes or scholarships and support other bodies in achieving their own objectives. The Volkswagen Foundation and German Federal Environmental Foundation provide good examples.
- Institutional foundations often aim at running some form of institution such as a nursing home, museum or hospital. These foundations generally have assets such as real-estate and land intended for a specific use. The Fugger Foundation and v. Bodelschwinghschen Anstalten Bethel are good examples of this kind of foundation.

Institutional foundations and project foundations can be grouped together in the category of "operating foundations". Approximately one fifth of German foundations belong exclusively to the group of operating foundations, whereas the share of promotional foundations is approximately one-third. Finally, about 15 per cent of German foundations are both promotional and operationally active. The following investigation entails a concentration on project foundations as operating foundations. If, in the following section, mention is made of operating foundations, this explicitly excludes institutional foundations, because the modus operandi of project and institutional foundations, apart from their operating orientation, reveals little similarity with respect to the considered object of investigation.

Foundations can be regarded as components of civic society in the context of societal development. They perform two main functions labeled in the literature as complementarity and innovation (Anheier 2003; Toepler. 1996, 74). On the one hand, they may promote where, because of pressure on budgets or a lack of interest on the part of firms, the needs of societal groups are insufficiently satisfied. Complementary activities in the area of welfare services and care or promoting education, have a long tradition in the German foundation sector. On the other hand, when they are regarded as particularly innovative and often as similarly risky, plans can be promoted or carried out by the foundation itself, without placing demands on public funds or the providers of capital. This substantial potential of the foundation sector can be seen, in comparison with the other actors, to derive from their large degree of economic and political independence. Because of this characteristic, foundations are well suited to assume an initiating role in innovation processes. For a substantial period of time, in American civic society, foundations have assumed a role as change agents in the societal innovation process (Toepler 1996, 82). The substantial contributions of American foundations to the "Green Revolution", minority issues or women's' policy, reflect this own understanding (Schmidt 2003, 89). The notion that German foundations could also assume the role of an innovator or "motor of change" can still be regarded as somewhat avant-garde. In the previous century, German foundations were exposed both to external attacks as well as to a devaluation of their financial resources (Brockhoff 2002, 277). Simultaneously, the Germans reveal a different attitude towards foundations and the state traditionally plays a dominant role. Furthermore, there has, so far in Germany, been a lack of the professional management generally obtained from extensive experience in the foundation sector. Nonetheless, there are currently a small number of operating foundations, which have the necessary critical mass to provide genuine structural intervention. In the following section, it will be shown how foundations use this intrinsic potential and, as initiators of innovation processes, make a sustainable and ongoing contribution to societal development.

3 Innovation in Operating Foundations

3.1 Organization of the Innovation Process

"An innovation is an idea, practice or object that is perceived as new by an individual or other unit of adoption." (Rogers 1995, 5). In the case of operating foundations, innovations are undertaken with the objective of providing model solutions for societal problems. For example, the Körber Foundation formulates the following for its own objective: "The Körber Foundation aims at meeting the challenges and creating an awareness of problems that emerge in our society and stimulating suggestions for solving such problems" (Körber-Stiftung 2003). In a similar manner, the Bertelsmann Foundation, which will be described later in this paper by means of an example of an innovation process, claims the following in its mission statement: "The foundation will provide an early identification of societal challenges and problems and provide model solutions which it will also implement." (Bertelsmann Stiftung 2002).

Figure 2: *The Life Cycle Model of Public Ventures*

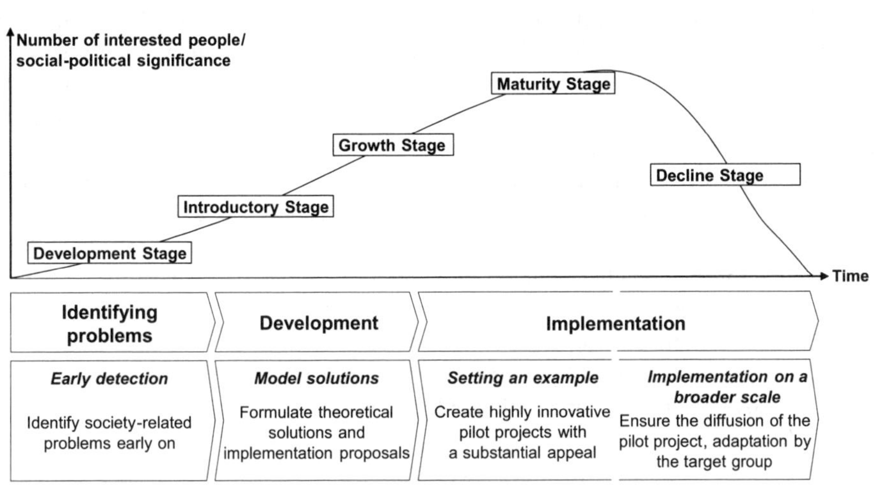

Within a social system, ongoing societal demands function in a certain life cycle (see Figure 2) and thus impact over time on ever more components of society. When foundations assume the role of innovators, they aim at recognizing societal problems at a very early stage, even before other actors within the social system have become aware of the problems. As the problem resolution progresses through the foundation and its partners, the number of interested parties and the socio-political significance of its responsibilities and activities will grow. On the one hand, this suggests that over time, problems will in any event come to light without any activity on the part of the foundation. In this manner, the solutions suggested by this foundation will make it easier to attract interest and the diffusion of its ideas will be more straightforward. On the other hand, foundations can influence the life cycle and this provides it with a catalyst function. By considering certain issues and questions itself, a foundation can bring closer the point in time of a reaction. A foundation can draw the attention of the public to specific issues and ensure that these find a wide audience. Public awareness of a particular problem is thus enhanced and the five phases of the life cycle - development, introduction, growth, maturity and decline - occur earlier than would otherwise be the case. Furthermore, problems will also be resolved more rapidly, than if there was no foundation intervening.

In principle, operating foundations follow a series of market and environmental observations which are familiar from innovation management. These range from problem identification to the generation of ideas, evaluation and selection of alternatives as well as the subsequent project implementation (Bodenstein 1987, 15).

Apart from those affected directly, employees of the foundation, members of the board of trustees or related officers as well as politicians and decision makers with whom the foundation is constantly in communication, serve as sources of an initial generation of new ideas in the case of problem identification. Operating foundations cater for societal needs for reform, generally together with those people affected by the particular problems. This necessitates constant dialogue with all societal stakeholders, not least, in order to win the confidence of the public upon whose attention and creativity the foundation is dependent in the implementation of its suggested solutions. Partners of operating foundations are, for example, political decision-makers, those in business and other societal functions, public and academic institutions and other related bodies. Furthermore, internationally oriented operating foundations particularly foster active exchange with representatives of other cultures and other societal systems. The gathering of ideas which arises in this process is reduced through an initial filter, to those ideas which are characterized by a high level of compatibility with the image or mission and the overall strategic orientation of the foundation.

Figure 3: *Dimensions of Project Work Within the Bertelsmann Foundation*

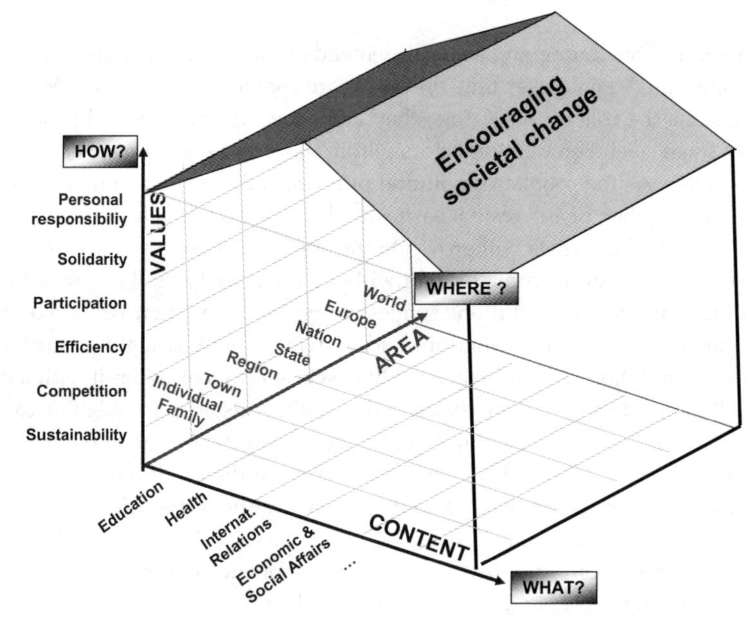

The example of the Bertelsmann Foundation makes it clear that project ideas must support the anchored values in the mission or broader image of the foundation. Likewise, in the sphere of private enterprises, the goal orientation of the innovation process must be derived from the general corporate or foundation objectives (Brockhoff 1999, 197). Apart from the content-related anchoring within the existing spectrum of activities and operational fields, attention must be paid to the transformation of society and its order. The overall innovation process of the Bertelsmann Foundation can be depicted by means of three dimensions (see Figure 3). The first dimension forms the anchored value system in the mission of the foundation. The subject areas and fields of competence which reflect the thematic organizational structure of the foundation, form the second content dimension. The third dimension characterizes the diffusion of innovation which reflects the particular implementation levels.

In order to generate a project portfolio that conforms to strategy, a consistent filtering of a large number of project ideas is necessary. The Bertelsmann Foundation uses a continuous strategy dialogue which is directly responsible to the board so as to ensure that this filter is a reliable component of internal foundation innovation processes (see Figure 4).

Figure 4: *Innovation in Non-Profit Organisations*

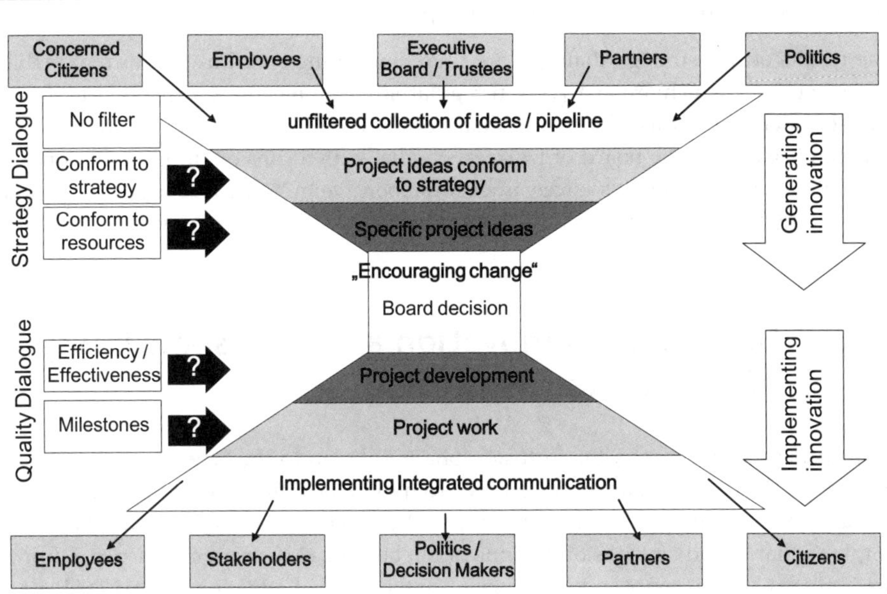

The following steps should be understood simultaneously as a platform for "inter-subject" exchanges about possible means of implementing the project ideas which have been generated and evaluated. By integrating the input of experts who have been brought in to the various projects of the operating foundation, the strategically appropriate project ideas are evaluated in terms of their ability to be implemented. In this context, particularly the question of required resources from the financial budget, employee capacity and potential cooperation with external partners, form the focus of attention.

Furthermore, at this point in time, securing the sustainability of the prevailing projects is an issue which must be clarified. The objective is to guarantee the long-term impact of intended investment in the context of the future society towards which the foundation strives. In this respect, preparing for decision-making, potential for an independent continuation of the initiated ideas after the successful introduction of a particular project, for example in the form of transfer agencies, should be analyzed and taken into account.

After ensuring resource conformity and sustainability, it is also necessary that central criteria for evaluating the project be determined and appropriate evaluators suggested. Additional significant milestones throughout the course of the project must be anchored, which serve as the basis for an accompanying external project evaluation as well as for regular internal quality dialogue. Through these measures, a continuous quality control and assurance of subsequent project work is guaranteed.

The results of this strategy dialogue are presented to the board in the form of viable project outlines which are analyzed in regular strategic meetings, discussed in detail and considered in terms of granting final permission to go ahead. Only after such a decision is made by the board of trustees, parallel with a consideration of the content orientation and available resources, is a comprehensive project concept processed and allocated to the various subject areas in terms of the approved new project.

3.2 Diffusion of Innovation as the Responsibility of Foundation Marketing

As a socio-societal process, the diffusion phase links up to the actual introduction of innovation. The question arises as to how, from the innovation itself, a specific project can develop and, initially in the form of a pilot project, can be implemented as an example so that the advantages of the innovation become clear from experience. During these phases, effectiveness and efficiency form the focus of attention and are evaluated within the Bertelsmann Foundation and the context of an ongoing quality dialogue (see Figure 5).

Subsequently, the operating foundation is faced with the task of ensuring a sufficiently broad diffusion and implementation of a project. For innovating enterprises, this diffusion process determines the success or failure of a product or service. All too frequently, resistance during this phase is underestimated (Brockhoff 2003, 587). "Although innovation is the key event in the technological change process, the economic impact of new products and processes depends on the speed with which they are diffused among potential users" (Rosegger 1986, 177). The same applies to innovating foundations which are inevitably evaluated as services to society in terms of whether or not the developed innovation is widely accepted. In this context, diffusion is defined as "the process by which an innovation is communicated through certain channels over time among the members of a social system" (Rogers 1995, 5).

Figure 5: *Objectives of Quality Dialogue - Raising the Quality, Competence and Impact*

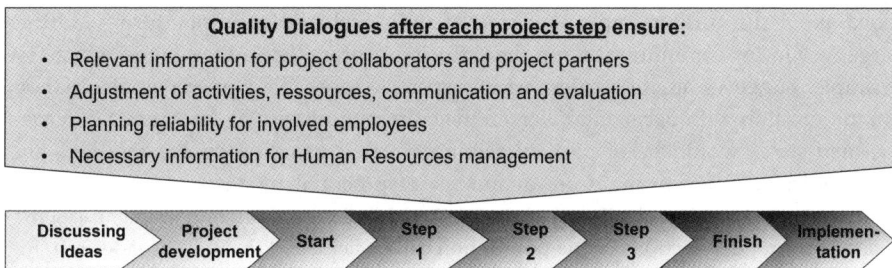

Quality Dialogues after each project step ensure:

- Relevant information for project collaborators and project partners
- Adjustment of activities, ressources, communication and evaluation
- Planning reliability for involved employees
- Necessary information for Human Resources management

From this definition, the four central elements of the diffusion process can be derived (Rogers 1995, 10). The first is the innovation itself, which, in the case of the foundation, generally takes the form of an idea or practice which is considered new by the adopting unit. This characteristic of concepts developed by foundations exerts a decisive impact on the speed of adoption. This includes:

- the relative advantage offered by the innovation, that is, the extent of improvement which can be achieved through the innovation
- the compatibility, that is the degree of conformity of this innovation with the values experiences and needs of the adaptors
- the complexity of the innovation
- the ability to test the innovation, which, in the case of operating foundations, is often evident in the implementation of a pilot project
- the extent to which the impact can be observed, that is, its consistent evaluation.

If foundations succeed in innovating and providing their adopters with what they regard as a substantial relative advantage, a high level of compatibility, a low level of complexity as well as sufficient testability and "observability", the products or services will be adopted rapidly.

The communication through various channels of the innovations in process, forms the second element of the diffusion process. In contrast to enterprises which strive primarily at finding potential users for their products, the communication task of foundations is more complex. Apart from employees whose acceptance of the new concepts must be ensured, the foundation communicates with different interest groups, each of which is concerned with the developed innovation. Furthermore, there will be communication with cooperation partners of the foundation. Also, an innovating foundation needs to succeed in creating sensitivity and acceptance of the innovation among broad sections of the population. Politicians or decision-makers who are located primarily in the various hierarchy levels of government institutions and can make decisions about the further implementation of the developed concepts, form a further target group for communication in the diffusion process. For a foundation which, for example, suggests an innovation with respect to prevailing university legislation, communication with decision-makers in the culture ministries of the various (internal) German states would be of particular importance. Depending on the receivers and communicated content, there are a number of potential modes of communication. While personal communication with important decision-makers is possible, the sensitization of broader sections of the population can be achieved through broader ranging campaigns.

Time forms the third element in the diffusion process. Initially, the question arises as to how long an individual needs, after noticing or becoming aware of an innovation, to make a decision as to accepting or rejecting it. Furthermore the time plan measures how long an individual needs in order to accept an innovation the level of innovation relative to other individuals Finally, the adaption rate refers to the time taken until the innovation is actually used by members of the social system.

The social system is the fourth element which must be investigated in the diffusion process. One of the main characteristics of diffusion is the assumption that social interactions exert a strong influence on this process (Meffert 1976, 97). The social structure exercises a quite significant influence on the diffusion process and simultaneously facilitates a certain predictability. For innovations which, for example, are implemented in the social system of a bureaucratic organization like a public authority, a very rapid adoption can be expected because of the high level of hierarchical structuring and regulation. This could be the case for a foundation which attempts to achieve a modernization of administration. Conversely, foundations which attempt to innovate in the preventative health sector, which is based on the voluntary participation of citizens, may find a slower adoption process, because it cannot be ordered or hierarchically organized.

There are also norms within the social system, that is, observable patterns of behavior which constitute relevant influences which give individuals an indication of the behavior that is expected of them. In this manner, an attempt is made to achieve a greater level of self determination of those insured within the health system in a system that is more strongly characterized by civic responsibility. This should hopefully achieve a more rapid adoption as well.

The promoters of particular innovations within the societal system are especially significant for the success or diffusion of innovations developed by foundations. Here, as in private enterprises, innovations often owe their success to the unconditional dedication of individuals (Hauschildt 1997, 53). In contrast to enterprises, foundations generally do not recruit such people from their own organization; they tend to belong to various units participating in the innovation process. In this context, subject or specialist promoters should be mentioned, who themselves are not involved in the diffusion process, but have both a high level of awareness of the problem and expertise in that particular area. These specialist promoters deal with innovations suggested by foundations, evaluate them and express their agreement or rejection to the various interest groups, the broader public or decision-makers and by so doing, influence the acceptance of the concepts. Furthermore, the "power promoters" from the group of decision-makers are of some significance. Power promoters have the necessary decision-making authority to facilitate the implementation process of innovations. By being convinced of the developed innovations which have proven their worth in pilot projects, beyond the actual giving of agreement by the specialist promoters, the power promoters commit themselves to a broader implementation of the innovation and also attempt to convince other decision-makers.

The success of diffusion depends very substantially on whether enterprises succeed, through their role as process promoters, in coordinating the co-operation of internal and external interest groups within the diffusion process and securing a commitment towards a common objective.

3.3 Significance of the Foundation Brand for the Innovation Process

The services provided by an operating foundation in the innovation process can be regarded as being provided for the good of society. As such, they have many confidence-related qualities. In order to overcome any possible resistance that may still occur, signals have considerable significance for services of this kind (Brockhoff 2003, 587). A clear brand profiling and the resulting confidence signals therefore support both co-operative work with external partners in the innovation process as well as the subsequent diffusion. The confidence aspect should be stressed, because the societal impact of the projects performed by operating foundations is influenced significantly by the level of conviction of the relevant decision-makers in politics and society (Meffert 2004).

In order to develop a consistent brand management concept, it is first necessary to specify clearly the self-image of the foundation. In this context, a mission statement has proven to be the ideal basis for developing a brand mission. As a future orientation, the mission statement defines the normative foundation and strategic position of the foundation. A good example is the mission statement of the Bertelsmann Foundation, which regards itself as a promoter of societal change and supports the objective of achieving a viable future society. The foundation aims at the early identification of societal challenges and problems as well as at the provision of model solutions, that is their development and implementation (Bertelsmann Stiftung 2002). In order to formulate the brand core, several workshops are conducted with employees in the communication area and with communication managers who are responsible for supervising the projects and their various subject areas. These workshops analyze and develop the brand core for the foundation. Along the following three central issues did we define our brand core in various zones.

- Where and how do we find subject areas?
- How do we develop these subjects?
- What do we expect as a result of our activities?

The very centre of the brand core is defined by the motto "encouraging societal change" (see Figure 6).

Figure 6: *Content of "Bertelsmann Foundation" Brand Core*

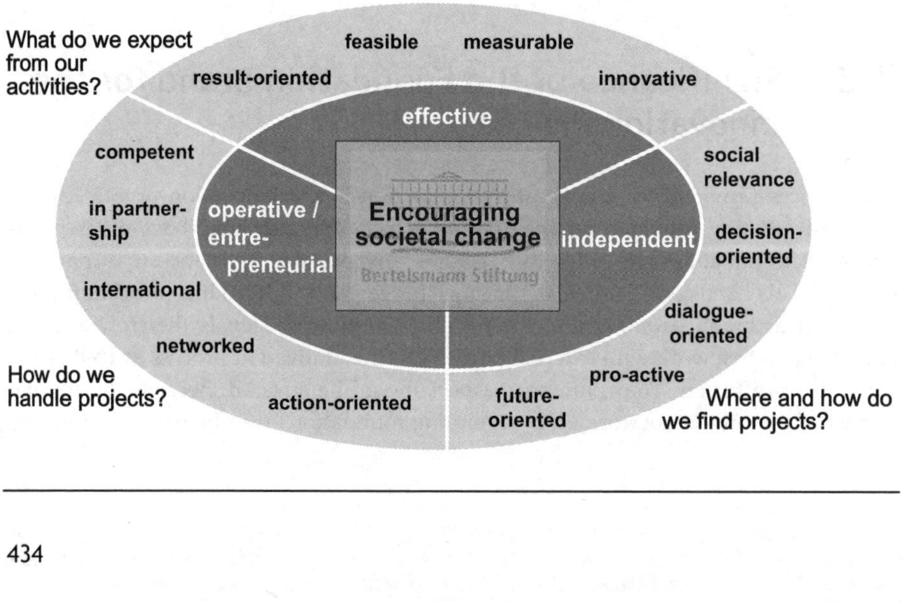

The first narrow definition zones of the brand core are characterized by the terms: pointing to the future, operational, entrepreneurial and demanding. In this context, topics and subjects that impact on society form the focus of attention. The Bertelsmann Foundation generates projects on these subjects which are carried out by its own employees. This relates to both operational and entrepreneurial modes of work. The results of these activities are intended to be demanding and intensive in every respect and to really exert an impact on society.

In the case of the Bertelsmann Foundation, because of the heterogeneous subject spectrum and large number of projects undertaken, this targeted brand profiling can only be conducted by means of a consistent and rigorous umbrella brand architecture. Only in this manner, does the Bertelsmann Foundation achieve clarity, coordinative power and discipline. The umbrella brand Bertelsmann Foundation is emphasized and implemented by means of specific projects and their associated activities. Through the umbrella brand, the "content" of the projects acquire a framework and thus a strategic mission or guidelines. The flow from the umbrella brand, which serves both as a door-opener and confidence-anchor (as well as the competence orientation of the umbrella-brand-related activities), must not be broken. For this reason, specific rules have been developed for applying the umbrella brand to different types of project (see Figure 7).

Figure 7: *Dynamics of Umbrella Brand Architecture of the Bertelsmann Foundation*

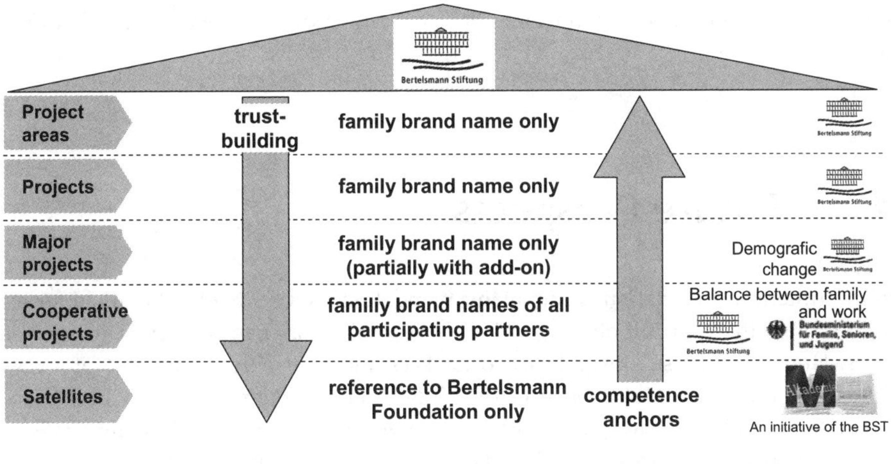

In this manner, the subject areas can be marked by the umbrella brand of the Bertelsmann Foundation. The Bertelsmann Foundation's activities are structured through four subject areas, three specialist areas and some large projects that cut across the different areas. Only rarely are exceptions from this convention allowed, for example some exceptionally large projects or those which are carried out with strong co-operating partners. In such cases, the project partners are cited in a similar manner to the foundation itself.

The actual implementation of the umbrella brand strategy is conducted in three steps. Firstly, a unified corporate design (CD) is established for all forms of foundation communication and these are set out as binding CD manuals. In this manner, not only logo, typeface and colors, but also the various internet presences of the projects, printed documents and so on are established including even the presentation documents. These CD manuals reflect the rules of the umbrella brand strategy. Based on the established corporate design, the umbrella brand concept and associated consequences for project communication are conveyed to all employees. As a third foundation, the communication for all new projects is formulated so as to provide an example or model within the context of the umbrella brand. In addition, major existing projects are analyzed to test their conformity with the umbrella brand and possibly adapted. A continuous communication control must be ensured, so that the consistent implementation of the umbrella brand strategy is maintained. With a similar priority, the content of all public relations and media work must be agreed upon centrally and the long-term consistency of communication ensured through an integrated approach to communication.

With a brand that is profiled in this manner, the external and internal interest groups serve as a confidence anchor, are able to create a substantial basis for foundations and support both the process of innovation development and its implementation or diffusion.

4 Future Prospects

In the American foundation scene, many foundations have already attempted structural change through self-developed innovations and this has succeeded in several cases. However, this self-insight has so far been manifest only in the case of a few German foundations. However, because of their large economic and political independence, foundations are particularly well suited to assuming an initiating role in societal innovation processes. Using the example of an operating foundation, this paper has demonstrated how such innovation processes and their subsequent diffusion can be formulated and what potential foundations can have, particularly when they are supported by a strong brand.

Recent investigations reveal that, as promoters of societal change, foundations are particularly effective when they develop a keen interest within the broader society through scientifically demanding ideas which focus on issues with strategic significance, coupled with an early recognition of a window of opportunity for change. A strong, integrated marketing approach can thus be combined effectively with credible and customized communication with various target groups (Thunert 2003).

5 References

Anheier, H.K. (2001): Foundations in Europe: a Comparative Perspective, in: Schlüter, A., V. Then., and P. Walkenhorst (Eds.): *Foundations in Europe. Society, Management and Law*, London, 35-82.

Anheier, H.K. (2003): Das Stiftungswesen in Deutschland. Eine Bestandsaufnahme in Zahlen, in: Bertelsmann Stiftung (Ed.): *Handbuch Stiftungen. Ziele – Projekte – Management – Rechtliche Gestaltung*, 2nd ed., Wiesbaden, 43-85.

Bertelsmann Stiftung (Ed.) (1999): *The Future of Foundations in an Open Society. Die Zukunft der Stiftungen in einer offenen Gesellschaft*, Gütersloh.

Bertelsmann Stiftung (Ed.) (2002): *Leitbild der Bertelsmann Stiftung*, Gütersloh.

Bodenstein, G. (1987): *Diffusion und Marketing*, Diskussionsbeitrag Nr. 98, Fachbereich Wirtschaftswissenschaften Universität Duisburg,.

Brockhoff, K. (1999): *Forschung und Entwicklung. Planung und Kontrolle*, 5th ed., Munich, Vienna, Oldenburg.

Brockhoff, K. (2002): Erhaltung eines Stiftungsvermögens, in: *Zeitschrift für betriebswirtschaftliche Forschung*, 54 (5), 277 – 284.

Brockhoff, K. (2003): Durchsetzung von Innovationen, in: Hungenberg, H. and J. Meffert (Eds.): *Handbuch Strategisches Management*, Wiesbaden, 579 – 593.

Bundesverband Deutscher Stiftungen e. V. (Ed.) (2001): *Verzeichnis Deutscher Stiftungen. Zahlen, Daten, Fakten*, Berlin.

Bundesverband Deutscher Stiftungen e. V. (Ed.) (2004): *Stiftungen in Zahlen 2003/2004.*

Deutsches Institut für Altersvorsorge (Ed.) (2000): *Erben in Deutschland. Volumen, Psychologie und gesamtwirtschaftliche Auswirkungen*, Cologne.

Hauschildt, J. (1997): *Innovationsmanagement*, 2nd ed., Munich.

Körber-Stiftung (Ed.) (2003): *Profile*, in internet from 05.04.2003 at http://www.stiftung.-koerber.de/allgemeines/profil/index.html.

Meffert, H. (1976): Die Durchsetzung von Innovationen in der Unternehmung und im Markt, *Zeitschrift für Betriebswirtschaft*, 46 (2), 77-100.

Meffert, H. (2004): Entwicklung einer Markenarchitektur für die Bertelsmann Stiftung, in: Riesenbeck, H. and J. Perrey (Eds.): *Mega-Macht Marke*, Munich, 174-179.

Rogers, E. M. (1995): *Diffusion of Innovations*, 4th ed., New York.

Rosegger, G. (1986): *The Economics of Production and Innovation – An Industrial Perspective*, 2nd ed., Oxford et al.

Schmidt, W. (2003): Stiftungen als Innovationsagenturen und Wohltäter der Gesellschaft, in: Bertelsmann Stiftung (Ed.): *Handbuch Stiftungen. Ziele – Projekte – Management – Rechtliche Gestaltung*, 2nd ed., Wiesbaden, 87-125.

Smith, J.A. and K. Borgmann (2001): Foundations in Europe: the Historical Context, in: Schlüter, A., V. Then., and P. Walkenhorst (Eds.): *Foundations in Europe. Society, Management and Law*, London, 2-34.

Thunert, M. (2003): Think Tanks in Deutschland – Berater der Politik?, in: *Aus Politik und Zeitgeschichte*, B51, 30-38.

Toepler, S. (1996): *Das gemeinnützige Stiftungswesen in der modernen demokratischen Gesellschaft. Ansätze einer ökonomischen Betrachtungsweise*, Munich.

Part 6:

Innovation and National Economic Performance

Heiner Müller-Merbach

Relative Export and Import Strength

Indicators of the State of Development of National Economies

Prof. Dr. *Heiner Müller-Merbach*, Department of Business Informations Systems and Operations Research, University of Kaiserslautern.

1 Reciprocity of Absolute and Per Capita Values

Management of innovation, management of technology, management of research and development (R&D) – i.e. Brockhoff's central fields of interest in the *Institut für betriebswirtschaftliche Innovationsforschung*, Kiel – are highly important arts, particularly in such countries the goods of which play an important rôle on the world markets. Is Germany one of these countries? This question will be answered here by means of three new indicators of foreign trade – with „Yes". This macro-economic consideration forms to some extent a frame around the micro-economic studies in R&D management by Brockhoff (1999) and his colleagues such as Hauschildt (1997) and Albers, Brockhoff and Hauschildt (2001).

Table 1: *Values of foreign trade 2001 of 37 countries with population, exports, per capita exports and RES versus imports, per capita imports and RIS; REID*
RES = exports • per capita exports; RIS = imports • per capita imports;
REID = RES - RIS

country	*population (million)*	*exports (billion $)*	*per capita exports (1,000 $)*	*RES*	*imports (billion $)*	*per capita imports (1,000 $)*	*RIS*	*REID*
Argentina	38.4	26.6	0.7	1.8E+13	20.3	0.5	1.1E+13	7.7E+12
Australia	19.7	63.4	3.2	2.0E+14	60.8	3.1	1.9E+14	1.6E+13
Austria	8.1	70.7	8.7	6.2E+14	74.6	9.2	6.9E+14	-7.0E+13
Belgium	10.3	188.1	18.2	3.4E+15	178.5	17.3	3.1E+15	3.4E+14
Brazil	178.5	58.2	0.3	1.9E+13	55.6	0.3	1.7E+13	1.7E+12
Canada	31.5	261.3	8.3	2.2E+15	221.5	7.0	1.6E+15	6.1E+14
Chile	15.8	18.6	1.2	2.2E+13	17.8	1.1	2.0E+13	1.7E+12
China	1304.2	266.1	0.2	5.4E+13	200.9	0.2	3.1E+13	2.3E+13
Denmark	5.4	50.8	9.5	4.8E+14	44.4	8.3	3.7E+14	1.1E+14
Finland	5.2	43.3	8.3	3.6E+14	32.7	6.3	2.0E+14	1.5E+14
France	60.1	323.0	5.4	1.7E+15	328.6	5.5	1.8E+15	-6.1E+13
Germany	82.5	571.5	6.9	4.0E+15	486.1	5.9	2.9E+15	1.1E+15
Greece	11.0	9.7	0.9	8.6E+12	28.1	2.6	7.2E+13	-6.3E+13
Hong Kong	7.0	189.8	26.9	5.1E+15	201.5	28.6	5.8E+15	-6.5E+14
India	1065.5	44.4	0.0	1.9E+12	51.9	0.0	2.5E+12	-6.7E+11
Indonesia	219.9	64.9	0.3	1.9E+13	38.8	0.2	6.8E+12	1.2E+13
Ireland	4.0	82.9	21.0	1.7E+15	50.7	12.8	6.5E+14	1.1E+15

Israel	6.4	29.0	4.5	1.3E+14	33.3	5.2	1.7E+14	-4.2E+13
Italy	57.4	240.8	4.2	1.0E+15	232.7	4.1	9.4E+14	6.6E+13
Japan	127.7	403.4	3.2	1.3E+15	349.1	2.7	9.5E+14	3.2E+14
Korea, Rep.	47.7	149.8	3.1	4.7E+14	141.1	3.0	4.2E+14	5.3E+13
Luxembourg	0.5	10.3	22.8	2.4E+14	12.2	26.9	3.3E+14	-9.1E+13
Malaysia	24.4	88.2	3.6	3.2E+14	73.9	3.0	2.2E+14	9.5E+13
Mexico	103.5	158.4	1.5	2.4E+14	168.4	1.6	2.7E+14	-3.1E+13
Netherlands	16.1	230.9	14.3	3.3E+15	208.7	12.9	2.7E+15	6.0E+14
Norway	4.5	57.6	12.7	7.3E+14	32.0	7.1	2.3E+14	5.1E+14
Pakistan	153.6	9.2	0.1	5.5E+11	10.2	0.1	6.8E+11	-1.3E+11
Portugal	10.1	23.9	2.4	5.7E+13	37.9	3.8	1.4E+14	-8.6E+13
Russian Fed.	143.2	82.5	0.6	4.8E+13	36.9	0.3	9.5E+12	3.8E+13
Sweden	8.9	74.1	8.3	6.2E+14	60.3	6.8	4.1E+14	2.1E+14
Switzerland	7.2	82.0	11.4	9.4E+14	84.1	11.7	9.9E+14	-4.7E+13
Singapore	4.3	121.7	28.6	3.5E+15	116.0	27.3	3.2E+15	3.2E+14
South Africa	45.0	21.6	0.5	1.0E+13	24.6	0.5	1.3E+13	-3.1E+12
Spain	41.1	109.0	2.7	2.9E+14	142.6	3.5	5.0E+14	-2.1E+14
Taiwan	22.3	122.9	5.5	6.8E+14	107.2	4.8	5.2E+14	1.6E+14
United Kingd.	59.3	268.5	4.5	1.2E+15	322.8	5.4	1.8E+15	-5.4E+14
United States	294.0	730.9	2.5	1.8E+15	1180.1	4.0	4.7E+15	-2.9E+15

Source: Statistisches Bundesamt (2003), Tab. 1.1 (pp. 176 et sqq.), 6.4, and 6.5 (pp. 250 et sq.).

Compared are the two countries A and B with an equal state of development and a similar geographical position, A accommodating four times the population of B. According to empirical evidence, country A will export (and import) only double the value of country B, i.e. the square root of the population ratio. But per capita, country B will export double the value of country A, the reciprocal square root, such as observed by Müller-Merbach (2002, 488-490, and Figure 9, 492). Thus, the "mathematical product" of exports and per capita exports will be identical for A and B. The same holds for the imports. France and Ireland are taken as an example (data as of 2001). France has a population of 60.1 million, exports of 323.0 billion US-$ and per capita exports of 5,374 US-$ (Table 1); the product is $1.7 * 10^{15}$. Ireland has a population of 4.0 million, exports of 82.9 billion US-$ and per capita exports of 20,725 US-$ (Table 1); the product is again $1.7 * 10^{15}$. The population of France is 15 times the population of Ireland; the square root is 3.876. The exports of France are pretty precisely 3.876 times the exports of Ireland. The per capita exports of Ireland are pretty precisely 3.876 times the per capita exports of France. The equivalent holds for any pair of countries with similar values of RES, such as the United States and Canada, or China and Portugal, or

Germany and Singapore, or Indonesia and Brazil, or Korea and Denmark, or Taiwan and Norway etc.

The reciprocity of absolute values and per capita values seems to be plausible:

- Large countries tend to export and import more goods than smaller countries, just because of their bigger size. On the other hand, large countries tend to have a higher degree of autarky than smaller countries, i.e. cover more climate zones, have a higher variety of natural resources and produce a larger variety of industrial products. Therefore, they are not so much dependant on foreign goods.
- In contrary, smaller countries are limited in their exports and imports by their smaller size. On the other hand, they have a lower degree of autarky such that they depend – per capita – much more on imported goods and tend to be more specialised in their goods to be exported.

2 Two Indicators to Balance the Reciprocity of Absolute and Per Capita Values of Foreign Trade

Therefore, the comparison of national economies by their absolute values of exports and imports does not make much sense, since it would lead to a comparison of population sizes. The comparison of per capita values makes as little sense, since the reciprocity of the population sizes would be compared. However, it seems to make sense to compare their (mathematical) products which leads to two indicators:

- $\mathbf{RES_j = E_j * (E_j / P_j)}$ as "Relative Export Strength" of country j and
- $\mathbf{RIS_j = I_j * (I_j / P_j)}$ as "Relative Import Strength" of country j; with
- j as index of the national economy (synonymously referred to as: country),
- P_j as the population of national economy j,
- E_j as the exports of national economy j (in $),
- I_j as the imports of national economy j (in $),
- E_j / P_j as the per capita exports of national economy j (in $), and
- I_j / P_j as the per capita imports of national economy j (in $).

The two indicators RES and RIS are to a high degree independent of the population. They seem to reflect well the strength of a national economy at the world markets. It is surprising that these indicators are not as yet used within the concert of macro-economic indicators related to foreign trade on the one hand and to economic strength of national economies on the other hand.

In addition to the indicators RES and RIS, a third indicator is suggested here, the difference of both:

- **REIDj = RESj - RISj** as "Relative Export Import Difference".

This indicator corresponds with the surplus or the deficit of the foreign trade of a country. This indicator does not immediately represent the state of development of a country. Instead, it reflects the country's discipline.

Again, France and Ireland shall be compared with one another. The exports indicator is almost identical: $RES_F = RES_{IRL} = 1.7 * 10^{15}$. The imports of France with $RIS_F = 1.8 * 10^{15}$ are much above the imports of Ireland with $RIS_{IRL} = 6.5 * 10^{14}$. In France, the imports are slightly higher than the exports which leads to $REID_F = -6.1 * 10^{13}$, while Ireland has a surplus with $REID_{IRL} = 1.1 * 10^{15}$.

3 Application of the Indicators to 37 National Economies

In order to justify the indicators RES and RIS as well as REID, the data of 37 national economies shall now be considered (all data for 2001, source: Statistisches Jahrbuch 2003 für das Ausland).

The data are collected in Table 1. More important are the diagrams, Figure 1 to 3. The diagrams (with logarithmic scales) show characteristic stripes of different states of development, such as (with respect to the exports indicator only):

- **Industrial countries** with $RES_j \geq 4*10^{14}$ (or $RIS_j \geq 4*10^{14}$, respectively), a kind of "milky way" (Müller-Merbach 1992), with: Hong Kong, Germany, Singapore, Belgium, the Netherlands, Canada, United States, France, Ireland, Japan, United Kingdom, Italy, Switzerland, Norway, Taiwan, Austria, Sweden, Denmark, Korea (including 10 out of 15 countries of the European Union before 1st May, 2004).

- **Semi-industrial countries** with $RES_j \geq 4*10^{13}$ (or $RIS_j \geq 4*10^{13}$, respectively) with: Finland, Malaysia, Spain, Mexico, Luxembourg, Australia, Israel, Portugal, China, Russian Federation (including 4 out of 15 countries of the European Union before 1st May, 2004).

- **Developing countries** with $RES_j \geq 4*10^{12}$ (or $RIS_j \geq 4*10^{12}$, respectively) with: Chile, Indonesia, Brazil, Argentina, South Africa, Greece (including 1 out of 15 countries of the European Union before 1st May, 2004).
- **Poor countries** with $RES_j < 4*10^{12}$ (or $RIS_j < 4*10^{12}$, respectively) with: India, Pakistan and many others.

The borderlines between these stripes are somewhat arbitrary; they could certainly be moved up and down, and the stripes themselves can be extended as well as narrowed. However, the borderlines with $4*10^x$ seem to be reasonable for that particular period of time, i.e. 2001 + /-.

Figure 1: *Relative export strength of 37 national economies (countries): Exports versus per capita exports, combined in the indicator RES*

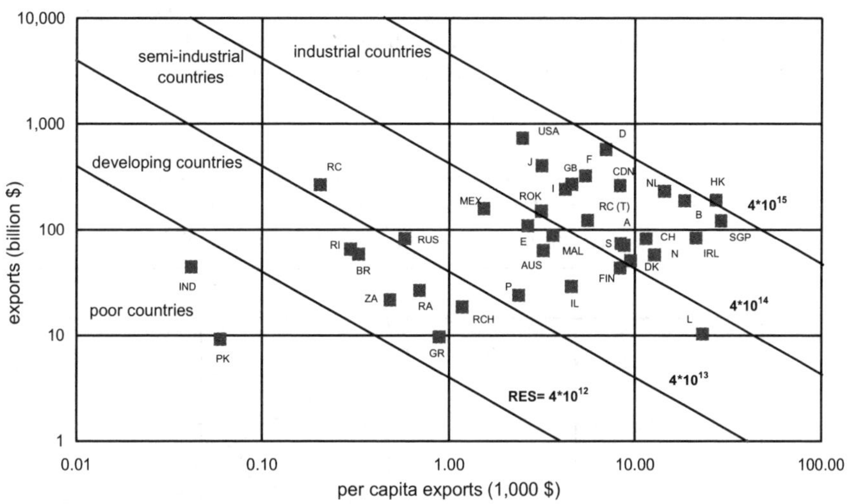

Source: Data from Table 1. The NW-SE diagonals represent the scale for the indicator RES and additional SW-NE diagonals would represent the scale for the population of the countries, China, India, United States, Indonesia, and Brazil in the leading positions.

Of central importance for the effect of RES and RIS are the diagrams in their particular structure. They are "two-dimensional" in the sense that both coordinates carry content information, opposite to the many diagrams applied to economics which use (or: "abuse") one dimension (mostly the abscissa) for time differentiation (e.g. 1985, 1990, 1995, 2000, ...) or object differentiation (e.g. B, DK, D, FIN, F, GR, ...) such that only one coordinate (mostly the ordinate) remains for content information. These "two-dimensional" diagrams are called "symplex diagrams" by the author (such as: Müller-Merbach 1988, 1991, 1994, 2002). Even if the denominations of the indicators RES, RIS, and REID are newly suggested here, the same kind of diagrams for exports versus per capita exports (as well as imports versus per capita imports) have been presented by the author several times (such as: Müller-Merbach 1988, 1989, 1992, 2002).

Such two-dimensional symplex diagrams tend to tell richer stories than the standard one-dimensional diagrams. For example in Figure 1,

- the ordinate represents the (absolute) export values with the sequence: United States (1), Germany (2), Japan (3), France (4), United Kingdom (5), China (6), Canada (7), Italy (8), the Netherlands (9) etc.,
- the abscissa represents the per capita exports and presents the sequence: Singapore (1), Hong Kong (2), Luxembourg (3), Ireland (4), Belgium (5), the Netherlands (6), Norway (7), Switzerland (8), Denmark (9), ..., Germany (13), ..., Japan (21), ..., and United States (24) etc.,
- in addition, the diagonals represent the indicator RES with Hong Kong (1), Germany (2), Singapore (3), Belgium (4), the Netherlands (5), Canada (6), United States (7) etc.

Figure 2: *Relative import strength of 37 national economies (countries): Imports versus per capita imports, combined in the indicator RIS*

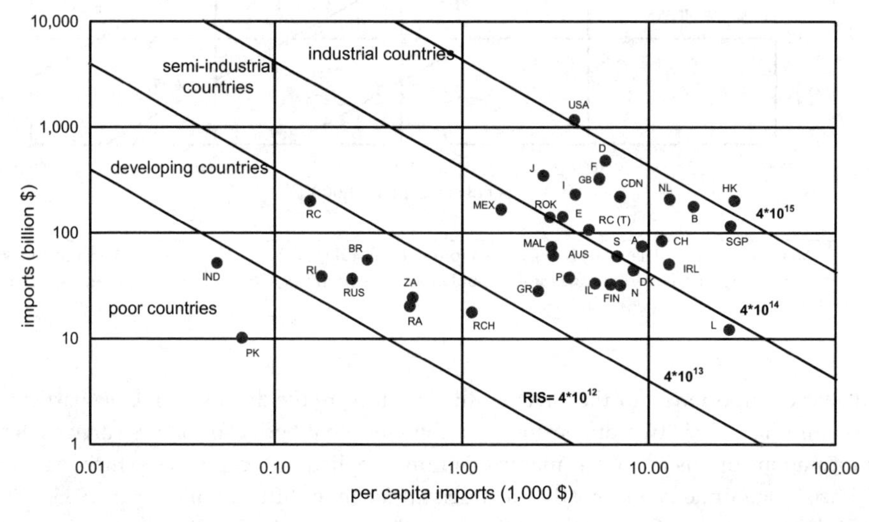

Source: Data from Table 1.

The equivalent applies to the imports (Figure 2): The greatest importers are: United States (1), Germany (2), Japan (3), France (4), United Kingdom (5) - large countries. The greatest per capita importers are Hong Kong (1), Singapore (2), Luxembourg (3), Belgium (4), the Netherlands (5), and Ireland (6) - small countries. Only the indicator RIS leads to a sequence which is size-independent: Hong Kong (1), United States (2), Singapore (3), Belgium (4), Germany (5), the Netherlands (6), France (7), United Kingdom (8) etc.

Figure 3: *Relative export and import strength of 31 national economies (countries): Exports and imports versus per capita exports and per capita imports, combined in the indicators RES and RIS, respectively.*

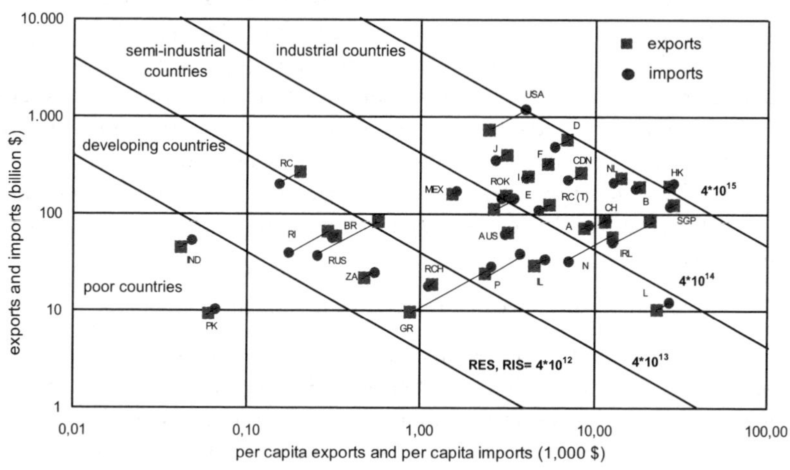

Source: Data from Table 1 (i.e. without DK, FIN, GB, MAL, RA, and S because of too high densities of positions).

The combination of export and import values (Figure 3) gives an impression of the foreign trade surpluses or deficits of the national economies. The distances between the exports and imports positions correspond with the indicator REID even if REID and the distance are not equivalent. The countries with the highest values of REID are: Germany (1), Ireland (2), Canada (3), the Netherlands (4), Norway (5), Belgium (6), Japan (7) etc. The national economies with the highest deficits are: United Stated (37), Hong Kong (36), United Kingdom (35), Spain (34), Portugal (33), Austria (32), Greece (31), France (30) etc. (Table 1, last column).

While REID is more or less an indicator of the country's foreign trade discipline, RES and RIS are mainly indicators of the state of development of the country. They correspond quite well with other strength indicators, such as the Gross Domestic Product per capita, the motor vehicles density per capita, the telephone density per capita, etc.

The positions of the 37 countries in the diagrams (Figure 1 to 3) within the stripes correspond with the image that most economists might have regarding these countries. There is no doubt that most member countries of the European Union, the United States, Japan, Switzerland and – to some extent – the "four little tigers" of Asia belong to the "milky way" of the industrial countries. However, the indicator RES (or RIS, respectively) serves the purpose of fine tuning with Germany, Belgium, the Netherlands, France, Ireland, United Kingdom, and Italy in the leading positions among the EU member countries with RES $\geq 10^{15}$. It may also correspond with one's expectation that Spain, Portugal, and Greece do not belong to the "milky way".

But what about Finland, Australia, Israel. Luxembourg, Hong Kong, the Americas etc. Do their positions (particularly in Figure 1) represent their techno-economics state of development? Not completely! RES and RIS suffer from the same deficiency as any other isolated indicator in that they only represent one single aspect, in this case: foreign trade. They do not reflect (i) the geographical location of a country: Australia and New Zealand are huge islands, far away from other industrial countries; Finland lies in the outskirts of the EU; Argentina, Brazil, Chile lack of industrial neighbour countries – certainly a competitive disadvantage; Germany, France, the Netherlands, and Belgium, on the other hand, are positioned in the centre of Europe – certainly a competitive advantage.

(ii) political isolation: Israel is isolated from its geographical neighbours.

(iii) the economic structure: Hong Kong and Singapore are traders and only to a small extent producers, therefore over-evaluated by RES; Austria and Switzerland (partly: Italy, Spain, Portugal, Greece) are vacation and recreation countries, therefore under-evaluated; Luxembourg accommodates several of the EU authorities; Switzerland and Luxembourg have their strengths in financial services.

The third deficiency (iii) can to some extent be overcome by replacing the data of the Balance of Trade by the data of the comprehensive Balance of Current Account. This would lead to an alternative set of indicators, equivalent to RES, RIS, and REID.

The first deficiency may be neutralised by a geographical factor for any country j. Such a factor could be the economic weight (such as the Gross Domestic Product) of any other country, divided by the geographical distance (such as from the capital city of country j to the capital city of the other country). However, such factors would tend to make the formulae of RES and RIS more complicated and less self-explained.

Thus, while using RES and RIS, one should carry in mind their limitations of interpretation.

The main advantage of the indicators RES and RIS over absolute values of exports (imports) or per capita values lay in their independence of a country's size. This is due to the reciprocity of absolute and per capita values of foreign trade. Thus, RES and RIS (as well as REID) are more or less independent of the population of a country.

Anyhow, it is not recommended here to replace other indicators of competitive advantage or state of development of nations by RES, RIS, and REID. Instead, it is recommended to include RES, RIS, and REID into the bouquet of indicators. Such bouquets are being used by several international institutions, such as the "International Institute for Management Development" (IMD), the "World Economic Forum" and many others (such as compared in a survey by Vogel 1996). Combinations of technological and economic indicators were suggested by Schmietow; (1988), Legler (1992), and Vogel (2000). Portfolio diagrams – frequently used for enterprises – may be included into the bouquet, such as suggested by the author (Müller-Merbach 1994).

4 Conclusion: The Top Position of Germany

Returning to the introductory question: Is Germany one of those countries the goods of which play an important role on the world markets? The answer is a clear: Yes. According to the exports indicator RES, Germany holds position 2 (after Hong Kong, Figure 1). According to the imports indicator RIS, Germany holds position 5 (after Hong Kong, United States, Singapore, Belgium, Figure 2). With respect to the surplus indicator REID, Germany keeps position 1 (Figure 3 and Table 1). Germany will maintain these positions only if it keeps the highest possible professionality of R&D management, technology management, and innovation management, the central topics of the *Institut für betriebswirtschaftliche Innovationsforschung*, Kiel, which was significantly coined by Brockhoff.

5 References

Albers, S., K. Brockhoff, and J. Hauschildt (Eds.) (2001): *Technologie- und Innovationsmanagement – Leistungsbilanz des Kieler Graduiertenkollegs*, Wiesbaden.

Brockhoff, K. (1999): *Forschung und Entwicklung – Planung und Kontrolle*, 5th ed., Munich, Vienna.

Hauschildt, J. (1997): *Innovationsmanagement*, 2nd ed., Munich.

Legler, H. (1992): Europa im Technologiewettbewerb: Stärken und Schwächen, *technologie & management*, 41 (4), 16-24.

Müller-Merbach, H. (1988): Wirtschaftsentwicklung in Symplex-Bildern, *technologie & management*, 37 (2), 52-58.

Müller-Merbach, H. (1989): EG-Länder im statistisch-graphischen Vergleich, *technologie & management*, 38 (1), 1 and 40-49.

Müller-Merbach, H. (1991): Entwurf zweidimensionaler Wirtschaftsgrafiken, *technologie & management*, 40 (2), 24-33.

Müller-Merbach, H. (1992): Die „Milchstraße" der Industrieländer, *technologie & management*, 41 (3), 1 and 4.

Müller-Merbach, H. (1994): Die Wettbewerbsfähigkeit der Bundesrepublik Deutschland - Eine Relativierung innerhalb der Triade, in: Schiemenz, B. and H.-J. Wurl (Eds.): *Internationales Management*, Wiesbaden, 61-93.

Müller-Merbach, H. (2002): Europe in symplex diagrams - From statistical tables to insight, *European Journal of Operational Research*, 140 (3), 482-498.

Schmietow, E. (1988): *Die technologische Wettbewerbsfähigkeit der Bundesrepublik*, Bad Homburg.

Statistisches Bundesamt (Ed.) (2003): *Statistisches Jahrbuch 2003 für das Ausland*, Wiesbaden.

Vogel, C. (1996): Studien zur Wettbewerbsfähigkeit Deutschlands, *technologie & management*, 45 (4), 189-193.

Vogel, C. (2000): *Deutschland im internationalen Technologiewettlauf - Bedeutung der Forschungs- und Technologiepolitik für die technologische Wettbewerbsfähigkeit*, Berlin.

Alok Chakrabarti and Mark P. Rice

Changing Roles of Universities in Developing Entrepreneurial Regions

The Case of Finland and the US[1]

Prof. Dr. *Alok Chakrabarti,* School of Management & Newark College of Engineering, New Jersey Institute of Technology (U.S.A.), and Prof. Dr. *Mark P. Rice,* Dean of the F. W. Olin Graduate School of Business and Jeffry A. Timmons Professor of Entrepreneurial Studies at Babson College (U.S.A.).

---

1 This paper was presented at the Babson Entrepreneurship Conference in Babson College. Some of the interviews reported in this paper were conducted with Professor Richard Lester and his students in the context of a larger project on Local Innovation Systems at the Industrial Performance Center. The authors thank Professor Lester for his support. The authors are responsible for the opinions presented in this paper.

1 Introduction

The competitive environment for most firms has been transformed by global competition, rapid changes in technology, diversity of product standards, and shorter product life cycles (Ali 1994; Bettis and Hitt 1995; Quinn 2000). Successful companies have reduced the cost of innovation and risks by outsourcing. A few scholars (Parkhe 1993; Pisano 1990; Shan, Walker, and Kogut 1994) have examined the inter-organizational collaboration in development of new technology. The problems of product development in a dynamic industry can be explained in terms of newness of the technology, customers and trajectory of the technology development. Classical models of product development assume the process to be a linear one. But as Leonard-Barton (1995) has shown the process of technology development differs with these parameters. The role of the company changes with the novelty of the technology and novelty of the market.

There are many compelling reasons for outsourcing innovation by a firm (Quinn 2000). Most of the major companies in Europe and Japan have set up R&D centers in places like the Silicon Valley, Boston in the US and in Cambridge UK. These centers are conduits for developing relationships with the premier universities in these regions. Better access to scientists and technologists in various parts of the world has provided great opportunities for outsourcing of technology development. The development of information and communication technology has helped effective interaction among the various individuals and coordination among geographically distributed groups. Finally, governments and the financial institutions are providing new incentives for inter-organizational collaboration.

2 Universities as Engines of Regional Development

With the growing importance of knowledge-based industry, policy makers in the private and public sectors have realized the importance of universities in regional economic development (Chakrabarti and Lester 2002). The role of Massachusetts Institute of Technology in growth of the industries in greater Boston area and Stanford University in the Silicon Valley area is quite well known.

After the economic collapse of its principal trading partner, Soviet Russia, Finland experienced a deep recession with high unemployment during the early nineties. Universities at that time became the important engines of economic development. Helsinki University of Technology became a major center for growth in wireless communication and information technology. The University of Oulu helped build up the Oulu region's capabilities in electronics and information technology. Tampere focused on electro-mechanical and automation industries. The University of Turku contributed to the development of pharmaceuticals and chemistry based innovations. The Finnish Innovation Foundation, a public organization has established Center for Technical Expertise with all major universities in Finland as shown in Figure 1.

Figure 1: *Cooperation between Finnish Invention Foundation & Universities*

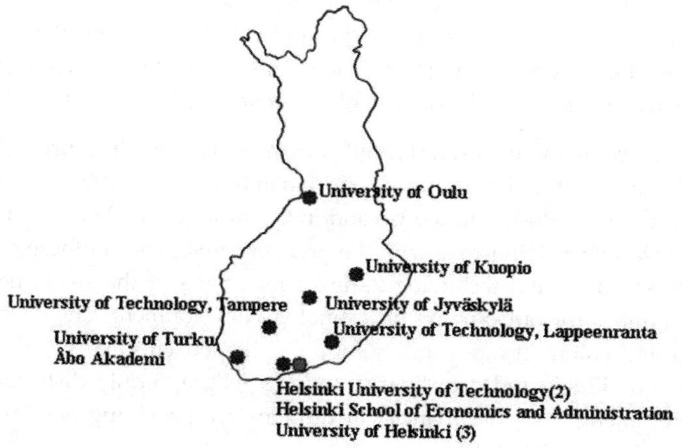

Each region in our study has had its share of economic crisis. Newark and its surrounding area have a long history of economic stagnation. New Jersey Institute of Technology (NJIT) has embraced economic development as one of its four central missions. Worcester Polytechnic (WPI) is located in central Massachusetts, a region that has experienced an erosion of its economic base with the demise of many mechanical and electrical manufacturing industries. WPI has been a stimulus to regional growth through its contribution to the development of new industrial activity in information technology and more recently in biotechnology. In the Bethlehem area, long disadvantaged by the decline of the steel industry, Lehigh University has become a facilitator of economic development in the region. Rensselaer Polytechnic Institute (RPI) is located in the capital district region of the state of New York, which has struggled through a series of economic cycles and where the dominant company, General Electric, has continued to downsize its local operations including the corporate research center. Both RPI and the nearby State University have set up incubators for new companies and other related activities.

3 University-Industry Relationship

University-industry relationship is not a new phenomenon. Germany was the pioneering country where university industry relationship helped create the pharmaceutical industry in the early 19th century. The United States has taken an active role in developing and fostering university industry collaboration. There are many mutual benefits to a close relationship between a university and an industrial firm. Firms gain access to not only leading edge technologies, but also highly trained students, professors and university facilities. A firm can gain prestige and acceptance in its stakeholder community though its association with a prestigious university.

Universities can augment their funding sources by working with the industry as public level of funding for higher education has become scarce. Working with the industry provides other pedagogical and academic value to the students and faculty, particularly in many emerging fields where academic research and publication usually lags industry.

The National Science Foundation in the US identifies four inter-related components in the university-industry relationships: research support, cooperative research, knowledge transfer and technology transfer. Research support involves contributions of both money and equipment to the universities by industry. Recently, a consortium of 23 companies has contributed 47 million Finnish Marks ($8M) to several Finnish technical universities to upgrade their programs in information and communication technologies.[2]

In the United States, the National Science Foundation has actively promoted formation of cooperative research through establishment of Engineering Research Centers (ERC) and Industry University Cooperative Research Centers (IUCRC). Contract research by a research center or a professor is often a vehicle for collaboration between university and a firm. In Finland, TEKES, the Finnish Technology Development Agency promotes the industrial collaboration by requiring all of its projects be collaborative. The policy implemented by Tekes not only promotes interaction between a firm and a university, but also decentralizes the control and monitoring of the projects.

Knowledge transfer involves many activities that include both formal and informal means of communication, interactions and personnel exchanges at student and faculty levels. Involvement of the firms in the academic programs of the universities is a major mechanism for knowledge transfer. Often students work on corporate problems for their theses and dissertations in many technical universities in Finland. Cooperative education programs, internships and job placements for students and recent graduates provide means for knowledge transfer.

---

2 Personal interview at Nokia Oy

Technology transfer is generally based on the collaborative research with the industry. The concept of "land grant" college was developed by an act of the US Congress in 1862 for "agriculture and mechanic arts, scientific and classical studies, and military tactics for the liberal and practical education of the industrial classes." Major public universities in the US have been established as land grant institutions with a clear mandate for knowledge and technology transfer. From that tradition, different models of interaction with the industry have evolved. Universities have taken active role in establishing various types of organizations, such as business incubator, science park, technology park etc. to foster entrepreneurship and business development.

Rice (2002) has shown that assisting entrepreneurs in business incubators is a complex process and depends on the strategic objectives of the entrepreneurs, their capabilities as well as managers of these incubators. Location in a business incubator offers great opportunity of networking as well as tapping the resources available at the sponsoring organization, often the university. The traditional view of the business incubator is overly focused on capital and infrastructure related resources. Our study in Finland shows that knowledge exchange is very important in developing unique value in university-linked business incubators.

4 Changing Role of the Universities and Nature of Scientific Research

Universities are traditionally viewed as bastions of learning and knowledge creation. The culture of academic freedom cherished by the faculty creates problems when a firm or an agency dictates the terms and conditions of support for research including the ownership of intellectual property rights and restrictions on publication. During the Second World War, universities and professors were active participants in developing and implementing knowledge that went into the war effort. Since then, the military has been a big supporter of research and graduate education in many universities in the US.

Discussions about the types of research suitable for universities often are focused on the continuum of basic to applied research and the complexity of the issues involved. Stokes (1997) developed a quadrant model of scientific research based on two dimensions of that inspire the research. These two orthogonal dimensions are: quest for fundamental understanding and considerations for use. Research in atomic structures by scientist like Nobel laureate Niels Bohr was driven by quest for fundamental understanding with little consideration for its commercial use. Work of Thomas Edison was driven by considerations for use and little by quest for fundamental understanding, if any. Louis Pasteur was concerned with both fundamental understanding as well as use. If the academic research needs to be more utilized, then one needs to be in Pasteur quadrant in Stokes' scheme.

To understand how the Finnish universities and institutions differ from the US universities and institutional structure, we can look at the nature and applicability of knowledge developed in Finnish universities and the US universities. One can categorize knowledge in two ways: theoretical and problem solving. In terms of applicability of knowledge, it can be either generic or context-specific. Finish universities tend to be high on problem-solving type of research and most often in specific situations. The institutional system in Finland promotes this. For example, Tekes, the technology development agency funds academic research only if one or more companies jointly sponsor it. In such projects, companies have great control over the intellectual property rights. Most of the theses and doctoral dissertations are focused on corporate problems. In developing technology policy and identifying priority areas for funding, Tekes often relies on committees that consist of both academics and corporate executives. Finally, the boundaries between the academic and corporate organizations are much more permeable than that in the US. Many of the top executives in the corporate and public organizations move from or to universities at different points in their career.

In the US, universities are motivated to work more on theoretical knowledge development. Reward system in the US academic institutions encourages faculty to be engaged in theoretical and more generic type of research. Public funds can seldom be used to further the interests of a specific company. There are some exceptions. The Small Business Innovation Research (SBIR) program at the National Science Foundation is aimed at rectifying such situation and is geared to help small companies to further their innovative activities. Such programs are too few and often the small companies are not properly equipped to tap into such programs. Most collaborative programs funded at the universities by public money are aimed at pre-competitive technology development. This means that the output of such programs needs further investment for development.

To further understand the differences in the roles that the universities in the US and Finland play in the knowledge exchange process, we look at the mode of transfer of knowledge and the nature of knowledge in terms of its communicability. Transfer of knowledge takes place either through personal or impersonal channels. Nonaka and Takeuchi (1995) differentiated knowledge as tacit or explicit. Explicit knowledge is codifiable and easily expressible. Tacit knowledge is not visible and difficult to formalize. It is not easily expressible and is often highly personal. In order to implement new technology in product or processes, industry needs tacit knowledge. Thus there remains a chasm between what industry needs and what universities are generally geared to offer. In Figure 2, we show that universities are often engaged in development of generic theoretical knowledge that is codified and transmitted through papers, patents and presentations. Industry needs tacit knowledge that can be applied and interpreted for specific problem situation. The chasm between the needs of the industry and what universities generally offer through their papers and patents can be described in three dimensions: structural, cognitive and informational. Traditionally, there is no structural mechanism for industry to interact with the academic professionals in universities. Cognitively, they also differ in terms of their priorities. Finally, the information that is conveyed to each other becomes not very meaningful.

Figure 2: *Knowledge Exchange between University and Industry*

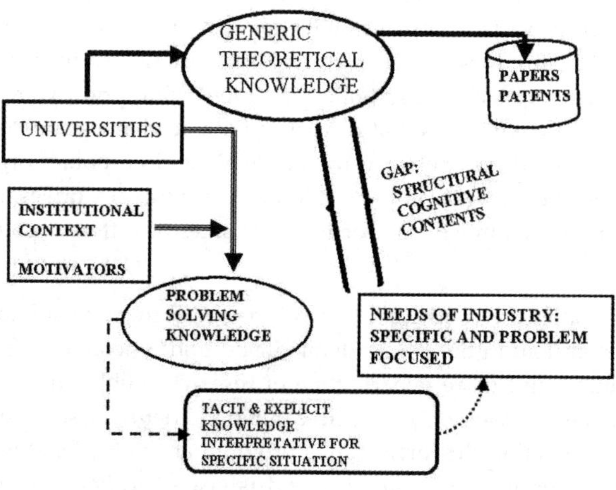

5 Social Capital and Bridging the Entrepreneurial Gap

For universities to be effective in fostering high technology entrepreneurship, one needs to bridge the gap as we have outlined above. The three dimensions identified are indeed three components of social capital (Nahapiet and Ghoshal 1998) that consists of "networks of strong, crosscutting personal relationships developed over time that provide the basis for trust, cooperation and collective action". Nahapiet and Ghoshal (1998) suggested, "social relationships – and the social capital therein- are an important influence on the development of intellectual capital". In defining intellectual capital, they acknowledged the importance of "contextually embedded forms of knowledge".

Combination and exchange of intellectual resources leads to the development of intellectual capital. This combination and exchange process depends on four factors: (1) access to the parties involved, (2) perceived value of such interactions, (3) motivation for engaging in such activities, and (4) creative capability of the parties. According to Nahapiet and Ghoshal (1998), much of this knowledge is socially embedded.

Entrepreneurial universities can create the social capital through various mechanisms that can sustain development of intellectual capital in their regions that will foster development and growth of high technology firms. Other public organizations can contribute significantly in development of such social capital. Universities in Finland have participated in building incubators or enterprise development centers to house the entrepreneurial firms. These incubators provide the opportunity to network with the university personnel. Helsinki University of Technology has Innopoli, the business incubator on its campus. Innopoli has been funded through various public and private sources. Technical University of Tampere has established Hermia, a business incubator on campus. The philosophy of Hermia is not to provide subsidized real estate, but the advantage of co-locating with the technical university. The success of Hermia can be seen how the employment in the Tampere region, a city of 300000 people has changed as shown in Table 1.

Table 1: *Employment in High Tech Industries in Tampere, Finland*

Industries	*1993*	*1998*	*1999*
Mechanical and Automation	20,000	24,000	25,000
Information & Communication	2,000	8,500	10,000
Media Services		4,600	5,000
Knowledge Intensive Business Services		5,500	6,000

In Turku, the bio-industry is being developed based on the long tradition of the knowledge base in chemistry at the Åbo Academy and the University of Turku. Pharmaceutical companies and companies dedicated to developing functional foods are agglomerated in the Turku area. Bio-Valley is the most recent business incubation program that has been initiated in 2001. The Bio-Turku Network consists of five types of organizations: biotechnology companies, university research organizations, discovery companies, integrated pharmaceuticals manufacturing and marketing companies, and service companies. It is important to note here that the Finnish system is predominantly based on organizational networks and collaboration.

It is also important to note here that other public organizations, Tekes, SITRA[3], a semi public venture investment organization, Finnish Foundation of Innovation, and agencies under the jurisdiction of other ministries are significantly involved in working with these incubators. The institutional infrastructure in Finland has developed the appropriate social capital conducive for development of business ventures.

Figure 3: *Number of New Technology Based Companies*

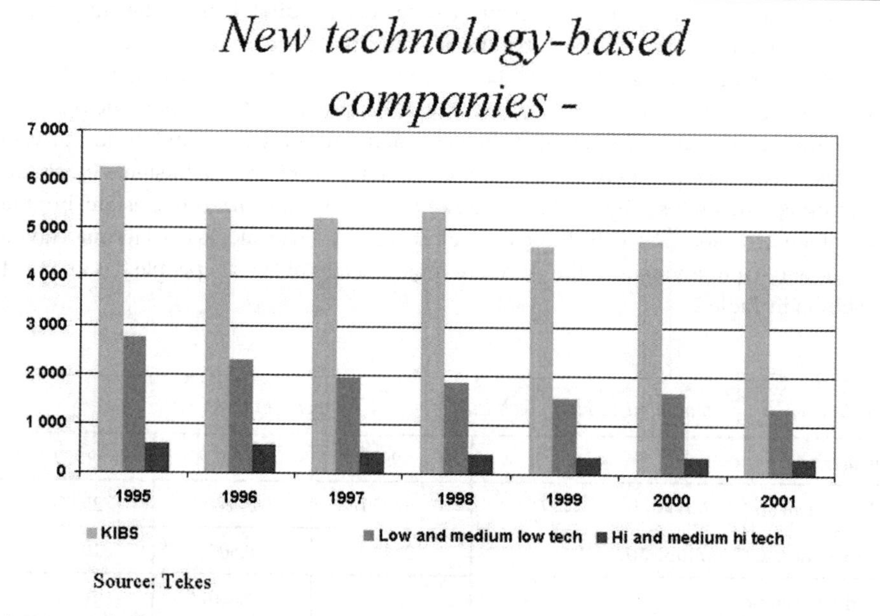

Source: Tekes

Figure 3 shows the annual growth of new technology –based companies in Finland. The explosive growth of the Knowledge Intensive Business Services (KIBS) companies is the culmination of the efforts that the Finnish organizations have made in recent years. Figure 4 provides estimated revenues that the Tekes funded or sponsored companies for next five years. The return on investment of the Tekes funds is indeed quite substantial in many respects including creation and retention of jobs.

[3] Sitra, the Finnish National Fund for Research and Development, is an independent public foundation under the supervision of the Finnish Parliament. The Fund aims to promote Finland's economic prosperity by encouraging research, backing innovative projects, organizing training programs and providing venture capital. Sitra aims to further economic prosperity in Finland by developing new and successful business operations, financing the commercial exploitation of expertise and promoting international competitiveness and cooperation.

Figure 4: *Estimated Growth of SME firms linked with Tekes in Finland*

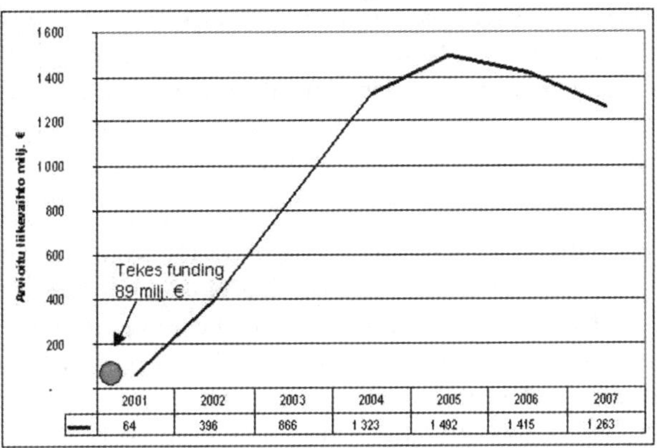

In the US universities have realized the role that they can play in stimulating growth in their regions. The southern tier of New York has suffered economic stagnation, although it had several reputable universities. In the early 1990s, several civic leaders and corporate executives pooled their resources and formed what is the Ceramic Innovation Corridor (CIC). It has two locations; one in Alfred adjacent to Alfred University and the other one in Painted Post near Corning Inc. The idea was to leverage the intellectual resources at Alfred University, renowned for its work in the ceramics and glass technology and the resources of Corning to help growth of business in this region. The CIC helped launch several companies and also provided the opportunity to Corning to pursue its telecommunication related activity. However, due to the recent debacle in the telecommunication industry and the investment climate in the US in general, the region is struggling hard.

The capital district of New York state has gone through some crisis with the decline of the activities of the major employer in the region, General Electric. Manufacturing related activities have significantly declined in other industries and thus have contributed to the economic malaise of the region. There are two reputable universities in the region along with a medical university. Rensselaer Polytechnic Institute (RPI) a nationally recognized technical university has taken the lead to establish a business incubator and a technology park to help foster entrepreneurial activities in the area. State University of New York at Albany (SUNY Albany) has also established an incubator with public funding. A center for research on nano-technology has been established in Albany with the cooperation of IBM, the State of New York and the SUNY. Although efforts are being made, the region is yet to become another Silicon Valley.

Similar experience can be observed in Newark, New Jersey. New Jersey Institute of Technology, a public research university has established several business incubators. The Public Health Research Institute that specializes on infectious diseases has recently shifted its operation to Newark. The City is also the home of the University of Medicine and Dentistry as well as one of the three major campuses of Rutgers University. Despite the agglomeration of these universities and research organizations, Newark has stagnated over a long period since the race riots of 1968.

The region around Oulu in northern Finland (close to the Arctic Circle) is a case of rapid growth in entrepreneurial firms. In its quest for economic development, a university was established. Major companies like Nokia and Sonera established their research centers. The close collaborations among the university, the university hospital and the companies have made Oulu region a major center in mobile communication technology. There are close to 500 wireless communications related companies in the region. Application of the electronic and communications technology to the medical field has created a new industry in *wellness*. There is a Mobile Forum in Oulu that is a platform for interaction and sharing of non-competitive knowledge among mobile communications companies in Oulu and elsewhere. Recently, the region has initiated a Wellness Forum that helps companies devoted to the wellness related products and services.

6 Observations on Practices in Finland and the US

Studies on regional development and agglomeration of high technology companies in certain areas have heightened the importance of universities as engines of growth. The recent advances in biotechnology and information and communication technology also have led to the development of knowledge intensive businesses. Importance of knowledge and highly skilled labor has influenced the location decisions of firms near research universities. Finland has made a conscious effort to utilize the universities as a major component of economic development.

Earlier studies have focused on the role of universities from a resource-based view. Most of the studies pointed out the universities as sources for knowledge, technology, and skilled employees. The importance of knowledge transfer has varied for different universities and also on the nature of the firms. Santoro and Chakrabarti (2002) observed that universities differ in terms of their strategic orientations. This study identified two types of university research centers: network-oriented and problem-oriented. Universities with strong reputations, as exemplified in their high ranking by the U.S. News and World Report, are network-oriented. Universities in the third and fourth tiers in US News ranking are problem-oriented. The level of interaction between a network-oriented center and its industrial collaborators remain at a low level and tangible benefit also remains low. The problem-oriented centers have a high level of interactions with their industrial collaborators and provide tangible outcomes. Generally large companies become associated with the network-oriented centers mostly for their non-core technology. Smaller sized companies on the other hand become associated with the problem-solving research centers in universities. Thus the university-industry relationship becomes dependent on the centrality of the technology for the business operations in one hand and the capability and reputation of the universities on the other hand.

The network-oriented centers, in fact are contributing to the building of the social capital for the firms that is not readily quantifiable in short term economic gains. But the close association with the research universities of international reputation helps these companies develop the structural mechanisms for interaction. Joint projects and sponsorship of research for thesis and dissertation bridge the cognitive gaps and develop the contextual conditions for meaningful interaction. Many international companies build relationships with organizations like Massachusetts Institute of Technology, Stanford University, and Harvard University. Novartis Corporation has recently established its Institute for Research on Bioscience on MIT campus. Nokia Corporation has close cooperation with most of the top ranked universities in the world. Building social capital has been the key ingredient for the Finnish companies to venture into international market quickly (Arenius 2002).

The experience of the regions like Tampere, Oulu, Helsinki, and Turku in Finland points to a symbiotic relationship among the corporations, public agencies and universities. Leadership at the local level is also an instrumental factor in building this social capital. In late 1960s, the City of Tampere realized the importance of an airport in the area. While the national government declined to build one, the local government took the initiative to build one from other sources of funds. Similar entrepreneurial initiative also helped build the Technical University of Technology in late 1960s as this was perceived to be critical in development of the region.

7 Conclusions

Universities are now increasingly recognized to have a broader role in the economic development and entrepreneurship. Smilor, Dietrich, and Gibson (1993) pointed out the factors that are the main driving forces for developing entrepreneurial universities in the US. Finland has been successful in building a tripartite collaborative relationship among universities, corporations and the public agencies. In the US, some regions have attempted to do so with limited success in sustaining that effort. We need further research to understand the cultural imperatives of Finland that help it to succeed. We have presented our observations based on qualitative interviews with the corporate executives, university officials and public agencies. One needs a more systematic investigation to understand the differences in the social capital that is built by universities in their regions and the contextual conditions supporting the process.

8 References

Ali, A. (1994): Pioneering versus incremental innovation: Review and research propositions, *Journal of Product Innovation Management*, 11, 46-61.

Arenius, P. (2002): *Creation of Firm-Level Social Capital, Its Exploitation, and The Process of Early Internationalization*, PhD Thesis, Institute of Strategy and International Business Department of Industrial Engineering and Management, Helsinki University of Technology, Espoo, Finland.

Bettis, R. and M. Hitt. (1995): The new competitive landscape, *Strategic Management Journal*, 16, 7-19.

Chakrabarti, A.K. and R.K. Lester (2002): Regional Economic Development: Comparative Case Studies in the US and Finland, *Proceedings IEEE Conference on Engineering Management*, Cambridge, UK.

Leonard-Barton, D. (1995): *The wellsprings of knowledge*, Cambridge, MA.

Nahapiet, J. and S. Ghoshal. (1998): Social capital, intellectual capital, and the organizational advantage, *Academy of Management Review*, 23, 242-266.

Nonaka, I. and H. Takeuchi (1995): *The Knowledge Creating Company*, Oxford, England.

Parkhe, A. (1993): Strategic alliance structuring: A game theoretic and transaction cost examination of inter-firm cooperation, *Academy of Management Journal*, 36 (4), 794-829.

Pisano, G. (1990): The R&D boundaries of the firm: An empirical analysis, *Administrative Science Quarterly,* 35, 153-176.

Quinn, J.B. (2000): Outsourcing innovation: The new engine of growth, *Sloan Management Review,* Summer, 13-28.

Rice, Mark P. (2002): Co-production of business assistance in business incubators: An exploratory study, 17, 163-187

Santoro, M.D. and A.K. Chakrabarti (2002): Firm size and technology centrality in industry-university interactions, *Research Policy,* 31, 1163-1180.

Shan, W., G. Walker, and B. Kogut (1994): Inter-firm cooperation and startup innovation in the biotechnology industry, *Strategic Management Journal,* 15, 387-394.

Smilor, R.W., G.B. Dietrich, and D.V. Gibson (1993): The entrepreneurial university: The role of higher education in the United States in technology commercialization and economic development, *International Social Science Journal,* 45, 1-12.

Stokes, D.E. (1997): *Pasteur's Quadrant: Basic science and technological innovation,* Washington D.C.

Ashok K. Gupta, G.L. Tembe, and Manjulika Koshal

Enhancing Industry Interaction with Publicly Funded R&D Labs in India

Industry Viewpoint

Prof. Dr. *Ashok K. Gupta,* Department of Marketing, Ohio University at Athens (U.S.A.), Dr. *G.L. Tembe,* Research Centre of the Indian Petrochemicals Corporation Limited (India), and Prof. Dr. *Manjulika Koshal,* Department of Management Systems, Ohio University at Athens (U.S.A.).

1 Abstract

Frequency and quality of interaction between suppliers and buyers of research is one of the most important ingredients in achieving the vision of building R&D organizations that meet industry needs. In this paper, perceptions of research buyers from Indian industry who have interacted with publicly funded R&D labs managed by the Council of Scientific and Industrial Research (CSIR) are presented. The industry viewpoint and perceptions are also compared with that of the interacting labs. The areas examined include: importance and frequency of industry's interaction with labs; barriers faced by industry in their efforts to interact with labs; and initiatives taken by industry to improve their interaction with labs. Recommendations are presented to improve lab-industry interaction by analyzing actions of industrial customers that are more successful in transferring labs' technologies to industry as compared to their less successful counterparts.

2 Introduction

2.1 R&D in India

With 400 state-run laboratories, 230 universities and 1,300 research and development units in industry, India has a huge scientific base (Rediff.com 2003). However, spending on R&D is meager; Rs. 14,164 crores ($3.15 billion) in 1999-2000 and 79.6% of it is by the government as compared to $292 billion in USA in 2002 and 38% by the government (Rediff.com 2003; Raj 2001). In GDP terms, India spends about 0.8% of its GDP on R&D activities compared to 2.7% in USA (Rediff.com 2003; Raj 2001). But, what is even more alarming is that out of India's 8,334 joint stock companies, 86% spent ZERO on R&D during the fiscal year 2001-02. Only seven Indian firms spent more than Rs. 50 crores [approximately $10 million] per year, while there are about 463 companies spending less than Rs. 1 crore [$200,000], according to a study done by the Hyderabad-based Administrative Staff College of India (ASCI) on `R&D in India' (The Hindu 2003). "On the one hand, during the era of license-permit quota raj, industry had little incentive to upgrade its processes or products," Prime Minister Atal Bihari Vajpayee told the gathering of 6,000 scientists at the annual Indian Science Congress in the technology capital of Bangalore. "On the other hand, many of our scientists viewed applied research and its commercialization as an inferior occupation" (Rediff.com 2003). In fact, 10 years ago the director of a Council of Scientific and Industrial Research (CSIR) laboratory declared at a press conference, "Asking scientists to do industrial research is close to prostitution" (Business India 1999). Besides the need to change attitudes of scientists in the labs and business people in industry, India has also realized that the low levels of R&D will adversely affect its competitiveness. Recently, Prime Minister Vajpayee released the new Science & Technology policy. The new policy aims to more than double R&D spending in India to two percent of gross domestic product by 2007 (Rediff.com 2003).

2.2 Publicly Funded CSIR Labs

In India a vast and diversified publicly funded R&D structure has been set-up, including 40 national laboratories employing about 10,000 highly qualified scientific and technical personnel under the Council of Scientific and Industrial Research (CSIR). The contribution of these labs can be measured in terms of economic, scientific and social benefits they provide such as: increase in industrial production and productivity, employment generation, enhancement of export potential opportunities, reduction in imported goods, boosting national competitiveness in world markets, building competence in the science and technology areas, and improving the quality of life of people of India (Gupta et al. 2000). In 1995, CSIR was amongst the first few organizations in India and the first publicly funded R&D organizations in the civilian sector to announce its vision, mission and quantitative goals/targets. CSIR's mission was enunciated as "to provide scientific industrial R&D that maximizes the economic (industrial), environmental and societal benefits for the people of India." Given the mission of CSIR and little R&D activity by Indian companies, one would expect a significant amount of industry-lab interaction to tap into the technological output of the publicly funded labs for industrial use as well as work on R&D projects and programs that would benefit society in general and economic development in particular.

2.3 Lack of Industry-Lab Interaction

An earlier paper (Gupta et al. 2000), highlighted the perceptions of lab directors and scientists with respect to their interaction with industry in terms of: the importance assigned by labs to industry interaction, frequency with which they interact with industry, barriers to industry interaction they face, initiatives they have taken to improve industry interaction. Significant gaps in industry-lab interactions were observed. Suggestions to improve interactions were presented to enhance labs' market-orientation. In this paper, we explore similar issues from industries' viewpoint.

3 Research Objective

A research study was designed to gain insights into the experiences "industrial customers" of publicly funded CSIR research labs have had with their interactions with the R&D labs. That is, what do companies, which have interacted with the labs in the past, think about:

- Importance of company interaction with the labs
- Frequency of company interaction with the labs
- Barriers to interaction with the labs
- Initiatives taken to improve company interaction with labs
- What do companies that are more successful in transferring technologies from labs do differently from their less successful counterparts?

4 Research Methodology

In the data collected for an earlier study (Gupta et al. 2000) of CSIR labs, 25 labs considered their primary mission to be one or more of the following:

- to conduct applied research focused on specific application
- to conduct contract R&D aimed at developing/modifying designs or products or processes
- to generate resources by providing scientific/technical services

These labs were designated as "Applied Labs" who would be expected to interact most with industry and the industry could benefit most from their interaction with them. Directors/Scientists from these labs who participated in an earlier study (Gupta et al. 2000) were contacted via mail. Each was requested to provide contact information of at least 3 industrial "customers or potential customers" with whom labs have interacted in the last three years. A list of 70 such industrial contacts was assembled. A questionnaire similar to earlier study (Gupta et al. 2000) was prepared and mailed to 70 industrial customers/potential customers of Applied Research Labs. After two follow-ups 37 completed questionnaires were received with a response rate of 53%.

Via a comprehensive questionnaire (Gupta et al. 2000; Baron 1990; Hughes 1993; Nordwall 1993; Roessner and Bean 1990, 1991; Thayer 1994), the industry respondents who have interacted with the CSIR labs were asked about their perceptions of:

- R&D mission of the company on a 5-point scale, where 5= Most important mission and 1=Not a mission.
- Level of satisfaction with their interaction with CSIR lab on a 7-point scale, where 7= very satisfied to 1= very dissatisfied;
- Company's success in transferring technology from lab on a 5-point scale, where 5= excellent and 1=totally ineffective;
- Commercial impact to company using labs' technologies on a 5-point scale, where 5=great deal of impact and 1=no impact;
- Future likelihood of seeking assistance of CSIR lab on a 5 point scale where, 5= Very Likely and 1= Very Unlikely;
- Importance of company's interaction with the lab on a 5-point scale, where 5=of great importance and 1=of little importance;
- Frequency of company's interaction with lab on a 5-point scale, where 5=very high and 1=very low;
- Barriers to interaction with lab on a 5-point scale, where 5=strongly agree that the given item is a barrier and 1=strongly disagree that the given item is a barrier;
- Initiative that company has taken to improve its interaction with lab on a 5-point scale, where 5=strongly agree that the company has taken this initiative and 1= strongly disagree that the company has taken this initiative.

5 Results

5.1 R&D Mission and Success in Technology Transfer

The most dominant mission of Indian industry participants in our study was to conduct R&D focused on bringing new products or processes into marketplace with an average rating of 4.05 out of maximum of 5 (Figure 1).

The least important mission for Industrial R&D was to conduct fundamental research in areas relevant for company's business goals with an average rating of 2.94 out of a maximum of 5. It is understandable that the goal of industrial R&D is to work on commercializable new products rather than science for science sake. Other objectives of conducting R&D included trouble shooting or achieving quality standards, modifying existing products or processes or application engineering, for import substitution, to reduce waste, and to utilize by-products.

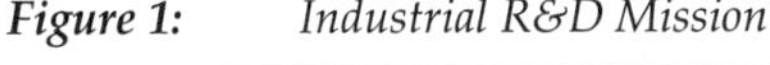

Figure 1: *Industrial R&D Mission*

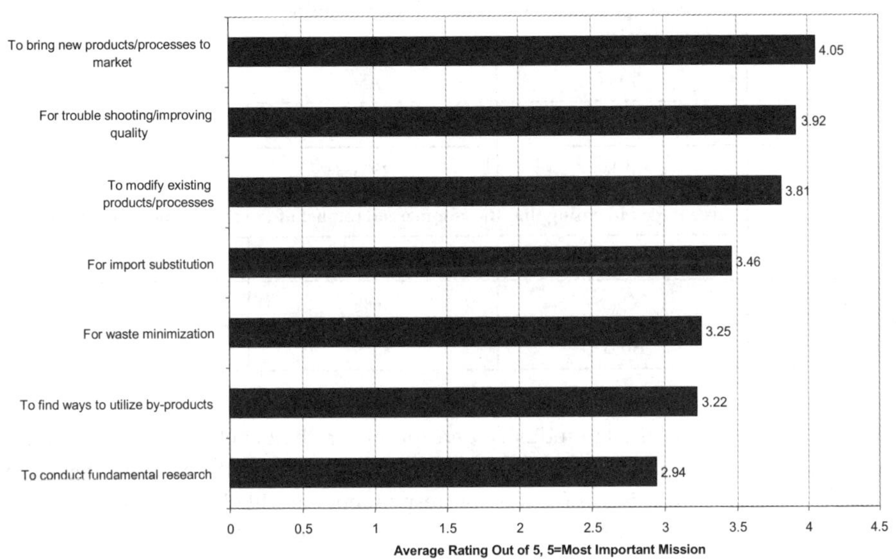

When industrial R&D mission is compared with the mission of Applied R&D Labs (Gupta et al. 2000), there is a great deal of commonality. The applied R&D labs indicated their mission: to conduct applied research focused on specific application, to conduct contract R&D aimed at developing/modifying designs or products or processes and to generate resources by providing scientific/technical services. Commonality in mission should facilitate interaction. However, when industrial respondents were asked about their overall satisfaction with CSIR labs, about 29% were satisfied and 34% were dissatisfied. Others were neutral.

The respondents were also asked to rate their company's overall success in the last three years on: (a) transferring technology from Government R&D labs, and (b) its commercial impact. Only 11% of the respondents rated technology transfer as a success (gave a rating of 4 or 5 on a 5 point scale) while none reported significant commercial impact of the technology transferred. Labs' scientists/directors however, paint a quite different picture. A majority of labs' respondents (58%) indicated that their laboratories had been successful (gave a rating of 4 or 5) in getting industry to avail the labs' outputs. In terms of economic benefit derived by industry, 50% of the respondents from labs felt that industry benefited well (a rating of 4 or 5).

Table 1: *Success in Technology Transfer*

	Percentage indicating that the success in transferring technology from lab to company is:		
	Good	*So-So*	*Poor*
Industry's View	11%	54%	35%
Labs' View	58%	29%	13%
	Percentage indicating that the commercial impact of the technology transferred is:		
	Good	*So-So*	*Poor*
Industry's View	0%	46%	54%
Labs' View	50%	32%	18%

There is a wide gap in the lab-industry perceptions on the benefits of interaction. Industry has a much grimmer view of the benefits they are getting from their interaction with the labs. However, 56% of industrial respondents are likely/very likely (gave a rating of 4 or 5 on a 5 point scale) to interact with or seek assistance of Government labs. Only 19% are unlikely/very unlikely (gave a rating of 1 or 2 on a 5 point scale) to interact with labs in future.

5.2 Importance and Frequency of Industry's Interaction with Labs

The importance that the industry accorded to their interaction with Government R&D Labs and the frequency of such interaction was analyzed on the ten areas where industry could interact with labs. The mean responses on importance and frequency of interaction with labs out of a maximum of 5 points where 5= importance of interaction is very high/frequency of interaction is very high are presented in Table 2.

Table 2: *Importance & Frequency of Industry Interaction with Government Labs as Perceived by Industrial Respondents on a 5-point scale*

Area of Industry Interaction with Government Lab	Importance of Interaction with Lab	Frequency of Interaction with Lab	Significance level of difference
Inquiring about the activities of Government R&D Labs	3.27	2.76	0.000
Informing labs of industry needs	3.11	2.64	0.000
Sponsoring projects to Government Labs	3.08	2.67	0.001
Seeking technical assistance/consultation from Government Labs	3.03	2.64	0.001
Jointly working on R&D projects with Government Labs	2.97	2.47	0.000
Transfer of technology from Government Labs to industry	2.89	2.39	0.000
Inviting Government Lab personnel to work with industry	2.22	1.89	0.016
Sharing industry's R&D findings with Government Labs	2.17	1.94	0.044
Sending industry personnel to work with Government Labs	2.11	1.80	0.014
Making pilot plants available to Government R&D Labs	2.06	1.72	0.000

(5= importance of interaction is very high/frequency of interaction is very high)

A significant gap was observed between the perception of importance of industry interaction with labs and the actual frequency of interaction. The differences between the mean importance ratings and the mean frequency ratings in each area were significant ($p<0.05$ level). The industry perceives that interaction with labs is important, however, actual frequency of interaction is significantly lower. The industry considers it most important to learn about the activities of Government Labs at the same time inform labs of industry needs. Also, industry will like to sponsor projects to Government labs and in return seek assistance and consultation from the labs on their technical problems. Hopefully working closely and synergistically on R&D projects will lead to transfer of technology from labs to industry. When these findings from industry are compared with the findings from an earlier study on labs' perceptions (Gupta et al. 2000), the Government labs in general assigned greater importance to interaction with industry than vice versa. Industry, in spite of little R&D activities, does not perceive as much benefit from their interaction with labs as the labs see with their interaction with industry. However, those companies which assigned greater importance to their interaction with labs also achieved greater interaction. [All correlation coefficients between importance of interaction and frequency of interaction were more than 0.75 and significant at $p<0.0001$]. The significant gap between the importance and the actual frequency of interaction indicates that there is a great deal of work ahead in helping industry see benefit from its interaction with labs.

5.3 Barriers to Industry Interaction with Labs

Fourteen common barriers to effective R&D lab/industry interaction were identified from literature and discussions with CSIR personnel. The degree of agreement was sought from the customer companies of CSIR labs whether a given item is a barrier to industry interaction on a 5-point scale, where 5=Strongly Agree that the given item is a barrier to interaction. Their responses are presented in Figure 2.

Figure 2: *Barriers to Interaction with Government Labs*

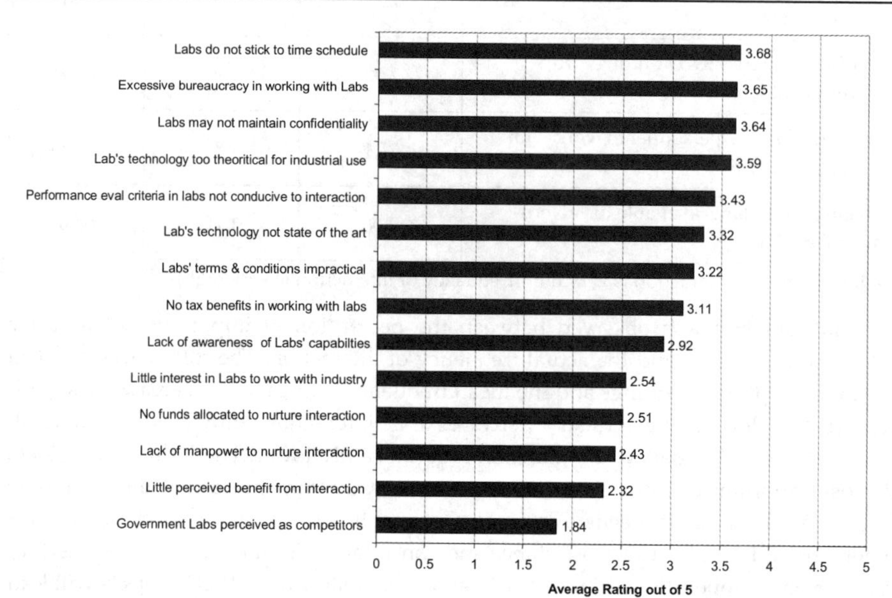

The biggest perceived barriers in the minds of industrial clients of Government research labs are (1) work-style of labs and (2) quality of technologies developed in the labs. Regarding labs' work-style, industry finds the labs' lack of commitment to sticking to agreed upon time schedules and excessive bureaucracy highly frustrating. They also fear that labs may not maintain the confidentiality of their work with industry which may lead to competitive disadvantage for them in the marketplace. Regarding the technologies developed in labs, industry is not convinced if it is the state of the art and considers it too theoretical for industrial use. Industry also believes that the criteria used to evaluate performance of scientists and engineers in the labs are not conducive to enhancing their interaction with industry. Lack of resources or interest or awareness of labs' capabilities is not cited as major barriers to interaction. On the other hand, when labs were asked about the barriers they face in interaction with industry the biggest barrier was cited the lack of funds to promote interaction between labs and industry. Labs attribute the poor state of industry interaction to lack of industry awareness of what the labs can offer. Interestingly, that is not the reason for lack of interaction from industry perspective.

5.4 Initiatives Taken by Industry to Improve Interaction with Labs

Our study findings indicate that 70% of the industry respondents agree that they need to improve interaction with Government Labs. About half of them have designated a person responsible to nurture contacts with labs of interest to their industry and 39% aggressively look at technologies developed by Government labs to reduce their own R&D costs. Based on the review of previous studies and discussions with CSIR personnel, eight potential initiatives that companies could take to improve their interaction with Government Research Labs were identified. Industry respondents were asked to indicate on a 5-point (5=Strongly Agree) scale if their organizations have taken each initiative to improve interaction with Government labs. In general, it was found (Table 3) that industry has not taken enough incentives to improve interaction with labs. About half of industry respondents indicate that they have designated an individual to nurture contacts with the Government Labs of industry interest. However, industry scientists/engineers working in their own R&D labs and facilities are not expected, at least via performance appraisal system, to interact with Government Labs or transfer technology from them.

When responses of companies more satisfied with their interaction with government labs (satisfaction score of 6 or 7) were compared with that of less satisfied ones (satisfaction scores of 1 to 4. Satisfaction score of 5=neutral were removed from analysis), it was found that more satisfied companies took more initiatives in each area presented in Table 3 than their less satisfied counterparts. However, the differences were statistically significant ($p<=0.05$) in four areas. Companies more satisfied with their interaction with Government Labs as compared with the less Companies satisfied with their interaction with Government R&D Labs agreed more strongly to:

Table 3: *Initiatives Taken By Industry*

Initiative taken by industry	Average rating out of 5	% who agree/ strongly agree
Realization of the need to improve interaction with Government Labs	3.86	70%
Designated an individual responsible to nurture contacts with Government Labs	3.03	49%
Invite Government Labs scientists/engineers to learn about industry problems	2.95	38%
Aggressively look at technologies developed by Govt. Labs to reduce cost of R&D	2.94	39%
Launched programs to make Government Labs aware of industry's technical problems or research needs	2.89	38%
Devoted part of the R&D budget to improve interaction with Government Labs	2.83	33%
Offer industry experts to review Government R&D programs for business relevance	2.76	30%
Criteria for performance evaluation of industrial scientists/engineers now include transfer of technology from Government Labs or efforts to improve interaction	2.05	11%

- Allocating budget to improve interaction (Average Agreement Rating for More Satisfied Group=3.40 vs. 2.0 for the Less Satisfied Group)
- Launching programs to make government labs aware of industry's needs (3.60 vs. 2.17)
- Aggressively looking to reduce R&D costs via collaboration with labs (3.40 vs. 2.45)
- Making industry experts available to review Government R&D programs and activities (3.40 vs. 2.25)

When these findings are compared with the initiatives taken to reduce barriers to industry interaction by Successful vs. Not-so-Successful Labs in an earlier study (Gupta et al. 2000), it was found that the 'successful' laboratories differed from their 'not-so-successful' counterparts in making efforts to reach out to industry by: launching programs to make industry aware of their capabilities and setting targets on budget to be met from external support. It appears that the 'successful' labs have launched cost-effective programs to enhance industry awareness: programs that do not require significantly more human or financial resources than their 'not-so-successful' counterparts.

6 Limitations

The study suffers from several limitations. First, in India a strong tradition of practical survey research is lacking. A great deal of wasteful correspondence and quite often personal efforts is required to encourage respondents to complete the questionnaire. The findings reported in this study are based only on a limited sample of 37 industrial respondents who have interacted with Government R&D Labs. A larger sample would have been more desirable. Second, most of the data collected in the study is perceptual in nature. In the absence of any objective data to compare with, perceptual data may have limited appeal to some readers. However, a great deal of published business management and marketing literature is based on perceptual data. Some may even argue that the perceptions are even more important than the reality. In spite of the above limitations, the current study on industry's perceptions when used in conjunction with the earlier study done from labs' perspective (Gupta et al. 2000) does provide important information on how industry can better use Government Labs as a resource for their technical and business needs as well as how labs' can better position themselves to serve industry.

7 Conclusions & Future Research

Research and Development in Indian industry is meager; out of India's 8,334 joint stock companies, 86% spent ZERO on R&D during the fiscal year 2001-02 (The Hindu 2003). While the dominant mission of conducting industrial R&D includes: bringing new products to market, improve product quality, and modify existing products or processes; how can industry achieve these objectives without committing adequate resources to R&D activities? Perhaps greater industry-lab interaction can provide much needed assistance to industry in achieving its R&D mission while keeping government labs market driven. This could be a win-win solution to both industry and publicly funded government labs managed by CSIR. The study findings reported in this article are based on the perceptions of 37 industrial clients of government labs. The industrial perceptions have also been compared with an earlier study (Gupta et al. 2000) of perceptions of government labs about their interaction with industry. Based on the analysis of the data and a comparison of 'satisfied and 'not-so-satisfied' companies some useful lessons can be learnt namely:

7.1 Bridge the Success Perceptual Gap

There is a great deal of commonality between the missions of applied R&D labs of CSIR and industrial R&D: to conduct research focused on specific applications and to conduct R&D aimed at developing/modifying products or processes. However there is a wide gap in the perception of success of transfer of technology from labs to industry and the commercial impact of the technology transferred. Only 11% of the industrial clients indicated success in transferring technology from labs while 58% of the labs perceived the transfer to be successful. On the other hand, none of the companies that transferred technology from the labs experienced significant commercial impact, while half the labs thought the commercial impact was good. Why such a wide gap in perceptions of success? Do labs have a pro-technology transfer bias? Is industry too skeptical about the value of technology it receives from government labs? Since no objective data was collected either from industry or labs about the success or commercial impact of technology-transfer, it is difficult to say what the reality is. Labs and industry need to maintain a database of their experiences. Success stories of technology transfer could be publicized and used as marketing tool to further enhance industry-lab interaction.

7.2 Translate Sense of Importance to Action

The Government labs in general assigned greater importance to interaction with industry than vice versa. The lowest importance rating given by labs for their interaction with industry was 3.27 on a 5-point scale (Gupta et al. 2000); this was the highest importance rating given by industry for their interaction with labs! Industry, in spite of little R&D activities, does not perceive as much benefit from their interaction with labs as the labs see with their interaction with industry. However, 70% industry respondents have started to realize that they need to improve interaction with government labs. A significant gap was also observed between the perception of importance of industry interaction with labs and the actual frequency of interaction. However, those companies, which assigned greater importance to their interaction with labs also, achieved greater interaction. The significant gap between the importance and the actual frequency of industry interaction with labs indicates that there is a great deal of work ahead in helping industry see benefit from its interaction with labs. When asked, "In future, how likely are you to interact with or seek assistance of Government R&D Labs," only 13% indicated that they are "Very Likely" to interact and 43% indicated that they are "Likely" to interact. Other 44% were neutral or unlikely to interact with Government Labs. The challenge is to move "Less Likely/Unlikely" to "Likely/Very Likely" to interact group.

7.3 Increase the Understanding of Barriers to Interaction

To enhance interaction between two parties one needs to have a better understanding of barriers to interaction. Labs attribute the poor state of industry interaction to lack of industry awareness of what the labs can offer. Interestingly, that is not the reason for lack of interaction from industry perspective. The biggest perceived barriers in the minds of industrial clients of Government research labs are (1) work-style of labs and (2) quality of technologies developed in the labs. Regarding labs' work-style, industry finds the labs' lack of commitment to sticking to agreed upon time schedules and excessive bureaucracy highly frustrating. Industry also fears that the labs may not maintain confidentiality of their work with industry that may lead to competitive disadvantage for them in the marketplace. Regarding the technologies developed in labs, industry is not convinced if it is the state of the art and considers it too theoretical for industrial use. Our study findings indicate that about half of the industry respondents have designated a person responsible to nurture contacts with labs of interest to their industry and 39% aggressively look at technologies developed by Government labs to reduce their own R&D costs. These actions should increase industrial awareness of labs' activities. Labs, on the other hand, need to become more user-friendly and market-oriented. Labs also need to demonstrate to industry that they can contribute to enhancing sustainable competitive advantage of industry by supplying them with the state of the art technologies for new products as well as product and process modifications. Those companies which expressed greater satisfaction with their interaction with labs tended to allocate more resources to enhancing interaction, keep labs aware of industry needs, aggressively look for technologies to reduce R&D costs via collaboration with labs, and make industry experts available to review government R&D programs and activities.

7.4 Future research

We suggest that the future research efforts be directed toward three areas. First, documenting the success and failure rates of technology transfer from labs to industry and their commercial impact. There seems to be a wide disagreement between labs and industry on the success of technology transfers. Labs perceive their efforts to be more positive than industry's experience. Second issue that needs to be researched is to develop some case studies of 'successful' and 'not-so-successful' labs. Why some labs are able to successfully interact with industry and transfer their technologies to industry while others lack this commercialization capability. Third, similar efforts could be directed toward developing case studies of successful and not-so-successful companies.

8 References

Baron, S. (1990): Overcoming Barriers to Technology Transfer, *Research-Technology Management*, January-February, 38-43.

Business India (1999): Catalyst for Change, *Business India*, June 28-July 11, 50-57.

Gupta, A., H.R. Bhojwani, R. Koshal, and M. Koshal (2000): Managing the Process of Market Orientation by Publicly Funded Laboratories: the Case of CSIR, India, *R&D Management*, 30 (4) October.

Hindu (2003): 86 Percent of Indian Companies Spend Nothing on R&D, *Financial Daily from Hindu*, March 20.

Hughes, D. (1993): Industry Seeks Expertise in Federal Lab Interaction, *Aviation Week & Space Technology*, November 8, 51-52.

Nordwall, B.D (1993): Many Civil Uses For Defence Technology, *Aviation Week & Space Technology*, November 8, 44-45.

Raj, N. Gopal (2001): India's Technology Priorities, *Hindu*, Thursday, Nov 1.

Rediff.com (2003): Government Unveils Plan to Double R&D Spending, January 3, http://www.rediff.com/money/2003/jan/03spending.htm.

Roessner, J.D. and A.S. Bean (1990): Industry Interactions with Federal Laboratories, *Technology Transfer*, Fall, 5-14.

Roessner, J.D. and A.S. Bean (1991): How Industry Interacts With Federal Laboratories, *Research-Technology Management*, July-August, 22-25.

Thayer, A.M. (1994): Companies Find Benefits and Barriers in Co-operative R&D with Federal Labs, *C&EN*, August 29, 17-19.

Part 7:

Klaus Brockhoff

Klaus Brockhoff

List of Publications

1 Books

B1. *Unternehmenswachstum und Sortimentsänderungen,* Köln and Opladen 1966 (=Schriften des Instituts für Gesellschafts- und Wirtschaftswissenschaften der Universität Bonn, Band 5).

B2. *Forschungsplanung im Unternehmen,* Wiesbaden 1969.

B3. *Forschungsprojekte und Forschungsprogramme: Ihre Bewertung und Auswahl.* 2nd, extended and modified edition of: Forschungsplanung im Unternehmen, Wiesbaden 1973.

B4. *Unternehmensforschung. Eine Einführung.* Berlin-New York 1973.

B5. *Gebührenbestimmung für die Abwasserableitung,* Essen 1973.

B5a) reprinted in: K.Brockhoff and J. Salzwedel: *Korrekte Maßstabsbildung für Entwässerungsgebühren. Rechtliche und betriebswirtschaftliche Aspekte.* Berlin 1978, 81-172.

B6. *Zur externen gesellschaftsbezogenen Berichterstattung deutscher Unternehmen. Eine Auswertung von Geschäftsberichten aus dem Jahre 1973,* Veröffentlichungen der Stiftung Gesellschaft und Unternehmen, 3, Cologne 1975.

B6a) partially reprinted in: E. Pieroth (Ed.): *Sozialbilanzen in der Bundesrepublik Deutschland,* Düsseldorf, Vienna 1978, 178-201.

B6b) *A Note on External Social Reporting by German Companies: A Survey of 1973 Company Report, Accounting, Organizations and Society,* Vol. 4, 1979, 77-85.

B7. *Prognoseverfahren für die Unternehmensplanung,* in: E. Gutenberg (Ed.): Reihe: Neue Wirtschaftswissenschaften, Wiesbaden 1977.

B8. *Delphi-Prognosen im Computer-Dialog. Experimentelle Erprobung und Auswertung kurzfristiger Prognosen,* Tübingen 1979.

B9. *Produktpolitik,* Stuttgart, New York 1981.
B9a) 2., modified and extended edition, Stuttgart, New York 1988.
B9b) 3., modified and extended edition, Stuttgart, Jena 1993.
B9c) 4., modified and extended edition, Stuttgart, Jena 1999.

B10. *Politica de Productos* (translated by S. Garcia Echevarria et al.), Madrid 1987.

B11. *Marketing durch Kundeninformationssysteme,* Stuttgart 1987.

B12. *Forschung und Entwicklung. Planung und Kontrolle.* Munich 1988.
B12a) 2. edition, Munich/Vienna 1989.
B12b) 3., modified and extended edition, Munich/Vienna 1992.
B12c) 4. edition, Munich/Vienna 1994.

B12d) 5., modified and extended edition, Munich/Vienna1998.

B13. *Kenkyukaihatuno Keieisenryaku* (Forschung und Entwicklung) (translated by M. Kuriyama, A. Mori, H. Nakahara, A. Takei), Tokyo (Chikura) 1994.

B14. *Schnittstellen-Management. Abstimmungsprobleme zwischen Marketing und Forschung und Entwicklung*. Stuttgart 1989.

B15. *Stärken und Schwächen industrieller Forschung und Entwicklung. Umfrageergebnisse aus der Bundesrepublik Deutschland.* Stuttgart 1990.
15a) partially printed in: W.P.J. Droege, K. Backhaus, and R. Weiber (Eds.): *Strategien für Investitionsgütermärkte,* Landsberg 1993, 303-307.

B16. *Management organisatorischer Schnittstellen - unter besonderer Berücksichtigung der Koordination von Marketingbereichen mit Forschung und Entwicklung,* Göttingen 1994.

B17. *Industrial Research for Future Competitiveness,* Heidelberg/New York 1997.
17a) partially printed as: Research in the Company of the Future, in: Hans G. Danielmeyer and Yasutsugu Takeda (Eds.): *The Company of the Future,* Berlin/Heidelberg/New York 1999, 49-90.

B18. *La ricerca industriale per la competitività nel futuro,* italian edition (with a preface of G. Petroni; translated by E. Vinassa de Regny), San Marino 2001.

B19. *Der Kunde im Innovationsprozeß,* Göttingen 1998.

B20. *Internationalization of Research and Development,* Heidelberg, New York 1998.

B21. *Geschichte der Betriebswirtschaftslehre – kommentierte Meilensteine und Originaltexte,* Wiesbaden 2000.
B21 a) Second, corrected edition, Wiesbaden 2002.

2 Articles*

1. Forschungsaufwendungen industrieller Unternehmen, *Zeitschrift für Betriebswirtschaft,* 34, 1964, 327-348.
   1a) printed in: H. Albach (Ed.): *Meilensteine der Betriebswirtschaftslehre. 60 Jahre Zeitschrift für Betriebswirtschaft,* Wiesbaden 1991, 193-214.

2. Zum Problem des optimalen Wertpapierbudgets, *Unternehmensforschung,* 11, 1967, 162-172.

* Mainly practically oriented articles

3. Unternehmenszusammenbrüche und Konjunktur: Zum induzierten Unternehmenswachstum, *Zeitschrift für die gesamte Staatswissenschaft*, 123, 1967, 654-667.

4. A Test for the Product Life Cycle, *Economometrica*, 35, 1967, 472-484.

5.* Steuerliche Abschreibungen in den USA, *Außenwirtschaftsdienst des Betriebs-Beraters*, 13, 1967, 464-471.

6. On a Duopoly with a Doubly Kinked Demand Function, *Zeitschrift für die gesamte Staatswissenschaft*, 124, 1968, 451-466.

7. Zum Problem der optimalen Betriebsgröße in einer sozialistischen Wirtschaft, *Zeitschrift für Betriebswirtschaft*, 38, 1968, 17-30.

8. Probleme und Methoden technologischer Vorhersagen, *Zeitschrift für Betriebswirtschaft*, (2. additional issue), 39, 1969, 1-24.
   8a) Problems and methods of technical forecasting, *The European Marketing Research Review*, European society for opinion and marketing research, 5 (2), 1970.

9. Ein Überblick über Modelle zur Bewertung und Auswahl von Forschungsprojekten, *Battelle Information*, 6, 1969, 5-15.
   9a) English Translation: ibid.
   9b) Romanian Translation: Modele de Evaluare A Proiectelor, *Viata Economica*, VIII, 1970, 47, 12 et sqq..

10. Steuerabzüge für Investitionen, *Finanzarchiv*, 29, 1970, 256-272.

11. Some Problems and Solutions in the Selection of an R&D Portfolio, in: J. Lawrence (Ed.): *Proceedings of the Fifth International Conference of Operational Research*, London 1970, 765-773.

12. Zur Quantifizierung der Produktivität industrieller Forschung durch die Schätzung einer einzelwirtschaftlichen Produktionsfunktion - Erste Ergebnisse, *Jahrbücher für Nationalökonomie und Statistik*, 184, 1970, 248-276.
    12a) slightly complemented English version: On the Quantification of the Marginal Productivity of Industrial Research by Estimating a Production Function for a Single Firm, *German Economic Review*, 8, 1970, 202-229.

13. Determinants of Research and Development Expenditure in Some Chemical Corporations in Germany, *Management International Review*, 4/5, 1970, 71-92.

14. (with H. Buck) Wirtschaftliche Konzentration und Betriebsgrößenoptimierung in sozialistischen Wirtschaften, *Deutschland Archiv*, 3, 1970, 225-266.

15. Zur Erfassung der Ungewißheit bei der Planung von Forschungsprojekten, zugleich ein Ansatz zur Bildung optimaler Gutachtergruppen, Entscheidung bei unsicheren Erwartungen, in: Herbert Hax, (Ed.): Beiträge zur Theorie der Unternehmung, Köln, Opladen, 1970, 159-188 at the same time: *Schriftenreihe der Betriebs-wirtschaftlichen Vereinigung Bonn e.V*, 3.

16.* Instrumentarual Matematic in Dirijarea Interprinderilor, *Viata Economica*, IX, 1971, 1, 10-11.

17. Methods for Management Training, *Acta Hospitalia*, 1971, 11, 105-127.

18.* Entscheidungsmodelle in der Forschungsplanung, *Wirtschaftswoche, No.* 49, 25, 1971, 35 et sqq..

19. On Determining Relative Values, *Zeitschrift für Operations Research*, 16, 1972, 221-232.
19a) printed in: R. Ackoff, (Ed.): *Systems and Management*, New York: petrocelli books, 1974, 459 et sqq..

20. Zur Dynamik des technischen Fortschritts, *Zeitschrift für Betriebswirtschaft*, 42, 1972, 283-292.

21. Ein Ansatz zur Abschätzung des Forschungserfolges, *Zeitschrift für betriebswirtschaftliche Forschung*, 24, 1972, 709-723.

22. Die Realisierung eines Zielsystems - dargestellt anhand eines Falles, *Zeitschrift für Organisation*, 6, 1973, 319-324.

23.* (with A. Sell) Unternehmensdispositionen bei Rentabilitätsbeschränkung, *WiSt, Zeitschrift für Ausbildung und Hochschulkontakt*, 1973, 309-313.

24. Zwei Fragen zum Einsatz der "Fallmethode", *Betriebswirtschaftliche Forschung und Praxis*, 1973, 313-318.

25. Vorhersagen über den technischen Fortschritt und Entwicklungsaufwendungen, *Zeitschrift für Betriebswirtschaft*, 43, 1973, 761-776.

26. Marktsättigung, in: B. Tietz (Ed.): *Handwörterbuch der Absatzwirtschaft*, Stuttgart 1974, 1401-1408.

27. Produktlebenszyklen, in: B. Tietz (Ed.): *Handwörterbuch der Absatzwirtschaft*, Stuttgart, 1974, 1763-1770.

28. Wachstumspolitik, marktorientierte, in: B. Tietz (Ed.): *Handwörterbuch der Absatzwirtschaft*, Stuttgart, 1974, 2139-2149.
28a) Spanish Translation: Politica de crecimiento de la impresa, in: S. Garcia Echevarria (Ed.): *Politica Economica de la Empresa*, 1, 1975, 479-489.

29. Planung und Organisation der Forschung und Entwicklung, in: E. Grochla (Ed.): *Handwörterbuch der Betriebswirtschaft*, Stuttgart, 1979, 1530-1542.
29a) Printed in: Erwin Grochla, (Ed.): *Betriebswirtschaftslehre, Part II: Betriebsführung*, Stuttgart, 1979, 166-171.

30.* Planung und Prognose in deutschen Großunternehmen: Ergebnisse einer Umfrage, *Der Betrieb*, 1974, 838-841.

31.* Innovationsprozeß und Unternehmenswachstum, in: K.H. Oppenländer (Ed.): *Technischer Fortschritt: Ursachen und Auswirkungen wirtschaftlichen Handelns*, Ifo-Institut München, 1974, 301-310.
31a) Spanish Translation: Proceso de Innovacion y Crecimiento Empresarial, Estudios De Gestion Commercial y Empresa, (ESIC)-Market, 18, 1975, 115-123.

32. The Performance of Forecasting Groups in Computer Dialogue and Face-to-Face Discussion, in: H. Linstone and M. Turoff (Eds.): *The Delphi-Method: Techniques and Applications.*, Reading, Mass.: Addison Wesley, 1975, 291-321.
32a) 2nd edition 1977.
32b) 3rd edition 1979.

33.* Planung in mittelgroßen Industrieunternehmen, Ergebnisse einer Umfrage, *Die Unternehmung*, 29, 1975, 303-317.
33a) Partially printed in: C.H. Hanf (Ed.): *Vorträge zum 2. Forschungscolloquium 1976 des Lehrstuhls für Wirtschaftslehre des Landbaus*, 7, 1976, Institut für Landwirtschaftliche Betriebs- und Arbeitslehre der Universität Kiel, 1976, 21-29.

34. Ist die gesellschaftsorientierte Berichterstattung ein geeignetes Meßinstrument, um die Auswirkung gesellschaftlicher Veränderungen auf die Unternehmenspolitik zu messen? Die Bedeutung gesellschaftlicher Veränderungen für die Willensbildung im Unternehmen, in: H. Albach and D. Sadowski (Eds.): *Schriften des Vereins für Sozialpolitik*, 88, 1976, 837-864.

35. (with O. Dietrich and G.F. Rueck) DELPHI.F4 ein Dialogsystem zur Unterstützung von Prognosegruppen unter Benutzung einer Datenbank, *Angewandte Informatik*, 18, 1976, 429-437.

36. Erste Beobachtungen über die Informationsnachfrage von Prognosegruppen. G. Reber (Ed.): *Personal- und Sozialorientierung der Betriebswirtschaftslehre*, 4, Stuttgart 1977, 22-41.

37. Technischer Fortschritt, II: im Betrieb, in: W. Albers et al. (Eds.): *Handwörterbuch der Wirtschaftswissenschaft*, 7, 1977, 583-609.

38.* Bewertung und Kontrolle von Forschung und Entwicklung, in: Warnecke et al., (Eds.): *RKW-Handbuch, Forschung, Entwicklung, Konstruktion*, 1977, 1-36.

39.* Scoring-Modelle in der Forschungsplanung, Kontaktstudium. *Zeitschrift für betriebswirtschaftliche Forschung*, 28, 1976, 205-212.
39a) Printed in: *Betriebswirtschaftliches Kontaktstudium*, Wiesbaden 1978, 153-160.

40. Technischer Fortschritt (Einführung zu drei Beiträgen) , in: W. Albers et al. (Eds.): *Handwörterbuch der Wirtschaftwissenschaft*, 7, 1977, 567-569.

41. (with S. Albers) A Procedure for New Product Positioning in an Attribute Space, *European Journal of Operational Research*, 1, 1977, 320-328.

42. Experimente zur Nutzung einer Datenbank, *Zeitschrift für Betriebswirtschaft*, 47, 1977, 509-530.

43.* Zur Diskussion von "Sozialbilanzen" in Frankreich, *Der Betrieb*, 30, 1977, 922-923.

44. Zur Entwicklung der realen Forschungs- und Entwicklungsaufwendungen der industriellen Unternehmen, *Der Betrieb*, 1977, 2289-2295.

45. Zur Bedeutung und Problematik formaler Planungsmodelle für Universitäten, *Führungssysteme für Universitäten*, Stuttgart et al 1977, 275-283.
    45a) Slightly modified version in: *Christiana Albertina*, 7, 1977, 31-39.
    45b) the same in: *Mitteilungen des Hochschulverbandes*, 26, 1978, 49-54.

46. (with F. Vogel) Sozialpolitische Maßnahmen und Arbeitskonflikte in französischen Unternehmen. Ergebnisse einer Cluster-Analyse, *Schriften des Vereins für Sozialpolitik*, 98, 1978, 377-411.

47. (with H. Rehder) Analytische Planung von Produkten im Raum der Produkteigenschaften, in: E. Topritzhofer (Ed.): *Marketing, Neue Ergebnisse aus Forschung und Praxis*, Wiesbaden, 1978, 327-349.

48. Improving the Management of Technology. A. Gerstenfeld, R. Brainard, Technological Innovation: Government-Industry Cooperation (Wiley & Sons): New York et al. 1979, 186-1 95, 268-270.

49. Die Bedeutung von "Sozialbilanzen", *Wirtschaftsdienst*, 58, 1978, 119-122.

50.* Ökonomische Probleme industrieller Forschung, *die pharmazeutische industrie*, 1978, 323-318.
    50a) Printed in: R. Herzog, FuE-Management in der Pharma-Industrie, Aulendorf 1995, 220-228.

51. Zur optimalen mehrperiodigen Produktpositionierung, *Zeitschrift für betriebswirtschaftliche Forschung*, 30, 1978, 257-265.

52. The Present State of the Theory on R&D Management in the Federal Republic of Germany (in Japanese language, translated by Sh. Mori: Doitsu Renpo Kyowakoku ni okeru kenkyu kaihatsu kanri ron ni kansuru gakusetsu no genkyo), *Principles and Strategies of R&D Management* (in japanese: Kenkyu kaihatsu kanri no rifon to taikei), Maruzen Co., Tokyo 1978, 57-76.

53. Verbraucherinformation im Computerdialog, *WiSt Wirtschaftswissenschaftliches Studium, Zeitschrift für Ausbildung und Hochschulkontakt*, 1979, 1, 15.

54. (with S. Albers) A Comparison of Two Approaches to the Optimal Positioning of a New Product in an Attribute Space, *Zeitschrift für Operations Research*, 23, 1979, 127-142.

55. Alternative Approaches for Optimal Product Positioning, in: Allan D. Shocker (Ed.): *Analytic Approaches to Product Marketing Planning,* Cambridge/Mass.: Marketing Science Inst., 1979, 115-124.

56. Der Umfang der Hochschulforschung, *Wissenschaftsrecht, Wissenschaftsverwaltung, Wissenschaftsförderung,* 12, 1979, 185-191.
56a) Shorted version in: Hochschulforschung darf kein bloßes Anhängsel der Lehre sein, *Hochschulpolitische Informationen,* 10 (7), 1979, 3-5.

57. Entwicklungslinien der Betriebswirtschaftslehre, *Christiana Albertina,* 11, 1979, 5-14.

58.* Die realen Forschungs- und Entwicklungsaufwendungen der industriellen Unternehmen, *Der Betrieb,* 32, 1979, 2385-2386.

59. Betriebliche Sozialpolitik und betriebliche Leistung, *Die Betriebswirtschaft,* 39, 1979, 585-600.

60. Forschung und Entwicklung, Programmplanung für die... , in: W. Kern (Ed.): *Handwörterbuch der Produktionswirtschaft.* Stuttgart 1979, 652-671.

61. Wachstumsschwellen und Forschungsschwellen, *Zeitschrift für Betriebswirtschaft,* 50, 1980, 475-499.
61a) Printed in: W. Bierfelder and K.H. Höcker (Eds.): *Systemforschung und Neuerungsmanagement,* Munich, Vienna, 1980, 273-311.

62. (with S. Albers) Optimal Product Attributes in Single Choice Models, *Journal of the Operational Research Society,* 31, 1980, 647-655.

63. Produktpositionierung - Das betriebswirtschaftliche Konzept der Produktgestaltung, *IHS-Journal,* 4, 1980, 199-207.

64.* Die Produktinnovationsrate im Lagebericht, *Der Betrieb,* 34, 1981, 433-437.

65. (with K.-P. Schütt) Preis-Absatz-Funktionen bei Idealpunkt- *Präferenzen, Zeitschrift für Betriebswirtschaft,* 51, 1981, 258-273.

66. Planungskontrolle im Entwicklungsbereich. K. Brockhoff and W. Krelle (Eds.): *Unternehmensplanung,* Berlin, Heidelberg, New York 1981, 173-192.

67. Internationale Forschung über Forschung und Entwicklung, Internationale Betriebswirtschaftslehre, *Zeitschrift für Betriebswirtschaft-Ergänzungsheft* 1981, 98-104.

68. Comment (on: Competition, Innovation, Productivity Growth, and Public Policy), in: H. Giersch (Ed.): *Towards an Explanation of Economic Growth,* Tübingen, 1981, 180-186.

69. Entscheidungsforschung und Entscheidungstechnologie, in: E. Witte (Ed.): *Der Praktische Nutzen empirischer Forschung,* Tübingen 1981, 61-78.

70. Planungsrechnung (Allgemein): *Handwörterbuch des Rechnungswesens*, 2nd edition, Stuttgart 1981, 1309-1331.

71. Betriebliche Sozialpolitik und betriebliche Leistung: Eine Ergänzung, *Die Betriebswirtschaft*, 41, 1981, 279-283.

72. Standards für den Einsatz von Rechnern als Experimentierinstrumente, *Marketing*, 3, 1981, 259-266.

73. A note on product positioning, *European Journal of Operational Research*, 9, 1982, 90-91.

74. Soziale Kosten und negative externe Effekte, *Zeitschrift für Betriebswirtschaft*, 52, 1982, 282-286.

75. Forschung und Entwicklung im Lagebericht, *Die Wirtschaftsprüfung*, 35, 1982, 237-147.

76. A Heuristic Procedure for Project Inspection to Curb Over runs, *IEEE Transactions on Engineering Management*, 29, 1982, 122-128.

77. Consequences of new technologies: Research in business and its limits, in: O. Dietrich and J. Moorley (Eds.): *Relations between Technology, Capital and Labour*, Brussels (Commission of the European Communities), 1982, 113-124.

78.* Gute Prognosen weisen den Weg, *Blick durch die Wirtschaft*, 26, 7.2.1983, 3.

79. Informationsverarbeitung in Entscheidungsprozessen: Skizze einer Taxonomie, *Zeitschrift für Betriebswirtschaft*, 53, 1983, 53-62.

80. Group Processes for Forecasting, (Invited Review), *European Journal of Operations Research*, 13, 1983, 115-127.

81. The measurement of goal attainment of governmental R&D support, *Research Policy*, 12, 1983, 171-182.

82. Prognosen, in: F. X. Bea, E. Dichtl and M. Schweitzer (Eds.): *Allgemeine Betriebswirtschaftslehre*, 2, Stuttgart, 1983, 357-396.
   82a) 2nd modified edition, Stuttgart 1985, 360-400.
   82b) 3rd modified edition, Stuttgart 1987, 413-454.
   82c) 4th modified edition, Stuttgart 1989, 413-454.
   82d) 5th modified edition, Stuttgart 1991, 551-592.
   82e) 6th modified edition, Stuttgart 1993, 560-599.
   82f) Prognosi. Ekonomika Predpriatija, Tom 2, Glawna 4, Moscow 1997.
   82g) 7th modified edition, Stuttgart 1997, 653-696.
   82h) Yosoku. Ippan Keieikeizaigaku (japanese translation), 2, Stuttgart 1999, 202-226.
   82i) 2nd russian edition, Moscow 2001.
   82j) 8th modified edition, Stuttgart 2001, 715-752.

83. Kontrolle und Revision der Forschung und Entwicklung. *Handwörterbuch der Revision*, Stuttgart 1983, 421-437.

84.* Neue Werkstoffe als Problem der unternehmerischen Technologiepolitik, (short version), *ÖIAG Journal*, 4, 1983, 3-7.

85. On the Relationship between R&D and International Competitiveness in the Case of Denmark 1970-1980 (Comment) , in: Centre National de la Recherche Scientifique et al (Eds.) : *Actes du colloque sur l'économétrie de la recherche*, Paris, 1983, 481-487.

86. Probleme marktorientierter Forschungs- und Entwicklungspolitik, in: J. Mazanec and F. Scheuch (Eds.): *Marktorientierte Unternehmensführung*, Vienna, 1984, 337-374.

87. Gebührenregelung für den Tiefseebergbau nach der Seerechtskonvention, *Zeitschrift für Betriebswirtschaft*, 54, 1984, 448-461.

88. Vergütungen für die Nutzung von Erstanmelder-Informationen in Zulassungs- und Registrierverfahren, *Zeitschrift für Betriebswirtschaft*, 54, 1984, 997-1015.

89. Forschung und Entwicklung, in: M. Bitz et al. (Eds.): *Vahlens Kompendium der Betriebswirtschaftslehre*, Munich, 1984, 159-186.
89a) 2nd modified edition, 1989, 163-191.
89b) 3rd modified edition., 1993, 171-201.
89c) Isseldowanie i raswitie. Kratkii kurs pa ekonomike predpriatia, Russian translation, Kiev, 1998, 7-34.

90.* Forschungs- und Entwicklungscontrolling, *Die Betriebswirtschaft*, 1984, 44, 681-682.

91. The production ceiling according to the United Nations Convention on the Law of the Sea, *Weltwirtschaftliches Archiv*, 120, 1984, 541-557.

92. Technologischer Wandel und Unternehmenspolitik, *Zeitschrift für betriebswirtschaftliche Forschung*, 36, 1984, 619-635.
92a) short version printed as: Die wachsende Bedeutung des technologischen Wandels für die Unternehmenspolitik, *Jahrbuch für Betriebswirte 1985*, Stuttgart 1984, 36-44.

93. Forschungs- und Entwicklungsproduktivität als Aufgabe des Forschungs- und Entwicklungsmanagement, in: M. Domsch and E. Jochum (Eds.): *Personal-Management in der industriellen Forschung und Entwicklung (F&E)*, Cologne et al. 1984, 1-15.

94. Controlling in Forschung und Entwicklung, *Zeitschrift für betriebswirtschaftliche Forschung*, 36, 1984, 608-618.

94a) Printed in: *Betriebswirtschaftliches Kontaktstudium, Finanz- und Rechnungswesen. Beiträge aus Wissenschaft und Praxis,* Stuttgart 1985, 172-182.

95. (with B. Waldeck) The Robustness of PREFMAP-2, *International Journal of Research in Marketing,* 1, 1984, 215-233.

96. (with S. Albers) Die Gültigkeit der Ergebnisse eines Testmarktsimulators bei unterschiedlichen Daten und Auswertungsmethoden, *Zeitschrift für betriebswirtschaftliche Forschung,* 37, 985, 191-227.
   96a) short version: Testmarktsimulator zum Produkttest in kleinen und mittleren Unternehmen, in: H. Albach and Th. Held (Eds.): *Betriebswirtschaftslehre mittelständischer Unternehmen,* Stuttgart 1984, 413-427.

97. Forecasting Quality and Information, *Journal of Forecasting,* 3, 1984, 417-428.

98.* Innovation im Spannungsfeld zwischen Hersteller und Handel, shortened version entitled "Das Angebot muß vielfältig werden", Lebensmittelzeitung vom 18.1.1985, F24/F25.

99. Die Produktinnovationsrate als Instrument der strategischen Unternehmensplanung, *Zeitschrift für Betriebswirtschaft,* 55, 1985, 459-476.
   99a) short version: Produktinnovationsrate als Planungsinstrument, in: D. Ohse et al. (Eds.): *Operations Research Proceedings* 1984, Berlin et al 1985, 63-70.

100. Optimal Compensation for Data Sharing in Registration Processes, *Management Science,* 31, 1985, 1142-1149.

101.* Wie effizient sind Forschung und Entwicklung?, *Blick durch die Wirtschaft,* 5.9.1985, 3.
   101a) Printed in: E. Staudt, (Ed.): *Das Management von Innovationen,* Frankfurt , 1986, 343-355.

102. Die optimale Ausgleichszahlung für die Datennutzung in Zulassungsverfahren, *Betriebs-Berater,* 40, 1985, 488 -490.
   102a) same in: *Pharma Recht,* 8, 1985, 59-63.

103.* Produktpolitik zwischen Einzel- und Gesellschaftsinteresse, short version printed in: Produktpolitik, Schädlicher Nutzen, *Wirtschaftswoche,* 39, 17.5.1985, 80, 85, 86, 90, 92.
   103a) Printed in: *Marketing im Spannungsfeld von Wirtschaft und Gesellschaft,* Stuttgart 1995, 44-51.

104.* Marktbearbeitung im Spannungsfeld zwischen Herstellern und Handel: Ändert sich der Stellenwert von Verkaufsförderung und Verkaufstraining? *BDVT intern,* 84, 1985, 8-20.

105.* Produktpolitik - Spannungsfeld zwischen Herstellern und Handel: *Markenartikel,* 7, 1985, 355 et sqq.

106.* Computergestützte Informationssysteme: Gebrauchtwagen über Bildschirm anbieten. *Absatzwirtschaft*, 8, 1985, 56-61.

107. Produktinnovationsrate und Unternehmensentwicklung, in: G. Bombach, B. Gahlen, and A.E. Ott (Eds.): *Industrieökonomik: Theorie und Empirie, Schriftenreihe des wirtschaftswissenschaftlichen Seminars Ottobeuren*, 14, Tübingen 1985, 87-101.

108. Experimental test of MCDM algorithms in a modular approach. *European Journal of Operational Research*, 22, 1985, 159-166.

109. Abstimmungsprobleme von Marketing- und Technologiepolitik, *Die Betriebswirtschaft*, 45, 1985, 623-632.

110. Erfahrungen mit einem Austauschverfahren der Clusteranalyse für gemischtskalierte Daten, *Jahrbuch der Absatz- und Verbrauchsforschung*, 4, 1985, 357-370.

111. Beiträge der Marketing-Wissenschaft zur Strategiediskussion, *Marketing ZFP*, 7, 1985, 212-213.

112. Überlegungen zu einem Qualifizierungsprogramm "Innovationsmanagement", in: Bundesminister für Bildung und Wissenschaft (Ed.): *Wissens- und Technologietransfer aus deutschen und britischen Hochschulen, Schriftenreihe Studien zu Bildung und Wissenschaft*, 30, 1986, 170-175.

113. Die Produktivität der Forschung und Entwicklung eines Industrieunternehmens, *Zeitschrift für Betriebswirtschaft*, 56, 1986, 525-537.

114.* Mit Marketing Erträge sichern. Was die Marketing-Wissenschaft dazu beitragen kann, *Marketing ZFP*, 8, 1986, 136-141.

115. (with U. Andresen) Verbundanalyse zur Gestaltung von Preisausschreiben, *Zeitschrift für betriebswirtschaftliche Forschung*, 38, 1986, 779-787.

116.* (with U. Andresen) Preisausschreiben - lohnt sich das? *Absatzwirtschaft*, 29, 1986, 8, 92-97.

117. Zur Zweitantragstellerfrage im Regierungsentwurf des Arzneimittelgesetzes, *die Pharmazeutische Industrie*, 48, 1986, 736-740.

118. Marktsättigung, (DBW-Stichwort) *Die Betriebswirtschaft*, 46, 1986, 514-515.

119. Decision Quality and Information, in: E. Witte and H.J. Zimmermann, (Eds.): *Empirical Research on Organizational Decision Making*, Amsterdam 1986, 249-265.

120. Spitzentechnik, *WiSt Wirtschaftswissenschaftliches Studium*, 15, 1986, 431-435.

121.* Markentreue hat ihren Preis. Der Zigaretten-Preiskampf von 1983 aus heutiger Sicht betrachtet. *Lebensmittel-Zeitung*, 45, 7.11.1986, F36.

122. Die Produktivität der Forschung und Entwicklung eines Industrieunternehmens: Eine Erwiderung. *Zeitschrift für Betriebswirtschaft*, 57, 1987, 81-85.

123. Anforderungen an das Management in der Zukunft, *Zeitschrift für Betriebswirtschaft*, 57, 1987, 239-250.

124. Wettbewerbsfähigkeit und Innovation, in: Dichtl, E., W. Gerke, and A. Kieser (Eds.): *Innovation und Wettbewerbsfähigkeit*, Wiesbaden 1987, 53-74.

125. Budgetierungsstrategien für Forschung und Entwicklung, *Zeitschrift für Betriebswirtschaft*, 57, 1987, 846-869.

126.* Absatzwirtschaftliche Anforderungen an die Fleischwarenindustrie. *Fleischwirtschaft*, 8, 1987, 910-919.

127. Der Innovationsaufwand in Unternehmen der forschenden pharmazeutischen Industrie, *die pharmazeutische Industrie*, 49, 1987, 1109-1117.
127a) printed in: Arzneimittelforschung - um welchen Preis. *Neue Untersuchungen zu Kosten und Nutzen der Arzneimittelforschung*, Aulendorf 1988, 5-21.
127b) printed in: R. Herzog, (Ed.): *FuE-Management in der Pharma-Industrie*, Aulendorf 1995, 287-300.

128. Die Förderung der Meeresforschung und Meerestechnik durch den Bund, *Technologie & Management*, 36, 1987, 4, 42-50.

129. Price Indexes to Calculate Real R&D Expenditures, *Management Science*, 34, 1988, 131-134.

130. Einige einfache ökonomische Regeln zur optimalen Ausstrahlungsdauer für Werbesendungen, *Werbeforschung & Praxis*, 33, 1988, 89-91.

131. Die Bewährung von Gutenbergs Preis-Absatz-Funktion im Zigarettenmarkt, *Zeitschrift für Betriebswirtschaft*, 58, 1988, 828-838.

132. Marktstruktur und Marktzugangsbedingungen in europäischen Offshore-Märkten, *Die Betriebswirtschaft*, 48, 1988, 477-487.

133. Beschränkungen des Marktzutritts in den europäischen Offshore-Märkten, *Christiana Albertina*, 26, 1988, 5-12.

134. Werbeblocklänge und Werbereichweite, *Werbeforschung & Praxis*, 33, 1988, 162-164.

135. (with A. Chakrabarti) R&D/Marketing Linkage and Innovation Strategy: Some West German Experience, *IEEE Transactions on Engineering Management*, 35, 1988, 167-174.

136.* (with T.G.J. von Ghyczy, W. Wilhelm) Die großen Drei im Test (F+E Enquête), *Manager Magazin*, 18, 1988, 185-197; 1988, 219-229; (with W. Wilhelm); 1989, 84-89.

137. (with Ch. Urban) Die Beeinflussung der Entwicklungsdauer, *Zeitmanagement in Forschung und Entwicklung*, special edition *23 der Zeitschrift für betriebswirtschaftliche Forschung*, 1988, 1-42.

138. (with H. Braun) PED - Ein Programm zur optimalen Planung der Entwicklungsdauer, *Zeitmanagement in Forschung und Entwicklung, Sonderheft 23 der Zeitschrift für betriebswirtschaftliche Forschung*, 1988, 74-85.

139. Wettbewerbsvorteile durch Informationstechnik. Ein Gebrauchtwagen – Informationssystem und sein Einsatz für das Marketing. *WiSt Wirtschaftswissenschaftliches Studium*, 17, 1988, 526-527.

140.* Das Marketing der ausgezeichneten Unternehmen. Leistungsmerkmale und Erfolgsfaktoren, in: Deutsche Marketing Vereinigung (Ed.): *Die Ausgezeichneten. Erfolgswege und Leistungskriterien Deutscher Marketing-Preisträger*. Stuttgart 1988, 14-39.

141. (with N. Dobberstein), Zapping: Zur Umgehung von TV-Werbewahrnehmung. *Marketing ZFP*, 11, 1989, 27-40.

142. (with H. Braun) Optimierung der Sendezeit im Werbefernsehen, *Zeitschrift für Betriebswirtschaft*, 59, 1989, 609-619.

143. Forschungs- und Entwicklungscontrolling, *Controlling*, 1, 1989, 123.
143a) printed in: *Controlling-Lexikon*, München, 1991.

144. Some Thoughts on a Qualifying Programme for Innovation Management, in: R. Miège and F. Mahieux (Eds.): *Training in Innovation Management, Commission of the European Communities*, Brüssel, Luxemburg 1989, 51-54, 145.

145. Forschungsförderung für das Technologie- und Innovationsmanagement, *technologie und management*, 38, 3, 1989, +33-37.

146. Research and Development. *Handbook of German Business Management*, 2, Stuttgart, Heidelberg et al. 1989, 2120-2134.

147. Funktionsbereichsstrategien, Wettbewerbsvorteile und Bewertungskriterien. Eine empirische Untersuchung am Beispiel der Biotechnologie. *Zeitschrift für Betriebswirtschaft*, 60, 1990, 451-472.
147a) printed in: H. Albach (Ed.): *Industrielles Management*, Wiesbaden 1993, 470-491.

148. Innovationsmanagement als Ausbildungsaufgabe, in: H.J. Schuster (Ed.): *Handbuch des Wissenschaftstransfers*, (Springer) Berlin et al., 1990, 565-575.

149. R&D and Marketing Productivities from Cross-Sectional Data: A Study of German Chemical Corporations, *R&D Management*, 20, 1990, 255-259.

150.* Forschung und Entwicklung. Blick durch die Wirtschaft (*Frankfurter Allgemeine Zeitung*): part 1: 26.2.1991; part 2: 1.3.1991.
150a) printed in: K. Küting and A. Schnorbus, (Eds.): *Betriebswirtschaftslehre heute*. Frankfurt am Main 1992, 35-39.

151. Koordinationsprobleme zwischen Forschung und Entwicklung und Marketing. *F&E und Marketing, Dokumentation eines Workshops (Wissenschaftliche Gesellschaft für Marketing und Unternehmensführung e.V.),* Münster 1991, 4-22.

152.* Ursachen mangelnder Effektivität und Effizienz, *F+E Jahrbuch* 1991, 30-33.

153.* Forschungs- und Entwicklungscontrolling zur Steigerung der Forschungs- und Entwicklungs-Effektivität, *Controlling*,3 , 1991, 60-66.

154. Competitor Technology Intelligence in German Companies, *Industrial Marketing Management*, 20, 1991, 91-98.

155. (with A.K. Gupta and Ch. Rotering) Inter-firm R&D Cooperations in Germany, *Technovation*, 11, 1991, 219-230.

156. Zur Optimierung der Entwicklungsdauer neuer Produkte, in: K.-P. Kistner and R. Schmidt (Eds.): *Unternehmensdynamik. Horst Albach zum 60. Geburtstag*. Wiesbaden 1991, 19-32.

157. Indicators of Firm Patent Activities, in: D. F. Kocaoglu and K. Niwa (Eds.): *Technology Management. The New International Language. (Proceedings of PICMET 91),* Portland/OR 1991, 476-481.

158. The Production Regulation of the Law of the Sea Convention: An Assessment and Alternatives, in: R. Wolfrum (Ed.): *Law of the Sea at the Crossroads: The Continuing Search for an Universally Accepted Régime*, Berlin 1991, 251-262.

159. R&D Cooperation Between Firms: A Classification by Structural Variables, *International Journal of Technology Management*, 6, 1991, 361-373.

160. Überwachung der Forschung und Entwicklung. *Handwörterbuch der Revision*, Stuttgart 1992, 567-583.

161. (with A. v. Boehmer and A. Pearson) The Management of International Research and Development, in: Buckley Peter J. and Michael Z. Brooke (Eds.): *International Business Studies: An Overview, Blackwell Publishers*, Oxford 1992, 495-509.

162. Unternehmer im Übergang zur Marktwirtschaft, *Wirtschaftswissenschaftliches Studium*, 21, 1992, 93-97.
162a) printed in: *Marketing im Spannungsfeld von Wirtschaft und Gesellschaft*, Stuttgart 1995, 144-152.

163. Instruments for Patent Data Analyses in Business Firms, *Technovation*, 12, 1992, 41-59.

164. (with A.K. Gupta, U. Weisenfeld) Making Trade-Offs in the New Product Development Process: A German/U.S. Comparison, *Journal of Product Innovation Management*, 9, 1992, 11-18.

165.* (with P. Bauer) Kennzahlenberechnung für Forschung und Entwicklung. *RKW Handbuch Forschung, Entwicklung, Konstruktion (F+E)*, Kennzahl 4070, Berlin 1992, 1-22.

166. R&D Cooperation Between Firms - A Perceived Transaction Cost Perspective, *Management Science*, 38, 1992, 514-524.

167. The Measurement of R&D Program Effectiveness at the Firm Level, Proceedings, *The First International Federation of Scholary Associations of Management Conference*, Tokyo 1992, 160-165.

168.* (with H. Krawinkel) Sponsoring für Museen, *Museumskunde*, 57, 1992, 119-126.
168a) shortened version in: *Absatzwirtschaft*, Oktober 1992 (Sondernummer), 220-226.

169. (with A. Pearson) Technical and Marketing Aggressiveness and the Effectiveness of Research and Development, *IEEE Transactions on Engineering Management*, 39, 1992, 318-324.

170. Zur Nutzung der Gewinn- und Verlustrechnung nach "neuem Recht" für die Analyse von Inventions- und Innovationspotentialen, in: K. Boysen et al. (Eds.): *Der Wirtschaftsprüfer vor innovativen Herausforderungen. Festschrift für Hans-Heinrich Otte*. Stuttgart 1992, 1-16.

171. Technologiemanagement - Das S-Kurven-Konzept, in: J. Hauschildt and O. Grün, (Eds.): *Ergebnisse empirischer betriebswirtschaftlicher Forschung. Zur Realtheorie der Unternehmung. Festschrift für Eberhard Witte*. Stuttgart 1993, 327-334.

172. Zur Erfolgsbeurteilung von Forschungs- und Entwicklungsprojekten, *Zeitschrift für Betriebswirtschaft*, 63, 1993, 643-662.

173. (with J. Hauschildt) Schnittstellenmanagement - Koordination ohne Hierarchie, *Zeitschrift Führung und Organisation*, 62, 1993, 396-403.
173a) shortened version, translated by J. Guan. Zhong, Wai Ke Ji Zheng, Zhe Yu Guan Li (Science and Technology International) 1997, 17-21, titled „Jie Mian Guan Li - Wu Deng Ji De Xie Tiao".

174. Produktpolitik, *Handwörterbuch der Betriebswirtschaft*, 5th ed., Stuttgart 1993, 3530-3545.

175. (with A. v. Boehmer) Global R&D activities of German industrial firms, *Journal of Scientific & Industrial Research*, 52, 1993, 399-406.

176. (with A.W. Pearson, A. v. Boehmer) Decision parameters in global R&D management, *R&D Management*, 23, 1993, 249-262.

177.* F&E - Projekte rechtzeitig abbrechen, *Frankfurter Brief für Unternehmensführung*, 4, Oktober 1993, 1-4.

178. (mit C. Zanger) Meßprobleme des Neuheitsgrades - dargestellt am Beispiel von Software, *Zeitschrift für betriebswirtschaftliche Forschung*, 45, 1993, 835-851.

179. (with V.R. Rao) Toward a demand forecasting model for preannounced new technological products, *Journal of Engineering and Technology Management*, 10, 1993, 211-228.

180. (with J. Hauschildt) Plädoyer für eine bedürfnisgerechte Differenzierung der Ausbildung in der Betriebswirtschaftslehre, *Zeitschrift für Betriebswirtschaft – appendix issue*, 3, 1993, 27-40.

181. (with K. Warschkow) Conditions for government support of private research and development, *European Journal of Operational Research*, 71, 1993, 454-462.

182. Forschungs- und Entwicklungsaufwand und Umsatzwachstum - eine Ergänzung zu Gierl/Kotzbauer, *Zeitschrift für betriebswirtschaftliche Forschung*, 46, 1994, 171-174.

183. Forschungs- und Entwicklungsfinanzierung als Wachstumsschwelle?, in: H. Albach (Ed.): *Globale Soziale Marktwirtschaft. Ziele - Wege - Akteure. Festschrift für Professor Dr. Dr. Santiago Garcia Echevarria aus Anlaß seines sechzigsten Geburtstages*, Wiesbaden 1994, 339-356.

184. R&D Project Termination Decisions by Discriminant Analysis - An International Comparison, *IEEE Transactions on Engineering Management*, 41, 1994, 245-254.

185. (with J. Guan) Stochastic Factors Affecting the Diffusion of a Technological Innovation - A Sytematic Review, *Journal of Systems Science and Systems Engineering*, 3, 1994, 241-256.

186. (with A. Pearson) The uncertainty map and project management, *Project Appraisal*, 9, 1994, 211-215.

187. Zur Theorie des externen Erwerbs neuen technologischen Wissens, *Zeitschrift für Betriebswirtschaft, appendix issue*, 1, 1995, 27-42.

188. Management der Schnittstellen zwischen Forschung und Entwicklung sowie Marketing, in: E. Zahn (Ed.): *Handbuch Technologie-Management*, Stuttgart 1995, 437-453.

189. (with Th. Teichert) Cooperative R&D and partners' measures of success, *International Journal of Technology Management*, 10, 1995, 111-123.

190. F&E und Umwelt, in: Junkernheinrich, M., P. Klemmer, and G.R. Wagner (Eds.): *Handbuch zur Umweltökonomie*, Berlin 1995, 30-37.

191. Innovationsmanagement. *Handwörterbuch des Marketing*, 2. edition, Stuttgart 1995, 981-995.

192. Marktsättigung. *Handwörterbuch des Marketing,* 2. edition., Stuttgart 1995, 1793-1802.

193.* (with R. Balachandra) Are R&D Project Termination Factors Universal? *Research Technology Management,* 38, 4, 31-36.

194. Generic Drug Approval, in: H. Albach and St. Rosenkranz (Eds.): *Intellectual Property Rights and Global Competition, Towards a New Synthesis,* Berlin 1995, 215-230.

195. Value Generation by industrial research, *Technovation,* 15, 1995, 591-599.

196. (with J. Guan) Das Diffusionsmodell von Bass als Ankunftsprozeß-Modell, *Marketing ZFP,* 17, 1995, 255-258.

197. Forschung und Entwicklung. Handwörterbuch der Produktionswirtschaft, 2. edition, Stuttgart 1996, 539-554.

198. (with J. Guan) Innovation via new ventures as a conversion strategy for the Chinese defense industry. *R&D Management,* 26, 1, 1996, 49-56.

199. (with R. Balachandra, A.W. Pearson) Career Consequences and Communication of Project Termination Decisions, *Journal of Product Innovation Management,* 13, 1996, 245-256.

200. Technology Management in the Company of the Future, *Technology Analysis & Strategic Management,* 8, 1996, 175-189.

201. (with Bernd Schmaul) Organization, Autonomy, and Success of Internationally Dispersed R&D Facilities, *IEEE Transactions on Engineering Management,* 43, 1996, 33-40.

202. Anforderungen an eine wissenschaftliche Ausbildung in der Betriebswirtschaftslehre und ihre Konsequenzen, *Zeitschrift für Betriebswirtschaft-Ergänzungsheft* 1, 1996, 41-53.

203. (with A.K. Chakrabarti, J. Hauschildt, A.W. Pearson) Managing Interfaces. Gerard H. "Gus" Gaynor, *Handbook of Technology Management,* New York et al 1996, 27.1 - 27.17.

204. Forschung und Entwicklung, in: W. Eversheim and G. Schuch (Eds.): *>Betriebshütte< Teil 1: Produktion und Management,* 7.A., Berlin, Heidelberg, New York 1996, 6.-1 bis 6.-14.

205. Strategic Issues of Technolgy Management, Rencontres Internationales de la Gestion. La gestion de l'immatériel. *IFSAM,* Paris 1996, 87-94.

206. Reaktionen von Unternehmen auf Wechsel staatlicher Technologiepolitik, in: K. Pinkau and Ch. Stahlberg (Eds.): *Technologiepolitik in demokratischen Gesellschaften,* Stuttgart 1996, 9-22.

207. R&D management in German companies, in: W. Krull and F. Meyer-Krahmer (Eds.): *Science and Technology in Germany*, London, 1996, 165-180.

208. Steuerung der Forschung durch abgestimmten Potentialaufbau, *Zeitschrift für Betriebswirtschaft*, 67, 1997, 453-469.

209. Wenn der Kunde stört - Differenzierungsnotwendigkeiten bei der Einbeziehung von Kunden in die Produktentwicklung, in: M. Bruhn and H. Steffenhagen (Eds.): *Marktorientierte Unternehmensführung, Festschrift für Heribert Meffert zum 60. Geburtstag*, Wiesbaden 1997, 351-370.
209a) 2. edition, 1998.

210. (with G. Koch, A.W. Pearson) Business Process Re-engineering: Experiences in R&D, *Technology Analysis & Strategic Management*, 9, 1997, 163-178.

211. Ist die kollektive Regelung einer Vergütung von Arbeitnehmererfindungen wirksam und nötig? *Zeitschrift für Betriebswirtschaft*, 67, 1997, 677-687.

212. Necessary Conditions for Successful Company Research, in: D. Kocaoglu et al. (Eds.): *Proceedings of PICMET '97*, Portland, OR 1997, 508-511.
212a) the same as: Papers Presented at *PICMET '97*, CD-ROM.

213. Betriebswirtschaftliche Erkenntnisse und rechtliche Normsetzung, *Zeitschrift für Betriebswirtschaft - special issue*, 4, 1997, 1-6.

214.* Management betrieblicher Forschung und Entwicklung, FuE Info, *Stifterverband für die Deutsche Wissenschaft*, 2, 1997, 14-15.

215.* (with A.K. Chakrabarti) Take a Proactive Approach to Negotiating Your R&D Budget, *Research .Technology Management*, 1997, Sept./Oct, 37-41.

216. Indirekte Aktivierung von immateriellem Anlagevermögen als Beitrag zur Unternehmenssanierung: Die Fälle Philips und Fokker, in: H.U. Küpper, and E. Troßmann (Eds.): *Das Rechnungswesen im Spannungsfeld zwischen strategischem und operativem Management. Festschrift für Marcell Schweitzer zum 65. Geburtstag*, Berlin 1997, 89-104.

217.* Kunden als Entwicklungspartner - ein Königsweg zum Markterfolg? *Signale aus der WHU Koblenz*, 4, 1997, 5-7.

218. Technology management as part of strategic planning – some empirical results, *R&D Management*, 28, 1998, 129-138.
218a) printed in: *Readings in Technology Management*, Enschede 2000, 23-42.

219. (with J. Leker) Zur Identifikation von Unternehmensstrategien, *Zeitschrift für Betriebswirtschaft*, 68, 1998, 1201-1223.

220. Patentierung von Hochschullehrererfindungen, in: N. Franke and C.-F. von Braun, (Eds.): *Innovationsforschung und Technologiemanagement*, Berlin et al., 1998, 49-61.

221. (with A. Pearson) R&D Budgeting Reactions to a Recession, *Management International Review*, 38, 1998, 363-376.

222. Strategieidentifikation und Strategiewechsel, in: Wagner, G.R. (Ed.): *Unternehmensführung, Ethik und Umwelt, zum 65. Geburtstag, Hartmut Kreikebaum*, Wiesbaden 1999, 210-225.

223. Steuerkreise schaffen, in: Stifterverband für die deutsche Wissenschaft (Ed.): *Public Private Partnership. Neue Formen der Zusammenarbeit von öffentlicher Wirtschaft und privater Wirtschaft*, Essen 1999, 40-45.

224. Zur Dynamik technologischer Kompetenzen, in: Albach, H., Eymann, E., Luhmer, A. and Steven, M. (Eds.): *Die Theorie der Unternehmung in Forschung und Praxis*, Berlin, Heidelberg 1999, 475-495.
224a) Dynamics of technological competencies, in: Albach, H., et al. (Eds.): *Theory of the Firm*, Berlin et al. 2000, 185-209.
224b) Dynamics of technological competencies, in: Brockhoff, K., Chakrabarti, A.K. and Hauschildt, J. (Eds.): *The Dynamics of Innovation*, Berlin et al. 1999, 31-56.

225. Theorien für Unternehmen – Erich Gutenbergs Leistungen, in: Albach, H., E. Eymann, A. Luhmer, and M. Steven (Eds.): *Die Theorie der Unternehmung in Forschung und Praxis*, Berlin, Heidelberg 1999, 1-6

226. Innovationen in Gruppen quasi-homogener Investitionsgüter, *Zeitschrift für Betriebswirtschaft – special issue* 2, 1999, 23-34.

227. Leistungen der Betriebswirtschaftslehre für Wirtschaft und Gesellschaft, in: A. Egger, O. Grün and R. Moser (Eds.): *Managementinstrumente und – konzepte. Entstehung, Verbreitung und Bedeutung für die Betriebswirtschaftslehre*, Stuttgart 1999, 27-61.

228. (with J.W. Medcof) Cooperation, participation, planning and performance in internationally dispersed research and development units, in: Nitsch, D. (Ed.): *Proceedings of the Annual Conference of the Administrative Sciences Association of Canada, International Business Division*, 1999, 20(8): 1-9.

229. (with A.K. Chakrabarti, M. Kirchgeorg) Corporate Strategies in Environmental Management, *Research Technology Management*, 42, 4, 26-30.

230.* Wissensbereitstellung einüben – Transfer von Ergebnissen aus der Grundlagenforschung in die wirtschaftliche Anwendung steht im Mittelpunkt vieler Debatten, *Wissenschaftsmanagement*, 5, 1999, 17-19.

231. (with H. Ernst, E. Hundhausen) Gains and Pains from Licensing. Patent-Portfolios as Strategic Weapons in the Cardiac Rhythm Management Industry, *Technovation*, 19, 1999, 605-614.

232. Zum Transfer von Ergebnissen öffentlicher Grundlagenforschung in die Wirtschaft, *Zeitschrift für Betriebswirtschaft*, 69, 1999, 1331-1350.
232a) printed in: Wirtschaft und Wissenschaft – eine Allianz mit Zukunft in Deutschland? *Max-Planck-Forum*, 1, 1999, 21-42 (discussion 43-50).

233. Zur Entstehung der Innovationsforschung in Deutschland, in: K. Pinkau and Ch. Stahlberg (Eds.): *Wie finden Innovationsprozesse statt? Zehn Jahre Karl Heinz Beckurts-Stiftung*, Stuttgart, Leipzig 2000, 19-28.

234. Technological progress and the market value of firms, *International Journal of Management Reviews*, 1, 1999, 485-501.
234a) printed in: *Readings in Technology Management*, Enschede 2000, 43-62.

235. Die Auswahl von Patentdatenbanken für das Technologiemanagement, Häflinger, in: G.E. and Meier, J.D. (Eds.): *Aktuelle Tendenzen im Innovationsmanagement, Festschrift für Werner Popp zum 65. Geburtstag*, Heidelberg 2000, 93-102.

236. Innovationsmanagement als Technologiemanagement, *Betriebswirtschaftslehre für Technologie und Innovation – eine Leistungsbilanz*, in: S. Albers, K. Brockhoff, and J. Hauschildt (Eds.): Kiel 2000, 17-64.
236 a) printed in: *Technologie- und Innovationsmanagement*, Wiesbaden 2001, 17-78.

237. (with J. Langholz) Überwachung des technischen Fortschritts: das Beispiel der Klassifikationsgesellschaften im Schiffbau, *Die Betriebswirtschaft*, 60, 2000, 336-349.

238. Problems of Evaluating R&D Projects as Real Options, in: Frenkel, M., Hommel, U. and Rudolf, M. (Eds.): *Risk Management – Challenge and Opportunity, Festschrift für Günter Dufey zum 60. Geburtstag*, Berlin/Heidelberg/New York 2000, 203-212.
238a) 2. edition, Berlin/Heidelberg/New York 2001, 203 - 212

239. (with A.W. Pearson) Technology Management – where do we stand, *Readings in Technology Management*, Enschede 2000, 7-21.

240. Produktinnovation, in: Albers, S. and Herrmann, A. (Eds.): *Handbuch für Produktmanagement*, Wiesbaden 2000, 25-54.
240 a) 2. edition, Wiesbaden 2002, 25-54.

241.* Technologiemanagement bei Unternehmenszusammenschlüssen, *Industrie Management*, 16, 2000, 5, 14-18.

242.* Innovationswiderstände, in: Dold, E. and Gentsch, P. (Eds.): *Innovationsmanagement*, Neuwied 2000, 115-126.

243. (with S. Albers, J. Hauschildt) Erwartungen, in: S. Albers, K. Brockhoff and J. Hausschildt (Eds.): *Technologie- und Innovationsmanagement* Wiesbaden 2001, 1-16.

244. (mit D. Tscheulin) Studentische Einstellung zum Unternehmertum, *Zeitschrift für Betriebswirtschaft*, 71, 2001, 345 – 350.

245. Neue Herausforderung an die Berichterstattung über Forschung und Entwicklung, in: K. Boysen, C. Dyckerhoff and H. Otte (Eds.): *Der Wirtschaftsprüfer und sein Umfeld zwischen Tradition und Wandel zu Beginn des 21. Jahrhunderts, Festschrift zum 75. Geburtstag von Hans-Heinrich Otte),* Düsseldorf 2001, 49 – 66.

246. (with J. Gerwin) Nicht länger im Verborgenen – Jahresabschlusspublizität von Forschungszentren, *Wissenschaftsmanagement*, 7, 2001, 8-13.

247* Die neuen Medien erfordern neue Strukturen, *Stifterverband für die Deutsche Wissenschaft, Campus online: Hochschulen, neue Medien und der globale Bildungsmarkt,* Essen 2001, 8-19.

248. Verlässlichkeit von Praktiker-Prognosen von Forschungs- und Entwicklungsbudgetänderungen, in: W. Hamel and H. G. Gemünden (Eds.): *Außergewöhnliche Entscheidungen, Festschrift für Jürgen Hauschildt, Munich* 2001, 579-596.

249. Die Erzeugung neuen technologischen Wissens als unternehmerische Aufgabe, in: D. Sadowski, (Ed.): *Entrepreneurial Spirits, Horst Albach zum 70. Geburtstag,* Wiesbaden 2001, 5-30.

250. (with U. Weisenfeld-Schenk, O. Fisscher, and A. W. Pearson) Managing Technology as a Virtual Enterprise, *R&D Management*, 31, 2001, 323 – 334.

251. Forschung und Entwicklung, in: G. Festel, A. Hassan, J. Leher and P. Bamelis (Eds.): *Betriebswirtschaftslehre für Chemiker,* Berlin et al., 2001, 151–166.

252. Technologie und Technik in der Dienstleistungsmarketing-Forschung, *Die Unternehmung*, 56, 2002, 50 – 54.

253. Forschung an privaten Hochschulen. Das Beispiel Wissenschaftliche Hochschule für Unternehmensführung Vallendar, *Wissenschaftsmanagement*, 8, 2002, 2, 16-19.

254. Erhaltung eines Stiftungsvermögens. *Zeitschrift für betriebswirtschaftliche Forschung*, 54, 2002, 277 – 284.

255. FuE-Controlling. *Handwörterbuch Unternehmensrechnung und Controlling,* Stuttgart 2002, 597 - 606.

256. Ökonomische Aspekte der Bedeutung der Gentechnologie, in: K. Köchy et al. (Eds.): *Gentechnologie als Wirtschaftsfaktor – Definitionen und Bewertungskriterien,* Heidelberg/Berlin 2002, 62 – 67.

257. Technologie- und Innovationsmanagement – Zur Entfaltung einer betriebswirtschaftlichen Teildisziplin, E. Gaugler and R. Köhler (Eds.): *Entwicklungen der Betriebswirtschaftslehre*, Stuttgart 2002, 387 – 409.

258. Aufgaben für die Controlling-Forschung – Versuch einer Außensicht, in: Weber, J. and B. Hirsch (Eds.): *Controlling als akademische Disziplin. Eine Bestandsaufnahme.* Wiesbaden 2002, 449-465.
258 a) printed in: *Zeitschrift für Controlling und Management*, 47, 2003, 33 - .40.

259. Technologiemanagement als Wissensmanagement. *Berichte und Abhandlungen der Berlin-Brandenburgischen Akademie der Wissenschaften*, 9, 2002, 11 - 32.

260. A utopian view of R&D functions, *R&D Management*, 33, 2003, 31 – 36.

261. Customers' perspectives of involvement in new product development, *International Journal of Technology Management*, 26, 2003, 464 – 481.

262. Management privater Hochschulen in Deutschland, *Zeitschrift für Betriebswirtschaft – special issue*, 3, 2003, 1 – 23.

263. Optimierung der Vermögensanlage einer Stiftung, in: H. Kötz, P. Rawert, K. Schmidt and W. Walz (Eds.): *Non Profit Law Year Book*, Köln 2003, 221 – 234.

264.* Nur nicht in den blauen Himmel hinein, *Wissenschaftsmanagement*, 9, 2003, 26-34.

265. Durchsetzung von Innovationen, in: H. Hungenberg and J. Meffert, (Eds.): *Handbuch Strategisches Management*, Wiesbaden 2003, 579-593.

3 Editor

Schriftenreihe: Betriebswirtschaftslehre für Technologie und Innovation, Wiesbaden 1994-1999.

Management von Innovationen - Planung und Durchsetzung - Erfolge und Mißerfolge, Wiesbaden 1995.

Marketing im Spannungsfeld von Wirtschaft und Gesellschaft, Stuttgart 1995.

4 Co-Editor

Vorträge am Institut für Betriebswirtschaftslehre der Universität Kiel, (Issue 1-9).

German Economic Review (2000 -).

International Journal of Entrepreneurship and Innovation Management (2001 -).

International Journal of Management Reviews (1999 -).

Journal of Enterprise Management (Vol. 1-3).

Journal of Engineering and Technology Management (1992 - 1995).

M@n@gement (1997 - 2001).

Management Science (Associate Editor) (1985-1991).

Marketing ZFP (1978 -).

R&D Management (Editorial Committee) (1991-).

Research Policy (1996-).

Schriftenreihe Forschung-Entwicklung-Innovation (with M. Domsch), Vol. 1, 1984.

Schriftenreihe Management von Forschung-Entwicklung-Innovation (with M. Domsch), Vol. 1 - , (1989 -).

Technology Analysis and Strategic Management (2000-)

RKW-Handbuch für Forschung, Entwicklung, Konstruktion, Berlin 1976 - .

(with W. Krelle) *Unternehmensplanung,* Berlin, Heidelberg, New York 1981.

Feature Issue: Empirical Decision Theory, *European Journal of Operational Research,* 22 (2), 1985.

Die Zukunft der Betriebswirtschaftslehre in Deutschland, *Zeitschrift für Betriebswirtschaft,* Special Issue 3,1993.

Die Bedeutung der betriebswirtschaftlichen Ausbildung für den Standort Deutschland, *Zeitschrift für Betriebswirtschaft,* Special Issue 1, 1996.

(with A. Chakrabarti and J. Hauschildt) *The Dynamics of Innovation. Strategic and Marketing Implications,* Berlin et al. 1999.

(with O. Fisscher et. al.) *Readings in Technology Management,* Enschede 2000.

(with S. Albers and J. Hauschildt) *Technologie- und Innovationsmanagement, Leistungsbilanz des Kieler Graduiertenkollegs,* Wiesbaden 2001.

5 Case Studies

(with U. Weisenfeld) *Preiskrieg am Zigarettenmarkt*, 1986.

(with J.N. Nommensen) *"Croissant" Marketing-Reaktion auf eine Produktinnovation*, 1987.

Synthesekautschuk, 1990.

Management von Innovationen, Wiesbaden, 1995.

(with H. Sattler) Markenwert und Qualitätszeichen, in: E. Dichtl and W. Eggers (Eds.): *Markterfolg mit Marken*, Munich 1996, 207-224.

Klaus Brockhoff

List of Supervised Dissertation and Habilitation Theses

1 Dissertation Theses

Schmalen, Helmut (1971): *Individuelle Berufswahl auf der Grundlage ökonomischer Analysen : eine Darstellung dieser Verhaltensweise und ihrer Bedeutung im Hinblick auf die langfristige Arbeitsmarktentwicklung*, Kiel.

Sell, Axel (1974): *Unternehmensdispositionen bei Rentabilitätsbeschränkung*, Meisenheim am Glan: Hain.

Steinmeier, Friedrich (1975): *Die Planung der Zuteilungsliquidität bei Bausparkassen.*

Martschinke, Siegfried (1975): *Aspekte der dynamischen Produktions- und Kostentheorie, dargestellt insbesondere am Problem des optimalen Potentialtimings*, Kiel.

Rehder, Heino K.K. (1975): *Multidimensionale Produktmarktstrukturierung: Theorie und Anwendung auf einen Produktmarkt*, Meisenheim am Glan: Hain.

Fenneberg, Günter (1979): *Kosten- und Terminabweichungen im Entwicklungsbereich: eine empirische Analyse*, Berlin: Schmidt.

Dietrich, Ottokar (1980): *Gemeinsame Auswahl von Forschungsprojekten und Absatzstrategien für Neuprodukte*, Hamburg: Dietrich.

Kröner, Arthur (1980): *Relationen zwischen Größe und Zielsystem des Unternehmens: Die doppelte Funktion der Unternehmensgröße dargestellt anhand von Daten aus Brauereien*, Düsseldorf: Mannhold.

Waldeck, Bernd (1981): *The sensitivity of a multidimensional unfolding technique: a simulation study of PREFMAP-2 (phase 2)*, Ann Arbor, MI: University Microfilms Int.

Schütt, Klaus-Peter (1981): *Wahrscheinlichkeitsschätzungen im Computer-Dialog : Theorie, Methoden und eine experimentelle Studie zur Schätzung von subjektiven Wahrscheinlichkeiten*, Stuttgart : Poeschel.

Neumann, Hans-Wolfgang (1984): *Entscheidungsunterstützung bei mehrfachen Zielen durch freie Algorithmenwahl im Computerdialog: Realisierung und experimentelle Analyse*, Frankfurt am Main: Lang.

Gutberlet, Kurt-Ludwig (1984): *Alternative Strategien der Forschungsförderung*, Tübingen: Mohr.

Hertrich, Roland (1985): *Die Reihenfolge der Informationssuche von Konsumenten*, Frankfurt am Main: Lang.

Huttegger, Thomas (1986): *Die steuerliche Behandlung von Einkünften aus Erfindungen : ein internationaler Vergleich*, Frankfurt am Main: Lang.

Gedenk, Gerlind (1987): *Einflussfaktoren auf den Imitationswettbewerb im Arzneimittelmarkt der Bundesrepublik Deutschland: eine theoretische und empirische Untersuchung*, Frankfurt am Main: Lang.

Hannig, Rüdiger (1988): *Robustheit von Produktpositionierungsalgorithmen*, Kiel.

Hets, Johannes (1989): *Kommunikative Marketingplanung bei Werbebeschränkungen*, Kiel.

Weisenfeld-Schenk, Ursula (1989): *Die Einflüsse von Verfahrensvariationen und der Art des Kaufentscheidungsprozesses auf die Reliabilität der Ergebnisse bei der Conjoint Analyse*, Berlin: Duncker & Humblot.

Rotering, Christian (1990): *Forschungs- und Entwicklungskooperationen zwischen Unternehmen : eine empirische Analyse*, Stuttgart: Poeschel.

Nommensen, Jens Nicolai (1990): *Die Prägnanz von Markenbildern: Prüfung der Kommunikationsstrategie bei Produktrepositionierung*, Heidelberg: Physica.

Bredehorn-Hiemenz, Saskia (1990): *Quantitative Werbeerfolgskontrolle am Beispiel der Tiefkühlkost-Lebensmittelindustrie*, Hamburg: Lottbek.

Sattler, Henrik (1991): *Herkunfts- und Gütezeichen im Kaufentscheidungsprozeß : die Conjoint-Analyse als Instrument der Bedeutungsmessung*, Stuttgart: M & P für Wissenschaft & Forschung.

Dobberstein, Nikolai (1992): *Technologiekooperationen zwischen kleinen und großen Unternehmen*, Kiel.

Warschkow, Kai (1993): *Organisation und Budgetierung zentraler FuE-Bereiche*, Stuttgart: Schäffer-Poeschel.

Preukschat, Ulf (1993): *Vorankündigung von Neuprodukten - Strategisches Instrument der kommunikationspolitischen Markteinführung*, Wiesbaden: DUV.

Lange, Edgar (1993): *Abbruchentscheidung bei F&E-Projekten*, Wiesbaden: DUV.

Teichert, Thorsten (1994): *Erfolgspotential internationaler F&E-Kooperationen*, Wiesbaden: DUV.

Lange, Veronica (1994): *Technologische Konkurrenzanalyse*, Wiesbaden: DUV.

Hilbert, Anette (1994): *Industrieforschung in den neuen Bundesländern - Ausgangsbedingungen und Reorganisation*, Wiesbaden: DUV.

Mordhorst, Claus (1994): *Ziele und Erfolg unternehmerischer Lizenzstrategien*, Wiesbaden: DUV.

Murmann, Philipp (1994): *Zeitmanagement für Entwicklungsbereiche im Maschinenbau*, Wiesbaden: DUV.

Schmaul, Bernd (1995): *Organisation und Erfolg internationaler Forschungs- und Entwicklungseinheiten*, Wiesbaden: DUV.

Hermes, Michael (1995): *Entscheidungshilfen für den Fremdbezug von technologischem Wissen*, Kiel.

Schirm, Karsten (1995): *Die Glaubwürdigkeit von Produkt-Vorankündigungen,* Wiesbaden: DUV.

Hansen, Tor Borgar (1995): *Beteiligungsstrategien zur Erschließung von Innovationen,* Wiesbaden: DUV.

Leptien, Christopher (1996): *Anreizsyssteme im Bereich der industriellen Forschung und Entwicklung,* Wiesbaden: DUV.

Ernst, Holger (1996): *Patentinformationen zur strategischen Planung von Forschung und Entwicklung,* Wiesbaden: DUV.

Reinhardt, Hans Christian (1997): *Kapitalmarktorientierte Bewertung industrieller F&E Projekte,* Wiesbaden: DUV.

Bochert, Alexander (1997): *Erfolgsfaktoren für die Lizensierung von Technologien der Großforschungseinrichtungen an Unternehmen,* Hamburg: Kovac.

Brinkmann, Jochen H. (1997): *Betrieblicher Innovationsprozess und Innovationserfolg – am Beispiel medizinisch-technischer Hilfsmittel,* Sternenfels: Wissenschaft & Praxis.

Boyens, Karsten (1998): *Externe Verwertung von technologischem Wissen - Möglichkeiten und Grenzen,* Wiesbaden: Kovac.

Bender, Alexander (1998): *Budgetierung von F&E - Das stochastische Simulationsprogramm RADBUDGE,* Wiesbaden: DUV.

Pieper, Ute (1998): *Wirkungen von Unternehmensakquisitionen auf Forschung und Entwicklung: eine empirische Untersuchung aus der Perspektive des erwerbenden Unternehmens,* Wiesbaden: DUV.

Bardenhewer, Justus (1999): *Zur Integration der Industriellen Forschung in ihr Umfeld - Empirische Ergebnisse aus Europa und Japan und ein Versuch der Wirkungsmessung,* Hamburg: Kovac.

Gerwin, Joachim (1999): *Regelmäßige, externe Rechenschaftslegung der deutschen Großforschungseinrichtungen,* Kiel.

Langholz, Jens (1999): *Klassifikationsgesellschaften im Schiffbau - Promotoren technischen Fortschritts?,* Frankfurt am Main: Lang.

Mehrwald, Herwig (1999): *Das "Not-Invented-Here"-Syndrom (NIH) in Forschung und Entwicklung,* Wiesbaden: DUV.

Scharffenberg, Malte (1999): *Die Aufnahmebereitschaft des Handels für neue technologische Gebrauchsgüter unter Berücksichtigung von Produkt-Vorankündigungen,* Frankfurt am Main: Lang.

Vanini, Sven (1999): *Halbwertszeit von technologischem Wissen: Meßkonzepte und Implikationen für die Technologieplanung,* Hamburg: Kovac.

von Boehmer, Alexander (1999): *Internationalisierung industrieller Forschung und Entwicklung, Typen, Bestimmungsgründe und Erfolgsbeurteilung*, Wiesbaden: DUV.

Höcherl, Ingrid (2000): *Das S-Kurven-Konzept im Technologiemanagement: eine kritische Analyse*, Frankfurt am Main: Lang.

Rüdiger, Mathias (2000): *Erfolgsbedingungen der Vertragsforschung in Deutschland*, Wiesbaden: DUV.

Schnoor, Anje (2000): *Kundenorientiertes Qualitäts-Signaling. Eine Übertragung auf Signaling in Produkt-Vorankündigungen*, Wiesbaden: DUV.

Ipsen, Christof (2002): *F-&-E-Programmplanung bei variabler Entwicklungsdauer*, Hamburg: Kovac.

Jochims, Marc (2002): *Diffusion innovativer Dienstleistungen - eine empirische Analyse*, Hamburg: Kovac.

Klinger, Raffaela (2002): *Schutz von Dienstleistungsinnovationen gegen Imitationen*, Frankfurt am Main: Lang.

Poser, Timo (2002): *Impact of Corporate Venture Capital on Sustainable Competitive Advantage of the Investing Company*, Wiesbaden: DUV.

Solf, Markus (2002): *Ressourcentransfers und Unternehmensfinanzierung als Erklärung der Unternehmenskooperation - Das Beispiel der Biotechnologie*, Vallendar.

Zillmer, Peter (2003): *Going Private - der freiwillige Börsenrückzug in Deutschland*, Wiesbaden: DUV.

2 Habilitation Theses

Schmalen, Helmut (1979): *Marketing-Mix für neuartige Gebrauchsgüter - Ein Simulationsmodell zur Wirkungsanalyse alternativer Preis-, Werbe- und Lizenzstrategien*, Wiesbaden: Gabler.

Albers, Sönke (1989): *Entscheidungshilfen für den Persönlichen Verkauf*, Berlin: Duncker & Humblot.

Weisenfeld, Ursula (1995): *Marketing- und Technologiestrategien: Unternehmen der Biotechnologie im internationalen Vergleich*, Stuttgart: Schäffer-Poeschel.

Ernst, Holger (2001): *Erfolgsfaktoren neuer Produkte. Grundlagen für eine valide empirische Forschung*, Wiesbaden: DUV.

Teichert, Thorsten (2001): *Nutzenschätzung in Conjoint-Analysen*, Wiesbaden: DUV.